Contents

SECTION 2: NATURE OF TOURISM

Case Studies

Hosts and Guests Revisited:
Tourism Issues of the 21st Century

Hosts and Guests Revisited:
Tourism Issues of the 21st Century

Copyright © Cognizant Communication Corporation 2001

Cognizant Communication Offices:

U.S.A.   3 Hartsdale Road, Elmsford, New York 10523-3701
Australia P.O. Box 352 Cammeray, NWS, 2062
Japan   c/o OBS T's Bldg. 3F, 1-38-11 Matsubara, Setagaya-ku, Tokyo

Library of Congress Cataloging-in-Publication Data

Hosts and guests revisited: tourism issues of the 21st century / co-edited by Valene L. Smith and Maryann Brent.
    p. cm. — (Tourism dynamics)
    Includes bibliographical references (p.).
    ISBN 1-882345-28-2 (Hard bound). — ISBN 1-882345-29-0 (pbk.)
    1. Tourism. 2. Tourism — Social aspects. I. Smith, Valene L. II. Brent, Maryann, 1944-
III. Series.

  G155.A1 H67 2001
  338.4'791—dc21

                                              2001042292

Printed in the United States of America

Printing: 1 2 3 4 5 6 7 8 9 10 Year: 1 2 3 4 5 6 7 8 9 10

Travel is fatal to prejudice, bigotry, and narrow-mindedness, and many of our people need it sorely on these accounts. Broad, wholesome charitable views of men and things cannot be acquired by vegetating in one little corner of the earth all one's lifetime.

—Mark Twain, *The Innocents Abroad*, 1869

SECTION 3: CHANGES AND IMPACTS

Case Studies

Case Studies

SECTION 5: CULTURE BROKERS

Case Studies

Chapter 29. The Commodificatin of Culture   380
Dean MacCannell

List of Figures

List of Tables

Preface

The creation of *Hosts and Guests Revisited: Tourism Issues of the 21st Century* has been a challenging experience. A review of the published tourism literature since 1974 was the minimum requisite, which only served to point up the many differences between the study of tourism "then" and "now." In 1964, when I proposed study of the impacts of tourism on the Inuit of Kotzebue Sound as a dissertation topic, the doctoral committee denied the request because there was no tourism literature. In 1974, when the first national tourism symposium convened at the American Anthropological Association meetings in Mexico City, there were a scant dozen individuals in the United States interested in the phenomenon of tourism and no academic departments (other than those affiliated with Schools of Business, and Hotel and Restaurant Management). The request to edit the papers from that meeting, as *Hosts and Guests: The Anthropology of Tourism* (1977), left virtually no literature to cite. For principles to organize the text, I looked within— to a background that included 15 years as owner/manager of a travel agency, 20 years of experience as a tour escort on six continents, a Ph.D. in anthropology, and 12 years teaching tourism courses at the local community college. The classification of tourists, from elite to mass, the interests of tourists as ethnic or environmental, and discussion of the role and extent of tourist impacts all derived from that pool of observer–participant data. Twenty-five years later there are more than 415 universities and colleges providing training for employment in the world's largest industry, more than 1200 individual researchers, and more than a dozen scholarly journals that publish academic research in tourism.

The present volume benefits from the participation of co-editor Maryann Brent, who, as a 1997 Ph.D. in geography and tourism, is a product of the recent important scholarly interest in the leisured and sustainable use of planet Earth and the space beyond. Her expert editing and graphic skills are evident throughout this book. Together we have read, sifted, distilled, and discussed the many facets of tourism. Our goal is to bring together into one volume the breadth of tourism issues in contrast to the single-topic volumes that dominate the literature. We have read widely but, by virtue of space limitations and philosophy, citations are minimal and the narrative is almost jargon free. The case studies, all of which were invited, were selected to illustrate what we believe to be the central issues of tourism, now and in the future.

The book is intended as an introductory text of value and interest to students coming into the field of tourism, to provide an understanding of the role of tourism in human lives. The World Tourism Organization conference, "Human Capital in the Tourism Industry of the 21st Century" (WTO, 1997b) set the tone. Those authors all spoke to the need to move beyond the present fragmentation of departments, to develop the "tourismification of the industry" (Jafari, 1997a, p. 210). Everyone engaged in tourism, as scholar or employee, needs exposure to the "big picture," to understand the significance of globalism as the dynamic economic and political process that has propelled tourism into front rank as the world's leading industry. The 21st century seems destined to enlarge the global network for travel, to include tourists who are more knowledgeable about world destinations, and to increase the competition soliciting tourism and tourist revenues.

Before radio and television widened our vision, *National Geographic Magazine* brought photos and narratives of the faraway places and amazing discoveries into millions of homes and offices around the world. Their appointment of a senior editor at *National Geographic Traveler* magazine to "cover the burgeoning field of sustainable tourism for the *Traveler*" (Tourtellot, 1999, p. 98) is heartening, and indicative of the growing public interest and knowledge about tourism. Jenkins (1997) suggests that our challenge is to use our knowledge base to devise education and training programs that are "relevant to the 21st century and which equip people to work effectively and efficiently in these areas . . . so that industry entrants are not taking a job but rather the first step on a career ladder" (p. 220).

The orientation in this volume is cross-cultural and eclectic, especially in the identification of tourism among preindustrial societies, in its statement of the economic and political threads that historically shaped the development of tourism in the last half-century, and in its projection into the next millenium. Much of the data may be not be new to professional colleagues but the integrative interpretation is different from the traditional tourism text.

The text is not intended to be inclusive but rather to suggest topics that could be further elaborated with additional references, for which the lengthy bibliography is supplied. The case studies have broad theoretical links to many aspects of tourism, in addition to the chapter with which they have been identified, again to promote discussion and further reading. We have also chosen to follow Weaver (1998) in the use of descriptive terms that allude to the process of development, with the *more developed countries* (MDCs) referring to Western Europe and Russia, Japan, South Korea, Taiwan, Australia, New Zealand, Canada, and the US. The *less developed countries* (LDCs) include all of Latin America, Africa, Asia, and former Soviet republics such Uzbekistan and Tajikstan.

We are indebted to our many colleagues for their assistance in the preparation of this volume, and beg forbearance for our sins of omission. Many excellent articles and fine scholars whose work has influenced our thinking simply could not be credited due to space limitations. I spoke of tourism as "then," with no literature to cite; the "now" is too many.

Valene L. Smith

Introduction

Valene L. Smith and Maryann Brent

The Qikqiktarukmiut Inuit of northwest Alaska have lived around Kotzebue Sound for several hundred years as seminomadic hunters who summered in seaside fishing camps and in winter also hunted in the interior (Figure 1). Their travels were important time-markers, as they visited relatives and other camps for sports competitions, games, and songfests. They hosted guests (including Siberian Inuit) at the annual midsummer trading rendezvous, and occasionally warred with Indians to the south.

Otto von Kotzebue (1816) made the first recorded European sighting but Captain Beechey on the HMS Blossom (1826) reached shore and reported that some 150 men in skin boats came out from a large camp to trade (Figure 2). In the 1850s the whalers came, followed by government officials, missionaries, and goldminers. These strangers also became tourists. Their letters, journals, and books describing northern adventures eventually inspired others to come North after World War II to tour arctic Alaska and to see "the Eskimo," as they were then termed.

In 1946, the first modern tourists arrived at Kotzebue on Wien Alaska Airlines, on a pilot-inspired package tour launched to create revenue for this fledgling airline. Guests were housed in an old warehouse dormitory and were guided about town by the station agent. The Inuit came to the dirt runway to see the eight passenger-tourists and laughed at their appearance, strapped with cameras and binoculars. However, these guests were welcomed because their presence translated into $1 per visitor for each Inuit who danced that evening. This seasonal summer income was important to a cash-poor economy.

In 1955 Wien Airlines hired the charismatic Chester Seveck to make winter tours to "the lower 48" and later to Mexico and Europe, to sing, dance, and "sell Arctic tourism." By 1965, Kotzebue had two airlines with daily jet service and 3000 summer tourists, slightly exceeding the permanent winter population of the community. The participating Inuit, now mostly elders from the northern village of Point Hope, received $10 each per visitor and were pleased with this easy source of income. Younger Inuit resented tourists who roamed the beach, photographed subsistence activities such as seal butchering, and sneered at the odor of fish drying on racks in the sun. These modern-oriented youths posted graffiti that urged "Tourists, Go Home."

The Alaska Land Claims Settlement Act of 1971 ushered a new day for native self-governance, and Northwest Alaska Native Association (NANA) gave priority to guest housing needs, including potentials of summer tourism, and built a

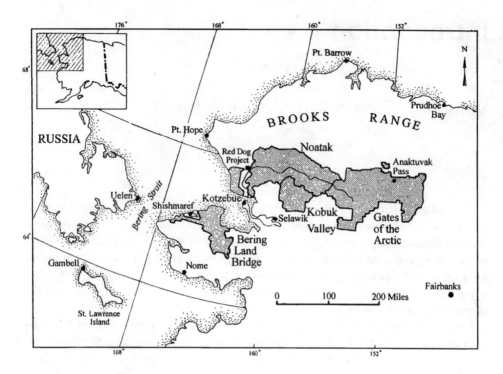

Figure 1. Map of Northwest Alaska.

Figure 2. Choris (1882), artist on the Kotzebue Expedition, sketched Kotzebue Sound Eskimo males wearing labrets and a female with a tattooed chin.

modern hotel. In 1976, NANA built the Museum of the North, a popular tourist attraction of indigenous history and land use. With the 1980 creation of several new US National Parks in the area, the Visitor Center was located in Kotzebue. Ultimately, NANA purchased the white-owned tour company, acquired their own buses, created a heritage village, and in 1997 initiated small-scale touring to outlying villages. The 1999 visitors numbered some 6000, including tourists and adventure travelers interested in trekking, kayaking, and sports fishing. It is not an overstatement: it has been the most successful tourism program in the North. (Valene L. Smith)

Anthropology and Tourism

The hallmarks of anthropology are its commitment to a holistic view of human society and its methodology of cross-cultural analysis. Different cultures develop physical and social survival mechanisms, or customs, that are dependent on their habitat, resources, and heritage. The Inuit miniethnography reflects the philosophy of this book and the tenets of the anthropology of tourism. It illustrates that tourism is a universal of culture—a culture trait found in every society but often in different form. Members of every human group, from aboriginal to post-Industrial, travel to visit relatives, to find entertainment in carnivals, fairs, and parties, and to see and learn how other people live. With global interest focused on the 21st century, in a world of ever more rapid technological change, it is important to recognize the universality of work and leisure, and the human need for travel and tourism. As world population and urbanization increases, and as cyberspace and robotics provide more leisure time, tourism seems destined to retain its leadership as a significant industry and an important component of everyday life. The social and economic values inherent in tourism are best understood by examining the past and studying the present. This knowledge will provide tools for tourism management that will create employment for hosts and enjoyable experiences for both hosts and guests.

To travel, derived from the French *travail*, is often hard work, but to use a modern term, it is also often *fun*. The enjoyment one experiences before, during, and after touristic activities provides a counterbalance for the stresses and boredom in the everyday world (see Graburn, Chapter 3). Tourism also mirrors society, as the available modes of transportation and the destination choices become part of prevailing travel fashions, personal preferences, and the degree of flux in that society. Inuit developed two seasonal modes of transportation: dog sledges in winter and *umiaks* (walrus hide boats) in summer. Inuit males traveled widely in their hunt for large mammals, both as subsistence food and for the furs and oil to trade at the rendezvous. It was their "job" and they were "business travelers" who often overnighted with distant family and friends to have a longer visit (Weyer, 1969). Information shared with other hunters was equivalent to the modern day "trading tips about the stock market" exchanged on a golf course. Many such cultural parallels exist between postmodern and aboriginal lives, including work and recreation.

The style of tourism reflects hosts' and guests' economy, their age and gender, as well as the appropriateness and motivations for travel (Figure 3). In centuries past,

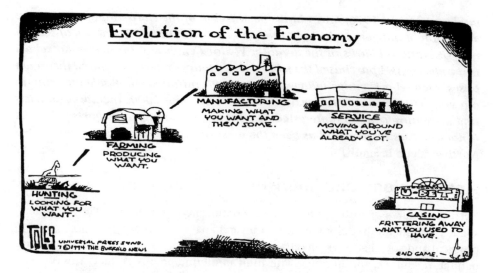

Figure 3. Evolution of the economy. (Toles © 1994 *The Buffalo News.* Reprinted with permission of Universal Press Syndicate. All rights reserved.)

Paleolithic hunters traveled in pursuit of game, and met at rendezvous to trade; Neolithic farmers and herders traded their surplus products and socialized in market towns (see Heath, Chapter 11); and individuals traveled for religious reasons (the Crusades). Many of these latter activities seem to have covert values, for as early as 1097 AD Jacques De Vitry (quoted in Sumption, 1975) wrote

> Some light-minded people go on pilgrimages not out of devotion but out of mere curiosity and love of novelty. All they want to do is travel through unknown lands to investigate the absurd, often exaggerated stories they have heard about the east. (p. 275)

The Age of Metals generated factories, urbanization, and more leisure, prompting travel for education (the Grand Tour), and for business and health. The service industries formalized host–guest relations into a travel industry, and established new centers for the redistribution of wealth in casinos and gaming (see Urbanowicz, Chapter 5).

In the contemporary scene, the economic transactions of tourism are major factors in the redistribution of wealth from guest to host, as payment for experiences, enjoyment, and informal education. Despite the 20th century creation of the global village with visibly homogenized, franchised urban culture, the styles of tourism have expanded proportionately to the technological changes— Fantasylands of virtual reality theme parks, high-speed "thriller rides" that can pull as much as 4 Gs, and "party cruises" to nowhere; "hard and soft" adventure including flights to the South Pole; ballooning in France or Kenya; and descending 5 miles to the ocean floor in a submersible to view the sunken wreckage of the *Titanic*; for US$50,000 a tour operator will get a visitor guest to the top of Mt. Everest.

Indigenous Peoples and the Ethnographic Present

Descriptions of indigenous cultures, written in an "ethnographic present," select a time frame that is a static interpretation. Such accounts often veil the ongoing internal process of change inherent in societies, and highlight only the changes in material culture due to outside contacts. The issues of time and authenticity have become significant anthropological and tourism concerns, now that national entities focus on heritage to support hegemony, and ethnicity is increasingly synonymous with identity. What was the "real culture," and when did it exist? The brief Inuit ethnography is a case in point.

Most of the first aerial tourists to Kotzebue anticipated seeing the supposedly traditional lifestyles of fur-clad Eskimo living in igloos (as their elementary schoolbooks had described). Even as late as the 1960s, visitors were often surprised (and somewhat disappointed) to discover that Inuit were living in framed houses, wore blue jeans, and that they owned electric refrigerators and freezers that had been delivered by air cargo. Prior to their visit, most such tourists had little real knowledge of arctic Alaska or the tundra carpeted with summer wildflowers.

Chester Seveck worked for 25 years as resident Eskimo guide in summer (Figure 4), and traveled with his wife Helen in winter to "sell" Arctic tourism. His real role was cultural mediator, as a "living museum" with one foot in the past and one

Figure 4. Umiak with tourists aboard. (1963 photo by Frank Whaley. Reprinted with permission from Arctic Enterprises.)

in the future (see Chapter 21). Often described as "marginal men," such individuals know through affiliation, residence, and/or employment the traditions and customs of two or more societies. They serve tourism as insightful interpreters of culture content and differences. Chester's identity was outside Kotzebue Sound. He grew up in Point Hope where he learned their whaling traditions, then worked for the US government as a reindeer herder for 46 years.

Chester was a *tareurmiut* ("salt water" Inuit) with a long, successful moneyed career in Western bureaucracy, and he recognized the values and limitations of both. In Hollywood, Chester and Helen appeared many times on radio and television shows. "Once, on the Groucho Marx TV show, Groucho asked, 'Chester, do Eskimo people loan or trade their wives?' I think about this and then say 'Yes, I think about all same Hollywood.' Many people laugh long time when I answer Groucho this" (Seveck, 1973, p. 44).

Although Europeans first visited the Kotzebue Inuit in 1826, the wage/barter economy was introduced with the whalers in 1850, and has subsequently been the preferred lifestyle. Trade and barter supplied guns more reliable than spears for subsistence hunting, and metal kettles that were far better than skin containers. The post-War air service brought fresh food and opportunities to work in the cities of Fairbanks or Anchorage (600 miles or an hour by jet flight). Simultaneously the introduction of the snowmobile to replace dog teams was dramatic because the increased speed shortened a 1-day sledge trip of 40 miles to 1 hour, and greatly extended the subsistence hunting range. This time/distance phenomenon (Figure

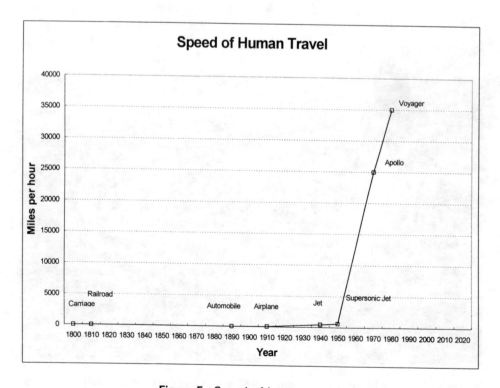

Figure 5. Speed of human travel.

5) continues to accelerate and dominate tourism, as the travelers who once walked, then rode, now fly, ultimately orbit to their lunar holiday (see Figure 27.1).

By contemporary standards, a successful modern Inuit male holds a wage job and hunts by snowmobile and fiberglass boat during paid vacations. Many Inuit women are employed full-time but the heritage of women as gatherers still persists, and several friends may occasionally charter an airplane to a favored berry patch for a summer afternoon excursion. The charter cost is exorbitant compared with the value of the berries but the outing is nostalgic and fun. Thanks to their multinational linkages, members of the Inuit Circum-Polar Conference regularly fly to attend political conferences in Alaska, Greenland, and Scandinavia, to participate in intramural games, and to perform their songs and dances for international audiences.

At what point in time does cultural heritage begin or end? For Kotzebue Inuit, is it at first contact, in 1826 (for which there is only an imperfect archaeological sequence, and the cultural description is at best a reconstruction from an unrecorded, often forgotten past)? With the whalers? Or the missionaries? These questions are highly relevant, as museums struggle with issues of authenticity. If indigenous—or historic—culture is commodified and used as a tourist attraction for profit (in a public showing, as at the Museum of the North or on a sightseeing tour), to whom does the cultural heritage belong? To the Inuit? To the culture brokers? Tourism now raises issues of ethical concern, as does Swain (see Chapter 17) in her discussion of induced culture change in China.

As this book will continually show, tourism was an important element in the ethnographic past, whether one writes of Inuit and trading trips, of the Melanesian *kula* ring (Malinowski, 1922), or of Mayan gambling at their ball courts (Fash, 1991; see Urbanowicz, Chapter 5). Tourism, then and now, is a culture construct, fashioned by the behavior and customs of each society, as it best fits in their habitat and lifestyle.

The purpose of this book is threefold: first, to recognize the cross-cultural nature of tourism and its social importance to members of society at all technological levels; second, to consider the changes that have taken place in tourism research in the past 25 years; and third, to project the use of this acquired knowledge to the analysis of tourism issues in the 21st century.

The Study of Tourism

The academic study of tourism, and especially the eclectic anthropology of tourism, is generally dated to the 1974 American Anthropological Association meeting held in Mexico City. The edited papers were initially published as *Hosts and Guests: The Anthropology of Tourism* (V. Smith, 1977), and are representative of the Advocacy and Cautionary Platforms (see Jafari, Chapter 2). Subsequently, each author restudied his/her topic and the second edition (V. Smith, 1989a) provided a significant new database. Most authors reversed their assessment of tourism impacts and became supportive. Two additional volumes in the mid-1970s, namely DeKadt (1976), *Tourism: Passport to Development*, and MacCannell (1976), *The Tourist: A New Theory of the Leisure Class*, provided additional impetus for the academic study of tourism. At that time, North American tourism research was considered

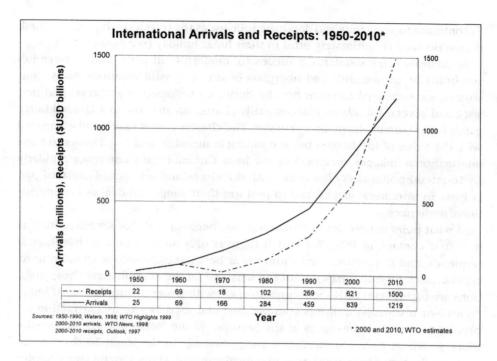

Figure 6. International arrivals and gross receipts: 1950–2010.

frivolous (perhaps a way for university faculty to pay for their vacations?) even though Europeans have been writing about the nature of tourism for nearly a century (cf. Towner, 1996).

Economic Growth and Impacts of Tourism

Subsequent to World War II, tourism has grown rapidly to become the largest global industry (Figure 6), as the number of international arrivals in this last half-century has increased from 25 million in 1950 to 663 million in 1999. Arrivals are forecast to continue upward, increasing to 1.04 billion in 2010 and 1.6 billion by 2020 (World Tourism Organization [WTO], 2000a). The receipts from international travel (not including transportation costs) reflect economic issues. The dip in the curve in the mid-1970s accents a period of gasoline shortages. The trend then climbs steadily to 2000 AD, when it is projected to rise more rapidly, as the increased numbers of travelers are expected to spend more per capita for their vacation. In 2000, tourism receipts were 10.8% of the world Gross Domestic Product (GDP) and employed 192 million people. As a provider of profits for industry and salaries for employees, following many career paths, tourism is without peer. By 2011 the global workforce in tourism will generate 260 million jobs, or 9% of the total employment or 1 in 11.2 jobs (World Travel and Tourism, 2001). Simultaneously a smaller workforce and an aging population will affect career choices. In the US, in 1998 travel and tourism was the third largest retail industry with an economic impact of US$1.3 trillion including 7 million jobs with payroll of US$128 billion and an additional 9.2 million supporting a payroll of US$189 billion. The industry also generated US$871 billion in tax revenues for federal, state, and local governments (Cook, 1999, p. 90).

Commensurate with this growth, the World Tourism Organization (WTO) headquartered in Madrid, Spain, has achieved notable leadership as an international body representing over 100 member nations. Dedicated to improving the quality of travel as well as extending its economic benefits to a wider audience, WTO assists with training programs, tourism assessments, and convenes conferences to consider issues such as Senior Tourism, Youth Tourism, Tourism Taxation, Child Prostitution and Tourism, Sustainable Development, Tourism and Security Issues, and Cultural Tourism. Numerous aspects of WTO activities are referenced throughout this volume.

Placing the economic benefits of tourism in perspective, by 1991 tourism had become the world's largest employer (P. Quick, 1991), and as a labor-intensive service industry, the sales/employee ratio is significant. In the US, each US$1 billion of gross travel and tourism sales supports more than 5000 jobs. By contrast, a similar US$1 billion sales in petrochemicals supports fewer than 300 jobs (P. Quick, 1991, p. 72). The use of tourism as a developmental economic tool, especially in less developed countries (LDCs), is directly related to statistics of this type. In addition, the US Department of Labor estimates that 80% of the new entry employees into the US work force are nonwhite, female immigrants who find employment in minimum pay jobs such as hotels and catering. This employment is particularly important in terms of the increasing urbanization throughout the world.

"Tourism Needs More Respect": The Statistical Dimension

Despite the economic magnitude of tourism, the travel industry continually asks for more respect, especially in the form of infrastructure and training programs. Most government leaders of past decades grew up and attended university in the era when their professors lectured that industry and agriculture were the kingpins of economic stability and commerce. Because tourism is recreation and fun, the travel industry had not received the serious attention or support that it deserves. The problem was exacerbated by the limited statistical data, and especially the extensive intra-European auto and rail travel, and the comparable visitor auto traffic between Canada, US, and Mexico. These impressive figures were hard to measure and, in their absence, the real volume of tourism was not accurately counted.

WTO Tourism Satellite Accounts

In June, 1999, WTO organized the "World Conference on the Measurement of the Economic Impact of Tourism." Delegates from 120 countries launched a new series of indicators, titled Tourism Satellite Accounts (TSA), which will for the first time include domestic tourism in relation to gross domestic product (GDP), and also distinguish between inbound and outbound tourism on the international level. By definition, "a Tourism Satellite Account runs alongside national accounts, drawing from each sector that has a tourism component without disturbing the totals . . . [the TSA statistics] measure Tourism's true contributions to GDP and allows tourism to be accurately compared to other economic sectors listed in national accounts" (WTO, 1999a). This new accounting established for tourism the respect it has earned as an employer and as a major contributor to the world economy. Although full accounting performance is still several years distant, the initial statistics are impressive. WTO tabulated in 1998 international arrivals at 635 million (Table 26.1) but, with the addition of domestic travelers, a more accurate assessment of total tourist arrivals for 1998 is more than 3 billion. Similarly, the 1998 international tourist receipts as published amounted to US$438 billion but the all-inclusive travel revenues for 1998 were an estimated US$1.7 trillion. WTO estimates that domestic tourism accounts for up to 70% of stays in hotels and supports 115 million direct tourism jobs worldwide, or 4% of the world total. Further, creation of new tourism jobs has been 1.5 times faster than the world average over the past 15 years. In 1999 the economic value of travel and tourism was 11.7% of total GDP and represented 8.2% of the global workforce (WTO, 1999a, p. 8).

The Tourism Satellite Accounting promises to provide the respect needed to ensure development of tourism infrastructure. "Tourism Satellite Accounts are not just an instrument of statistical comparison or economic analysis, but also a tool for policy making and this is where its true value lies" (Geoffrey Lipman, President, World Travel and Tourism Council, 1999).

Early tourism studies were oriented toward international tourism for the sake of its infusion of hard currencies. However, in the decades ahead, there will be greater need and demand for local tourism, to serve the burgeoning urban population (see Figure 26.1). The editors of this book feel that the current United Nations definition of tourism, involving an overnight stay at a destination away from one's home, is too restrictive. The category of domestic tourism should include, for example, the 56.2 million tourists who in 1999 spent the day at one of the five largest theme parks (The Magic Kingdom at Walt Disney World, 15.2 million; Disneyworld, Anaheim, 13.4 million; Epcot, 10.1 million; Disney-MGM Studios at Walt Disney World, 8.7 million; and Animal Kingdom, Disney World, 8.6 million). Psychologically many visitors consider this as vacation, and with admission (US$48 per adult at Walt Disney World, summer 1999) plus meals, snacks, and souvenirs, a family day at a theme park is often more costly than much longer camping trips. Similarly, a day of skiing, using the "3Ls" (lifts, lunches, and lounges) is expensive with the inclusion of transportation and equipment rental.

Many theme parks and ski resorts function as local attractions but seek the destination status of Orlando, FL, with its multiple theme parks, or Vail, with expenditures for lodging and other services. Individual attractions can share advertising and promotional costs, and may achieve *place marketing*, where the name alone defines the destination image and the anticipated activities. Place marketing is now true of Las Vegas and Cancún (see Pi-Sunyer, Chapter 9) or the Barrier Reef (see Parker, Chapter 18).

Economic Value Versus Sustainability

The economic importance of tourism has tended to outweigh all other values, but there is increasing and valid concern for its social, cultural, and environmental impacts. Landscape degradation and physical pollution demand serious reflection, as even the most basic survival resources are strained by tourism demands: tourists' breath has necessitated the closing of historic caves such as Lascaux in France; tourist "trails" around the base of the Stonehenge monument in England mandated its enclosure behind a glass wall; water for resort use in toilets, swimming pools, and grass lawns strains local supplies in many areas.

Ecology is a cultural construct that must be learned and is often many-faceted in principle and operation. The maintenance of animal preserves to support safari tourism in Africa is a major concern, given indigenous population increases and their need for arable land (see Heath, Chapter 11). The use of the Inuit miniethnography to illustrate indigenous tourism does not ignore the widespread problems of unemployment, welfare, alcoholism, and identity that plague northern peoples (Williamson, 1999). The International Whaling Commission (IWC) receives widespread public support for its protection of endangered species, but the Inuit see the IWC

> as hypocritical because they support indigenous self-determination at the global level, but they oppose whaling. And animal rights and environmental groups, the Inuit argue, are city dwellers who don't understand the subsistence life. In Nunavut [NB. an Inuit "state" in eastern Canada], a "greenpeace" is a derogatory term for someone who has a purely emotional bond with animals, and doesn't recognize northerners' dependence on them. (Mastny, 2000, p. 33)

The American ban on the importation of seal skin handicrafts is a useful example for tourism research. The Inuit of Greenland and Canada have retained more of their traditional subsistence lifestyle than in Alaska, but to help them obtain needed cash income, the respective governments provided training in the fur industry. Inuit, at a factory in Narsaq (Greenland), produced fashionable fur coats for an upscale European market. However, in 1982 the European Economic Market placed an embargo on the importation of sealskin garments and souvenirs fabricated from leftover pieces, which proved financially disastrous. The value of the Canadian pelts used in 1980–81 was $890,000, and 5 years later it dropped to $17,801. The monetary loss has had deep social consequences in the loss of hunting as a subsistence activity and as an element of cultural esteem, and had an adverse effect upon their nutrition (Williamson, 1999). The European ban has been lifted but the American legislation still stands. Because fewer seal are being taken, the commercial fish harvest also dropped significantly, representing yet another loss of revenue. The Inuit Circum-Polar Conference is aggressively campaigning to lift the embargo and reactivate this important craft industry, citing a global seal population that numbers at least 60 million.

It is the growing economic dependence of many nations and regions on tourism, together with the sociopolitical–cultural changes that tourism has generated (and will further magnify in the decades ahead), that necessitates this reexamination of the anthropology of tourism, as *Hosts and Guests Revisited: Tourism Issues of the 21st Century*.

SECTION 1

STONE AGE TO STAR TREK

Chapter 1

Stone Age to Star Trek

Valene L. Smith

Archaeology confirms that Inuit occupied the shores of Kotzebue Sound for several centuries during which time a trading rendezvous became a well-established annual event (Giddings, 1960). The Sound was a rich habitat, flanked by three major river valleys that supported inland Inuit (see Figure 1), who came to the coast in late June and stayed until early August. Offshore, the farthest north salmon run in the world easily filled set-nets and baskets every day, and the surplus fillets were dried and stored for winter. Schools of beluga *(white whale) and seal augmented the diet, together with tomcod, Arctic char, rabbits, geese, and ducks. Although they were working part-time, sociability overshadowed their labors; the festivities made it seem like a vacation with family and friends. No other site in the Alaskan arctic has a resource base to host such a large seasonal influx, which in 1884 Cantwell (1889) estimated as 1400 Inuit camped together, their skin tents grouped by family and dialect (Figure 1.1).*

To go to the rendezvous was everyone's dream; one stayed home only because of old age or illness. Memories of the six weeks of feasting, competitive sports and story telling for which the Inuit are famous filled ten winter months with a mix of nostalgia, then anticipation while new clothes were made and new songs practiced. The trade itself was a shopping expedition—a trip to an aboriginal mall—for inland Inuit had salmon skin bags and boots, beaver pelts and grey-brown caribou hides, and jade for jewelry and tools. Coastal Inuit had supplies of muktuk *(whale blubber), seal oil, walrus hides and ivory, mammoth ivory, and whale ribs for house supports. The Siberian Inuit brought umiaks laden with sable pelts, black-and-white reindeer hides and, most precious of all, leaf tobacco and tea. The men formed trading partnerships, women gossiped and children played. The social bonding reinforced their kinship networks in the event of failure in the winter food quest, and the need to seek aid beyond the immediate family.* (V. Smith, 1966)

Definitions of Tourism

There are as many definitions of tourism as there are disciplines and investigators, but all share commonalties. From an anthropological perspective, a tourist

Figure 1.1. Summer camp, Hotham Inlet 1884. [Photo by Edward Nelson in *The Eskimo About Bering Strait* 1899. Reprinted by permission of the Smithsonian Institution (SI-6387).]

was originally defined as "a temporarily leisured person who travels away from home for the purpose of experiencing a change" (V. Smith, 1977). This simple definition has stood the test of time, and remains in wide usage. From the same era, but oriented toward the management perspective, R. McIntosh (1977) defined tourism as an industry catering to tourist needs, or "the science, art and business of attracting and transporting visitors, accommodating them and graciously catering to their needs and wants." Wahab (1975), a professor of law and tourism policy, observes that the "anatomy of tourism is composed of three elements: man, the author of the act of tourism; space, the physical element to be covered; and time, the temporal element consumed by the trip and the stay" (p. 8). These three social science definitions of tourism remain academically useful to convey the diversity of tourist motivations and activities. D. Pearce (1992) describes the many organizations including governments, carriers, and industry (termed in this volume the culture brokers) who motivate and manage tourism. He conceptualizes tourism as an "origin-linkage-destination system involving the temporary movement of people from an origin to a destination and usually back home again after at least one overnight stay" (p. 4).

Tourism Elements

All forms of tourism—international, domestic, business related, pilgrimage, or family visits—require participants to have three essential elements, best expressed as an equation: tourism = leisure time + discretionary income + positive social sanctions.

Leisure is the time when an individual is neither employed at gainful work nor attending to essential daily tasks. At leisure, one has a choice to do virtually nothing, such as lie in a hammock and read, or meditate. Or one could participate in recreational activities that are usually close to home, such as dining with friends, playing ball, swimming, or "jamming." Tourism, however, requires money to spend for lodging, meals, entertainment, and shopping. Discretionary income refers to those funds not needed for basic survival and available for optional items that are a cultural choice. The individual could buy a car, take a cruise, invest in the stock market, or repaint the house. Leisure and funds are essential prerequisites but the individual choice may be decided at least in part by prevailing local social sanctions. In the pre-World War II era, an American of modest means who traveled overseas for pleasure was subject to community censure for violating the Puritan work ethic that sanctioned "saving for a rainy day." In contemporary America, to stay home because you lack ready cash is "old-fashioned" because travel costs are so easily charged to credit cards. To "fly now, pay later" is the modern philosophy. However, approval for tourism is still sometimes rooted in the appropriateness of the travel activity, considering, among others factors, the age and gender of the travelers, and the social milieu. Examples from the travel industry that might have different sanctions include family travel, singles travel, senior travel, gay and lesbian travel, handicapped (or physically limited) travel, pilgrims, conventioneers, business travel, and youth travel. Sanctions are silent but powerful cultural constructs that vary geographically, temporally, and socially.

Tourism Through Time

A definitive history of tourism is waiting to be written. Towner (1996) has set a high standard for sociopolitical interpretation but the time frame is limited. Sigaux (1966) is difficult to access and lacks the broad perspective. This chapter provides a brief historical analysis of the socioeconomic foundations and the emerging technologies and philosophies that have made tourism a global business leader as well as a dominant recreational mode, and a potential avenue for peace.

Tourism parallels the process of acculturation (culture change and adaptation), particularly in terms of technological innovation. As noted in the Introduction, as speed increases, relative distance is shortened (see Figure 5). Dramatic changes in culture and tourism can be directly correlated with the development of new sources of industrial power or energy, including The Industrial Revolution (coal–steam) of the 1700s, the Nuclear-Synthetic Revolution of the 1940s, and the Electronic-Cyberspace Revolution, circa 2000. The travel and tourism activities in each era can be best defined in terms of the available modes of transportation, and thus human mobility. Each technological revolution is identified with a progressively larger population, more urbanism, and more stringent education and skill requirements for lucrative jobs, discretionary income, and opportunities for travel.

The Pre-Industrial Era

The Inuit vignettes describe the travel and tourism of one aboriginal group, with a theme that could be replicated with variations in style for other indigenous tribes. For example, the main trade route of Mayan communities—*La Ruta Maya*—linked Central America from Yucatan south to Honduras (D. Brown, 1999). Religious motivations built the great Mayan ceremonial centers and their shopping plazas to which the devout traveled with gifts and trade goods. For hundreds of years, Mayan market towns were the social hubs and source of regional news. The major Eurasian caravan route, the *Silk Road*, stretched from Rome to Xian (China), along which moved goods (and ideas) to the famous bazaars of Damascus, Samarkand, and Urumchi. African commerce spanned the Sahara for centuries and also dealt in the slave trade, bringing unfortunate victims to coastal markets for sale and export to the New World, in what is now termed the *Slave Route*. These three highways of history, where the traveler once walked, are now promoted by the World Tourism Organization (WTO) as agendas for economic development. Air routes, paved highways, and modern hotels provide 21st century travelers to these destinations with history combined with a standard of comfort unimaginable three centuries ago.

The Industrial Steam Revolution: 1700 AD

The Industrial–Steam Revolution, circa 1700 AD, fathered mines, factories, and the railroad, and introduced the use of nonrenewable resources, especially coal and petroleum. In so doing, it also translated the value of an hour of labor into a monetary unit, based on the worker's skills and expertise. Time literally became money. Men (or women) could sell unlimited weekly hours of labor for whatever wage they could obtain, and keep or spend the earnings as they chose. The concept of "time off," shifts, and workweek crept into vocabulary, as did "paid vacations." Industrialization created new mine and factory towns peopled by in-migrants from rural farmsteads to live in cramped unsanitary housing. The first railroads carried freight but soon these "horseless carriages" were carrying small numbers of passengers, for the new service was cheaper, faster, and more comfortable than stagecoaches.

In 1841, Thomas Cook, a Baptist missionary, persuaded the Midland Counties Railway Company (UK) to operate a special train over a 40-mile distance for a 1-day Temperance meeting. He had no difficulty finding passengers for this Sabbath day, as it was a morally sanctioned cause (and a day of fresh air!). With this initial success, other day trips followed. The rail company agreed to offer tours regularly—if Cook would provide the passengers, which he did. In the 1860s, Cook opened a travel agency, for which he invented the first travel vouchers, so clients could prepay at his office and not have to carry large sums of money to pay on-site for accommodations and meals. He also created Traveler's Checks as a safe means to carry funds, and designed sleeping cars (Wagon-lits Cook) for long-haul passengers. He soon had tours operating to Egypt, Asia, and North America. An ambitious and worldly entrepreneur, he almost single-handedly created the basic operations of today's travel industry. In addition, he became so knowledgeable about world affairs that Queen Victoria once commented that Cook knew more about the colonies than her own Foreign Office.

Rail travel also revolutionized agricultural Europe, whose population lived in dispersed, farm villages, many no more than 1 mile apart. Larger market towns, with churches, shops, and schools, were an hour or two away by foot. With the advent of the train, myriad small rail lines developed throughout Europe, linking farm villages to urbanizing market centers. These lines gradually became the modern network of convenient rail connections that still serve Europe's densely populated countries as well as the mass tourism supported by Eurailpass traffic.

In the US and Canada, a few major rail lines spread westward from their eastern hubs, to service growing cities on the West Coast, and some intermediary centers such as Chicago, St. Louis, Denver, Winnipeg, and Calgary. Distances were great, and the trip was long, tiring, and expensive. Short feeder lines served local coastal and mountain resorts near the populous east (see Brent, Chapter 7). However, even today entire states in the US, and most of Canada, have no rail service (Figure 1.2).

In 1908, Henry Ford introduced his "Tin Lizzie" (the black Model-T Ford), which literally put Americans on the road. Gunn (1995) reports

> To say that the proliferation of Ford cars in the 1920s was the sole cause for the travel boom in American may be taking some license with the truth. But undeniable was the detonation that occurred when the insatiable desire to experience the West fused with the new mass ability to get there. The resulting explosion in tourism had never happened before, and has never been equaled since. (p. 73)

By 1927, 15 million Model-T Ford cars had been built and there were 200 auto factories in 28 Michigan towns involved in automobile production. Despite a "great Depression," in 1935 the American Automobile Association estimated some 40,000,000 Americans (roughly one third of the population) took motor tours each year. They drove to see their national parks, including Yellowstone (established in 1872), Yosemite (1890), Mesa Verde (1906), and Grand Canyon (1908). Americans were soon addicted to their cars and were nostalgic about their highways, including Route 66, which "led from Chicago to LA."

Pioneering airlines had been established during the 1930s, most notable among them was Juan Trippe's Pan American Airways, which was the world's largest mail carrier by 1930. In 1935, the Pan-Am four-engine flying boat, the China Clipper, departed from San Francisco, where 150,000 people (including President Roosevelt) gathered to watch the take-off. It completed the Pacific crossing in a 7-day, 60-hour inaugural flight, stopping overnight at US naval bases mid-Pacific, and was greeted in Manila by 200,000 cheering Filipinos, celebrating a half-holiday. The world audience was ready for air travel but they lacked the technology, and a war intervened. The first American architect to design a noteworthy overseas hotel, Frank Lloyd Wright, was already setting the stage for the new tourism with the construction (1917–1922) of his Tokyo hotel, incorporating the stylistic details of Japanese

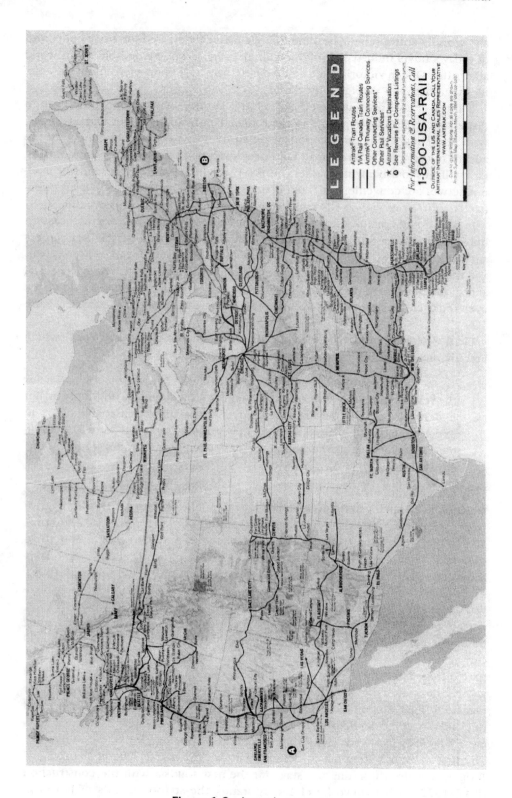

Figure 1.2. Amtrak route map.

printmakers. It survived the 1923 earthquake unscathed, giving credence to American construction, but was razed in 1968 for a high-rise with more guest capacity.

The Nuclear–Synthetic Revolution: 1940 AD

The military technology, including nuclear firepower developed to win World War II, spawned many peacetime innovations in communication, manufacturing, and travel. When World War II ended, experienced military pilots returned home, looking for jobs and, finding none, bought surplus war aircraft at bargain prices and started airlines, including Wien Alaska, Eastern Airlines, and Flying Tigers (Figure 1.3), the latter destined to become the world's largest freight carrier and merge into Federal Express. Underfunded, these neophyte companies needed revenue, and added charter services to fill passenger seats. For two decades, during the 1950s and 1960s, many American universities maintained summer programs in Europe, using cheap charter flights. Their counterpart campuses in Europe welcomed these visitors, who were an entirely new element of American tourism. Today many of these youths are matured "baby boomers," entering senior traveler status, and are frequent fliers because their overseas college experience sanctioned travel as a way of life. Commercial jet air service in 1959 marked the advent of mass tourism, which did not fully develop until the mid-1970s.

After World War II, it was soon apparent that the assembly lines of war could produce more goods than a peacetime society could consume. Consequently, the postwar workweek was shortened from 48 hours to 44 hours, then to 40 hours and a standard 5-day week. From this time forward, the employment trend has

Figure 1.3. Flying Tigers Squadron over Salween River Gorge (Burma), May 28, 1942. Returning to Kunming, China, from a strafing over the Burma Road. (© R. N. Smith, courtesy of his family.)

consistently moved to limit the weekly work schedule including "part-time" employment and more paid holidays and 3-day weekends. The Puritan work ethic
was replaced by the philosophy that "work is for play," and the seeds for consumerism had been laid.

Women had responded to the wartime demand for labor, and postwar they became the "taste-makers" of tourism, thanks to the double-income families they generated (V. Smith, 1979). By the mid-1970s, the baby boomers (children born during
or just after World War II) were out of college and working, and their parents were
retiring. Their demographics favored leisure, recreation, and a desire to travel. Without fanfare, and little public recognition, travel became essentially a human right.

The Electronic–Cyberspace Revolution: 2000 AD

At the millennium, a new technological revolution is clearly in progress, involving the use of new fuels (fusion), new synthetic materials, and new travel frontiers—in space, in virtual reality, and in a deeper awareness of the need to conserve and protect our planet and our human heritage. If peace—so essential to
personal safety and psychological well-being—is preserved, the potential for expanded tourism is vast (see Chapter 26).

Global Trends

What most Americans did not yet perceive in post-World War II was their new
status as a superrich global superpower. The US became the role model of Western
industrial society, especially in less developed countries (LDCs), although within
the US the shift to a service-oriented economy was already under way. The significance of these impacts on tourism seems to have escaped clear articulation elsewhere, including the scholarly tourism literature. However, to develop tourism
policy and management plans for 21st century tourism, it is imperative to understand the newly evolving global philosophies of this post-Industrial era. Three key
issues that will dominate the structure and marketing of travel in the next few
decades include: consumerism, globalization, and urbanization (discussed further
in Chapter 26).

Consumerism

Consumerism is a social and economic outgrowth of World War II, born in the
US in an Age of Affluence—in a country that benefited economically from the
manufacturing of war materiel and escaped the physical military destruction in-
curred in Europe and Asia (see Packard, 1960). The war itself displaced millions of
residents in Europe and Asia, redrew political boundaries that divided Europe,
created two Chinas, and, in spin-off revolutionary wars, divided Korea and splin-
tered Southeast Asia.

In the process, tradition and family ties to ancestral land in much of Europe and
Asia were fractured beyond repair. Individuals best identified themselves with their
place of origin rather than their homeland, as the latter in many instances no
longer existed. Adrift, they sought new bonds in associative organizations in cities,
in social and service organizations, and in activist health, political, and human
rights groups. Increasingly, these landless migrants traveled in search of a better

life, and returned home for family visits. The emerging synthetics industry altered agricultural production, as nylons replaced silk hosiery and polyesters displaced cotton and woolen textiles. Unless they could modernize, old factories closed, people moved, and towns and churches died. Port facilities closed as air cargo replaced shipping. New cities formed, filled with strangers. Megalopolis corridors such as *San-San* sprawled from San Francisco to San Diego, and ethnic enclaves from former colonies formed in many European cities. In eastern Europe and Asia, where land was scarce and valuable, urban housing went skyward in 1000-unit concrete blocks served by school, market, and small shops. Only the world's wealthy could afford a home, a garage, and a garden.

Consumerism has become a major personal identifier in the West (and is a growing trend in the Orient, evident in Japan by the 1990s). Individual worth is measured by possessions, for which one must often work very hard and, if not attainable by work, the alternate avenues are corruption or theft (for which tourists are "soft targets"). Although statistics are difficult to establish, it is generally conceded that shopping ranks high if not number one as a travel activity. Within tourism, the trip itself is a consumable to be discussed with all who will listen. The farther one goes and the more frequently one travels, the "best" trip and the "worst experience" are often more important to ego enhancement than the purchase of a new car, new home, or the establishment of a "new relationship." Research probably would establish that the "fashions" in tourism destination develop from consumptive travel. Informal observation reinforces the subjective comment that once several friends have traveled to and returned from a particular "in" destination, individuals are motivated to visit that destination, too. Tourism is often a "keeping up with the Joneses," and the ability to share the chatter of name-dropping about hotels, cafes, handicrafts, and even "experiences." Tourism at the millennium is a prestigious consumable commodity for salaried singles, dinks (double income, no kids), and the upwardly mobile, in all industrial spheres worldwide. The destinations, the duration and frequency of their travels, may be currently restricted among the LDCs but this global behavior pattern is only latent there.

The Shopping Malls

When customers could not find parking space in the crowded urban core, entrepreneurs moved their shops to new suburban citadels of commerce. Consumerism has turned many shopping malls into mercantile pleasure parks, with food courts and weekly free "shoppertainment" (see Figure 28.2). Advertising promotions of "dinertainment" capture evening shoppers, and "edutainment" lure customers to the bookstores (with lecturers offering free advice on "how to write and sell a travel article"). These blandishments are increasingly more important to counter the growing trend to shop on the Internet, to "save time" by catalog or mail order purchases, and then "spend time" on travel. Millennial consumerism focuses on the acquisition of cars, condos, clothes, and travel that have replaced, for many, the decaying traditions of home, church, and land. Durning (1992, p. 8) observes, "Shopping centers have become the centers of our public life, and consuming has become both our primary means of self-definition and our leading pastime" (p. 8). Malls have matured into international destinations, especially the enclosed Edmonton Mall (Alberta, Canada), noted for its sandy beach, heated water, and a wave machine (Butler, 1991). When February temperatures drop to subzero, a weekend spent there is vastly cheaper and almost as satisfactory as a comparable weekend in Florida, but without the multiple theme parks of Orlando.

The Mall of America in Minneapolis is also situated in the winter snow belt of North America, and is more easily accessible by international air carriers than Edmonton. Said to be the largest completely enclosed mall, the three-storied complex surrounds a huge play area complete with roller coaster, Ferris wheel, Camp Snoopy, wild animals show, and Legoland, In 2000, it was the epitome of shoppertainment and, unlike theme parks, admission is free. The annual visitation is consistently 42 million and is a mix of domestic tourism plus tour groups from the Orient and Europe who come for a week to shop, to be entertained, and to dine. The economic impact on the surrounding area is impressive. Study estimated the Mall had a US$1.4 billion impact on the Minneapolis–St. Paul (Twin Cities) economy, and that 80% of the impact came from out-of-state tourists. Of that amount, only 20% resulted from shopping. Instead, another 20% was generated by the mall in the form of payroll and taxes. The remaining US$840 million supported the ancillary hotels, restaurants, and transportation *outside* the mall (Simon Property Group, 1995). This impact study attracted international attention and supports the belief that the many small malls already conspicuous in Europe, in major Latin American cities, and in South Africa will expand, diversify, and further serve the objectives of the industries that fuel consumerism. Industrial Japan shunned the malls to conserve farm land, but Shirouzu (1997) predicts malls will "blossom in Japan" in the next 4 to 5 years because of clogged roads, lack of city parking, and the loss of jobs in suburban areas. For the future (both global and interplanetary), Kowinski writing in the *Malling of America* (quoted in Durning, 1992) predicts

> Someday it may be possible to be born, go from preschool through college, get a job, date, marry, have children . . . get a divorce, advance through a career or two, receive your medical care, even get arrested, tried and jailed; live a relatively full life of culture and entertainment, and eventually die and be given funeral rites without ever leaving a particular mall complex—because every one of those possibilities exists now in some shopping center somewhere. (p. 131)

Economic Globalization

Globalization is described by Short and Kim (1999) as the new meta-narrative for the third millennium. It is a concept with both a process of economic, political, and cultural change, and a discourse of globalism. The upbeat and optimistic view promises "foreign products and investment increased economic efficiency, political transparency and overall competitiveness" (p. 6). The negative interpretation of economic globalization describes the process of change as mechanisms to:

> discipline workers to accept lower wages [NB. sometimes through part-time work], increased workloads and changing labor practices. Globalization, downsizing and restructuring are terms used not only to describe but also to justify and legitimize changes in capital-labor relations. (Short & Kim, 1999, p. 5)

Economic globalization is most immediately apparent in transnational mergers and in the relocation of Western (MDC) manufacturing plants in LDCs to take advantage of cheaper labor. By saving production costs, the product can be competitively marketed at home or abroad. Newly employed LDC workers benefit from discretionary wages to buy their own products and/or to travel. The manufacture of the traditional little Volkswagon "bug," now built only in Mexico for Mexicans, at a 1999 cost per car of US$7000 is a case in point. By intent, as the "have not" nations industrialize and mainstream into consumer behavior, their labor force will attain both the leisure and the discretionary income to travel. The aspirations and sanctions favoring tourism are already established. The implications of globalization for increased 21st century travel and tourism are profound.

Cultural Globalization

The nature of cultural globalization is important to tourism in relation to the issues of the tourist gaze, and to heritage and authenticity. The homogenized global village emerged as the initial specter as the Americanization of the world spread via CNN and by construction of some 23,000 Golden Arches in 110 countries. Why travel when there is a Benetton in every French village? Subsequent analyses, however, by Appadurai (1990, 1996), suggest that the rampant display of American culture had formed a globalized culture of homogeneity with five dimensions of flow, including: (1) *ethnoscapes* (the movements of tourists, immigrants, refugees, and guestworkers); (2) *mediascapes* (the worldwide distribution of information through newspapers, magazines, and TV programs and films); (3) *technoscapes* (the distribution of technologies); (4) *financescapes* (global capital flows); and (5) *ideoscapes* (the distribution of political ideas and values, such as the master narrative of the Enlightenment). This is accompanied by a "global babble" of connectedness associated with international organizations, with international spectacles (such as the opening and closing ceremonies of mega-events, like the Olympics, World Cup), and with a rising global consciousness about human rights, the UN Year of the Child, International Day of Tourism, and the important 1992 Rio Conference on Environment and Development. Barnet and Cavanagh (1996) termed this process of homogenization as cultural imperialism.

Deterritorialization

When popular culture traits spread from their country of origin, changes of *deterritorialization* occur. As the trait is adopted into a new culture, it changes through a process of *reterritorialization*. Disneyland is a case in point: the Japanese welcomed it, and many visit several times a year; the French received it, some with visible distaste and refused to visit at all. In Japan the franchise agreement required Disneyland-Tokyo to be constructed exactly like the Anaheim model but the lease agreement failed to allow for climatic and cultural differences. California enjoys winter rain, and during the busy summer season rainfall almost never occurs. In Tokyo the busy summer season coincides with almost-daily heavy monsoon rains. The Tokyo property had to renegotiate (i.e., reterritorialize) their theme park lease to enclose Main Street with an expensive glass roof and to construct rain gutters on other buildings. Japanese visitors, tired of hamburgers and fries, demanded a Japanese food concession. Another lease negotiation permitted the addition of a large second-floor restaurant that remained unsigned except for the traditional blue-white curtain at the entry, recognizable to Asians. Warning signs, such as "Watch Your Step" and "Hold Hand Rail," are printed only in English and Chinese and not Japanese. According to Tokyo-Disney public relations personnel, "only Americans and Chinese sue; if a Japanese falls and is injured, he accepts personal responsibility for the accident as a matter of his own clumsiness." Disneyland was deterritorialized for Japanese to enjoy but reterritorialized to meet Japanese preferential customs (including a preponderance of "Eastern" toilets in the restrooms). Language similarly adjusts, as Minnie Mouse became Minaku-Mouse.

Cultures are historically resilient, however, and traditions often persist long after the events that initiated them. Their resilience suggests that globalization leads to cultural heterogenization, engendering local and regional responses to external stimuli. McDonald's originally enforced rigid franchise stipulations for their Golden Arches but now allows architectural variations to meet local zoning laws. In Austria and Germany, beer is sold to accompany a "Big Mac" and in the new McCafes, the tira misu dessert is advertised as "tira mac su."

A number of governments, prompted in part by segments of the tourism industry, have responded to the challenge of "global Americanization" by actively stressing a program of renationalization, based on traditional values and heritage. Reterritorialization of immigrant ethnicity is the foundation for many folk festivals that promote multiculturalism and simultaneously involve residents in community activities. Street fairs and cultural shows provide low-cost recreation for the urban poor in the world's mega-cities (see Chapter 26). This positive trend needs to be nurtured and should figure prominently in future tourism planning and marketing, for it is repeatedly shown that "culture sells" (see Fagence, Chapter 15, and Shackley, Chapter 24).

The Media

The media have played a major role in the development of global tourism, even as Durning notes (1992) "the wildfire spread of the consumer life-style around the world marks the most rapid and fundamental change in day-to-day existence the human species has ever experienced" (p. 36). America started the motion picture industry and made Hollywood glamorous, where tourists could buy a map or take a tour to see where "the stars" lived. Initially, the themes featured lavish living, cops and robbers, and Western gunfights between cowboys and Indians. These movies became the dominant theater fare the world over, including Friday nights in an Inuit village schoolhouse, and established the national character image of "gun-totin" wealthy Americans. Even in the 1960s, these visual images were so real that some educated New Yorkers feared to travel "out West" lest they encounter Indians on the warpath.

"Half the television programs aired outside the United States are American reruns, so aspirations everywhere are defined by the norm in the United States" (Durning, 1992, p. 127). The effect of American television on global culture has been profound, and although the Westerns, murder mysteries, war films, and musicals are still produced, there has been a perceptible change in Hollywood scenarios in the past three decades. Subsequent to Woodstock '69, the first major televised rock music festival, which proved to be the defining event for the sexual/ social revolution and "hippie" era of the 1970s, films reflect the use of narcotics, violence, and obscenities as first screened there. Thirty years later, Woodstock '99, advertised as a festival of Peace, Love, and Music, ended in destructive carnage, nudity, and violence. A participant interviewed by a *New York Times* reporter, July 26, 1999, responded to a question, "Violence? That's what my generation is about—violence!" The event raises an important question: if the world's role models—the Americans—smash and burn, what is wrong with hooliganism, or fights at the World Cup? Or violence in a schoolyard? Or randomly shooting tourists in an Egyptian temple to prove a political point? And lead to unprovoked bioterrorism? These are tourism deterrents.

Concurrently the expanding video technology has sharply reduced production costs for films of wilderness travel (such as African safaris and polar bear viewing), participatory adventure tours (including kayaking, river rafting, and scuba diving), and cultural and historical events. TV channels with 24-hour programming of these themes are constant and persuasive incentives to travel, and the accompanying advertising is standardizing consumer tastes, as Pi-Sunyer documents (see Chapter 9). By this process, English has become the global language and the agent for transmission of American culture. Crystal (1997, p. 61) estimates that at least one fifth of the world population has a working knowledge of English, and 75 countries recognize it as either the primary or secondary language.

Summary

Consumerism and mass tourism are fraternal twins, both born in the mid-1970s from common parents—the social revolution and the commercial shift from manufacturing to service industries. Americans physically exported their styles of tourism overseas, when Conrad Hilton founded his hotel chain and central reservations system in 1948, and opened the Caribe Hilton in December 1949 as an entrée into a sound business venture in tourism, "combining American standards of efficiency and modern comfort with the best traditions of hotel keeping abroad" (Comfort, 1964, p. 219). Pan-American, then the premier round-the-world airline, inaugurated Inter-Continental Hotel chain to house airline crews and passengers. The American architect, Pete Wimberly, launched a long and successful career designing overseas hotels to fit local landscapes and incorporate indigenous motifs. In general, these new hostelries were well received in the LDCs for they were visible and validating proof of their progress toward Westernization. Europeans and Japanese whose postwar economies created personal wealth are following the American manufacturing mode and adopting consumption as the organizing principle of their lives. The wealthier citizens of poor nations already emulate this orientation as their status symbol, even as many of their poorer neighbors are already (largely unrecognized) domestic travelers in the patterns of their ancestors, visiting families, going to markets, and making pilgrimages. The major culture brokers (Chapter 21) clearly recognize these trends, and are designing larger aircraft, longer landing strips, bigger hotels, and more cruise ships to accommodate an ever-expanding travel clientele—and space tourism is plainly on the horizon.

Chapter 2

The Scientification of Tourism

Jafar Jafari

Perhaps few industries have transformed as rapidly as tourism—and all that, despite its age-old origin, mainly during recent decades. As communities and countries discovered its economic prospects and mustered their efforts to tap on its potentials, tourism suddenly evolved into an invigorating business, an international trade, and a global mega-industry. In a short time span, it was first elevated to the rank below that of oil, then at par with it, suddenly above it, and it is now being positioned as the largest industry in the world. In turn, this impressive growth and transformation stimulated efforts to develop a multidisciplinary body of knowledge that can understand it and guide its planning and development in all phases and spheres: locally, regionally, and internationally. This new field, with its scientification process also in rapid progress, is today recognized as a legitimate and important area of investigation in many scholarly communities worldwide.

The purpose of this chapter is to provide retrospective and prospective views on tourism's scientific journey. More specifically, the aim is to identify some of the past conditions that have helped tourism to assume its present scholarly dimensions and depth; to sketch the formation of this landscape of knowledge, to selectively extract from this context emerging central socioeconomic issues; to suggest research crossroads for advancing to new frontiers; to sample the richness of the state of knowledge—along with challenges and opportunities ahead—that, in turn, can guide present and future planning and operation of this diverse mega-industry. Conceptually informed and practically enriched sustainable strategies, now rooted in this body of knowledge, can and will benefit all those directly and indirectly involved in tourism: the entrepreneurial and public agencies committed to its development; the tourists who invest their leisure time and disposable income to see near and far peoples and places; the host whose communities and resources are mobilized and affected by the needs of tourists and the very industry that accommodates them; and academic institutions involved in research, delivery of education, and advancement of scholarship in this field, now housed on many university campuses worldwide.

Evolution of Thought on Tourism

Today, tourism is acclaimed as a major global economic force and a giant industry worldwide. Many publications of the WTO, among others, testify to its steady growth since World War II. For example, in 1950, 25.3 million international tourist arrivals resulted in $2.1 billion receipts. Close to the end of the 20th century, in 1998, 625 million international tourists generated $445 billion receipts. In the same year, worldwide spending on both domestic and international tourism surpassed $3 trillion. The latter is, according to an analyst, several times larger than what the world spends on defense; or said differently, world spending on tourism exceeds the gross national product of any country in the world with the exception of the US and Japan. The estimates on the volume of tourism for the years ahead into the 21st century remain impressive.

The steady growth of tourism since World War II, and especially during more recent decades, has brought much attention to it, both as an industry and as a phenomenon. A review of the literature sheds light on the growth and popularity of tourism. To reveal this pattern, the writings and insights of the last few decades can be aggregated into four groups, each suggesting a distinctive position or platform of thinking. These, the Advocacy, Cautionary, Adaptancy, and Knowledge-Based Platforms, as will be discussed, have emerged chronologically, with the text and position of one leading to the next, but without being replaced by it; and indeed all four platforms coexist today.

Advocacy Platform: The Good

This first position was formed by those individuals or firms and institutions— including private businesses, public agencies, and trade associations, among others—directly or indirectly concerned with tourism's economic prospects. These "interest" groups often argue that tourism is a labor-intensive industry; that it benefits sectors beyond its operation; that it is a viable economic alternative for many communities or countries; that it generates foreign exchange badly needed to sustain membership in the global community; and more. To place tourism under an even brighter light, these advocates also emphasize other attributes: that tourism preserves the natural and built environments; that it revives traditions of the past; that it actively promotes cultural performances; and that it facilitates cross-cultural communication and the prospects for global peace. These combined socio-economic perspectives (Table 2.1), when placed under such an aggrandized spotlight, have fueled its development and promotion in near and far destinations.

Cautionary Platform: The Bad

With the passage of time, casual observations as well as serious research findings on touristic issues and influences began to challenge the advocacy position. This new voice, barely audible before or during the 1960s, grew to become the Cautionary Platform in the 1970s. Members of the research community, and especially those (private and public) concerned with the protection of culture and nature, contributed to the formation of this cautioning or alerting position. Their message has not been limited to economic disbenefits, arguing that the industry generates mostly seasonal and unskilled jobs; that it benefits only firms and big

Table 2.1. Advocacy Platform on Tourism Influences

Economic Benefits	Sociocultural Benefits

• Can be labor intensive, generating:
    Full-time jobs
    Seasonal jobs
    Part-time jobs
    Unskilled jobs
• Can generate foreign exchange
• Can be built on existing infrastructure
• Can be developed with local products
• Can spread development
• Can complement production of other economic activities
• Can have high multiplier effects
	• Can broaden education
	• Can promote international understanding/peace
	• Can reduce:
	    Language barriers
	    Sociocultural barriers
	    Racial barriers
	    Political barriers
	    Religious barriers
	• Can reinforce preservation of heritage/tradition
	• Can promote worldview and membership in the global community
	• Can enhance appreciation of one's own culture

corporations; that it destroys nature and scenic resources; that it commoditizes people and their cultures; that it disrupts the structure of the host society. Today, as before, this second stand ranges from outright rejection of the earlier position to calculated pronouncements about undesirable consequences of tourism.

As subscribers to these two platforms still express their respective positions (though not in an organized fashion or unified voice), cross-firing between them, which was at its height in the 1970s, has been inevitable. These encounters, often charged with emotion, include exchanges of views and opposing stands as well as sharp criticism of each other's position. For any claim of the Advocacy Platform (Table 2.1), there has been a counterclaim by the Cautionary Platform (Table 2.2), a situation potentially not conducive to fruitful dialogues or discourses.

Table 2.2. Cautionary Platform on Tourism Consequences

Economic Costs	Sociocultural Costs
• Can cause inflation • Can result in high leakage • Can have seasonality and contribute to unemployment • Can be susceptible to change, rumor, spread of disease, economic fluctuation • Can result in unbalanced economic development • Can lead to extraneous dependency • Can increase demonstration effects • Can destroy resources and create visual pollution	• Can contribute to misunderstanding • Can generate sterotypes • Can lead to xenophobia • Can result in social pollution • Can commercialize the community and its culture, religion, arts, and more • Can threaten family structure • Can contribute to prostitution • Can increase instance of crime • Can induce conflicts in the host community

Adaptancy Platform: The How

Because the polarized debates between the Advocacy and Cautionary Platforms have been mainly concerned with the *impacts* of the industry, one then could argue that some alternative forms or adapted types of tourism would have lesser or fewer negative consequences than other options. Therefore, attention was gradually drawn to its alternative forms of development. This proposition fostered the formation of a third position in the 1980s: the Adaptancy Platform.

Armed with the earlier separate perspectives, this third position emerged by favoring those forms that are especially responsive to the host communities and their sociocultural, built, and natural environments and, at the same time, that provide tourists with new choices and rewarding experiences. The prescribed strategies have variously been known as agritourism, appropriate tourism, community-based tourism, controlled tourism, cottage tourism, cultural or ethnic tourism, ecotourism, farm tourism, green tourism, indigenous tourism, lifeseeing tourism, nature tourism, paratourism, responsible tourism, rural tourism, sensible tourism, small-scale tourism, soft tourism, and sustainable tourism; the list is still growing, with "no tourism" even named as an alternative by itself.

In general, the Adaptancy Platform argues that these forms are community centered, employ local resources, are relatively easier to manage, are not destructive, benefit host and guest groups alike, and even improve communication between them. Adapted tourism, regardless of its nature or scope, is presented as an informed set of alternative options to the present mass, commercialized, out-of-control, hard forms practiced almost everywhere. One of the latest alternatives, known as ecotourism, has attracted the attention of operators and governments, as well as researchers and academicians, with the former exploiting this for quick profits. However, these and other "alternative" forms, exploited or not, have emerged as partial remedies. But strategies of the Adaptancy Platform cannot accommodate the mass volume of tourists generated globally. While forms and practices can be influenced, the tourist volume can no longer be curtailed.

Knowledge-Based Platform: The Why

The collective positions of the Advocacy, Cautionary, and Adaptancy Platforms were among the main conditions and forces fostering a number of developments in the thinking about tourism. First came a general recognition by all, independent from their positions, that this is a *giant global industry*, that it caters to millions of tourists *daily*, and that both tourism and tourists *are here to stay*. Second, any development, tourism included, generates both desirable changes and unwanted consequences; and it is the *relationship* between the costs and benefits that should matter. Third, the general foci of the Advocacy and Cautionary Platforms on *impacts* and of the Adaptancy Platform on *development forms* represent only a *partial or limited* view. Fourth, therefore, if tourism is taken as a *whole* or a *system*—for an understanding of its underlying structures and functions— this would contribute to the formation of knowledge in this field. In turn, this would aid in further development of theoretical constructs on a phenomenon now evolved into a global institution and on a business turned into a mega-industry. It was due to these interrelated, processual, and assimilating insights that a fourth position, the Knowledge-Based Platform, emerged in the last decade of the 20th century.

This final platform, mostly occupied by members of the academic/research community, has been aiming at positioning itself on a scientific foundation and, at the same time, maintaining bridges with the other three platforms. For a balanced view, the resulting knowledge landscape upholds objectivity, with the bridges intended as accesses, not attachments, to other perspectives. Further, it systematically studies tourism's own structure; annexes it to various fields of investigation or disciplines; defines its place in this larger multidisciplinary context that generates and accommodates it; examines its functions at personal, group, business, government, and systems levels; identifies factors that influence and are influenced by it; and more. This all is meant to contribute to a *holistic* treatment of tourism—not just its *impacts* or *forms*. The main goal is the *formation of a scientific body of knowledge on tourism.*

With these processual developments almost simultaneously in progress, the early definitions of tourism, generally concerned with the number of miles traveled, reasons for travel, and money spent (an orientation typical to the Advocacy Platform), have continuously evolved. This shift has been in favor of framing holistic definitions that would include, among other things, the tourist-generating and -receiving systems and their interdependence and the total text and context that bring them to vitality. For example, tourism may be defined as the study of man away from his/her usual habitat, of the touristic apparatus and networks, and of the ordinary (home) and the nonordinary (touristic) worlds and their dialectic relationship. This, and even more recent articulations, as is the intent, have departed from the earlier notions designed to mainly measure tourism traffic or its economic magnitude, to instead view it as a total system, with economics as only one of its significant constituent dimensions. Such systemic attempts will undoubtedly continue into the next century, aiming for more refined definitions and holistic treatments of tourism as a scholarly field of investigation. Presently, this foundation and orientation is in its solidifying stage: the work of the Knowledge-Based Platform is gradually paying off.

The Scientification of Tourism

The Advocacy, Cautionary, Adaptancy, and Knowledge-Based Platforms, seen together, provide an overview of the formation and transformation of insights on tourism. But hidden in this general sketch are the specific conditions (catalysts, agents of change) that have contributed to this evolution and to the development of tourism knowledge. A review of this scientification process shows that tourism now has almost all properties and tools typically associated with the more established field of investigations.

Tourism as a University Subject

As is apparent from this discussion, the interest of the academic community in research has continued to increase with the passage of time. But research is one valued aspect of the academic world; instruction is another. Many universities have gradually expanded their course offerings to include tourism. In the early part of this century, several European universities had already established professorial chairs in tourism. Universities in the US and elsewhere discovered tourism much later. At the outset, it was the hotel management programs that added tourism to their curricula. Soon after, it also penetrated such programs or departments as business, leisure, recreation, and even social sciences. Today's offerings range from a single course/subject to minors and majors in tourism, at both undergraduate and graduate levels. Significantly, the number of universities offering advance degrees is on the rise. For several years now, some universities worldwide have even expanded their existing doctoral programs in such fields as education, recreation, and urban/regional planning to include tourism, with a few now offering independent doctorate degrees in tourism. Examination of degree programs and dissertations written on tourism reveals that this truly multidisciplinary field (Figure 2.1) is enjoying a growing rate of popularity on campuses, as both areas of instruction and research. But these developments did not take place in isolation. Other conditions and change agents also have been present.

Research Journals

The scientific role that *research* journals play in their respective fields requires no elaboration. In tourism there are several, of both older and more recent origins: (from North America) *Journal of Travel Research, Tourism Analysis, Annals of Tourism Research, Tourism, Culture & Communication*; (from Europe) *The Tourist Review* and *Tourism Management*; (from Asia) *Tourism Recreation Research* and *Asia Pacific Journal of Tourism Research*; (from the South Pacific) *The Journal of Tourism Studies* and *Pacific Tourism Review*; and this is only a small sample of English language periodicals. Today the number of English language academic journals in hospitality, tourism, and leisure is about 40. While each, with its wide range of contents and treatments, intends to meet certain objectives, together they structure and are structured by research efforts of a multidisciplinary community of scholars whose contributions can also appear in other forms and places. Their occasional special issues on specific themes provide added focused perspectives, still reinforcing tourism's connection to and dependence on other fields of investigation (Figure 2.1).

Publications

There is certain regularity about journals, assuring a continuous flow of research contributions. Through them, findings appear more frequently and more quickly, and hence contain more up-to-date information: the continuous and cumulative flow of knowledge is reassured. But books, monographs, references, and other publications serve similar purposes and their contributions to the advancement of knowledge are of paramount importance. The number of such publications was insignificant in the 1960s, more appeared in the 1970s, with still many more published in the 1980s, and the 1990s has already been a decade of abundance. Publishers, some of them among the most prestigious houses internationally, even produce book series committed to tourism. The latter, because of their thematic continuity, also assure the type of regularity inherent with journals' cumulative process. Free-standing books and the series, along with major reference books—

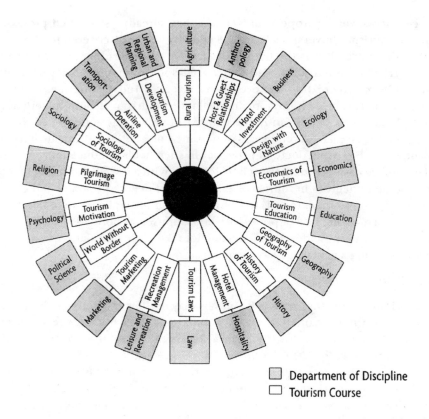

Figure 2.1. The multidisciplinary foundation of tourism studies.

such as the *Encyclopedia of Tourism* (Jafari, 2000)—are among significant contributions that collectively advance the scholarly position of tourism worldwide.

Research and Scholarly Groups

Still another structuring and structured force for this scientification process has been the formation of research interest groups, which come in many sizes, with varied systems of operation. In tourism, the number of such groups is not very large, almost all are membership associations, and they have somewhat similar goals and objectives. To build upon the existing efforts and past research accomplishments, such as those started in 1951 by Association Internationale d'Experts Scientifiques du Tourisme and in 1970 by the reorganized Travel and Tourism Research Association, the idea of a tourism academy was materialized with the formation of the International Academy for the Study of Tourism in 1988. The Academy, with its membership coming from the many fields represented in Figure 2.1, is naturally a body committed to the Knowledge-Based Platform, and hence it directly relates to the theme of this chapter, and therefore another tool and means of scholarship is now in place.

Operational Forces

For decades now, governments have recognized the importance of tourism. Though this has been mainly due to its economic potentials (Advocacy Platform), this stand has nevertheless enhanced its image in circles small and large, private and public. This, in turn, one can argue, has provided some of the impetus at work in the areas already noted. Further, as another set of forces or developments that has helped the scientification of tourism, one should acknowledge the works and functions of those organizations in or closely affiliated with tourism as a business. Such establishments are indeed very large in number and range from local to international levels. Chief among them is the World Tourism Organization, an intergovernmental agency affiliated with the United Nations. While its original raison d'être can be traced to tourism as a trade (and hence its connection to the Advocacy Platform), during recent years it has made giant strides in both recognizing and promoting tourism research and education. Its recent commitment to the latter, including establishment of formal ties with some 15 universities in Europe and elsewhere, speaks to this point.

Tourism Seminars

Still another set of active change agents advancing this scientification course is seminars or symposiums organized by many associations and interest groups, especially those committed to research and scholarship in their respective fields. Thus, the importance of conferences organized by tourism associations or institutions should also be recognized. They bring together researchers and industry experts with diverse disciplinary and professional backgrounds. Their seminar reports, some of which are published in journals, speak to this point, with the resulting proceedings and volumes sustaining the discourse well beyond the conferences themselves. Efforts of anthropology, geography, and sociology associations, as well as the academy, should be acknowledged here.

Training and Education

The scientification process and the use of the resulting body of knowledge directly relate to both of tourism's fields of theory and practice. One of several subjects or themes that concretely connects them together is training/education. At this juncture, it seems appropriate to use this subject to suggest how the knowledge as a whole and its two fields of theory and practice can best guide the present and future human resource development task, which is nowadays more and more assumed by colleges and universities worldwide—the very institutions that in the first place contributed to the development of the knowledge foundation in tourism. Their training and education mission (on the top of their research and scholarship roles) is not a minor task, as it directly relates to the work/performance of a workforce over 6 million strong in the US alone or over 120 million worldwide. The task does not become any simpler when knowing that this workforce is mostly unskilled and semiskilled, with only a small percentage placed in the management-administration-leadership cadre. Together the workforce forms a pyramid with the latter occupying the top and the former the middle and bottom layers

(Figure 2.2). In order to make the scope of this discussion manageable, only training and educating of the future generations is kept in mind, but without failing to
realize that the same body of knowledge can guide the fine tuning and upgrading/
updating of the present workforce at all layers.

In tourism, the training and education terms are used interchangeably, but here
"training" covers what is given to those who want to occupy "hands-on" jobs and
"education" to those interested in "minds-on" positions. As Figure 2.2 suggests, the
top and bottom positions stand in contrast to one another, and thus by commenting on one, the other is also defined. Recognizing the nature of the industry, the
top cadre's education must ingrain those multidisciplinary theories and tools that
best prepare for the diverse leadership and top-level management tasks in the
private and public tourism sectors. Figure 2.2 further suggests that education must
provide a "field vision," including a comprehensive understanding of the industry
sectors, of their interrelationship, of shifts and trends, of how these all relate to
broader sociopolitical systems that shape and control tourism, and more. In contrast, in the bottom, as shown, this vertical bar is narrowed downward to a minimal level; instead these workers (say, those who set tables in the banquet halls of
a convention hotel) are expected to simply perform a given task(s) prescribed to
them at their "work station."

Moreover, Figure 2.2 shows some other categorically distinctive differences
between these two opposite ends. For instance, the curriculum designed for the
"education" of this upper level must result in "conceptual ability," again nurtured

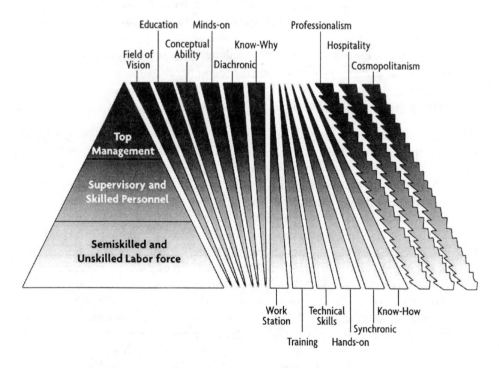

Figure 2.2. Tourism education–training continuum.

in appropriate multidisciplinary contexts. On the other hand, the bottom layer's "training" would teach "technical skills," whose bar is widest for this group and comes to a point for their counterparts on the top. Other paired bars include "minds-on" vs. "hands-on," "diachronic" (a vision of the future *à la* present and past) vs. "synchronic" (now and today), and "know-why" vs. "know-how"—a set of bars that, despite their apparent separations, are part and parcel of what constitutes education vs. training and distinguishes them from one another.

The third row of vertical bars relates more closely to whether people are to be placed in front or back positions of the industry, regardless of whether they enter the top or bottom layers. Obviously those prepared to deal with tourists need to have added education and training for this not-easy function. That is why the bars do not narrow up or down, but their scope throughout the pyramid reflects the degree of contact with tourists. "Professionalism" is important to the entire workforce, but manifests itself more in contact situations, as does "hospitality." To enlarge on the latter, it must be recognized that the mega-industry of this chapter is an art-and-science field at the same time, with hospitality being its "art" (or soul) and tourism its "science." But regardless of how this distinction between them is argued, still those who are in direct contact with tourists must have mastered the art of hospitality, to appropriately attract, receive, accommodate, and serve their customers coming from many regions, with diverse cultural backgrounds and expectations. Finally, "cosmopolitanism" further defines the concept and practice of hospitality. Education and training of those being prepared for front positions must include an understanding of the cultures of their tourist-generating markets, so that they feel comfortable to operate beyond their own immediate home culture. Cosmopolitanism here also suggests that the front people need to speak at least one of the languages of their main markets, again regardless at which layer of the pyramid they function.

In fact, Figure 2.2 makes more sense when it is viewed in the light of the earlier discussion on the four tourism platforms and the outlined evolutionary process. For instance, typically the advocacy groups show more interest in training and the knowledge-based show more interest in education of the workforce; the trade associations emphasize hands-on and academic circles emphasize minds-on; the industry pushes its trade publications and scholarly circles push their refereed journals, etc. Benefiting from this perspective, Figure 2.2, despite its simplicity, offers insights into curriculum development, range of subjects to be taught, degree of abstractness, techniques of instruction, types of fieldwork, and more. But, even more significantly, this education/training example becomes a commentary on what the new knowledge base is offering to tourism, whether regarded as an industry, as a field of investigation, or both—a distinction that can begin to blend as the landscape of knowledge is being better mapped, marked, and populated. This multidisciplinary foundation provides what is needed to study all tourism aspects, individually yet coherently, including education and training issues that have been discussed for decades. To mention here a newer research theme, the debate on sustainable tourism development is also getting its inspiration, force, and substance from the very evolutionary foundation that can now advance this development theme. Education/training, sustainable development, cultural issues, costs and benefits of tourism, etc., all are becoming even more promising themes as the landscape of knowledge grows in size and sophistication in years ahead, with the old, new, and still unrevealed dimensions of tourism begin to unfold more fully.

The Awaiting Future

The above discussion on the four platforms, the transformative forces or catalysts, the text and context of these in structuring and shaping training and education efforts and outlooks, provide informative retrospective and ongoing insights on tourism—both as a realm of concepts and as a field of operations. This may now be coupled with a prospective view beyond the present scholarly footholds and operational matters, toward scientific and developmental horizons ahead.

Tourism as a Scholarly Field

The cumulative process of building a scientific foundation for tourism—brick by brick, block by block—will continue. As in the past, the social sciences will make substantial contributions to its formation and solidification. Other fields related to the study of tourism will also further define and refine their areas of commonality with tourism. Because it relates to several phenomena and because its study utilizes theories and methods of many disciplines, tourism will assume a truly multidisciplinary position in the academic world. With this foundation in place, its own emerging theories and methods will be borrowed by the same disciplines that earlier on had generously contributed to the formation of its scientific corpus. Furthermore, tourism research will be used at a growing rate in other disciplines' publications and journals in order to illustrate issues native to their own domains. This will be so because tourism has special and unique perspectives to offer, and even more so as it becomes a common phenomenon to which people can readily relate (due to the growing awareness about its place in society and the economy). Moreover, a larger number of Ph.D. dissertations, dealing with old and new dimensions of tourism, will continue to be produced by students majoring in a variety of established fields, as well those doing tourism by itself.

Presently, some disciplinary associations have established tourism interest groups within their formal organizational structures. With the growing importance of tourism, more disciplinary associations will establish bridges with it. These will include formation of additional interest groups by associations dealing with anthropology, ecology, economics, history, leisure, marketing, management, political science, psychology, and more (again, some of these are already in place). As the numbers of these disciplinary interest groups increase, they will begin to sponsor joint seminars or congresses. It is indeed at such gatherings that creative minds will have the opportunity to truly advance this multidisciplinary tourism discourse.

With these and other scientific achievements in progress and with sustained growth in tourism jobs, additional universities will commit to offering undergraduate and graduate programs in this field. Offering doctoral degrees will attract the attention of even more prestigious universities. Many universities will offer their tourism programs within the presently typical departments/schools, with leisure and recreation departments paying closer attention to tourism for an eventual integration. More university departments, such as those in the social sciences, will first offer tourism courses, then minors, and later majors. This could partly be due to their present lack of ability to attract sufficient numbers of students to their own majors and partly due to the relevancy and attractiveness of tourism to their fields. On the other hand, additional universities will establish free-standing tourism schools or colleges. Their offerings would include general tourism degrees, with specialization options in hospitality management, marketing, planning and development, public administration, tourism in developing countries, and international tourism, to name a few.

The privilege of enlarging the scientific base horizontally and vertically will turn into an obligation—for the tourism faculty to regularly utilize the existing body of knowledge and to productively contribute to its growth. This expectation is already in place in all established fields, and tourism will not be the exception. The present de facto publish or perish rule in tourism will assume a more prominent position among its faculty for retention, promotion, and tenure decisions.

A few universities have already established endowed tourism hospitality chairs. The scientific developments as well as further growth in the industry will increase the prospects of establishing additional chairs in many countries, developed and developing. As in the past, some of the new chairs will be created mostly with direct support from various segments of the industry. Further, as the scientific layers increase and as tourism becomes an even more recognized socioeconomic phenomenon, granting institutions would favorably consider research proposals in tourism, a noticeable shift from the present situation. This change will be both in respect to funding requests for dissertations and for independent research projects. Such favorable developments will be augmented with establishment of prestigious awards recognizing research scholarship in this field. These developments will boost tourism's reaches to a new height, alongside other established fields.

Tourism as an Operation Field

Ironically, the industry itself has not yet fully recognized and supported tourism research and scholarship. This will happen, but more gradually, especially as the number of decision-makers holding tourism degrees increases and as the industry begins to witness more progress through research. As well, responsible governmental bodies and trade associations will not only incorporate more scientific substance and tools in performing their tasks, but will also produce more quality research works with application beyond their immediate parameters. This prospect will be further magnified as they favor hiring employees with advanced training in tourism. Both the industry and public agencies will pay closer attention to the noneconomic dimensions of tourism, with a growing percentage of their research budget set aside for nonmarketing studies. In general, the present wide gap between the research and operation camps will be desirably reduced and concretely bridged. The tripartite tourism academic–industry–government relationship will also further solidify.

Collaborative research and action between the operation and concept camps is also one of the desirable and expected outcomes. Many ongoing and emerging themes will be pursued in this joint fashion, including research on and application of, for example, shifting lifestyles and trends. It is often assumed that the future will be a natural extension of the past. But not exactly: people change, societies change, values change, needs and expectations change, and so do lifestyles. Such shifts in turn will define and redefine the future of the industry and its many products, as tourism reflects societal shifts.

Another example of joint research/action effort will be in the area of health and tourism. The new and emerging lifestyles encourage people to be, for example, more health conscious. People are exploring various alternatives to extend their lives, to live a healthier life, and to enjoy it fully. Right here an automatic connection between lifestyle à la health and tourism is made. Many alternative forms of tourism are favored because of this "healthy" notion, as this practice contributes to a healthier mind and body.

Work on the senior citizen market, as still another instance of collaboration, comes to mind. Changes in the lifestyle and the desire for a healthier body and mind are universal trends, cutting across race, class, gender, and age. Dealing with now such an enlarged scope, crowded with many variables, complicates the task of research. Still, lifestyle and health, both boosted with advancements in medicine, technology, and welfare systems, among others, have in turn led to another phenomenon: a sudden increase in the population of the third age, or senior citizens. Today senior citizens are much greater in number, they enjoy an invigorating lifestyle, and they are healthier. Further, many choose to retire at an earlier age in order to move on to the next phase of their lives sooner. With family and professional commitments left behind and prospects of a good life seen ahead, pursuits of a healthy, leisurely life—fueled with saved resources and an "unlimited" supply of just-accessed leisure time—becomes their new profession or religion, with tourism as the main means and end of this living journey. This suggests a massive movement of senior citizens endlessly zigzagging the globe. Studying this ever-increasing population—with its own mindset and philosophy, which "is not willing to die" but is instead "eager to enjoy life," as put in public media, both at home and away for home, at near and far away destinations—would now mean connecting tourism to still other fields such as medicine and gerontology. Significantly, because away from home is where they mostly want to be, as often as possible, with the saved disposable income available to them, challenging, new, and creative alternatives emerge, in both fields of theory and practice. Tourism, this convoluted phenomenon, begins to unfold, with often less-than-apparent dimensions brought to new multidisciplinary focus.

To conclude, in a short period of time, the study of tourism has taken several major strides, lifting off from a mainly practical/applied springboard and landing on a small but growing scientific foundation. This transformative process has been benefiting from the insights of four schools of thought: Advocacy, Cautionary, Adaptancy, and Knowledge-Based Platforms. The latter, influenced by several favorable conditions and change agents, armed with multidisciplinary means and tools, has maintained its forward move on a definitive scientific course, now with a rather clearer sense of direction.

Today, as the new century is starting, it is quite evident that tourism is finally assuming its scholarly position among research and academic circles. All signs suggest that this trend will continue, toward new frontiers of knowledge. This development will further enhance tourism's status among formal institutions and in society at large. But attainment of the ultimate scientification goal will depend on the support and the type of influence exerted by the scholarly community itself, grant institutions, government bodies, associations, and the tourism industry. "A journey of a thousand miles," a Chinese proverb says, "begins with a single step." Obviously tourism is already beyond the initial steps, its scientific journey is clearly in progress, aiming at new frontiers, heading to new horizons. The tourism landscape of knowledge is now sketched, as demonstrated by the contents of the 25th anniversary issue of *Annals of Tourism Research* and *Encyclopedia of Tourism*, among others.

The prime beneficiaries of this achievement will be the tourism industry itself and governments who, on behalf of their constituencies, capitalize on it as it utilizes the growing store of basic and applied knowledge to everyone's advantage, especially the total host system. Informed holistic research and operational strategies—which think future, but act today, which project globally but develop locally—provide necessary principles, practices, and philosophies guiding the process. The field, though, is mindful that its scientification course is a journey, not the destination. The goal remains the development of a body of knowledge that is thematically organized and coherently synthesized, which defines and consumes a distinct phenomenon of related concepts and actions, fields of theory and practice, called tourism.

Acknowledgments—This chapter is based on the author's earlier (joint) publications, particularly Jafari (1990, 1994, 1997a, 1997b), Jafari and Aaser (1988), Jafar and Ritchie (1981), and Jafari and Pizam (1996). In particular, in his capacity as Editor-in-Chief (1973–2000) of *Annals of Tourism Research*, he has benefited from the offerings of its past volumes (see *Annals* special 25th anniversary issue 1999). Earlier versions of this chapter have been presented at three international conferences. The author has also benefited from the interactions and comments received at these gatherings.

Chapter 3

Secular Ritual:
A General Theory of Tourism

Nelson H. H. Graburn

Tourism, defined by the sentence "a tourist is a temporarily leisured person who voluntarily visits a place away from home for the purpose of experiencing a change" (Smith, 1989b, p. 1), may not exist universally, but in many ways it is functionally and symbolically equivalent to other institutions—calendrical festivals, holy days, sports tournaments—that humans use to embellish and add meaning to their lives. In its special aspect—travel—tourism has its antecedents in other seemingly more serious institutions such as medieval student travel, the Crusades, and European and Asian pilgrimages.

It is my contention that tourism is best understood as a *kind of ritual*, one in which the special occasions of leisure and travel stand in opposition to everyday life at home and work. This general theory applies to all forms of tourism. Therefore, we have to understand the nature of tourist travel and experience in terms of the *contrasts* between the special period of life spent in tourist travel and the more ordinary parts of life spent at home while working. Tourism experiences are meaningful because of their difference from the ordinary and they reflect the home life from which the tourists stem. Thus, any one kind of tourist experience (e.g., a week in Paris) can mean something very different in the life of tourists from, for example, urban New York, metropolitan Tokyo, or rural California. Indeed, for some people a week in Paris would be too ordinary and boring, whereas for other people, from very different social backgrounds, it might be too daunting and exciting and they would never undertake such a vacation. Thus, we can see that the tourists' gender, class, occupation, and life stage are all significant in determining where tourists choose to go and what they think of the experience when they have been there.

Tourism: Rituals of Reversal

The ritual theory of tourism proposes that the motivations and compensations of tourism involve "push" and "pull" factors. Tourists leave home because there is something that they want to get away from, and they choose to visit a particular place because they believe that they will experience something positive there that they cannot easily experience at home. This kind of explanation involves the "ritual reversal" or "ritual inversion" of some aspects of life. Simple examples would include the winter migrations of Eastern Canadians to the Caribbean and of Scandinavians to the Mediterranean, when these northerners seek some warmth away from home, or when lower middle class Californians go to large hotels in Las Vegas or Reno at any time of the year and "live it up" by occupying large, well-appointed rooms and being served lavish meals (Gottlieb, 1982). Middle class Japanese who vacation in the hotels of Southeast Asia in the wintertime seeks both touristic goals: seasonal warmth and a luxurious style of life (Beer, 1993)—inversions of their cramped lives in cold Tokyo.

The felt needs of tourists, the things that they look for and forward to in their travels, are never the complete opposites to their home class position and lifestyle. For instance, erudite people don't want to become ignorant, although they may want a relaxing break, and good athletes don't try to become physically incompetent. The felt needs are indeed the product of, or an inherent part of, the values of the home class and lifestyle. Scandinavians and Canadians value sunshine and warmth; American college professors value culture and history and may seek more of it on their vacations; many obese people value thinness and may visit a special reducing establishment; and gourmets may partake of simple foods in their travels, but never bad foods—not willingly! So the temporary reversal sought is rarely an antithesis of their values but is a product of their cultural background, and the promised reward is supposed to satisfy the need in a direction of further enhancement of these values, not turn the tourist into an entirely different kind of person.

The claim that tourism is a secular ritual, embracing goals or activities that have replaced the religious or supernatural experiences of other societies, was strongly suggested by a recent television advertisement in the San Francisco Bay area (1997). It showed exciting scenes of young, fit people diving off cliffs into the sea, skiing down steep slopes, bungee jumping, and so on. At the end of these came a voice-over, "If you want a religious experience, why don't you try a **religious** experience!" as the scene moved to a shot of the Protestant evangelist the Rev. Billy Graham, who was about to bring his crusade to the area.

Tourism, Ritual, and Time

Tourism in the modal sense emphasized here is but one of a range of choices or styles of recreation or vacation. All of these ritualized breaks in routine define and relieve the ordinary. There is a long tradition in anthropology of the examination of these special events and institutions as markers of the passage of time. Vacations involving travel (i.e., tourism) are the modern equivalent for secular societies to the annual and lifelong sequences of festivals and pilgrimages found in more traditional, God-fearing societies. Fundamental is the contrast between the ordinary/compulsory work state spent "at home" and the extraordinary/voluntary metaphorically "sacred" experience away from home.

The stream of alternating contrasts provides the meaningful events that mark the passage of time. English anthropologist Leach (1961) suggested that celebratory events were the way in which people without clocks and calendars used to measure the passage of time, implying that those who have scientific calendars and other tacit reminders such as newspapers, TV, and radio rely only on the numerical calendar. I believe that even "scientific, secular" Westerners gain greater meaning from the personal rather the numerical in life. We are more satisfied and better recall loaded symbols marking the passage of time: for example, "that was the year we went to Rome" or "that was the summer our dog drowned at Brighton Beach" rather than "That was 1988," because the former identify the nonordinary, festive or sorrowful, personal events.

Our two lives—the sacred/nonordinary/touristic and the profane/workaday/at-home—customarily alternate for ordinary people, and are marked by rituals or ceremonies, as should be beginnings and ends of lives. For instance, after a period of work we celebrate with TGIF (Thank Goodness Its Friday), "happy hours," and going away parties, to anticipate the future state and to give thanks for the end of the mundane. The passing of each year is marked by the annual vacation (or by Christmas or a birthday); something would be wrong with a year in which these events didn't occur, as though we had been cheated of time! These repetitive events mark the cyclical passage of time just as in traditional Christian societies weeks would be marked by Sundays and church-going and the year would be marked by Easter, Harvest Festival, Advent, Christmas, and so on. These rituals have been called "rites of increase" or "rites of intensification" in agricultural or forager societies (Durkheim, 1912), but are generally better thought of as *annual cycle rites*. The types of holidays and tourism that fill these functions may be family occasions at home but, when they involve travel (e.g., weekends spent skiing or fishing, weeks spent on the beach or even longer trips traveling abroad), they are usually of the seasonal or "annual vacation" type, a form of re-creation, renewing us and making the world go round.

Life is not only cyclical, with the same time-marking events occurring again and again, but it is also progressive or linear, as we all pass through life by a series of changes in status, each of which is marked by different but similarly structured rituals. These life-stage marking events are called *rites of passage* and were first analyzed by French folklorist Arnold Van Gennep (1960); it his model that we shall follow in our analyses of tourism as ritual. Just as rites of passage (e.g., births, graduations, marriages, and funerals) are usually more significant rituals than ordinary cyclical events such as birthdays, Thanksgivings, or *Días de Los Muertos*, so rites of passage-type tourist experiences may be unusually intense (e.g., semesters abroad, honeymoons, or retirement cruises). But in the relatively individualistic, informal lives of the contemporary Euro-Americans, many rites of passage as kinds of tourism may be purposely self-imposed physical and mental tests (e.g., college-aged people trekking across continents trying to go as far as possible with little expenditure) (Cohen, 1973; Teas, 1988) or when recently broken up, divorced, or laid-off middle-class persons take "time off," for long sailing, walking, or cycling trips or other adventures (Frey, 1998; Hastings, 1988).

The Structure of Ritual and Tourism

For the present discussion our focus is consciously on the prototypical examples of tourism, such as long-distance travel to famous places or to visit exotic peoples, all in unfamiliar environments. However, even the most minimal kinds of tourism, such as a picnic in the garden, contain elements of the "magic of tourism." The food and drink might be identical to that normally eaten indoors, but the magic comes from the movement and the nonordinary setting. Conversely, a very special meal in the usual but specially decorated eating place may also, by contrast with the ordinary, be "magic" enough for a special celebration.

The alternation of sacred and profane states and the importance of the transition between them were first shown by the French sociologists Hubert and Mauss (1898) in their analysis of the almost universal ritual of sacrifice. They emphasized the sequential process of leaving the ordinary, that is, the sacralization that elevates the participants to the nonordinary state where marvelous things happen, and the converse of desacralization and return to ordinary life. "Each festival [and each tourist trip, we contend] represents a temporary shift from the Normal–Profane order of existence into the Abnormal–Sacred order and back again" (Leach, 1961, pp. 132–136). The flow of time has a pattern, represented in Figure 3.1.

Each festive or tourist event is a miniature life, with a happy anticipation, A–B, an exciting middle, C–D, and a bittersweet ending, D–F. The periods before A and after F are the mundane, everyday life, expressed in "That's life." The period C–D, the metaphorically "sacred," the "liminal" (see below) out-of-the-ordinary period, is the time of pilgrimage, travel, and tourism. These holidays (formerly "holy days") celebrated in vacations and tourism might be expressed as: "I was living it up, really living . . . I've never felt so alive." These changes in moral and spatial states are usually accompanied by aesthetic changes and markers. This is most obvious in the case of religious rituals and rites of passage, where colorful dresses and strikingly decorated settings are accompanied by chanting, singing, and music. In tourism, too, there may well be aesthetic and sensory changes, in clothing, settings, and foods, and even in touch and smell in the case of tropical beach holidays or Japanese hot springs tourism (Graburn, 1995b).

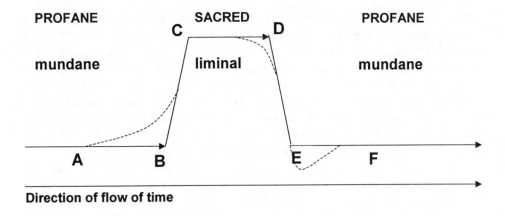

Figure 3.1. The ritual of tourism (modified from Feyerabend, 1997, p. 11).

Entries and Exits

The experience of being away on vacation (or going on pilgrimage) has important effects on the life of the traveler *outside* of the actual time spent traveling. Just as there are rituals of preparation, cleansing oneself, changing garments, perhaps putting on perfumes, or getting into the right frame of mind before undertaking religious rites such as pilgrimages, sacrifices, or Christian communion, so for the tourist and travelers there are rituals of preparation. These routinely involve not only planning, booking, and getting new clothes, gear, or luggage, but also social arrangements such as getting someone to water the garden, to look after the house and pets, to collect the mail, to leave numbers for emergencies, and often having parties for saying goodbye.

All of these necessary actions produce the pleasure of anticipation in the period A–B, the weeks and months before the actual take off B–C, but the feelings are also ambivalent. There may be misgivings about having made the right decisions, having laid out so much money, or having chosen the right traveling companions. There is also the remote possibility that one is saying goodbye forever, especially for long journeys to more distant places for greater lengths of time, as well as for the elderly or infirm either as travelers or those left behind. [For instance, when I went to graduate school in Canada (by ship) my mother at home in England died unexpectedly before I had my first trip home.] Nevertheless, this period of anticipation is extremely important: the pleasure being looked forward to itself shines on many of the preparations and is often what people "live for" in their workaday lives.

Going home, the journey D–F, the reentry process coming down from the "high" C–D, is equally important and fraught with ambivalence. Most people are reluctant to end a vacation, to leave the excitement and new friends, and to have to go back to work. In fact, a desire to get home and end the vacation might be seen as an admission that it didn't turn out to be as good as expected—that the recreation did not re-create. Some travelers even have twinges of sorrow during the period C–D, for instance on reaching the furthest point away from home (Frey, 1998), as they anticipate "the beginning of the end," the loss of new friends, or of the "paradise" visited.

The work of Berkeley undergraduate Amanda Feyerabend (1997) on the rituals and experience of the reentry and the reincorporation into normal society explains what is called "reverse culture shock." The term is a corollary to the notion of "culture shock"—the feeling of strangeness and inability to cope—that travelers feel when first in unfamiliar environments, such as tourists at point C in Figure 3.1. The reverse of this is the unhappiness felt when the tourist first gets back into his/her home and working environment (the period E–F in Figure 3.1). Feyerabend's informants suggested that while their normal home and work lives might be quite satisfying most of the time, that life suffered by comparison with the excitement, the out-of-the-ordinary special experiences that they had just left behind; thus, the lowered state of feelings at E–F is a relative measure of happiness.

Feyerabend also found that, in general, the length of time this ambivalent reverse culture shock lasted was approximately *half the length of time* the traveler had been away. For instance, after a 2-day weekend of skiing in the nearby Sierra

Nevada range, Berkeley students felt the next day (Monday) was a real let down, but they would feel OK by Tuesday. On the other hand, a student who returned from a year abroad in a foreign country might feel ill at ease and not quite at home for the whole next semester back in the US.

The Tourist Experience: Liminality and Communitas

Van Gennep (1960), building on the work of Hubert and Mauss, gave us the model commonly used for the analysis of rituals in general. While Hubert and Mauss emphasized the micro-rituals of preparation, separation, and reincorporation in their look at sacrifice, Van Gennep focused on the central period of the ritual, C–D, and the nature of the participants' experience. In his analysis he labeled the "sacred" out-of-the-ordinary period "liminal," meaning "on/over the threshold," following the European custom where a groom has to carry his bride over the threshold of their new home. At this liminal point the participants are neither in nor out, or as V. Turner (1974) put it, they are "betwixt and between." In some societies this special period is likened to a temporary death; the person in their old status dies, then follows the liminal period where they are bracketed off from ordinary time (or their ordinary place in the case of tourism), out of which they are reborn with their new status, e.g.,

> Bachelor → [groom @ wedding ceremony] → husband
> Single → [bride @ wedding ceremony] → wife

Victor Turner (1974) and his wife Edith Turner (Turner & Turner, 1978) further examined this period of *liminality* in African rituals and Christian pilgrimages, and they noted: "If a pilgrim is half a tourist, then a tourist is half a pilgrim" (p. 20). Turner stressed that for the participants, those to be transformed in the ritual or the travelers as pilgrims and tourists, the normal social structure of life, work, and family roles, age and gender differences, and so on tend to become looser or disappear. This leveling he called "anti-structure" though, of course, these participants are always surrounded by others carrying out their usual structured roles (e.g., priests or shamans at rituals, and guides, hoteliers, and food workers for pilgrims and tourists). Turner suggested that this leveling of statuses ideally sought outside of home and work structures produces a special feeling of excitement and close bonding among the participants, which he called *communitas*. This state is often signaled by a reduction in marked differences, with all pilgrims wearing the same clothes or all Club Med clients in their beach wear, and with people addressing each other as equals, and sharing the same foods, drinks, accommodations, pleasures, and hardships. While consulting for Club Med, I explained this ritual model to a number of *chefs de villages* and *G.O.s* (*gentils organisateurs*) who replied with a flash of understanding: "Of course, and the hard part of our job is to keep our customers 'up' in the state of communitas for their seven days non-stop!"

This liminal state, this special human feeling of communitas, may be examined and understood in a variety of ways. In lay language "going on a trip" usually refers to a journey but it can refer to a an "altered state of consciousness" (ASC) brought on by drugs or alcohol, and a special religious or magic experience; "trip" literally means away from the ordinary. Such experience may be called "a high" after which there is a "let down" or a "come down" (i.e., period C–D followed by D–F in Figure 3.1.), and a "high" is opposed to a feeling of depression or a "low," the negative ASC experienced in period E–F. The special state of consciousness experienced during a "trip" was illuminated when I was discussing Feyerabend's findings with my undergraduate class on tourism. Some students pointed out that the "reverse culture shock" (E–F), lasting half as long as the period of absence (C), paralleled the students' common belief that the time it takes to get over a serious love affair or a broken friendship is half as long as the relationship lasted, putting the "magic" of tourism and pilgrimage into the same emotional category as love and friendship!

Variations on a Theme: Different Strokes for Different Folks

Our analysis of tourism as ritual and the equation of the feelings and meaning of the trip with other human experiences does not mean that all tourism experiences are the same any more than all rituals are the same. Turner and others have characterized the state of communitas as being: "high," "liminal" (or liminoid when not part of a truly religious experience,), a state of homogeneity, equality, and humility among the participants, a period of transition, magic, or otherworldliness. For today's tourists, the vacation away from home might be described as above, but may also be described as "away," "timeless," a time of freedom, play, mindless spending, and attention to the past or the future (cf. Dann, 1996).

The range of tourist experiences has best been outlined by Israeli sociologist E. Cohen in his "Phenomenology of Tourist Experiences" (1979a). Here he takes into account the equation I have suggested between today's tourism and more spiritual pursuits such as pilgrimage, by placing such serious pursuits at one end of his continuum. At this serious end, the traveler is seeking a very important or "sacred" experience or place "out of this world," a sacred center spiritually more important than anything at home. These "existensional" tourists or pilgrims are on a true exploration and many are so moved by the experience attained or the place visited that they stay there and never go home or, in a more practical sense, they never want to go home. Thus, American Jews, having visited Israel, may emigrate there; North American mainlanders may retire to Hawaii or San Franciscans to the Mendocino County coast. The nature of such tourists' experiences may well be spiritual rather than patently religious; one may feel deeply moved by "communing with nature." Others, atheist or agnostic, might follow the old European pilgrimage way through northern Spain, the Camino de Santiago, and have profoundly moving, even life-changing experiences both along the way and on reaching the cathedral in Santiago (Frey, 1998).

At the other end of Cohen's continuum are the mere diversionary or recreational tourists, who never seriously doubt their commitment to their home lifestyle, but just want a simple change—perhaps a change of climate or season, a temporary change of recreation or sports—and have very little desire to explore or seek new experiences. And in the middle of the continuum are the more exploratory tourists, who may make considerable efforts to go to out-of-the-way places, may try to learn foreign languages, or may live temporarily like foreign peoples. These "experiential" and "experimental" tourists are fascinated by difference, like to get close to others, and like to immerse themselves in different environments (e.g., jungle ecotourists, Middle Eastern *souks*, or visitors to remote Nepalese villages). Such people, often young adults without much money or work experience, but probably well educated by their home standards (Cohen, 1973; Teas, 1988), have the exploratory urge and the *cultural self-confidence* (Graburn, 1983) to get out of their shell and experiment with different lifestyles.

Plus ça Change, Plus c'est la Même Chose (The More Things Change, the More It's the Same Thing)

This chapter claims that tourism is a manifestation of a need for a change, and that the change the tourist seeks depends on what perceived touristic attractions would satisfy something not fully met at home. In this concluding section, this general proposition is explored by some specific cases, pointing in particular to the social historical contexts.

In the contemporary Western world and in modern Japan, tourism is the opposite to work; it is one kind of that recent invention: re-creation. It is a special form of play involving travel and "getting away from it all" (i.e., from work, including homework and housework). There is a symbolic link between work + staying and play + travel. Most people feel they ought to go away when they have holidays, and never to go on a vacation might be an indication of sickness or poverty, or extreme youth or old age. Able-bodied adults who don't take holidays might be thought of as poor, unimaginative, or the "idle rich." For the middle classes, this going away on holiday is supposed to be a worthwhile, even a stimulating, creative, or educational experience (see below); for such people staying at home can be "morally excused" by participating in some creative activity, such as remodeling the house, redoing the garden, or seriously undertaking painting, writing, or sports.

Sociologist Dean MacCannell (1989) has powerfully expressed another instance of this theory in *The Tourist: A New Theory of the Leisure Class*, claiming that the educated middle classes are the sector of our present population who are the most alienated, contrary to Marx's 19th century assertions. MacCannell shows that the urban and suburban middle classes feel that their lives are overly artificial and meaningless, lacking deep feelings of belonging and authenticity. These are thought to exist elsewhere, especially in the simpler lives of other peoples such as family farmers, manual workers and craftsmen, and "primitive peoples." This missing authenticity is thought to lie, above all, in the past, as indicated by English geographer David Lowenthal (1985) in *The Past is a Foreign Country*. Thus, historical, cultural, and ethnic forms of tourism have become increasingly popular, all of them catering to one form or another of modernity's nostalgia for the premodern (Graburn, 1995b). MacCannell also shows us that the producers of tourist packages and displays understand these longings and are capable of "manufacturing" authentic Others and Pasts, so that the unfortunate tourists are once more faced with the artificial and commercial in their quest for "reality" and the untouched. One popular arena for getting in touch with the true and the pure is Nature itself, which is often sought in its wilder forms by Euro-American campers, backpackers, and ecotourists, and in more managed versions by the equally alienated urban

Japanese (Graburn, 1995a). The world's tourist industry, in its advertising and its packaged offerings, must paradoxically create the illusion that the tourists are, by purchasing their services, getting satisfaction of their needs.

While MacCannell's work is a brilliant analysis of educated Westerners, it is not a universal theory. Many people in Europe and North America are not necessarily seeking the particular ritual inversion from "fake to authentic culture"; indeed, it has been shown that this "moral" concern with authenticity correlates with years of education. This search for the pure and the Other, which Urry (1990) has called the "Romantic" gaze, is supplemented by a more direct, communal, and, some would say, unsophisticated (perhaps a better term is unpretentious) kind of enjoyment he calls the "Collective" gaze. The latter is typical of the "working classes," who are more gregarious and derive as much pleasure from the company they keep as the places they visit. Indeed, R. Campbell (1988) has shown that city bus drivers often return to their places of work on their days off, just to socialize with their coworkers. Similarly, Japanese *salarymen* and other groups of male workers often go on trips together, leaving their families at home. Hence, Japanese women often travel in single-sex groups, and children travel in school groups.

The research focus on the "gaze"—the visual practice of sightseeing—has also been challenged by those whose research shows that the changes desired may be sensual or tactile. Selänniemi (1994a) found that Scandinavians wintering in the Mediterranean or elsewhere in the "south" want a thoroughly Scandinavian vacation, but one in which they can soak up the sun, lie on the beach, or play simple sports. Jokinen and Veilola (1994) have criticized tourism theorists in general for overemphasizing the visual, the sightseeing quest, because that is the touristic goal of the educated class to which the tourism theorists themselves belong.

In conclusion, this chapter has taken care in using the ritual model not to see all tourism as one individual might experience it, nor should it be expected that ritual reversals are all-encompassing. In fact, tourists on holiday are seeking specific reversals of a few specific features of their workaday home life, things that they lack or that advertising has pointed they could better find elsewhere. Other than obtaining some straightforward goals, whether they be warmth for northerners, weight loss for the overweight, history for the culturally hungry, or immersion in nature for bored urbanites, tourists generally remain unchanged and demand a lifestyle not too different from that at home. Rarely do the timid become bold, the neat become messy, the educated become dumb, the monolingual become polyglot, the frigid become sexy, or the heterosexual become gay, except when these are the specific goals of the trip. Gottlieb (1982) has shown how tourists may play "Queen [or Peasant] for a Day" with temporary changes in life or class style, and E. Cohen (1973, 1979b) and Frey (1998) have described some of the more rigorous touristic choices for the young or the alienated moderns, but most tourists on their seasonal and annual vacations want to enjoy their own chosen pursuits and come back refreshed as better versions of their same old selves.

SECTION 2

THE NATURE OF TOURISM

Chapter 4

The Nature of Tourism

Valene L. Smith

The ice has frozen on Kotzebue Sound, and only a few "salt water" families are still at the coast, where we hunt seal at breathing holes and fish for tomcod through the ice. The sod-covered igloos are warm but we miss our friends. The "fresh water" Inuit left before freeze-up, going upriver to winter homes to hunt caribou and to set trap lines. But someone will come later by dog team and invite us to their camp, maybe up the Noatak (River) for a visit . . . we can be the guests, and our sledges will carry muktuk and fish as gifts. With our good dog teams, we can arrive in two sleeps. We love to travel in winter, in the clear, cold nights when the stars sparkle and sheets of color swish across the sky. We hear the sound, and know it is the Spirits playing football.

If it is a good year, with enough food, maybe we will stay 5 or 6 sleeps . . . and dance and sing. We look forward to these visits with our ilyaga *(relatives) and our friends. They have stories to tell, and new babies to see, and so do we. . . .*

Anthropologists describe the events of birth, marriage, and death—with their respective rites of passage—as the age markers of an individual life. Often one has little control over these rituals—in much of the world even marriage was arranged or spousal choice limited by population size, as was true for Inuit. The events of travel were the social time markers of Inuit lives, just as tourism defines our lives today. As Graburn noted in Chapter 3, our journeys are often our best remembered events. Aboriginal tourism, with its activities of the journey, the visiting, the socializing, and the learning, provided the same break in the monotony of their lives as does the weekend "get-away" or vacation for modern society.

The term to *tour* derives from a Latin origin: to make a circle trip and return to one's home. To vacation comes from a verb, *vacare*, meaning to vacate the house. To *travel*, from *travail*, means to labor or to work and, by contrast, a *holiday* is a day exempt from work. Although these subtle meanings are now blurred, some individuals readily admit that travel is "hard work," involving hours of waiting for transportation, sleepless night, poor food, and uncomfortable conditions. The range of experience between luxury and discomfort is often great, at least in activity if not in price. Some adventure travelers—especially those making long treks in high mountains, rock climbing, and river rafting—seek hardship as a form of physical or mental self-testing. Other tourists anticipate vacation as a time for *fun*, to be carefree, and to socialize, and disdain rigorous activity to relax on a beach or to sightsee. The travel industry has developed an enormous range of options, to meet all tastes, but many maintain the essence of the social time markers. An American travel agent (Tansey, 1999) adopted for her agency the slogan, "Memorable Vacations to Recreate Yourself," because a vacation is "a time of re-creation . . . a journey of the mind and spirit."

Tourist Motivations

The recreational travel that now spans all seven continents provides multiple levels of comfort and exertion. It involves transportation ranging from supersonic jets to camel safaris and walking tours. This vast contemporary diversity is the by-product of consumer interest, and forms the *demand* side of tourism. The vast array of products, including modes of transportation, types of accommodation, large- and small-boat cruises, and literally thousands of tours, stems from the *supply* side of the industry. These offerings are constantly adjusted as tourist motivations change, under the aegis of fashion, crisis, new technology, and world view. The motivations for travel rest on the basic philosophical foundation (Dann, 1981) that tourists are simultaneously "pushed" from their homes by the desire to escape what Graburn terms the "profane" and are "pulled" by the destination and its attractions, to fulfill some vague illusory expectations. Tourist motivations are thus a mix of push–pull and multiple other factors, including the role and the influence of the culture brokers (see Chapter 21). Motivations are also influenced by time (calendrical, historical, and generational), by age and gender, by the ethnicity of the guest and also that of the host. Other motivational influences include the nature of the attractions, the destination, and the strength and nature of the media, including motion pictures, advertising, infomercials, and the available descriptive literature including travel magazines and guidebooks (Dann, 1996). The media and the Internet are progressively more important elements in the decision-making process. The combined magnitude of these factors contributes to the difficulty of defining and describing travel motivations.

Research Interests

The "why" of travel and the choice of destination are important topics for the planning and management of tourism. The scholarly community has broad interests in human behavior, and it seeks data about the psychological and social processes involved in travel motivation and destination decision-making. Three examples of motivational research—descriptive, psychological, and quantitative—are presented below.

By contrast, the travel industry strives to meet visitor demand and satisfy expectations with product diversity suitable for a range of ages and interests. The preferred industry data are usually obtained from market surveys, which are largely conducted in-house or by consulting agencies. Unfortunately, most surveys are not published or are copyrighted because they are product specific in a highly competitive market environment. However, Travel Industry of America (TIA) holds an annual Travel Outlook conference at which industry speakers summarize the year's business and forecast the year to come. A published summary appears annually as *(Year) Outlook for Travel and Tourism* (the 2000 volume is US$195). TIA also undertakes industry-level research on requested topics. Their publication, *The Minority Traveler* (TIA, 200), is an update of a focused study (non-TIA members US$195) that surveys education and occupation in relation to travel habits of three ethnic minorities: African-Americans, Hispanic-Americans, and Asian-Americans, compared with all Americans (dominantly white). Combined, these three minorities represent 26% of the US population. The sample included 50,000 US households. Summary data identified the Asian-Americans as the minority group that traveled the most, spent more money per trip, stayed longer in a single hotel, traveled less frequently with their children, and spent the least amount of time shopping. However, distinctions in travel behavior among the three named minorities and the general population were all almost negligible. Linking historic origins, the primary domestic destinations for African-Americans were southern states such as Texas and Georgia; Hispanic Americans went to California, Texas, and Florida, while Asian-Americans who were more likely to gamble than all others listed their top destinations as California and Nevada. This information assists industry carriers to develop special fares of interest to ethnic travelers.

A 2001 TIA publication, *The Profile of Travelers Who Participate in Gambling* (nonmembers US$195), noted that gambling accounts for 7% of all US travel, or 72.8 million person trips in 2000 (see Chapter 5). Research of this type identifies market niches and helps direct advertising funds to appropriate peer and special interest publications

Other research interests include the preferred travel modes of older versus younger travelers. Why are some people nontravelers, and how could they be encouraged to travel? What factors support the popularity of cruises? Is there a significant market for space tourism? Answers to these questions are marketing guidelines and are specifically useful in the allocation of advertising funds. The identified market niches—whether youth travel, singles travel, senior travel, or business travel—focus advertising copy into peer group publications.

The travel agent researches individual clients. In a single meeting, the agent must try to satisfactorily match the stated interests (or vague ideas) of a previously unknown client with a specific product. Here, observation and intuition depend on a rapid assessment of the would-be traveler in terms of the "three As": Age (a potential guide to gender and peer group interests); Ability (to pay, which suggests a recommended category of services); and Agility (mental and physical appearance, indicative of mobility, stamina, and health). The agent thus becomes the *initial* mediator between the client, his/her motivations for travel and expectations, and the selection of an appropriate product. Sometimes termed "dealers in dreams," the agent as culture broker is often the first to be blamed for a poor choice or a bad experience.

The three interest levels—academia, travel industry, and travel agent—support the need for research as a planning tool but with due regard for the enormous diversity of people. All tourist-travelers are individuals whose ideas have been shaped by heritage and education, and whose personal and professional lives are structured by training and occupation. Their motivations are often time and place specific. Riley, Baker, and Van Doren (1998) document that movie-induced tourism frequently draws increased visitation to the site of a motion picture scene, with the percentage of visitors increasing annually after its release. Conversely, a terrorist act or war can have an immediate and chilling negative impact upon travel (see Chapter 26). Mega-events such as the World Cup or Olympic Games often spur habitual nontourists to travel as sports spectators, although they might deny they were "tourists." Whatever the motivation for travel, efforts to understand travel behavior have both theoretical and practical value.

Academic Motivational Research

The Descriptive Approach

Early in post-World War II travel, the psychologist authors of *Individual in Society* (Krech, Crutchfield, & Ballachey, 1962) undertook an analysis of tourist behavior and drafted a 12-point approach based on the travel appeals to the visitor and the resulting experiential rewards (Table 4.1). The concept is historically signifi-

Table 4.1. Twelve Types of Travel Appeals

Types of Potentially Rewarding Experience	Rationale	Potential Type of Reward		
		Sensory	Social	Ego-Satisfying
Direct-result experience	Northwest: fastest way to the Orient	Arrive relaxed and refreshed	Pleasant people await you in Mexico	Virginia is for lovers
In-use experience	You'll never wait in line at Hyatt	Escape the winter's cold in warm sunny Florida	Fly the friendly skies of United	Equatoriana's attractive, mutilingual stewardesses are chosen and trained to pamper and please you
Incidental-to-use experience	Coming or going nobody gets you out of the airport faster than Hertz	Just to dig a toe into the soft sand of Bermuda is to feel young	You'll want to be seen in Barbados	A tour for the discriminating traveler

Note: The peak of an earlier main class of wants must be passed before the next "higher" want can being to assume a dominant role. Generally, as psychological development takes place, the number and variety of wants increase.
Source: Reproduced from D. Krech, R. Brutchfield, and E. Ballachey, 1962, *Individual in Society*, p. 77, with permission from McGraw-Hill Book Company.

cant, as the era predates mass tourism, and the content phrases are essentially advertising slogans of destinations or carriers.

Soon after, J. Thomas (1964), writing in the journal of the American Society of Travel Agents (ASTA), offered to the travel industry a list titled "Eighteen important travel motivations" (Table 4.2). The time frame again predates mass tourism, and the topics were useful classificatory devices for an industry at the threshold of new growth.

In 1973, Stanley C. Plog published his first diagram, Distribution of Population by Psychographic Types (Figure 4.1), shown here in its 1991 format. The descriptive bell-shaped curve, rooted in demographic data, has become a much-cited indicator of tourist types and associated destinations.

In brief, allocentrics are the travel doers, ready to try new products, and they exercise more intellectual curiosity about the tourism experience. The psychocentrics prefer hospitality that is more like home and activities that are physically less challenging. The case study on the Finnish tourists (see Chapter 6) is a near-classic example of psychocentric tourism.

Plog (1998), as Chief Executive Officer (CEO) of Plog Research Inc., updated his nomenclature of tourist types, substituting Venturers for Allocentrics, and Dependables for Psychocentrics. Further, and somewhat parallel to the Resort Cycle (Figure 7.1), Plog suggests that the rise and fall of destinations is related to the

Table 4.2. Eighteen Important Travel Motivations

Education and Culture
To see how people in other countries live, work, and play
To see particular sights
To gain a better understanding of what goes on in the news
To attend special events

Relaxation and Pleasure
To get away from everyday routine
To have a good time
To achieve some sort of sexual or romantic experience

Ethnic Heritage
To visit places one's family came from
To visit places one's family or friends have gone to

Other
Weather
Health
Sports
Economy
Adventure
One-upmanship
Conformity
Participation in history
Sociology, a desire to get to know the world

Source: Reproduced from J. Thomas, 1964, "What Makes People Travel," in *ASTA Travel News*, p.65, with permission.

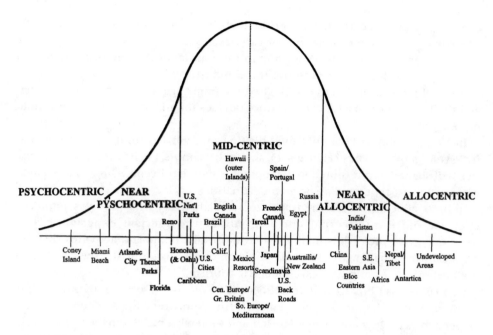

Figure 4.1. Psychographic positions of destinations. (Reprinted from Stanley C. Plog, 1991, *Leisure Travel*, with permission of John Wiley & Sons, Inc.)

interests and activities of these two tourist types. Venturers are usually frequent travelers who also spend more income on travel and, having visited an area once, they move on to new adventures. The Near-Venturers follow, and they are described as the "destination planner's dream" because they have plenty of money to spend, like what they find, and are welcome guests. However, when they leave due to excessive commercialization, they are followed by the Centrics and Near-Dependables, who prefer to visit the touristy well-known spots "because the very image of popularity suggests to them that it must be a good place or it wouldn't attract so many people" (Plog, 1998, p. 262). The Dependables follow, stay fewer days, and spend less per diem, so the type of guest has changed.

In summary, as the quality of the experience changes, the number of visitors initially increases but the per person visitor yield (or income) declines (Plog, 1998, p. 262). As numbers increase, it literally "wears out" the physical and social environment. This sequential development is singularly important because it is the usual progression of *ecotourism* (see Chapter 14) that initially attracts the up-scale adventure market but, following the adage that success breeds success, as more facilities are constructed to service more visitors, the pristine area devolves into mass tourism. The profitability associated with consumerism often destroys the original product.

In the US, residential address lists are compiled (and available for purchase by advertisers) based on census data, and can detail household income, ethnicity, household size, number of children, and/or other statistics as needed. To tie his

Venturer/Dependable categories with actual tourist markets, Plog (1994, p. 254) links the annual Venturer household income level with specific travel industry suppliers, as airlines target annual household incomes above US$60,000; first-class and luxury hotel chains target US$80,000; distant travel operators target US$100,000; and luxury cruise lines target US$125,000. Tourism to Antarctica exemplifies the Plog model, as it was a Venturer destination beginning with the first annual cruise season in 1966 (Headland, 1994) with small ice-reinforced vessels carrying about 70 passengers. In 1981, the cruise ship *World Discoverer* pioneered the route from Chile to New Zealand via Antarctica. Minimum tariff for this 30-day voyage was US$11,000, identified in a front-page *Wall Street Journal* article (January 11, 1981) as "the world's most expensive cruise." Seventy venturesome Allocentrics were aboard (V. Smith, 1994). By 1999 there were 12 ships regularly cruising Antarctica each austral summer, some with 500 passengers and occasionally one with 1200 passengers. The cost is now sharply reduced to US$4000–5000 but the Dependable Psychocentrics seem not to mind that the vessels pass like ferry boats and passengers wave to each other.

The Psychologic Approach

The American psychologist Abraham Maslow (1970) developed the theory of self-actualization as a succession of incremental steps through which an individual could achieve his/her full potential (although few actually did so). P. Pearce (1993) suggests that "like a career at work, people have a career in their tourist behavior" (p. 125). Using a Maslow-type diagram, the Tourist Career Ladder (Figure 4.2) is a

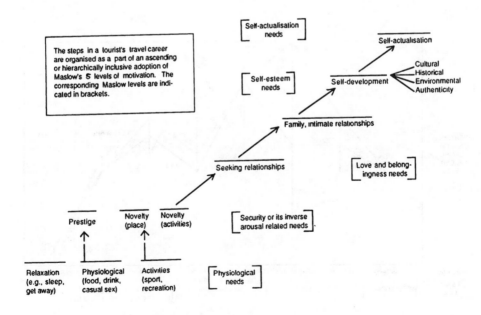

Figure 4.2. Suggested steps in tourists' travel careers. (Reprinted from P. Pearce, 1988, *The Ulysses Factor: Evaluating Visitors in Tourist Settings,''* p. 29, with permission from Springer-Verlag.)

series of steps that show an individual's concerns for biological needs, safety and security needs, relationship development and extension needs, special interest and self-development needs, and, finally, fulfillment or self-actualization. Tourists can enter the hierarchy at different stages, assuming that "while tourists initially enjoy physiological type experiences, more experienced travelers may use travel for the development of relationships, self-esteem purposes and even self-actualization motives" (P. Pearce 1988, p. 28).

Pearce further examined the relation between tourist motivations and their attitudes and behavior in relation to the chosen activity or destination. It is relatively apparent, for example, that even allocentrics, looking at a destination as distant and forbidding as Antarctica, would have different motivations and select their itinerary accordingly. Young, hardy adventurers might opt to ski across the continent, as some have done; the young but not so hardy might be content to fly into the South Pole, another realistic option. Able-bodied but older visitors might choose to explore aboard an ice-breaker whereas the mature sightseer would select a comfortable cruise ship that offered a casino and nightly entertainment. All four options are currently available. Age and gender are obvious variants in travel motivation but so are education, affluence, prior travel experience, and the all-important, word-of-mouth information provided by friends and travel companions.

Theme parks are an important domestic travel destination, with particular appeal to youths (an age group whose tourist motivations are seldom considered). In a theme park adaptation of the five stages of the travel career ladder, Pearce (1993, p. 127) collaborated with the management at Dreamworld, a Townsville, Australia theme park. Using a 4000-person survey, the data were divided into three

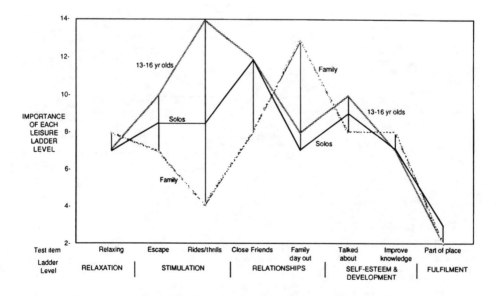

Figure 4.3. *Dreamworld* demographics: Recent levels of enjoyment. (Reprinted from P. Pearce, 1993, "Fundamentals of Tourist Motivation," in *Tourism Research: Critiques and Challenges,* p. 126, with permission from International Academy of Tourism.)

demographic segments: youths (age 13–16), single adults, and family groups (Figure 4.3). Youths were excited and stimulated by the rides and thrills, whereas the family most valued the day of togetherness, but few attendees came away "really feeling a part of the place," inasmuch as "place" was a virtual reality. This psychological research illustrates the dynamic aspect of tourist motivations. Further, using this example as model, the authors were able to explain and predict attendance at three competitive theme parks, and successfully evaluate new development proposals.

The Quantitative Approach

Visitor surveys, conducted in person, by phone or by mail, have considerable attraction because they represent human input, not just an assemblage of numbers or vague theorizing. However, C. Ryan and Glendon (1998) openly acknowledge that the results of their survey are less than perfect because of human diversity. These authors reviewed numerous quantitative studies by other investigators on travel motivation, using the much-tested Beard and Ragheb (1983) Leisure Motivation Scale. The survey instruments consisted of 113 questions relevant to recent holidays, which were mailed to 6000 residents in the East Midlands of UK, using a well-tested geodemographic database. The usable replies numbered 1127 (or 18.8%) of the sample. From this, the authors identified 11 cluster groups (Table 4.3), and their stated preferences for Holiday Destination Attributes (Table 4.4).

Ryan and Glendon note that their sample proved to be somewhat overweighted in terms of one cluster (young families with children) but that this group is known to be an important purchaser of British holiday packages. Therefore, the study distinctly has marketing validity for British tour operators. Replication of this study in other British locales could identify other clusters with significantly different holiday preference.

Table 4.3. Social Characteristics of Cluster Groups

Cluster	Characteristic
Friendly discoverers	Male, young
Relaxed discoverers	Married, middle aged
Competent intellectuals	Youngish, tendency not to be married
Relaxing moderates	Tend to follow the characteristics of sample population (i.e., not particularly young or old, high or low income)
Social relaxers	Middle age, lower income, slight tendency to be single
Positive holidaytakers	Akin to relaxing moderates
Active relaxers	Tend to be male, with higher income
Unimaginative holidaytakers	Tend to be married
Intellectual active isolates	Skewed to higher income groups
Noisy socializers	Male, young, low income
Mental relaxers	Married, male, with children

Source: Reproduced from C. Ryan and I. Glendon, 1998, "Application of Leisure Motivation Scale to Tourism,", p. 180, in *Annals of Tourism Research*, with permission from Elsevier Science.

Table 4.4. Mean Scores of Holiday Destination Attributes

	Nightlife	Bars	History	Scenery	Accommodation	Comfort	Locals	Culture	Get Away	Child Facil.	Mix With Others	Need Courier Input	Climate
Friendly discoverers	2.9	1.8	6.0	6.7	6.3	6.1	5.7	6.1	5.6	1.7	4.4	4.5	6.6
Relaxed discoverers	2.2	1.8	5.7	6.6	6.3	6.4	6.1	5.8	6.4	2.6	3.2	4.2	5.9
Competent intellectuals	4.3	3.1	4.9	5.8	5.1	5.3	5.7	5.3	5.0	2.3	4.4	3.1	4.9
Relaxing moderates	3.1	2.6	4.2	5.9	6.2	6.3	5.8	4.7	6.3	3.6	3.8	3.9	6.0
Social relaxers	2.4	2.3	4.1	6.0	6.4	6.1	6.0	4.0	5.9	1.9	5.2	3.1	6.8
Positive holidayakers	3.3	2.6	5.5	6.5	6.3	6.3	6.2	5.8	6.3	3.2	4.8	4.7	6.1
Active relaxers	1.8	1.5	4.3	6.2	5.3	5.5	5.4	4.6	6.2	1.9	1.7	3.0	5.6
Unimaginative relaxers	1.9	1.6	5.1	6.1	5.9	5.9	5.6	5.3	5.8	2.9	2.7	3.7	5.8
Intellectual active isolates	2.0	1.7	5.4	6.2	5.4	5.4	5.3	5.5	4.9	2.3	2.2	2.9	5.3
Noisy socializers	4.1	3.9	2.6	4.2	5.3	5.4	4.8	3.0	3.8	2.3	4.3	3.0	5.4
Mental relaxers	1.8	1.4	3.5	5.3	5.7	6.1	4.9	3.2	5.6	3.2	1.6	2.7	5.2
Total smaple score	2.5	2.0	4.9	6.1	5.9	6.0	5.7	5.1	5.8	2.9	3.2	3.7	5.7

Source: Reproduced from C. Ryan and I. Glendon, 1998, "Application of Leisure Motivation Scale to Tourism,", p. 181, in *Annals of Tourism Research*, with permission from Elsevier Science.

The three investigative styles—descriptive, psychologic, and quantitative—illustrate the interest and need for knowledge of tourist motivations and behavior. Taken together these data have immediate value in marketing and long-term value in planning. However, P. Pearce (1988) correctly observes that "all such studies are socially and culturally bound in a time frame; tourists of the 1970s are different from the tourists of the 1990s—due to changes in perceptions, transportation, better health, greater longevity and multiple other factors" (p. 220). One cannot build a tourism industry without the knowledge of the special, unique defining characteristics of the tourist, which are the core of each traveler's interests, activities, and desired experiences. The rise and demise of tourist centers, described by the Butler Resort Cycle model, is built upon this premise and is well illustrated in the case study of Atlantic City in 1886 (see Chapter 7).

Tourist Classifications

Classification systems are linguistic shortcuts. A tourist classification describes a population group, or cluster, whose members share some preferences or characteristics that differentiate that group from other clusters. Many classificatory terms are now in use, and are commercially used to segment the travel market. For example, business travelers, from World War II to the late 1980s, were predominantly male. As women have broken the glass ceiling into middle and upper management positions, the percentage of women business travelers has soared. Metropolitan hotels now solicit this market niche, and advertise special rooms, or even special floors, for businesswomen. The latter want rooms with more security, more in-room amenities such as hair dryers, coffeepots, and irons, and sometimes semi-public lounges for committee meetings or entertaining.

Traditional Classifications

E. Cohen (1972) published one of the first post-World War II tourist classifications, based on research in Thailand. He identified four categories. First were the noninstitutional travelers, as "drifters," who searched for exotic and strange environments, and "explorers," who arranged their own travel, to visit places "off the beaten track." Second were the institutional travelers, which included the "individual mass tourists," who made arrangements through a travel agency to visit popular destinations, and the "organized mass tourists," who traveled in the security of the environmental "bubble" of an organized tour.

Cohen's definition was excellent in its day, for it expressed the interaction between visitor and destination at a time when the options for tourism were much less extensive than is true today. Subsequently, V. Smith (1977), in the original *Hosts and Guests,* elaborated a similar theme, using the broad spectrum of international travel to reflect the greater differentiation in modes of travel, and the significant increase in tourist numbers, including mass and charter tourism. In both the Cohen and Smith classifications, the orientation was patently Western. In the early 1970s, the proportion of non-Western travelers was very small.

The 1977 V. Smith classification is compared with its updated 2000 counterparts (Table 4.5). The terminology is now essentially international, for all travelers, regardless of country of origin, participate in most designated categories, although

Table 4.5. Comparison of Tourist Type Classifications: 1977– 2000

1977 Tourist Types	2000 Market Terms	Numbers of Tourists	Desired Tourism Characteristics	2000 Cost[a]
Explorer	Adventure travel	Very few	Unusual: space tourism, submersibles, skiing in Antarctica	$1000 +
Elite	Soft adventure: upscale, "high end"	Increasingly "high end"	Deluxe resorts/cruises: exotic destinations	$1000 +
Off-beat	Off-beat	Uncommon	Unusual destinations: backpacking in Tibet, camel safaris (ecotourism?)	$500–1000
Unusual/ Incipient mass	Special interest tours: FIT/DIT	Diverse, numerous, and seasonal	Usual destinations in unusual style: small group walking, wine, music tours	$300–500
Mass	Mass, bulk tours	Continuous influx	Popular destinations; package tours	$200–300
Charter	Charter	Massive arrivals	Place marketing: Cancun, Canary Islands	Under $200

[a]Costs per day (excluding airfare) in US dollars.

their costs are sometimes less than the US dollar amounts listed. In general, Asian tourists are reported to spend less money on hotels and meals than Westerners but proportionately more on shopping (Mok & Lam, 1997). Some original 1977 terms have been redefined, such as *explorer* and *elite*, by the industry creation of new terms: *Adventure travel* and *high end* or *upscale*. There are few areas on this planet left to "explore," and "elite" seemed pejorative. Other terms, particularly *mass tourism* and *charter tourism,* are now commonplace and are routinely used in both scholarly literature and industry publications. Other categories have changed, commensurate with changes in the global economy. For non-Western readers, the daily cost seems excessive—often 1 day of travel is equivalent to a month's salary in some LDC destinations. However, the costs must be correlated with American earnings. For perspective, using US data, in 1998 1.3 million Americans earned more than US$200,000, of whom 86,000 earned more than US$1 million. According to a *Wall Street Journal* survey, 1999 MBA graduates from leading US universities (Harvard, Pennsylvania, and Stanford, among others) may expect a starting salary of US$130,000 per year in the high-tech industries and as entry-level stockbrokers. These young employees are current examples of a 10-year-long trend associated with the burgeoning US economy and bullish Wall Street. Combined, it has created a substantial market for what is now termed upscale or high end. Until the 1997–1998 Asian financial crisis reduced Asian travel, the Japanese had been a major source for upscale travel, and the Taiwanese and Koreans were entering that market in growing numbers (see Chapter 8).

Adventure travel now replaces most explorer travel, leaving to the latter principally the emerging space travel and use of submersible vehicles as the only areas left to be, expensively, "explored" (see Chapter 26). Several American tour operators market (and fill) a 2-week jet charter flight around the world, with selected stops, for US$50,000 (1999 prices)—as a trip that meets the travel interests for high-salaried management with limited vacation time. Luxury travel also includes numerous five-star resort properties and several cruise companies, using small vessels with all-suite cabins, and a high ratio of guest/service personnel, at a minimum cost of US$1000 per person per day. *Travel Weekly* (April 29, 1999, p. 56) reports an industry survey of data from 3500 affluent clients (defined as those who spent an average of $6000 per trip) that 35% prefer adventure travel, 21% favor family travel, and bus and group tours are on the decline. For the younger affluent travelers (ages 34 to 52), cruises on luxury and expedition ships are highest in priority (31%) followed by adventure travel (22%), with a further emphasis on more frequent shorter trips, and biking and walking trips abroad. Similarly, what was originally described as "off-beat" travel has now become a variant of more traditional routes. Grand Circle Travel, the travel division of the American Association for Retired Persons (AARP), operates extended stay vacations and middle-income tours for senior citizens. They expanded in 1998 with OAT (Overseas Adventure Tours) with a maximum group size of 15 persons and include itineraries such as Tibet and desert camping (in Outer Mongolia and Morocco). This company has popularized many former "off-beat" and "unusual" destinations for the travelers who have "been everywhere else," and thereby reduced costs to US$200 per day. Incipient Mass Tourism is now best described in terms of Foreign Independent Travel (FIT) or Domestic Independent Travel (DIT) that includes Fly-Drive packages and Hotel Vouchers available at a fixed price per night. Mass tourism continues with package tours and cruise vessels with 1000–2000 passengers. The 1979 deregulation of American airlines and subsequent airline mergers brought about more competitive pricing. Further, the global population is progressively more knowledgeable about travel, thanks to multiple daily television programs that showcase documentary travel footage.

Business and Convention Travel

Business travel, built on the principle that a one-on-one relationship best cemented commercial relationships, has gradually shrunk during the 1990s, due to tightened fiscal budgets and more effective video-conferencing. However, demand for centrally located hotels and fine restaurants were the mainstays for many metropolitan facilities. Hotels added conference centers and trained staff so that small group meetings are now characteristic of many industries, to showcase products, provide consumer support, and inform potential customers. Site selection is important to convention success because attendees are drawn toward attractive venues, such as to cities noted for: their hospitality qualities such as Atlanta or Amsterdam; their dramatic setting as in San Francisco or Sydney; their cultural composite as in New Orleans or Singapore; or for the outdoor amenities as at

Whistler in British Columbia or Orlando. The opportunity for attendees, and quite possibly their spouses and family members, to extend their visit beyond the stipulated agenda in order to enjoy environs is an added incentive to attend, and generates increased cash flow to the host area. The tourist value of the site is often at least as important as the topic as an influence for attendance. Staff at metropolitan Convention and Visitor Bureaus (CVBs) are usually expert at presenting their community as the hub from which to visit a hinterland with a broad spectrum of varied activities.

Incentive Travel

Incentive travel is a socially important variant of the commercial travel industry. Capitalizing on the motivational power of travel, sales managers in large companies often set promotional sales targets. Individuals who meet or exceed the stipulated goals are rewarded with group tours in lieu of a cash bonus. The travel award is usually preferred in lieu of a cash bonus because it is nondiscretionary income, whereas the family might choose to spend a cash award on utilitarian needs. A farm machinery distributor sold 14 new tractors one winter, at $100,000 each, by offering a free week in Hawaii to each farmer and his wife as a thank you gift for their purchase. The salesman and his wife accompanied the group as a free bonus for his promotional efforts.

Pilgrimage Travel

A pilgrimage is a long journey to a historical place (*Webster's 1988 New World Dictionary of the English Language*, 1988), which could be either sacred or secular. V. Turner and Turner (1978) neatly defined the potential duality of behavior, noting that "a tourist is half a pilgrim, if a pilgrim is half a tourist." This theme is rooted in the philosophical context that a traveler's journey is in part a ritual quest, during which time the individual is (1) separated from his/her past, and distanced or freed from the normal social milieu; the individual then (2) crosses a cognitive threshold, into the period of *liminality* oriented toward a *Center* "in which the structured necessities of ordinary life dissolve into a destructured, nonordinary state, which can have a sacred aura around it" (D. Nash, 1996, p. 41); and he/she (3) develops a sense of *communitas* with other individuals (tourists or pilgrims) sharing the same process. Returning home following the journey, the individual often perceives him- or herself as "different" or in a new light, somewhat comparable to having experienced a rite of passage. The Finnish tourists (see Chapter 6) exemplify secular pilgrims who, in this instance, have already found their spiritual Center, shared *communitas* with their friends, and annually seek this *liminoid* state through their return pilgrimage to the beach on the Canary Islands.

The differentiation between tourist and pilgrim prompted E. Cohen (1979a) to draft another classificatory system to distinguish between modern pilgrims and pleasure seekers. The former seek values in their journeys, either as (1) *existential pilgrims*, who leave modern life to become absorbed in a new spiritual setting; as (2) *experimental pilgrims*, who quest for an alternative lifestyle, especially through engaging in its authenticity; or as (3) *experiential pilgrims*, who look for meaning in the life of others through an enjoyment of its authenticity. All three variants are prominent in Asia (see Chapter 20), including Buddhist groups in Japan, the millions of Moslems who journey to Mecca each year, and the throngs who gather at holy sites in India. By contrast, Cohen identifies the mass tourists who have become pleasure seekers either as (1) *diversionary* tourists who seek escape from the route or (2) *recreational* tourists for whom the trip is entertainment. The classification is explanatory but fails to incorporate the duality of sacred–secular behavior often characteristic of the pilgrim tourist.

The French *Lascaux* Cave was undoubtedly a religious shrine for Paleolithic ancestors 25,000 years ago, and probably constituted a gathering place somewhat like the Inuit rendezvous. Modern visitors were so awed by the religious artwork that the government was forced to close the site for preservation, and construct a mediated replica next door. The Mayan temples in Yucatan 1000 years ago were impressive pilgrimage sites for thousands of worshippers, who also shopped in the adjoining markets and gambled at the ball games (see Chapter 5). Pilgrimage, like tourism, has ancient links with aboriginal people who, probably like modern pilgrims, traveled to sacred sites for religious purposes and for what some scholars term "knowledge-based tourism" (Jackowski & Smith, 1992).

Poland is the most practicing Catholic country of Europe, and the monastery at Czestochowa is the most famous of its 11 shrines. The little town of 250,000 people hosts some 4 million visitors each year, almost one third of whom strive to be on site for the Feast of the Assumption (August 15). In 1989, in the only remaining foot pilgrimage in Europe, 150 groups walked to Czestochowa—some were as much as 20 days en route and covered 600 kilometers (Figure 4.4). The groups formed in their parish (home communities) and, as working people, planned this to be their vacation. Sometimes their pilgrimage was scheduled several years in advance, to ensure leisure and discretionary income. A truck carried camping gear to the selected night stop, and as the "pilgrims" passed farms and villages wellwishers came out to bring fruit, cookies, and juice to cheer them on.

Most Poles make such a trip once in their lifetime (except during World War II occupation when only the daring few attempted it, including Pope John Paul, then not even a seminary student). Singing as they walk, these knowledge-based pilgrims tour their country, bond with their peers (for most will remain friends thereafter), and have a fun-filled holiday under a summer sun. They are the living example of what Vukonic (1996) has termed *Homo Turisticus Religiosus*.

Tourism in Perspective

In the past half-century, tourism has become a way of life for millions of people and a future dream for many more millions. Tourism is essentially a peaceful process that silently and subtly alters public opinion and also coerces behavior. Codes for Travelers are widely published with a central theme such as "Take Only Pictures, Leave Only Memories." As a consequence, the big-game hunters who formerly displayed their mounted trophies on walls are now largely displaced by far greater numbers of travelers who protest killing elephants for ivory and donate funds to wildlife preservation. The generations that once mocked tribes who practiced cannibalism and sent out missionaries to "save the savages" are now replaced

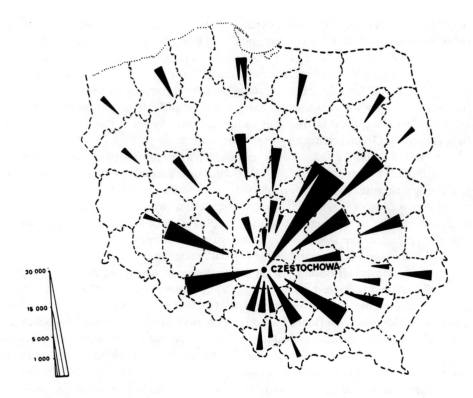

Figure 4.4. Main pilgrimages on foot (over 1000 pilgrims) to Jasna Góra in August 1987 (the triangle surface is proportionate to the pilgrim numbers). (Reprinted from A. Jackowski and V. Smith, 1992, "Polish Pilgrim Tourists," in *Annals of Tourism Research*, p. 100, with permission from Elsevier Science.)

by a larger generation that condemns "ethnic cleansing" because they have visited African villages or vacationed in the Balkans.

Travelers in the 21st century have a broader perception of humanity, both from their personal and their media experiences; yet their world becomes ever smaller as transportation speed increases and costs diminish. The prevailing Western philosophy of multiculturalism tends to negate the ethnic categories of "them" or "us" and substitutes the belief that a threat to peace anywhere is a threat to peace everywhere. Taken together, these two concepts support the increased importance of tourism in a plural society, and the power of tourism as a peaceful agent of change within ongoing increased globalization.

Chapter 5

Gambling Into the 21st Century

Charles F. Urbanowicz

America is witnessing the most widespread liberalization of casino gaming entertainment in its history. Although permitted in the United States since it was legalized in Nevada in 1931, casino-style gaming is expanding at an unparalleled rate (Satre, 1993, p. 5). This chapter addresses the major sources and development of American gaming, and it questions the impact of gaming on society (see Figure 5.1).

Four events contributed to this acceleration of gambling in the second half of the 20th century in the US: (1) lotteries became a part of the American scene; (2) the Holiday Inn Corporation, acting on changes made by the Nevada Legislature, made it respectable for average stockholders to be part of the gaming industry; (3) the passage of the Indian Gaming Regulatory Act (IGRA) by the United States Congress caused phenomenal growth in Native American facilities; and (4) human nature.

The British novelist and playwright J. B. Priestly (1894–1984) was noted for his shrewd human characterizations. During his days in England in the 1920s, he wrote book reviews and sold the book afterward. He describes the emotions accompanying the book sales in an essay entitled "Money for Nothing":

> At this shop, where human nature was understood, one was always paid at once and always paid in cash, generally in exquisite new pound notes. And of all the money I have ever handled, this gave me the most delight. Money for Jam, Money for Old Rope, Money for nothing. When we receive our wages, salaries or fees, we may be content, for that is what we have earned, but we are a long way from delight. It is money that we have not earned, the windfall, the magical bonus, that starts us capering. (J. Priestly, 1951, pp. 349–350)

This "magical bonus" is what drives the guest-as-gambler to take risks at various host destinations that offer this form of entertainment. Anthropologists identify gambling as one of the several forms of redistribution of wealth, together with gift giving, taxation, and theft. Ethnographic research for more than two decades has convinced me not to gamble. Consider the words of Steve Wynn, Chairman of Mirage Resorts Inc. (cited in Spanier, 1992, p. 17) concerning gambling as a way to earn money: "If you wanna make money in a casino, own one."

Figure 5.1. The "crazy girls" of the Riviera Hotel and Casino (photo by Charlie Urbanowicz).

Research indicates that individuals go to casinos (1) to gamble (or take risks), (2) to regain some control over their lives, and/or (3) to feel that they are important! Priestly wrote that he earned a great deal of money elsewhere but that it all was "lost in a dreary maze of bank accounts, stocks and shares, tax certificates, cheques and bills and receipts" but, the book sale money, that was something else:

> But when I used to hurry out of that shop with five or six new pound notes singing in my pocket, for quarter of an hour or so I felt like a tipsy millionaire or the man who broke the bank at Monte Carlo. Money to Burn! And the only comparable moments I have known since then have been on the certain very rare occasions when I happen to have been fortunate in playing those fruit machines [or slot machines or "one-armed bandits"], which were so popular in the American southwest when we were there. (Priestly, 1951, pp. 349–350)

This unexpected windfall, achieved through a perceived control of the situation, is why people really gamble. Potential guests look to various host destinations to get that adrenal "rush" to remove the boredom from their lives. Romero, an industry consultant, had the following perceptive words about the role that human nature plays in gambling activities:

> Why do they come to gaming tournaments? After 15 years of Casino tournaments, I've come to a melancholy conclusion. They come because they're lonely. Sure, price, prize list and free play mean something but those are the

intellectual reasons, not emotional reasons. Look carefully at your tournament customers and you'll see most are middle-aged to elderly, living a generally quiet existence (read boring). All this changes at tournaments when they become the center of attention. For brief moments at the slots or tables, they're the stars. It's easy to become addicted to recognition, which is why the best way to keep them as customers is to meet them, learn their names and show them a good time. Did you think they came because of the brochure? Naw. (Romero, 1993, p. 8)

Gambling has evolved into a respectable entertainment industry that is attempting to draw as many new guests as possible to an ever-increasing number of host destinations. On a typical day in the early 1990s, people wagered about US$627,000 every minute of every day on all types of commercial gambling in the US, and all of these commercial gaming ventures made a profit of about US$57,000 per minute! Data from 1997 indicate that in 1995 the "win" was about US$84,000 per minute in the US (or an increase of US$27,447 per minute from the early 1990s). This revenue underscores the reason big business and corporations are willing to invest a "small fortune" in refurbishing establishments in order to attract consumers for this highly profitable form of entertainment now, and it is predicted to continue into the 21st century. The gaming industry continues to proliferate, adding new sites to compete with the increasing expansion from Indian operations on tribal lands (see Lew & Van Otten, 1998).

Background

We all gamble. The term "gambling" has several definitions, including "to play at any game of chance for stakes" and "to stake or risk money, or anything of value, on the outcome of something involving chance; bet; wager." Ambiguity surrounds the use of the terms "gaming" and "gambling." As someone once remarked, "if you bet on a horse, that's gambling. If you bet you can make three spades, that's entertainment. If you bet cotton will go up three points, that's business. See the difference?" (Orkin, 1991, p. 1). Although the industry executives use the euphemism of *gaming*, our use here is *gambling*. This chapter points out that whereas the outsider (or guest) might think gambling is entertainment, the insider (the hosts, owners, or management) views gambling as a volatile, profitable, competitive enterprise. "Winners" and "losers" exist from the industry or "host" perspective as well as from the perspective of the guests! Not only do "gaming guests" lose money, but certain casinos have also disappeared in past years. For example, in the late 1990s the downtown area of Reno, NV, was literally littered with the "shells" of empty casinos that had prospered when the town was a railhead and served the mining camps at the turn of the last century. These old casinos failed because of their inability to meet market demand for new luxury hotels, big-name entertainers, in-house amusements, and lavish but inexpensive food buffets.

Competition

The competition between the gambling industry casinos to attract guests to their respective locations around the world is multifaceted and occurs as: Nevada vs. New Jersey (and the rest of the nation), northern Nevada (Reno) casinos vs. southern Nevada (Las Vegas) casinos; Las Vegas "strip" vs. downtown Las Vegas; the land-based casinos vs. riverboat casinos; and even table games vs. machine games. And in 2000, competition is seen between visiting a casino and Internet gambling (which does not mitigate the loneliness). Technology has allowed various host destinations to change gambling machines from old-fashioned mechanical machines to newer electronic machines with random-number-generated computer chips. These computer-linked machines do pay off and the casinos love the publicity when a relatively modest investment hits a jackpot.

Competition also exists between players or guests (those seeking entertainment) and casino operators or hosts (who have the statistical advantage). At the end of 1996, the Reno-Sparks Convention and Visitor Authority (RSCVA) made the following statement:

> More tourists are visiting Reno this year than last, but more of them are also visiting Indian casinos and Las Vegas—a potentially significant shift, say market analysts. . . . "The product in Reno is pleasing a lot more people . . . but it's disturbing that we have so much competition," he [Buddy Frank, RSCVA member] said, emphasizing Reno's need to continue improving its product. If it doesn't, he said, "we could lose (business) far more quickly now than we ever could in the past." Visits to Indian casinos appear to be rising because more casinos are now located in key Reno feeder markets, like the Pacific Northwest and Northern California. (Stearns, 1996, p. 1E)

In a hotly contested November 1999 election, California voters affirmed casino-style gambling, with entertainment, on Indian reservations within the state because of the job creation and employment that this tourist industry would provide for native Americans.

Specifics

State and local governments are looking at gambling to pay for social services. Legalized state-authorized gambling began in 1931 in Nevada and was then legalized in Atlantic City, NJ, in 1978, a move to rejuvenate an almost derelict resort (see Chapter 7). The 20th century legalization of gambling in the US, however, does not mean that gambling was brand new to the continent. Native Americans partook of games of chance long before Europeans arrived in 1492. Patolli was a board game involving competitors throwing dice. In the Yucatán of Mexico (Chitchén Itzá), Native Americans made bets at the largest ball court in all of Mesoamerica, measuring some 83 meters in length (272 feet). The following description of the game is interesting:

> This game was both a sport and a sacrificial ritual. It was played throughout Mesoamerica, using a large rubber ball that could be hit by the elbows, knees, or hips, but could not be touched by the hands or feet. The game required the players to wear heavy protective equipment, and much paraphernalia was developed during the Classic period. It was often played in masonry courts, and rings or other markers were used for scoring. (Kelly, 1993, p. 41).

The US has a long and lengthy history of gambling (Findlay, 1986). In a delightful and fascinating book, *Big Deal: A Year as a Professional Poker Player*, Anthony Holden (1990) made the following perceptive statement:

> In retrospect, it seems inevitable that games of chance should have played so large a role in the development of the American character. By the time of the American War of Independence, financed in large part by lotteries, public auctions had been a routine alternative to taxation since Queen Elizabeth I sanctioned England's first raffle in 1566, to finance harbor improvements. In the early seventeenth century, it was a lottery that funded the first permanent English settlement in North America at Jamestown, North Virginia. . . . Risk-taking, by definition, is a fundamental aspect of any pioneer or frontier ethic. (pp. 217–218)

During the 18th and 19th centuries, the prevailing American "Puritan ethic" did not sanction public gambling. It was primarily identified with pool halls and saloons, especially around the Gold Rush mining camps, and later with organized crime. The American musical, *Showboat* (Rogers and Hammerstein, 1927), characterized the gambler as an irresponsible "drifter" and opportunist.

The Effect of Communication Technology

A recent addition to the worldwide accelerating growth of gambling, however, comes via cyberspace. The gambling industry is well aware of this cyberspace potential, as one article pointed out:

> The electronic superhighway now under construction . . . has profound implications for USGI [U.S. Gambling, Inc., "a fictional holding company for the nation's casinos and slot machines and video poker devices and racetracks and lotteries and other gambling businesses"]. How will commercial games adapt to the fast approaching interactive future? (Christiansen, 1993a, p. 28)

Gamblers no longer need travel but can be entertained in the comfort of their homes. The fiscal effect on the huge casinos is as yet unclear, given the legal issues that have recently been raised. The families of gamblers who "lost" their entire assets have sued the casinos for permitting these individuals to "borrow" money on their credit cards to continue their gambling spree. The courts have yet to decide whether the casino "hosts" have a financial as well as a moral responsibility to monitor guest behavior. Harrah's, the oldest and largest casino conglomerate, now advertises the motto, "Know when to stop before you start." Large casinos electronically track the wins and losses of their regular clients, using an in-house ID card with an imbedded chip; these data can be then be compared with their personal credit record, as a matter of self-protection. Given this potential liability, even the "Internet gamers" asked for regulations at the March 1998 International Gaming Business Exposition in Las Vegas:

> We believe regulation is needed to legitimize the market and grow the market'. . . . Internet gambling is here and it is not going to go away, the experts

said. . . . Three weeks ago, federal prosecutors in New York announced in-
dictments against 14 American managers of off-shore companies set up to
accept bets over the Internet. (Wilen, 1998, p. 10B)

Sources of Gambling

State-sanctioned lotteries began on March 12, 1964, when the Governor of New
Hampshire purchased the first sweepstakes ticket in New Hampshire. *International Gaming & Wagering Business*, an extremely influential trade publication,
had the following statement in 1994:

> It was a simple act, exchanging $3 for ticket number 0000001, but one that
> would set into motion a juggernaut that, 30 years later, would be a US$25
> billion per year industry comprising 36 states and the District of Columbia.
> (Dworin, 1994, p. 8)

Corporate America entered the industry in 1978 when the Holiday Inn Corporation made gambling legitimate to stockholders. The following is a clear statement
of this aspect:

> That [1978] vote [by the Holiday Inn Corporation] marked a significant turn-
> ing point not just for Holiday, but for the country and the lines that distin-
> guish legitimate business from that which is illegitimate. Throughout history
> gamblers could earn fortunes, but not much else. If they wanted the status of
> legitimacy, if they wanted respect, they had to take their money and get
> themselves or their children out of gambling and into businesses that were
> respectable because they added some value to society. (D. Johnston, 1992, p.
> 49)

Prior to corporate America becoming involved in the gaming industry, the expansion of Nevada casinos had come from a questionable source of money:

> Throughout the 1960s and well into the 1970s, most of that investment
> money came from the Teamsters Central States Pension Fund, which pro-
> vided the money to make Las Vegas the capital of gaming at a time when
> most financial institutions still steered clear of casino investments. Las Ve-
> gas would not be what it is today without the Teamsters Union. . . . All the
> casino loans, however, seemed to come with strings
> attached. . . . [Eventually] In 1969 the Nevada Legislature passed a corpo-
> rate gaming control law that permitted corporations to enter Nevada's gam-
> ing industry without requiring each shareholder to submit to individual
> licensing. (S. Lalli, 1997, pp. 14–18)

These cumulative events have been powerful contributors to the acceleration
of gambling in the 1990s. Not only can a "guest" be entertained in a gaming establishment, he/she can also "invest" in various industry stocks, such as: Alpha Hospitality Corporation, Aztar Corporation, Circus Circus Enterprises, Inc., Colorado
Casino Corporation, Grand Casino Inc., Harvey's Casino Resorts, Harrah's Entertainment Inc., Hilton Hotels Corp., MGM Grand Inc., Mirage Resorts Inc., Station

Casinos Inc., and Winner's Entertainment Inc. (just to name a few); one can also invest in various industry suppliers, such as Acres Gaming Inc., International Gaming Technology, Shuffle Master Inc., and Video Lottery Tech, Inc.

Eventually the US Congress passed the 1988 Indian Gaming Regulatory Act (IGRA), and this continued the acceleration. Prior to 1988, federally recognized Native American tribes and individual states had the authority to enter into various agreements dealing with taxes as well as tribal social services. It was the United States Supreme Court decision in *California v. Cabazon Band of Mission Indians* (begun in 1986 and eventually decided in favor of the Cabazon in 1987) that resulted in the passage of IGRA. McKay (1991) pointed out that "the primary issue in Cabazon was whether the State of California had authority to enforce its gambling laws within the reservation occupied by the Cabazon Indians" (p. 472) and the resulting court decision on the Cabazon "allowed unregulated gambling to flourish on Indian reservations" (Weissmann, 1993, p. 124).

Not everyone is pleased with all aspects of Native American involvement in gambling, called the "new Buffalo" by some (Hill, 1993, 1994). In the mid-1990s the following statement was made by a Representative from the state of New Jersey: "We have seen created 296 Indian casinos in a US$7.5 billion industry that is untaxed, unregulated and out of control" ("Lawmakers Aim to Bar Indian Lottery," 1995). The legal situation is so volatile and changing so quickly, one can only cite a 1997 commentator on Native American gambling establishments in North America: "Tribes are groping for ways to deal with immovable state governments" (Connor, 1997, p. 62). According to Connor, IGRA provided "the framework by which games are conducted to protect both the tribes and the general public. Its goals are tribal economic development, self-sufficiency and strong tribal government" (1993, p. 9). IGRA may have provided a statutory basis for the creation and operation of Indian gambling establishments in the US, but the results from IGRA are still evolving (and for an excellent short overview, see J. Davis & Otterstrom, 1998). The Mashantucket Pequot Tribal Nation Casino in Mashantucket, CT, is the most successful casino (Indian Nation or not) in the Western Hemisphere. An article in the *Pequot Times* points out:

> Tribal leaders at Taos Pueblo say their gaming operation is in "dismal financial condition" and it can afford to pay only $4,516 of the $169,000 it owes the state. In Washington, one of the 12 tribal casinos was forced to close last summer and at least three more have stopped making required community-impact contributions. "I don't think anybody expected this," said Carrie Tellefson of the state Gambling Commission. "We never thought they might be unprofitable." Many tribes, with casinos in isolated rural areas, are finding that gaming is by no means a sure bet. ("Indian Gaming Offers No Assurance of Success," 1998, p. 10)

Symptomatic of the Times?

From 1910 to 1931 Americans did without legal gambling, but that changed because gambling was already such a major portion of American life and history. Now the availability of various destinations is getting stronger as marketing becomes increasingly creative. A new "family" approach (see Figure 5.2) at destinations makes Las Vegas Americans' destination of choice (Stearns, 1997a, p. 1).

In addition to getting the "complete family" to the destination resort, the industry is working on everything to get individuals to various destinations, including the increasing popularity of tournament lures by featuring poker, slot machine, Caribbean Stud, Let-It-Ride, and blackjack tournaments. "High rollers" have traditionally been rewarded with complimentary items. The industry is also looking at other ways of encouraging gambling, such as discounts, specialized memberships, monthly mailings, and the related electronic tracking of various gamers. Readers of this chapter should consider the words of industry analyst Byron Liggett in *The Reno Gazette-Journal* in the mid-1990s in response to the question "Is it true that casinos use certain fragrances to induce customers to gamble more?" The complete answer follows:

> A year-long study at the Las Vegas Hilton in 1992 indicated that certain aromas caused slot players to spend as much as 45 percent more. Since then, numerous casinos have used the science of scents to create a comfortable, conducive environment. Scent manufacturers and casinos consider the use of aromas to be no different than the employment of lighting, sound and decor to create a positive gambling environment. (Liggett, 1995, p. 19)

Figure 5.2. Treasure Island Hotel (photo by Charlie Urbanowicz).

Gaming guests should be aware that the chemically produced pheromones just might have a greater effect than "lighting, sound and décor" in encouraging gambling. Certain casinos might create a "gaming environment," which is designed to unconsciously manipulate the gambling behavior of individuals in order to increase their profits: it is a business to the industry and not a game! The "risk-taking" atmosphere is further encouraged when guests are offered "free" drinks by their convivial hosts while being "'entertained" or gambling. The effect of alcohol can lead to fuzzy thinking and increase the risk-taking quotient.

Meeting the Competitive Challenge: Las Vegas

The gaming industry fully understands the changing patterns of tourism, described by Butler (1980) as the resort cycle (see Chapter 7), and modifies their investment program to meet new interests. Despite its isolation in the Nevada desert, Las Vegas grew to become the gaming capital of the world, and held that status for almost 50 years. Their long-term legal monopoly, heightened by the glamour of lavish Paris-style revues and headliner stars such as Elvis Presley and Liberace, made Las Vegas an important international destination. To maintain that preeminence, as TV brought more entertainment to homes, the city faced stiff competition and carefully restructured its focus with three innovations:

1. the creation of international "theme" hotels such as New York, Luxor, the Venetian, the Bellagio, Mandalay, and Paris!, with lavish decor, fine dining, and boutiques (see Figure 5.3);

Figure 5.3. Luxor Hotel (photo by Charlie Urbanowicz).

2. extremely high occupancy rates (85.8%) in its 109,365 hotel rooms through promoting Las Vegas as a convention town (with an average nightly room rate of only US$66); and

3. construction of seven major shopping malls, catering to every purse, to keep visitors occupied and amused.

The city of Greater Las Vegas has a population of 1.2 million (1999) but attracts 31 million visitors per year. The Las Vegas News Bureau (May 1999) tabulates the 1998 economic impact as US$24.6 billion based on 3900 conventions, hosting 3.3 million delegates. The gross gambling revenues for Las Vegas amounted to US$5 billion, which averaged US$469 per person per trip. A serious shortage of air traffic capacity suggests an urgent need to construct a high-speed rail link to southern California to service that large market.

Las Vegas will host the American Society of Travel Agent (ASTA) convention in 2000. With new hotels under construction, there will be 126,000 rooms available, but to maintain the high occupancy level the challenge is to attract an additional 6 million visitors per year. Toward that goal, the casinos seek diversification because only 60% of their revenue is derived from gambling (Much, 1998). The owners of the Bellagio Hotel purchased a small collection of Impressionist paintings by artists such as Degas, Renoir, Cézanne, Manet, and Gauguin for US$260 million, installed as an art gallery exhibit for US$10 admission. The Nevada Division of State Parks is reconstructing the 1855 Old Mormon Fort with Paiute Indian exhibits and re-created pioneer ranch life. Las Vegas has grown into a brand name resort destination with enough attractions to keep guests active for several days, not just the overnight gamblers or conventioneers, and directly supports over 700,000 jobs.

Conclusions

Security is mostly a superstition. It does not exist in nature, nor do the children of men as a whole experience it. Avoiding danger is no safer in the long run than outright exposure. Life is either a daring adventure, or nothing. Helen Keller (1880–1968)

Living is risky and as social scientists we have the obligation to make others aware of some of the risks involved in various aspects of life. Legalized gambling in the US (1) generates a great deal of revenue, (2) has a great deal of visibility, (3) is creating some interesting partnerships, and (4) is a risky business for both hosts and guests. The visibility and the competition in the industry are obvious. From the bombarding messages of the state lotteries to the development of mega-resorts in Nevada, there is demand for the guest dollar.

From 1931 until 1978, Nevada was alone. Since then, there has been growth and competition; today, Reno/Sparks/Tahoe and Las Vegas must all compete with numerous activities and destinations all across the US (see Meyer-Arendt & Hartmann, 1998). Some establishments will survive and some will fail. In contrast to the fairy tale of Las Vegas (which is not without potential failure at some point), in 1995, Harold's Club closed in downtown Reno, NV, and as of late 1998, six additional casinos in Reno closed their doors since that closing: Holiday-Hotel Casino, Horseshoe Club, Nevada Club, The Riverboat, Riverside, and The Virginian, while only one new resort "gaming" destination opened, The Silver Legacy (in 1995). The potential guests for all of these destinations (and across the entire US) should realize that gambling is not entertainment. Gambling is a very big business and these hosts always have the advantage! Gambling is very expensive entertainment.

Gambling is here to stay. The long-term future in the US is debatable because there are numerous problems concerning expansion and growth of the gambling industry. Eadington (1992) pointed out that "observers, such as I. Nelson Rose, have argued that the proliferation [of gambling] carries with it the seeds of its own destruction" (p. 12) and this could be true. There is growing concern about "addictive gambling," labeled by the American Psychiatric Association as "an impulse control disorder" said to affect about 11% of all gamblers. Rose (1991) expects that after the boom of the 1990s and the first two decades of the 21st century, gambling will be outlawed again. Whether satiation or legislation ends the current unlimited growth is a question for the future!

Chapter 6

Pale Skin on Playa del Anywhere: Finnish Tourists in the Liminoid South

Tom Selänniemi

The Finns have been eager travelers since the emergence of mass tourism in Finland, beginning in the late 1960s and the early 1970s. The Finnish airline, the Kar-Air, opened the first "sunline" from Helsinki via Gothenburg, Luxemburg, and Barcelona to Malaga on April 8, 1961, and the planes were quickly sold out. Since then, there has been a steady increase in the annual number of Finnish tourists traveling abroad. The zenith in Finnish international charter tourism occurred in 1989 when sales topped more than 1 million charter flight package holidays. This statistic is significant for a country with about 5 million inhabitants. A subsequent economic recession in 1993 profoundly reduced the number of sun vacations by half—to 500,000 charter trips. There has been a slow recovery in the number of holidays abroad, again reaching almost 1 million charter trips in 1998 (excluding scheduled flights and boat, train, and auto travel).

This chapter examines tourism from Finland to Playa del Ingles on the island of Gran Canaria. The description and analysis also draw on data from field research in Athens (1991, 1992), Rhodes (1993), Bodrum (1993), and Aqaba (1994) for comparison. Throughout, my role as a tourist among tourists facilitated participant-observation in various touristic activities, from suntanning to barhopping, while recording tourists' behavior and my own reactions.

Thematic interviews proved to be almost impossible to perform because tourists did not wish to spend valuable holiday time answering research questions. The strategy of "spontaneous chats" with the tourists proved to be a good solution, so I talked with tourists wherever I met them, and made notes afterwards. I was better accepted by the tourists when I was "one of them," even though all the Finnish tourists who participated were aware of my research. To deepen the introspective view of tourist culture I requested written diaries of their holiday experience. In addition to the qualitative data, notes, diaries, and photographs, statistical data from questionnaires and structured time-use surveys were utilized.

Playa del Ingles

Gran Canaria is an almost circular island of 1532 square kilometers located just 115 kilometers from the Moroccan coast and north of the Tropic of Cancer. Since the early 1970s the island has been one of the most popular winter destinations for Finnish tourists. Tourism was initially directed to the capital city of Las Palmas but today Playa del Ingles in the southern part of the island, and nearby Maspalomas and Puerto Rico, host the majority of Finns (Figure 6.1). In 1991, the peak year to date, a total of 283,003 Finnish tourists traveled to the Canary Islands by charter planes.

Playa del Ingles on Gran Canaria is an excellent example of minimal cultural authenticity. It is one of the most popular winter holiday resorts among Finnish tourists. Indigenous habitation never existed in the area of Playa del Ingles or nearby Maspalomas. The hotels and restaurants were constructed on the sand dunes of Maspalomas in the early 1960s, when there was nothing but sand, sea, and a few fishermen's huts. In those early days of tourism, tourists hired a taxi from Las Palmas to Maspalomas to enjoy the natural scenery and privacy. Now 200,000 hotel beds occupy the area.

Today, the town center of Playa del Ingles appears clean, with newly paved streets and bungalows of a very international style, and almost all restaurants and shops are located along its principal streets. The town still has many hotels, but in the more recently developed Maspalomas area, large apartment-hotels dominate. These apartment complexes may feature multiple swimming pools, tennis courts, restaurants, bars, and shops (supermercados) as well as a gym and/or a sauna. Considering the array of services and opportunities for recreation, tourists need not leave the apartment-hotel complex during their vacation, and some tourists never go to a restaurant for dinner. Finnish tourists often make coffee and prepare meals in their apartments. They bring foodstuffs with them, mainly Finnish dark rye bread and, of course, Finnish coffee. Finns are absolutely convinced that nobody can roast and grind coffee beans as well as the Finnish companies. One eld-

Figure 6.1. Map of Gran Canaria.

erly Laestadian man—a member of a conservative Finnish Christian revivalist movement—had elk meat in his luggage. Because these apartment-hotels are self-contained, there is no need to venture beyond them unless one wishes.

The sand dune area of Maspalomas is clearly the most important single attraction in the Playa del Ingles region, where the large sand dunes offer a privacy
barrier to nearby nudist beaches. This desert-like environment within a stone's
throw from tourist facilities and the Atlantic Ocean also provides opportunities
for long strolls or camel "caravan" rides amidst the dunes. Other regional attractions include two theme parks: Sioux City and Palmitos Park. Sioux City is a Western theme park located outside the hotel area. Its flyer, available everywhere in
Playa del Ingles, uses the following text as a visitor inducement:

> Come on over and visit us! Every boy is a cowboy. "Sioux City," the authentic
> Western Town. Ride back into the days of the "Roaring West" and find your-
> self in the middle of a bank holdup or a sudden shootout between cold-
> blooded cowpokes and the lawman of Six Gun.

It is not difficult to image what a MacCannellian view on authenticity and tourism would have to say about Sioux City (see MacCannell, Chapter 29). The other
theme park, Palmitos Park, is a subtropical oasis with 50 different types of palm
trees and 230 species of birds from all over the world. In addition to these, there is
a butterfly house and a very popular parrot show. Sioux City and Palmitos Park, as
well as Playa del Ingles, entertain and cater to tourists without disturbing elements of locality or reality.

The cleanly paved streets of Playa del Ingles are lined with supermarkets, fast
food stalls, pubs, restaurants, and hotels. Several shopping malls exist in the area
of Ingles and Maspalomas. The town caters to Finnish tourists by availing them
with Finnish shops, bars, restaurants, and nightclubs such as Casa Finlandia with
karaoke singing in Finnish. At Tiffany, Finnish popular music artists perform almost
every night. These services and the large number of Finnish tourists make Finns
very comfortable in Playa del Ingles. One is able to eat Finnish food, drink Finnish
coffee and beer, and speak Finnish with neighbors in a very favorable climate
compared with winter in Finland! In a way, Playa del Ingles is an extension of the
tourists' home culture (see Hanefors & Larsson, 1989, 1993) and could be considered the southernmost province of Finland. Similarly, and contiguous with "little
Finland," in Playa del Ingles there are "little" Swedens, Englands, and Germanys.

Alongside "little Finland," comprised mainly of middle-aged and retired Finnish
tourists together with other extensions of the tourists' home cultures, Playa del
Ingles accommodates the touristic subculture of sexual minorities. From a superficial point of view it is difficult to understand coexistence of "little Finland"—
tourists that are predominantly middle aged to elderly, relatively uneducated, and
apparently conservative—with the blooming culture of transvestites, transsexu-
als, and homosexuals in Playa del Ingles. The big shopping center, Yumbo, frequented
by strolling and shopping tourists during the day, turns into an archipelago of gay
bars and transvestite clubs at night. The two worlds meet only occasionally. On
several nights I witnessed the performance of a Finnish male transvestite in the
Finnish karaoke bar, which was very popular among the "typical" Finnish tourists.
Some intermingling of these two worlds occurs even in "little Finland."

Table 6.1. Age Comparison of Finnish Tourists

Age	Rhodes (n = 150)	Bodrum (n = 58)	Playa del Ingles (n = 118)	Total
16–25	22%	24%	8%	12%
26–35	27%	36%	15%	20%
36–45	17%	17%	15%	20%
46–55	21%	16%	30%	28%
56–65	12%	5%	24%	14%
66–75	1%	2%	6%	5%
76–85			2%	1%

The Southbound Masses

Questionnaires were distributed to Finns arriving in Gran Canaria on a charter flight for a short-term visit (1–2 weeks) in January 1994. Longer stays by Finnish tourists are not supported by my data because those tourists had already arrived before January. An age comparison (Table 6.1) with two additional holiday destinations (Rhodes, Greece and Bodrum, Turkey) shows that the tourists traveling to Playa del Ingles are clearly older than tourists traveling to Rhodes or Bodrum. These Mediterranean destinations are popular with young Finnish tourists, who party until dawn and live according to this rhythm. In comparison, Playa del Ingles and Maspalomas are rather sleepy bungalow areas where parties occur at concentrated spots while the rest of the tourist community sleeps around them.

A comparison of Finnish tourists who traveled to Athens, Greece, shows that the education level of tourists to Playa del Ingles is distinctively low (Table 6.2). This suggests that there is still a distinction in tourism types by class. The upper levels of the social strata form the typical cultural tourists who travel to authentic historical and cultural sites (see E. Cohen, 1988) while the lower educational levels form the southbound masses. The democratization of tourism has not necessarily led to crowding in the places formerly frequented by the elite but rather in places that were selected for touristification relatively recently—in this case Playa del Ingles (Selänniemi, 1994b).

The level of education among tourists traveling to Athens is very high compared with Playa del Ingles and the general level of education in Finland. The

Table 6.2. Comparison of the Educational Levels of Finnish Tourists

	Basic School or Equivalent	Upper Secondary Education	Higher Education (MA, Equivalent or Higher)
Athens (n = 127)	15 (12%)	40 (31%)	72 (57%)
Playa del Ingles (n = 118)	59 (50%)	54 (46%)	5 (4%)
Total	168 (29%)	284 (50%)	122 (21%)
Level of education in Finland (as of 12/31/91)	49%	41%	10%

tourists with advanced degrees seek destinations that offer more than the sun and the beach, which are the main attractions (sometimes the only ones) of Playa del "Anywhere" around the world. In support, Athens is popular among educated Finnish tourists (Selänniemi, 1994a, 1994c).

Despite their low level of education, the Finns who holiday in Playa del Ingles are relatively experienced travelers. Of the sample polled, 51% had made more than 10 holiday trips abroad and only 4% were experiencing their first vacation abroad. In Athens these figures were 70% and 1%, respectively. The statistics are deceiving on this point. Of the Finnish tourists who returned the questionnaire, 74% were repeat visitors to the Canary Islands, and many were repeat visitors specifically to Playa del Ingles. What is more significant in comparison with the tourists at the other destinations is the fact that 9% of these tourists had never traveled to a destination other than the Canary Islands (Table 6.3).

A statistical comparison (although samples are small) clearly illustrates travel preferences. Tourists at Playa del Ingles favor Spain as their holiday destination, whereas Finns contacted in Rhodes clearly favor Greece. However, tourists in Athens demonstrated a wide variety of equally favored destinations with a high percentage of trips to central Europe and long-distance tourism (Asia, Africa, and Oceania).

A Diary: Days in Playa del Ingles

The following diary, written by a Finnish tourist, provides deeper insight into a holiday in Playa del Ingles. The diary was, of course, originally written in Finnish. Translated and shortened here, it is unfortunately bereft of the misspellings and style that contributed to the impression of a happy holiday in Playa del Ingles. Written by a 52-year-old woman who worked in a farmer's locum in a small municipality in central Finland, she was on holiday with her husband. Both were relatively inexperienced tourists (fewer than 10 holiday trips).

Table 6.3. Frequency of Visitation Choices: Athens, Rhodes, and Playa del Ingles

Destination	Athens (n = 49)	Rhodes (n = 150)	Playa del Ingles (n = 118)	Total
Spain	89 (7%)	207 (14%)	470 (31%)	766 (18%)
Scandinavia	257 (21%)	341 (22%)	400 (26%)	998 (23%)
Greece	125 (10%)	339 (22%)	105 (7%)	569 (14%)
Other Southern Europe	175 (14%)	155 (10%)	94 (6%)	424 (10%)
Central Europe	218 (18%)	150 (10%)	151 (9%)	519 (12%)
East Europe	118 (10%)	192 (13%)	171 (11%)	481 (11%)
Great Britain	67 (5%)	57 (4%)	26 (2%)	150 (4%)
US/Canada	48 (4%)	27 (2%)	31 (2%)	106 (2%)
Other long distance (Asia, Africa, Oceania)	128 (11%)	49 (3%)	92 (6%)	269 (6%)
Total	1225	1517	1540	4282
Trips per person	25	10	13	13

The Chronology

Day 1. We took a bus from Jyvaskyla to Tampere. From there we flew to Las Palmas. We have been here before, so it isn't so strange for us. At the airport girls dressed in green showed us the way to our bus that would takes us to Ingles. We made some coffee and took a shower and went to bed. It is nice to come from the winter to the summer.

Day 2. The morning was warm and sunny. After drinking our morning coffee we went out to take a look at Ingles. We looked for the way to the beach and found it. After 4 hours of sunbathing we came back to our hotel. We sat down in the sun and had a drink. In the evening we just wondered that here we are again.

Day 3. The morning was windy but warm. We have already been on all the daytrips, so we won't go this time. We walked down to the beach to look at the sea. It was impossible to stay there because the wind was blowing so hard. We came back to the pool to sunbathe, and stayed 4 hours sitting and lying and dipping into the pool at times. We got hungry, so we went to Casa Finlandia for a meal. Then we took a nap and in the evening we went to sing karaoke. It was a good day.

Day 4. The morning came windy, but it was nothing compared with the winds of Finland. We strolled in the malls. When the sun rose higher the beach and the sea started to tempt. We walked first to the beach and then to the dunes and to Masapalomas. It was wonderful to walk barefoot in the hot sand just like when I was a child. Tired but happy we returned to the hotel. It feels strange when it is summer and the evening gets dark so quickly.

Day 5. The morning was warm. Today it is going to be a nice weather for sunbathing. Many people came to the pool. We lay down at the pool. The sun warmed nicely. It's wonderful that after a few hours' flight you can be and feel like this. This is a place where all worries disappear. After 4 hours we were "ripe," so we went to make coffee. To celebrate Sunday we went out for dinner. The smorgasbord at Casa Finlandia offered a good meal.

Day 6. The sun kept hiding all day. Still we had lots to do. We walked around and strolled in the mall. We took photos and wondered how many species of plants and cactuses grow here. We looked for our travel agent's office and finally found it. We strolled in the center and shopped a bit. In the evening we went singing karaoke. The Finns were having a party there. It was February when we returned to the hotel.

Day 7. The sun was shining again. We went straight to the pool to sunbathe. The water in the pool was getting warmer. We stayed til afternoon, making coffee in between. In the afternoon we heard that we will have to change hotel tomorrow.

Day 8. Today we moved. It felt a bit sad to leave the places that had already become familiar. We packed our bags and went for our new home. We settled down soon and found a nice sunbathing place on the roof. The travel agent has treated us well. The things happen and they can't help it. After we had finished our tax-free bottle we were ready for bed.

Day 9. The first morning without a cloud in the sky. Today is going to be hot, and it felt wonderful. We started to get to know other Finns. We went to the same restaurant to eat as earlier. At night we walked back to the same place to watch the karaoke contest. We know people there also.

Day 10. Today we went to the sea in the morning. The sun was shining brightly but it was rather windy. We started walking along the beach and there were a lot of people coming and going. My skin started to burn so I took a quick swim in the sea. After 4 km we felt that today's exercise and sun was done. Tomorrow we will go on a sea trip. I hope it will be warm.

Day 11. A bus picked us up at the agreed spot. We didn't understand a word during the whole trip, we were the only Finns. After the return we went to look at the action in town.

Day 12. Sunday came with sunshine. We got a message that our neighbors from Finland had come here too. We went for a visit. Then we went walking together. They had not seen the camels so we took a look at them. We came back and had coffee together. We decided to go out to dinner together. The food is good here and I eat a lot. We sat chatting together until midnight.

Day 13. I woke up at the same time with the sun. After coffee we went to the roof balcony to sunbathe. We had an invitation to visit our neighbors. We went to the shops before the siesta. We telephoned home, where the freezing cold had not eased yet and had broken the water pipes so the cows had to be watered by carrying the water from the well. This did sink the holiday mood a bit, but you thought that you cannot do anything from here. With our friends we sat in the sun and felt very relaxed.

Day 14. The first thought today was that tomorrow we will return home. The presents and souvenirs had to be bought today. We bought jogging suits. The other one's zipper broke right away. We have kept close contact with our neighbors. We had coffee together and talked about going home. We agreed that one week is too short for a holiday over here. We hope to come back next winter.

Author Interpretation

The writer experiences Playa del Ingles mainly synesthetically with her senses of feeling and sight. The sun is a very central issue in the diary, except for the last day, when thoughts are already directed to the return. Playa del Ingles is sensed mainly as heat on the skin and under the bare feet, warm and beautiful weather, and a cooling sea. Alongside these primarily tactile sensations some visual percep-tions also add to the picture of the place visited. Hearing, taste, and smell have been largely filtered out.

The writer's perceptions of Playa del Ingles mainly include things that strike the writer as most different from her home environment—which echoes Urry's (1990) view on tourism resulting from the basis of binary opposition between the ordinary and nonordinary. These observations deal with climate, the sea, the sand dunes, and also the hotel area, which are compared with home. The only places that are named in the diary are shopping centers, hotels, restaurants, and the sand dunes of Maspalomas. With the exception of the sand dunes, the perceptions of Playa del Ingles are interchangeable with any holiday resort in the "south."

The diary implies altered meaning for spatial, temporal, and even social bound-aries for tourists in the "south." In some cases they even cease to exist or are at least very ethereal, as in the case of the boundary between inside and outside. The writer does not differentiate between these, even though she refers to the hotel as "home." The ambiguity of these boundaries also affects the experience of the south, as well as culturally determined patterns of perception. This emerges in the sentence where she writes that it feels so strange when nightfall arrives so early in summer. The only time a Finn experiences a warm night is at midsummer, when it is light almost 24 hours a day.

The writer expresses the journey to Gran Canaria as a journey to summertime, away from the arctic winter in Finland. The thought of the south as eternal summer, like the summers of childhood when it was always warm and one seemed to have almost unlimited time, is clearly present in this diary. She expresses her return to childhood memories when she writes about the enjoyable feeling of heat under one's bare feet, just the way it was when she was a child. These tourist pleasures are derived from tactile stimuli of a very basic nature, to which we do not pay attention in everyday life, nor can we afford the time to stop to enjoy them. As Pasi Falk (1994) has written:

> the human body as a sensory and sensual being presupposes always (already) its counterpart, the 'sensible' body, that is, a body subsumed to a cultural Order—both symbolic and practical—defining its boundaries and its position in the larger whole (community or society). (p. 2)

Perhaps the transition from home to the south in sun tourism can be understood as a crossing of the boundaries of the sensible body.

The diary of the 52-year-old woman from the countryside of central Finland, together with diaries from other destinations (Rhodes and Bodrum) relating to this case study, accentuate the point made by Soile Veijola and Eeva Jokinen that the tourist's physical body is largely absent in tourism research. *The Tourist Gaze* (Urry, 1990) or MacCannell's (1973, 1989a) theories approach tourists' perceptions visually. They become powerful tools for the analysis of sightseeing, cultural tourism, and "secular pilgrimages" to sites like the Acropolis in Athens (cf. Selänniemi, 1994c). However, they are inadequate in the analysis of sun tourism at beach resorts. Tourism research has long focused on one sense—sight—while negating an entire spectrum of human senses, perhaps as a result of the Aristotelian hierarchy of the senses where only sight and hearing were human senses, the rest animal senses. In this sense [sic!] one might see the pleasures of sun lust tourism result from "letting the animal loose" (not necessarily in the stereotypically negative meaning) in oneself to enjoy sensual pleasures. Thus, the cultural elite (including many tourism scholars) are given the means by which to create a distinction (cf. Bourdieu, 1989) between the "high" culture/tourism (looking and hearing) and "low" culture/tourism (feeling, tasting, smelling) but they seldom do so. This bias—or even elitism—is apparent in much scholarly work on tourism (Selänniemi, 1996a).

In spite of the monotonous daily rhythm of this tourist's holiday, she appeared to be very happy. The change from the cold countryside of central Finland with hard agricultural labor seemed to be absolutely wonderful. She did not express any wish to gain contact with local people, or even to see other ways of life. She and her husband even dined either at their apartment or at the Finnish restaurant Casa Finlandia! This tourist was happy with the "south" where she could do as she pleased at her own rhythm. The diarist expresses almost daily how wonderful the climate and warmth is. Another interesting feature in the diary occurs on day 8 when she implies an attachment to the apartment as a home in "little Finland" with their actual neighbors from central Finland. The recurring social activity of coffee drinking, for example, is very typical of Finns and creates an atmosphere of safety and familiarity by structuring the sojourn and forming a link to the cultural practices of home. The diary quoted above, together with other field material from Playa del Ingles and other holiday destinations, confirms the comment by Richard Butler (1992) that people in fact seem to enjoy being mass tourists:

> They actually like not having to make their own travel arrangements, not having to find accommodations when they arrive at a destination, being able to obtain goods and services without learning a foreign language, being able to stay in reasonable and sometimes considerable comfort, being able to eat relatively familiar food, and not having to spend vast amounts of money or time to achieve these goals. (p. 32)

Ambiguous Places at Curious Times

Playa del Ingles is clearly a holiday destination that is located in the ambiguous zone labeled "the south." Finns often refer to their holiday destinations simply as *etela* (south) without clarifying the exact geographical destination. Common phrases are *kavimme etelassa lomalla* (we went south on our holiday) or *lahden etelanmatkalle* (I will go south). In fact, the term *etelanmatka* cannot be translated into English without losing some connotations. Literally it means a "trip to the south," but the term refers to a specific trait in modern Finnish culture: a charter trip to a holiday destination where the climate is more favorable than arctic Finland. The concept *etela* also is widely used in tourism marketing, especially in newspaper advertisements, sometimes without any identification of where the "south" is. This type of marketing is directed to attract tourists wishing to get away from everyday life for a short time to somewhere where it is "nice and warm"—*Playa del Anywhere*.

The Liminoid South

These southbound Finnish mass tourists do not fit neatly into Valene Smith's (1989b) definition of a tourist: "in general, a tourist is a temporarily leisured person who voluntarily visits a place away from home for the purpose of experiencing a change" (p. 1).

Yes, they are temporarily leisured persons who do voluntarily take a charter flight to a holiday destination in the south. But *do* they really visit a place? The south, the holiday zone, is away from home, but can the tourists be said to *visit* a place if they have no interest in the destination's distinctiveness? They do intend to experience a change, but the change is not extended to the full experience of a place. It is much more a question of *getting away* from work, home, and negative aspects connected with everyday life to a holiday zone with few attributes of a distinctive place. If the holiday destination has too many characteristics of a real place, the tourist will be reminded of everyday life or challenged by the intricacies of cultural difference. Playa del Ingles is a perfect place for tourists who just wish to experience a change, to recuperate, to "charge the batteries," by traveling *from a place to*, in a sense, *nowhere.*

The holiday for the southbound mass tourist is a vacation *in the liminoid zone.* The south is a zone where the sun always shines and produces a nice tan. The climate is warm, and the norms and sanctions are much more relaxed than at home, to the degree that tourists feel "free" to do things or behave in ways that they would not consider when at home. This *antistructure* is to be found in a resort that is often familiar to the tourist in some way. When the principal motive for travel is to get away from everyday life, a destination that has familiar aspects is tempting. In such a familiar, safe place, one can order meals and drinks in Finnish from a Finnish menu. This is especially true for older Finnish tourists, with less education and limited foreign language skills. These extensions of the home culture, the "little Finlands," can be found in many Mediterranean mass tourist destinations as well as in Playa del Ingles.

A re-statement of Graburn's model (see Graburn, Chapter 3; cf. Leach, 1982a, p. 134) with a focus on the ritual process (V. Turner, 1978; van Gennep, 1960) allows an analysis of liminoid tourism (Figure 6.2). In contrast to Graburn's and Leach's models, I consider liminal (or sacred) time to be a flow of events, where the ritual subject glides from one condition into the other.

In transition rites, the ritual subjects pass through phases from preliminal (the normal profane state of things), through the liminal (the sacred, abnormal, anomalous, dangerous time), then back to the postliminal (normal and profane). Victor and Edith Turner (1978, pp. 249–250) describe the liminal as a state and process in the transition phase, during which the ritual subjects go through a zone, which has few if any attributes of the pre- or postliminal phase. They are *between.* Liminality has often been compared to death, invisibility, darkness, bisexuality, and wilderness (Turner & Turner, 1978, pp. 249–250). The stage in tourism that resembles the liminal phase in rites of passage could be called the liminoid or quasiliminal by Turner's terms.

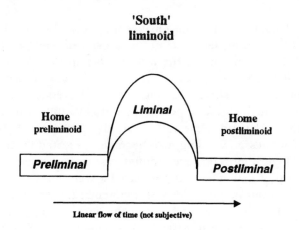

Figure 6.2. The charter trip as a journey to the liminoid.

The liminoid is related to the ritually liminal, but is not identical with it. The liminoid of tourism is *produced and consumed by individuals* while the liminal is believed by the members of society to be of divine origin and by nature anonymous. The liminoid is also fragmentary compared with the liminal. Often elements of the liminal have been separated from the whole to act individually in specialized fields like art (Turner & Turner, 1978, p. 253.) In art, popular culture, entertainment, and tourism products are made for consumption by individuals and groups that promise to remove the consumer away from the everyday experience into a stage that resembles the liminal for a limited time span. The attraction of traveling to the south, "to nowhere," lies in the opportunity to be transported and transformed for a moment into the liminal or liminoid where "everything is possible."

The liminoid phase in tourism has a very diffuse beginning. The individual glides into the tourist role with thoughts about a holiday away from home. When the potential tourist enters the liminoid, fundamental changes occur: normal social time stops. People are no longer confined to everyday timetables; they sleep late, eat whatever it suits them, follow no time schedules, and party until they drop. A freedom of the "south" is that one does not have to do anything.

Social antistructure or the so-called *communitas* (undifferentiated, democratic, direct, and spontaneous social bonds or contacts) is characteristic of liminality. Communitas is a temporary state in which common norms are relaxed and social structure partly loses its significance (Turner & Turner, 1978, pp. 249–250). The communitas-type social contacts become evident when the normally (stereotypically) shy, stiff, and laconic Finns chat eagerly with total strangers, even though these strangers most often are other Finnish tourists. Social bonds are created without obligations. In the holiday resort tourist couples may jointly hire a car and go on excursions, dine together, or invite each other for a drink on the balcony of their apartments, and even exchange driving directions to each other's summer cottages on the plane before landing. But when the plane has landed at Helsinki airport and the "posttourists" have collected their luggage, there is no obligation to contact the people met on holiday, even less to drive up to their summer cottage. It would probably be interpreted as impolite. On another level, it would mix the "south" with "home," that is, the liminoid with the postliminoid.

The liminoid character of the south makes it possible for people to behave in ways they would not consider at home. It is even possible to think that the antistructure of the south entices the *latent other* in the tourist self to come forth. The anti-self (the boozing, destructive, sexual, or adventurous) or the ideal self (social, creative, or sensitive) may take over and even alternate in the same person. In Playa del Ingles I met a person who was happily drunk. At home this person had a rather strict and conservative attitude towards alcohol consumption. And in Rhodes I witnessed a young man become interested in the medieval old town and archeological museum, even though he was supposed to party day and night with a group of pals who had purchased a week in the "party zone." This altered state of mind during liminoidity or fragmental antistructure of the "south" explains why the overt homo- and transsexuality does not raise havoc among the relatively conservative Finnish tourists. In this state, they regard the "south" as a *warm playground* where everything is possible. People are inclined to either accept or close their eyes to normally intolerable behavior, and also to stretch the limits of their own behavior.

Conclusions

The Finnish diarist experienced the south mainly synesthetically with her senses of sight and feeling. The trip to Playa del Ingles was a surrogate return to childhood, to pleasures derived from simple but very profound visual and tactile sensations. The "otherness" of the south compared with home was expressed in binary opposites, with only the positive experience actually mentioned and the negative experience implied in the diary. Thus, the recurring mention of the sun implies the lack of sunshine in the winter of arctic Finland; warmth is compared with the extremely cold temperatures, which even broke the water pipes back home; relaxed time use and the easiness of falling asleep implies structured time and even possible insomnia in everyday life; the repeated visits to the Finnish karaoke bar imply the reality of countryside Finland with few leisure opportunities and perhaps even negative sanctions connected with alcohol use.

Location seems to be of little importance to sun tourists as long as the visited resort has all the attributes of the "south," which could be described as liminoid zone or not located exactly anywhere. The attractiveness of sun trips lies partly in the promise of liminoidity; not explicitly, but in the expectation of the freedoms of the south. Playa del Ingles is familiar, either by virtue of prior visit or by word of mouth. The tourists import their cultural habits and practices with them, like the preparation of Finnish coffee, and interact mainly with other Finnish tourists in bars and nightclubs with Finnish hosts and artists. Finns traveling on an *etelanmatka* visit a familiar culture outside time and place, "like fish in water." In essence, the Finns (and probably many others) are psychocentrics who travel *with and in* their culture, but by changing location they leave sanctions behind and gain the freedoms of liminoidity. Thus, cultural authenticity of the destination is of little importance. In this type of tourism *how* you experience is more important than *what* you experience (Selanniemi, 1996b, 1997). The transition to the liminoid alters our sensual awareness.

In image-oriented sun tourism people buy time as much as they buy a place to visit. In modern society, time is a marketed commodity; to relax from everyday life, a person must "buy time" at ever-increasing cost. It may be one hour in the gym, a season ticket to the hockey matches, or any other preferred activity, including to *be home*. The most conspicuous form of time buying occurs in tourism. Anything from spa daytrips to 24-hour cruises "to nowhere" or charter tourism to the south provides a way of escaping the normal, profane, everyday time to a state of mind where even time loses its importance. The data collected from Finnish tourists indicate that in tourism there are different degrees of the liminoid, which partly supports E. Cohen's (1979a) phenomenology of tourist experiences. However, Cohen uses the degree of alienation from the individual's home society as a measurement of the depth of the tourist experience, and this is open to question (Selänniemi, 1996a). As Tom Selwyn (1996, p. 6) argues, Cohen's classification is built on *a priori* grounds and one may doubt its ethnographic justification.

Sun tourists do not travel with an expectation of something new or strange. Confrontation with the "other" is not even an attractive thought to them. They want the same safe and familiar extension of home culture with better climate and liminoid features every year. Even people who can otherwise be termed cultural tourists may buy a trip to Playa del Anywhere for relaxation every now and then to avoid the sightseeing obligations involved in cultural tourism. Individuals who have fulfilled a secular "pilgrimage" to a place like Athens, Istanbul, Rome, or Paris know the exhaustion of the touristic rituals of a cultural liminal "high." In fact, the sun lust tourist may find authentic pleasure in the inauthenticity of a tourist attraction, or as D. Brown (1996, p. 38) puts it, "the tourist seeks out the inauthentic Other in the quest for the authentic Self" (p. 38).

The key to an emic understanding of Finnish sun lust tourism lies in seeing the *fourfold transition* that takes place during the trip. The *spatiotemporal transition* from place to, in a sense, placelessness (cf. Relph, 1986) and similarly from time to timelessness are the first two transitions that seem prerequisites for the following two. The trip from everyday life, home, work—the profane to the liminoid south—brings with it a *mental transition* whereby the tourist leaves the everyday Self behind and becomes the holiday Self. The fourth transition—the *sensory/sensual transition*—becomes the shift in how we sense our surroundings.

The critics of mass tourism often say that it cannot provide personal, unique, and strong experiences. But for the diarist, the charter flight, package tour, and sightseeing are only a means to an end. They do not imply superficiality and triviality, as often stated. The phenomenon called tourism must not be expressed solely in quantitative terms as one kind of tourism, or as the largest industry in the world (cf. Davidson, 1994; Theobald, 1998). The qualitative interpretation of Finnish mass tourism to Playa del Ingles (and the other destinations studied) shows that a charter trip to a mass tourist resort in the south can be a very significant experience for the tourist. It is important to know the motives of the tourists who prefer the ready-built resorts of the Mediterranean region and Canary Island as their destinations. Additionally, this type of charter tourism can actually be nonthreatening to the local culture and natural environment. Charter flights transport large numbers of tourists with relatively low environmental impact compared with the same number of "individual tourists" flying to the jungles of Borneo. If the tourists are content with inauthenticity—and many are—they will have minimal contact with local people and a relatively low cultural impact on the host culture (compared with so-called "cannibal tourists"). As soon as tourists step outside the fenced area the trouble begins.

Chapter 7

Time and Space: Atlantic City in 1886

Maryann Brent

The board game Monopoly, appearing near the height of Atlantic City's popularity (1930s), revisits the successes and pitfalls of entrepreneurial activity in coastal resort towns. Built uniquely for tourism, the seaside resort of Atlantic City was a genial success while the railroads prospered (1856–1963). Most recent visitors will agree that Atlantic City is no longer a seaside resort. It is a gambling resort by the seaside. This case study converts a selected year of real time into a map of organized space while pursuing two objectives. The first locates a heyday within Atlantic City's evolution. Heyday is defined as the time when essential tourism infrastructure is complete, hosts are prospering, guests are enthusiastic, and the *rate of tourism growth has recently peaked.* The second objective reveals the relationships between selected heyday recreational land uses (transportation, tourist public space, tourist accommodations) and permanent residences. The goal of this exercise is an assessment of the transportation (railroad) impact on resort land use.

Context

Funnell (1975) described Victorian Atlantic City as a Disneyland for adults. This coastal resort town resides on a barrier island belonging to a system of islands and salt marshes on the east coast of New Jersey in the United States. Approximately 10 miles long, it is located in the southern half of a peninsula whose western border is the Delaware Bay and whose eastern border is the Atlantic Ocean. Atlantic City did not emerge from a fishing industry or any industry. It was a planned resort.

In the mid-19th century, Jonathan Pitney, a physician from the mainland town of Absecon, envisioned a health spa for his patients and friends on the neighboring barrier island. Pitney was so convinced of the success of a resort that he persuaded a group of Philadelphia investors to embrace a development plan. The investors constructed a railroad from Philadelphia to Absecon Island and immediately established a land company there. Begun in 1852, Absecon Beach (or Absecon

Island) adopted the name of Atlantic City and was operational by 1856. Investors planned the street grid, transportation access, internal transportation, and a large hotel before any construction occurred. While land company investors and small businesses flourished early on, all of the original railroad investors went bankrupt because they could not combat the political influence and incorporation of the much larger Pennsylvania and Reading railroad companies.

In order to find a year representing heyday, it was useful first to apply the benchmarks of Butler's evolutionary stages to Atlantic City's tourism chronology (Table 7.1). This exercise located the approximate conclusion of development and the onset of consolidation, which was subsequently compared with data illustrating the resort's cumulative growth and rate of growth. The goal was the creation and analysis of a land-use map of Atlantic City's heyday, marked by the *recent peak of the rate of growth.*

Time: Atlantic City Heyday, 1886

Cyclical Time and Real Time

Urban scholars of various perspectives have described the cyclical nature of cities since the 1920s. The concept of destination evolution most frequently referenced in tourism research bases itself on the product life cycle. British geographer Richard Butler (1980) described the evolution of resort towns in a unique way by proposing that successive phases of a single destination present different "places" during the maturation process. The phases—"places"—range from a total absence of tourist amenities (exploration) to a conspicuous overbuilding (stagnation). Each "place," like sequent occupancy, attracts different types of tourists ranging from explorers to mass tourists. Thus, the phases of a single destination correspond to changes in tourist types and changes in the tourist landscape.

A thorough understanding of Butler's original essay is essential for two important reasons. First, while the article is enjoyable to read, it is conceptually denser than it appears. Butler's findings are based on earlier (1974) work. Second, the "resort cycle," as the concept is informally known, enjoys relationships not only with tourist type, but also with landscape and activity type (Lavery, 1974), resort type (Meyer-Arendt, Sambrook, & Kermath, 1992), distance decay (Travis, 1993; G. Wall 1974), cost–distance (Stansfield, 1983), resort morphology (Meyer-Arendt, 1987, R. Smith, 1992), responsible tourism (Wilkinson, 1997), and others. The resort cycle is important in its own right and by its association with other concepts.

The two aspects of growth employed in the resort cycle—cumulative growth and rate of growth—have not always been well understood. Butler's well-known evolutionary chart based on tourist arrival data illustrates cumulative growth (Figure 7.1). The maximum popularity of a destination occurs late in evolution but does not correspond with the highest rate of growth. The highest rate of growth occurs during late development and the beginning of consolidation.

Butler (1980) bases evolutionary progress upon visitor response: the number of tourist visits. When tourist arrival data are not available, it is reasonable to substitute appropriate surrogate data. Because the author could not find dependable

Table 7.1. Chronology of Atlantic City's Evolution

1840s	Stage or jersey wagon to Absecon Island; Leed's and Ryan's boarding houses (Wilson, 1953)	**Involvement?**
1850	Absecon Island inhabited by lighthouse keeper and a few fishermen	
1852	Dr. Pitney secured rail charter for C&A	**Development**
1854	First train arrives in Atlantic City (Coop & Coxey, 1980); all east–west blocks are the same length (Rose, 1878)	Changes in physical appearance
1856	Regularly scheduled passenger trains to Atlantic City (Stansfield, 1978)	
1863	City ordinance prohibits sand, seaweed, and grass removal to avoid recurrences of beach erosion (Butler, 1954)	
1870	First bridge for horse-drawn vehicles (Stansfield, 1983); first boardwalk along the ocean	Man-made/imported facilities
1877	Original C&A investor, Richards, builds second railway (Cook & Coxey, 1980); significant erosion of north beaches, expansion of south beaches (Rose, 1878)	
1883	C&A and P&AC railroads now controlled by Pennsylvania and Reading Lines, respectively (Cook & Coxey, 1980)	Tourist market open to working classes
1886	Residents plan Chelsea suburb (Funnell, 1975)	**Consolidation;** Discontent among permanent residents
1887	Iron Pier (later the Heinz Pickle Pier) opened	
1890	Rate of permanent population growth begins to decline	Height of the resort's rate of growth
1920s	Rise of automobile access to Atlantic City (Funnell, 1975)	
1933	All trains owned by the Pennsylvania and Reading Lines merged in South Jersey (Butler, 1954)	
1941–1945	World War II	**Stagnation;** Economic decline
1963	Passenger train service ends	
1975	Gambling is legalized	**Rejuvenation attempt**

visitor arrival data for the closing decades of the 19th century, population census data were substituted. In this particular case study, the substitution is reasonable because Atlantic City's only industry was, and is, tourism. Thus, one can assume that changes in permanent population reflected demand (tourist visits).

Cumulative Growth and Rate of Growth

Rate of growth can be derived from cumulative growth. The population data (1860–1990) shown in Table 7.2 portray the cumulative growth of Atlantic City's tourism.

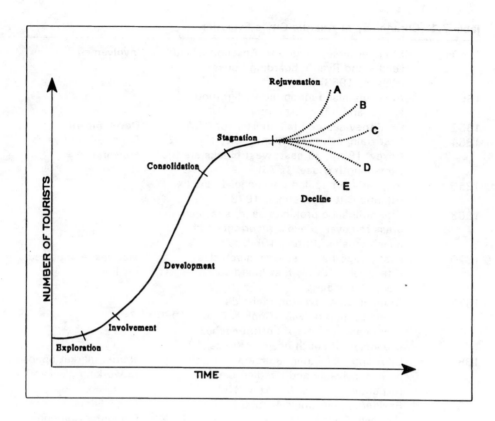

Figure 7.1. Butler's resort cycle. (Reprinted from Butler, 1980, *The Canadian Geographer, 24*, with permission.)

Table 7.2. Atlantic City Population Data

	Year	Resident Population
A	1860	687
B	1870	1,043
C	1880	5,477
D	1890	13,055
E	1900	27,838
F	1910	46,150
G	1920	50,707
H	1930	66,198
I	1940	64,094
J	1950	61,657
K	1960	59,544
L	1970	47,859
M	1980	40,199
N	1990	37,986

Rate of growth can be determined by applying the following equation to the cumulative data: if A = population in 1860 and B = population in 1870, then the percentage of change at 10-year intervals (or rate of growth) is:

B - A/A
1043 - 687/687 = 52%, the starting point
C - B/B = percentage of change from 1870 to 1880
5477 - 1043/1043 = 425%

One can continue in this manner through all of the data (i.e., A, B, . . . X, Y, Z) to record rate of growth. Figure 7.2 illustrates cumulative population growth and the rate of population growth.

The rate of growth from 1880 to 1890 declined in relation to the previous decade. This was so even though the increase in visitor arrivals from 1880 (5477) to 1890 (13,055) was much greater (7578) than in the previous decade (4434). The percent of change necessary for an increase in the rate of growth between 1880 and 1890—or any other decade of Atlantic City's history— would have to exceed 425%. As shown above, it is merely 52%.

The beginning of the consolidation stage corresponds with the height of the rate of growth (Butler, 1980). Figure 7.2 identifies the years between 1880 and 1890 as heyday—just past the peak in the rate of growth. The creation of a landuse map of Atlantic City's heyday required the location of historic records for the period between 1880 and 1890. The discovery of an 1886 Sanborn map of Atlantic City (New Jersey State Library) and Gopsill's 1886 Atlantic City Directory (Atlan-

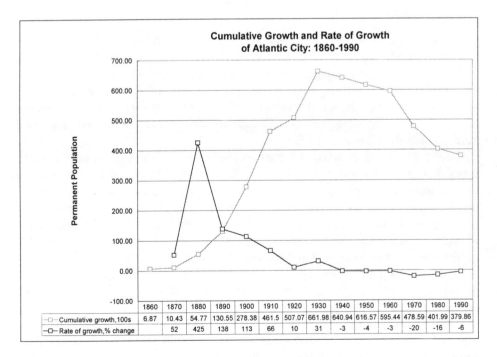

Figure 7.2. Cumulative growth and rate of growth of Atlantic City: 1860-1990.

tic City Free Public Library) proved fortunate in this regard. The map and the city
directory complemented each other and permitted the creation of a new land-use
map portraying the tourist culture.

Space: Selected Atlantic City Land Uses in 1886

Transportation

Construction of the Camden and Atlantic Railroad (C&A) began in 1852 when
the state of New Jersey granted a charter to investors. The right of way followed a
straight line from Philadelphia, PA, across the Delaware River and the state of New
Jersey to the ocean. In fact, the directness of the route ignored the marshy landscape and attendant engineering problems. When the engineering was resolved,
on the other hand, the conservation of time was very fortunate for tourists. In
1879, a second railroad introduced competition for the C&A. After only 5 years
(1883), this renegade was taken over by the Reading Railroad, which initiated
ticket prices that were lower than those of the C&A. Thus, tourists were lucky to
have a very good ticket price—50 cents—and a mere 90-minute ride to the beach
from smoky, steamy Philadelphia.

The train tracks for Atlantic City's internal transport spanned the town from
east to west, occupying the main street, Atlantic Avenue. Therefore, upon reaching
Atlantic City, the C&A continued eastward on Atlantic Avenue toward the Inlet so
that wealthier tourists could disembark at the large hotels. Daytrippers from
Philadelphia's factory workforce continued directly to the beach and the boardwalk on the southwest side of town.

Public Space

The dominant public space in 1886 was the beach. Symbolically, the beach represents a buffer zone between culture (human constructions) and wilderness (nature) (Jeans, 1990). Original entrepreneurs envisioned a wealthy clientele who
would take elegant carriage rides on the beach, a custom followed in resort towns
such as Cape May to the south. However, Philadelphia factory workers delighted
in taking donkey rides (Figure 7.3) and wore daring bathing costumes that reached
only as far as their knees!

Atlantic City's boardwalk was the second public space and paralleled the beach.
It began as an 8-foot-wide path along the beach in 1870 but quickly transformed
into commercial space, perfectly representing the classic recreational business
district (RBD) (Stansfield, 1971; Stansfield & Rickert, 1970). It was characterized
by many mechanical amusement rides (Figure 7.4). Such amusement rides, origi-
nating from the great expositions and pleasure parks of North America and Europe, continue their existence in contemporary theme parks and amusement parks.
Well-off tourists who became fatigued during boardwalk promenades hired wicker
rolling chairs (Figure 7.5). Both amusement rides and boardwalk trams are familiar components of resorts more than 100 years later.

The boardwalk and the beach were separate places. In 1886, the boardwalk was
a partially roofed structure that made ocean views difficult or impossible from
some locations. More importantly, the boardwalk symbolically turned its back to

Figure 7.3. Tourists riding donkeys. (Courtesy of the Atlantic County Historical Society, Somers Point, NJ.)

Figure 7.4. Epicycloidal diversion. (Courtesy of the Atlantic County Historical Society, Somers Point, NJ.)

Figure 7.5. The boardwalk and rolling chairs. (Courtesy of the Atlantic County Historical Society, Somers Point, NJ.)

the water by virtue of its intense commercial nature. Besides mechanical amusements, Atlantic City's boardwalk RBD included food and beverage services, candy concessions and souvenirs, skating, shooting galleries, water slides, photography stalls, and bowling. At first a novelty that rapidly gained popularity locally, boardwalks contribute to resort landscapes across the United States.

Tourist Accommodations

Accommodations existed south of Atlantic Avenue. The large hotels, served by the first railroad (C&A), catered to upper-middle-class tourists and occupied the eastern side of the resort. The large hotels required spacious grounds because they offered RBD functions immediately on the premises (Brent, 1997). In addition to private room accommodations, the large hotels included a dining room, facilities for entertaining friends, concerts, social functions such as balls and hops, as well as archery, tennis, and quoits outside on the lawn.

Although a great deal of space was required for the hotels, larger profits were gained from the crowded boarding houses and guest houses that clustered south of the second train terminal on the western side of the resort. These accommodations were simpler, more limited in amenities, and much less expensive than the hotels. Although the original investors hoped that the resort would rival other elite resorts on America's east coast, such as Long Branch, Cape May, and Monmouth Park, Atlantic City was favoring lower class mass tourism resort by 1886.

Permanent Residences

Gopsill's Atlantic City Directory 1886 and the Sanborn Map of Atlantic City 1886 permitted an understanding of both employment locations and home addresses of Atlantic City's permanent residents. Seventy-five percent of the usual retail goods and services occupied the main street, Atlantic Avenue (Gopsill's Atlantic City Directory, 1886; Sanborn Map & Publishing Ltd., 1886). A node near the original C&A terminal located Atlantic City's Central Business District (CBD). Permanent residents lived on, or north of, Atlantic Avenue, and their demographics reflected the distribution of tourist accommodations south of Atlantic Avenue. Servants and poorly paid workers lived on the west side. These included waiters, wheelwrights, drivers, porters, and other low-wage workers. However, the northeast was less homogeneous socially and economically. It housed servants as well as professional individuals who lived and worked from the same location. The principal residents listed in the northeast quadrant included engineers, engravers, grocers, oystermen, printers, upholsters, roofers, and real estate agents. Thus, the town was divided on both axes by the railroads (Figure 7.6). East and west generally separated rich and poor while north and south divided residents from the tourists.

It is significant that in 1886 many successful merchants were eager to live in a new residential community in adjacent Chelsea. Atlantic City's business families no longer wished to maintain their homes in the cluttered, noisy, and hectic town that had become a recreational suburb for Philadelphia's factory workers (Funnell, 1975).

Discussion

Historiographical evidence indicates that the dominant class of tourists changed after 1883. The change of tourist type is a direct response to transportation prices, market proximity, and acceptable profit for the railroads, hotels, and small business entrepreneurs. Very simply, transportation was a critical element in the success of Atlantic City's tourism. Further, it has been shown elsewhere (Giuliano, 1986; Hoyt 1939) and reemphasized here that transportation influences urban land-use patterns.

It is reasonable to assume that when one transportation technology is eclipsed by another, former land-use relationships may no longer apply. As a result, the destination can experience crisis. After World War II, railroads encountered a decline as automobile use increased dramatically. Atlantic City's demise followed the disappearance of the trains because it was planned for rail arrivals, not automobiles.

Atlantic City declined as the use of automobiles increased. While there were only two train termini, each automobile required its own individual terminal—a parking space. Besides parking spaces, maintenance, repair, and fuel services were required for automobiles, which crowded out residents and even tourists and the land use created for their enjoyment. There was no means of isolating Atlantic City from the predominant transportation technology apart from going back in time and disallowing the automobile bridges constructed from 1870 onward. While the physical tourism infrastructure remained, the merchant population finally closed their businesses in the 1950s and 1960s. Without an active merchant population and enough tourist parking, the original resort died.

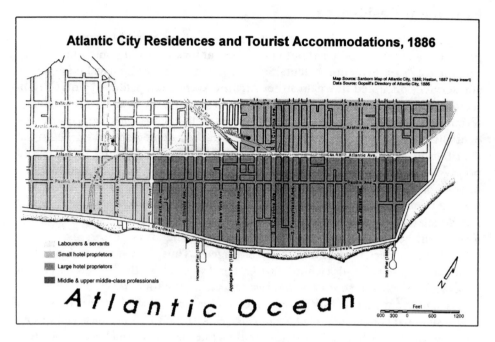

Figure 7.6. Map of Atlantic City residences and tourist accommodations, 1886. (©1997 M. T. Brent and the University of Waterloo.)

From the example of Atlantic City, one can consider rate of growth as a series of points, each calculated from the previous point. Cumulative growth, on the other hand, reflects change occurring between the initial and concluding points of data. Cumulative growth data are more compelling in later stages of evolution than those from the rate of growth. For this reason, marketers often promote cumulative growth when the rate of growth is slowing down or declining. It is important for both the community and industry to understand the implications of slowed *rate of growth*. While large corporations use growth concepts routinely for marketing, tourism communities normally understand little about it and are thus vulnerable to negative consequences when their destination is no longer the "in" tourist location.

Understanding evolutionary stages is significant for the economic survival of resort towns. Tourist destinations are vulnerable to a cyclical nature attributable to all cities. In addition, they are often subject to a seasonal nature. They are exceptionally responsive to external events such as terrorism, economic recession, and crime. While a given destination may appear to be robust, the link between appearance and reality might in fact be fragile. Host communities, local entrepreneurs, and large hospitality corporations all benefit from recognizing the current evolutionary phase at their destinations. The tourism industry is skillful at determining when to enter and retreat from investment opportunities. Host communities, on the other hand, have been uninformed. Community members could benefit from applying the descriptive markers of the resort cycle and rate of growth information as tracking tools. This practice could lead to appropriate planning at their destination.

Conclusion

This chapter study has identified a stretch of real time—a heyday—and converted it to a land-use map. Further, it has discussed the influence of transportation upon tourist types and the permanent population. It provides an explanation for the relationships between land uses, both natural (the ocean beach) and constructed (the boardwalk, retail businesses, tourist accommodations, and permanent residences). Transportation technology determined the location of the tourist RBD (Stansfield, 1978) and changed the nature of beach activities. Transportation infrastructure physically divided permanent residences from tourist functions from north to south. At the same time, it bisected the town with an invisible class barrier on the east—west axis. This research has demonstrated the powerful influence of transportation technology in determining land-use borders, shapes, and relationships at tourism destinations. It has also shown that the resort cycle has become integrated into many aspects of tourism theory and has the potential of contributing practical applications in tourism communities.

SECTION 3

CHANGES AND IMPACTS

Chapter 8

Tourism Change and Impacts

Valene L. Smith

"Thar she blows . . ." came the cry from the crow's nest, as the first whaling bark, Superior, *ventured into the Arctic Ocean (1848) in search of a new harvest, and took so many bowhead whale that the following year, 154 whaling vessels cruised north of the Bering Strait (Oswalt, 1979, p. 206). These sailor guests bartered for Inuit services with sugar, cloth, kettles, rifles and, ominously, with rum. Whaling crews needed manpower, warm clothing and food. Inuit men were hired as sailors (or 'shanghaied') aboard the whaling ships, or they hunted for game. Inuit women sewed skin clothing, dried fish and meat, and also became "seasonal wives" for men aboard vessels that over-wintered. The sailors taught Inuit to distill liquor from the potatoes and molasses brought as trade goods. The effects of culture change were immediate and major, especially the introduction of tuberculosis, that spread as the ravages of liquor sometimes reduced subsistence hunting to near starvation levels. The subsequent purchase of Alaska (1867) introduced government officials. The gold-miners of 1898 were another intrusion of exploitative newcomers, who often turned to Inuit hosts for food and clothing. The influence of the Friends' Mission (1898) was predominantly positive, and provided elementary schooling in English, and became a much-needed new surrogate social network in a rapidly changing world. Four distinct types of foreigners: whalers, government officials, miners, and missionaries had significantly changed aboriginal culture in the hundred years before tourism began in 1948.*

More than 50 countries attained independence after World War II (Table 8.1), a list that spans all but two continents (Australia and Antarctica). Their colonial history and subsequent acculturation all bear resemblance to the Alaskan Inuit example. Explorers charted their shores, alien governments accessed their lands, and colonial managers exploited their resources with extractive industries. The Victorian mind-set often deemed the lifestyle of the indigenous people "primitive" and they introduced elementary schools and clinics from the outside, industrial world. Some of these newly independent nations have prospered as important tourist destinations, either as sunbelt centers (Bahamas and Cyprus),

Table 8.1. Independence of Former Colonial Possessions: Post-World War II

Europe		Africa	
1949	Ireland	1951	Libya
1960	Cyprus	1953	Egypt
1964	Malta	1956	Morocco
1990	Lithuania	1956	Sudan
		1956	Tunisia
North America		1957	Ghana
1961	Jamaica	1958	Madagascar
1966	Barbados	1958/9	French West and Equatorial Africa
1968	Bermuda	1959	Zaire
1973	Bahamas	1960	Chad
		1960	Mali
South America		1960	Mauritania
1966	Guyana	1960	Nigeria
		1960	Somalia
Asia		1961	South Africa
1945	Indonesia	1961	Sierra Leone
1946	Jordan	1962	Algeria
1947	India	1962	Burundi
1948	Sri Lanka	1962	Uganda
1948	Burma	1964	Tanzania
1948	Israel	1964	Zambia
1953	Cambodia	1964	Kenya
1956	Pakistan	1965	Gambia
1957	Penang	1966	Botswana
1957	Molucca	1966	Lesotho
1958	Iraq	1974	Guinea-Bissau
1963	Malaysia	1975	Angola
1965	Singapore	1975	Mozambique
		1980	Zimbabwe
Oceania			
1970	Fiji		

Source: Wetterau (1990).

wildlife safaris (Kenya, Tanzania), or historical and cultural treasures (Israel, Egypt). By contrast, Libya, Angola, and Guyana have languished for political reasons. The list is instructive because it recognizes the role of governments as culture brokers in tourism development and culture change (see Richter, Chapter 22). The influences of colonialism and the subsequent importance of the media have usually far outweighed the role of tourism in effecting economic and social change. McElroy and de Albuquerque (1998) astutely summarize this process of economic development,

> The post-1960 restructuring . . . from colonial export staples to tourism has been facilitated by a confluence of forces: metropolitan affluence, multinational investment by invitation, aid-financed infrastructure, and the advent of low-cost jet travel. (p. 145)

Additional factors important to post-Industrial tourism include the progressive sophistication of communication technology and marketing, with a shortened workweek and a changing work ethic.

Tourism: Blessing or Blight?

In the 1980s, individuals questioned whether tourism was a blessing or blight, but the issue is now essentially academic, given the value of tourism as the world's largest industry and its role as a global employer and customer. However, stresses are still evident in the interface between the *supply* and *demand* sides of tourism. The *supply* side of tourism becomes the assets of the culture brokers (see Chapter 21) and also provides service employment. Modern consumer society creates many "aspirational wants" in contrast to "needs" and, for the unemployed, these "wants" may become incentives for crime: car theft, shoplifting, and mugging. Unemployed youths in crowded cities are a frequently untouched labor pool, overshadowed by aggressive in-migrants. An important activity of the World Tourism Organization (WTO) is the impetus to establish training programs to assist young people, especially in Less Developed Countries, to qualify for tourist industry jobs.

The *demand* side of tourism reflects contemporary travel motivations, which in 2000 presses for great travel diversity, including a search for knowledge, for self-identify, and for *fun*. Given the 21st century lifestyle of "hyperculture" (Bertman, 1998), in the Westernizing world the speed of cyberspace has changed the work place, altered family life, and induced greater bodily stress. We work harder, longer (Lardner, 1999), and the pace is quickly absorbed by children born into the microwave culture. Vacations become an essential therapy beyond reach of a cell phone to restore personal equilibrium.

The impacts of tourism reflect incompatible philosophies between demand and supply. On the demand side, the tourist who wants a private beach and the amenities of a fully staffed five-star hotel is unrealistic, because she/he disregards the basic economics of hotel keeping. From the supply side, residents in some rural or suburban communities prefer to limit tourism yet their municipal leaders may be committed to the growth machine philosophy that "bigger is better." Disney Corporation wished to establish a war-related theme park, somewhat in competition with Gettysburg National Cemetery. Supporters included real estate brokers and concessionaires who would benefit financially from this new virtual reality attraction. When the contentious issue was finally brought to a vote, residents overwhelmingly rejected the Disney plan. Their action clearly showed the importance of community input in tourism planning.

The role of tourism as blessing or blight may be assessed by a consideration of its costs and benefits. Table 8.2 summarizes the most basic economic, sociocultural, and environmental influences (or impacts) of tourism, all of which are subject to extensive elaboration.

Tourism income usually benefits a community economically but the associated development often serves as a magnet that attracts labor from outside the area. When Cancún was developed, individuals with greater sophistication and travel industry skills quickly recognized the opportunity for new jobs, and they moved to Cancún. Too much tourism, or the wrong type of tourism, can despoil a commu-

Table 8.2. Selected Cost–Benefit Factors of Tourism

Positive Aspects
  Economic
    Influx of "hard" currency
    Multiplier effect
    Labor-intensive service industries
    Better infrastructure: roads, water, sewage, airports, recreation opportunities
    Income from residents' use of amenities
  Sociocultural
    Widening of social perspective
    Preservation of family ties
    Upward mobility
    Appreciation of heritage and ethnic identity
    Folklore stimulation (or stimulus?); creation of museums
  Environmental
    Awareness of conservation needs
    Establishment of eco-labels
    Awareness of global resource limits
    Establishment of land use limits

Negative Aspects
  Economic
    Seasonality
    Economic leakage
    In-migration of outsiders as managers/labor
    Cost of security to offset crime
    Loss of receipts owing to external economic crises/terrorism
  Sociocultural
    Coca-colaization
    Loss of culutral identity in the Global Village
    Commodificatin of tourists as "things"
    Deterioration of historic sites owing to overuse
    Fearfulness from terrorism and crime
    Commodification of culture
    Misuse of intellectual property rights
  Environmental
    Preservation costs
    Transformation of national parks and zoos
    Loss of wilderness
    Pollution
    Overuse of habitat from the ecotourist fad

nity and marginalize the residents. The case studies in this section detail some of these issues. The Norwegian resorts still fight "turf wars" to attract and maintain their tourist influx but elsewhere, as in the beach resorts of Cancún and Boracay, communities are overwhelmed by mass tourism. However, even a cost–benefit analysis can mask fundamental societal issues including the self-enhancement and greed of individuals who, like Philippine president Marcos (see Richter, Chapter 22), identified the development of tourism as a contribution of his/her leadership.

Tourist Culture: Bridging the Gap Between Resource and Consumer

Our accumulated knowledge of culture change can facilitate two important goals in the decades ahead: finding the "best use" of the tourism resource for consumers and creating proactive tourism management policies. Best use of resources and good policies can "bridge the implementation gap" (Pigram, 1993). The intent of tourism development will achieve what Selwyn (1996, p. 249) terms *tourist culture*. Ideally this local hegemony over economic and political institutions would permit hosts to cope with tourism by "providing some cultural space for tourists while simultaneously preserving other, more private space for themselves." The significance of this space dimension was defined by Goffman (1967) as the *front* and *back* stages of communal life. The front is the meeting place between hosts and guests, including main streets, plaza, and beach; the back region is the private zone such as the little stores where locals shop and eat. Puijk (Chapter 13) describes the problems of violated space in Norwegian life. Each tourist community could develop a unique tourist culture that reflects the ethnographic portrait it wishes to display, including public festivals. Some communities in Europe have long-standing traditions for wine festivals, Christmas markets, and other events that are openly advertised. The sites may not be much visited at other seasons except as place markers (an Olympic host city, or a former World's Fair location).

An alternative approach to tourist culture might also be viewed in terms of effective management of the local carrying capacity (P. Williams & Gill, 1998). Investigation of carrying capacity became fashionable in tourism research a decade or more ago, when carrying capacity was defined as "the level of visitor use an area can accommodate" (WTO/UNEP, 1992). The criteria included statistical data about the volume of tourists (bed nights, visitor days, etc.), their density (numbers of persons per unit of space or activity), and the market mix (the ratio of visitor to resident use of a facility). Farrell and Runyan (1991) note, "the concept is attractive in its simplicity, yet difficult to employ as a basis for a management system" (p. 31) because of the complexity in trying to quantify social and environmental quality. Acknowledging that it is a neat sounding phrase, Lindberg, McCool, and Stankey (1997) echo many of the criticisms directed against carrying capacity and suggest that the concept is inadequate to measure the complexities of tourism. Many social scientists share skepticism about digitizing human behavior as "garbage in, garbage out."

Greater scientification of community ability to better cope with mass tourism depends upon increased sophistication in assessing the host resources and the guest preferences and linking them more carefully through *place marketing*. Cities (and many towns) are becoming particularly adept at creating distinctive self-images, as Las Vegas proclaims it is "the entertainment capital of the world," Vienna is the "city of Strauss," and Manchester, England is "the gay village" (Short & Kim, 1999). The creation of a public culture, by designing open space with artwork, attracts tourists and simultaneously invisibly defines the "front stage" boundaries.

Ethnography of Tourism

The identification of culture change, the management of impacts, and the development of a tourist culture requires breadth and depth of data, best accomplished by envisioning the "big picture" or an ethnography of tourism. Van den Berghe (1994) has provided a rare model in *The Quest for the Other: Ethnic Tourism in San Cristobal.* The case studies in this volume are mini-ethnographies descriptive of one major facet of a larger whole. Ideally, every community should draft its own tourism ethnography, as a description of the lifestyle and values of a group of people united by a culture. If done as a self-analysis, the ethnography elicits knowledge of local strengths and weaknesses in their tourism program, and identifies strategies for development of their tourist culture. Toward that goal, the 4 H's of tourism are outlined here as a field technique for gathering, organizing, and analyzing the essential data for a local tourist ethnography. The 4 H's provide a time-depth, cross-cultural methodological tool that fills a gap in tourism research.

They can be effectively used at various levels, including: (1) introductory workshops to solicit *local input* from residents concerning their tourist resources, and their interest and ability to participate in tourism; (2) an *assessment* mechanism that identifies new opportunities to refocus existing tourism that is approaching decline (on the Butler model); (3) *analysis* of potential sociocultural conflicts in the existing program that may require remediation; (4) provision of a *database* in association with other contiguous destinations to form a regional tourism program (see Zimmermann, Chapter 25); and (5) identification of *potential tourist market(s)* in terms of existing psychographic guest profiles (see Table 8.4).

The 4 H's of Tourism: Habitat, History, Heritage, and Handicrafts

The 4 H's of tourism—habitat, history, heritage, and handicrafts—pinpoint host assets and liabilities in the market mix for initial tourism development (Table 8.3). The same method can also be employed to examine new strategies related to psychographic profiles among the guests, and may reveal previously unrecognized but usable resource assets.

Habitat

Habitat refers to the physical landscape and its tourist attractions: the Great Barrier Reef of Australia, the beaches of the Philippines, or the marshes of Lake Balaton. Critical questions pertinent to habitat areas include: (1) access of the area to tourist markets by reasonable (inexpensive) transportation (this may be a limiting issue for remote islands and for many communities in the sparsely settled

Table 8.3. Analysis of the 4 H's for Tourism

Habitat	Heritage	History	Handicrafts
Access	Museums	Decision-makers	Heritage crafts
Appeal	Ceremonials	Conflict resolution	Innovations
Climate	Experiential	Modern showcase	Authenticity?
Landscape	Ethnnic centers	Marginal man	Miniaturize?
Resources	Folk villages	Honorifics	Artisans

exotic locations such as northern Canada and Greenland); (2) visitor seasonality due to climate; and (3) recreational and participatory activities available for the visitor.

History

History, as used here, is delimited to the record of prior contact with *outsiders*. Exploration and colonialism differ in their degree of cultural disruption, but the nature of those early contacts may predispose an interest in, or success with, modern tourism. For Kotzebue Inuit, most early contacts were relatively benign and hosting outsiders had historically been profitable. By contrast, farther south, the Russian invaders and settlers all but annihilated the Aleuts, and residual resistance to outsiders is still evident in a disinterest in tourism. In 1993, an east Greenland village, Scoresby Sound, refused landing permission to a Russian icebreaker with more than 100 American and German tourists aboard, fearing their presence might endanger local wildlife (as had earlier nontourist vessels, intent on trophy hunting). Hours later, and too late for the icebreaker to return, the decision was reversed when Inuit learned by phone that passengers on this cruise had purchased more than US$10,000 in handicrafts the preceding day, at the neighboring village of Angmagssalik. Both craftsmen and tourists were disappointed at this lost opportunity for sales. Here the roles of decision-makers and marginal men (who may be bilingual and function as cultural intermediaries) are often of critical importance.

The history function provides insight in assessing potential conflicts between government and individuals in decision-making. Some cultures have successfully sustained leadership roles and authority even within a colonial structure. The Maharajahs of India retained most of their lands and privileges intact for nearly a century under British rule. Today many of their palaces are still privately owned and operated as hotels for the benefit of their original owner families. Other groups, such as Aboriginals in Australia, have successfully reasserted tribal authority in conjunction with a supportive government, and are making their culture an integral part of the Australia travel experience at Alice Springs, the Atherton Tableland, and Kakadu National Park (Zeppel, 1998).

Heritage

Heritage refers to the analysis *by the resident population* of the traditional culture in terms of appropriateness for display and manner of display. Museums, folk villages, ceremonial events, and festivals are among the options. Such decisions are often rooted in cultural sanctions, as the Amish have tried to preserve their traditions in private, despite the external commercial interests that commodify their religion. In the American Southwest, the Indian pueblo of Acoma has a history of visitor hospitality, and now welcomes Western guests to their annual festivals (V. Smith, 1996b). Potters display their wares on stands outside their homes, and purchasers may photograph artisans with their work. The adjacent Zuni have strong religious sanctions that ban outsiders, and their pueblo is closed to tourists (Mallari & Enote, 1996). The Zuni are world-renowned silversmiths, but sales of their jewelry are handled by a tribal Co-op at the entry to the pueblo and by retail jewelry and curio stores throughout the region. Such decisions regarding tourist access are politically sensitive and reflect a growing awareness of indigenous autonomy and identity.

Elements of cultural heritage, including traditional knowledge, when commodified and publicly shared, have an obvious monetary value to the host culture, but there are few mechanisms to realize payment and equitably distribute the income. Acoma charges an admission fee, provides trained guides for a short tour of the pueblo, and the earned income is used for community projects and social services. Zuni forego the tourist income for high moral purpose, remain poor, and face increasing internal disruption from consumer-oriented youth who value money more than philosophy. The Amish case study (see Fagence, Chapter 15) highlights the fact that Amish culture is the tourist attraction but non-Amish entrepreneurs reap the benefits. The Chinese government has recognized the importance of their minority peoples and encourages the creation of folk villages and folk arts to augment the national treasures, including the Great Wall (see Swain, Chapter 17).

Heritage, as history, language, and custom, is a powerful culture marker that differentiates and unites nations, tribes, ethnic enclaves, or even neighborhoods. The travel industry recognizes and markets heritage tourism as niche travel. The identification and development of heritage assets is crucial to sustainable tourism.

Handicrafts

The production and sale of handicrafts depend on the availability of raw materials and a craft tradition. The aboriginal Inuit in Kotzebue Sound worked well with skins and sinew and wove willow baskets but seldom carved ivory, which was only available through trade with Bering Straits people. The Canadian Inuit are now widely identified on the world art market with stone carvings and block prints. Neither craft is aboriginal in origin but was introduced into the Arctic villages at mid-20th century by Canadian artisans and representatives of the national government, to create a source of wage employment. The introduction of new art forms to create income and serve the tourist market, as was true in this Canadian example, now raises questions of ethics and authenticity (see Swain, Chapter 17). Native images, when screened onto a T-shirt, usually do not protect the owner-rights or provide income to the designer. The development of marketing cooperatives, with logos that guarantee authenticity and quality, protects the integrity of artisans as well as the purchaser.

The manufacture of artifacts is one issue, while their sale to tourists is another. Many world cultures are noted for their aesthetic creativity in fine pottery and porcelains, large stone carvings, and well-designed furniture, but massive or heavy items are difficult to transport, especially for air travelers. Market demand commonly generates heterogenization of tourist art including miniaturization of traditional forms and proliferation of new styles (well illustrated by the Acoma potters who created small animal figures—including penguins!—decorated with age-old Mimbres designs). Over time, these innovations may achieve a status of "assumed authenticity." E. Cohen (1993c, p. 160) carefully notes that authenticity is not a theoretical concept by which the status of a craft article can be "objectively" evaluated but rather depends on the criteria by which authenticity is conceived. When tourists choose to purchase modern innovations for reasons of size, price, or style, they have stimulated the market and become "culture brokers" (see Section 5). In the American Southwest, traditional Indian designs that originally decorated large pottery vessels now appear on pottery earrings and necklaces. Large (and expensive) Navajo wedding baskets have been miniaturized to wearable brooches and earrings. The bulky and fragile spirit figures, or *kachinas* of the Hopi Indians, are now available as refrigerator door magnets or even earrings.

The Kotzebue Inuit: A 4-H's Assessment

The introduction to each section in this volume incorporates a mini-ethnography of Kotzebue Inuit. Using the Inuit example, the 4 H's assessment illustrates the claim that this is the "most successful tourism program in the (North American) North" (p. 3).

Habitat

The Arctic and its indigenous Eskimo sparked curiosity and admiration for several centuries among early European and American explorers. The lure of the "midnight sun" and the hardy fur-clad dwellers, made famous in Flaherty's documentary film *Nanook of the North*, were reasons enough for many travelers in the 1950s and 1960s to venture North. In 2000, a two-day excursion to Kotzebue cost only $500 for airfare, hotel, and guided sightseeing. The trip was highlighted by regional diversity. The hour-long jet flight from Anchorage to Kotzebue passes close to Denali, the highest peak in North America, with a dramatic view of the glaciated Alaska Range. The routing then descends to the Bering Sea coast over the broad treeless tundra dotted with lakes and meandering streams. The summer days are warm and the tundra is a "Persian carpet" of wildflower blossoms. Tourists are thrilled to watch the sun circle the horizon at midnight, so light they can be photographed reading a paper with their watch showing the hour. NANA's Musuem of the North, generally listed as one of the four leading Alaskan museums, provides an interesting educational display of landscape and resources. The addition of a sightseeing stop in Nome, to visit the 1898 Gold Rush town, adds further regional interest as tourists pan for gold. Nome is the terminus of the famous Iditarod sledge race and tourists are treated to a sled ride (on wheels), pulled by a team of Huskies or malemutes. The afternoon return flight to Anchorage often affords a final photo op, in a sunset view of Denali. Only one other North American location, Iqaluit (the capital of Nunavut, on Baffin Island, eastern Canada), offers access to comparable scenery but at far greater cost and with less historical interest. On a grading scale of +, 0, -, *Kotzebue rates a + in Habitat, for access, interest, climate.*

History

Details of local history have already shown that the Inuit of this area have had a long exposure through the intercontinental trade with Siberia, as a source of tea (termed *chai* from its Chinese origins) and tobacco, glass beads, and iron knives, the latter fabricated from Ural Mountain ore and associated with the 1000-year old Ipiutak site at Point Hope, north of Kotzebue (Rainey, 1947). Using Kotzebue Sound as the hub, local Inuit traders profitably exchanged goods far upcountry. Kotzebue Inuit history reflects an openness in dealing with outsiders, in contrast to the frightened Canadian Inuit who saw the beleaguered and starving sailors of the ill-fated Franklin Expedition but failed to approach or assist them. *The history of Kotzebue tourism merits an analytical +.*

Heritage

Cultural traditions may be suppressed by outside influences but they can survive and resurface, within a generation or two. The Friends Mission in Kotzebue in 1898 banned native dancing, shamanism, and use of the Inupiaq language in school. Much Inuit lore gave way to the modernization of airplanes, snow machines, and supermarkets in lieu of dog teams and subsistence food. Following the 1971 Alaska Land Claims Settlement Act, which awarded to indigenous tribes their aboriginal lands and some money, Inuit leaders expressed the view that the claims were awarded in recognition of their traditional culture (of which the younger generations knew very little). NANA hoped to restore pride in heritage to offset welfare dependency and alcoholism (and to expand tourism for its job benefits). In 1976, NANA leaders obtained a matching State grant, and with US$60,000 brought together into their Nullukvik Hotel all NANA Inuit above age 65, for a 2-week *Inupiat Paitot* or Elder's Workshop (V. Smith, 1976). Of the 80 original participants only two dropped out, for reasons of health. Numerous youth participated as recorders and became deeply involved in cultural revitalization. Subsequent small workshops followed for two additional years. Combined, the data generated three published volumes (Lore of the Inupiat, 1989/1990/1992) of historical and educational value. The 2 weeks of social networking renewed group solidarity and restored the summer games, once an important part of the aboriginal trading rendezvous. Significantly, it was the Inuit who initiated this recovery of their cultural traditions, and hired their ethnographer to organize the workshop and elicit the information. Subsequently, NANA received a US$150,000 Ford Foundation award for this innovative effort, which has subsequently encouraged other Northern peoples to look more closely at their heritage. *For Heritage, Kotzebue clearly deserves a +.*

Handicrafts

Handicrafts virtually disappeared in the Kotzebue Sound area after World War II, with the subsequent importation of sneakers, then Nikes and Eddie Bauer parkas. The brackish waters of the Sound do not support a walrus population and thus there was no aboriginal source of ivory, except by trade. A few older Kotzebue Inuit women made small fur items—pins of Inuit faces surrounded by a fur ruff or pairs of Eskimo yo-yos. Eskimo dolls by Ethel Washington became the only collector items of note. *Inupiat Paitot* influenced other women to again make, for the tourist trade, traditional-style willow baskets, wolf-roarers, and wooden snow goggles. The Visitor Center at the US National Park Headquarters has encouraged their production and proudly markets such items in their gift shop. *Kotzebue handicrafts merit a + for cultural revitalization.*

The 4 H's as a field tool are equally applicable to rural tourism, to enclave and ghetto tourism, and to the analysis of special interests such as sport tourism, historic homes, or ethnic festivals. The 4 H's provide information to identify impacts, and can suggest avenues to effect change in the tourism product. However, the analysis is best utilized when matched with the appropriate tourist market(s).

Psychographics: The Five Generations

From the anthropological perspective, tourism involves transactional relations between hosts and guests. Tourism's success can be enhanced when hosts use the 4 H's to fully understand their assets and form partnerships with the culture brokers to market their product to the clientele who will most enjoy it. American travel suppliers, especially tour operators and experienced travel agents, recognize psychographics as an important tourism marketing tool. The research has been largely undertaken in the last decade by several firms including Plog Research of Redondo Beach, CA, and API Travel Consultants of Seattle, WA, to name two of the best known American firms, and whose data appear occasionally in trade journals. Until recently, quantitative questionnaires and surveys have provided data about styles of travel (Taylor, 1998). Psychological "ladders" have defined motivations, but tourism is experiential and involves individual thoughts and emotions (A. McIntosh, 1998). These psychographic perceptions are not solely demographic, expressed in age or gender, but reflect aspects of the culture and time frame in which individuals were reared, schooled, and employed. In the year 2001, there are five age levels of travelers whose life experiences and education have differed quite markedly, with a consequent effect on their destination choices and their styles of travel. The data presented here are taken from US sources but seem to have some parallels among other travelers. Elderly (senior citizen) American women, mostly widows, travel on motorcoach tours, Elder Hostel, or on cruise vessels (especially those that employ male "social hosts" as dancing partners). Many German and Japanese women of the same age group never married due to high male mortality rates during World War II, or are now widowed. These women all share similar travel requirements, of "safety in numbers" and companionship.

Psychographic Evaluation: The Five Generations

The widening tourist market, created by population growth and supported by increased global affluence and heightened consumer orientation for travel, now includes multigenerational travel. Gebhart (1999) identifies five distinct American generations whose lifestyles are based "mostly on what they experienced during their formative years into high school" (pp. 9–10) (Table 8.4). These market segments are well described in American travel industry literature, have quite different tourist profiles, and make different demands on the same destination or attraction. K. Jones (1999) observes, "an old Arab proverb states 'Men resemble their times more than they resemble their fathers.' " The five generations include the following.

The Depression Kids were the first generation of jet setters. Born in the late teens and 1920s, they lived through the "Great Depression," were proud they finished high school, served in the military or worked in defense plants during World War II, and established most of the post-World War II traditions in travel (V. Smith, 1998).

The Swing Generation, born in the 1930s to 1945, was strongly influenced by the frugality of their parents and the rationing of food and gasoline during the war. They now tend to follow the travel patterns of their parents.

Table 8.4. Five Generations of US Travelers

Generation Name	Birth Years	Economic Profile	Travel Style
Depression Kids (now mature seniors)	1915–1930	25% of total population; 50% of US discretionary income	30% of domestic travel; 80% of RV travel; 65% of cruise travel
Swing or Silent Generation	1931–1945	Inherited money and substantial incomes	Moving into travel patterns of parents and elder siblings
Baby Boomer Generation	1946–1964	Indulged by parents; Vietnam and dissent; Woodstock '69 is the defining event of sexual revolution	Self-indulgent, want luxury; now middle-aged; seek nonstressful vacations and sports
Generation X	1965–1980	Fewer in numbers; from broken homes; seeking personal identity	Self-testing sports: surfing, skiing, trekking; "backpackers"; sanctions gay and lesbian travel
Echo Boomers	1981–present	Children of the Baby Boom; torn between doting parents and a soulless society; Woodstock '99 is the defining symbol of violence	Dreaming of travel, not yet independent travelers; a few are "protestors" wearing chic T-shirts of riot city origins

Source: Gebhart (1999), K. Jones (1999), and S. Mitchell (1998).

For the decades of the 1950s to 1980s, most visitors to Kotzebue were Depression Kids and the Swing Generation, who drove their RVs to Alaska (because they remember the construction of the Alaska Highway as an "engineering marvel" during World War II) and wanted to "experience" both it and the "North." When the cruise industry to Alaska expanded in the 1980s, more Depression Kid travelers came in increased numbers.

These mature travelers now represent "a little over 1/4 of the population . . . make up more than half of all discretionary spending and account for well over a third of all domestic travel. People above age 50 account for 4/5 of all RV trips, 65% of all cruise trips, spent 74% more on a typical vacation, more nights away from home and travel farther distances on every trip than any other age group" (Ahlsmith, 1999). However, they are aging and progressively moving into nursing homes.

The Baby Boomers, born between 1946 and 1964 and now aged 35–54, were the dominant travel market in the 1990s and 2000, and are the largest travel market in history. According to K. Jones (1999), in North America (and also in select areas of Western Europe),

Boomers are the most educated generation ever—a third of the men and a quarter of the women have college degrees; nearly 20 percent of the 45-54 year olds households have incomes in excess of US$100,000. Women are the primary decision-makers . . . and make 80 percent of the leisure travel decisions. By 2007 Boomers will control US$12 trillion in assets, fully half of the wealth of the USA. (pp. 9-10)

Boomers consider travel an entitlement and their largest stress reliever. Many live in a centrifugal family (Bertman, 1998), and "it's not uncommon for Boomers on their second or third marriage to have children the same age as grandchildren from their first marriage" (Mancini, 1999, p. 16). Boomers have seen Alaska on TV documentaries. They will take their children or grandchildren on Inside Passage cruises to Alaska to introduce them to shipboard life. As individuals they are more interested in "experiencing the North" by an adventure icebreaker cruise in the Canadian High Arctic, or kayaking the rivers in the new Arctic Alaska national parks.

The American Association of Retired Persons (AARP), in a recent poll (Ahlsmith, 1999, p. 38), found that 80% of the Baby Boomers plan to continue working beyond the normal retirement age of 65 (compared with only 12% of people over 65 who are currently employed). These "extended careers" mean more frequent and shorter vacations, more luxury vacation travel, and will extend the Boomer travel market for at least another decade.

Generation X, born 1965 to 1980, were children during the Sexual Revolution that followed the first Rock festival, *Woodstock '69*, and the "hippie era." Often a product of dysfunctional families and poorly defined life values, they seek personal identity and are drawn to social experimentation in the "backpacker" lifestyle or to physical self-testing in sports. Those who can afford it (and many Americans and Europeans can) fashionably trek in Nepal, bicycle in New Zealand, or become active "danger tourists" in war zones.

Echo Boomers, children of the Baby Boomers, were born since 1981. They are generally in school but a significant number have generous allowances from parents or inheritances from grandparents, which provide funds for vacation travel. Many are already frequent travelers, as young as age 5, shuttling airborne between divorced parents on custodial visits. Rock music and the violence of the media, motion pictures, and video games influence this high school age group. Two hundred thousand music lovers gathered at *Woodstock '99*, which ended in a fiery riot "while naked men and women danced around and jumped through the flames" (Strauss, 1999). The *New York Times* reported on July 27, 1999 that "Mark Szcerbiak, 20, a body piercer from New Hampshire, walked away from the flaming trucks in a gas mask he had brought to the festival: 'Our generation isn't about peace and love anymore; they're all about destruction and hostility. This is to show everybody that we're young and we don't care, just burn everything.' "

These comments must not be taken lightly by tourism planners, especially the convention and visitor sector, given the mobility of jet travel and youthful incentives to be "where the action is." Many Echo Boomers have money to quickly join political protests in Indonesia or Timor, Seattle or Vienna, and proudly wear riot-theme T-shirts as trophies to impress and inspire their peers. In balance, their forebears joined the French Foreign Legion, rioted against the Shah of Iran, or fought in the Spanish Civil War, but that commitment was longer term, not the "smash and grab" philosophy of some Echo Boomers.

Looking Ahead

The progressive increase in Western affluence in the past 50 years has given millions of people the opportunity to travel who, as Depression Kids, never expected to leave their farm, their town, or their country. The media and tourism have made us all world minded, even as the television sequence of the December 31, 1999 Millennial celebrations demonstrated the universal human desires for peace, goodwill, and prosperity.

The supply–demand disparities and the impacts of tourism will take new directions in the decades to come—first as the present LDCs attain new status based on higher standards of living for their citizens, second as the Asian economic "tigers" rebound and provide more discretionary income for their citizens, and third

Figure 8.1. New Guinea native with a ballpoint pen through his septum. (Photo by V. Smith)

as space tourism moves from dream and drawing board to eventual reality. Each new stage will require increased sophistication in tourism assessment, implementation of program, and mitigation. It will also necessitate renewed effort to develop psychographic profiles of new travelers from different cultural backgrounds.

In 1963, at the Sing-Sing (Highland Show) in Goroka, New Guinea, a tribesman pointed to my ballpoint pen. When I handed it to him, he removed a boar's tusk from his nose and substituted the pen (Figure 8.1). When I pointed to a landing helicopter, I was told, "him big mixmaster belong Jesus Christ now." What is his psychographic profile?

The stereotypes of host–guest impacts that have dominated academic analysis for a quarter century, starting with *demonstration effect*, the *tourist bubble*, and classifications of tourists as *ethnic, cultural,* or *historical,* must now be cojoined with both the host ethnography and the psychographic guest profile. Multidisciplinary research has advanced the scientification of tourism, even as case studies continue to illustrate the importance of the historical sequences of culture and their varying effects on tourism.

Chapter 9

Tourism on the Maya Periphery

Oriol Pi-Sunyer, R. Brooke Thomas, and
Magalí Daltabuit

Tourism is not just about escaping work and drizzle; it is about power, increasingly internationalized power. (Enloe, 1989, p. 40)

Cancún, the resort city on Mexico's Yucatan peninsula, is a location closely identified with the 4 S's of mass tourism: sun, sex, sea, and sand. It has become a major holiday destination famed for sugar-fine beaches, turquoise seas, and scuba diving along a 280-kilometer coral reef. From the guest's perspective, it offers good and predictable hotels, an exotic ambiance of margaritas and mariachis, lush tropical forests, and Maya ruins. Cancún is composed of two distinct spaces: the hotel zone on what was once an island, and the city proper with a population of more than 310,000 inhabitants, many involved in the tourist trade. This destination is the entry point for more than 2 million visitors annually, an increasing number of which come to stay and play along the coastal strip of the Cancún–Tulum Corridor fronting the Caribbean (Figures 9.1 and 9.2). The "Riviera Maya," as it has now been rebranded, had a 1998 room count of 7600 units, but has attained such popularity with European charter tourists and vacationing Americans that new investment capital plans the construction of an additional 2400 rooms in the course of next 3 years. These developments reflect the 1990's trend towards a tourism oriented to environmental concerns and cultural interests—but without a loss of comfort. A parallel project centers on the transformation of Puerto Morelos, formerly a fishing village, into a major yachting destination with a marina capable of accommodating 300 boats. Other plans include two golf courses and an expansion of soft-adventure activities including scuba diving, sailing, fishing, and outings to archaeological sites. Developers promote a goal of creating attractive resorts in a Quintana Roo "riviera" that will provide sustainable employment to the people of the area. Whether expansion of this type and magnitude is compatible with the well-being of local populations is a central concern of this chapter.

The indigenous Maya have occupied Mesoamerica for several thousand years, working the land as slash-and-burn (*milpa*) horticulturists, sustained by a diet of

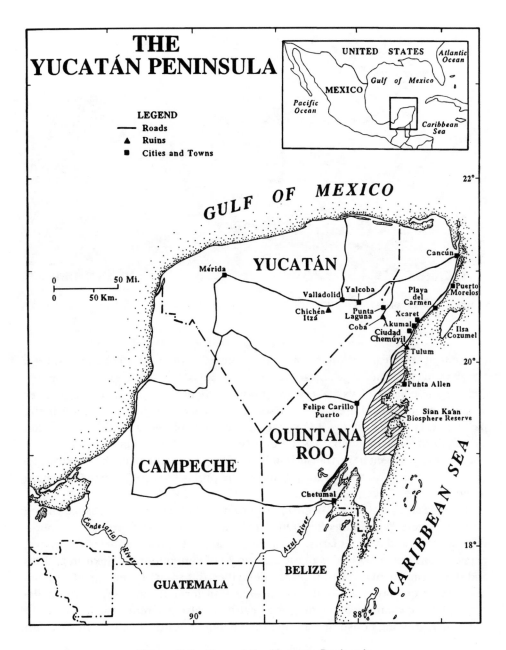

Figure 9.1. Map of the Yucatan Peninsula.

maize, beans, squash, and garden vegetables. The surrounding forest provided them with game animals, and wood and thatch for fuel and housing. The rise of state systems governed by deified kings led to the construction of dramatic ceremonial complexes such as Chichén Itzá and Uxmal in Yucatan, Tikal in Guatemala, and Copán in Honduras. Now marketed by the travel industry as Mundo Maya, originally termed "La Ruta Maya" (W. Garrett 1989), this promotional partnership joins

Figure 9.2. Tourists at Tulum. (Photo by R. Brooke Thomas and Oriol Pi-Sunyer)

the Central American nations from Mexico south to Honduras, all of which share a Mayan indigenous heritage and archaeological ruins. Most foreign visitors come to Quintana Roo as holidays-makers, and are virtually unaware of the consequences for local inhabitants of the rapid touristic development that has taken place in the past 30 years. The Quintana Roo situation is remarkable because the penetration by a modern tourist industry has not only been fast and recent but also massive in scale. These changes have transformed a territorial periphery of the Mexican republic into a First World playground and in the process led to the marginalization of much of the native population.

This case study describes the process of tourism-induced culture change among Mayan villagers in Quintana Roo. Our informants were mostly ordinary people— wage workers and peasant farmers—whom we asked to position their lives, hopes, expectations, and fears in the all-too-real world of contemporary Mexican politics and development plans. The research describes the specific impacts of tourism penetration on Mayan life, and how this has transformed social organization, demography, wage employment, diet, and health; we also examined the influence of the media, growing consumerism, and the changing political climate in southern Mexico.

The Development of Quintana Roo

A generation ago, Quintana Roo remained one of the most inaccessible locations in Mexico, an economic and political frontier where the institutions of the state were minimally represented. From the beginning of our research more than a decade ago, it was clear that local people were reluctant to fill roles designed for them by the politically powerful (Daltabuit & Pi-Sunyer, 1990). Specifically, they recognized that for them the drama of modernization seldom offered more than the lowest paid (and generally uncertain) wage labor. In most instances, there was little choice respecting matters of livelihood, but limited options should not be interpreted as satisfaction with conditions of life and work. Our informants, however, tended to be practical people less concerned with dismantling the structures of state and capital than with working the system to their minimum disadvantage.

In 1939, during an official tour of the then territory of Quintana Roo, President Lázaro Cárdenas made it a point to assure the Maya villagers that the government would grant no land concessions to private companies (Quezada, 1940, cited by Villa Rojas, 1945, p. 35). Ten years later, in 1950, the total population of the territory still numbered only 26,967 inhabitants (up from just over 10,000 in 1930), a figure that would increase to 50,169 by 1960 (Villa Rojas, 1969, pp. 247–248), and Cancún was a village of only 600 persons. By 1990, the state's permanent population (i.e., not counting tourists) had risen almost 10-fold to 493,605 (Instituto Nacional de Estadística, 1991, p. 207). Thus, until the advent of mass tourism in the early 1970s, Quintana Roo (which became a state in 1974) remained pretty much what it had been for centuries: an extensive region with very low population density inhabited by Maya forest dwellers in the interior and small mixed and non-Indian enclaves along the coast. To geographical distance can be added a cultural and conceptual peripherality from the national world.

The Spanish tried to colonize this extensive area, but Quintana Roo proved inhospitable, and as time went on "almost the entire region . . . was deserted by the Spanish, leaving it to those unsubdued and 'idolatrous' Indians who continued to hold fast to their traditions" (Villa Rojas, 1945, p. 15). Fundamentally, Quintana Roo became what Aguirre Beltran (1979) has so aptly termed a zone of refuge, first for Indians fleeing Spanish control and, following independence, for Maya villagers equally disinclined to come under Mexican rule. The 1847 native uprising in Yucatan known as the Caste War, and the many smaller insurrections that followed, further isolated the region (N. Reed, 1964). Draconian campaigns by federal troops well into the 20th century reinforced the prevailing Mayan belief that the agents of the state were both brutal and untrustworthy. The other side of the coin is that for generations the directing classes of Mexico—to the extent that they gave the matter much thought—regarded Quintana Roo as a worthless and barbarous land that contributed nothing of value to national society. Typical of this perspective is the opinion voiced by a former Mexican army doctor interviewed by the American journalist John Kenneth Turner (1969) in the early 1900s: "Quintana Roo is the most unhealthy part of Mexico. . . . For every soldier killed by a Maya at least one hundred die of starvation or sickness" (p. 123). At issue here is not the accuracy of the statistic, but the sense of the territory as a jungle waste, graveyard for soldiers and would-be settlers.

When did the conquest of Quintana Roo really end? Following their failure to take the city of Mérida in the Caste War, the Maya insurgents retreated east and south and established a capital at Chan Santa Cruz (now Felipe Carrillo Puerto), which only fell to the Mexican army in 1901. The Maya, for their part, never conceded defeat. Farriss (1984) offers her consideration that "perhaps the conquest was not complete until 1969, with the death of the . . . last of the Caste War leaders" (p. 19). Coincidentally, this date for the end of Maya autonomy is the threshold of the tourist boom. The region, and particularly its coast, rapidly became redefined as a tropical paradise and the tourism industry now perceives the natural and archaeological properties of the state to be vital and threatened resources. Both tourism in its more typical sun-and-sea formulation and the new ecological discourse limit the access of local populations to a diminishing stock of natural resources.

Contested control over resources represents a significant part of the broader issues that decide the roles of small-scale agriculturists and similar groups within national and global political and economic structures. When regions such as Quintana Roo undergo modernization, local populations (still generally perceived by the dominant society as "backward") are assigned subordinate roles in the drama of development—sometimes to the point of invisibility. As Geertz (1994) points out, modernizing states "do not bring all their citizens equally with them when they join the contemporary world of capital flows, technology transfers, trade imbalances, and growth rates" (p. 3). Today, the Quintana Roo Maya find themselves part of a totalizing experience driven by the exigencies of modern tourism. In common with many other previously isolated people, they are marginalized in their own land by a rapid displacement and redefinition that is not only economic and cultural but, in many instances, also demographic. Furthermore, the expansion of tourism has stimulated such an influx of job seekers from other parts of Mexico that the indigenous population now constitutes a minority in its own land. The Maya must compete with more urbane and aggressive employees from the capital and other overcrowded areas.

Under these circumstances, the cultural landscape of the state is not easily defined. Even the use of such conventional terms as "the Maya," which may carry the implication of organic cultures and self-contained communities, has to be used with care. The reality on the ground is complex, fluid, and socially and culturally blurred. Some people are trying to make sense of overwhelming forces by holding on to elements of their past, their language, and their identity. In this dynamic cultural arena, both adaptation and resistance are part of the response. Some villagers live in what are still predominantly Maya-speaking communities heavily dependent on subsistence agriculture; other individuals try to move between several worlds. A growing number of former peasants now inhabit squatter settlements that, in the case of Cancún, are partially screened by trees but begin only a few blocks inland from five-star resort hotels. Many employee communities resemble colonial company towns, created by the demands of the tourist industry. These enclaves of marginality have very little in common with traditional Maya peasant life as conceptualized by Redfield (1947): "folk societies" of small, isolated, homogeneous village dwellers underpinned by a strong sense of group solidarity. Now, in Quintana Roo, factionalism is common and often expressed in the language of religion; there is high physical mobility and many locations, not simply the urban centers, have a heterogeneous population. What is occurring, and with extreme rapidity, is the penetration of a hegemonic order that tries to frame and define social concepts, priorities, and directions. The authority to do this does not go unchallenged, but these forces are backed by the power of the state and by a mystique of development that assumes: (1) the inevitability of economic transformation; (2) the benefits of this process; and (3) the primacy of national goals over local claims and needs (Escobar, 1995).

To understand how such policies and positions came to impact so strongly, and so suddenly, on Quintana Roo necessitates a brief review of Mexican development policies during recent decades. It illustrates how the "global" and the "local" come together and are reconfigured in this corner of Mexico.

Mexico and the Price of Progress

For all practical purposes, Mexico has been a one-party state since 1928. Every president elected has completed his term of office, then transferred power to his handpicked successor. In terms of political control, state and party are virtually the same. The ruling party, the Partido Revolucionario Institucional (PRI), began as the heir of the Mexican Revolution—the first social revolution of the 20th century. In the 1930s (and to some extent later), the PRI undertook development programs, not unlike those of the New Deal in the US, with policies crafted to correct social inequities and bring education and health services to the peasantry and the poor. Later, centralized policies and a political culture of authoritarian control became a screen for quick profits and the emergence of a new economic and political elite. The system is esoteric in the extreme, but functions as a mechanism for dispensing favors, grand and petty.

Because of this long history of single-party government, the political and the economic domains are particularly closely linked. Discussing this situation and its relationship to economic liberalization, the opposition presidential candidate Cuauhtémoc Cárdenas commented on how the benefits and costs of development should be apportioned: "The issue is not whether the country should be modernized and opened up," he stated, but rather "who should pay the unavoidable costs of restructuring." To date, the Mexican workers—through sharply lower real wages and dramatic cuts in education, health, and housing expenditures—have carried a disproportionate share of the burden. "For Mexico, Freedom Before Free Trade" (Cardenas, 1990). Any political order dominated by centralism, paternalism, and corruption is unlikely to make much headway in reforming itself.

Demographic Pressures

The Mexican economic dilemma is often expressed as a race between development and population, although earlier in the century population grew remarkably slowly. The first modern census (1895) counted only 12.5 million Mexicans, a number that may have approximated the size of the indigenous population at the time of Cortés' conquest (1519). By 1950, the population had doubled to almost 26 million, and had tripled to 77 million by 1984. In 1998 Mexico ranked 11th in population size among world nations, with 98 million people, and is projected to increase another 60% to 154 million people by 2050 (United Nations, 1996). This surge is most often attributed (sometimes exclusively) to a sharp decline in the mortality rate, but whatever the cause, rapid growth is clearly related to modern social processes and is a pressing issue. In the early 1970s, 2 million Mexicans were born every year, a statistic that would later translate into an enormous gap between a plentiful supply of labor and a lack of jobs. Approaching the millenium, the workforce was still expanding at the rate of 3% per year, and some 35% of Mexicans were under 15 years of age with a full 80% under age 40.

Development Models

In the four decades following World War II, the conventional yardsticks of Mexico's productivity, gross national product (GNP) and gross domestic product (GDP), kept pace with population, rising about 6% per year, which translates to a 10-fold increase. Optimists could argue that growth was winning the race, but these measures are notoriously deceptive. Neither GNP nor GDP measures the welfare of a society or assesses the aims and ultimate uses of goods and services. Similarly, these indices offer no information about environmental and resource issues. To use a local example, the heavy commercial logging and forest clearance in southeastern Mexico, which have devastated the ecology of the region, are included as an added GNP and GDP.

In Mexico, even the most favorable growth statistics commonly obscure unresolved problems. The post-World War II development model has minimally improved the living standards for the majority of the population. Its benefits have primarily accrued to the political and economic elite and, to a lesser degree, to the expanding middle sector of society and, of course, to foreign investors. Income distribution is so skewed that the top 10% of the population receives 39.5% of the national income, and the bottom 20% of the population shares a scant 4.1% (World Bank, 1995, p. 221).

Traditional economic plans solicit intensified investment and development with the expectation that these inputs will, in due course, improve the general standard of living and in the process reduce demographic pressure (Rohter, 1990, pp. 1–6). However, it makes a great deal of difference how such investments are allocated. Twenty years ago, the president of the World Bank observed that "if the growth in national income does not result in improvements of the living conditions of the lower income groups, it will not help to reduce fertility throughout the society" (D. Gordon, 1978, p. 3). In general, improvements in the material welfare of poor people lead to important demographic consequences. However, what has occurred in Mexico is that during these decades of industrialization and expanding urbanization, the population has tripled, unemployment has become more acute, and the labor force is increasing more rapidly. There have never been more billionaires in Mexico, but about a third of the population lives in poverty.

Tourism Development in Yucatan

Tourism is a key component in the Mexican development strategy. It is typically presented as a sort of internal export industry; what are sold are the various national "attractions," whether archaeological, natural, or cultural. In the process, a flow of foreign exchange is generated and one can balance the money coming in against the money going out. The figures are very favorable. In 1990, Mexico hosted 16.7 million international visitors, ranked eighth in the world for tourist arrivals, and earned US$5,467 million. By 1999, Mexico ranked seventh among all nations with its 20.2 million tourists, and benefited from earnings of US$7.9 billion (WTO, 2000). In global and regional terms, Mexico ranks second only to the US in numbers of international tourists coming to the Americas. Tourism differs from other export sectors in that both production and consumption take place at home, which is another way of saying that it is labor intensive, an attractive feature for a country that suffers high rates of unemployment and underemployment.

Where does Quintana Roo fit into this picture? In many respects, tourism patterns here are similar to those encountered elsewhere in Mexico. Tourism is predominantly a business that takes place in special tourist enclaves, in resorts such as Cancún, and, increasingly, in gated complexes that provide accommodation and recreation within highly controlled, secured, environments. Fundamentally, First World guests are ensconced in what is still very much a Third World country. A middle-class Mexican informant offered his opinion that the lifestyle of Quintana Roo resort dwellers "has more in common with the ways of south Florida than with anything Mexican."

The dominant influence in Quintana Roo tourism remains Cancún, the port of entry for the majority of foreign tourists, of whom 91% are American. Most foreign visitors are relatively young—average age 36 years—with an annual income between US$65,000 and US$75,000 (FONATUR, 1993, p. 12). From its inception, Cancún tourism projects have been large scale, capital intensive, and highly concentrated with respect to ownership. Most are owned by foreign nationals—chiefly in the form of major hotel chains—or Mexican investors. The ability of Mexican national and local elite to exercise substantial influence over Yucatecan tourism has long been noted (R. Lee, 1978). The financial structure dates to a development plan initiated in 1969, ostensibly dependent on a trust fund administered by FONATUR (Fondo Nacional de Fomento al Turismo), the agency charged with planning. In theory, FONATUR was underwritten by the Mexican government, but in reality, of the total initial investment amount of US$70 million, some US$30 million came from the Inter-American Development Bank and a further US$20 million from private, mostly foreign, investors. Fundamentally, this translates into "big tourism" centered on the construction of large first-class facilities, but offering few benefits to small entrepreneurs and local wage earners (L. Turner & Ash, 1976, p. 203).

According to initial plans, Cancún island was to be the primary tourist zone with hotels and guest services. "Ciudad Cancún" was supposed to develop as the secondary tourist zone or service city, and to benefit the locally employed population with utilities, roads, schools, and health facilities. Public assurances promised that strict zoning regulations would be followed and environmental protection diligently enforced. Very early in the building of Cancún, Mexican government officials asserted they had had an anthropological team help lay out the city—its hospitals, its schools and its houses—and were taking pains to avoid social tensions later. Alas, this integrated tourist planning effort was never really put into effect, and FONATUR essentially became a tool of tourism promotion. Ciudad Cancún remains woefully short of public services, and environmental safeguards are often disregarded.

To these inadequacies should be added the sense that Cancún is hardly a Mexican city, but one catering to the strange ways of foreigners. Other observers have remarked on this alienness—and the cultural separation that accompanies it: "Begging was banned on the streets of Cancún to minimize tourists' exposure to the poverty of local workers. While wealthy vacationers cruise in taxis to classy restaurants and 'spring-breakers' transit to the discos downtown, hotel employees are packed like lemmings into lurching diesel buses that ferry them home to humble colonias north of the city" (Celaya & Owen, 1993, p. 441). In addition, the hours of work are long and hard, wages are poor, and, for the slightest infraction, they may not be paid at all. Many employees work split shifts, with no place to go in the interim; they may not use the hotel-owned beaches or patronize local cafes or shops.

Two further features of Cancún warrant comment. The first is the near-absence of a modern cultural heritage. To fill this void, the individual resorts have concocted images of faked authenticity, including Caribbean adventure and countless designs vaguely attributable to the ancient Maya. Given this Disneyland-like version of the archaeological past, foreign guests commonly believe that the Maya are "extinct." Second, Cancún reflects the 1960's development concept, with its emphasis on massive investment and huge buildings. The world has changed significantly since Mexican technicians used the magic of the computer to plan the resort. For tourism, probably the most important change is ideological and perceptual, with a much greater interest in, and concern for, the environment. This newfound ecotourism interest has clearly influenced tourism promotion. The following passage from Passport Cancun (1994) is an enticement to experience the natural while it is "still around," and describes the "still crystal-clear waters and virgin beaches" south of Cancún: "This is a land that still belongs to nature, where ocelots, kinkajous and spider monkeys still roam wild in their native habitat, and where giant sea turtles—almost extinct in other parts of the world—still flood the coast each spring to lay their delicate eggs in the moonlit sands" (p. 9).

The Maya and Marginality

Our extensive fieldwork involved four village locations that represented progressive levels of tourism impact: isolated and traditional Punta Laguna; intermediary Cobá (described below); Akumal (destroyed by hurricane in 1995); and Ciudad Chemuyil, the most un-Maya settlement. Daltabuit (1992) had previously conducted extensive research on health and nutrition in the communities of Cobá and Yalcob. The primary research goals were to understand and document (1) the role of tourism as the agent of rapid cultural change and (2) the penetration of state institutions and market forces that were impacting a peasant population.

Cobá seemed a particularly appropriate place to initiate this study. A substantial village of 819 inhabitants (Daltabuit, 1996, p. 21), Cobá has several features that would appear to place it in the category of the quintessential Maya peasant community. It had been settled by a small group of Yucatecan Maya agriculturists some 60 years ago when those living in the Quintana Roo interior were pretty much left to their own devices. Later, the village was granted *ejido* communal tenure to some of the land it worked, but other areas—especially those in and around the extensive archaeological zone—were designated as protected federal lands. All the evidence, both in the literature and from field data, indicates that Cobá was representative of traditional Maya communities that, until recently, had been intimately linked through mechanisms of reciprocity and agricultural practices that reinforced social solidarity. In the 16th century, Diego de Landa (1941) described the Maya as having "the good habit of helping each other in all their labors" (p.

98). Kintz (1990), writing chiefly of the recent past, notes the same spirit of reciprocity:

> Collection of goods and the redistribution of items (particularly food) was an economic pattern that enhanced security for all families. . . . The economic web that collected and centralized goods and redistributed the excess ensured that no one starved. This redistribution system of economically important goods was formalized under ritual circumstances that traditionally occurred throughout the yearly cycle. (p. 138)

Communal agricultural work, particularly slash-and-burn cultivation (*milpa*), has been gradually superseded by wage labor jobs that now threaten household cooperation. Individual household plots are still part of the communal land grant (*ejido*) that includes *milpa* and an undivided forest (*monte*) to which villagers have, until recently, enjoyed unhindered access. In Cobá, the minimum land needed to maintain a single family through the slash-and-burn cycle is some 50 hectares of rainforest (about 123 acres), to which should be added space for kitchen gardens and the raising of pigs and chickens. Now many of these holdings are reduced to 20 hectares per household, or even less. The restrictions on forest use are increasingly onerous, and are greatly resented. In Cobá, one must go 4 kilometers into the forest, and it may take up to 50 round-trips to obtain the building materials for a single traditional thatch and hardwood house.

There is a pervasive belief that as each year passes agriculture is becoming more unpredictable. Given the pressure on land and resources, it is not surprising that at least one third of the able-bodied men must now seek employment outside the community. During our stay in 1994, at least 50 Cobá men found work helping to excavate and reconstruct an archaeological site inside the extensive Xcaret eco-theme park (Figure 9.3).

What is distinctive of Cobá is the location of the village at the very edge of one of the largest archaeological complexes in the Yucatan—a Classic Maya site from which the community takes its name. Since the late 1970s, Cobá has become an important tourist destination. Busloads of tourists, totaling 70,000 annual visitors, arrive daily and make their way to the archaeological remains and the surrounding rainforest. The presence of visitors stimulated the making of handicrafts and the opening of small stores, while the development of the ruins into a destination for adventure tourism led to a greater interest in ethnic tourism. The ecotourism literature promises that tour visits can protect the social, cultural, and psychological characteristics of the local communities, and that in authentic Indian villages everything is as God intended it to be—natural, healthy, away from the stress and the lights and glamour; an area where tourists can relax, be themselves, see the wonders, and help the Indians.

This external modernization has worked to intertwine the world of international tourism (exemplified by the Club Med hotel overlooking Lake Cobá) with the lives of one-time subsistence farmers. Although an estimated 40% of working-age Cobá population derive some income from tourism, this employment pulls the youngest and strongest from the fields. That the people of Cobá are trying to navigate their way through a rapidly changing and contradictory world is also apparent from the religious–communal dimension. Some 20 years ago, religious

Figure 9.3. Workers reconstructing a Mayan site. (Photo by R. Brooke Thomas and Oriol Pi-Sunyer)

practice in Cobá was a variant of folk syncretism that joined elements of Catholic ritual to a Mayan cosmology in which the *milpa* and the forest represent a model of the universe. The task of the ritual practitioner was to help maintain the various components, and their keepers and spirits, in order and balance. Something of this belief remains, but Cobá is now an arena for competing congregations. There are five—some claim six—different religious groups. Sectarian balkanization has reinforced individualism and tended to deauthorize communal ties and rituals. New belief systems are congruent with a sense of the individual as consumer and autonomous economic agent.

The growing reliance on outside employment and changes in patterns of village reciprocity can be broadly applied to other Quintana Roo communities. Common themes and processes differ in magnitude rather than in subject, and our analysis of ongoing culture change draws on the other three villages as well as on Cobá. While tourism has clearly been the engine of economic and social transformation in Quintana Roo, from the beginning it was linked to official development plans responding to national, rather than local, initiatives and priorities.

This history, this process, has relevance for our research design and the issues that it addresses. Perhaps even more so than elsewhere, in Quintana Roo one cannot examine "tourism" as something separate from the many other changes that accompany it. To cite a couple of examples, the construction of the highway linking Cobá with the coast not only put this interior village on the tourist itinerary but was chiefly responsible for bringing it into the orbit of powerful market forces.

The same road that transports busloads of foreign tourists to visit the Maya ruins also carries the trucks that deliver the soft drinks, prepared foods, and other items destined for local consumption. Electrification—another facet of rural moderniza-tion—has done much more than improve lighting: in the course of a decade it has helped transform virtually everyone in Cobá into an avid television viewer. In turn, exposure to television entails exposure to the mass-mediated messages of adver-tising. To interpret changes of this type as simply individual consumer choices misses the consequences they have for an array of communal issues, including social structure, cultural practice, and public health. The decline of kitchen gar-dens—a general trend to be sure—marks not only a growing dependency on wage labor and commercial foodstuffs but real erosion of local knowledge respecting herbal remedies and their application.

The Elements of Social Change

A major challenge was how to deal systematically with such interlinked pro-cesses and influences, and to obtain a sense of the political economy of tourism, especially as it affected: (1) social relations and cultural systems; (2) food con-sumption; (3) environmental adaptation and resource control; and (4) women's health. A common thread of commodification was apparent in all four settlements, in which most people, in the space of a generation, had been transformed into a class of wage earners. The loss of land instilled a deeper fear of crop failure. Many people felt poor, and spoke of the shortage of cash and the lack of decent jobs.

To assess the broader aspects of these processes, use of a household question-naire provided information on a range of issues, among them employment, con-sumption patterns, education, attitudes towards tourism, and cultural identity. A total of 82 households was sampled, with the largest sample (34) from Cobá. We also carried out anthropometric surveys in two schools (most of the elementary school pupils) and a pilot study of food consumption habits. Henry Geddes (1996), a co-investigator, researched the impact of radio and television. The sample—about a quarter of the villagers—is more than sufficient to provide a solid database and suggest trends in social and economic change. For example, the open-ended in-quiry, "Who benefits most from tourism?" was often greeted with astonishment (the answer apparently being self-evident) but was followed by a catalogue of such responses as "the hotels," "the bosses," and "the rich." Clearly, the majority of our informants view themselves as exploited, people who receive minimum wages (about $10 a day) for low-skilled tertiary work. Sometimes, this condition is ex-pressed in the most unambiguous terms, as one man described construction work on the coast as "slave work" (Geddes, 1996, p. 5). But this recognition of exploita-tion does not mean a desire to revert to subsistence agriculture and the old forms of rural life. It is instructive to trace the responses to the question, "Would things be better without tourism?" Seventy-eight percent of the sample responded in the negative. There is clearly a nostalgia for the past, combined with a fear of losing language and identity, but the only alternative to greater poverty is employment in tourism—however badly paid and demeaning.

A particular example may give human shape to the complexity of such atti-tudes. One of our most articulate respondents is a woman in her middle thirties, a single parent who works in one of the largest new resort complexes on the coast. When we visited her home we were struck by her "modern" appearance and demeanor—crisp white shorts with matching tee shirt, brand-name sneakers, trimmed and styled functional hair. Her house is a *palapa* with wooden walls and palm-thatch roof, with a cement floor that keeps it dry and easy to clean. Inside, she had tastefully arranged the spaces and contents, and while hardly lavishly furnished, it was comfortable in all respects. The overall impression of house and owner was of modernity—a traditional structure containing a harmonious mix of old pieces and contemporary appliances.

Born in a Maya village in Chiapas, she described her parents as "good people of the pueblo, of the older generation." She had married at a young age—"much too young"—to a man who had turned out to be a drunk and a wife-beater. In her own words, she managed to "escape misery and torment." Leaving her children in her parents' care, she headed for the coast and sought work in tourism. A decade later, she had saved enough money to buy a house of her own and regularly sent a third of her wages to support her children and help out her now-aging parents.

This is a story of liberation—no less than the reconstruction of a life—in the face of adversity and poverty, and our respondent made it abundantly clear that her material and emotional independence, and the well-being of her children, had been achieved as a result of employment in tourism. With the same analytical clarity, however, she detailed the grueling work schedule, the extent of corporate control over the life of workers, a work environment permeated with racism and sexism ("we don't exist as human beings"), and the tremendous disparity between wages received and the wealth of clients. In this resort it was mandatory for workers to carry two types of identification (one pinned to the company uniform), and they were not allowed to stray from strictly designated areas. Her job in the huge laundry, "a place of steam and noise," paid more than chambermaid work, but it left her completely wrung out at the end of the shift. Still, since she needed the money, it was her intention to continue working in this unhealthy and enervating place for as long as she had strength. This biography is not idiosyncratic. The author is remarkably articulate, and her discussion of industrial disciplinary practices echoes Foucault's (1980, p. 39) observation that such power seeks to reach "into the very grain of individuals." She also stands out as a single mother in a rural area where this status is still somewhat uncommon. But what she speaks about, the strategies of making a living, and the pains and opportunities that have accompanied the development of mass tourism, has been related by many other people [see also Madsen Camacho's (1996) discussion of the hotel industry in Huatulco].

Social Relations and Cultural Systems

Society is undergoing a veritable reordering of cultural meanings and priorities that is externally driven and over which local people have little control. Quite evidently, much of the population is becoming wage dependent, and landless Indians (as well as non-Indians) are moving into the coastal zone in search of employment. The Maya of the interior, who still control significant resources, are increasingly pressured to alter their livelihood and collective identity. As the old structures of community and subsistence experience increased stress, the sense of group membership suffers and local discontents mount. Only a generation ago, property was identified with locality in a system reinforced by an egalitarian ethos and a sense of justice that considered exclusive property rights as selfish individualism. Today, much communal property has been privatized or has come under government control. This shift is paralleled and reinforced by the new emphasis on the individual. The government deals in citizens and voters; for entrepreneurs, Maya villagers are treated as consumers or would-be consumers, and as a labor supply to fill servile jobs.

These changes have profound consequences for the fabric of social life. Thus, in what was once rural Cobá, a new local bourgeoisie has emerged composed of merchants, shopkeepers, ranchers, and restaurant owners—stakeholders in tourism and community leadership. Similar processes of class segmentation have been documented in several other indigenous Mesoamerican communities (Annis, 1987, pp. 60–74). These changes are not limited to the material and economic, for increased social stratification often correlates with cultural differentiation: the well-to-do are noticeably more comfortable in the Spanish language and other markers of national culture than are poor peasant farmers. Religion is not without a cultural component, and Cobá has become a zone of religious conflict. Evangelical congregations typically conduct their services in Spanish and host visiting Spanish-speaking preachers and musical groups. The ideology they espouse stresses the centrality of individual salvation and the dyadic link of person and God.

The family network is also changing. Young couples were outspoken in their preference to live separately from their parents, and have smaller families. They emphasized the greater freedom (personal and economic) that nucleated arrangements are supposed to facilitate, but it is also possible that such an orientation reflects partly understood metropolitan models, perhaps derived from the media. This apparent trend towards nuclear family structures suggests that support from the extended family in childcare and related activities may become less readily available in the future. Also, we noted that in Cobá, some elderly people now live lonely lives of extreme poverty.

Consumerism

Throughout rural Quintana Roo, increased contact with tourism and the national culture correlates with soaring consumption norms. Only money buys the long list of commodities that forms part of the new requirements and aspirations: food and household supplies, agricultural tools and products, building materials, furnishings, and electronic equipment. School children need proper clothes and supplies. Quintana Roo is not a rich agricultural or manufacturing region. Virtually all the staples necessary to feed tourists and resort workers must be shipped in from distant places, at prices high by national, not to mention local, standards. Electricity and butane have to be purchased. Men want new bikes and adolescent boys eye used cars. Younger people are more and more concerned with style and all males now wear some variant of Western casual attire. The *huipil*, the traditional Maya women's dress, is seen much less often, particularly in coastal communities. At times, a substantial portion of household income is spent on medical care and health expenses, especially commercial drugs, a reflection of how drastically the authority of h-men, the Maya curer-priests, has eroded.

The Role of the Media

No single artifact of modernizing society has such far-reaching effects as television, introduced into the villages within the past 15 years or so. According to our household inventory, 67% of Cobá households owned sets, and many families watch TV 6 hours per day. As Kottak (1990) has noted with reference to both Brazil and the US, "television is one of the most powerful information disseminators, public opinion molders, and socializing agents in today's world" (p. 9). Television and other mass media exercise their power in diverse ways. They restructure the context of social relations, both public and private; bring about changes in beliefs, values, and types of knowledge; profoundly influence popular culture; impact on political views; and most certainly act as powerful commercial agents (Pace, 1993).

Television dominates the mass media environment and plays a critical role in two spheres: the construction of images and symbols of national society, and the propagation of a culture of consumption. Contemporary nation-states use visual mass media to help constitute "imagined communities" in the sense first elaborated by Anderson (1991). Such communities are imagined because even the members of the smallest nation "will never know most of their fellow-members, meet them, or even hear of them, yet in the mind of each lives the image of their communion" (Anderson, 1991, p. 6). In the process of image making (Hamilton, 1990), television functions as a "national imaginary": a mirror of society in which we see ourselves while we think we are seeing others. It matters a good deal what the viewer sees in this mirror.

Television in Mexico is concentrated in ownership, closely linked to the institutions of political power, and homogenous with respect to message— particularly at the level of mass culture. The themes and images to which Maya households are exposed seldom relate to indigenous peoples, or to such pressing social problems as emigration, unemployment, or poverty. Television portrays a national society where everyone speaks Spanish and forms part of a common culture; the message is one of assimilation. This national myth is reinforced through cultural practices that are now highly ritualized (Geddes, 1996), and linked to national stereotypes that celebrate dramatic hypermasculinity and individualism. The principal carriers of these forms are the Mexican-produced soap operas, the telenovelas, which depict a distant fantasy world peopled by men and women engaged in a succession of tragedies, triumphs, and misdeeds. It is a universe that is generally violent and unpredictable, and whose values are often in conflict with the Maya ideals of community, reciprocity, and marital fidelity. Since television is relatively new, the appeal at this juncture is probably as much the medium as the message. But, nevertheless, the message is followed closely. People will discuss at length the plot and subplot of popular telenovelas. Miller (1994), who studied the nearby village of Yalcobá, supports our impression that television makes young people feel impoverished and deprived.

The link between television and the growing acceptance of consumption values is particularly strong. For Maya peasants and unskilled workers, television projects into their lives new forms of being and belonging—metropolitan, competitive, driven by materialism—that are only being experienced at the edges. As it parades an outside world of wealth and power (the world from which the rich tourists come), some Maya sense their marginality and dissatisfaction with the status quo. However, they generally lack the power to question the contrasts, let alone reject this new materialism. TV sets are expensive and powerful status symbols and commonly the focal point of living spaces; a shrine-like arrangement in which the set is surrounded by family pictures, flowers, stuffed animals, or other mementos is not unusual. And certainly the price of ownership is high. A black-and-white set costs the equivalent of some US$200, with a hook-up fee of US$230 and a monthly charge of US$6–7.

The theme of consumption is implicit in programs and blatant in commercials. For Mexico as a whole, television has become the major advertising agent, especially for national and international products such as Bimbo bread, Coca-Cola, Nestle, pharmaceutical products, Sabritas snacks (PepsiCo), alcoholic beverages, and cigarettes. The mix of programs and commercials received in Quintana Roo is similar to the rest of Mexico but the audience is largely unlettered. Products are presented in such a manner as to seem accessible, convenient, not too expensive, and the markers of modernity.

Food Consumption

Both television and tourism are expressions of consumption. Much of what is visibly consumed is various kinds of food and drink. These worlds merge: tourists consume, and consumption is valorized on television. Many products such as Coca-Cola are easily obtained, often within reach of a child with only a few pesos, from a store in an adjoining house. In villages like Cobá, women often operate a refrescos store as a source of supplemental income.

To estimate the degree of dietary change, we used different techniques of measurement, including counting deliveries to town, interviews with storeowners, talking to children, and 24-hour recall. The data are all approximations, but point in much the same direction. A 24-hour recall study in Akumal (McGarty, 1995) found the three most commonly consumed foods at meals to be tortillas, Coca-Cola, and beans. Snacks included white and sweet breads (*pan dulce*) and various types of cookies and potato chips. Combined, they made up a large part of almost a quarter of the meals. Recalled soft-drink consumption (during and in between meals) was on the order of two to three drinks a day, and in actuality may well have been significantly higher. Altogether, this adds up to a lot of sugar, and when cola consumption is combined with coffee for breakfast and a variety of chocolate-flavored snack foods, the amount of caffeine is also quite elevated. The biological consequences of this changing diet, now high in sugars and fat, is a marked increase in dental caries, including secondary dentition erupting with already serious decay. Babies are sometimes given Coke in a feeding bottle after 6 months, and they come to prefer this to mothers' milk. Overall, the pattern is one of dietary deterioration rather than deprivation. Essentially, the shift is not from subsistence farming to a well-stocked supermarket, but from food production to reliance on cheap commercial foods with a long shelf life. Canned Spam-like meat and Vienna sausages, both high in fat and salt, are substitutes for homegrown chicken and pork, and canned tomatoes and tomato paste replace garden produce. These dietary changes are the result of wage employment and diminished resource control.

Environmental Adaptation and Resource Control

Historically, the transformation of peasantry into a proletariat involved the loss of control of the means of subsistence, as was the case in early modern Europe (De Vries, 1976, pp. 30–84) and later in various Latin American societies (Valdez, 1996). In Quintana Roo, however, the situation differed in at least two ways. First, as previously noted, much of the state was a "zone of refuge," and inland populations lived in relatively autonomous enclaves; second, the pace of change has been precipitous. Taken together, these two features shed light on some of the stresses that we witnessed. To offset loss of cropland, some Maya agriculturists are turning to cash crops, especially raising cattle. But the meat is sold to urban centers and seldom consumed locally. For dispossessed farmers wage employment is the only solution.

A complex rearrangement of access and rights is under way. Beachfront areas (including reserves and sanctuaries) are essentially under the full control of government agencies and the tourist and recreation industry. Local people have virtually no access. The forests are still very extensive, and 80 miles south of Cancún the Sian Ka'an Biosphere Reserve protects 1.3 million acres of the "ecological cornucopia" (W. Garrett, 1989) that provided so well for generations of indigenous Maya. Privatization—including changes in agrarian reform legislation—threatens much other federally protected land.

Quintana Roo may, in some respects, be moving in the same direction as Costa Rica, where controls have helped improve environmental protection—in designated areas—but also profoundly affected local communities. In Tortuguero National Park (Place, 1991) villagers formerly relied heavily on animal protein from the forest, beach, and river. With the advent of tourism, and strict controls on local subsistence, the increase in visitors to Tortuguero has left the local inhabitants with no visible means of subsistence. Likewise in Quintana Roo, beachfront owners have declared themselves protectors of the environment and employed patrols to discourage "poachers." Thus, the specifics of Quintana Roo, as analyzed here, are issues important to regional planning in southern Mexico and Central America, all of which share the mix of cultural tourism and ecotourism. These projects, in particular Mundo Maya and Paseo Pantera, are designed to stimulate regional integration and "soft-path" tourist development. On paper, they call for broad-based community participation, but if the past is any guide, local involvement will be minimal.

Women's Health

Does tourism have an impact on household demography and women's health and diet? The changing diet of the Maya foreshadows serious cardiovascular risks, although high blood pressure does not appear to be a problem at this juncture. Part of the reason may be that pork is still regarded as something of a festive food and that the total consumption of meat is relatively low, even if potted meats and similar products are high in fat and salt. Likewise, infant mortality rates are reported to be low, and young mothers and their babies are not at higher risks according to local nurses and physicians. In all probability, this mixed picture reflects the relative novelty of "convenience foods" and the fact that older people were brought up on a much healthier diet. In keeping with expectations, there is a positive association between a later age of having children and the degree of involvement in wage labor. Thus, in response to the question, "What is the best age to start having children?" the answers clearly reflected the individual's employment status. The linkage between wage labor and fertility may be one of the most important changes taking place in the less traditional sectors of Quintana Roo society. Obviously, people living semiurban lives (with little or no possibilities for farming and gardening) can only make limited use of child labor, and children cease to be an economic asset. Another consideration is the changing employment pattern with its growing emphasis on feminized labor. As tourism shifts from construction to services and maintenance, a greater percentage of jobs is opening up to women—however poorly paid these positions may be.

Conclusions

Our Maya informants were well aware that the benefits of tourism have been very unevenly distributed. They had heard messages of "economic development" and "progress" from the media and visiting politicians, but the language always seemed remote, not really directed at them. Education was deemed an asset, but it spoke more of the outside world, not their own. Nothing in the Mexican system of education reinforces or dignifies the identity of present-day indigenous people. Economically, their stake in tourism is generally limited to the kinds of jobs that they have been allowed to fill, nothing approaching "local involvement in the decision-making process" or "host control or ownership of touristic infrastructure," which Mansperger (1995, p. 93) describes as desirable in effective tourism development in small-scale economies. The full impact of many variables discussed here is difficult to measure, but the evidence indicates that the greater the disruption in land tenure systems and forms of land utilization, the more harmful the impacts of tourism.

How have local people reacted to the advent of tourism? The answer—the only answer that can be given—is that the response has been mixed. There has been accommodation as well as resistance. Some local people have benefited, most obviously the merchants of Cobá, by virtue of proximity to a large-scale tourist attraction. We have tried not to present a picture of a romanticized indigenous society as unitary and in undiluted opposition to the outside world. As Ortner (1995) notes with reference to the colonial Maya, "such groups have their own politics—not just between chiefs and commoners and landlords and peasants but within all the local categories of friction and tension: men and women, parents and children, seniors and juniors . . . and on and on" (p. 177).

Resistance to the dominant order exists, but it is often passive and difficult to interpret. When a poor peasant steals from a rich man, or "poaches" game that the state has defined as protected, is this a form of resistance or simply survival? Many such minor infringements of the law take place. At another level, the vast majority of our informants felt that their culture was being undermined—although what they most feared varied considerably from person to person. There was consensus that education for their children would ultimately improve their income through better jobs, but the school did not teach anything about Mayan culture, even though the villagers of Cobá lived adjacent to superb ruins. Our impression, especially in the context of the uprising in Chiapas, is that "Maya" is being generalized to stand for all peasants and workers, all poor people. One of our informants in Ciudad Chemuyil, whose "European" features and light hair were inherited from Spanish emigrant grandparents, responded to the question of her origin, "I'm not Maya in ancestry, but I understand the condition of the poor and the campesinos; I feel Maya."

Acknowledgments—This chapter is based on two summer field seasons in Quintana Roo (1993, 1994) and a number of other visits. We are very grateful for the support provided by the Wenner-Gren Foundation for Anthropological Research (grant No. 5618) and the University of Massachusetts (Faculty Research Grant, Summer 1994). Our essay is based on data and insights obtained by the whole Yucatan Project team whose other members were Marne T. Ausec, Henry Geddes Gonzáles, Guillermo Iranzo, Catherine McGarty, Markéta Sebelová, and Ellie Zucker. Without the help of many different people in the communities it would have been impossible to piece together this picture of present-day life in Quintana Roo. We are particularly indebted to the Centro Ecológico Akumal for invaluable assistance. Any errors or misperceptions are entirely our responsibility.

Chapter 10

Power and Ethnicity in "Paradise": Boracay, Philippines

Valene L. Smith

Boracay has often been termed a tropical "paradise"—a beautiful little island with a white beach of "talcum powder" sand fringed by palm trees arching around a crystal blue bay of warm water. This relatively flat island, only 4.5 miles long and 1.7 miles wide, lying on the west coast of the Philippines (Figure 10.1), was a tourist "discovery" 30 years ago. In 1997 it was a crowded Asian "Waikiki" hosting mainland Asians for whom, at present, there is a dearth of inexpensive resorts of this type. The transition from farming community to world-famous resort has been locally painful, resulting in degradation of the physical landscape and marginalization of the indigenous hosts. The demand–supply trend demonstrated here raises important issues concerning power and ethnicity in future Asian tourist areas.

Filipino Heritage

It is important at the outset of this study to understand that although the Philippine islands are geographically positioned off the coast of Asia, the Filipinos do not consider themselves Asian, either genetically or culturally. The Filipino population is descended from several waves of immigrants who peopled the islands over a period of many millennia. They included proto-Malaysians (who probably were also the first settlers in Polynesia), and ultimately Malaysians, Chinese, Indians, Arabs, and Indonesians, all of whom predated Magellan's "discovery" of the islands in 1521 AD. Soon after his report to Spain, Spanish conquistadors and their accompanying friars occupied large tracts of land, and converted the population into the Spanish-Catholic tradition. After nearly 400 years of Spanish influence, educated Filipinos spoke Spanish as well as their native Tagalog. Filipinos looked to Spain as their colonial model during the centuries that China and Japan were closed to outsiders and Manila was a friendly port of call for sailing vessels. The Philippines has long been recognized as the "most Western" country of Asia in language, philosophy, and lifestyle. Following the transfer of the islands to the

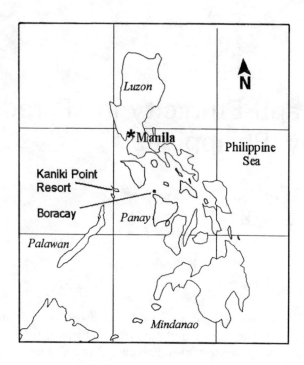

Figure 10.1. Map of the Philippines.

United States in 1898, English became the dominant language of commerce and government. The tenure of the United States until World War II continued this Western orientation and intermarriage, and elementary schools were established in rural areas. With the introduction of radio and television in English, most contemporary Filipinos speak Tagalog as a primary language but are equally fluent in English. Their European culture orientation is manifest in their lifestyle and in their arts (as their folk dances include flamenco), and the traditional cuisine is more Continental than Asian. The residents of Boracay share this Euro-American heritage, and as farmers they raise more field crops than rice.

Boracay: The Development of Tourism

The Early Phase: 1970–1984

After supporting a farm population of some 3000 persons until World War II, Boracay was "discovered" as an inexpensive vacation locale in the early 1970s. These first tourists were American and European families from the diplomatic corps stationed in Asia. The hospitable English-speaking Filipino landowners built thatched cottages to house them, provided fresh fish, chickens, and garden vegetables, and pocketed with pleasure this modest cash income. By the mid-1970s, the rustic setting with only kerosene lanterns for light made Boracay a near-ideal family vacation spot at very low cost. Word-of-mouth recommendations about this island paradise—where a cottage was US$5 per night, a main meal cost US$1, and a can of beer only US$0.10—spread to young, single, European backpackers. A few began to drift into Boracay in the late 1970s to spend a few weeks in winter, and more cottage complexes were constructed to house them. By the early 1980s Boracay had attained an international reputation among these dominantly European "drifter" tourists. The salubrious winter climate from November to March brought gentle breezes to warm the fine coral sand beach, and palm trees shaded the thatched cottages.

National Government Interest

The 1970s was the era of World Bank support for tourism development, and the Philippine government eagerly turned to international tourism as a panacea for its sagging unemployment. The Philippine economy had been shattered during World War II by the Japanese occupancy of the archipelago. The fragile postwar independence economy was further shaken by a series of disastrous typhoons that destroyed many coconut plantations and greatly reduced copra production. Copra, or dried coconut meat, had long been an important Philippine agricultural export as a nutritious stock feed. This revenue disappeared when copra was replaced on the world market by other products. Adding to the economic woes, the Huk insurgencies were politically disruptive and discouraged tourism. While continental Asian economies began to blossom, the Philippines was infused by corruption and cronyism.

By 1975, consistent with a national tourism policy (see Richter, Chapter 22), the presence of even these few tourists prompted then-president Marcos to declare Boracay a Tourist Preserve, and its future development was vested in the Philippines Tourism Authority (PTA). This announcement was a silent signal to some wealthy Manila families that the purchase of land on Boracay would be a good long-term investment, as beach frontage was then selling for only US$1 per square meter. With assistance from the PTA, a Cottage Owner's Association was formed in 1979, and the bylaws restricted membership to Filipino Cottage Owners (V. Smith, 1992a). This body established development standards, including a 30-foot (10-meter) setback from the beach for all construction to preserve the tropical panorama of palms and sea. All powered vehicles were to be banned. Seemingly, local governance was in place.

Growth and the Quest for Funding

In 1981, the Ministry of Tourism declared the entire island a Tourist Zone and established a Tourist Office (1983) to assist arriving guests and collect statistics (Figure 10.2). By then, enough "backpackers" had targeted Boracay as a destination to support a French-operated sports center, which rented motor scooters (a powered vehicle). To further meet tourist demand, several refreshment stands (nightclubs) installed gasoline-powered generators to refrigerate beer and to provide juke boxes and neon lights at night. The chickens still crowed at dawn but the bucolic quietude of Boracay had been shattered.

It is to their great credit that the Philippine Department of Tourism recognized the uniqueness of Boracay and its tourism potential in the early 1980s. Based on

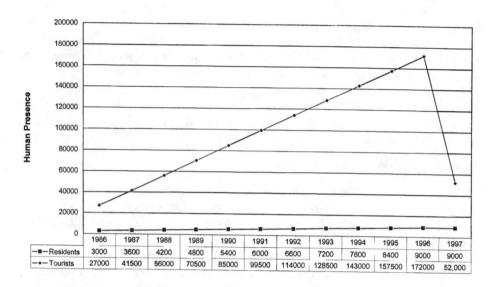

Figure 10.2. Growth of permanent residents compared with tourists in Boracay: 1986–1997. Data are averaged. Source: Trousdale (1999).

only visitor statistics of 14,277 annual visitors, the PTA commissioned a well-known Hawaiian resort development company to determine the resort capability of this tiny site. Their proposal included construction of a resort with golf course and horse trails but set occupancy limits of 1700–1900 rooms, a daily employee count of 2400–2600 persons, and a total permanent population of Boracaynons between 4000 and 4600. However, the report clearly stipulated the resort required an off-island water source (pipeline), sewage system and solid waste disposal, and electricity (Helber et al., 1984). The unstated cost for these services vital to sustainable tourism implied millions of pesos and the project was not implemented.

The Philippine government could not support their essential national social service programs and also fund tourism projects on one small island. Rumors spread quickly around the island but no government officials came to explain the project or their inability to implement it. Cottage owners were uncertain what would happen to their business when the big resort was built. Concern about culinary water and sewer did not trickle down to either the tourist market or to the island residents.

The Middle Phase: 1984–1997

The tourist count, initially recorded in 1984 as 14,277, nearly doubled in 2 years to 27,000 in 1986, and doubled again to 56,000 in 1988, and continued to spiral upward. In 1987, Long Beach on Boracay was glowingly described in newspapers as distant and as small as the *Chico Enterprise Record* (March 8, 1987, p. 4C), the hometown paper of this volume's editors. An avant-garde travel book, *BMW Tropical Beach Handbook* (Hanna, 1989), listed Long Beach as "the world's best beach." More tourists arrived!

Officials at the PTA were not unaware of the deteriorating environment and potential health problems on Boracay but lacked funds to remedy them. They also lacked the fortitude to limit tourism to a resident population who were benefiting from the income. For perspective, not far from their Manila office and within daily view (still true in 2000) are the hundreds of "real life" families who literally dwell in the fetid-smelling garbage dumps, which they comb daily for their food and saleable salvage. And on the streets are thousands of young Filipinos who hold bachelor's degrees from one of some 60 colleges in Manila but have no job. By contrast to the urban problems, Boracaynons were well off (and they realized it!).

PTA hoped to make of Boracay their "model tourism project" to be replicated for the economic benefit of other islanders in the archipelago. Toward this goal, PTA solicited a 1987 World Tourism Organization (WTO) study to assess the island tourism potential (V. Smith, 1992a). Provided with fresh data confirming both the potential and the infrastructure requirements, the government appealed (unsuccessfully) for United Nations Development Project (UNDP) funds. Unfortunately, to UNDP funding agencies Boracay in 1987 seemed inconsequential in the face of pressing urban and agricultural needs throughout Asia. Later, in 1996, the British Department of International Development (DID) also undertook a study (Nicholson, 1997). In 1997, a partnership project of the Philippine Department of Tourism (DOT) with the Canadian Urban Institute (CUI) further confirmed the significant land-use problems in Boracay, related to inadequate culinary water, sewage, garbage, litter, and power for essential services (Trousdale, 1999).

The 1986 visitor count included a high proportion of European and American visitors numbering 8563 (Figure 10.3). It must be noted that a high percentage of

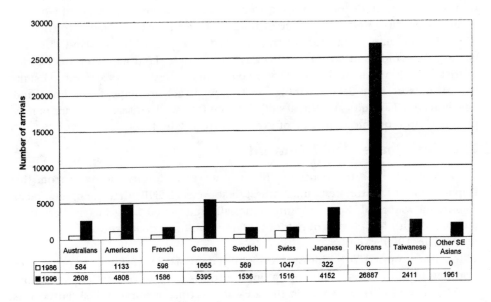

	Australians	Americans	French	German	Swedish	Swiss	Japanese	Koreans	Taiwanese	Other SE Asians
☐ 1986	584	1133	598	1665	569	1047	322	0	0	0
■ 1996	2608	4808	1586	5395	1536	1516	4152	26887	2411	1961

Figure 10.3. International visitor arrivals in Boracay, selected nationalities: 1986 and 1996. Source: Philippine Tourist Authority; 1986 data, V. Smith (1994, p. 145); 1996 data, Nicholson (1997, p. 22).

the nearly 19,000 domestic visitors registered were not tourists but residents and family members going back and forth to adjacent islands on business, to shop in the markets, to visit the hospital, and to see family and friends. It also included outsiders (meaning non-Boracaynons) who were already migrating to the island to build cottages and open businesses. As foreigners they were ineligible for membership in the Cottage Owners Association (COA) nor did any of them follow COA guidelines. Concerned members wrote letters of complaint to the PTA in Manila and locally called meetings to ask, "Why doesn't the government do something? They support tourism, so why don't they help us (with the violations of the setback zoning and the construction of rental units by non-Filipinos)?" No guidance was forthcoming.

Most cottage owners were unaware of the fundamental issues involving waste management and water supply, as the island had never experienced a problem. In 1986 raw sewage drained at one point across the beach walk into the bay. A German visitor engineered a school construction project to bridge this area but it did not abate the contamination. The medical staff at the adjacent island hospital shared my concerns about potential epidemics from mounting piles of garbage and rat infestation.

Tourism continued to expand. In 1988, the DOT in Manila sent in demolition crews to remove buildings that violated the setback (and despoiled the view). The crews were recalled because of protests staged by the in-migrant owners of these offending structures. The increasing community divisiveness prompted the PTA in 1990 to hire consultants to identify new bases for sustainable development but, again, their findings were not publicly shared or implemented.

In 1991, as the prevailing ideas of the 1987 Brundtland Report spread across the world, Philippine national legislation supported the philosophy of administration by local input, or "bottom up" government. The newly passed Local Government Code transferred governance of Boracay from the PTA in Manila to the Municipality of Malay, a small administrative town on adjacent Panay Island. This legislation also voided all *land titles* because the entire island had been declared a tourist zone. In the land rush that followed, as more newcomers arrived to establish businesses, boundary squabbles arose over beach frontage, fence lines, and beach access. Lawsuits and threats of violence followed. (Interested readers may pursue this incredible sequence of events in Trousdale, 1999.)

The Final Phase: 1997 Onward

"On June 30, 1997, the people of Boracay were shaken by the news from the Department of Environment and Natural Resources (DENR) that the crystal clear swimming waters off Boracay's internationally renowned Long Beach were contaminated with high levels of coliform blamed on inadequate sewage treatment" (Trousdale, 1999, p. 840).

Tourism dropped 70% almost overnight (Figure 10.3). The decade of neglect crippled local industry and gave Philippine tourism a bad reputation. According to Trousdale (1999), who was in the area at the time, a Boracay Task Force was activated to coordinate the government's "solemn promise of increased spending on much needed physical infrastructure." This Task Force was to oversee the further expansion of tourism, including sewer lines to support three new resorts being developed on the north end of the island, which would double the 1996 capacity to 300,000 tourists (or an average of 25,000 per month).

Trousdale (see Chapter 19) provides an alternative case study of another Philippine island, Kaniki Point, in which the environmental impact studies will (hopefully) avoid the Boracay-type problems, thus demonstrating the advantage of prior planning.

The water pollution edict that dramatically curtailed the tourist influx was, however, only the tip of the iceberg. Common to many areas where "new" tourism is introduced, as at Huatulco (Long, 1993b) and Cancún in Mexico (see Pi-Sunyer, Thomas, and Daltabuit, Chapter 9), the social problems may be as acute as the physical degradation but remain unresolved because they are not so readily apparent. In Boracay, community divisiveness between the original inhabitants and new business owners shattered social integration and mutual dependence, to breed "them" and "us" as hostile neighbors. The changed guest ethnicity further widened this schism, as foreign capital investment poured into the island and foreigners gained control of the local economy. The bases for widespread Boracaynon discontent are well illustrated by a comparative 10-year assessment.

Boracay Compared: 1986 and I996

Boracay 1986

The physical assets of Boracay in 1986 were its beautiful beach and the uncluttered beach walk. Cottage units were small, surrounded by gardens, and were almost entirely family owned and operated. Tourism impact was quite limited and the guests were almost exclusively European or American, virtually all of whom spoke English and were friendly. Some stayed for months, others came every year for a few weeks, and others drifted in and went on. In general, life was a pleasant routine.

The elementary school changed class hours so upper grade students were free during lunch hours to work in the family kitchen or wait tables. Some families had small souvenir stands and made T-shirts and shorts, mostly on order. Earned income went directly to the service providers and was commonly used to pay high school tuition so children would have a better life. Above all, residents enjoyed the stability of their land, their community, and their heritage.

Boracay 1996

Nicholson (1997) did field work in three Filipino villages and provides an on-site description of the 1996 transition from the previous pattern of long-stay Europeans to a "mass Asian market for short-stay visitors in high standard facilities" (p. iii). The new, largely foreign-owned and foreign-staffed, hotels opened with 30 or more units and included on-site restaurants, karaokes, bars, gift shops, and for-hire bicycles and sports equipment. They rapidly filled with tour groups who stayed only 3–4 days, and who ate and shopped at the hotel. There was far greater leakage of income and employment to non-Filipinos.

The 1996 visitor arrivals (Figure 10.3) document that of the 52,880 international guests, over half were Korean (26,887), and combining all Asians, the ratio increased to 67%, most of whom did not speak English or patronize local businesses. To cater to this vacation market, the beach walk was soon lined with Asian vendors selling Asian goods from their tricycles, as is customary in crowded Asian markets. This new package tour orientation with its rapid guest turnover changed the leisurely resort pace, and the European and American "regulars" began to move out, vacating the cottages. The financial security of the cottage owners faded, due to diminished business and an inflationary trend induced by the increased need to import food, water, and other essentials. Even though construction jobs and employment as porters and boatmen increased, wages for unskilled labor were very low, even by Filipino standards. A tourism skills training program, originally intended to assist Boracaynons, was not implemented. (An economic analysis of the leakage to foreign investors would be very instructive here, to assess the impact of foreign investment in a small indigenous community.)

The Future

The 1997 government promise to build infrastructure and increase the tourist potential to 300,000 visitors offered virtually nothing to the Filipino Boracaynons, for they lacked capital with which to build competing hotels. Families had hand-built their thatched cottages, and they served meals al fresco in a cabana-like structure. Some had lacked money to install electricity when the service was introduced (1991), and most did not have funds to connect their units to the sewer when it was provided. The prospect of a jet runway on Panay Island to provide nonstop charter air service from Seoul, Tokyo, and Taipei would only create more service jobs and the probable in-migration of outsiders from Manila to fill them. To the Boracaynons who had abandoned farming and fishing for the cash income from tourism, the future is discouraging in terms of landlessness and loss of identity.

Power and Ethnicity

This Boracay case study offers an opportunity to consider two significant issues that will arise as globalization increases: namely, *political power* as the controlling force in tourism development, and the *ethnicity of the guests* rather than the hosts.

Political Power

Much of the contemporary literature devoted to tourism development suggests that "good tourism" (sustainable and thus beneficial to all) is rooted in community empowerment. The first decade of tourism in Boracay appears to have successfully followed this pattern and is consistent with the model of small-scale tourism and privatization with tourism under control and profits directly feeding providers (Dahles & Bras, 1999). But the in-migration of outsiders displaced traditional leadership networks. Thus, there appears to be a threshold of locality and size, which, when breached, requires at least some external intervention. By independently commissioning the first resort survey (the Helber project), the national government adopted the "top down" political approach and established the priority that, in tourism, "bigger is better."

Sofield (see Chapter 20) has had extensive administrative experience in community empowerment in the Pacific Rim, as shown in his case study of Nepal. His six-tier multidimensional process offers potential guidelines for fieldwork, to reinforce local participation. However, it is initiated with outside expertise, and thus closely parallels the Appropriate Tourism Impact Assessment (ATIA) described by Trousdale (see Chapter 19). The 4 H's of tourism, previously described in Chapter 8, are yet another form of assessment and can be initiated either as a self-assessment or with outside expertise.

The Community Empowerment model (Sofield) provides the following sequence:

1. a consultative process often characterized by the input of outside expertise;
2. the opportunity to learn and to choose;
3. the ability to make decisions;
4. the capacity to implement and apply those decisions;
5. acceptance of responsibility for those decisions and actions and their consequences; and
6. outcomes directly benefiting the community and its members, not diverted or channeled to others.

Tourism brought modernization to Boracay in the form of electricity, television, and a cash economy, but it was purchased at the price of heritage and place. This case study suggests that planning and effective governance could have mitigated many of the existent problems but the greed of numbers dominated the Philippine goals in their role as culture broker. Therein lies an important lesson: the *objectives of governance* (and governments) are crucial to the development of *appropriate tourism*. Confronted with pervasive globalization, privatized small-scale tourism cannot survive but must be shielded by stringent monitoring and aided when necessary by regulatory bodies or it will be displaced.

Once the *imported* infrastructure (water lines, sewer, and electricity) are in place, thereby making Boracay essentially an artificial *built* island platform on which to construct hotels, cafes, and shops, tourism will probably be sustainable but the quality can only be assured by monitoring. The larger process, sustainable tourism development, will have reached a dead end. The island will no longer be Boracay, for its aesthetic essence and physical attractiveness will have been destroyed. This sanitized bit of land could be named "Anyplace." The Philippines gained a client but lost an asset and, as Trousdale thoughtfully asks: Is Boracay approaching the stagnation phase of the Resort Life Cycle?

Ethnicity

Ethnicity in Asia has been recently and extensively discussed by Yamashita, Din, and Eades (1997) in *Tourism and Cultural Development in Asia and Oceania*, and by Picard and Wood (1997) in *Tourism, Ethnicity and the State in Asian and Pacific Societies*. Essentially all the research identified by these authors and their stimuli address only one side of the issue: namely, host ethnicity as it is commoditized, dramatized, or even recreated as a readily marketable, highly profitable guest attraction. The exotic aspects of indigenous cultures provide strong motivations for tourism, and tribal symbols are sources for "market art" in T-shirts and fabrics. If heritage has faded, authenticity can be reconstructed into "model cultures" such as the new Alaskan Native Heritage Center in Anchorage (see Chapter 21).

The ethnicity of the guests is almost never mentioned—possibly because a hint of discrimination might lurk in the shadows (or some other deviation from political correctness?). More likely the omission reflects the fact that no other case study has as yet demonstrated such a rapid and enveloping community transformation as shown in little Boracay. Indian businesses dominate Nepalese tourism, and the Chinese traders control Tibetan tourism, but these facts are seldom mentioned.

The study of national character has been out of fashion among anthropologists for several decades, yet it is clear from the psychographic profiles (Table 8.4) that discernible tourism differences occur among people based on the economic and social milieu during their maturation. N. Graburn (1977) observed that different nations take to their countryside differently, and Jafari has noted that in international travel, people take their cultural baggage with them. In confirmation of these generalities, McGahey (1994) analyzed Korean behavior in 34 countries, in which the data indicate that all local hosts found that Koreans are often rude and discourteous, "more demanding of service staff and less understanding when things go wrong" (cited in Trousdale, 199p, p. 849).

The differences in cultural heritage between the Filipinos and continental Asians are considerable, and ethnic irritation may be dismissed as a phenomenon of tourism but it could decay into deeper resentment and serious antipathy. There is a clear and pressing need to investigate the relation between ethnic differences and host–guest satisfaction. Ethnicity often lends itself to cartoons, including those created by Africans, who ask, in the book *Touristes-Rois en Afrique* (Dieng, 1982): How are tourists in Senegal viewed by those who serve them?

Research regarding the world's largest industry serves many masters: scholars, the industry itself, government and its agents, and hosts and guests. The American travel industry has benefited from the studies by Plog and others, which define the five generations of American travelers (Table 8.4). Comparable profiles of other nationalities could be of value in alleviating misunderstandings and alienations involving tourist ethnicity.

Tourist Culture and the Product Life Cycle

When international tourism was introduced into Boracay 30 years ago, the community inherently defined comfortable public and private space. Visitors occupied cottages and beach; the beach walk was common space; and homes, gardens, and inland farms were private. It was the ideal *tourist culture*, destroyed by overloading the carrying capacity of the island. The concept of tourist culture closely parallels the Butler resort life cycle (see Brent, Chapter 7), and Walle (1998) has elaborated it into a marketing model for culture tourist professionals engaged in planning and development (Figure 12.5). It is instructive to examine Boracay in the light of this model of Classes of the Consuming Public (Figure 10.4).

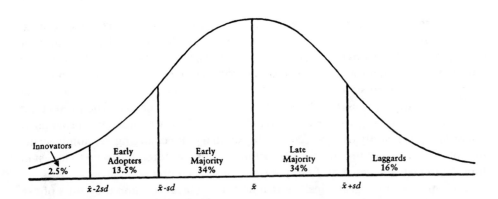

Figure 10.4. The classes of consuming public. (Adapted with permission of the Free Press, a division of Simon & Schuster Inc., from *Diffusion of Innovations*, 4th ed., by Everett M. Rogers. Copyright 1962, 1971, 1983 by the Free Press.)

The five classes of Consuming Public closely parallel the four categories of tourists who have visited Boracay to date:

> **The Innovators** are generally young, upscale, and educated (as was true of the international diplomatic corps families first to visit Boracay).They correspond to the allocentrics defined by Plog (see Chapter 4).
>
> **The Early Adoptees** are also young, affluent, educated, and near-allocentrics (the "backpackers") who ventured to Boracay with advance knowledge of the tourist amenities, as an alternative to other popular Asian beach resorts such as Goa (India) or Phuket (Thailand).
>
> **The Early Majority** are mid-centrics (the increased European influx from 1987 onwards) who came to Boracay as a "destination," described in guidebooks and by international travel writers.These guests knew in advance which accommodations had concrete "ocean view bungalows" and electricity.
>
> **The Late Majority** are near-psychocentrics (the Asian visitors) on package tours with bulk airfares and all-inclusive land prices.They are generally a less affluent market who buy into a destination that is possibly declining in quality.
>
> **The Laggards** are the unknown future in Boracay.Will the new resorts rejuvenate the island, or will it become the cheap vacation locale for psychocentric Asian workers?

Conclusions

Boracay is a microcosm, but may be predictive of future Asian travel. Half the world's population lives in Asia, and as their economies rebound from a late 1990's economic crisis, there will be an outpouring of new tourists.This vast population has viewed the world on television; they now want to *experience* it. Many are curious to see snow. Others who live in the northern areas of Japan, Korea, and China will seek sunbelt vacations just as the Europeans and Americans have for decades.

Areas like Boracay can meet the aspirations of the deterritorialized Western vacation with beach experience and shopping at very low cost. The proximity of Philippine and Vietnamese beaches to Korea, PRC, Japan, and Taiwan benefits the 1-week vacationer, for air travel is fast and comparatively cheap. The Asian desire to travel in "Western style" prompted the world's largest cruise operator, Carnival Cruises, to station a vessel in Korea for exclusive all-Asian cruises. The project did not materialize owing to the 1998 financial crisis, but a comparable program is operating successfully from Singapore. In summary, the changing economic structure of Boracay is not unique. Globalization encourages foreign capital to invest in tourism infrastructure to profitably service their traveling compatriots.

Governments must realistically examine their role, determine the limits of use in conjunction with their residents, and develop effective plans. The Filipino hosts of 30 years ago were proud of their properties and their hospitality, and the income was a positive change in their lives. Trousdale (1999) concluded that the case study of tourism on Boracay Island "supports the assertion that governance is the critical issue in moving development towards sustainability" (p. 843). And the contemporary generation expresses their present dissatisfaction as, "tourists work for dollars and pay in pesos; we work for pesos and pay in dollars (for imported food, water and other essentials)" (Nicholson, 1997, p. 24).

Chapter 11

Wilderness Tourism in Zimbabwe

Robin Heath

Attractions in Zimbabwe range from spectacular mountain scenery, waterfalls, rivers and lakes, to large concentrations of wildlife of all types. Zimbabwe holds protected areas and wildlife resources that compare favorably with any equivalent area in Africa. Activities available to tourists include game viewing, hunting and nonhunting safaris, white-water rafting, canoeing, angling of all types, water sports, hiking and mountain climbing, as well as the more urbanized activities of golf, horse riding, gambling, and even steam-train safaris. The infrastructure is reasonably developed, with good highways providing easy access to most tourist destinations. Regular domestic flights also serve the most important tourist centers. Most hotels are of a relatively high standard while the Parks and Wild Life Estate provides a range of reasonably priced self-catering accommodations.

The government of Zimbabwe recognizes tourism as an important source of foreign exchange but not at the expense of local social values or natural resources (Chitepo, 1986). The current strategy demands catering for the upper end of the adventure and wildlife market. Safari and hunting operations are largely in the hands of local entrepreneurs, as are most hotels, and there is a serious attempt to limit economic leakages.

The Resource Base

The Parks and Wild Life Estate and other commercial operations form the nucleus for the tourist attractions. Lands managed by this organization extend some 5 million hectares, covering about 13.1% of the country, and are located largely on the periphery, in sparsely populated areas (Figure 11.1).

Apart from world-famous Victoria Falls, most visitors to Zimbabwe come for safaris and for the excellent game viewing and hunting. Hwange National Park, for example, contains 35 species of large mammals including some 25,000–30,000 elephant (reputedly the largest herd in the world), 13,000 buffalo, 3000 sable antelope, 2000 giraffe, 2000 wildebeest, 1700 zebra, 150 black rhino, and unknown numbers of impala, eland, warthog, lion, leopard, and cheetah, as well as over 400 different species of birds (Pitman, 1987). Hippopotamus and crocodile are plentiful along the Zambezi River and in Lake Kariba. The Estate is divided into six classes of protected area, offering a variety of tourist experiences.

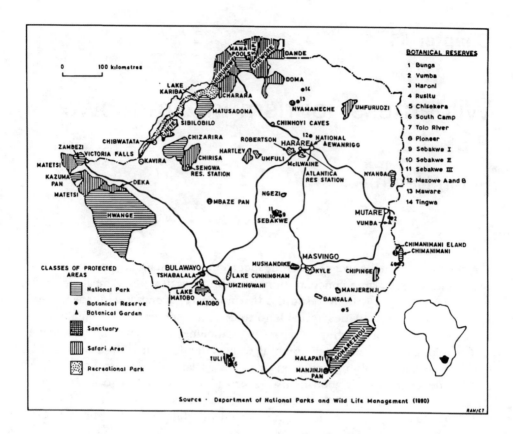

Figure 11.1. Map of the Parks and Wild Life Estates in Zimbabwe.

National Parks and Safari Areas

Eleven national parks, comprising approximately 2.7 million hectares (6% of the country), enjoy the highest protection status of any land in Zimbabwe. In the parks there is minimal interference with natural processes, and visitor activities are strictly controlled in order to protect all flora and fauna.

Zimbabwe's 16 safari areas (1.9 million hectares), on the other hand, permit recreational hunting, nonhunting safaris, hiking, and other forms of recreational activity. There is currently more freedom of action in safari areas although at some point they may be upgraded to National Park status.

Recreational Parks

These are generally associated with large impoundments (lakes) near major urban centers. The conserved area around the water body is aimed at protecting and prolonging the life span of the impoundment. Natural features and the rural atmosphere are preserved and protected, but a wider range of recreational activities is allowed than is possible in the National Parks and Safari Areas. At present, there are 15 recreational parks in Zimbabwe. Additionally, the government determines the recreational potential of each new large dam with a view to deciding whether it should become the nucleus of a recreational park.

Sanctuaries, Botanical Reserves, and Botanical Gardens

Sanctuaries have been created for the protection of individual animal, bird, or plant species or of unique biotic communities and have similar objectives to those of national parks. Some sanctuaries are managed for educational or other specific purposes. The objectives of botanical reserves are similar to those of sanctuaries but the reserves protect only plant communities. Botanical gardens are managed to propagate Zimbabwean species or particular exotic species of plants. These classified areas of conservation and propagation reflect the importance of nature and the land.

Zimbabwe also has substantial wildlife resources outside the Parks and Wild Life Estate. These exist in the protected areas of the State Forest Lands and on privately owned farms and ranches. They also exist within the communal lands where indigenous farming communities hold land under communal tenure, with management vested in Rural District Councils. The Councils issue hunting permits, lease hunting concessions to safari operators, and generally control the use of wildlife within their areas. Over 30% of Zimbabwe is now under wildlife conservation in some form or other and these areas are being increasingly utilized by both hunting and nonhunting commercial safari operators.

The Growth of Foreign Tourism to Zimbabwe

Foreign tourism to Zimbabwe grew slowly until the 1960s, when jet service shortened travel time and visitor numbers began a marked increase. After the unilateral declaration of independence (UDI) in 1965, there was a temporary drop in tourist arrivals but the industry soon revived and has been steadily increasing ever since. In 1990, for the first time, the number of visitors exceeded 500,000 and earned approximately US$100 million. Growth continued to 1.9 million tourists in 1997 with a revenue of US$250 million (WTO, 1997a). Prior to 1980, South Africans dominated the tourist market but, in the years immediately after independence, their importance was greatly reduced and they were superseded by visitors from Zambia and Botswana (Zinyama, 1989). However, since 1987, with the depreciation of the Zambian *kwacha* and increasingly stringent currency controls in that country, the number of visitors from Zambia has dropped while the number of South African visitors has increased rapidly to regain market domination. Africa continues to be the major tourist-generating region for Zimbabwe, contributing more than 75% of all visitors.

Tourism Within the Parks and Wild Life Estate

The Department of National Parks and Wild Life Management offers a variety of accommodation types, ranging from exclusive bush camps through fully equipped lodges and partially equipped cottages to chalets with shared baths and outdoor barbecues. In 1994, the total visitor count to the parks was 710,502. However, there is a seasonal factor that causes bed occupancy rates to fluctuate from 66% to 80% during the high season of July, August, and September.

It is not only the domestic and regional market that prefers fairly low-cost, simple, self-catering accommodation. When international visitors become aware of the smaller properties, with individual cottages, that are also available within the Parks and Wild Life Estate, many of them indicate a preference for that type of accommodation as opposed to conventional hotels.

Safari Operators and Professional Hunters

Both hunting and nonhunting safaris are a major component of wildlife-based tourism in Zimbabwe, and the number of operators concerned has grown rapidly since 1980. In 1995 there were 198 tour operators and 127 professional hunters. Hunting safaris are widely criticized, especially in the US, by radical environmentalists who have very little understanding of the reality of African wildlife and their habits. An article, "Too many elephants," published in the influential *Wall Street Journal* on July 17, 1997, states the issue as it impacts Hwange National Park,

> A single elephant knocks down 1,500 trees per year, and drinks 13 gallons of water per day. Soon smaller animals, deprived of shade and water, will be forced to flee the park as elephants trample Zimbabwe's distinctive grasslands into deserts. . . . Elephant overpopulation is a threat to other species and to the environment . . . and also threatens human lives and livelihoods. . . . one elephant herd consumes nearly 10 acres of cropland in an evening–often the annual food supply for an entire family. (Miniter, 1997, p. A22)

Hunting safaris are the most reasoned solution to the problem (Figure 11.2). The article continues,

> Without hunting, wildlife managers have only two choices: to do nothing and let the animals die from starvation, or employ the park rangers to selectively kill elephants, which robs money from other needed services, and diverts the employee time from wildlife protection. Either way, the animals die (Miniter, 1997, p. A22).

Safari operators and professional hunters operate in the Parks and Wild Life Estate, on state Forest Lands, on communal lands, and on privately owned farms and ranches. While recreational hunting remains an important component of the safari industry, photographic and walking safaris are increasing in popularity, as are canoeing, white-water rafting, and water-based game viewing.

Revenue earned from hunting safaris for foreign visitors increased from US$4 million in 1985 to US$12.8 million in 1993 while the value of trophies rose to US$5 million. For 1997, the estimated revenues from hunting safaris was US$15.9 million (personal communication with World Wide Fund for Nature). Most of the trophy fees (81%) are earned from a limited number of species, namely elephant, leopard, buffalo, sable, kudu, zebra, eland, lion, and waterbuck. During 1997 Zim-

Figure 11.2. Too many elephants. (Photo by Betty Porter, Chico, CA)

babwe supported over 16,500 days of hunting and, together with other Southern African countries, provided about 86% of all safari hunting in Africa.

Wildlife-Based Tourism Benefits for the Rural Economy

During the past decade, two important developments have taken place in Zimbabwe's tourism industry. The first is the growth of wildlife ranching and associated tourist activities on commercial ranches and farms. The second is the growing interest in the Communal Areas Management Programme for Indigenous Resources (CAMPFIRE) program.

Ranchers and commercial crop farmers now devote large areas entirely to wildlife management that were utilized previously for cattle rearing. In addition to recreational hunting, photographic and walking safaris, many sites offer lodges and self-catering chalets at reasonable rates for tourists who opt to travel by rented car or drive in from adjoining South Africa. The sustainable use of wildlife, through various types of tourism, has become an important economic activity for many commercial farmers. This success led to the formation in 1985 of the Wildlife Producers Association in an attempt to structure the industry. It now has 480 members, of whom some 240 are actively involved in promoting the utilization of wildlife on their farms and ranches. Half of these are also involved in tourism of some sort or other. In October 1990, 76 of these farmers formed the Wildlife Producers

Co-operative, which markets "tourism on the ranch" and acts as a travel agent for its members. This development has had the positive effect of dispersing tourists and tourist activity over large parts of Zimbabwe rather than allowing them to concentrate within and around the Parks and Wild Life Estate. The potential benefits to the rural economy accruing from the provision of tourist facilities of this nature appear to be high. The CAMPFIRE program was instituted by the Parks and Wild Life Act (No. 14 of 1975) and deals holistically with the management of all natural resources, including wildlife, within communal lands (Figure 11.3).

Nyamaphene (1985) states that the CAMPFIRE plan was based on several occurrences. The rapid increase in rural population caused competition between agriculture and wildlife for the land. It is possible for local people to continue farming arable land while simultaneously collecting profits from wildlife management. Wildlife management in lands that are marginal for agriculture demonstrates better economic returns for individual landowners and improved standards of living for the community. Specifically, wildlife foraging on native grasses survive and produce a better animal yield than cattle. The CAMPFIRE program in Zimbabwe

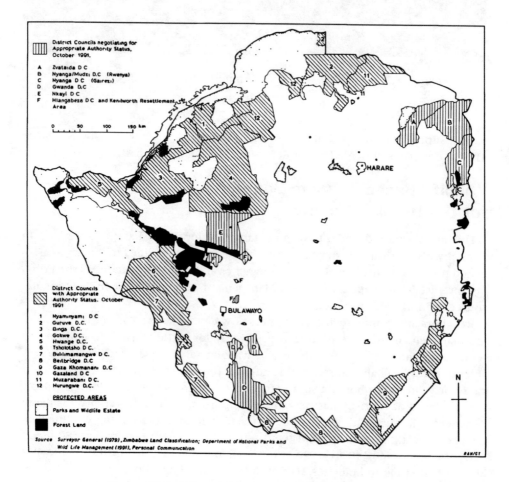

Figure 11.3. Map of Zimbabwe's CAMPFIRE projects.

may protect the native animals here from the land depredation that occurs in Kenya, where open space in the Masai Mara is being plowed and planted for barley to make beer. These developments represent efforts to manage wildlife on an economic basis and to secure benefits for local communities from both recreational hunting and nonconsumptive safaris.

Hunting is an integral part of the CAMPFIRE program. The World Wildlife Fund and the African Wildlife Foundation both support the CAMPFIRE initiative and the government's sale of hunting licenses in the Safari Areas of the Estate. CAMPFIRE funnels 70% of the hunting license fees to villagers involved in the program, who may elect to spend some of the money on community needs but will retain the remainder as individual household incomes. Overall, it is an exciting proposition, offering not only direct revenue from wildlife-based tourism for poverty-stricken marginal communities but also the promise of economic multiplier effects in the future. In 1997, CAMPFIRE projects earned US$1,384,083 (Z$20 million) and, consistent with their intent, funds provided rural residents with community needs including drilled wells for clean drinking water, construction of schools and health clinics, fencing for residential lands, and the installation of grinding mills (Gunther 1999). If domestic tourism expands in the future, modest accommodations and services could be provided in these peripheral areas to spread the economic and employment benefits more widely through the country.

Pricing Policies and Domestic Tourism

Child and Child (1990) point out that "wildlife is a renewable resource which, like others, must be conserved and used wisely. Its continued existence outside protected areas will depend on its competitive ability in terms of landholder benefits" (p. 18). A fundamental issue, when considering wildlife-based tourism in Zimbabwe, relates to pricing policies in the Parks and Wild Life Estate, which reflect the Western attitude that protected areas should be available to the public free or at a nominal charge. This raises the moral issue of whether a developing country can afford to subsidize the leisure of its more affluent citizens and of foreign visitors (Child & Heath, 1990). This policy is also directly opposed to Zimbabwe's current foreign tourism marketing policy, aimed at the up-market, and places the Estate in the position of undercutting private enterprise, particularly that of commercial farm and communal landholders. Furthermore, this policy results in a loss of potential revenue to the annual Estate. Visitor services, including those that are labor intensive, have had to be curtailed and opportunities for creating new attractions have been lost (Child & Heath, 1990). On the other and, it is important that pricing policies in the Estate do not lead to the exclusion of the majority of Zimbabwean citizens from their own resort areas. Many tourism planners believe that a dual pricing policy within the Parks and Wild Life Estate—one for outsiders, the other for local residents—is entirely fair because the latter are also local taxpayers.

Many of the larger hotels are located adjacent to the National Parks. For example, the Hwange Safari Lodge with its 94 deluxe rooms is very popular, offering Continental cuisine, boutiques, and a night viewing platform, and was priced in 1998 at US$200 per night. The daily traffic with Hwange National Park has necessitated the paving of principal routes through the park, particularly those that connect the most frequented waterholes where game viewing is generally assured. Prolonged drought combined with an increasing elephant population forced the creation of artificial waterholes. Hwange Safari Lodge offers an excellent wildlife experience in what is termed "soft tourism" (with comfortable amenities).

Regional Development

Little national attention has been given so far to the possibility of integrating wildlife-based tourism in Zimbabwe to the wider Southern African region. Within the framework of the Southern African Development Community (SADC), Lesotho has been tasked with developing the tourism sector but little has yet been achieved. A SADC Federation of Travel and Tourism Association has been established, and the need to develop a comprehensive tourism strategy for the region is widely acknowledged. South Africa has an aggressive tourism training program, to provide employment in all sectors of the industry. Many tour operators include Botswana, Zimbabwe, and South Africa in their tour packages because of the diversity of attractions. South Africa offers the Garden Route along the eastern coast, Table Mountain and the harbor at Capetown, and the popular Wine District. Botswana also features wildlife in the Okavango Delta. In combination, this circuit for a 2- to 3-week stay justifies the long-haul air expense from Europe and North America. Thus, the SADC countries, including South Africa, are in a position to offer a wide-ranging package of natural, historical, and cultural attractions in a regionally integrated program. However, before this can become a reality, the political instability and violence in the region must come to an end. The image of danger and violence in Southern Africa has a serious effect on international tourism to the region, even in peaceful countries like Botswana and Zimbabwe. A major international marketing program is essential if the regional image is to be improved.

Conclusions

Africa receives only about 3.8% of international arrivals, and Zimbabwe receives only 8% of that total (WTO, 1997a). Zimbabwe does not have glorious beaches, coral reefs, giant cities, or important religious or cultural centers. However, it does have large numbers of wild animals and can offer a wilderness experience. However, wildlife-based tourism cannot survive under mass tourism. There is a limited carrying capacity for tourists as well as for wildlife in any given location. Plog (1974) warns that "Destination areas carry with them the potential seeds of their own destruction, as they allow themselves to become more commercialised and lose the qualities which originally attracted tourists" (p. 13). Uncontrolled numbers of visitors will damage the wilderness experience that attracted tourists in the first place, leaving Zimbabwe with very little to offer as a tourist destination. What is needed currently is a long-term strategic plan and a comprehensive tourism policy that will guide the future development of tourism for domestic and international tourists alike.

Chapter 12

Pamukkale:
Turkish Homestay Tourism

Anne Marie Van Broeck

This case study describes the social changes in the traditional farm village of Pamukkale, Turkey, during five periods of residence in the community between 1983 and 1990, when Western tourists were first attracted to the area in increasing numbers. The author originally went to Turkey on unrelated research, and became an intermittent guest of the family through whose eyes this study is documented. The changes in the community were initially subtle and modest but, by December 1988, the progressive tourism-related changes in Pamukkale suddenly became marked. Although it was winter (off-season), a stroll through the town revealed the recent construction of numerous new hotels, restaurants, and discotheques. What was tourism doing to the village and its inhabitants? What was tourism offering, and what was it destroying? These questions prompted the decision to focus on Pamukkale as a case study and to examine the consequences of tourism in a small, formerly homogeneous Moslem farm community.

Background

Pamukkale is a small town (*koy*) located in a fertile valley in southwestern Turkey. The nearby bluff, almost pure white in color, is visible from far across the valley, and is sometimes described as the "cotton castle." The geological formation is unique, a karst landscape, shaped by water seeping from a fault line. As the water drains down the face of the bluff, calcium oxide deposits form ledges and impond turquoise blue pools of the thermal waters, interspersed with stalactite-like pillars. The beauty of the site together with the therapeutic quality of the warm springs attracted the Romans to Hierapolis around 190 BC. It became a Roman pilgrimage center and sacred city (or *hieron*) dedicated to Leto, the Great Mother of the Gods. The elegant Roman buildings of Hierapolis included temples, theaters, bathhouses, a gymnasium, an agora (marketplace), and a necropolis (cemetery) (Figure 12.1). The thermal waters were believed to cure many ailments including rheumatism and skin diseases (Figure 12.2).

Figure 12.1. Roman theater of Hierapolis near Pamukkale. (*Pamukkale: Hierapolis-Aphrodisias,* Akşit Kültür Turizm Sanat Ajans Ltd., 1994, p. 22)

For nearly a thousand years, Hierapolis was a much-visited holiday, health, and pilgrimage center. Consuls, kings, and philosophers attended festivals, bathed in the water, and generally enjoyed rest and relaxation (Kekeç, 1990). German archaeologists did some preliminary work beginning in 1887 but the community was little changed until after World War II. Excavations by Italian archaeologists beginning in 1957 resulted in a Turkish awareness of the city's former grandeur, and domestic tourists rediscovered the therapeutic benefits of the mineral spa. The community became a popular site for weddings and honeymoons where visitors found accommodations in small local pensions and "Turkish-style motels" (large structures with interior corridors, whose rooms face outward).

In 1980, international tourism was small scale. A Turkish-style motel had been constructed adjacent to the largest Roman bath, where tourists swam and lounged in warm water amidst the ruined columns. Foreign tourists "discovered" Turkey during the mid-1980s and inspired the construction of several Western-style hotels featuring on-site swimming pools and hydrotherapy with water piped from the springs. In recognition of the dramatic terraced landscape formed over a period of 14,000 years, UNESCO added the Roman settlement of Hierapolis to the World Heritage List in 1988. At this point, tourism began to replace the traditional economic activities, such as the cultivation of cotton, wheat, corn, and grapes.

Figure 12.2. The thermal pools near Pamukkale. (*Pamukkale: Hierapolis-Aphrodisias*, Akşit Kültür Turizm Sanat Ajans Ltd., 1994, p. 6)

Methodology

Mathieson and Wall (1982, p. 176) wisely suggested the need to focus on residents' perceptions when assessing tourism change, and the Kaya family (the name is fictitious) graciously took me into their home to share their lifestyle and, with great patience, to teach me their language. The role of participant-observer came easily, with the opportunity to document, through their eyes, their transition from farm family into hotelkeepers. With five periods of residence—1983, 1984, 1986, 1988, and 1990—the relationship with the Kayas became familial. The family included *Anne* and *Baba* (mother and father) and their nine children, seven sons and two daughters. *Anne* and *Baba* addressed me as *kiz* (daughter), and among the Kaya children, everyone was *kardesler* (siblings).

From 1983 to 1990, there was growing involvement in tourism both in the village and in the Kaya family. Day-to-day living facilitated numerous informal conversations with family members and some formal interviews, especially with Faruk Türkoglu, another hotel owner. Supplemental sources included the regional and local directors of tourism, and Hasan Zafer Dogan, director of the Aydin Turizm Isletmeciligi ve Otelcilik Yüksek Okul (a small regional tourism and hotel school in the community of Aydin).

Perceptions of the Kaya Family

By 1984, following my initial visit, the Kaya family began to convert parts of their houses into pensions, nearly doubling the number of available beds. After a veritable invasion of tourists during summer 1985, despite the well-known summer heat, the construction of modern hotels increased in their rate of growth. Many had their own swimming pools and restaurants. Shortly thereafter villagers began to open carpet shops, pubs, discotheques, and other businesses serving the tourist trade. What DeGroote (1982) termed the pioneering phase of tourism had ended.

In 1985 the Kayas took in more guests. *Anne* and *Baba* lived together with their unmarried children, while Hasan, the second son, his wife, Hanife, and their child lived in a separate house constructed within the courtyard of the parents' residence. Hanife and Hasan converted a room of their house (previously a small grocery store) to a tourist rental. Furnished with three beds, the room had a separate entrance. When needed, Hanife also placed Turkish mattresses on the floor of one room within her own house in order to accommodate more tourists, and therefore derive more income.

By 1986, the Kayas had erected signposts at the entry to the village indicating the way to the Gül Pansiyon (Gül Pension, as they now named their facility), and Hanife's house had been remodeled by converting the former family rooms into guest bedrooms, and by constructing a terrace restaurant on the roof. Because no modern bathroom existed on-site, tourists washed in a small outdoor basin and used a squat toilet at the edge of the garden. Hanife managed the small family-run operation almost single-handedly, and it provided many opportunities for personal contact between the hosts and guests.

By December 1988, to expand their family-run pension, the senior Kayas had started construction of a formal hotel that incorporated the original houses (those belonging to *Anne* and *Baba*, and to Hanife and Hasan). This step significantly altered both the character of the property and the interpersonal relations with guests. While showing me around the construction site, one of the sons pointed to a neighbor's traditional house, saying with some contempt, "Look how they live!" as if the Kaya family themselves had not lived that same way only a few years before. Because their hotel (previously a farmhouse) was located on the outskirts of the village, the enterprising Kaya family also opened a restaurant in the center of the town to take advantage of the greater concentration of tourists. By 1990, Gül Pansiyon had evolved into the Gül Motel, a modern, two-story building with 33 rooms and 80 beds (Figure 12.3). The additional buildings spanned three sides of the original courtyard, and a kiosk, which served as a small bar, and tables and chairs (restaurant) occupied the fourth side. A swimming pool replaced the area where chickens once ran and garbage had been thrown. The entry to the inner yard between Hanife's house and that of her in-laws was roofed by a second story, and the passageway was fitted with wide glass doors that separated the courtyard from the street, creating a formal reception hall. The former family house had completely disappeared, leaving the Kaya family without a home. Faruk, a local village tourism pioneer, described a similar evolution in his property: "I began by using the first floor of my house, and then the second floor of my house. I even gave up

Figure 12.3. The modern Gül Motel transformed from a homestay. (Photo by Anne Marie Van Broeck)

the rooms which belong to me; I slept in the car or anywhere outside, just using a mattress."

Before their tourism involvement, the Kaya family subsisted primarily by farming. Townspeople considered them prosperous, for they owned a car and good farm equipment. In 1990, the family still owned most of their fields, and, aided by a few seasonal farm laborers, they still grew small crops of cotton, wheat, and tomatoes. But the motel and restaurant businesses now occupied most of the men's time. The Kayas did sell one small parcel for 60 million Turkish Lira (about US$23,000) and this money, supplemented with a bank loan, financed the motel construction. They planned to repay the bank with the income from the upcoming tourist season. Clearly the family invested all of their energy and a great portion of their personal resources into tourism.

The Entrepreneurial Spirit

This entrepreneurial spirit was not new to the Kaya family. In addition to their agricultural activities, the family had ventured into other business enterprises. As noted above, the small room in which tourists were first lodged had at one time been a small grocery store run primarily by one of the Kaya daughters. In addition to farming and storekeeping, Hanife's husband, Hasan, and a cousin (the son of his maternal aunt) had also owned and operated a minibus shuttle for local residents and visitors between Denizli and the village. Although the cousin continued to run the minibus, by 1990 Hasan had dropped out to pursue his involvement in the tourist industry.

In 1990, the entire Kaya family (except for married daughters and the oldest married son) worked at the Gül Motel and the town-center restaurant. Age and gender marked the division of labor. *Baba* oversaw both businesses and functioned as "the banker," because he kept the key to the safe and controlled most of the money. Refik liked to call himself the "director" of the motel, although it was his brother's name, Omer, that appeared on the invoices. Outgoing and very sociable, Refik enjoyed spending time with tourists, which reinforced his position as the driving force in the family enterprise. Hasan was responsible for bank interactions and public relations, including the promotion of the Gül Motel among tour operators in coastal resorts. Two younger brothers were often posted near the bus stop to approach newly arrived tourists and persuade them to stay at the Kaya's motel. Most of the brothers also worked, as needed, in the restaurants.

The daughters-in-law, assisted by *Anne*, mainly took care of the laundry. At first the women did all laundry by hand but by 1990 a cleaning company collected the sheets each day. Still, every morning the women took turns at washing tablecloths and towels by hand and hanging them to dry on the roof. Occasionally, they also gave a helping hand in the kitchen of the hotel restaurant (Figure 12.4). Grandchildren helped by washing, hanging clothes to dry, sweeping the reception hall, or welcoming the guests. None of the family members received a monthly wage for their work. Whenever a person needed money, he or she simply asked for it.

In addition to the family, seven other people were employed in the motel: two female cousins and five men including a cook, a dishwasher, and waiters. For their work cleaning rooms, the two female cousins split 500,000 Turkish lira per

Figure 12.4. Woman washing utensils. (Photo by Anne Marie Van Broeck)

month (about US$192).The cook received 600,000 lira monthly (about US$230).
On occasion, a belly dancer was also contracted to perform for the tourists in
the hotel.

The Impact on Family Life

The Kaya family voluntarily entered the tourist industry for economic benefit.
As they added to the hotel, they destroyed the family home and altered their
lifestyle. Upon the completion of the new motel in Fall 1988, the Kayas essentially
lived in the hotel. During the following tourist season, the family used a room off
the reception hall to visit with relatives and personal friends, but when business
considerations led them to convert that room into a gift shop, family social intercourse was on public view in the reception hall (Figure 12.5).

In summer 1990, Hanife and her family were reduced to living in the old grocery store (one room and a small bathroom). When the hotel was fully occupied,
Anne, who normally slept in a vacant guestroom, had to go either to her sister's
home, a few blocks away, or to the home of some other relative. Male family members had fewer problems finding a place to sleep; some slept in the small room
next to the reception hall or in the hall itself. According to the Kaya sons, from
time to time one of them might not return home at night, and when that happened, he was rumored to be staying with some tourist girl.

At this point, the rhythm of domestic life was controlled by the demands of the
family's tourist businesses. Conflicting work schedules in the two restaurants,
searches for new hotel clients, and other tourism-related activities made it difficult for the family to socialize. They visited less frequently.

Figure 12.5. Reception desk and gift shop. (Photo by Anne Marie Van Broeck)

Before the boom, young people worked mainly in their parents' fields or small businesses, where parents could watch and control their children. Tourism brought new work opportunities for the younger generation, as wage earners in other pensions, or at hotels. With their income they also gained personal independence. According to Faruk,

> Before tourism, parents watched over their children and knew where they went in the evening. But now that a boy works away from home, his father or mother can no longer check on him.

"As a consequence, young people feel empowered to choose their own lifestyle and are less dependent on their families and less willing to listen to them" (Refik).

Tourism diminished family contact, weakened family control, and resulted in a loosening of familial bonds. "The Turkish family is very strong . . . perhaps the strongest." The bond among the Kaya seems enduring, possibly because they still live together and generally worked side-by-side. Traditional family structure, authority, and control prevailed because the subordinate members of the family had not achieved financial independence (Dogan, 1990). In contrast, other villagers appear to have escaped familial authority, and experienced more financial and social independence, with more opportunities to dictate their lives.

The Social Position of Women

Tourism development offered supplemental cash income to women who, prior to the tourist boom, had worked primarily in family fields or at domestic chores. Domestic activities were now extended to "visitors," who also had to be cared for. According to Faruk, Islamic doctrine typically allowed women to work only if their work environment was "safe"—that is, monitored and protected. In family-run pensions or businesses woman's behavior was still circumscribed by family and community pressures. Women's economic independence was limited because they commonly did not receive wages. If they were paid, the money might be given directly to a male relative.

With the expansion of tourism, some women began to work for a salary in the newly opened pensions, hotels, or gift shops. Ultimately, this may empower them to gain more independence. However, even though access to wage employment may influence their social position, the work itself does not necessarily emancipate them. The determining factor for female emancipation is the degree to which the income endows her with greater economic and social independence.

Women are often responsible for the tourists in the family-run pensions but, as tourism has become more institutionalized, the position of women has shifted, and the men have taken over. The Kaya family is typical in this respect. Hanife initiated the family involvement with tourism, and provided much of the impetus while it was still a family-run pension. However, when the business grew, her husband and brothers-in-law assumed the management roles. Hanife remained an important figure in the administration of the hotel only because of her leadership in establishing the business and her years of hard physical work that ensured her continued participation.

Outside cities and institutional tourism, Middle Eastern women rarely interact directly with tourists, except in family-run pensions where tourists and family members interact more casually. In communities like Pamukkale, where tourism is somewhat institutionalized, the men are the spokespeople who receive, wait on, and entertain the guests. Women rarely appear in public venues, such as restaurants or bars. Instead, women are commonly relegated to roles as maids and cooks, and almost never serve as waitresses or cashiers, or handle money. Although some expressed a desire to meet foreigners, village women are usually reserved and seldom initiate contact with outsiders. The Kaya women often sat on the rooftop terrace from where they could observe and comment on the guests below. In the center of town, women watched tourists from the balconies of their houses. Thus, without leaving the security of the home, a woman could participate vicariously in the touristic activities. The Islamic moral code reinforces the gendered division between the male public sphere and the private sphere of women. Many local men, like *Baba*, spoke only Turkish but were successful in their active search for new patrons.

The advent of European tourists to Pamukkale reinforced new roles for women, as a kind of demonstration effect of women shown on TV. Hanife observed: "Women are much freer now; you can go any place, even during the night . . . in earlier days you could only go to the neighbors, but now you can also go to the center of the village, to a shop." Moreover, local residents, especially couples, had begun to stroll in the evening along the streets, mixing with the tourists.

Despite this momentum for change, social sanctions still prohibit Kaya women from going to a discotheque, with or without their husband, or swimming in public, even in the motel pool. Refik declared that husbands feared that if their wives went to discotheques, other men might become interested in their wives. They believed that the women themselves did not want to frequent such places. Hanife publicly agreed with her husband, that "a discotheque is not a place for women," but privately she was ambivalent, and more than once expressed her desire for a visit.

Most village women seemed comfortable with the traditional Turkish values. Hanife observed, "Every woman practices proper control. Family control exists, but good, decent women practice self-control." Hanife objected to single Turkish women who engaged in love affairs or even just friendships with Turkish men. The Kaya women were ambivalent about the new freedoms and the contrasting behaviors they saw among local women.

Nevertheless, tourism had brought certain comforts to their daily lives. Before tourism, Hanife rose at sunrise to milk the cow, clean the house, or do other household chores. With tourism, she sometimes slept until 9 a.m. Another "comfort" was a big, industrial washing machine. While washing the hotel's towels and tablecloths by hand, the women often discussed with great authority the features of the various brands of washing machines in anticipation of someday buying one. By 1990, Hanife and her husband owned a car and enjoyed a few days as tourists in Bodrum, a Turkish coastal resort. The improvement in their living standards led Hanife to hope that she might stop working in the hotel. She dreamed of having a residence somewhere away from the motel.

Relationships Between Villagers and Female Tourists

Pamukkale men, whether single or married, were eager to get involved with female tourists. According to Refik, "Foreign women remain an attractive opportunity for the Turkish man. . . . Foreign women, if they are older than thirty, generally come to Turkey for a Turkish man. . . . And Turkish men like adventure; if female tourists are near, they forget everything and only think of very beautiful things." In my 6 years of observation, a behavioral shift was apparent. Turkish men became bolder and propositioned foreign women more frequently and easily than they had only a few years earlier. Refik and Faruk believed that the desire of Turkish men to socialize with foreigners might be attributed to the restrictive Islamic moral code imposed on local women. This aspect of tourism proved divisive within families and occasioned arguments between spouses "when a husband comes home very late at night, or does not come home at all."

Community Bonds

Tourism and the existence of the cash economy contributed to a loss of family and community sharing. In contrast to the former reciprocity, villagers were now selling goods and services. To make and have money were of paramount importance. Faruk claimed (and the Kayas confirmed) that there was also a decrease in village solidarity, and tourism introduced new conflicts among community members. Villagers competed to attract as many tourists as possible. Rivals gossiped about the pensions and their owners, saying such things as, "Their prices are very high." "They have tour groups everyday; it is very crowded." "There are many mosquitoes (or rats or lice or mice)." "She's a divorced woman and sleeps with all the men; I would not take my family there." Some hotel owners accused each other of "stealing" guests by intercepting them upon their arrival at the bus stop.

Hanife and Faruk complained of the noise and litter caused by tourism, which led to quarrels among neighbors. In general, those who participated in and benefited from tourism tolerated its negative effects better than those who reaped little benefit from the influx of foreigners.

> The people who live close to the pensions and hotels suffer from noise. For instance, they work very hard on their farm during the day. They want to be in bed at 9 or 10 o'clock in the evening. But nearby, people continue until 12, 1 or 2 a.m. playing music, wandering in the streets, and driving their cars past villagers' houses. The people who are not participating in the tourist industry are not happy. (Faruk)

Declining Hospitality — Rising Commercialism

Turkish people have typically been renowned as friendly hosts who can be counted on to give visitors a warm reception. However, tourism is frequently identified with more commercialism, and business interests have superseded the former personal friendly spontaneity. Turks seem to be losing traditional values of hospitality as their desire to obtain money increases. In this respect, throughout Turkey tourism appears to have greater influence among the younger generation, and Pamukkale is no exception.

> Turkish people are very hospitable towards foreigners . . . before 1986, when the people saw a tourist walking in the street, they might have given them fruit or invited them to drink tea. After they drank tea or after they treated them to food, they did not expect money, nor did they try to sell something. . . . But now, when someone invites a tourist off the street to drink tea, he might be thinking about selling something, a scarf, carpet, hand-bag, or anything else. . . . We can say that now people are less hospitable. It's the nature of human beings, as long as they can earn more money; they want more and more. But that is not our character. Money is affecting everybody, not only here, but also everywhere in the world. (Farouk)

Tourists are no longer treated as true guests. Instead, as Refik explained, a tourist is *altin yumurtali tavuk* (the "chicken" with the golden eggs). If they are warmly welcomed, it is because no one in the village likes to see empty beds. Walking in the streets has actually become annoying: shopkeepers use intrusive sales pitches and compete aggressively with each other, and a tourist can no longer stroll about without being called, or even pulled, into a shop.

Changes in Food, Clothing, and Lifestyle

Over the years, the Kaya family changed their diet. Before tourism, women cooked the meals. In 1984, Hanife began cooking for her tourist guests as well as for her family. By 1990, the women rarely cooked for the family; instead, everyone chose their food from the meals that the hotel cook prepared for the guests. The fare was also different, for now there was more meat, and *yufka*, a flat bread traditionally made on a weekly basis by the Kaya women, was rarely eaten. Some of these influences were apparent as early as 1984, when Hanife's children were eating spaghetti almost every day. At first, she explained they simply enjoyed it, but upon further questioning, she responded that since she cooked spaghetti for the tourists, she fed it to her children as well. The food service also changed. Previously, the Kayas ate together seated in a circle on the floor around the *sini*. By 1990 the men rarely joined at mealtime and those who did, sat at a table, each person with his own plate.

Clothing also became Westernized. The new styles were considered more *açik* ("open"), a deviation from the expected norm of *kapali* ("closed"). By Turkish tradition a woman wore a headscarf, and covered her shoulders; she would not wear short skirts or a bra. If they did wear Western dress, they wore pantyhose. Women were also expected to refrain from using makeup or wearing ostentatious jewelry. In general, in 1990, women still wore traditional dress for work but, on occasion, younger women wore Western-style skirts or dresses or went without headscarves. When Hanife visited relatives, she dressed up, used cosmetics, and wore golden jewelry. *Anne*, in contrast, continued to wear traditional clothes at all times.

Both Refik and Hanife judged one important lifestyle change as positive: formerly they were farmers, now they were *kültürlü*, or "having more knowledge and cultural background." For them, this distinction meant acquiring external forms or aspects of behavior, such as wearing "open" clothing and going to the center of the town.

> Life is very different now. . . . You get to know more and different people, and can more easily distinguish good from bad. Before we were a farmer's family, a village culture. Now it is a city culture. . . . Before, I was a farmer, and I had not seen any European country; now I run a hotel, I'm a businessman, . . . and I've traveled a lot in Europe. You know, the advantage tourism brought, the more you travel, the more you enlarge your culture. You possess more knowledge and culture, and you become *kültürlü*. (Refik)

Thus, tourism introduced the Pamukkale villagers to many different cultures. The profits from their businesses permitted them to travel abroad, and they considered the broadening of their cultural knowledge a positive effect of tourism.

Elders and Tourism

The senior citizens did not welcome tourism in Pamukkale lest they lose Moslem traditions and values. Older people view most of the changes with regret, yet they tolerate them and have reconciled themselves to what cannot be avoided. Grandmother *Anneanne* (who had made the *Haj* to Mecca) refused to drink anything out of the motel refrigerator because alcoholic drinks, such as beer and wine, are stored there. She also feared that eventually no one would be left to work in the cotton fields because they would all be employed in the hotels. However, the elders who had been positively involved in tourism, and realized it as good business, voiced some approval, especially because people did not have to work as hard as they had before the tourist boom.

Tourism as the Cause of Observed Changes

Tourism is an agent of sociocultural change, but probably it only strengthens the effects of other ongoing processes. To separate tourism from the other agents of change in terms of their magnitude or effectiveness is critically important but difficult to execute because of the dominance of the mass media, education, urbanization, industrialization, increased mobility, economic aid and development, visits by businessmen, or even migrants who return to the village.

The informants in Pamukkale recognized that the influences of education and television have been significant in addition to tourism, and that they intersect in mutually reinforcing ways. According to Refik, speaking to the author:

> In previous days the girls stayed home. Now they attend school. So, they have more freedom and they escape the control of the parents. And what happens with them? They come to know different people. Besides, then they see and meet also the tourists [in our village] and they see the freedom the female tourists are having. You, for instance, are a very free woman: You can do what you want, you come and go as you please, you decide when and where you go on holidays. So, when the girls [in the village] see this, they wonder why they can't do that? Your behavior leaves an impression, an im-

print. And what happens next? On television they also see different movies [with behavior different to the traditional one]. So what happens? The girls open up completely and lose their blindness. And a similar evolution is happening to the boys as well.

With sage insight, Faruk noted, "No matter what you see on television, young men cannot get a girl through the television, but when they see lots of foreign girls [face to face], there is a mutual attraction [and a possibility for a real interaction]." Thereby he illustrated the importance of tourism: the influence of the media is reified by the presence of the tourists.

Women informants judged television and education to be neutral or perhaps positive influences on people, whereas the influence of tourism is negative especially on the behavior of many women, whose behavior in going swimming in a pool is *ayip* or shameful.

Mathieson and Wall (1982) suggested that guests from similar cultural backgrounds had less impact on the host society than outsiders, but the research in Pamukkale suggests otherwise. Turkish tourists have had a great impact on their Pamukkale hosts. In certain aspects, interactions between villagers and domestic tourists seem indeed more troubling and influential than meetings with Westerners. The interactions with domestic tourists raise questions concerning the villagers' values, in contrast with their fellow nationals who share a common heritage yet who behave in Western ways and exhibit attitudes that violate traditional norms. Foreigners from outside Turkey are *expected* to have different religious and cultural beliefs and practices. Their behavior is not deviant as much as it is different. Therefore, the behavior of foreigners is more easily accepted and leaves less impact on the host community than the behavior of domestic Turkish tourists.

Conclusions

The villagers of Pamukkale initially welcomed tourism. Even in 1990, they often judged the industry positively because of the money and the material well-being that it brought, but other changes aroused ambivalent feelings. Tourism had indeed changed the village, including family lifestyle, the social position of women, community bonds, and, to some degree, traditional values and customs. However, some residents fear that increased competition will make the future less lucrative, especially for the family. There are also worries about community integrity.

Epilogue

The senior editor of this volume visited the Kaya family in November 1994. Because of a recent snowfall, tourism was minimal and my arrival was expected. The family had gathered to welcome me, and to send pictures to Anne Marie. Visiting in their reception hall, it was evident that the family had prospered. They showed off their hotel and their swimming pool. Their good car was still in use as a taxi. With great pride, the women pointed to wall photos of former guests, and especially the framed clippings from American and German newspaper articles written by former tenants who attested to the quality of their services. The message was clear: Gül Pension is famous abroad!

What had the family gained, and at what cost? Having lived and taught in the Moslem world, the reticence of the women peering from behind half-drawn shawls was not surprising. Neither were their drawn faces, and worn hands, which silently spoke of long years of hard physical labor. They smiled and sent good wishes and photos to Anne Marie, but the body language betrayed exhaustion.

The men who now spoke some English and our bilingual interpreter who was from Pamukkale openly answered the direct question: Has your family benefited from tourism? "Yes . . . we have kept our family together; that is the main thing! Other families have lost their young people, who have gone to Istanbul and Ankara for money jobs. Parents don't know where their children are, whom they marry, and even if they are all right. All our family is here; we all have money; we have our land and our business; our children and our grandchildren have a future here."

Acknowledgments—The author of this chapter would especially like to thank the Kaya family in Pamukkale and all the other informants, without whose experiences and information this research could not have been realized. The initial English draft for this chapter was revised by Patricia Rosas, to whom I owe my deepest gratitude. I also thank Robert Dover for his comments. To all those who stimulated me, believing in this work, I express my thanks.

Chapter 13

Tourism in the Fjords and Mountains: A Case Study From Western Norway

Roel Puijk

Ulvik, Norway, is a scenic and historic community to which tourists have been attracted for nearly 150 years. In retrospect, tourism has modernized the community, although modernization is not an inevitable consequence of tourism. Some segments of the community thrive while others complain that new attractions violate Norwegian traditions. As a consequence, the municipality is divided over conflicting social values. This chapter identifies the locally divisive issues and is instructive as an illustration of the role of local power and the political process.

Tourism in the 19th Century

Ulvik, Norway, is situated in the inner part of the Hardanger fjord, a 114-mile-long glacial embayment that penetrates the Norwegian coast. The scenic beauty has attracted summer tourists since the mid-19th century. The Hardanger vidda (the plateau that lies at the eastern end of the fjord) is the largest plateau in Europe and a renowned and majestic natural landscape that includes green slopes, the rough, steep mountains, high waterfalls, and blossoming fruit trees in the spring. Salmon fishing and cruises along the fjord are very popular visitor activities (Figure 13.1).

Development in the tourist sector was closely related to the expansion of communication and transportation networks. The 19th century access to Ulvik was by boat, and between 1861 and 1890, steamship, ferry, and tourist boat routes were established. The historic steamer that plyed the fjord, the *D/S Voring*, was named for the area's best known attraction, the Voring waterfall (B. Kolltveit, 1980). Prior to 1860, travelers to Ulvik could board overnight with the local priest, but that year an enterprising local blacksmith constructed a forge, then a two-story building with five rooms to accommodate overnight visitors. This establishment soon evolved into a posting inn. Enlarged to a 50-room hotel, it became one of

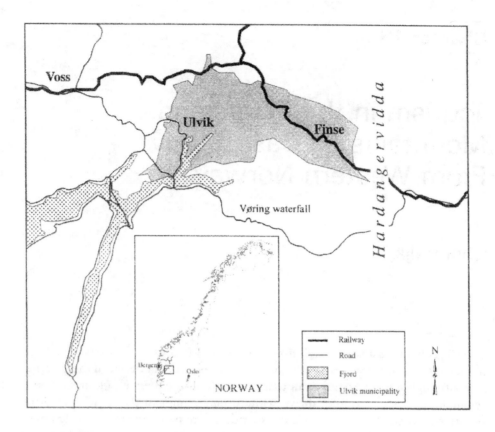

Figure 13.1. Location map of Ulvik, Norway.

Norway's original fjordhotels. Three additional hotels opened in the early 1890s. Tourists began to arrive by land with the completion of the Bergen–Oslo railway in 1909 (and the connecting Voss–Ulvik national road). Both were considered engineering marvels at their opening, and still rank among Europe's finest scenic routes.

Host and Guest Relations

Before World War I, the 1400 inhabitants of Ulvik were divided in their perception of the growing tourist industry. Some, especially farm families, felt that tourism was demoralizing. The superior attitudes and social insensitivity of affluent visitors caused a loss of self-respect that tempted Ulvik residents to sell their land and move away. From a different perspective, tourists provided jobs and income through the increased local sale of agricultural products. Residents who traditionally moved to their summer cottages higher in the hills during the tourist season were able to rent their Ulvik homes to Bergen visitors. Despite the cash incentive, employment in the tourist sector was considered inferior to independent farming. There was also a certain fear that local girls working in the tourist sector would acquire new habits in their association with wealthy guests and that they would no longer be available as spouses for the farmers.

By 1920, the permanent residents of Ulvik had grown to 1700, and that figure remained fairly stable until the 1980s when it gradually declined to 1250. By that time, many European tourists had been to Norway and, with jet air service available, were vacationing overseas. Agriculture remained the predominant occupation, and the emergent new tourist sector simply added more wage jobs and created a further expanded market for agricultural goods. Pronounced class differences between the tourists and the permanent residents can be inferred from comments relating to local attire by Bårtvedt (1984) from tourist diaries and traveling accounts in her study of a neighboring village:

> They (the locals) are not described as simple peasants. Instead there is a tendency to focus on 'Sunday' side. They are beautiful, nicely dressed and proud. The people are in harmony with the beautiful nature. (p. 51)

The use of the local folk-costume, the *bunad*, depicts a local adaptation to tourist demands (Figure 13.2).

In the Romantic turn-of-the-century period, the rural population and folk dress became prime symbols of Norway's aspiration towards independence (Norway separated from Sweden in 1905). Each region typically adopted different *bunad* for sacred occasions, such as marriages, Sunday church, and Holy Days, to signify the difference between everyday life and feast. Thus, the traditional use of *bunad*

Figure 13.2. Ulvik residents dressed in the bunad. (Photo by R. Pujik)

symbolized both Norwegianness and the local rural community. Hotel owners introduced *bunad* as the work dress. Although tourists appreciated the new custom for its authenticity and photographic style, farmers considered this use of ceremonial attire as disrespectful or even morally wrong. Local newspaper articles described the changed use of *bunad* as one of the disadvantages of tourism, editorializing that when the folk costume was used to attract tourists, it no longer functioned as a unifying symbol for the local population.

Another source of cultural disunion relates to the Norwegian landscape. The natural environment was the prime tourist attraction, and tourists employed local guides for excursions to waterfalls and glaciers. While these visitors were greatly impressed by these natural features, the local people took them for granted, illustrating two distinct perceptions of what Urry (1990) terms "gaze."

The late 19th century tourists from the relatively flat terrain of England had a distinctly Romantic perception of the Hardanger fjord landscape (K.Thomas, 1983). Many Norwegians, even from Ulvik, had never taken the trouble to visit the waterfalls (Bårtvedt, 1984). This philosophical schism reflected the business-as-usual local values and the tourists' romantic admiration for the wild Norwegian landscape and traditional way of life.

Towards a New Tourist Structure

During World War I, British visitors vanished and were replaced by other Scandinavians who were not permitted to travel to the continent. After the war the greatly reduced traffic slowly rebuilt during the crisis years when the Depression of the 1930s paradoxically made travel much cheaper. Boat connections, Bergen–Newcastle and Bergen–Rotterdam, provided the hotels with both British and Dutch guests, many of whom were repatriated Norwegians.

During World War II, most centrally located Ulvik hotels were ruined by a German bombing attack. In addition to the three hotels that remained, two new hotels opened during the 1960s and a guesthouse was added during the 1970s. Subsequently, summer tourism has remained relatively stable, weighted heavily with British tourists. Accommodations still number three to five hotels, a boarding house, a campground, and rental cottages. However, during the 1980s and 1990s, tourism sagged somewhat due to the declining value of the British pound sterling. Consequently, the ownership of the three largest hotels (Brakarnes, Strand, and Ulvik) ultimately merged, accompanied by a shift in the nationality of the guests (Table 13.1).

As British, Dutch, and American guests decreased in number, the percentages of Norwegians, Germans, and others (mainly French, Italian, and Japanese) increased. The number of Norwegian visitors, however, is questionable because statistics do not differentiate between tourists and guests visiting Ulvik to be with family, or in conjunction with second-home ownership. In the past two decades, the dominant visitor nationalities have changed, and so has the tourism structure. Prior to the 1980's arrival of circuit bus tours, many visitors stayed several days to fish, hike, and enjoy the setting. In the last decade, the summer tourist visit was frequently only overnight and often the guests merely passed through.

Table 13.1. Ulvik Hotel Guests' Nationality

	1967	1997
Norwegians	15%	44%
Other Nordic countries	1%	1%
United Kingdom	53%	12%
Netherlands	7%	1%
Germany	7%	23%
United States	16%	3%
Others	1%	25%

Source: 1967 (D. Kolltveit, 1987); 1997 (Ulvik Tourist Office).

Tourism-Related Activities

Tourism often generates considerable activity beyond hospitality, especially in heritage tourism. The Ulvik tourist office can arrange guided tours to the impressive natural phenomena—fjords, mountains, water falls—as well as flightseeing by small airplanes. Farm tourism is popular and provides some farmers with additional income. The hotels and tour operators provide cultural performances with local accordionists or a recently revived folk dance group. Nevertheless, the trend towards cultural tourism and farm tourism is relatively weak in Ulvik despite these initiatives.

The long-standing economic pattern of rural Norway, with its well-established agrarian base, is changing. International treaties such as General Agreement on Tariffs and Trades (GATT), implemented in 1967, and plans for the economic unification of Europe into the European Economic Community (EEC) create new economies. Norway is a major oil producer, and young people find lucrative jobs in this industry. These global forces trickle down, altering the prevailing Norwegian government subsidies on farm products. Nationwide, Norwegian agriculturists have complained that their standard of living and their livelihood are threatened. Some Norwegians also watch with anxiety the in-migration of Pakistani and other non-Europeans, wondering if newcomers will maintain rural architecture and lifestyle that have been the basis of the Norwegian visitor attraction.

The municipality of Ulvik, with its stable population of 1200, has to date fared rather well, thanks to a tax income from a major hydroelectric power station within its boundaries. A municipal fruit-growing industry also compensated somewhat for the deterioration of national subsidies. In an effort to forestall uncertainty about the future, several farmers developed plans for additional income. Activities vary from the redecoration of houses and the construction of summer rental cabins for Europeans who drive to Ulvik, to the presentation of handicrafts and traditions, such as weaving, rosemaling (traditional furniture decoration), beer brewing, and traditional hay harvests. Additionally, two small art galleries have been opened and added to the list of tourist sightseeing amenities.

Despite these efforts, negativism towards the tourist presence persists even though the underlying reasons have changed. Initially, social cleavages arose as a result of class distinctions between the local population who were "working" and the traveling elite—the divisiveness was linguistically and blatantly expressed in terms such as "them" (foreign elite) and "us" (free farmers). The available employment in the tourist sector was predominantly in service jobs that farm owners considered unpleasant. Many residents took great pride in their well-kept homes and fields, and resented the commercialization of their attractive landscape resources. Further, their lives were already almost fully committed to several income-producing activities such as timber production, sheep raising, government administration, teaching, carpentry, and milling, which have sustained them for generations. They have had little time or interest for the additional business of tourism because they have no real need.

Although seldom discussed openly, the distasteful sentiment among landowners for tourism in their community reflects the ethnic soul of Norwegian nationalism. Although Norwegians have occupied this isolated peninsula in northern Europe for many generations, dating long before the Vikings, the nation attained independence only in 1905. The long period of political subjugation under Sweden and Denmark imprinted Norwegians with a strong sense of nationalism. The loss of the mountain *seters* or meadowlands traditionally used as summer pasture for sheep and autumn hunting grounds provoked fear that the presence of tourists was counter to the welfare and pleasure of the local population. A horse owner made this point explicit, explaining that although he might occasionally use his horse in tourist-related activities, he never did so in the mountains because the horse (although less than the tourists and their dogs) could easily disturb the sheep that wander freely through unfenced meadows. In addition, the mountains supply Ulvik with culinary water in a quantity that roughly equates to traditional use. The town site could not support greatly increased tourist traffic, except at major expense for infrastructure. In essence, he summarized, the landowners fear that tourism would make the area less valuable for their own recreational purposes. Many, if not most, farm families own a mountain cabin as a second home, for weekend and holiday use in summer and as a winter ski lodge.

Local Tourism Initiatives

Although Ulvik shopkeepers did not share the rural sentiments of indifference to, or rejection of, tourism, neither did they benefit financially to the degree that many would have liked. Their failure to do so was in part self-inflicted, by a failure to develop local initiatives that would bring more business to their doors. Norwegian tourism is principally marketed to international visitors as summer sightseeing on circuit tours, and to domestic tourists as winter conferences (augmented with some skiing). The foreign escorted group tours generally stay in Ulvik only one night. They arrive by bus in the afternoon and depart the early the next morning for another destination. During the short time before or after dinner, passengers may walk through the village and purchase a souvenir. The two-night option features local sightseeing, including a visit to the waterfall and a boat trip on the fjord, both of which are outside the municipality. Or depending on itinerary, tourists could take the popular "Norway in a Nutshell" train tour and go into Bergen for the day, which would give them the highlight of Finse en route. Because of these time constraints, the market for alternative cultural activities has been limited. It should be said that the tourist office has not had widespread community support to publicize the concept of Ulvik as a source of day tours and local activities. If the community was unified in support of well-designed day trips, then the culture brokers (the tour operators) might well change their itineraries to take advantage of a community-specific heritage offering.

Conference participants usually have little contact with the local businesses because of their conference schedule, and the attendees dine and shop on the hotel premises. The hotels are often marginally profitable because of the short summer season, and thus have little incentive to send visitors away from their own doors. Tour operators, both outside and within Norway, usually organize the group sightseeing tours as well as the conferences. Participating tourists have little control of packaged hotel arrangements and cannot alter their itineraries. This pattern of close cooperation between large hotels and major tour operators is common throughout Norway. Local entrepreneurs are frustrated and seem virtually powerless in the ability to develop local initiatives.

Tourism at Finse

The municipality of Ulvik has two faces. Fifty-seven percent of the land area is mountainous, lying above 900 meters. Within this sector, and inaccessible to motorists at an altitude of 1200 meters, is the tiny settlement of Finse, with only 12 officially registered inhabitants. Finse originated with the construction of the Oslo–Bergen railroad around the turn of the century. Until recently, the population consisted of railroad employees who kept the tracks free of winter snow. The surrounding landscape is steep and the climate so harsh that, in 1911, Captain Robert Falcon Scott prepared for his Antarctic–South Pole expedition here. Several motion pictures with polar expedition theme have also used this site, as did part of the film *Star Wars*. Beginning in 1909, a state-owned Mountain Lodge, adjacent to the railway station, hosted both Norwegian and foreign elite visitors. In 1914, an indoor ice rink provided a venue for skating and curling during winter. The famous Norwegian figure skater, Sonja Henie, trained at the Finse rink. In summer, the ice rink is converted to tennis courts. Now advertised as a "sports hotel," implying that accommodations are somewhat rustic, the Mountain Lodge (later known as Finse 1222) is marketing itself as "The high mountain lodge on the top of Norway" and as "a rough, no-nonsense, real Norwegian hotel."

Another tourist accommodation, the Tourist Association Lodge, is the trailhead for many cross-country skiers who follow trails from one mountain lodge to the next. The clientele is predominantly students and middle-class Norwegians. The guests at the Tourist Association Lodge share a common cultural background with guests in the Hotel Finse 1222, but are often younger and less affluent. Ninety percent of the Finse tourists are Norwegians. The lodges operate with two distinct seasons: winter season is February to May, and summer season spans from July until September. The hotel is increasing its summer conference bookings, and summer occupancy rates now exceed those of winter.

Conflicts Between Finse and Ulvik

The relations between tiny Finse and the parent municipality of Ulvik are ridden with conflict. The Norwegian State Railroad (NSB) is a federal operation, and all decisions concerning it and the lodge are made at the national level. The only person committed to the local Norwegian perspective is the manager of the hotel, who incidentally played a prominent role in the development at Finse.

The conservation-minded Ulvik residents perceive Finse as a rural resource that has been used for generations as summer pastures for their animals and as hunting grounds for wild reindeer. The number of reindeer in the immediate surroundings of Finse has been reduced to avoid overgrazing, but the hunt is important. Originally it was for subsistence, but in contemporary society it is a Fall outing, a time to enjoy the autumn colors and to be freed from stress. To protect the area, the Ulkvik council is very restrictive of new tourism activities—especially bicycling along the old construction road during summer. To urban-oriented Finse, Ulvik is physically and mentally far distant. Just to accomplish one-way transportation involves both a rail and bus trip, and a minimum of 3.5 hours. This separation makes it difficult to maintain reasonable working relations with Ulvik and its travel association/tourist office.

The Finse mental map does not include the agricultural fjord municipality of Ulvik. Local residents orient themselves much more in an east–west direction following the railroad towards urban centers. In their efforts to display the heroic railroad past, people from Finse are doubly supported by those who have a personal connection to Finse through the ownership of second homes in the area, and by national-level interests in heritage protection.

Norwegians maintain their strong tradition for spending leisure time in the mountains, and some feel drawn to nature in a religious relationship. Among the rural population, strong sentiments are voiced in favor of their traditional rights and against overuse by tourism and even urban "second home" owners. The rationale is both economic and as compensation for the disadvantages of life in the rural areas. One of the fiercest defenders of the landowners' rights said: "we who live in the periphery should have some privileges; we want to keep the area to ourselves."

Conclusion

At the millennial milestone, Ulvik is still attempting to integrate several types of modern tourism with its farm community and more traditional values, all within one municipality. The 19th century tourism was positive in many respects: it established needed economic relationships between the tourists and the local population; it generated capital in the hotel sector; it augmented job opportunities especially for women; and it created an additional source of income for local farmers. However, class difference—between wealthy upper class tourists and farmers and wage laborers—in combination with language problems prevented more intimate social relations. Tourism was profitable but not comfortable.

The foreigners who now travel on group bus tours through Norway represent the most "industrialized" form of tourism. Organized by tour operators, they support the hotels and other infrastructure during the summer and, although they generate the greatest percentage of tourists and money, they have the least contact with local Norwegians. Ulvik has failed to establish the cultural/historical markers that would identify its heritage. A display of heritage in the form of folk festivals, museums, and local history can become a source of local pride and can stimulate cross-cultural communication. Guidebooks written and sold in the US, for example, simply dismiss Ulvik as a pretty little town (with nothing in particular to commend a visit).

By contrast, tiny Finse has capitalized on its location and history, and is a recognized center for hiking and for cross-country skiing (with published information about equipment rental). Their Randermuseet features exhibits of prehistoric occupancy, reindeer hunting, and railroad history. Most visitors are Norwegians from the urban centers, which, in turn, heightens interpersonal bonding. For these guests, to visit Finse is a positive example of returning to tradition and "being Norwegian." The power struggle between the two entities is nominally said to be over tradition, but it would be misleading to dichotomize the issue to modern vis-à-vis old-fashioned. All so-called traditions (such as reindeer hunting) have evolved into new forms. The defense of new quasi-traditions is part of the rural cognition. Young people who cannot find employment in stagnant villages emigrate to urban centers where their skills are marketable. Unfortunately for the people of Ulvik, their persistent failure to showcase their culture history has worked to their economic disadvantage and threatens their future in light of the political and economic reorganization of Europe.

The Ulvik example highlights the importance of time as a variable in tourism—a topic that to date has received little attention in the tourism literature. The use of time is an important mechanism in the role of the travel industry as a culture broker. Time should be considered in the host–guest relationship for getting acquainted both with the geographical space and, more importantly, with people from the host community. In Ulvik, time is so limited that it prevents organized tour participants from using most of the geographical space. Extended visits in this instance at least would strengthen the host economy and benefit the visitor with a greater enjoyment of Norwegian landscape and culture.

SECTION 4

SUSTAINABILITY

Chapter 14

Sustainability

Valene L. Smith

Inuit (we the people) are said to have migrated from Asia into Alaska several thousand years ago, as hunters and gatherers with the survival skills to support our families through the long cold winters of "dark nights." Using resources of both land and sea, the food supply was adequate for our small and widely dispersed families. We believed that all animals had spirits, and whenever a sea mammal was taken, the hunter's wife always poured fresh water from a special small basin into its mouth. She thanked the animal for giving its life that Inuit might live, and thus returned its spirit to the sea. Many such customs ensured our survival, and we respect our traditional knowledge.

If the food quest failed, everyone knew some person had broken a behavioral taboo with respect to the animal(s). The wisdom of an angakok (shaman) might be needed to determine the cause and try to restore environmental harmony. Our oral history is filled with stories of starvation because men and women, and evil spirits did not respect our land.

When the early nineteenth century European explorers first saw us, they were impressed by the skills and customs that enabled us to live for generations in this difficult and fragile land. Our warm fur clothing, our boats made of seal and walrus hide, our tools made of bone and stone prompted some to say "Eskimo use everything but the squeal." We loved our homeland but also knew its limitations, for wood was precious and came to us only as drift wood or by trade (or war) with the Indians who lived in the forest to the south of us. The annual salmon run was the single season that could briefly support the important summer rendezvous—vital both as a source of trade goods to augment local food and fur, and as a time to be with our extended families and friends upon we must depend for help in times of need. The much-loved winter visits and feasts were possible only when stored food resources were abundant.

For a century, we, the Qikqiktarukmiut of Kotzebue Sound have attended American schools and universities including Chukchi College, a branch of the University of Alaska-Fairbanks that now has classrooms in Kotzebue. Some of us are now physicians, lawyers, legislators, teachers, pilots, entrepreneurs and tour guides but we still cherish our heritage. Many of us still hunt and fish part-

*time, on vacations and weekends but life in a modern small town (including
the Arctic) depends heavily on wages (or welfare). The 1971 Alaska Land Claims
Settlement Act was awarded to sustain Inuit heritage and our land-based
economy. That stewardship is an on-going challenge.*

Sustainable Tourism

Sustainable tourism is a cultural construct, or a set of ideas, inspired by the
concept of environmental or "green" tourism from books such as *Nature Tourism*
(Whelan, 1991) and *Ecotourism: The Potentials and Pitfalls* (Boo, 1990). Sustainable tourism has multiple goals, namely to create and maintain successful industries including tourism, and to conserve appropriate levels of the natural and cultural environment, with due regard for time and place. D. Pearce (1988) states so
simply, sustainability is "making things last," whether it is an economy, an ecostystem,
or a culture.

A second concept, *sustainable tourism development*, has been coined to ensure that environmental conservation accompanies tourism growth or change. This
multidimensional issue is difficult to define because sustainable and development
are not necessarily compatible concepts. Murphy (1998) draws a working definition from Tourism Canada (1990) that envisions sustainable tourism development
as "leading to the management of all resources in such a way that we can fulfill
economic, social, and aesthetic needs while maintaining cultural integrity, essential ecological processes, biological diversity, and life support systems" (p. 179).
The editors support this broad-based definition as a usable platform for research
and as a test for planning, particularly because it details further avenues of investigation. As Murphy notes, this concept provides for seven dimensions of multidi-
mensionality and interdisciplinary concerns:

- need for resource management,
- economic opportunities to benefit the community,
- fulfills social obligations,
- addresses aesthetic appeal,
- sets ecological parameters,
- maintains biological diversity, and
- reaffirms the industry role of tourism.

Concepts of land use and heritage change as a consequence of history and technology, and these dynamics must also be factored in the process of planning and
implementation.

The Historical Roots of Sustainability

The study of sustainable tourism has historic origins that are important to an
understanding of the "big picture" of tourism and the individual ethnographies of
destinations. The roots of sustainability date to 19th century Romanticism, particularly in the United States after the Westward movement reached the Pacific
Ocean. The 1864 book, *Man and Nature or Physical Geography as Modified by
Human Nature*, by George Perkins Marsh was widely read and so influential

throughout the English-speaking world that it is now considered the foundation for the conservation movement. Marsh's scholarly concerns gained support in the aesthetic writings of American authors Thoreau and Emerson, who viewed nature in terms of its perfection, and saw its ruin at the hands of man. These powerful literary arguments supported conservation and tourism, as did the paintings of Yellowstone by Thomas Moran (Figure 14.1), which became instrumental in the Congressional decision to create the world's first national park.

Hall (1998) observes, "tourism was the driving force behind the creation of the first national parks and conservation reserves . . . tourism gave value to lands that were otherwise useless in terms of other forms of economic exploitation" (p. 17). This concept of worthless waste lands with little value other than for tourism holds equally true today for many of the physical sites now named to the United Nations World Heritage List, including Grand Canyon in the US, the desert Tassili n'Ajjer of Algeria, and Ireland's Giant Causeway.

The contemporary interest in conservation stems from a heightened awareness of our finite global resources and their human abuse. A popular 1962 book by Rachel Carson, *Silent Spring*, criticized the environmental hazards of toxic agricultural chemicals, and was widely read by two generations of Americans. The 1972 United Nations Conference on the Human Environment held in Stockholm drew attention to the problems of underdevelopment in areas of Asia, Africa, and Latin America. The urban air pollution and degraded forests and fisheries of the LDCs were directly identified as important causal factors to environmental deterioration at the global level.

Figure 14.1. 1872 Painting of Yellowstone by Thomas Moran.

This "Stockholm conference" established an imperative for action to reduce degradation, and mandated global monitoring of climate, transboundary air pollution, and toxic chemicals. However, subsequent reports were dismal, and indicated further environmental decline in the LDCs. As Nazim and Polunin (1993) observe with reference to their poverty cycle,

> no amount of environmental logic or reasoning can prevent a poor and needy man from cutting a tree for fuel, or cultivating unsuitable slopes for food to succour his otherwise starving family. Everyday necessity forces him to exploit whatever is near at hand, no matter how short-lived and precarious the basis may be. (p. 5)

Europeans began to observe that the Black Forest of Germany was dying from air pollution and fish were disappearing from a polluted Mediterranean Sea. Africans in Sierra Leone saw Saharan sands blowing into the Sahel, and Ghanaians pulled empty nets from depleted fishing grounds. The media reported global warming and the discovery of an "ozone hole" over Antarctica. These issues became a cause for action.

Task Forces and Guidelines

The United Nation created the first global task force in 1983, to deal with sustainability, known now as The World Commission on Environment and Development (WCED), headed by Norwegian Gro Harlem Brundtland. Their guidelines for future development prescribed further growth without sacrificing environmental resources. Their report, *Our Common Future* (WCED, 1987, p. 43), commonly known as the Brundtland Report, introduced the term, sustainability, and five applicable principles:

1. the need for holistic planning and strategy making;
2. the importance of preserving essential ecological processes;
3. the need to protect both human heritage and biodiversity;
4. to develop in such a way that productivity can be sustained over the long term for future generations; and
5. achieving a better balance of fairness and opportunity between nations.

The Bruntland Report was widely discussed and stimulated great interest in the Rio Earth Summit (The 1992 UN Conference on Environment and Development or UNCED), attended by 10,000 delegates representing 178 governments, 1400 nongovernmental organizations (NGOs), 50,000 spectators, and 9000 journalists. The extensive media coverage popularized global awareness of environment and conservation. Thus, after some 30 years of jet travel and mass tourism, the 1990s created a quest for tourism that is less consumptive of global resources. Tourism should seek to: (1) protect the physical environment and biodiversity to ensure human survival; (2) maintain cultural heritage and ethnic diversity in support of multiculturalism in a plural society; and (3) sustain the continued prosperity of the world's largest industry on which many national and local economies now depend. This section, with five case studies, addresses varied aspects of this psychological rush to "save the earth" to which tourism, through its culture brokers, has responded at several levels, including privatization, industry self-monitoring, and ecotourism.

The Challenge of Sustainability

To introduce sustainable tourism development into contemporary tourism is difficult because of the widespread ignorance about the realities of tourism. As Butler (1992) observed, "few people, even decision makers, are aware of its true magnitude, economic and social linkages, and political significance" (p. 33). The Rio Earth Summit identified Travel and Tourism as one of the key economic sectors that could make a positive contribution to achieving sustainable development (World Travel and Tourism Council [WTTC], 1999) and spurred a number of important initiatives.

Local Agenda 21 (LA21): Agenda for the 21st Century

At the succeeding (1992) Earth Summit, the 179 participating governments endorsed Local Agenda 21 (LA21) as a "cross national agreement working towards 'sustainable development' " (Jackson & Morpeth, 1999). LA21 is the first document of its kind to achieve total international consensus, especially since "it challenges action on the part of *local* authorities to adopt ways to involve their communities in defining their own sustainable futures." This theoretical landmark is notable because it clearly shows the philosophical shift from 1960s tourism development in which governments had been principally concerned with tourism *growth*. Using an administrative style now referred to as "top down" management, governments provided funds, donated land, and gave tax incentives to entities that would provide infrastructure, thereby creating markets and attracting guests. LA21 suggests that "we will only achieve sustainable development through planned, democratic, cooperative means including community involvement in decisions about the environment and development" (Jackson & Morpeth, 1999, p. 3). Thus, Agenda 21 introduces privatization at the government level as a new basis for managerial decisions, influenced by local input or a "bottom up" administrative approach. The tourism development strategy should protect local culture, respect local traditions and promote local ownership and management of programs and projects, so as to foster community stewardship of the natural resource base. Agenda 21 also recommends use of Environmental Impact Assessment (EIA) as a strategic tool for tourism planning (see Trousdale, Chapter 19).

Attendees at the April 1999 meeting of the UN Committee on Sustainable Development further defined LA21, assigning to the travel industry the task of educating travelers about sustainable tourism practices. In-flight "edutainment" such as videos could inform travelers and reinforce the need to respect the rights of indigenous peoples (United Nations Committee on Sustainable Development [UNCSD], 1999). This concept was tested more than a decade ago by a small Germany company (Institute fur Film und Bild), on outbound *charter* flights. To Kenya, the topic was sex tourism and prostitution. En route to Sri Lanka the themes were respect for Hindu temples and to discourage giving money to children who "begged" at popular tourist stops. The film documented that some youngsters successfully obtained more money in 1 day than their employed parents earned in a month.

The children's "wealth" negated school attendance and undermined family values; the families were not destitute, as the children's behavior implied. The film shown en route to Yucatan highlighted the archaeological significance of the Mayan ruins and the need to protect them, not collect "pieces of them." The 20-minute films were relatively well received by vacationers on the charter flights but not equally successful on scheduled services with a mixed (often business) audience. This idea remains valid, however.

Case studies in this volume illustrate the complexities involved with definitions of terms and reveal the problems encountered when trying to implement the "bottom up" policies of sustainability. Most travelers are pleasure seekers, not environmental reformers, and often pay little attention to local issues. Thus, the jurisdiction of government agencies so apparent in the management of Australia's Barrier Reef (see Parker, Chapter 18) does not concern the catamaran swimmers. Many day-trippers on catamarans are first-time snorkelers, not trained divers. Lacking expertise, they stand on coral to rest or adjust a mask, with little real concern, let alone an understanding of their damage to the reef. Zimmermann's case study (Chapter 25) highlights the historical cleavages of age-old but not forgotten wars, whose specter now compromises efforts to achieve transboundary tourism in Europe (or elsewhere, as in Kashmir and Israel-Palestine).

Other Industry Initiatives

The Local Agenda 21 proposal did not initially name tourism, but the travel industry quickly recognized the implied role. In 1990, as Agenda 21 was being discussed, the Chief Executive Officers (CEOs) from 90 leading worldwide travel suppliers (carriers, hotels, tour operators, car rentals, etc.) created the World Travel and Tourism Council (WTTC) to advance the quality of travel and to represent the industry in public policy forums. In 1996 WTTC allied with WTO to form the Earth Council (EC) that represents, respectively, private enterprise, government, and civil society. A summary of their sustainable development program is posted on the Earth Council Web site (www.ecouncil.ac.cr/rio/focus/summary/business.htm). By intent, EC is concerned with issues that "threaten to bring about economic and ecological catastrophe, and presents a strategy for transition to more sustained development practices" (WTTC, 1996). The adopted theme, "Think global, act local," urges local priorities such as creation of local tourist boards to actively involve all stakeholders, and to especially cooperate with grassroots organizations.

> Protecting the environment is both a moral obligation and a business imperative for the Travel and Tourism industry. As the world's leading industry, it can effectively reach millions of customers with a coherent, compelling environmental message. And industry can and must persuade their members to adopt ecologically sound business practices. (Strong, 1993, p. 8).

In March 2000 at the International Tourism Berlin (ITB is the largest travel exhibit gathering in the world) a number of tour operators from different parts of the world launched the Tour Operators Initiative. Developed by Tour Operators with the support of UNEP, UNESCO, and WTO, all of whom are members of the Initiative, this is an industry commitment that sustainable tourism shall form the core of their business activity, and that they will *work together* [their emphasis] through common activities to promote and disseminate methods and practices compatible with sustainable development. The Web site lists participating members and the initiative goals: http://www.toinitiative.org/home/html.

Tourism Training

WTTC (1999) "forecasts that travel and tourism will generate some 100 million new jobs world-wide over the next 12 years. The challenge will be to ensure that a well-trained workforce can meet ever-increasing visitor expectations in a globally competitive environment." Towards this goal, WTTC maintains study links with programs offered by George Washington University in Washington, DC, on a business school network, with particular interest on distance learning. WTTC has established a Human Resource Center with Capilano College in Vancouver, BC, and has a strategic alliance with "Reach and Teach" in South Africa to supply tourism education packages. WTTC is also in partnership with www.ttjobs.com as an Internet-based recruitment center to highlight the number and array of job opportunities. Their goal is to expand educational bridges between government and industry.

Green Globe and ECoNETT

WTTC launched Green Globe, an Agenda 21-based industry improvement program, in 1994. Green Globe provides a certification process, and presents annual awards to participating companies. Their Debt for Nature provides funds for improvement projects and has, to date, purchased for conservation millions of acres of land in the Amazon Basin, provided money to stabilize the travertine pools at Pamukkale (see Chapter 12), and also funded conservation efforts for the threatened Rwandan mountain gorilla. In 5 years of activity, Green Globe (1999) had set primary global environmental standards and had enlisted 500 members in 100 countries. WTTC also created "ECoNETT," a Web site that contains advice on good practices and is considered a focal point for environmental education.

Many travelers, especially ecotourists, want to know if their travel suppliers are practicing so-called "green tourism," to protect the environment. A number of leading hotel chains visibly promote ecological policies, in part because conservation is also good economy. Eco-labeling includes signs posted in guest bathrooms that suggest it may not be necessary to wash every towel every day: "put only the towels you want replaced into the tub (or basket)." Hotels point to alarming statistics associated with the daily waste of water and accumulated detergent.

The US National Park Service created a Sustainable Information Directory available at http://www.nps.sustain/. This site solicits information from government agencies, universities, nongovernmental organizations, and commercial entities, and is updated annually. Their philosophical goal is "bottom up"—with input from the consumer to assist making appropriate choices.

Ecotourism: Benefits and Costs

By our definition, *ecotourism* is nature-based tourism that reputedly supports environmental conservation, social responsibility with respect for indigenous cul-

Table 14.1. Hypothetical Costs and Benefits of Ecotourism

Environmental Impacts
Direct benefits
- Provides incentive to protect environment, both formally (protected areas) and informally
- Provides incentive for restoration and conversion of modified habitats
- Ecotourists actively assisting in habitat enhancement (donations, policing, maintenance, etc.)

Direct costs
Danger that environmental carrying capacities will be unintentionally exceeded, due to:
- rapid growth rates
- difficulties in identifying, measuring, and monitoring impacts over a long period
- idea that all tourism induces stress

Indirect benefits
- Exposure to ecotourism fosters broader commitment to environmental well-being
- Spaces protected because of ecotourism provide various environmental benefits

Indirect costs
- Fragile areas may be exposed to less benign forms of tourism (pioneer function)
- May foster tendencies to put financial value on nature, depending upon attractiveness

Economic Impacts
Direct benefits
- Revenues obtained directly from ecotourists
- Creation of direct employment opportunities
- Strong potential for linkages with other sectors of the local economy
- Stimulation of peripheral rural economies

Direct costs
- Start-up expenses (acquisition of land, establishment of protected areas, superstructure, infrastructure)
- Ongoing expenses (maintenance of infrastructure, promotion, wages)

Indirect benefits
- Indirect revenues from ecotourists (high multiplier effect)
- Proclivity of ecotourists to patronize cultural and heritage attractions as "add-ons"
- Economic benefits from sustainable use of protected areas (pharmaceuticals, research) and inherent existence (e.g., flood control)

Indirect costs
- Revenue uncertainties due to in situ nature of consumption
- Revenue leakages due to imports, expatriate or nonlocal participation, etc.
- Opportunity costs
- Damage to crops by wildlife

Table 14.1 continued.

Sociocultural Impacts

Direct benefits
- Ecotourism accessible to a broad spectrum of the population
- Aesthetic/spiritual element of experiences
- Fosters environmental awareness among ecotourists and local population

Direct costs
- Intrusions upon local and possibly isolated cultures
- Imposition of elite alien value system
- Displacement of local cultures by parks
- Erosion of local control (foreign experts, in-migration of job seekers)

Indirect benefits
- Option and existence benefits

Indirect costs
- Potential resentment and antagonism of locals
- Tourist opposition to aspects of local culture (e.g., hunting, slash-burn agriculture)

Source: Reprinted, with permission from CAB International, from David Weaver, *Ecotourism in the Less Developed World*, 1998, p. 21.

ture, sensitivity to the economic balance sheet. It derives its popularity from a natural science term—ecology—that confers *psychological righteousness* upon travelers who elect this as a vacation style. Some vacationers preferentially select vacation destinations such as Costa Rica or Belize because they are advertised as ecotourism centers and said to be environmentally sensitive.

> Ecotourism draws much of its potential from a dichotomy of riches: the industrialized world is rich in cash, but the tropical world has the lion's share of the planet's animal and plant species. Ecotourism is a plausible way to apply some of the financial wealth of the developed world toward protecting the biological wealth of the developing world. (Jones, 1993, p. 54)

Unfortunately, most holidaymakers do not read the scholarly literature, such as *The Other Side of Paradise* (Stonich, 2000) or "How sustainable is ecotourism in Costa Rica?" (Place, 1998). The land developers and their salesmen responsible for subdividing coastal marshlands in Belize for sale as time-shares and condos see only the income from more tourism and not "best practices." Research has generated an impressive list of hypothetical costs and benefits of ecotourism (Table 14.1).

Unfortunately, well-intentioned travelers and even some officials advise indigenous villagers or remote rural residents, "you ought to develop ecotourism—it will create jobs and cash income." Such statements are often irresponsible and a disservice to residents because these well-intentioned advisors fail to fully comprehend sustainability and its complexities, particularly in marginal environments.

In isolated Arctic villages, for example, proposed ecotourism projects must consider the expensive transportation-induced costs to import food and construction materials by air freight, to build lodges, and to develop a water system and sewage

and garbage disposal. Tourist facilities customarily have a minimal 2–3-month seasonal use. To repay the large capital outlay necessitates high per diem charges
plus the expensive air flights or charter service. The demand side for this type of
wilderness tourism is narrowly defined. Inuit across Arctic North America share
the problems of the Pamukkale villagers: they want to keep their families at home
but they need income to satisfy the aspirational wants of snowmobiles, computers and Internet access, and vacations in the "South," as the Finns do (Chapter 6).
To counter massive underemployment and consequent alcoholism and suicide
among youths, tourism seems full of promise. Ecotourism is not a widespread panacea nor is it necessarily sustainable in the Arctic.

The several excellent books on ecotourism (Cater & Lowman, 1994; Hall & Lew,
1998; D. Weaver, 1998a) are replete with case studies that are both positive and
negative. The recurring danger in ecotourism is the matter of size—a small but
very successful initial project often expands for additional income and soon becomes what many critics term "eco-nomic" tourism, not ecotourism. Boracay in
the 1970s would have been an ecotourist resort had the term then been known.
Elsewhere, a small attractive jungle lodge originally started and operated by a US
Peace Corps worker or by an anthropologist who longs to remain "near his/her
people" may be environmentally friendly and a rare opportunity for the tourist to
"get close to the people" (see Borman, 1999). However, when the benign adminis-
trator departs, new management is often not equally committed or conscientious.
Ecotourism often grows into mass ecotourism, as is now true in numerous African
safari locations where the former dirt game trails are now paved roads and 200-
room resort hotels have replaced tented camps. In Kenya, each park lion is said to
generate in its lifetime ecotourist revenues in the amount of US$515,000 (Aveling
& Wilson, 1992), and a herd of elephants is worth US$615,000 income per year for
the country. Sadly, a "protected" animal in a game park has more "rights" than the
Masai cattle on which this indigenous tribe depends for livelihood, and the tribe
is marginalized as their lands are confiscated for bean and hop cultivation (Fratkin
& Wu, 1997). This East African dilemma highlights the merits of the CAMPFIRE
program in Zimbabwe (see Heath, Chapter 11).

Observing a single lion resting on a knoll, surrounded by 27 safari vehicles each
with four to six passengers shrieking above the click of their cameras, "Look at the
lion," prompted the Amboseli National Wildlife Park Superintendent to shake his
head and mutter, "even the lion has no privacy." With more than a little editorial
cynicism, the path to sustainable ecotourism is strewn with rocks labeled greed,
profit, and "bigger is better" left by avaricious individuals and governments whose
sole interest has been the tourist receipts, labeled economic development, and
not the sustainability of the planet.

Heritage Tourism

Interest in cultural heritage emerged as a tourist attraction during the 1990s,
and was embraced as an important economic asset and a mechanism to preserve
ethnicity. History and its tangible markers in the form of buildings, cemeteries,
folk music, and literature have quietly survived for centuries. All too often they
were denigrated as "old-fashioned" or outmoded as towns and people strove to-

wards modernity. Europe has a long tradition of historical remembrance, as do some parts of Asia, but the recent shift toward heritage has been particularly striking in the US. This nation is a vast landscape whose Northwest was explored by Lewis and Clark only 200 years ago, and is peopled by immigrants from many lands all of whom originally sought to "be American." The plural society and multiculturalism are essentially new concepts. Previously, to talk of a former heritage was neither fashionable nor popular. However, when museums and tour operators discovered that attractively packaged commoditized ethnicity had commercial tourist value and would "sell," public and private funds initiated the upgrading of museums and historic sites.

Heritage is not history. History records facts (sometimes also pseudo or assumed facts) but heritage augments this information, and provides what Kirschenblatt-Gimblett (1998) terms the "value added" interpretations that create virtuality and "hereness." Heritage makes history come alive, as is well demonstrated in the "living museums" of Scandinavia's *skansen*, and in the US at the reconstructed reality of Plymouth Plantation and Williamsburg. A day spent at one of these historical sites is an educational experience for the tourist and a source of community revenue. The goal of modern museums is to judiciously design their exhibits (the supply side of tourism) to generate demand. Increasingly, statistics indicate their success. In a 1996 study undertaken on behalf of the 94 museums in the State (and islands) of Hawaii, the visitor count was 20.1 million persons, of which the out-of-state visitors accounted for 58% of the paid attendance. Overall, the museums generated US$154 million in operating revenues, and supported 3302 jobs. Liu (1999) summarized the study, noting that museums and cultural attractions are a valuable and cost-effective community resource that create income and jobs and enjoy "tremendous popularity with visitors in providing a highly satisfying experience at bargain prices" (p. 13).

Heritage and Authenticity

Hawaii's Polynesian Cultural Center (PCC), which opened in 1963, was the first model culture, built as a reconstruction of aboriginal lifestyles (Stanton, 1989). The original complex consisted of seven reconstructed "villages," each with one or two "thatched" huts built in the architectural style of the culture it represented, as Tahitian, Fijian, Samoan, Maori, Hawaiian, and Tongan. The PCC goals were three-fold: (1) to preserve the cultures of each individual island; (2) to provide employment for students from those islands who attending Brigham Young University, adjacent to the site; and (3) to provide direct financial aid to BYU-Hawaii for its scholarship program for island enrollees. Although stringent efforts were made to create "authentic" villages, the administration freely acknowledged that the individual villages did not represent a specific date but, rather, a time frame. The public accepted the virtuality of the complex, and for more than two decades the PCC received upwards of 1 million visitors a year and ranked second (after the *USS Arizona* Memorial) among Hawaiian attractions in total attendance.

Initially the visitors were primarily "mainland" Americans vacationing in Hawaii, and many repeated their PCC visit whenever they came to the islands. Although the individual students who staffed the respective villages changed from year to year, the activities in general did not. Guests walked from one "village" to the next (perhaps half a city block), saw a demonstration typical of each culture and had time to informally visit with the native hosts.

Revisiting these "hosts and guests" in the late 1990s, the visitors now are increasingly Asian, as Hawaii is a favored honeymoon locale for Japanese, some of whom do not speak fluent English. The *allocentric* Americans who had "been there, done that" had moved on to newer island attractions. The PCC found it economically expedient to redesign their format to service this new clientele, and constructed an outdoor amphitheater at each village, seating 200–300 guests. Visitors are now given a printed time schedule from which they can make selections, as "shows" are staged at 1.5-hour intervals (and most guests do not have time to visit them all in a single day visit). At each village the Master-of-Ceremonies uses a microphone to welcome the assembled crowd in English and Japanese (and possibly also in Korean and/or Taiwanese). A scripted performance invariably involves guests who "volunteer" from the audience (and are presented with small token gifts). The narration includes many jokes (in Japanese and English) in each half-hour "show," to keep the audience laughing, but the content has very little relation to the native culture on display.

The original small gift shop that had stocked quality handicraft items of original workmanship has been expanded into a square block of "villages," selling trinkets of dominantly Asian manufacture that somewhat resemble real wares: cellophane grass skirts, plastic leis, plastic shell jewelry, and T-shirts. Dinner has been modified into a 1000-person "luau" with modern entertainers. At an average cost of US$40 for the day plus transportation and meals, attendance has dropped below the magical "million."

The PCC changed their format, substituting lesser levels of authenticity in response to the perceived educational and interest level of the predominant audience. The original one-on-one interaction between a South Pacific native host and an American "guest" is now the outdoor equivalent of a television production and *mass heritage tourism*.

The PCC example illustrates the contemporary role of heritage as a management tool, to secure income and meet operational costs for the model culture or museum (Hall & McArthur, 1996). Heritage, as "value-added" history, can be manipulated by culture brokers and displayed at varying levels of sophistication from an exhibit of original documents to a fanciful Nottingham statue of Robin Hood (Shackley, Chapter 24).

Heritage Tourism and Indigenous Peoples

An important but seldom recognized correlation links three essentially wilderness habitats as the only geographic regions still occupied, at least in part, by indigenous people. In these three geographical areas—the arctic, the dry deserts, and the rainy tropics—sustainable environment issues coalesce with the sustainability of traditional tribal inheritance or heritage culture. The arctic Inuit, the desert dwellers (including, among others, the Indians of the American southwest, the Abo's of Australia, the San of Africa's Kalahari desert, and the Bedouins, Rifs, and Taureg of the Saharan areas), together with the tropical tribes living in

New Guinea, in sub-Saharan Africa, and in equatorial South America are all "endangered cultures" that have been marginalized by Westernization ("*Cultural Survival Quarterly*," 1999). Many of these tribes are now refugees displaced from homelands that have been targeted for hydroelectric dams, open pit mines, and oil exploration. "Once self-reliant populations have been transformed into small-scale and powerless actors in the global economy. . . . ecotourism has the best chance of being a boon to indigenous peoples where they have control over their lands, and tourist developments are in accord with their own visions of their future" (I. McIntosh, 1999, p. 3). In disagreement with this idealism, it is true that although often exploited in the name of tourism, their collective voice is slowly gaining volume, demanding to be heard. Their commoditized culture has economic value, as does their heritage in the form of traditional knowledge. However, provision for compensation is haphazard at best and nonexistent at worst. Some individuals earn small sums by performing in tourist troupes at hotels or nightclubs, by selling cheap handicrafts (in such sites as the San Blas Islands, when the cruise ships arrive), and by soliciting money for photographs, as do the Masai. It is demeaning to many. Some individuals escape by becoming "marginal men" (see Chapter 21) as tour intermediaries or guides; others may eventually drift off to a city for a poorly paid service job where at least they no longer feel "on display."

The creation of indigenous states such as Nunavut in Canada (April 1, 1999) is one potential solution. It is a daring economic experiment that is being closely watched by many indigenous groups (V. Smith, 1996c). One factor seems certain: tourist demand for new destinations, especially for adventure tourism, will bring tourist traffic into these remaining remote areas. Visitor numbers to Antarctica, for example, nearly doubled from 6585 in 1992–1993 to over 12,000 in 2000–2001, including 800 passengers aboard a single vessel. This latter is no longer adventure cruising but a luxury cruise with casino and floor shows; to put 800 people ashore by zodiac to visit a penguin rookery defies the imagination. A tourist-free wilderness safari in Africa is also almost impossible as tourism doubled from 13.8 million in 1989 to 27.2 million in 1999.

Conclusion

The decade of the 1990s was marked by two major thrusts. First was the ongoing participation of international agencies in issues pertaining to environmental concern. Increasingly their awareness of the indisputable economic importance of tourism has focused discussion on sustainability. Conferences produced paper guidelines but so far there are very little concrete data to demonstrate results. It appears that the real stakeholders in tourism—the hosts, the guests, and the tourism facilitators (the industry)—are the prime movers in effecting innovation and change. Hosts, especially indigenous groups, have begun to speak out, to provide "local input" about self-determination. Some guests are responding to suggestions of environmental and social conscience, if nothing more than using a towel a second day. Industry takes greater pride in the promotion and certification of sound ecological practices, admittedly because in many instances they are also cost-effective. When governmental discourse catches up with the grassroots action, and develops and implements policies that can be monitored, all who deal with tourism will benefit.

The second strength to emerge from this decade of change has been the role of World Tourism Organization. WTO has demonstrated sound leadership in a broad range of topics, including education, crime and terrorism, regional sector analysis, and age and gender issues.

Environmental safeguards are easier to implement—oil spills, polluted rivers, forest fires—for they are television visible and they adversely affect tourism. Therefore, government and industry both take prompt action. Sustaining culture, especially indigenous culture, has far less priority; the population base is small, often somewhat remote, and it may serve the tourist industry to perpetuate the "Noble Savage" image. Waitt (1999) writes about the Australian Tourist Commission, "adventure, escape and ecotourism are signified by the Anglo-Australian constructions of Aboriginality defined upon antiquity. Aboriginals are, therefore, stereotyped as stone-age peoples, clad in loin cloths, decorated with body paints, bearing spears and boomerangs, and located in arid environments of the outback or mythical frontier" (p. 157). This illustrates the imposition of Eurocentric cultural forms, meanings, and values.

An important consideration in the structure of this volume was the effort to counteract those Eurocentric views in relation to Inuit, by recounting aspects of their lives. The further challenge in sustainable tourism lies ahead, well stated by McLaren (1999):

> The Globalization of tourism threatens indigenous knowledge and intellectual property rights, their cosmovision, technologies, religions, sacred sites, social structures and relationships, wildlife, ecosystems and basic rights to informed understanding—reducing indigenous peoples to simply another consumer product that is quickly becoming exhaustible. (p. 3)

Chapter 15

Tourism as a Protective Barrier for Old Order Amish and Mennonite Communities

Michael Fagence

As tourists wish to extend the range of their experiences, intrusiveness by visitors into the everyday life of cultural groups has increased. This intrusion has two origins: first, the visitation to countryside areas adjacent to metropolitan areas, especially at weekends; second, an outcome of the growth of special interest tourism. The visits that target the Anabaptist communities of Amish in the US and Mennonites in Canada include both of these origins and introduce an opportunity to indulge in shopping expeditions. After a brief discussion of these special communities and the likely focus of tourist interest, this chapter concentrates on a revisit to the concept of protective boundaries (Buck, 1978). It also examines the proposition that tourism activity may provide a protective barrier by focusing the attention of visitors on superficial trappings and by deflecting tourist disruption away from the core of these communities.

The Anabaptist Communities

It is first necessary to describe briefly who and what these communities are. The diffuse groups that are referred to generically as Anabaptist comprise the Amish, the Mennonites, the Hutterites, and a few other subgroups identifiable by their particular social and religious codes and behavior (see, e.g., Hostetler, 1968; Kraybill, 1989). These groups evolved in the period of social and religious chaos in the 17th century in Europe. They developed unique ideas about the church, the state, the family, and the person. This development contributed to the creation of a particular code of behavior regarding dress, conduct, and association with people outside of their community and the maintenance of a peculiar language. Besides producing these characteristics, it led the groups to high levels of skill and self-sufficiency in rural crafts. It also contributed to a fortress mentality of separation from mainstream society. The various groups of Anabaptist migrated across Europe in the 17th and 18th centuries seeking a safe haven for their practices, and some eventually traveled to North America with several arrival points on the east coast of the US and Canada. Since the early arrivals in the 18th century and later arrivals from Russia in the 19th century, the Anabaptists have spread out across the continent, with distinct concentrations in, for example, Pennsylvania and Ohio in the northeastern US, and Ontario and Manitoba in Canada.

The tendency for these groups to concentrate in rural areas that lie within a few hours' drive of major urban centers has contributed to their emergence as a legitimate target for visitor interest. In addition to the reputations for quality of agricultural produce, of domestic crafts including furniture, and of integrity, the special character of the people themselves seems to act as a magnet for the inquisitive tourist.

Tourism Interest in the Anabaptists

One of the first points to be made is that the Anabaptist groups are not homogeneous in lifestyle or commitment to underlying religious beliefs. One of many complicating issues in unraveling the impact of visitor interest in the Anabaptist communities is the existence of many different orders (congregations). The Anabaptist communities are not uniform in their modus operandi. In the case of the Canadian Mennonites, for example, there are possibly as many as 14 identifiably different groups (Redekop, 1988). However, the highest level of tourist interests focused on the conspicuously different Old Order Anabaptist people, who have maintained a rigorous lifestyle base upon their religious code. There is anecdotal evidence of disappointment by some visitors when they realize that not all members of the Anabaptist groups maintain the same dress or exclusivity as the Old Order congregations. To the mass tourist, the subtleties of difference are of little consequence.

A second point to be made is that the independence, self-sufficiency, and particularly the commitment to strongly held beliefs of the Old Order groups causes them to eschew the use of technology (such as electricity) that modern society considers indispensable. This tends to increase the admiration of the tourists for the quality of the craft production of the Anabaptist communities, and leads to heightened degrees of inquisitiveness. One response to this has been that some congregations of less strict orders of these communities have adopted an interactive practice of sharing their quality crafts, goods, and services with the general community. The resultant cottage industries have been described as the potential Trojan horse for Amish society (Olshan, 1994). The manifestations of this relaxation include the farmer's markets (especially food products and crafts), the roadside stalls of Amish quilts, maple syrup, the living museums of Amish farms, and the visitor centers, which purport to exhibit authentic evidence of Amish and Mennonite history and lifestyles. These are some of the trappings to which the recreational tourist is attracted.

The special features of touristic interest include, for example:

- the somber dress code of plain colors, free of decoration and embellishment, with a style that is reminiscent of the puritanical forms of the 17th century;

- the horse and buggy transport;
- the focus on agrarian and agrarian-related skills;
- the pursuit of simple agricultural practices (such as the use of horse-drawn farm machinery and the avoidance of chemical fertilizers);
- the simple architectural forms for farm buildings (sometimes described as the Dutch barn) and houses, with the readily identifiable additions to farmhouse structures to accommodate an increase in family members and especially the grandparents;
- the communal telephone boxes, the lack of electrical power cables, and sometimes ingenious substitute engineering devices to generate power and distribute water;
- the range of quilts, wood and other craft items;
- the peculiar language.

With this potential scope of touristic interest it is hardly surprising that "it is safe to say that any sizeable Amish settlement within several hours driving time of large cities is being affected by tourism" (Luthy, 1994, p. 129).

Intrusion, Invasion, Exploitation

It is the relative ease of access to these communities from major urban centers that contributes to the potential intrusion by tourism. The evidence is especially conspicuous in two particular major concentrations of tourists in Anabaptist communities in Lancaster County (Pennsylvania, US) and Waterloo County (Ontario, Canada). These two examples will provide a basis for the discussion of intrusion, the outcomes of that intrusion, and the responses of the local Amish and Mennonite communities to that intrusion. This discussion leads to interpretation of the following proposition: high levels of tourist interest in the activities of the Anabaptist communities is bounded by a protective cordon, behind which the conservative Old Order Anabaptist communities shelter and sustain their lifestyle.

Intrusion (invasion) takes many forms. For example, the mere fact of "gazing" at people is an intrusion upon their "personal space"; in some societies, that mere fact could lead to acts of belligerence. The penetrating gazing by tourists at people for their differences in dress or mode of transport is tantamount to disrespect for their privacy; this act of gazing sometimes extends to the physical invasion of the privacy of Anabaptist homes, businesses, farms and churches. The Amish hold a religious belief that they should not be photographed. Yet there are many occasions when tourists disregard this belief. For example, in the case of some Canadian Mennonite churches, the tourists wait in readiness for the Mennonites to leave their service and then line up to photograph the worshippers in the church or as they ride homewards in horse and buggy transport. Other examples of invasion include photographing Amish workers plowing the fields or using the communal phone boxes and local retail stores.

These actions of intrusion are generally concentrated into nodes of activity. The touristic interest in the Old Order Mennonites in Waterloo County, a 1-hour drive west of metropolitan Toronto in Ontario, lies in staged authenticity in the village of St. Jacobs. Here there is a representation of Old Order Mennonite communities in an easily accessible form with farmer's markets, craft stores, produce stores, interpretation centers, and a number of retail outlets that purport to have at least some Mennonite associations. The Mercedes Corporation manages the enterprise in St. Jacobs. This agency has adopted a self-generated charter to safeguard the integrity of the Waterloo Mennonites while providing a quasi-authentic experience for visitors. It commits only the less strict "orders" to contact with visitors. The outcome has been a tourist shopping village that contributes a recreational resource for metropolitan Toronto and provincial Kitchener–Waterloo, attracting in excess of 1 million visitors annually. Added to the expected Mennonite-related craft and food stores have been art galleries, antique shops, restaurants, lodging houses, and precincts of "designer label" outlet stores.

One of the principal fears of St. Jacobs is that development may escalate to the levels manifest in Lancaster County, Pennsylvania. The Amish attractions in this county are located about 2 hours' drive from metropolitan Philadelphia, Baltimore, and Washington, DC. Various state and regional tourist agencies have claimed visitor levels of about 4 million per annum to Lancaster County, with an exceptional concentration during the summer months and at the long weekend holiday periods. The dilemma for the "Amish experience" in Lancaster County is the extremism of the commercialism. In order to cater for and maintain the interest levels of the visiting hordes, the general community has become committed to commercial exploitation of the Amish theme. These developments include allegedly authentic Amish farm visits, horse-and-buggy rides, Imax presentation, tours of the district with stopping points at Amish businesses, "villages" of Amish businesses, and static displays in one-room schools. The exploitation of the Amish theme uses the conventional symbolism of the horse and buggy or the distinctive dress code to advertise some of the major hotel chains (such as Best Western and Holiday Inn), major shopping malls, entertainment venues, restaurants, and road houses. Local intelligence suggests that one almost invariable clue to authenticity is that if the enterprise uses an Amish symbol in its advertising then it is not authentic "Old Order" Amish. However, some of the less strict orders are entitled to use the logos of the Amish because, in fact, the entrepreneur is a committed Amish-man or Mennonite. Because of the religious underpinnings of the Anabaptist beliefs, there is a general acceptance that the businesses of these groups operate at high levels of integrity.

Outcomes of Invasion, Intrusion, Exploitation

In his assessments of the impact of outsider interest in the Old Order Amish communities, Buck (1978) referred to the action of retiring behind a "boundary" that afforded some protection from the tourist invasion. This invasion is a product of both intrusion and exploitation, and it is manifest in several ways, including, for example:

- pressure on the rural landscapes and rural land use, with the progressive expansion outwards of the urban centers on to land farmed by the Anabaptists, creating a reducing pool of land available to those groups to maintain their traditional rural lifestyle;
- accompanying that pressure, land values experience a general creep upwards so that, first, the Anabaptists may be unable to avoid selling off the

family farm and utilizing the financial return to purchase less expensive land elsewhere, and second, the Anabaptists are being squeezed for farmland that can be passed to later generations of family members as viable farm lots;

- the creation of opportunities for alternative Anabaptist employment in the service and craft industries to meet the insatiable demand from "outsiders," thereby creating a potential rift in the family structure where the occupational opportunities for all family members had been previously prescribed by convention and tradition;
- the competition for road space between the increasing number of tourist vehicles and the horse-and-buggy transport;
- the persistence of the "goldfish bowl" syndrome (tourist gaze) into the personal space of the Anabaptists;
- the "demonstration effect" on the young members of Anabaptist groups of the material culture of the visitors.

The tourists have an expectation that a drive into Amish or Mennonite territory will be rewarded with evidence of the special activities, dress, crafts, behavior, and produce usually associated with those communities. To meet this expectation, there are breaches of authenticity and manifestations of staged authenticity that seem, at least prima facie, to satisfy the tourists. This point is addressed later.

The responses of the Amish and Mennonite are dependent upon the level of the order. The Old Orders try desperately to maintain their lifestyle, their particular language/dialect, their patterns of activity, their ownership of farmlands, and their reluctance to participate in the government and commercial activities of the "English." As far as tourism is concerned, the Old Orders try to retain a detachment, while recognizing that their actions are being scrutinized by an inquisitive public. The less strict orders have become drawn into the commercialism of tourism with the development of souvenir and retail outlets, information and interpretation centers, tour and transport services, entertainment venues, multimedia staged events, commercial lodgings, restaurants, and especially the outlet stores for the famed quilts and furnishings and woodwork. Individual scruples shape the level and nature of involvement of the less strict orders, and it may be the actions of this group that provide the barrier that safeguards the integrity of the Old Order communities.

The Focal Concentrations of Tourist Activity

Some sources have suggested that the tourist intrusion on the Amish and Mennonite community "space" has contributed to a deterioration of the quality of the special cultures. The following discussion challenges that assumption, advocating that the presence of the tourism phenomenon may be beneficial as a protector rather than a destroyer of the culture, and formulates a research hypothesis that would be capable of examination. This is a restatement of the conjecture posed by Buck (1978).

In the absence of published records of visitor systematic interviews, it is not unreasonable to assume that the principal motivation for the visits is recreation rather than a wish to learn about the meaning of the Anabaptist culture. Most evidence points to the satisfaction of these touristic needs within one long day visit, or a one-night stopover. It is largely the recreational shopping and the general ambience of the Amish and Mennonite communities that are the principal attractions.

St. Jacobs

The motivation for the visits is clear in the case of St. Jacobs in Waterloo County (Ontario), where the evidence lies in the food and produce farmer's markets. Attendance at the Mennonite information center (The Meeting House) has been recorded at less than 2% of the estimated 1 million visitors each year. The same low level of crowd interest is evident at the open craft workshops and the Maple Syrup Museum. Shopping and recreation as the major tourist motivations are supported by concentrations of visitor activity at the refurbished St. Jacobs Country Mill and its former storage building, the Riverworks Retail Center. These and various craft and art shops front the main shopping street (King Street). The spatial pattern of visitor activity has two nodal concentrations. One straddles the main village street to a depth of one block and the second, outside the village, contains the principal farmer's markets. It should be noted that these markets act as one of the principal produce outlets to meet the demand for vegetables, fruit, dairy, and meat for the Kitchener–Waterloo urban center. Therefore, many visitors to the markets are local residents engaging in normal provisioning and food shopping. A successful proposal to link the downtown area of the nearby urban center of Kitchener–Waterloo with St. Jacobs by a refurbished steam locomotive is indicative of new attempts to market the village as a visitor destination for retailing and entertainment. Recent research has highlighted the principal focus of St. Jacobs as a "tourist shopping village" servicing the Toronto metropolitan area (Getz, 1993; Mitchell, 1993).

Lancaster County

A second, demonstrably more commercialized example is Lancaster County in Pennsylvania. The reputation of the county as an Amish "exhibit" is based upon the pervasiveness of the symbols of the Amish lifestyle. The Lancaster example is less concentrated geographically and extends astride two major highways (US Route 30 and State Route 340). In this example, the scale of the Amish connection is large, with commercial shopping malls, many motels, restaurants, entertainment centers, static exhibits, and a general ambience replete with horse-and-buggy transport, the severe dress styles, and the Dutch-barn architectural styles. In addition to the strip developments along the highways, there are small concentrations at villages with beguiling names such as Bird-in-Hand and Intercourse, where precinct developments (such as Kitchen Kettle on Route 340, the Old Philadelphia Turnpike) include shops and restaurants focusing on Amish and Mennonite themes. It is the level of commercialism evident at Lancaster County that is of concern to Waterloo County, where efforts are being made to temper the attractiveness of the Mennonite theme while capitalizing upon it as a regional tourism destination. In the case of Lancaster County, the strategic planning agency has revised the Amish theme to focus on heritage as an attraction of the county (Hovinen, 1995).

Tourism Planning to Provide Protection

Anabaptists and some tourism and government agencies are concerned that visitors experience a tourism product whose level of authenticity is relaxed. Because visitors are unlikely to achieve a deep experience of genuine Anabaptism and because tourism is a leisure-bound activity, a reasonable degree of pseudo-realism is acceptable to most visitors. The crass and trash will not be acceptable. In order to sustain the reasonable expectations of visitors, the "zones" of tourism attraction concentrate among nodal village centers or extend along arterial routes. These concentrations differentiate the tourism activity zones from the areas that require protection for the Old Order lifestyles.

Deliberate tourism development strategies can facilitate both concentration and protection. Buck (1978) has referred to "boundary maintenance" by which the Old Orders protect themselves from the tourist gaze. Testa (1992) has described a *cordon sanitaire* of tourist attractions that could protect the Amish from the invasion by the millions of annual visitors. This cultural commoditization has spatially segregated the staged authenticity of tourist attractions from the rural, authentic Old Order lifestyle zones. This has achieved some reduction in the intrusiveness by tourists into the Old Order territory.

Formal tourism planning strategies could achieve the same end in a statutory form. Clare Gunn (1994) has proposed a most sympathetic approach for sustaining a fragile environment or a sensitive cultural group. In this strategy, the spatial organization of tourism attractions and services is distributed into four zones. The first zone accommodates the retailing, entertainment, and services; the second is the isolated tourism attraction, such as a theme park or a major static exhibition; the third is the route system that links the various other spatial components together; and the fourth is the nonattraction hinterland, or tourism "no-go" area, which provides a geographical context in which the other three units are set. It is this fourth unit that could be the protected area of Old Order farms and communities and could be accompanied by sets of ordinances that would preclude forms of development that would be intrusive and incompatible with the Old Order landscape. Derived strategic planning forms could provide spatial guidelines for separating sensitive natural environments and cultural groups. For example, national parks employ environmentally protective strategies that could be adapted to the Anabaptist communities. Defined route systems could link isolated attractions and prevent serious digression into rural by-ways of Anabaptist communities. Additionally, trail systems could be constructed to meander through interesting landscapes in such a way that the travel is serviced at nodal points that do not impinge on sensitive natural environments or communities. Encompassing all of these various spatial strategies is the creation of visitor routes and patterns that are concentrated at nodal points (such as villages, or clusters of attractions) or are dispersed along defined routes.

In both of the cases reviewed briefly in this chapter there is a high potential for "fitting" one or more of the available spatial forms to tourist areas so that tourism "no-go" areas can be delimited. To some degree, the planning agencies in both locations are attempting to do that. In the case of St. Jacobs, the strategy has been to define the limits of the shopping village and to accommodate visitor services within a defined envelope. There is an outlier of attraction, including the farmer's markets and outlet mall, but this is defined as a distinct nodal point. In addition to the linkage of these components by conventional road systems, a tourist train route complements the linkage. Accompanying this nodal and linear strategy is a consideration to importing from an adjacent county the special land use ordinances that are designed to facilitate Old Order Mennonite farming styles and to prevent other forms of development in the nominated districts. These formal strategies should provide at least a basis for protecting Old Order rural landscapes. The strategies adopted in Lancaster County are different. Because tourism-related attractions have already penetrated Old Order Amish farmlands, the planning commission supports an attention-deflecting strategy. This strategy would embrace the attention on the Amish landscape and lifestyle in a broadly based heritage strategy that adds the Amish component to interest in natural environments, other cultural environments, and modern tourism attractions facilitated by a series of travel routes complete with interpretation. These routes encourage tourist penetration to non-Amish attractions through rural by-ways to village centers, to historic buildings, and to craft centers.

The tourism planning strategies in both of these examples afford some protection for the Old Order areas from intrusive penetration by hordes of visitors. This is accomplished partly by focusing attention on sites and settings, facilities and amenities, and attractions that are Anabaptist related but that do not require face-to-face contact with genuine members of the Old Orders. There is no recorded research that suggests tourists to St. Jacobs and Lancaster County are dissatisfied. Whether by design or by unfolding circumstances, these various strategies achieve three objectives: first, they provide a "tangible" zone in which the Old Order lifestyle can be pursued with continuity; second, they create a means of protection of the Old Order activities from the trespass of unsympathetic and disruptive forms of development; and third, they provide a development zone in which tourism and tourism-related activities can be pursued without the concern that the integrity of the Old Order activities will be jeopardized.

Conclusion

The general case for the impact of tourism on special cultural groups often bears a negative outcome (Boissevain, 1996). The case being made here is that Anabaptist communities have managed to adapt to the demands and expectations of tourism in at least two ways. Some have deliberately sought to distance themselves from the materialism of tourism while maintaining their lifestyle behind a protective barrier of tourism development. Others have, with equal deliberation, engaged the tourism industry as another facet of economic and social life that needs to be serviced. One outcome of this differentiated response is that participants supply a protective barrier to those who elect not to do so. This differentiated approach may contribute to the sustainability of the traditional and Old Order Amish and Mennonite lifestyle behind a protective boundary established by members of those same groups that share some of the same fundamental beliefs. This circumstance is reinforced by the tendency for commercial tourism activity to be nucleated at particular locations or along traffic highways, thereby contributing to "fortuitous and unanticipated boundary maintenance" (Buck & Alleman, 1979, p. 19).

Tourism development may not be as disastrous as is sometimes surmised. This is particularly likely if tourism industry strategies correspond to the wishes and lifestyles of the special groups they promote. In addition, careful tourism planning can achieve appropriate levels of tourist–Old Order interaction. There is an axiom in tourism planning that is appropriate to the circumstances discussed in this chapter: "in tourist regions only certain areas are absolutely necessary for tourist development." The corollary of this is that "certain areas" could be delimited, thus affording protection from visitor intrusion. In the case of the areas of tourism interest in Old Order Amish and Mennonite communities, there are opportunities to protect the integrity of these communities by defining tourist zones and cultural "no-go" zones. In both of the cases considered here, there is evidence of industry self-regulation and of deliberate tourism planning to provide protection.

Chapter 16

Tourism to the Anne Frank House

Rudi Hartmann

The Anne Frank House in Amsterdam holds a unique place among the numerous memorials and museums honoring the victims of Nazi Germany in Europe. It focuses on the life of one individual, Anne Frank, her writings and ideals, her immediate family and the group in hiding, as well as the helpers at the house *263 Prinsengracht* in Amsterdam. In a wider sense, it exemplifies and highlights the human spirit trying to overcome adversity and hostility. Although the omnipresent political situation of then Nazi-occupied Holland and the fate of Jews living in the underground is at the core of the visitor experience at the Amsterdam historic site, it largely leaves out the "topography of terror" so evident and stirring at the former concentration camps.

Despite this and other basic differences here, many parallels can be drawn between the historic site of the Anne Frank House in Amsterdam and the concentration camp memorials of, for instance, Dachau or Auschwitz. Getting these infamous locales established as historic sites in postwar Europe was difficult and usually accompanied by local or national controversies (Marcuse, 1990, 1999). By the 1970s and 1980s these and many other Holocaust memorials and museums appeared on most tourist maps; many of them have become major historic attractions and tourist destinations (Hartmann, 1992, 1998). Millions of people from Europe and overseas have visited the grounds of the former Nazi concentration camps as a first-hand opportunity to learn of the historical events at the museums and facilities established there. The initiatives of the many active groups and individuals to give the public access to the former places of terror and tragedy and to provide educational programs have been marked—with few exceptions—by success. At times, the magnitude of visitor volume was overwhelming, the challenge of education staggering, and the lack of official support appalling (Distel, 1993; Marcuse, 1999; J. Young, 1993).

New Challenges in the 1990s

Now, at the millennium, many of the memorials—among them the Anne Frank House in Amsterdam, also Dachau and Auschwitz—are confronted with considerable if not massive changes in site management. What reasons caused the officials to reconstruct the historic sites, to reorganize and rearrange the educational environment and, thus, to redefine the visitor experience in a profound way? Three main considerations support the ongoing changes:

1. The intention to create—at last—a more authentic environment at the memorial sites, many of which were changed in the years immediately after the war and continue to show those physical alterations and modifications.
2. Efforts to update the outmoded educational facilities and to fundamentally upgrade the museum technology for the 21st century and when World War II Holocaust survivors are no longer present.
3. The need to integrate volumes of new research data and add important thematic aspects to the long-neglected exhibits, which were created before the changed political and social reality in central and eastern Europe in the 1990s, or showed distorted versions of the fate of the gypsies, homosexuals, or other oppressed minority groups.

This chapter principally focuses on the continued responsibilities and changing situation at the Anne Frank House. First, the process that led to the establishment of the historic site and museum is examined; second, the growth and change in visitors are analyzed; and third, the plans for completely restructuring the site and the adjoining buildings are discussed.

The Anne Frank House: From a "Secret Annex" to a Showcase Historic Site

The house at *263 Prinsengracht*, with its gray three-story front, hardly stands out along a canal in the mixed-use Westermarkt neighborhood of Amsterdam (Figure 16.1). In 1940 and the few years after, it served as the production site of spices for a small business venture (Opekta) owned by Otto Frank, originally from Frankfurt. Like many other German Jews he, his family, and business associates had left to seek refuge in neighboring European countries after 1933. Amsterdam had a large colony of immigrants living in or near the Jewish quarter of the city. As the persecution of Jews started to expand to Nazi-occupied territories during the war years, many went into hiding. It is estimated that in the Netherlands alone some 16,000 Jews went "underground" in the early 1940s when restrictions for Jews mounted and the threat of being deported, first to an outlying transit camp (Westerbork) and eventually back to Germany or farther east, became more and more a reality. The annex of the three-story house provided a hiding place for eight individuals, including the Frank and VanPels families, over a 2-year period (1942–1944) before they were betrayed and deported.

The events that occurred at *263 Prinsengracht* reflected in many ways the social, political, and economic life in Nazi-occupied Amsterdam. Little would have been known, however, without the diary of the younger daughter, Anne Frank, who died in the Bergen-Belsen concentration camp in March 1945. Secretary and helper Miep Gies saved her diary pages after the raid. In 1947, Otto Frank, the only survivor of the group, published the diary in book form: *Het Achterhuis (The Secret Annex)*. Subsequently, the book has been translated into more than 50 lan-

Figure 16.1. The Anne Frank House in 1940 (left) and 1998 (right). (The 1940 photo courtesy of the Anne Frank Museum; the 1998 photo by Rudi Hartmann)

guages, has been adapted as a theater play and musical, and has served as theme for numerous exhibits shown worldwide.

By the mid-1950s the unassuming house on the canal was known to Amsterdam citizens, literature experts, and a growing circle of fans of the deceased young writer. A new literary landscape had taken shape, and the newly recognized meaning of the locale saved the old house from demolition. When a clothing factory sought the entire block for construction of a new plant, the Anne Frank House Foundation was formed. With support from the City of Amsterdam, the landmark house and an adjoining building were saved. In 1958, plans for the partial restoration of the building and the establishment of a small museum materialized. The museum entrance was at the front of the building (former spice production site), which led the way through the revolving door to the now famous annex. The Anne Frank House officially opened on May 3, 1960.

Visitors to the Anne Frank House in Amsterdam 1960–1998

Visitation figures in the first half of the 1960s increased from 9000 to 70,000. As the numbers continued to rise rapidly through the 1960s, to about 180,000 visitors in 1970, capacity problems became evident (Figure 16.2).

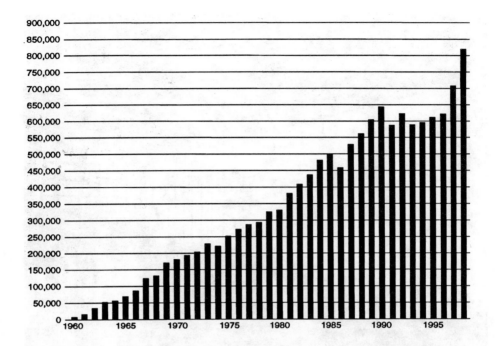

Figure 16.2. Visitation to the Anne Frank House 1950–1998.

The beams and walls of the heavily used building had to be repaired, and a one-way route was established by using the attic at the front of the building. In the early 1980s the number of visitors surpassed 400,000, and first plans for a completely rearranged museum route and historic site surfaced. By the 1980s the Anne Frank House was widely perceived as an important Amsterdam cultural institution and a leading tourist attraction. Eventually, it became clear that the private Anne Frank House Foundation (which operated the museum) needed public support to realize its far-reaching goals. In 1993 the Amsterdam City Council approved the "Maintenance and Future of the Anne Frank House" project, which would provide for redesign of the house *263 Prinsengracht* and the structural inclusion of the neighboring buildings for an expanding museum concept. The plan restored the front building to its authentic war time condition, as former production site of Opekta, thus giving the visitor a more complete experience and a better understanding of the living space in hiding. The adjoining structures (in totally rebuilt form) serve as additional museum space for new exhibits and facilities (with the most modern museum technology including interactive media), administrative offices, and additional meeting rooms, as well as a student housing area. The completed project (late 1999) is a truly reconstructed historic site embedded in a showcase museum and educational center (Figure 16.3). The 1998 statistics of 822,000 visitors showed an increase of some 15% over 1997 and supported the new magnitude and intended scale of service. Amsterdam's growing tourism industry and the Anne Frank house as one of the city's landmark attractions form a symbiotic relationship for the decade(s) ahead.

Figurer 16.3. The Anne Frank Museum 1999. (Photo by Rudi Hartmann)

Holocaust Memorials: Individual Experiences or Group Fates?

Literary landscapes like Anne Frank's "Secret Annex" in Amsterdam or Krakow's Jewish Ghetto and Auschwitz that are more recently associated with the book and movie *Schindler's List* have changed the visitor dynamics to memorial sites honoring the millions of victims of Nazi Germany. Although *Schindler's List* has promoted a greater interest in the sites and events, a new "Schindler tourism" has led to greater commercialization (and thus, profanity) in places with sad and painful memories for many. Visitors to present-day Oswiecem in southern Poland, and the nearby sites of the former Nazi death camp, find themselves in the midst of a new tourist environment nicknamed "Auschwitzland."

Another debate in the management of Holocaust memorials surrounds the question of whether selected individual fates should be given a more prominent role in the representation of the historical facts, and if so, how. Traditionally, museums and memorials at the former concentration camps used to practice exclusively a "group approach." Affiliations with political parties, social, racial, and ethnic groups were at the center of explanations of the historical events. These affiliations dominated the display of statements and statistics underneath oversized black-and-white photographs of people. Victims were largely portrayed as representatives of the major groups oppressed and persecuted in the years 1933–1945. On the other end of the educational spectrum, the exhibits at the Anne Frank House tend to emphasize the individuality of the young author. Her life story and tragic fate are explained, and her legacy, in form of the writings and humanistic ideals, is presented to the audience, whereas a more general analysis of the historical developments seems to cut short—perhaps because of the lack of space.

The 1998 publication of *Anne Frank: The Biography* (Mueller, 1998) sheds light on both dimensions: the personal development of young Anne Frank (including the time before and after the hiding period) and the specific sociocultural context and general political developments that would shape some of her life experiences—in Frankfurt, Aachen, Amsterdam, Westerbork, Auschwitz, and Bergen-Belsen. It is not pure coincidence that all the marked stations along her life path (with the exception of Auschwitz) are within a relatively short distance in central Europe (Figure 16.4).

Hundreds of Anne's peers, young German-born Jews who were raised in a secular, middle or upper-class environment, were eventually forcibly moved with their parents to refuges in Europe and all ended up in Bergen-Belsen. Many of the 10,000 concentration camp prisoners who succumbed to the hostile and merciless envi-

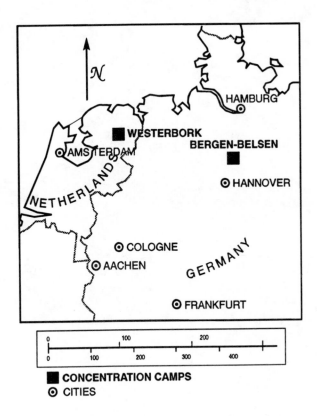

Figure 16.4. Map of selected Holocaust sites.

ronment at the Bergen-Belsen concentration camp of March 1945 came from Holland and most—like Anne Frank—died young. Memorial sites like the ones in Westerbork and Bergen-Belsen and the Jewish community museums in Frankfurt and Amsterdam may stress more effectively the group fate. The powerful story told by Anne Frank shows the historical events from a different perspective and puts a human face on the tragic outcome. To place her compelling message within the confines of a very complex historical context is the ultimate challenge in the future management of the Anne Frank historic site in Amsterdam.

Chapter 17

Ethnic Doll Ethics: Doing Tourism Research in Southwest China

Margaret Byrne Swain

Tourism researchers working in developing economies often have the opportunity to do some applied anthropology, to intervene in the situation in which they are engaged. Many have not, but some of us, including myself, have approached a project with possible interventions in mind. This chapter explores the rationales, perceived issues, and outcome of a research decision made during 1993 fieldwork with Sani women producers of tourist arts in Yunnan, China. I chose to introduce a new idea—making dolls—into the repertoire of Sani women's tourism goods, and now weigh the ethics of my action.

At the time, I rationalized my decision with both altruistic and pragmatic motives. One rationale was a desire to "give something back," in the form of an idea that might sell, to the people from whom I extracted so much time and information. Showing them how to make a different product—cloth dolls—using their strong repertoire of needlework skills and aesthetics could introduce a profitable new commodity. Another rationale was to conduct a research experiment. This action might also create a new category of goods to trace dissemination, production, and marketing in the Sani ethnic minority and Han Chinese community of tourism artisans and peddlers. Ethnic and gender relations involved in Sani doll commoditization could illuminate these relationships in a larger social context of tourism development.

A discussion of theoretical and ethical issues encountered in the project form the core of this chapter, proceeded by a brief description of the research site's background and the actual implementation of doll making. Some of these issues arose at the time of research, while others became apparent in reflection. They fall into three linked categories. First, issues are addressed surrounding the idea itself, a doll, as a gendered ethnic icon, cultural artifact, and souvenir commodity. Second, issues are raised about indigenous tourist arts as a strategic response to global exchange, representations of authenticity, and innovations affected by animateurs and intellectual property rights. Third, ethical issues in the relationship between researcher and her research community in this project are examined. In conclusion, the outcome of this research decision affects its unique context and also encompasses broader issues in tourism social science.

Tourism and the Sani Yi in Yunnan, China

Yunnan Province, situated in the southwest corner of China, is a major asset in China's tourism industry due to its geographic and unique cultural diversity (Swain, 1990). While the majority of Yunnan's people are ethnically Han Chinese, approximately one third of its population of 38 million people belong to 25 minority nationality groups, mainly indigenous peoples living in mountainous regions. In all there are 55 state-recognized minority nationalities in China compromising 8% of the national population. Historically, some of China's ethnic minorities migrated into or were formed in Han-dominated regions, such as some (but not all) Islamic peoples. Other ethnic minorities are indigenous peoples, groups that were settled in an area before Han Chinese expansion incorporated their homeland into the nation-state. Chinese tourist literature for domestic and international markets emphasizes this diversity and promotes images of idyllic experiences in places where scenic variation is enhanced by the presence of local non-Han living quaint premodern lifestyles.

In Yunnan, these factors can also be interpreted as remote regions and impoverished indigenous communities, thus marking Yunnan in the early 1990s as home to some of the most economically underdeveloped people in contemporary China (YINGOS, 1993). Efforts to address one of Yunnan's greatest problems, rural poverty, with one of its potentially greatest economic resources, tourism, is a government development strategy. Foreign exchange income generated in Yunnan by tourism rose to US$16.43 million in 1990. These figures leaped to US$63.79 million in 1991, a 388% gain, and stabilized at US$67.51 million in 1992 (Yunnan Sheng Luyouju, 1993, p. 53). Certainly the province's cultural attractions were an important reason for this growth (Swain, 1995). Whether benefits of this income actually reach Yunnan's poor is an open question.

The selling of Yunnan indigenous peoples' culture can be seen as a "commoditization of ethnicity" (Swain, 1990). Rather than the marketing of cultural things per se, there is an added politicized dimension of "otherness" marking ethnic goods, lifeways, and performance as products traded across economic and ethnic boundaries. As in many other parts of the world, ethnic tourism in Yunnan is built on an us–them dynamic, in this case contrasting the majority Han Chinese society with the exotic (but now modernizing) minorities for both domestic and international tourist consumption (Swain, 1995; van den Berghe, 1995).

In Yunnan, the Minzucun or Nationalities Village constructed on the outskirts of the provincial capital of Kunming is a popular new tourist attraction. Representations of the architecture and folklife of many distinct peoples are marketed here with ethnic souvenirs for sale. A little further from the capital in Lunan County is a primary site of intense in situ tourism development. It is an easy day trip from Kunming to see the Shilin (Stone Forest) karst formations and the Sani minority group living there (Swain, 1995).

Lunan Yi Nationality Autonomous County (Lunan Yizu Zizhixian) is building a complex web of tourism facilities, transportation, and attractions with provincial support, centered around the Shilin national park. Clearly, significant increases in tourism were expected for the 1990s. In 1992, there were 1.48 million visitors to Lunan scenic districts, including 104,800 international tourists (Wang, 1993). Local tourism employment in administration, service, and infrastructure is growing rapidly, but was not quantified in provincial reports for 1992–1993.

Shilin used to be Sani ancestral lands belonging to this Tibeto-Burman group that settled in the region more than 500 years ago. The Sani are one of 28 designated subbranches of the state constructed "Yi" nationality (minzu). The Yi nationality is a macro-linguistic group of over 5 million people. Sani language, social system, and material culture are distinct from other Yi groups, and are very different from Han Chinese. Lunan County population in the late 20th century was about 31% Sani (60,000 people) and 67% Han Chinese. It is ironic, from an outsider's point of view, that one of the primary images used to promote the region by the government draws the Sani folktale heroine "Ashima," a maiden who was turned into stone while resisting a rapacious interloper (Swain, 1993).

"Welcome to Ashima's Hometown" proclaim signs in English and Chinese along the new superhighway from Kunming to Lunan County. For several generations, a few Sani youth have worked as state-trained "traditional" entertainers and official "Ashima" guides to lead tourists through the park's labyrinths. Following national economic reforms and the opening of Shilin to international tourism in 1980, Lunan County residents have become more involved in tourism by providing services and souvenirs. They manufacture and sell distinct types of handiwork: marketing simple bags to domestic tourists and more intricate expensive "ethnic" work based on Sani material culture to international tourists.

While only a few of the local population work directly in tourism, county-wide employment is stimulated by the tourist trade. Furthermore, examples of economic gain from tourism fuel the strategies of individuals at household and village levels of organization. An ethnic group dichotomy of Sani versus Han is generally true in the county, but local Sani government officials carry out the Han-run state project, and local Han also produce Sani/Ashima/Lunan images for tourism as guides, authors of poetry, prose, and guidebooks in the popular press, manufacturers of pseudoethnic goods, and marketers of their own and genuine Sani goods.

Among the Sani, the gender division of labor in handicraft production has remained consistent, with embroidery generally done by women, but machine sewing construction often done by Sani men. The primary sites of Sani ethnic handicraft marketing are in and around Shilin and Kunming in shops and government outlets, or peddled on the streets. Handicraft marketing at Shilin started from the village of Wukeshu, which was a nondescript Sani village until the mid-1980s, when the state started to actively administer tourism development. Three periods of handicraft commoditization at Wukeshu can be seen from 1981 to 1994 (Swain, 1995). The first era, 1981–1986, was village family based, marketing indigenous goods mainly to international tourists. Sales were usually conducted by local Sani women in the park or by leading tourists into their nearby homes where they plied their guests with sunflower seeds, tea, and a hard-sell.

From 1986 to 1992 during the second era, the government's Shilin Tourism Bureau become involved in controlling the handicraft trade by setting up stalls within the park's gates, where all trade must be conducted. These stalls rented for 10 yuan (Renminbi, RMB) per month in 1990 and 10 yuan per 10 days in 1993, money collected by the county tax bureau. Up to 125 stalls were rented out, often with two to four women sharing a stall. While the trade had been organized mainly along family ties, now some unrelated women from other villages were also renting stalls, and a new marketplace developed outside the park gate specializing in generic manufactured tourist souvenirs. Within the park, purchased manufactured goods, ranging from tablecloths to plastic bead bags emblazoned with "Seattle" or "Jerusalem," were gradually added for domestic tourists.

From 1992 on, the third era of Shilin handicraft marketing has continued to develop. Tourism Bureau control has again reshaped the face of handicraft marketing. A 1992 ruling made it possible for only citizens of Wukeshu to sell at stalls within the park, as a compensatory arrangement along with various service work for villagers who are steadily loosing their agricultural base to tourism development. Eighty-eight families officially worked as handicraft marketers in Shilin. They rented their stalls by 10-day lottery, as some were much better located than were others. Their average monthly earnings were self-reported at 400 yuan (RMB) per woman. They also had a number of expenses, due to extensive purchasing of piecework and manufactured items to sell. All in all, there was a noticeable decline in the general quality of goods; there were fewer traders, and pessimism existed among the locals about the future of Sani marketing of handicrafts in Shilin.

The Tourism Bureau has constructed a cement and tile shopping plaza just outside the park gates and planned by 1995 to remove the handicraft stalls in the park, forbidding any trade there, and renting out little shops to Wukeshu residents along with a number of outsiders (Sani and non-Sani alike) running restaurants and souvenir shops. Many of the approximately 20 Wukeshu women sellers who are over 50 years old have said they will not make this transition but will retire rather than compete with younger, multilingual local women once Wukeshu's special privileges in the park are removed.

Economic competition and cooperation across ethnic boundaries is another factor in the production and sale of Sani artifacts. Han tailors (mostly men) from as far away as Sichuan have moved into Wukeshu during the past few years to craft "Sani" goods to sell themselves or for Sani traders to sell in the park or on the streets. Fourteen Han families lived in the village in Fall 1993, producing vast quantities of piecework bags and children's Ashima costumes for Sani and Han retailers. Many Wukeshu women say they have no time to make all the goods they can sell.

Sani Handicraft Production

Sani handicrafts, based on women's embroidered arts, are forms of "Fourth World" tourist arts. These indigenous ethnic arts and crafts are produced for an external audience often unknowledgeable of the objects' everyday use and the producers' shared cultural aesthetics (N. Graburn, 1976, p. 8). The mixture of terms "arts" and "crafts" is intentional in this discussion because some tourist products are standardized crafts while others are individual artistic expressions (see Phillips, 1995). Sani tourist arts can be chronologically categorized into four groups (Swain, 1995):

a. Indigenous products for their own use, such as hand-woven hemp cloth bags, women's clothing, baby pack carriers.
b. Tourist goods of their own manufacture using indigenous Sani products, such as pillow cushions from baby packs, simplified shoes, hats, and aprons adapted to tourist tastes.
c. Invented forms, adapting nonindigenous goods to their cannon of embroidery motifs, such as money belts, tableclothes, and purses; and newly introduced goods such as Japanese tourist-introduced "pulseras," modeled on braided cotton bracelets in a style often sold in Guatemala (A. Horner, 1993), missionary-requested bible/book markers made with indigenous motifs, and anthropologist-inspired dolls.
d. Mass-produced goods using machine embroidered ribbons, wholesaled Sani hand-embroidery, and machine-made components in items such as children's souvenir clothing and coin purses made only of ribbons.

This is not so much an evolutionary process ending in debased pseudoethnic goods as it is a range of responses to commercialization conditions (E. Cohen, 1993b). In general, new forms of goods have been added to the basic inventory of Sani items. A survey of urban Sani women selling baskets in Kunming during 1992 revealed high percentages of b and d products, the small, quickly produced sure sellers, valued between 2 and 20 yuan. Their inventories averaged about 90 pieces, including a few higher priced unique, "traditional" items and/or self-valued fine embroidery from a and c categories.

Sani women urban sellers have been working in Kunming since the mid-1980s. Most of them migrate between their homes in Lunan and a guest house in Kunming. Over the years, up to 100 women have been in the city during the summer high tourism season, at times when there is little agricultural work. Throughout the year, there averaged about 40 Sani women peddlers in the city at one time, selling in many locations where tourists may be found. These women's backgrounds are varied, as is the amount of time they spend peddling, and the sources of the goods they sell. Many were also engaged in the black market money changing trade between "soft" Chinese (RMB) and "hard" Chinese and foreign currencies, fueled by tourists and government agencies alike until mid-1994 when China went to one hard standard currency. In 1993 there were officially 5 yuan to US$1, or 8 to 10 yuan on the black market.

Making Dolls

In January 1993 I initiated this experiment, introducing the idea of fabric "ethnic" dolls as a new handicraft item. First I showed a group of Sani women photos of various "ethnic" dolls while sitting daily on the streets of Kunming with them as they made and sold their wares. Then I hand-sewed a cotton doll over several days in front of my embroidering companions. By turning my doll over to one woman who asked to dress it, interest in a new artifact was sparked and later owned. On the following day, the original doll was given back to me dressed in an intricate miniature Sani outfit.

Subsequently, there were a few rough moments when I refused all requests to make more dolls, but I was willing to show them how to cut out fabric, using a pattern as they also do for some embroidery motifs, and demonstrated how to stuff their own products. Soon doll parts were being produced on sewing machines back home, assembled by peddlers waiting in the streets, and wholesaled among Lunan peddlers for sale to tourists in Kunming. The dolls were sold primarily to Western and Japanese tourists for prices the peddlers deemed good for the work and materials invested. Local Han were curious, but very rarely thought the dolls were worth their asking price, or a reasonable thing to buy at any price.

By Spring, my street companions, referring to the Sani dolls or *buwawa* (cotton babies), would say, "*xie xie Laushi, ni bangzhu womende shenghuo*" ["thanks 'teacher' " (what some women have called me since asking my occupation when we met in 1987), "you have helped our livelihood"]. Chinese-speaking foreigners reported back to me that when peddlers were asked why they started selling dolls, the answer was invariably "*meiguo laushi jiao women*" ("the American teacher taught us"). I was most severely criticized for my intervention into Sani culture by German students studying Chinese at Yunnan University, who assumed I was a missionary. Any discomfort from this critique of meddling with an indigenous culture was relieved months later in Lunan when I found an elderly Sani doll maker whose "independently invented" products were on display in the County Archives. I had not known, however, that there were Sani dolls when I began my project.

From my experiment I learned about Sani handicraft wholesaling, by observing that dolls made by some women were being sold by other peddlers. Individual styles were more readily traced in this new handicraft as unique patterns of production and products developed. Cooperation and competition developed around doll manufacturing, much as it was evident in other handicraft production. Certainly doll making quickly fell into the gender and ethnic divisions of labor found in other Sani tourist arts production. Virtually all handwork was done by women, especially the embroidery and assembly work that could be done either at home or on the street. Machine sewing construction of doll bodies and clothes was often done by men or other women in the household. Ethnically, most doll makers were Sani, but a few Han women, Lunan natives from Sani–Han mixed villages, also made and sold dolls in Kunming.

The original group of doll makers, who sold their goods and changed money outside of the Yunnan University Guest House, numbered seven women in January 1993. By summer's end, there were 20 to 35 women actively making and selling dolls at any one time. The income these women earned from dolls had become significant. A Sani vendor was making about 400 yuan in a good month, which was comparable to the monetary part of a subsidized (with housing and other benefits) urban salary. The per capita poverty level in Yunnan in 1993 was 200 yuan and 200KG of rice per year. Clearly, Sani women peddlers were earning a respectable income. Some doll makers were earning more than 200 yuan per month in dolls alone. They sold the dolls at a market price that tourists were willing to pay. The asking doll price was often 20 yuan, a value suggested by myself and other Westerners based on other Sani handicraft market values, but it could be bargained down to 10 yuan by tourists. If a doll was of average quality, it usually went for 15 yuan.

Material costs for doll production were minimal, as scraps and leftovers from other projects or recycled clothes were used. A few doll makers purchased special fabric and stuffing to make the doll itself. The average time to make a cotton doll was about 2 days of intermittent, cooperative work according to doll makers' own estimates. This was much less time compared to embroidering a panel used in an item for sale at 15 to 20 yuan. After about 6 months of producing this new tourist art, some doll makers began wholesaling their mid-quality dolls to other peddlers. This activity was consistent with other wholesaling of handicrafts among Sani.

Sani dolls were a firm part of the urban peddler's inventory by late 1993. In mid-1995, a few Sani women, including all of those discussed below, began taking a 3-day train ride to Beijing to stay for at least 20 days of selling on the streets. Dolls sold for more than 50 yuan there, and could sell for almost as much to foreign tourists back in Lunan County's Stone Forest. Sani doll production had taken off, just as the money changing business had declined (but was still going on in Fall 1995). Whether doll sales fill a niche similar to profits made from the money black market and what this means to the Sani women peddlers are questions for future study.

Doll Makers

The range of Sani doll makers' backgrounds and products were as varied as the peddlers' in general. Many were Lunan residents, but some had lived in the city for years. Some were illiterate, while others had Middle School degrees. A few were either Catholic or Communist Party members. Some were teenagers, while others were grandmothers. In several sketches of Sani doll makers, we can see these individual qualities, as well as innovations and standardizations in their work. These women are referred to by fictitious last names, not their genuine Chinese or Sani language full names.

There was Li, the most exacting of doll makers who was the first to produce a doll all by herself and quickly developed a distinctive, standardized style (Figure 17.1). She made and sold dolls, for 20 yuan apiece, in female and male pairs, because that was the way they should be, she said. Only after it was clear that tourists preferred the more colorful female dolls did she make a few single dolls. At this initial stage of Sani doll making my colleague, Laurel Bossen, had joined me. She actually commissioned Li to produce the first Sani dolls, and helped negotiate the relatively high market price, which, as we will see, has fluctuated widely both up and down. Li has become the "Ford" of Sani doll making, developing a technique of sewing doll components, then assembling them when she had time. She had plastic bags of tiny Sani clothes, doll heads, and doll bodies. Li was an urban Sani who lived with her family at her husband's work-unit, apart from many of the migrating vendors living temporarily in a guesthouse. Illiterate herself, Li was saving money for her daughter's college education. She was shy by habit, but willing to give her fellow vendors a hand in working out sewing details.

One guest house resident, who Li worked with in vain to improve her doll technique, was a feisty entrepreneur called Zhang. This woman bought wholesale in Lunan, then peddled her wares in Kunming, wearing poor clothes and an attitude. Zhang had been raised Catholic and was quick to identify with European and American tourists. She was an intriguing mix of Sani, Chinese, and Western ways.

Figure 17.1. The first Sani doll. (Photo by Margaret Swain)

Zhang was a reluctant convert at best to Sani doll making. An imperfectionist in all her handicraft work, she was satisfied with crude ill-made dolls that her colleagues disparaged. Zhang persisted in producing and selling her inferior dolls for as low as 5 yuan, severely undercutting other more detailed doll makers. She has also had major disputes over money changing practices, and was often very marginal to the group when selling on the streets.

Pu, another woman who commuted back and forth from Lunan to Kunming, became one of the innovators in Sani doll making. Her first efforts were to her own mind comical, but she persisted and perfected a style as well as a number of ideas for construction and costuming. In the Summer of 1993, it was always Pu who introduced regional variations in Sani clothing displayed on the dolls, and then slowly branched into making dolls that represented Sani neighbors such as the Ashi and Hei Yi ethnic minority groups. After a few months of doll making, Pu showed up at her usual selling place with a bag of plastic "Barbie" style dolls, dressed in Sani style clothing she had made. To a one, her peers were very negative about this new idea. It was not the right thing to do. Pu quickly put the plastic dolls away and soon went back to making her own fabric dolls to dress. It was a very interesting moment in the evolution of an introduced tourist art when an innovation could be so soundly judged as inauthentic by the producers (Figure 17.2). While Sani children may play with modern plastic dolls, during the first year of manufacture I never saw a Sani child play with a "Sani bu wawa." These dolls were products for sale.

Figure 17.2. Doll makers en groupe. (Photo by Margaret Swain)

Doll Issues

Dolls are a distinct form of human culture. These portable representations of people can be used as playthings, gendered icons, ethnic artifacts, and souvenir commodities. Since the rise of mass tourism in the 20th century, dolls have been part of a global tourist arts industry (see Phillips, 1995). Dolls are cultural symbols, products of popular culture, and collectible material culture. They can evoke strong responses such as a child's affection toward a doll or some feminist repudiations of Barbie dolls as icons of racialized patriarchal culture and consumption (Ducille, 1994). In her study of the commercialization of American girlhood, Formanek-Brunell (1993) maintains that dolls "can be seen as texts that shed light on the intentions of producers" (p. 2), and proceeds to illustrate gender differences in the motivations, aesthetics, and techniques of female and male doll makers over a century of American history.

Likewise, ethnic dolls, representations of specific ethnic groups, can be read for commentary on ethnic and gender relations, social conditions, material culture, and motivations of their makers. Sometimes ethnic dolls portray racial/ethnic stereotypes promoted and produced by the majority society, as seen in manufactured black "pickaninny" dolls in America, or the featureless generic "ethnic minority—shaoshuminzu" stick dolls of Yunnan. Dolls are part of a transnational trade in the portrayal of difference. From factories licensed in the US, multicultural Barbies are produced in identical idealized form, with different skin shades and costumes. As

Anne Ducille (1994) wrote: "Barbie is just a piece of plastic, but what she says about the economic base of our society—what she suggests about gender and race in our world—ain't good" (p. 66). Through out the 20th century, global capitalism, gender relations, nationalism, racism, world travel, and ethnic arts markets have affected the development of indigenous/ethnic dolls from both outside and within the group.

Some modern ethnic dolls have evolved from a cultural heritage of doll making, as seen in the work of contemporary Oglala Sioux doll artist Charles Chief Eagle. Chief Eagle (1990) writes: "I would like to note most emphatically the traditional art form I currently render was originally the creative expressions of the Lakota women and it is to them that I proudly dedicate my work, My greatest source of inspiration are my two grandmothers. . . ." Personal interest may also lead to more varied doll making, as is the case of Native American doll artist Nadine Van Mechelen (1991). She carefully researches the clothing she creates for dolls representing various tribes. Another example of this genre is the highly individualized and valued Alaska native dolls made by a number of artists of indigenous materials. These dolls have developed as a specific kind of cultural artifact sought by collectors.

Ethnic doll production may evolve out of political conflict situations. Refugee Maya in the US and Tibetans in India have produced dolls as both a commoditized reminder of their cultural heritage embedded in a homeland denied, and a vehicle to teach others about themselves. Maya dolls made and sold in California grew out of individual women doll makers' childhood playthings and experiences (Swain, 1993). Tibetan dolls made by monks of the Drepung Loseling monastery, relocated from Lhasa to India, are a new craft that developed after a guild to market monk products celebrating Tibetan culture was started by an American-Tibetan couple in 1983. Demonstrations of "Losel" doll making by visiting monks were part of a 1991 museum exhibit in New York City (Wolff, 1992).

Religion, in the form of missionary projects, has also implemented ethnic doll making in many parts of the colonial and postcolonial world. One of these efforts, now very collectible, was the Door of Hope wooden dolls produced in Ningpo, China from the early 1900s until World War II. They were dressed by young girls who had been taken in from the streets by American missionaries. These dolls portray people in a wide range of Chinese social positions and occupations, and were sold to tourists in China and worldwide through a network of outlets. The girls earned a small salary, with most of the proceeds going into the mission (M. Lalli, 1994).

In contrast to these highly organized efforts, individual ethnic doll makers, like Maya women who recycle old clothes into tourist souvenir dolls in Chiapas, Mexico (Rosenbaum, 1993) and Sani women in Yunnan, pace their production to meet market demand. In the 1990s this international market even included organized tours of doll collectors traveling to "exotic" corners of the world (B. Johnston, 1995) in search of their favorite indigenous or tourist art.

Issues in Indigenous Tourist Arts

The Sani engagement in tourist arts production for the world market has followed a similar scenario found among indigenous peoples in Latin America and elsewhere. Small-scale, often fairly isolated, indigenous groups whose recent history includes marginalization in remote areas by cultural, class, and ecological criteria now find themselves living in regions of state tourism development where they are one of the exotic attractions. Pierre van den Berghe's (1995) work on Maya ethnic tourism in Mexico's highlands has lead to his analysis of four factors that he argues makes Mexico a "uniquely interesting case for the study of ethnic tourism . . . especially for an analysis of the role of the state in marketing its indigenous population" (p. 568). All of these factors (see below) can also be found in China's marketing of its ethnic minorities for tourism. Therefore, it can be argued that they form a pattern of ethnic tourism as postcolonial internal colonialism played out in various nation-states' distinct histories, cultures, and physical environments.

These factors outlined by van den Berghe (1995) are:

1. The nation is a major tourist destination. Tourism is the largest noncommodity component in China's trade and, like Mexico, has comprised as much as 3% of the GNP (Swain, 1990).
2. The national government is extremely tourism conscious.
3. Postrevolution ideology promotes a nation defined by genetic and cultural blending and acculturation to the language and the culture of the conquerors (Spanish or Han Chinese), while indigenous cultures are romantically idealized.
4. About 8% (in China and Mexico) of the national population are categorized as minority, indigenous people, based on linguistic and cultural criteria.

Indigenous minorities are thus a marketable resource for the national good. Local elite, members of the majority, are often best positioned to profit from this ethnic tourism as middlemen between indigenous producers and tourists. National governments' efforts to integrate indigenous people through infrastructure, schooling, and market reforms have opened up areas for further tourism development. One of the aspects of this development has been the growth of artisanal craft production and its integration into the world capitalist market.

In an edited collection of essays subtitled "the impact of global exchange on Middle American artisans," June Nash (1993) focuses on handicraft commercialization impacting gender and other social relations in rural indigenous communities. Again, studies from the Americas can also inform conditions found in Asia. Rural men seek work as wage laborers, and women may go into towns to sell their crafts. As both new goods and roles evolve, these changes feed back into domestic relations and may challenge status in family systems (Nash, 1993, pp. 6–7).

Indigenous craftswomen draw from their heritage and everyday material culture, and also respond to market forces including consumer tastes and available raw materials, as we can see with the Sani, Maya, and many other embedded and refugee groups around the world (Swain, 1993). Consumers of their work include the state, nonprofit outlets, buyers for artisan stores in industrialized nations, and tourists. Nash (1993) comments that:

> . . . commercialization of artisan production bridges the contrasts in gift giving and commoditized exchange that are often posed as polar

opposites. . . . Tourism epitomizes the newly monetized yet culturally embedded encounters that characterize the value of these exchanges as the culture of the artisans is packaged along with the product. . . . But this process may indeed involve a renewed colonization as these semi-subsistence farmers become even more dependent on distant markets. (p. 12)

Their actions may be "desperate efforts to escape the poverty brought on by overpopulation and ecological degradation, and the exploitation characteristic of the patriarchal social system. This escape leads to the alienation of local handicrafts for commercial production for tourists and export, as an alternative to migrant labor or proletarianization in large cities" (N. Graburn & Delugan, 1995, p. 215). Factors in this reconfiguration could include assistance from state-run agencies (the National Indian Institute in Mexico or the Women's Federation in China, for example) or various outside activists and advocates, from missionaries to Peace Corps volunteers, who introduce new craft forms and marketing strategies.

Lynn Stephen's (1993, pp. 25–57) work on craft commercialization among the Zapotec indigenous group in Mexico raises important issues of ethnic identity and authenticity applicable to the production of many tourist arts. As everyday use objects become transformed into handicrafts, ethnic group control over production may be challenged within the community and in the global market. Stephen views this process from a fluid understanding of ethnic identity as a dialectic, counter-hegemonic response of a self-defined and externally categorized group of people to dominant culture. She argues that "because the content of ethnic identity is flexible and changes through time according to the cultural material available to a particular group of people to work with, there is no such thing as 'real' or 'genuine' ethnic content" (pp. 27–28). Within the Zapotec ethnic textile market, American importers "cross-fertilized" designs and materials from around the world to develop market demands (p. 47). Such efforts resulted in "Zapotec" textiles being produced in India, and Zapotec weavers refusing to produce Oriental rug designs for their buyers. Stephen interprets this refusal as assertion of ethnicity-based claims to their textiles in both a bid for economic control and defense of a particular ethnic identity. The international division of labor in handicraft production does not distinguish "authenticity" in this case, but local ethnic group production often claims this distinction.

The role of outsider innovation for the world market and its acceptance or rejection by a handicraft-producing ethnic community is a central question in this exploration of Sani doll production as tourist arts. Among the Sani, various "animateurs," primarily the state as government souvenir buyers, the tourism bureau, and the Women's Federation, have animated or stimulated the production of tourist arts. Innovation from within the group may also be accepted or rejected. The "Ford" assembly techniques developed by one artisan, producing batches of tiny doll components much like batches of "Sani bags" ordered in huge consignments by state buyers, does not appeal to some doll makers who create individual works.

My act of introducing dolls as a new idea to Sani craftswomen raises questions of authenticity and intellectual property rights—mine and theirs. I voluntarily gave up my claims to "inventing" Sani dolls the moment Sani innovations took over.

Authenticity is a topic well discussed by tourism researchers, as a quality of experience and artifact defined by tourist consumers (see Littrell, Anderson, & Brown, 1993). Are Sani dolls authentically Sani ethnic/tourist art? Even if tourists got so far as to learn that an American had taught Sani women how to make dolls, they were buying an authentic doll, made by Sani. For most Sani producers, the primary issues were income and product aesthetics. Dolls made by Sani, wearing replicas of Sani costumes, were Sani dolls, icons of Sani identity, as seen in the tale of innovator Pu and her Sani "Barbies." A few craftswomen in the urban peddlers' group were reluctant to make animateur products. Interviews indicated that one factor for some of them may have been an issue of authenticity in their desire to produce only things generated by Sani people. As artifacts, Sani dolls are both products of outside intervention and Sani material culture.

In the world marketplace, application of intellectual property rights to indigenous knowledge or handicrafts is occasionally discussed (Posey, 1991). Intellectual property, the products of individual and community thought or knowledge, has been commoditized in Western industrial society for centuries by patents, copyrights, trade secrets, and trademarks. These protections of intellectual property rights may actually inhibit collective innovation by favoring individual inventions (Brush, 1993). The United Nations World Intellectual Property Rights Organization developed model provisions in 1984 for the "Protection of Expressions of Folklore Against Illicit Exploitation and Other Prejudicial Actions." As model provisions, member states are not required to adopt them, and subsequent international discussion has stagnated on identifying protected folklore and providing mechanisms to settle disputes.

Language in the model provisions recognizes individual and collective folklore traditions as expressions and productions rather than as work. This distinction "removed folk expressions from the necessity of having the 'personality' of a creator or artist as required by copyright law" (Posey, 1991, p. 31). Despite these provisions, it is ironic, as Brush (1993) has noted, that proponents of intellectual property rights for indigenous knowledge "seek to address problems caused in part by the expansion of capitalism by employing a tool of capitalism" (p. 666). Brush concludes that "other ways of constituting rights, such as guaranteeing human, cultural, or land rights, might be more effective in meeting the goals of conserving indigenous knowledge and providing more equitable treatment for indigenous people . . ." (p. 667).

Ethical Issues

What were the ethics of my chosen role of animateur in Sani ethnic goods production? My choice was based on my understanding of culture as mutable, adaptable, and not easily tricked into spurious deceit. My altruistic, advocate motive was based on the belief that valuing indigenous culture and promoting indigenous cultural rights are enhanced by offering new possibilities for cultural expression. If I had become an active partner in doll manufacturing and marketing, I would have larger issues to address. Consequently, I chose to make only an example doll, and would not produce dolls for my companions to all dress. It was the idea, not the artifact, that I wanted to give them.

In her summary discussion of anthropologists' ethics, Skomal (1994) argued that "by recognizing how ethical problems are culturally constituted, socially regulated and historically determined, . . . informed anthropologists help empower the peoples and communities studied to participate more actively in the world economy" (p. 4). Ethics, Skomal notes, is a means to deal with the way we ought to act, putting values on behaviors that cannot be empirically tested. Science, the study of what is, uses testable hypotheses to explain what is observed, and has been a primary tenant of anthropology. Now it seems that there is a "greater concern with what ought to be, . . . as more than detached observers of human nature" (p. 4). While some anthropologists will clearly position themselves as collaborators in their work, Skomal cautions that we must be able to differentiate between competing responsibilities of objectivity and advocacy in our research.

My low-risk doll project assumed that I could be a researcher studying the effects of what I advocated. Cleveland's (1994, p. 9) analysis of the ethics of sustainable development notes that while science allows us to predict the results of our actions, it cannot answer such value-laden questions as what is right and wrong. We need to keep open the dialogue between science and advocacy, acknowledging that our own cultural values shape our "objectivity." "How to interpret and use scientific information is a question of subjective value to be negotiated by . . . moving beyond cultural hegemony and cultural relativism, and in the process anthropologists become colleagues with the people with whom they work— they are no longer 'informants,' 'subjects,' or the 'other' "(p. 10). In the year that I worked with Sani doll makers, I very much wanted to see them move toward a cooperative organization to maximize their economic gains. But this was not something they would "naturally" do in a postcommunal, socialist market economy. It was not my mandate to effect such change, and my efforts to engage the state Women's Federation's interest in the doll makers were of no avail.

It was easier to do science, mapping the convoluted spread of doll making among the Sani peddlers in Kunming. However, there was always an "ethical dialogue" (Osborne, 1994, p. 1) between me, as the researcher, and the Sani doll makers, as the researched, in the community we formed. I adopted what I thought was a Sani women's work ethic, showing a new way of doing something, an innovation, that others could follow if they chose. It was in this context that I asked if Sani women could see that I had given them an idea, not a set thing. I believe the ethics of dialogue, advocacy, and science worked when Sani doll makers made it clear that I had "improved their livelihood," not given them piecework to do (Figure 17.3).

Conclusions

Members of the American Anthropological Association are enjoined to follow our "Principles of Professional Responsibility." We have a "first responsibility" to the people we study to be humane and careful of how we apply our personal and professional ethics. We also are expected to conduct our work, even if we are postmodern theorists, in a manner that is quantifiable, repeatable, objective—in a word, scientific. The research decision described in this chapter has been weighed in its unique context and in the broader issues it encompasses. The specific consequences raise general issues: dolls as a type of material culture that evoke reac-

Figure 17.3. Margaret Swain with Sani doll makers in Kunming. (Photo by Walt Swain)

tions across gender and ethnic lines; the parameters of tourist art as economic development and as material culture with conditions of authenticity, commodity, and intellectual property rights; and, finally, research ethics

Yes, in terms of research ethics, I would do it again. As a researcher I made a conscious decision to join in a process of change, becoming ethically engaged in a dialogue with the people I worked with, while also doing work that could be objectively measured. My position as a factor in my research is something to which both the "subjects" and I must respond. This applied tourism research also raises questions for further study among the Sani, as well as other situations of tourist arts development. Fluid definitions of ethnicity and authenticity, and the facts that new ideas and markets occur all the time over and through ethnic boundaries in the global economy, make this a challenging field of research. We are further challenged to advocate for the people who make the goods and from whom we extract our data.

Acknowledgments—I would like to acknowledge and thank the Committee on Scholarly Communications with China, National Academy of Sciences for their year-long fieldwork support. Laurel Bossen noted this correlation, when we discussed Sani dolls in late 1995.

Chapter 18

Marine Tourism and Environmental Management on the Great Barrier Reef

Steven Parker

The Great Barrier Reef (GBR) is a huge marine system composed of some 2900 individual reefs and approximately 900 islands, lying near the Equator in the state of Queensland on Australia's northeast coast (Figure 18.1). This most famous of coral reefs runs north–south for more than 2000 kilometers (1200 miles), parallel to the shore. Comparing distances with the US, to travel the full length of the GBR approximates the driving distance from New York City to Miami, FL, or from Los Angeles, CA to Seattle, WA. In addition to being very long, it is very wide, having an average width in excess of 100 kilometers (60 miles), and is equal in square miles to one half the state of Texas. If sheer size were not daunting enough, add to the complexity of its management the staggering diversity and variety of marine life found in these warm waters. The GBR is home to 400 different varieties of hard and soft corals, 1500 species of fish, 4000 different mollusks, thousands of different sponges and crustaceans plus countless other creatures.

For millennia this colossal ecosystem slumbered on, undisturbed by outside forces. The European discovery of Australia caused major changes whose pace has accelerated dramatically in the last quarter century. Fearing that this vast resource might be in considerable danger from human impacts, the Australian Commonwealth Government sought to permanently protect it by creating The Great Barrier Reef Marine Park in 1975. In this name, the term "park" should not be misunderstood, for in any discussion of resource management the term refers to a protected area, not to an amusement attraction. The enabling legislation created a management agency, The Great Barrier Reef Marine Park Authority (a.k.a. the Authority or GBRMPA), charged with the primary purpose and responsibility for conserving the natural resources of the Park. The 1975 law instructs the Authority to regulate the Reef while allowing for "reasonable use" for extractive activities such as commercial fishing. The same statute mandates that some areas be left completely undisturbed and that others be made available for the appreciation and

Figure 18.1. Map of Australia and the Great Barrier Reef. (Courtesy of URL http://www.theodora.com/maps)

enjoyment of the public. It is this last element that, of course, forms the connection with tourism, but the great boost for that particular use of the Reef occurred in 1981 when it was listed as a World Heritage Site under the international World Heritage Convention.

Today GBRMPA follows a multiple-use strategy that attempts to balance the values of conservation with those of four main user groups: the commercial fishing industry, Queensland recreational users, a sizeable Aboriginal population, and the commercial tourism industry. Each of these groups has different needs and puts different types of demands on both the Reef and the management agency, but tourism is the Reef's major commercial user. Commercial fishing ranks second, but the economic value of tourism is four times greater.

Reef Tourism

Visitation to the GBR Region is numerically high, and generates approximately 10% of the region's economic activity. Visitor use of the Reef itself has grown rapidly in recent years, rising from 900,000 visitor days in 1990 to 1.7 million visitor days in 1997. While many factors help to explain this phenomenal rate of growth, part of it is technology driven with bigger and faster boats that deliver far larger numbers of passengers to once remote areas of the Reef. If acceptable travel time for the day visitor is 2 hours in each direction, in 1985 most boats could

traverse 20 miles of ocean in that amount of time. By 1998 new high-speed catamarans could reach cays and islands 75 miles from port in the same 2 hours. It is
estimated that by the year 2001 newer craft will have a one-way range of 100
miles, enough to put almost the entire Reef within reach of the day visitor. Such
changes pose enormous challenges for the Authority in regulating certain components of the Marine Tourism industry.

Management Tools

Zoning is the broadest management tool available to GBRMPA. Most people are
familiar with this concept on land, grouping similar uses and activities together.
Houses and factories are placed in different zones and thus are not in direct conflict with each other. Thus, a single area can accommodate multiple uses with a
minimum of mutual interference. In a marine park, similar uses can be grouped
together, as commercial fishing areas are kept separate from conservation zones.
Because the GBR covers such an enormous area, the Authority began by first di-
viding it into four geographic sections: the Far North Section, The Cairns Section,
the Central Section, and the Mackay/Capricorn Section. In turn, each of these sections was divided into a number of activity zones such as the:

- Preservation Zone
- Scientific Research Zone
- National Park Zone
- Buffer Zone
- Conservation Park Zone
- Estuarine Conservation Zone
- Habitat Protection Zone
- General Use Zone

While not all zones are found in every section, the basic plan is to set an increasing level of limitation on human activity as one moves up this list from the
General Use Zone (least restrictive) to the Preservation Zone (where no unautho-
rized entry is permitted). Together these zones regulate a broad range of activities
such as aviation, shipping, trawling, recreational fishing, specimen collection, and
tourism. Certain dangerous activities such as mining and oil exploration are completely prohibited throughout the entire Park, but other highly destructive practices may be locally permitted. For example, nearly 1000 trawlers dredge for sea
scallops or drag the sea bottom for prawns in the Marine Park. Dragging a prawn
net across the ocean bottom has been likened to clear cutting in a forest. Everything in the path of the harvesting equipment is destroyed. Trawling vessels drag
huge nets hundreds of miles across estuaries, bays, and inlets, pulling up tons of
marine creatures, rocks, and mud. Catch that is not wanted is simply thrown over-
board. Because this practice cannot be legally stopped, zoning limits the areas
where it can be undertaken.

Zoning was initially useful, but because the zones are so broad and the reef is
so vast, it proved inadequate in the face of the increasing tourist use. The Authority has subsequently developed a new management approach called the Plan of
Management (POM). POMs have become essential because zoning could only

delineate areas for extractive activities like trawling. Tourism was never specifically addressed in the zoning plans simply because in the Park's early days, tourism levels were extremely low. Then, the Authority could regulate visitation through a permit system, and each proposed operation was examined in terms of its individual requirements. If an operator successfully obtained a permit, he was free to provide tourism activities in all zones except those restricted to Scientific Research or Preservation, which comprised less than 1% of the entire park.

The Cairns Section is the part of the Park most heavily used by tourists. It hosts over 60% of the Reef's annual visitors, and serves as a useful model to illustrate the structure of a POM. The Authority applies a four-level hierarchy: first, a management area like Cairns is divided into sectors, then further subdivided into localities and locations, and finally into sites. The Cairns area has six different geographic sectors, and within each sector there are a number of localities. For example, in the very popular Ribbon Reefs Sector, one of the localities is Cod Hole, a place seen in countless television documentaries with divers hand feeding the enormous cod that lurk there. The locations are the separate reefs and cays to which a tourist might be taken, and the sites are the very specific geographic points on the reef where the visitor might be allowed to dive or where a mooring might be placed. To appreciate how such an approach allows for very finely tuned resource management and protection, consider the following scenario involving two operators visiting the same reef location. The first operator is allowed to anchor at a site 25 meters from the reef, above a sandy sea bottom. He is allowed no closer because a thrown anchor explodes onto fragile coral like a wrecking ball. The heavy chain attaching it to the boat destructively rakes over other nearby coral for hours as the craft swings back and forth with the wind and tide. To avoid such impact, a permanent mooring buoy has been placed at an adjacent site and the other operator can stop there if he has the permit to use it. The two sites are side by side, but through the POM they are controlled in very different ways way, in contrast to the simplicity of the zoning plan.

Utilizing this hierarchical and spatial system, the Authority's planners now rely on a combination of scientific studies and site visitation data to assess the carrying capacities and vulnerabilities of major sectors, locations, and sites in the Cairns Area. The term "carrying capacity" refers to the ability of a site to absorb visitation without suffering undue degradation. Each reef or island can accommodate only so many boaters or divers per day before reaching an unacceptable impact level. The maximum sustainable "load" is the carrying capacity of the resource, and to manage this fragile resource, GBRMPA planners generate numerous regulations, all of which vary with location. There are maximum boat sizes, and capacity limits on the numbers of visitors who may be brought to a site. A reservation and booking system regulates the number of operators who can voyage to any one reef on any one day. For example, a specific popular location may have two public moorings, but 10 tour operators wish to use it the same weekend. The reservation system restricts mooring and prohibits nonreserved boats from the area. In addition, there are stipulations regarding the placement and operation of large, floating platforms called pontoons (Figure 18.2). These extensive, man-made structures (about the size of a bowling

Figure 18.2. Small reef pontoon. (Photo by Steven Parker)

alley) are permanently moored in one place, miles from shore. Many of the newer ones are floating, two-story buildings, complete with small theaters, underwater observatories, dining areas, and catering for several hundred people. Some also have helicopter pads to provide visitors with flightseeing excursions. These amenities are supplemental to the usual provisions for diving, snorkeling, and swimming.

Each day modern, high-speed ferryboats deposit hundreds of passengers on pontoons where they spend the day snorkeling, diving, riding in glass-bottom boats, and sun bathing. That evening they return to port, usually at Cairns. Obviously mass tourism mandates careful regulation and monitoring to minimize resource damage. Authorities therefore have a legitimate interest in everything on a pontoon from visitor behavior that may directly damage coral, to the structural integrity of a facility's wastewater holding tanks.

However, despite its best efforts at managerial innovation, it is doubtful that the Authority can deal effectively with an 11% annual growth rate in tourism, covering a geographic area larger than Britain. Some Reef locations are heavily used because high-speed boats bring hundreds of tourists to individual pontoons. And some islands are almost urban in character. The largest of these, Hamilton Island, is a miniature city that attracts thousands of visitors to its beaches, shops, restaurants, 20-story hotel, and high-rise apartment buildings. Even small cities produce enormous amounts of waste, which directly impact the Reef. Another heavily used site is Green Island, where ferry boats can deposit more than 1000 people daily on a single reef. In such cases, the term "enlightened marine resource management" really means "cutting your losses."

To decrease such damage, GBRMPA is now using the POMs to encourage tour operators to install permanent moorings instead of anchoring. Moorings are far less environmentally destructive because they rely on a one-time securing of a line from a floating surface buoy to the reef or sea bottom. With the buoy in place, the operator merely has to clip his boat to it each time he arrives at the site. Under the Cairns POM, the Authority has licensed the installation of more than 250 such devices with 115 more still planned.

The connection between individual operators and the POMs is the regulatory device known as the permit or license. Anyone who wishes to go into the business of transporting, or otherwise assisting, paying visitors out to the Reef must apply for a permit from GBRMPA. Before the advent of the POM (1998), when the only tool that existed was zoning, customized, lengthy permits and long waiting periods were normal. Owing to the standardization of acceptable practices, the licensing process has been greatly streamlined and coordinates with POMs and GBRMPA to reduce human impacts.

Enforcement and Implementation

Planning and regulation are the primary responsibility of GBRMPA, but enforcement responsibility on the GBR, the "wet end of management," rests with the Queensland Department of Environment (DOE). This agency operates patrol boats and surveillance aircraft to ensure compliance. With a staff of 106, it also develops and maintains infrastructure projects, such as island campgrounds, public moorings, and docks. As the only department with the personnel actually in the field, the staff is in a unique position to observe problems and report to other agencies. These reports are often instrumental in effecting operational change. For example, when existing rental boat regulations allow for unforeseen crowding on a certain island in an area known as the Whitsundays, the impetus for changing these regulations is likely to come from the DOE because it is the agency dealing with the problem on a daily basis.

DOE surveillance boats and aircraft in the Whitsundays have filed numerous reports on reef and island damage caused by inexperienced sailboat captains. The "bareboat" industry rents boats to customers without crew or captain and the customer sails the boat himself. Some individuals may never have sailed in the area before and thus do not know all of the dangers—either to themselves or to the Reef's flora and fauna. Coral may be damaged; islands are left in an unsanitary condition; nesting turtles and sea birds are disturbed. When patterns like this appear, the DOE initiates action. However, it must be remembered that there are a mere 106 employees to watch over the entire 1200 miles of reef. Inevitably many impacts go unreported.

The careful reader has undoubtedly noticed the existence of two levels of government involved in Reef management. GBRMPA is a federal agency reporting to a minister in The Commonwealth Government in the national capital, Canberra, while DOE is a state agency administered by the government of Queensland. The establishment of the federal Marine Park in 1975 sparked considerable conflict and debate between these two levels of government as to who would actually be in charge. The debate was resolved by The Emerald Agreement, which divided their activities: policy-making went to the national level, and administration went to the state. While easily distinguishable in theory, the two functions have always overlapped in practice. Nowhere is this more true than in the DOE budget, where each level provides half of the approximate US$55.3 million spent each year. The Emerald Agreement provides that each level is to contribute 50% of the DOE budget, management that assures continuity in funding. Despite changes in political party leadership, the aggregate budget has not been dramatically affected because the commitment of the other side has remained constant.

The Environmental Management Charge (EMC), a so-called user fee, generates much of the money used by both DOE and GBRMPA, and is collected either directly or indirectly from visitors. First levied at the Reef in 1993, the EMC is now $A4.00 per visitor per day (about US$2.50) with all proceeds earmarked for reef agencies. The funds are to be used for reef management and protection. Businessmen feared the fee would be a disincentive to travel, but when the $A4.00 fee is viewed in relation to the visitor's overall travel budget, the amount is minuscule. No existing data demonstrate that the charge has caused tourists to cancel their trips. The tour operators assume responsibility for collection and remittance of the fees, which for them is a matter of increased overhead expenses. However, the fee helps to conserve the resource upon which their businesses depend.

Industry Self-Regulation

The issue of moorings introduces another approach to regulation. When moorings are licensed, they belong to the licensee and are fully transferable and saleable. While individual operators own most moorings, the Authority has recently embarked on an approach that relies heavily on the free market and the private sector. Known as self-regulation, the system works as follows. In each area of the Reef, locally based marine tourism associations are comprised of businessmen whose boats have the same ports and visit the same geographic areas each day. Instead of issuing the mooring licenses exclusively to the individual businesses, the authority now dispenses a certain number of licenses to the associations. Once done, the site belongs to the association, and only "members in good standing" can use it. More than a quarter of a century ago, Garret Hardin wrote a famous article entitled "The Tragedy of the Commons." In it he argued that when everyone owns a resource, it is as though its ownership is vested in no one. All have an interest in overusing it. This problem is diminished through controls known as Codes of Practice, a technique of self-policing by "members in good standing," as a matter of mutual self-interest.

The Codes generally focus on matters such as mooring and anchoring procedures, visitor education, and safety and conservation practices. Boats operating in an ecologically harmful manner can be fined or even excluded from use of the moorings. An irresponsible operator is a threat to the group and the group now has the authority to punish. Of course, having this authority is not the same thing as actually using it, and thus the effectiveness of The Code of Practice approach is far from certain. The program is new, and the Authority does not yet have sufficient information on the extent to which these businessmen are actually regulating one another. On this matter, only time will tell. However, it is hoped that self-regulating activities and the efforts of the DOE will make an effective contribution to Reef conservation (Figure 18.3).

Research

Whether the regulations are public or private, the ultimate rationale behind the POMs is to protect the reefs by monitoring the cumulative effects of usage. To meet this goal requires a substantial scientific research capability, for which the Authority usually turns to an organization called the Cooperative Research Center-Reef (CRC-Reef). The group is a partnership founded in 1993 between industry (including marine tourism), James Cook University, the Commonwealth government, and the Queensland government, and has an annual budget of about US$5.7 million for offshore research. The research agenda includes marine ecology and biology, fisheries engineering design, tourism and its impacts, hydrodynamic modeling, and water quality analysis.

One of the most dramatic examples of this organization's importance dealt with shipping. Every year through the mid-1990s, some 2500 large commercial ships, about 10% of which were oil tankers, navigated the channel between the Reef and the mainland. More than 50 ships have run aground or collided since 1979 because the coastline boundary changes continuously. In 1995 CRC-Reef released a

Figure 18.3. Excursion boat. (Photo by Steven Parker)

study entitled "Shipping Risk Analysis for the Great Barrier Reef." In it scientists focused on the commercial bulk shipping allowed in the interior waters of the Marine Park. In the wake of accidents such as the *Exxon Valdez* in Alaska, there was a legitimate fear that a large oil spill could have devastating consequences for the Reef, and CRC-Reef was asked to do a risk assessment. As a direct result of this study, federal shipping policy was altered to require that most bulk shipping routes be moved outside the Reef. Loss of this inner passage route cost the maritime shipping industry both time and money, but the study clearly demonstrated it was environmentally too hazardous. Although this study did not deal directly with tourism it was indirectly of great value and relevance to it.

The Authority and CRC-Reef also monitor numerous ecological impacts specific to tourism. Coastal tourism infrastructure for tourism facilities such as resorts and marinas can cause massive environmental problems: loss of habitat, the dumping of dredge spoil, increased effluent discharge from resorts, plus spilled fuel and antifouling preparations from marinas. A good example of both the promise and the failure of tourism management in the Marine Park area is provided by the case of a planned resort development known as Port Hinchinbrook. During most of the 1990s, developers and conservation groups battled over this proposed mega-resort. Port Hinchinbrook was designed to be an integrated tourism and residential facility with both shopping/business areas and a central recreational core. An extensive marina provided access to the GBR. While the developers argued their plan was ecologically friendly, the Marine Conservation Society and the Australian Conservation Foundation opposed the resort. Ultimately the developers won, despite their need for the extensive dredging of mangrove and sea-grass areas. GBRMPA and DOE staffers opposed the project but were not politically powerful enough to overrule the favorable review from upper echelons at both the State and Commonwealth levels that solicit the tax and economic benefits of tourism.

Going beyond tourism, CRC-Reef claims that terrestrial development, in general, is the single greatest threat to this delicate ocean environment. Development changes land use, which, among other problems, can cause massive siltation when it rains. The addition of fertilizer and pesticide residues from agribusiness into the runoff creates enormous problems for reef sustainability. In addition, urban development increases the discharge of wastewater, poisoning inlets and nurturing the growth of algae that covers and kills coral.

Conclusion

This discussion of Australia's Great Barrier Reef is intended to sensitize the reader to the challenges that face management agencies in charge of marine tourism. While a primary goal is conservation, increasing numbers of global visitors want to experience first-hand this World Heritage Site. Australia is politically dedicated to principles of a free market economy, and businessmen must be allowed to operate in these waters. The commercial fishing industry and cargo shipping firms both place demands on the Reef Region as do tourism operators, aboriginal groups, and Queensland residents, who just want to go out for a day of fun in the sun. This high level of utilization inherently carries the danger of overuse and the consequent danger of resource degradation. The only solution appears to be informed management.

In Australia, on Australia's GBR, the Great Barrier Reef Marine Park Authority, assisted by the Queensland Department of Environment, is in charge of day-to-day management. These two agencies have primary responsibility for zoning, planning, and regulation, but they share some of these functions with private industry. Tourism operators have been given a substantial stake in their own self-regulation through the use of Codes of Practice. While this public–private partnership is a useful innovation, the rapid increase of visitor numbers, traveling farther and faster in new and larger boats, suggests new problems and obstacles will continue to surface. If the World Heritage site is to be saved, new protective measures must be established or visitor use may have to be curtailed.

Chapter 19

Appropriate Tourism Impact Assessment: A Case Study of Kaniki Point Resort, Palawan, Philippines

William J. Trousdale

There is a growing gap in the developing world between the accumulated information generated by tourism research and its practical application. Nowhere is this gap more apparent than in the relationship between tourism and its impacts on natural and human environments. This case study presents a practical model for impact assessment adapted for tourism development in LDCs, as a way to close the gap between knowledge (tourism research) and action (effective decision making and management). Appropriate Tourism Impact Assessment (ATIA) is a field methodology designed to assist decision-makers, project developers, and affected communities, to recognize local problems and assist in their remediation. ATIA can help create and maintain tourism sustainability in the developing world.

Kaniki Point Resort was a proposed ecotourism and scuba-diving project in the Philippines (Figure 19.1) The case study is a practical application of ATIA, to illustrate the opportunities and constraints of managing tourism impacts in a developing world setting. Impact assessment at an early stage of development is important to responsible tourism planning.

Tourism, Impacts, and the Developing World

Tourism researchers have conducted extensive research in tourism impacts (e.g., E. Cohen, 1978; Mieczkowski, 1995). Recently, academics and practitioners have come to a general agreement that these impacts should be addressed by applying a balanced planning approach to development: planning that incorporates public participation and issues of sustainability (e.g., Inskeep, 1991). Unfortunately, balanced planning in the developing world is rarely achieved (but see Long, 1993b; Trousdale, 1996), and the literature is still replete with developing world case

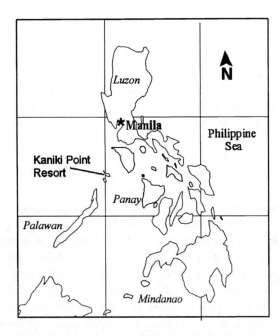

Figure 19.1. Map of the Philippines and Kaniki Point Resort.

studies chronicling failures in tourism development (e.g., R. Sofield, 1990). The fundamental reason for these failures is an ill-defined "messianic faith" in economic growth that negates the consideration of tourism's known adverse effects. Furthermore, developing countries often lack a participatory governance structure, strong regulations, enforcement capabilities, technical and managerial expertise, and the political will required to pursue a balanced planning approach. In an increasingly competitive marketplace, business promotion tends to displace the thoughtful anticipation of how to avoid tourism's negative externalities.

However, as countries gain experience with tourism, there is a growing recognition that anticipatory control of development impacts will lead to a better "quality of life," which is the underlying goal of development. This recognition is manifest as formal, informal, and ad hoc use of impact assessment applied within broader development processes (Abracosa & Ortolano, 1987). As a concept, impact assessment is familiar to many involved with tourism development (e.g., developers, funding organizations, professional planners, local governments, NGOs, community groups).

Impact Assessment: Trends and Opportunities

Impact assessment is a formalized set of procedures that seeks to identify, evaluate, and predict the sociocultural, biophysical, and economic impacts resulting from a proposed project, program, or policy. Recommendations are then made for appropriate mitigation and communicated to the appropriate decision-makers (unfortunately, not necessarily the public, as is the case in the Philippines where assessment documents are not made public). Impact assessment is often referred to as environmental impact assessment (EIA) or simply as environmental assessment (EA), although these labels tend to reflect procedures with a narrower focus on environmental and social impacts (World Bank, 1991).

The past three decades have seen a steady evolution in impact assessment, widening the range of techniques to include complex matrix analysis, expert systems, mathematical modeling, numerical simulation, quantitative risk assessment, and GIS applications. However, these increasingly sophisticated techniques are so expensive and often generate such voluminous reports that they obscure the assessment's use as a decision-aiding tool. Evidence from evaluations of impact assessment in developing countries suggests that expensive and time-consuming techniques are unlikely to be of much practical value in an operational sense (Bisset, 1987). Although strong regulations and policies may be in place, agencies are unlikely to have the budgets, staff, expertise, or political power to enforce them (Brillantes, 1993). As early as 1990, leaders in the field were recommending that impact assessments should regain focus on "the identification of ecological and social *issues* and *implications* of proposed directions in development" (original emphasis, Sadler, 1990). Impact assessment needs to be recast to reflect the reality that the regulations, policies, and laws in developed countries do not directly translate in the developing world. Faced with these limitations, agencies tend to concentrate their efforts on politically palatable projects or projects deemed to have potentially major impacts (e.g., heavy industry and dams), leaving many tourism projects relatively free of regulatory controls.

Without a realistic threat of enforcement, project developers simply comply with mandated procedures without substantive follow through, or else ignore impact assessment completely. This can be attributed to several perceptions:

- a general distrust of most environmental planning, which is often seen as an expensive regulatory nuisance needed for project approval that may also radically alter the project developer's "resort vision";
- ignorance about the beneficial impact assessment can make to project development;
- a desire to keep front-end costs at a minimum, especially when requisite engineering and economic analyses have been completed.

In other words, a cursory glance through the lens of a developer suggests that it often makes more sense to "ask forgiveness rather than permission" by developing first and addressing regulations later, if at all. In 1987, the Anuha Island Resort in the Solomon Islands was closed and later burned to the ground because indigenous concerns were subordinated to the will of a corporate resort owner (Roughan, 1990). In Mexico, the idea for a golf course and condominium development in Tepotztlan was abandoned after police shot a protester. On the coast of Quintana Roo (see Chapter 9), the construction of a cruise ship pier near Cancún is now an international environmental issue because of its potentially adverse impacts on the area's highly valued coral reef ecosystems (Patterson, 1996). Considering the growing influence of the tourism industry throughout the developing world, it is important to examine potential roles for impact assessment in tourism development.

ATIA as a Practical Alternative

The implementation of full-scale, conventional impact assessment processes is constrained by many factors that make ATIA an attractive alternative, particularly in less developed regions. The legal and practical reality of any impact assessment procedure typically involves considerable expense and is largely focused on the legislated requirements, regulated processes, and factual data. In addition, impact assessment often takes the place of a complete planning process. ATIA distinguishes itself from a standard impact assessment by considering both the technical issues and also the values of stakeholders (parties that are interested in, or affected by, the project). ATIA broadens the developer perspective through a partnership approach to assessment. Therefore, ATIA is unique. It dovetails the strongest recommendations from the impact assessment literature (focus on issues and implications) with the tourism planning literature (need for better planning that incorporates community interests). Combined, this approach is consistent with most legislated requirements (environmental certificates/permits) and has a high probability of being implemented (by educating and building the capacity of the developer in environmental management). The role of the impact analyst(s) in ATIA is critical in developing confidence from all stakeholders as to the value of the approach. In addition, the analyst(s) must have facilitation skills as well as knowledge of tourism and impact assessment. An ATIA analyst should:

- incorporate community participation and a focus on stakeholder values as well as technical data;
- make explicit efforts to incorporate learning for all stakeholders into the process;
- take a partnership approach with the developer, which not only educates but also informs and increases environmental management skills.

Simply put, ATIA can quickly and effectively provide a structured understanding of a project development that incorporates technical aspects and addresses the concerns and values of interested or affected parties. Within the national and local context, an ATIA: (1) provides a systematic overview of the site characteristics; (2) provides the current project status; (3) provides the probable impacts from alternative project options; and (4) outlines an appropriate monitoring and mitigation program from project inception through operation (see Asia Development Bank, 1991).

By using available resources and simple procedures such as checklists, matrices, and unstructured interviews, ATIA can help focus the dialogue surrounding a proposed project by providing a more informed decision-making environment that helps avoids shallow, polarized debate. Ideally, any impact assessment should occur at the prefeasibility stage before the final design and engineering is completed, when alternatives can still be considered. Nevertheless, consideration of impacts should never be discouraged. An ATIA can be performed at any point in time, or in discrete stages throughout the project development and operations (World Bank, 1991).

An essential ATIA task is to identify the most important impacts that warrant more detailed study or special attention from project management. To assist with this process of identification, Ahmad and Sammy (1985) have suggested six helpful impact criteria:

- the magnitude (amount of change);
- the extent (area affected);
- the significance (how important);
- the special sensitivity (country or regional concerns);
- the time frame (duration);
- the irreversibility (permanence of change).

The use of these criteria in the assessment can conserve valuable resources by concentrating on important information gaps and issues of critical community concern.

Using an Active Approach

Enforcement is a prominent issue. In the developing world, impact assessments are usually developer funded. For an ATIA to be effective it must seek the cooperation (or "buy in") by demonstrating to the developer the value to him, and to the community, of the assessment procedure, the study results, and subsequent recommendations. The impact analyst(s) should take an active approach to the project's positive impacts and promote the ATIA as a beneficial management tool, rather than simply a regulatory hurdle. This is contrary to a prevailing emphasis that regards impact assessment as a method to counter the adverse impacts of tourism (e.g., Ioannides, 1995). The ATIA provides a formal mechanism to demonstrate development benefits that would: (1) initiate local government and community support early in the process; (2) avoid costly environmental remediation or social compensation after the fact; (3) preserve the tourist product (the biophysical and sociocultural environment; (4) avoid costly delays in implementation due to unanticipated environmental problems or regulatory demands; and (5) increase goodwill and improve marketability.

The extensive tourism literature provides reasonable parameters to evaluate specific project impacts (Table 19.1). However, these general impacts, derived from field studies, must be sensibly contextualized with the type and scale of project being proposed and site-specific information (sociocultural, biophysical, economic, political, and regulatory). To achieve this, it is imperative to conduct physical site assessments, elicit information about local systems, and determine fundamental community concerns. Perhaps most importantly, an active approach to ATIA should foster learning, facilitate meaningful communication, and promote partnership between the developer, local governments, and communities.

The ATIA is an important step in beginning to address tradeoffs associated with change: what is likely to be gained and lost through different courses of action, and what is preferred from different stakeholder perspectives. The case study of Kaniki Point Resort describes a practical application of an active approach to an ATIA by detailing the anticipated impacts of the development and highlighting mitigation recommendations and management responses.

The Kaniki Point Resort Case Study

Kaniki Point Resort is being developed as a world class scuba-diving and ecotourism resort (see Figure 19.1). The development is located on the small is-

Table 19.1. Tourism Impacts Considered

Physical Environment
- Marine flora and fauna
- Terrestrial flora and fauna
- Soil
- Hydrology
- Climate
- Marine and fresh water
- Air

Sociocultural
- Anxiety over change
- Social and employment restructuring
- Migration patterns and changes in land values, use, and ownership
- Improved standard of living
- Changes in political–economic system
- Job satisfaction and income
- Growth in undesirable activities
- Change in value structure
- Receptiveness to change
- Culture as commercial commodity
- Growth in hostility towards tourists
- Access to resources and infrastructure use
- Human health and visual change

Economic Environment
- Job creation and employment increases
- Infusion of hard currency
- Economic diversification and regional distribution
- Seasonal employment
- Leakages
- Increased government revenues
- Lost opportunity costs
- Increased competition

land of Kaniki, near the larger island of Basuanga in the Calaman Group of Palawan in the Philippines. The proposed resort concept also included an agricultural component of primarily fruit-bearing trees (mangos, coconuts). Basuanga is rapidly becoming a popular tourist destination because of the high quality of the natural environment and excellent scuba diving.

In 1995, the developer of Kaniki Point Resort sought an environmental certificate in order to comply with government regulations (something not always done due to lack of government supervision). To obtain the certificate, the developer was required to complete a Project Description, a simplified impact assessment tailored to the Philippines. From a decision-making standpoint, the major constraint of the Project Description was that detailed site drawings were required, precluding the consideration of many design or project alternatives.

The developer attempted the assessment but viewed it as another step in the burdensome ladder of bureaucratic requirements. He perceived the assessment to be a request to justify the existing concept and not as opportunity to reevaluate and improve the project. Through a chance meeting between EcoPlan International and the developer, EcoPlan International was invited to take part in the assessment process for three main reasons: (1) the Project Description process was challenging and time consuming, (2) the developer felt that an objective expert opinion would hold more weight in the government decision-making process, and (3) the developer recognized potential improvements in the tourism product with expert evaluation.

Area Overview

The entire region of Northern Palawan is undergoing rapid socioeconomic and environmental change. The traditional slow–paced lifestyle is faced with an increasingly dynamic environment. Specifically, the municipality of Basuanga, a poor rural area with a population of just over 12,000, is saddled with high unemployment, compounded by in-migration of people from other resource-deprived regions of the Philippines. Stress on the existing social fabric is also seen in the poor health conditions and lack of adequate infrastructure (most serious being water, sewer, and roads). The primary causes of death include: malaria, acute respiratory infection, diarrhea, parasitism, and anemia or other nutritional deficiencies, all of which are preventable where poverty is reduced and medical access is adequate.

The ocean surrounding Kaniki Island has historically been a primary food source for local *barangay* (village) residents through the harvesting of fish and kelp. Like much of the Philippines, dynamite, cyanide, and illegal net fishing have been common in the area. Local fishers and business interests (i.e., pearl farmers) have successfully fought this illegal activity, preserving large tracts of the marine environment. The terrestrial environment is also beginning to feel the pressures of development, as deforestation is evident.

Site Description

The buildings of Kaniki Point Resort would occupy only 1 hectare of a 20-hectare privately owned waterfront land parcel. Roads and paths would traverse the parcel. Prior to acquisition by the developer, the site was used as agricultural land with poor production, due to lack of irrigation and unwise crop choices. An estimated 80% of the forest had been cleared. Remaining on the site were a few fruit-bearing trees (i.e., mango and coconut) and scattered indigenous trees (i.e., dapdap and fica). Hunting was also common on the site, putting stress on wildlife populations.

Kaniki Point Resort Objectives

The first activity of the assessment was to work with the developer to establish well-defined objectives for the development. The result of this exercise explicitly articulated a broad commitment to regional sustainability. It also created a development atmosphere that promoted a greater acceptance of the recommendations made in the final report. In this way, all recommendations could be validated by direct linkages to the developer's original set of objectives (Table 19.2).

Impact Assessment Constraints

One important consideration in the assessment was the fact that Phase I of the project was already under construction. This was clearly a limitation as there was

Table 19.2. Kaniki Point Resort Objectives

Kaniki Point Resort Objectives

- To furnish world-class accommodations in a natural/native setting for domestic and international clients.
- To supply jobs, education, and training opportunities to local residents in environmental construction, sustainable agriculture, scuba diving, resort service and management, and environmental management.
- To rehabilitate/reforest the island with valued ecosystem components such as fruit trees, hard wood trees, and other indigenous species.
- To provide nature trails for guest enjoyment and education.
- To provide skin-diving and scuba-diving facilities and instruction.
- To secure and help administer protected status for the coral reef–seagrass ecosystem to the west of the site and for the mangrove ecosystem to the east of the site.
- To assist local government units (LGUs) with community projects and events.
- To collaborate with LGUs in the eradication of illegal and disruptive activities (e.g., dynamite and cyanide fishing).
- To provide a secure livelihood for Kaniki Point Resort owners and workers.

little room for altering undesirable consequences from current construction practices. In a perversely positive way, the existing site work did help to ascertain the level of understanding and commitment by the developer to environmentally sensitive development before more building occurred. The Philippine government acts pragmatically in these cases by requesting a description of the current stage of development. Although this is not a desirable circumstance, because any construction will reduce future options, this approach does provide an additional opportunity for existing operations, like Kaniki Point Resort, to come into compliance.

Other limitations included the evolving regulatory environment, the inherent uncertainty in predicting impacts, lack of detailed local and regional data, and a general naiveté concerning tourism development displayed by the local communities. Furthermore, the analysis needed to be sensitive to the important issues and intentions of national legislation including the devolution of powers to local government promulgated through the Local Government Code of 1991 (see Brillantes, 1991) and the establishment of the Palawan Council for Sustainable Development. The new regulations played an important role in the report recommendations. For example, in 1993, the Palawan Council for Sustainable Development adopted "Guidelines for Tourism-Oriented Establishments in Palawan." These guidelines were meant to assist the local government units (LGUs) in developing and adopting their own regulations. When the ATIA report was written, however, no ordinance had been adopted in the Municipality of Basuanga.

Methods

Because very little baseline data existed and there were few financial resources available, costs were kept to a minimum by focusing efforts on critical issues of community concern, using analogous case study research and involving the resort staff and community members with data collection. Various rapid assessment methods and analytical tools were used to evaluate a broad cross section of potential impacts and integrated qualitative and quantitative predictions (Table 19.3). Critical were the use of formal and informal interviews and site inspections. Two site visits were conducted: the first in May, and a second in August. These visits were used to (1) provide a seasonal perspective (dry season/rainy season); (2) identify impacts; and (3) assess historical and existing environmental conditions. The second visit was also used to address gaps in the data.

Needs Assessment and Regulatory Overview

Tourism development in Northern Palawan was promoted at the national level. These national goals for developing tourism were articulated in *Philippine Tourism Master Plan*; the *National Physical Framework Plan, 1993–2022*, and the Palawan Council for Sustainable Development's *Guidelines for Tourism-Oriented Establishments in the Province of Palawan*. Executive orders recommended that tourism be promoted in less developed areas, such as Basuanga, in order to contribute to regional income distribution and economic diversity. Similar orders promoted foreign investment, and Kaniki Point Resort was a joint Filipino-American enterprise. Conversations with the developer suggested that Kaniki Point Resort's approach to tourism would reflect the intentions of these national mandates.

Locally, there was strong support for the development. Residents and officials were quick to point out that development of Kaniki Point Resort would help alleviate local poverty and economic hardship. Furthermore, some local residents felt that a window of opportunity existed for Kaniki Point Resort to contribute to

Table 19.3. Data Collection and Analysis Methods

Primary
1. Interviews with key governmental officials (both elected and technical experts at the national, provincial, municipal and *barangay* level).
2. Public participation through interviews with informal community leaders and interested or affected residents — often at local community gathering spots in order to incorporate a wide cross section of *barangay* members (gender and age).
3. Visual site inspection and initial resource inventory collection (both terrestrial and aquatic).
4. Ambient water quality sampling and subsequent laboratory analysis.
5. Continued dialogue with project developer, Palawan Council for Sustainable Development, and Department of the Environment and Natural Resources personnel.

Secondary
1. Research and collection of existing statistics, policy, guidelines, and other relevant data.
2. Compilation of documented case study work, focusing on the Philippine and Southeast Asian experience.
3. Interviews with Filipino and international experts.
4. Computer modeling and desk analysis.

long-term economic and environmental sustainability by helping to establish Basuanga as a world-class scuba destination (Figure 19.2).

Environmentally, local officials felt the Kaniki Point Resort development should be committed to Palawan's *Environmentally Critical Areas Network (ECAN)*. Residents and officials largely ignored the potential for negative social impacts, although a few voiced concerns about the rate of change caused by increased tourist influx in the area.

General Impacts and Regional Planning

Overall, the probable impacts from development of Kaniki Point Resort were expected to be beneficial, mitigable, or made insignificant by using appropriate technologies and responsible project planning and management. It was stressed that, above all, a commitment from the project developer to a philosophy of conservation and meaningful dialogue with the local communities underpinned the level of impacts. Many of the biophysical and social impacts identified by local residents and the author transcended the Kaniki Point Resort project, but posed a threat as indirect and cumulative effects of regional development.

Regional planning and management efforts, such as the ECAN, could contribute to sustainable resource use and help direct the local tourism development. Similar

Figure 19.2. Kaniki Point coral gardens. (Photo by Victor Organ)

proactive efforts are needed to combat impacts from tourism growth on regional and local systems. Growth pressures, only in part due to tourism growth, were already evident in shortages of goods, inflation, changes in land use, land values and ownership, and initial signs of crowding. Social as well as biophysical carrying capacity needs to be addressed through growth management controls, especially if the area increases in popularity as a tourist center. Clearly, the newly empowered local government units need to apply regional planning controls (not project specific regulations) to address many of the adverse impacts that were identified during the project assessment.

Matrix Overview of Impacts

Assessments of probable impacts from the Kaniki Point Resort development were detailed in a final report. However, in order to quickly communicate this information, an impact matrix (Table 19.4) was constructed (adapted from Rescan, 1993). This matrix is included in this chapter to illustrate one technique for highlighting impacts from a tourism development.

The table lists the *environmental component* under consideration followed by some of the *possible effects*. Then, the *stage and the associated activities* creating the perturbation are denoted. The fourth column *comments* on some of the potential mitigation measures or concerns specific to the impact. The fifth column denotes the *likelihood* (low, medium, high) of the impact occurring during the

Table 19.4. Sample of Impact Summary Matrix for Kaniki Point Resort

Physical Environment	Possible Effects	Stage	Comments	Occurrence Likelihood
Marine flora and fauna	Reduced illegal fishing through independent monitoring	S, C, O	Train employees and work with local authorities (Bantay Dagat—the local marine police)	High
	Sedimentation and stress on mangrove dependent species from bridge construction and operation	C, O	All in-water construction must be done with extreme sensitivity with use of existing technology (e.g., silt curtains) and depth of channel must be maintained to ensure boat traffic and water exchange needed for ecosystem health	Medium

S = site preparation: clearing, grading, landscaping, and agroforestry.
C = construction: structures, roads, trails, bridges, landscaping, and agroforestry.
O = operation: dining, lodging, scuba diving, hiking, boating, barangay tours, other water sports, and agroforestry.

identified stage, after recommended mitigation measures have been implemented. These measures have not been quantified and represent subjective impressions of impacts. Further scientific study and use of specific expert judgment could yield quantified probability distributions, but were considered inappropriate for this stage of analysis.

Often the likelihood is followed by the stage of the project it reflects (i.e., S = Site Preparation). These estimates are intended to communicate to the reader a qualitative expression of the impact analyst's judgment. No attempt was made in the analysis to assign discrete confidence factors, but very high confidence factors are associated with the high and low likelihood distinctions. Also no clarification was made between "actual risk" and "potential risk." More work would be required to specifically address the impacts from intensity and exposure (over time) with far more attention to cumulative probability of annual occurrence.

Enhancement, Mitigation, and Management Responses

Any human-induced change in the natural environment causes impacts. Even small-scale, environmentally sensitive "ecotourism" developments should be influenced by thoughtful consideration of their potential impacts. Careful design, planning, and the use of appropriate technology can greatly augment the potential benefits, and avoid or reduce potentially adverse consequences. This is clearly illustrated in the simple matrix analysis conducted for Kaniki Point Resort.

Based on the impact assessment recommendations, significant benefits should accrue to the biophysical environment (e.g., through reforestation and rehabilitation of the site), to the social environment (e.g., through increased income, livelihood, and cultural exchange opportunities), and to the economy (e.g., through infusion of hard currency, diversification). The most threatening adverse impacts were expected to come from building, road, and bridge construction. Many sociocultural impacts would not be specific to Kaniki Point Resort, although the resort would contribute to the cumulative effects of the rapid change in the region. To combat these potential impacts, recommendations were made for Kaniki Point Resort to promote meaningful dialogue with the communities and to become actively involved in regional planning, including the formation of strong regulations, effective enforcement by local government, and cooperation by tourism operators. The most important enhancement, mitigation, and management responses are listed:

- Erosion and sedimentation control techniques (silt curtains, retaining walls/seawalls, accommodating drainage patterns) should be utilized during all potentially disruptive construction and operation activities.
- Due to the uncertainty surrounding tourism development legislation actively being debated, consultation with local government officials should be conducted throughout the development process regarding scale, design modifications, and development standards.
- Employment and investment opportunities should focus on the surrounding communities.

- Substantive and responsive dialogue should be continued with the local communities to incorporate important indigenous knowledge and values in development and management of Kaniki Point Resort.
- Biophysical impacts (through simple surveys and observations) and social impacts (through continued dialogue with communities) should be monitored and managed.

Other, more specific, mitigation recommendations were also made (Table 19.5). The results of the impact assessment supported the issuance of an Environmental

Table 19.5 Specific Mitigation and Management Responses

Physical Environment
- Avoid disturbance or stockpiling materials in natural swales.
- Continue revegetation.
- Use of grading and sedimentation controls: drainage berms, settling basins, retaining walls.
- Special training for hazardous and toxic materials and proper storage facilities.
- Establishment and posting of tourist guidelines.
- For road construction: conduct major earthwork during dry season; follow contours of the land; provide for monsoon season drainage patterns; ensure compact or paved road surface to avoid sedimentation.
- For bridge construction: cut minimal number of mangrove trees; do construction sensitive to mangrove species life cycles; use sedimentation screens; allow for continued flow of water that will avoid scouring.
- For building construction: do major earthwork during dry season; use legal local building materials from a respected source where possible.
- Use standardized sanitation guidelines and facilities.
- Separate organic, inorganic, and toxic wastes and properly recycle, reuse, or dispose.
- Ensure that ecosystem components that depend on ground and surface water have access to resource and avoid excessive use of ground water that might weaken freshwater lens (use rain water collection if necessary).
- For all structures, roads, and bridges: appropriate scale and design standards should be used in conjunction with sensitive landscaping.
- Muffle motors (i.e., the developer had enclosed the generator in a scaled building and this had proven effective at eliminating noise).
- Follow the highest international and local standards concerning site design, planning, and construction.

Sociocultural Economic Environment
- Provide on-site medical facilities and communication/access to hospital.
- Follow the highest international and local standards concerning site design and planning.
- Provide cultural education opportunities for both host and guest populations.
- Train and hire local residents when possible, follow nondiscriminatory hiring practices and pay fair salaries.
- Work with local entrepreneurs to develop spin-off employment (i.e., local nature guides, boatmen, local crafts).
- Reinvest in local area.
- Make efforts to minimize economic leakages.

Compliance Certificate for the development of Kaniki Point Resort contingent upon the implementation of report recommendations.The most important factors contributing to this conclusion were:

1. the degraded existing biophysical environment and the willingness of the project developer to invest the requisite capital needed to rehabilitate the site and surrounding;
2. the fundamental orientation of the resort to ecotourism principles demands specific attention to an authentic and clean environment;
3. the high quality of existing ambient conditions (largely unstressed by excessive natural or man-made perturbations), which should minimize the risk of exceeding ecological system thresholds;
4. the scale of the resort would be sensitive to the natural and sociocultural surroundings;
5. the geographic isolation of the subject site would provide a buffer to both the natural and social environments and provide greater control for social stress–economic benefit tradeoffs;
6. the ability of the project to help alleviate the poverty level socioeconomic conditions of the surrounding rural *barangays*;
7. the area residents' strong support for the project;
8. the contribution of the resort project to national and provincial policy objectives.

Above all, this project was recommended for government certification based on the developer's demonstrated commitment to an ethos of equitable and sustainable development.

Conclusions

The systematic and active approach to the ATIA described in this case study served to: awaken new opportunities for community involvement; to alert the developer to modest changes in design that could have significant positive implications; and to introduce basic mitigation and monitoring programs that would have otherwise been ignored. Although the report was neither a highly technical nor data-intensive assessment, it effectively utilized existing information, perhaps the most important being community participation. Dialogue with the affected community facilitated an important two-way learning process wherein local information and values were expressed by the community and included in the assessment, and information regarding the potential effects from tourism were conveyed by the impact analyst to the communities.

By actively engaging the developer and involving the local government and host communities, the ATIA approach created opportunities to make the critical transition from knowledge to action. For example, by conducting follow-up research on the life cycles of local mangrove species, the project developer will be able to modify the design and timing of bridge construction in a more environmentally sensitive manner. Also, the developer is now working closely with the local governments. Besides contributing to the Environmentally Critical Areas Network, research for the assessment with local environmental officials revealed an opportunity to become involved with an integrated social forestry program. Finally, Kaniki Point Resort has expanded its communications with local communities. These represent only some of the sensible and inexpensive responses made by the project developer that will make a significant contribution to the sustainability of both the project and the region.

Whether or not all of the recommendations made in the final report will be followed remains unclear. It is equally unclear if a different, less responsive developer would have been as open, forward thinking, and proactive as the developer of Kaniki Point Resort. Nevertheless, the success achieved at Kaniki Point Resort suggests there is both the potential for similar achievements in the future for tourism development and potential applications to many other development projects.

An ATIA tends to be a discrete activity, in terms of both time and place, while human and natural systems are dynamic, change over time, and contribute to incremental movements that are difficult to determine in a "snap-shot" assessment (Hichcock, King, & Parnwell, 1993). Because of this, much legitimate criticism leveled at impact assessment is also true of ATIA and other methods for assessing tourism's impacts. This criticism includes assertions that too often conventional impact assessments are: reactive in nature; come too late in the development process; tend to be overly project or site specific; focus on immediate impacts; contain unconnected partial solution methods; and tend to have a single discipline bias (S. Holtz, 1990).

When impact assessment is effectively integrated with regional planning, however, it can be a valuable tool in the process of moving tourism planning away from anarchy and toward sustainability. Faced with the unique challenges of tourism growth in the developing world, applying an active ATIA approach can provide a practical alternative by making the most of "what is available" in order to encourage integrating, thinking, and learning about the environmental and social values inherent in pursuit of sustainability.

Chapter 20

Sustainability and Pilgrimage Tourism in the Kathmandu Valley of Nepal

Trevor H. B. Sofield

Nepal has many historic sites that are rich in built heritage, cultural distinction, or traditional significance. This diverse heritage reflects more than 30 indigenous groups whose unique languages, cultures, and religions have penetrated its mountains, hills, valleys, and plains. It has been said that Nepal has more temples and *gompas* (monasteries) per capita than any other country in the world, and the religious devotion of its Buddhist and Hindu populations has resulted in thousands of sacred sites. In this context, Nepal's rich history and religious monuments from Hinduism and Buddhism provide many places with considerable touristic potential.

For centuries, small indigenous communities have been responsible for the custodianship of sacred religious sites. In the past, relatively few pilgrims visited and the sites retained much of their environmental and religious integrity. However, modern transport now generates hundreds of thousands of visits per year, and the recent environmental degradation has created dissonance between the "host and guest" relationship. The fieldwork for this case study was conducted in 1998 and 1999 and supported by the Nepal Government and the United Nations Development Program (UNDP), in the context of research associated with two UNDP tourism projects at Svayambhunath and Changu Narayan. Fieldwork was supplemented by intensive library research and access to UNDP and Government of Nepal documentation. The case study examines the empowerment of the indigenous community as a legal and legitimate entity, able to sustain tourism development, tourism management, and tourism attractions at two sacred World Heritage Sites in the Kathmandu Valley of Nepal.

Empowerment

Empowerment of communities for tourism development requires a political framework that is either supportive (proactive) or at least neutral, not obstructionist. In situations of dual systems (traditionally oriented communities located in the social and political space of a modern state) there must be effective means whereby empowerment can be transformed from "legitimate" into legally sanctioned empowerment if it is to be a vehicle for sustainable development (Weber, 1978, p. 53). In his typology of power and domination, Weber drew a distinction between legal domination and legitimate domination. The latter is not necessarily dependent upon the existence of the state and is expressed through "traditional domination" in which personal relations are used as support for the political authority.

The processes leading to empowerment (the so-called institutional or "environmental change" of Wallerstein & Bernstein, 1988) depend on a shared willingness by community, individuals, and external entities (authorities) to initiate and undertake. A fundamental tenet is that the empowerment must be able to counter dependency. If it cannot or does not, then it cannot be defined as genuine empowerment. As Jacobsen and Cohen (1986) stated: "resources which cannot be applied to contended issues leave their owner impotent, while a position of strength without adequate resources to hold it under pressure is a temporary illusion of power, not its reality" (p. 110).

In the context of tourism development it is proposed that empowerment be regarded as a multidimensional process that provides communities with:

1. a consultative process often characterized by the input of outside expertise to which they have access;
2. the opportunity to learn and to choose;
3. the ability to make decisions;
4. the capacity to implement/apply those decisions;
5. acceptance of responsibility for those decisions and actions and their consequences;
6. outcomes directly benefiting the community and its members, not diverted or channeled into other communities and/or their members.

These proposals emphasize the necessity for positive support emerging from the public sector, working in partnership with peoples' organizations, if a project is to be sustainable.

Pilgrimage

In the literature of pilgrimage tourism, the seminal work of Turner (1973) provides a useful starting point. Shrines as major places of pilgrimage are visited by all the adherents of a religion, regardless of divisions into sects, ethnicity, or some other characteristic. Turner's concept was of sacred centers "out there," peripheral and remote, "excentric" to the centers of population and the sociopolitical focus of secular power, often located beyond a stretch of wilderness in the "chaos" surrounding the ordered, "cosmicized" sociopolitical world. While this may be true for many Christian shrines, it is less accurate in the context of Hinduism and Buddhism, and in the case of Kathmandu's shrines, E. Cohen's (1992) thesis, based on empirical observation of Buddhism in Thailand, is more opposite. Cohen suggested that where there is a fusion of religion and politics the same place will be the center for both, although the institutions are separate; there is thus a "concentric" rather than an excentric pilgrimage center. This thesis could be refined in a case such as that of ancient Nepal, when the Licchavi kings were considered reincarnations of Vishnu: both the religious head and the government head were combined into the one so that the pilgrimage would be to what we could term a "unicentric place of conjoint authority," a power place both spiritually and politically. Svayambhunath still retains an aspect of this in modern Nepal. Although the present king is constitutionally head of a Hindu state, every 12 years there is a great Buddhist festival called the *Samyak*, which draws together every single Newar in the kingdom over a 3-day period.

If we apply the Turner/Cohen theses to Kathmandu "geographe" we arrive at a concept I have termed "concurrence" concerning visitation to sacred sites. For a Buddhist from India, Sri Lana, Thailand, or Japan, the same journey could validly be regarded in Turnerian interpretation as a pilgrimage to an excentric place. For the secular non-Nepali tourist who visits Svayambhunath, the journey is also one to the periphery, away from the center of his/her society and its religious and sociopolitical institutions: it is the search for the "Other" (E. Cohen, 1992, 1998). Even in the 20th century with its superior technology of transport for the journey from Europe, the Americas, Africa, Asia, and Australasia, travel to Nepal is still distant, time consuming, and "out there." The same sites are also visited by nonbelievers for their historic or aesthetic qualities (Lewis, 1995, p. 68). Combining both theoretical approaches, visitation to the pilgrimage sites will *concurrently* include the sacred (pilgrim) and the profane (tourist). It simultaneously includes travel to both a concentric place (for national visitors) and an excentric place (for international visitors) (E. Cohen, 1992, 1998). The site, its temples, stupas, and history, intrinsically are both sacred and familiar (to the believer) and a place of religious significance but exotic (to the tourist). The behavior of the pilgrim is determined by religious protocol or *liminal* experience. It is a "power place" for pilgrims immersed in the cosmological significance of the site whereas for the tourist the site is a place of exoticism and curiosity, possibly fostered by a desire for an educational/cultural experience or some other secular rationale. The pilgrimage accommodates simultaneous participation and observation, the former by pilgrims in individual or collective acts of worship and religious ceremonies, and the latter by tourists. (Tourists as nonbelievers may occasionally also be participants depending upon the nature of the worship or ceremony, and may be able to participate at the margins.) In this context, a pilgrim may be clearly differentiated from a tourist by virtue of the motivation for traveling, which is intrinsically religious. Pilgrim actions are often accompanied by collective asceticism, sacrifice, and symbolic behavior; without the religious element, the journey would not be undertaken (Vukonic, 1996).

However, the distinction drawn between pilgrims and tourists by the International Workshop on Tourism held by the Christian Conference of Asia in Manila in 1981 is principled but not necessarily accurate: "The pilgrim steps gently onto holy soil: the tourist overruns holy places and photographs their remains. The pilgrim travels with humility and patience; the tourist travels arrogantly and in a hurry" (cited in Vukonic, 1996, p. 135). As will be noted below, the pilgrim rather than the tourist is, in the view of the management committee of Svayambhunath, responsible for most of the physical pollution and degradation of the site.

Heritage and Social Identity

The social significance of heritage lies in its association with identity: it is fundamental in helping individuals, communities, and nations define who they are, both to themselves and to outsiders. It provides a sense of "belonging" in a cultural sense and in terms of place. For the Newars of Kathmandu Valley, their custodianship of religious heritage sites such as Svayambhunath and Changu Narayan constitutes a key element in defining their sociocultural identity. In this context, "Place"—territoriality—has always been important for the Newar (Gellner & Quigley, 1995). The question of identity for the two communities at the two religious sites demonstrates with special clarity the intertwining of place and power in the conceptualization of "culture," as Gupta and Ferguson (1997) note, and the Newar tendency of "introversion" based on clearly defined and bounded territorial ownership, as described by Quigley (1995).

The UNDP Partnership for Quality Tourism Program

Through the agency of the UNDP, Nepal has been the location of an innovative experiment designed not only to identify but also to implement the elusive goal of quality in tourism. It has attempted this ambitious undertaking through the Partnership for Quality Tourism Project (PQTP). The three-tiered exercise incorporates local projects carried out between 1994 and 1998 at Svayambhunath and Changu Narayan in Kathmandu Valley. PQTP intervention enhanced touristic qualities of the two sacred sites of Svayambhunath and Changu Narayan by working in close cooperation with their indigenous communities.

Prior to the PQTP projects, both Svayambhunath and Changu Narayan exhibited significant physical degradation. Many of the buildings and monuments were dilapidated and in various stages of disrepair, with cracked walls, rotting timbers, missing windows, collapsing walls, and leaking roofs. Stairways and paths were also in a state of disrepair. Rubbish was strewn haphazardly everywhere, and in some places had accumulated so greatly over many years that smaller monuments and stupas had in fact disappeared under mounds of refuse. Additionally, the Harati Temple at Svayambhunath is used extensively for *pujas* (ceremonies to invoke the gods) on a daily basis, and after the *puja* a feast generally follows, which may involve several thousand pilgrims: all of the waste generated by the *pujas* was not disposed of by the pilgrims and simply accumulated in ever-increasing piles. On special occasions such as the Buddha Jayanti and Sri Panchami very large quantities of refuse were generated by the thousands of pilgrims for which no clean-up regime existed. Dogs and monkeys were a major hazard (both suffer from rabies), and hundreds of ravens also contributed to dispersal of garbage around the sites. Toilets were nonexistent and the surrounding forests were literally ankle-deep in fecal waste and garbage. There was a severe shortage of water on the hilltops, which compounded efforts to improve hygiene. Sanitation was the single greatest environmental problem associated with both sites.

Residents of the hilltops had once been able to manage the sites effectively, but that management had broken down and there was no single local institution able to assert its authority to maintain the sites. Physical degradation was accompanied by social degradation. The indigenous communities were unable to cope with the sheer volume of visitors. The PQTP realized that before any lasting rehabilitation of the sites could be attempted community involvement needed to be restructured to provide sustainable solutions to the degraded sites.

Other areas of concern included the way in which itinerant stall holders and hawkers were using the several hundred monuments as display sites over which they draped their products to sell to pilgrims and tourists. This practice commoditized and, in the eyes of some devotees, degraded the religious experience, obstructed pilgrims' and visitors' view of and access to the different monuments, and diminished their sacredness and significance. The spiritual experience and visual appearance of the entire complex and the environment had therefore been adversely affected. Tension between hawkers, pilgrims, and tourists over the aggressive selling tactics of the hawkers was also evident and was a major concern to the residents, especially because most of the hawkers were from outside the villages. Additionally, the complexes lacked appropriate signs and interpretation. Visitors to the area could not appreciate the full significance of the World Heritage Sites. According to local residents, many interpreters who accompanied tourists had extremely poor knowledge of the historical significance of the complexes as well as the monuments.

In view of the deteriorating state of the environment at this World Heritage Site the PQTP project goal for Svayambhunath was: "to establish and test an active, functioning and self-sustaining urban heritage site management model for possible replication in other sites" (UNDP, 1994). To be sustainable, the management framework had to empower the indigenous community, and "institution building" at the local level was to be an integral component of the project. The objective was to make qualitative improvements at Svayambhunath by assisting the indigenous Newari community to establish a social structure capable of managing the site on a continuing basis and to assist in undertaking activities such as waste collection and disposal, toilet construction, training of guides, provision of interpretive plaques, maps, brochures, a tourist information kiosk, reforestation, relocation of hawkers, and an awareness program for visitors.

The Indigenous Newar Community of Kathmandu Valley

The ethnically mixed residents of the Kathmandu Valley were fused into the kingdom of Nepal by Prithvi Narayan Shah in 1769. The Shah dynasty continues as the ruling dynasty to this day. The people of the Kathmandu Valley have practiced a mix of Buddhist, tantric, and animistic systems of worship. Hinduism has been the dominant religion of the kings; Buddhism has continued to flourish and was supported rather than suppressed by the rulers. It is often difficult to distinguish between the two main spiritual practices of Nepal because they are interwoven with "the exotica of Tantrism on a background of animistic cults retained from the distant past: and the result is a proliferation of cults, deities, and celebrations in variations unknown anywhere else on earth" (Locke, 1999, p. 98). In fact, Newars do not cease to be Hindus by virtue of being a follower of Buddha. This syncretism is reflected in religious sites, which encompass both Buddhist stupas and Hindu temples and statues of Lord Buddha and Hindu gods side-by-side within the same walled courtyard.

In the Buddhist and Hindu traditions of the Kathmandu Valley, the first residents settled around *pithasthann*, freely translated as "Power places of the gods," because the focal point of devotion and communication with the gods is at their residences (Dowman & Bubriski, 1995). Temples and shrines were erected at such power places and the Newar settlements clustered around them. Ever since, generations of the same extended families, the cornerstone of Newar indigenous society, have resided in such villages as priests and custodians of the sites, providing sustenance and welcome to pilgrims for hundreds of years (Bahadur Bista, 1999). The entire Kathmandu Valley is a "power place" of the gods and it has been called "Nepal Mandala," its shrines among the holiest places of pilgrimage in the subcontinent. The term "mandala" has two meanings. In Hindu/Buddhist cosmology it is a circle, a mystic diagram of varied form, and in this context the valley and its encircling hills symbolize just such a spiritual, powerful circle. The second meaning relates to Indian usage of the term to signify an administrative unit or country. "[F]rom the sixth century AD, in conjunction with the word Nepal, it signified to the Nepalese the Kathmandu Valley and its surrounding territory" (Slusser, 1982, p. vii). Throughout the centuries the Newar communities have exhibited "a pronounced territorial introversion—settlements were protected from the dangerous outside by a ring of deities and defensive walls" (Quigley, 1995, p. 300).

The rich Kathmandu Valley has benefited from stability. Agricultural wealth and trade with Tibet and India provided an environment in which the Newars were able to develop their vibrant artisan culture, which is universally acclaimed. They produced the intricately carved monuments, palaces, temples, monasteries, and courtyards that today constitute the built heritage of the Kathmandu Valley's villages, towns, and cities.

In due time, the Newar tribal society was replaced by the caste system of Hinduism and became hierarchically organized by occupational castes and subcastes with the priests at the apex. Newar caste divisions:

> make clear everyone's identity to everyone else and also mark out members of the community from outsiders who do not belong: Buddhist Newars no less than Hindu Newars are organized along caste lines. Caste divisions are underscored, as are all aspects of Newar social life, by pervasive ritual. While certain rituals bring together all the inhabitants of a particular settlement, many others are primarily oriented to a particular kinship group—a household for example, or a group of affines or perhaps a lineage. (Quigley, 1995, p.300)

The most distinguishing feature of Newar social structure is "its pervasively communal nature identified by compact urban settlements, with houses closely packed along narrow streets and lanes. Even the farmers are town dwellers, occupying special quarters of large towns or established in separate tightly knit villages surrounded by their fields" (Slusser, 1982, p. 9). The communal characteristics of Newar society are also conspicuous in their many socioreligious associations of common interest groups called *guthis*. The primary function of the *guthi* is to enable the individual Newar to fulfill his/her many socioreligious obligations through group action. Membership of a *guthi* may be voluntary in some instances and compulsory in others, it may be dependent upon common descent, or common locality, or a combination of both, and will entail a balance of privilege and responsibility. As a consequence it constitutes a basic element in-group identity and is a key integrative factor (Gellner & Quigley, 1995).

Traditionally, one of the chief functions of the *guthi* was the upkeep of monasteries, temples, and shrines through administration of proceeds from lands granted as endowments to certain deities and their temples and shrines. The unbroken continuity of Nepalese religious institutions and of the monuments themselves is quite closely related to the Newar *guthi* system (Slusser, 1977). However, the strength of this tradition has significantly weakened in the past 50 years or so, and many endowments were allowed to lapse with a marked adverse effect on the physical condition of the monuments of the Kathmandu Valley. Funds for their conservation must now be sought from other sources, hence the involvement of the UNDP in two of the most sacred sites: Svayambhunath and Changu Naryan.

Svayambhunath and Changu Narayan

Svayambhunath is a hilltop temple complex situated on the northwestern boundary of Kathmandu, with panoramic views of the valley and city. Its main feature is a Buddhist stupa, the Maha Chaitya, reputed to be more than 2000 years old. According to Nepalese legends, the site was once an island sustaining a blue lotus that contained the eternal flame of the Primordial Buddha. Manjushri, a reincarnation of the Buddha, came to worship here, and to make access from India easier for pilgrims he cut a passage through the Mahabharat hills with his thunderbolt sword and so drained the lake. This is the creation myth for the Baghmati River and Chobar Gorge. A fertile valley replaced the lake, the Newars settled there to farm and build their cities, and this became Nepal Mandala. Svayambhunath hill and its famous stupa on the summit mark the site of the original lotus island, the stupa being constructed over the eternal flame to shield worshippers from its searing light.

The permanent residential community who traditionally cared for this stupa now consists of 29 Newar households with a population of 212 people (November, 1998). Two historic *gompas* (monasteries) with resident populations of monks cared for the hilltop shrine. One *gompa* is run by Bhutanese Lamas and was established in 1780 at the invitation of the Gorkha king. The other *gompa*, established in 1954, is run by Tibetan Lamas, although Tibetan Buddhist links with Svayambhunath may be traced back at least to the 11th century. There is also an ancient Hindu temple, the Harati Temple, near the main stupa that attracts thousands of pilgrims per year and is the focus of daily *pujas* (religious ceremonies invoking the gods). Perhaps as many as 150,000 pilgrims and tourists visit Svayambhunath each year. They arrive every day of the year, although their numbers are greatest on festival days or auspicious days in the Buddhist or Hindu religious calendars. For Newar Buddhists, Svayambhunath is their preeminent sacred site and is regarded as the most important "power place" for the Valley and considered by many as the most powerful shrine in the Himalayas (Dowman &

Bubriski, 1995, p. 24). It is visited on a daily basis by many Newar associations from around the city (e.g., the *Uray* merchant caste from the Asan Twah market precinct of Kathmandu, Lewis, 1995).

Changu Narayan, with an ancient Hindu temple complex inside an enclosed courtyard, was the second site selected for PQTP intervention. Located approximately 13 kilometers east-north-east from Kathmandu, the temple is also on a hilltop, at an altitude of 1550 meters above sea level. Narayan, or Vishnu, is the preserver of creation to Hindus. His temple is often described as the most ancient temple in Kathmandu, based on a 5th century inscription on a stone pillar discovered inside the temple grounds. The Changu Narayan complex and associated statues, carvings, and artifacts cover 1600 years of Newari art and in effect chart the cultural development of the indigenous Newari people. The temple and surrounding buildings exhibit some of the finest stone, wood, and metal craft in the Valley. As with Svayambhunath the hill is forested, although the tree density has been severely reduced during the past decade with consequent erosion of the slopes.

Changu Narayan, a pilgrimage site for more than 1700 years, has become one of the three most important power places in Nepal for both Hindus and Buddhists. Of the 900 households (nine wards) in the village of Changu Narayan, 143 households are located on the actual temple hilltop, while the other wards are located in settlements up to 1.5 kilometers distant. About 80% of the village population are Newars and the other 20% are Chhetris, descendants of the warrior caste who had responsibility in ancient times for defending the fortress temple on the hilltop.

Institution Building at Svayambhunath

In 1994 no less than 17 different organizations were involved in a variety of different ways with Svayambhunath. Seven of these were *guthi* located within the Newar hilltop community. The other 10 were "outsider" (Buddhist and Hindu) organizations with specific interests in the site. In addition to these entities, the Department of Archaeology, the Department of Forestry, and the Urban Development through Local Effort (UDLE) department of the Ministry of Home Affairs were involved in physical aspects of the site rather than day-to-day operations and management. All of these organizations had their own agendas, worked independently from each other, and there was little or no cooperation between them. In the face of significant conflict between many of them, local people felt unable to control what was happening (Banskota, Sharma, Neupane, & Gyawali, 1995). Even something as basic as garbage removal had been taken out of their hands by a benefactor from New Delhi, who had paid a contractor living near the Bouddanath shrine some 12 kilometers away to keep the site clean. This contractor employed his own people from Bouddha who did not arrive at Svayambhu until after 10 am each morning. Banskota et al. (1995) found a strong resistance by the local Svayambhu people to assume responsibility for keeping the site clean as they had traditionally done for centuries because of the element of payment for "outside" sweepers. They considered they should "own" the task and any payment should be theirs. This attitude of resistance to outsiders reveals their disempowerment. The intertwining of place and power in the conceptualization of "community" was particularly apparent in Svayambhunath as the residents struggled to assert the control they had exercised for centuries.

The huge growth in visitation, both sacred and secular (touristic), had impacted in a number of ways on the social fabric of the custodian communities, and the traditional social structures were failing in attempts to maintain the integrity of the sites. The magnitude of the problem revolved around the presence of the sacred in which space was contested: sacred space versus secular space; private space versus public space; family space versus social space; leisure space versus work space; space controlled by community; commercial space controlled by hawkers; and bureaucratic space controlled by national government and its representative ministries. The distinction between these different spaces at times overlapped and clear demarcation lines were lost, so that pilgrims, tourists, and hawkers alike were contesting the spatial dimensions of the site, "invading" and cross-cutting each others' spaces. The private space of resident communities and monks was assumed in many ways to be public space, accessible to the curiosity and cameras of the tourists; family space became social space for visitors; the workspace of the resident community became the leisure space for visitors. Activities of the various organizations were on occasion mutually contradictory and inappropriate for some of the spaces, and tension was manifest between them. Some of the dissension may have been the result of contested hierarchies among the Newar castes (Gellner & Quigley, 1995). A more detailed ethnographic study than was possible in this framework of research would be required to examine caste issues in depth and is not pursued here, other than to note that caste itself may be seen as an allegorical reflection of the sacred/profane dichotomy contested over spatial dimensions of the sites.

To generate a more representative local organization and thus empower the indigenous Newar community, the PQTP utilized one of the 17 local organizations, the Maha Samiti (Buddhist Community Development Committee), as the recipient of its project funds to undertake the various tasks and activities mentioned above, provided it was able to widen its membership to include at least one representative from each of the 29 Newari households on the hilltop. This organization was an amalgamation of the Svayambhu Management Committee and the Svayambhu Conservation Committee, which had, 1 year prior to the establishment of the PQTP, attempted to increase coordination of effort by local institutions in order to prevent the continual decline of the site. It was therefore considered "tailor-made" by the PQTP to take up the challenge of growing into a viable local institution with the capability to take over the project on an ongoing basis.

Over the next 2 years the PQTP nurtured the Maha Samiti, assisting in drafting a formal constitution and having it legally registered through the UDLE as a local NGO (nongovernmental organization). It was necessary to hold a series of meetings to explore the understanding by all the different organizations of the situation, seek consensus on the need to take action, and formulate a plan of action. Subsequently, the Maha Samiti obtained support for a restructuring of community organizations that would implement that planning process. It was instrumental in bringing together the 17 different bodies and developing a single coordinated plan for the maintenance and upkeep of the stupas, temples, monuments, and grounds, in cooperation with the Department of Archaeology and the Forestry

Department. Its membership increased to include not only household representatives but a local women's group and a youth group. Training programs were initiated and the Youth Association of the Maha Samiti became the core for more than 20 trained guides, both male and female, as gender equity became an important aspect of the PQTP's work. Plaques, directional signs, and interpretive notices were displayed around the site. Seven toilets were constructed, five for local use and two for visitors to the site, and the UDLE provided a water tank on the hilltop for this purpose. A massive clean-up operation to remove the garbage that had encroached the outer perimeter of the stupa complex was successfully completed. Systematic cleaning of the complex was carried out by the Committee, and monuments were no longer buried in garbage.

The Maha Samiti developed a revenue base by charging car parking fees, an entrance fee (for noncitizens and nonpilgrims), a fee for using the toilets, guiding fees, rent from retail stalls and hawkers, and the sale of brochures, maps, and posters provided under the PQTP. It created the paid position of Site Warden and took over responsibility for hiring sweepers, collecting car park fees (40% of which went to the wages of the car park attendant), running an Information Kiosk, rostering guides, and supervising toilets. Cultural performances provide an additional opportunity for fund-raising. By December 1998, the Maha Samiti was operating smoothly and had held its first elections under its constitution in October of that year, with the community passing its judgement on the past performance of its office bearers by changing one third of them.

In terms of social (institutional) sustainability, the model of coordinating the 17 disparate bodies into a loose cooperative, with key responsibilities specifically tasked to designated subassociations and individuals, appears to have been successful. There might be significant tensions below the surface (there invariably are in collectives as diverse as this, especially when complicated by the vexed issue of caste and different religious emphases). But the administration by the Maha Samiti of the temple complex as an extremely important power place for pilgrimage by both Buddhists and Hindus, and as World Heritage site and a major tourist attraction for Kathmandu, it is functioning reasonably effectively. Due accord is being paid to the religious significance and integrity of the site by the management committee, so that certain practices and behavior are not permitted (e.g., photographing the interiors of some shrines and not allowing tourists physical access to others). This integrity and the distinction drawn between tourists and those visiting the site for religious purposes (citizens and pilgrims are admitted free of charge) are two vital components in setting the parameters for a degree of commercialization that will support rather than debase the site. Signage and the courteous instructions of the Youth Group guides assist in this objective. In addition, vendors are prohibited from displaying their wares against and over religious monuments and shrines (as was previously the case), although they are permitted to use the walls of monks' quarters. The space of the sites is now demarcated rather than contested. Dissonance is largely absent, the presence of tourists is mainly passive, the noncommoditization of festivals has minimized change to ritual, and so adverse cultural impacts from tourism at the present time are minimal.

The introduction of fees removed the need for subsidies or grants by government or donor agencies to cover wages. A degree of local employment was created and the residents of the hilltop were benefiting from the improved cleanliness, sanitation facilities, and more orderly management. Financial independence is a fundamental element of sustainability, and Svayambhunath satisfied this criterion in 1999.

However, while foundations for financial, social, and cultural sustainability had been achieved, environmental sustainability was still short of its goals. Two external factors, outside the immediate control of the Maha Samiti, were responsible. The first is that while rubbish removal and sweeping inside the temple complex was effective in keeping the site clean and garbage was deposited daily in a large container adjacent to the car park, the Kathmandu municipal authorities failed to empty the container regularly. Because the container had no lid, monkeys and ravens scattered garbage all over the place. The Maha Samiti designated a disposal site in the forest to handle the overflow, but it was located only 25 meters outside the perimeter wall of the temple complex and quickly reached capacity; monkeys, dogs, and ravens also scavenged there and garbage was once again being deposited just outside the perimeter walls. The community is dependent upon the municipal authority for removal of wastes from the hilltop and its inability to control this key aspect of environmental degradation threatened the site.

The second external factor that the Maha Samiti found difficult to control was the behavior of pilgrims and locals concerning disposal of waste, and toileting. No effective awareness program had been introduced to educate them not to discard rubbish wherever and whenever they liked, despite various attempts. The resident community was vocal in its complaints, especially of *Puja* worshippers who created significant piles of rubbish. The lack of general awareness about appropriate rubbish disposal among most worshipers was identified by the Site Warden as a major obstacle for greater effectiveness in maintaining site cleanliness. Hilltop residents said they preferred international tourists who were sensitive in this regard and as a general rule did not litter.

With reference to toileting, a small charge is levied for use of the toilets (2-5 rupees) and in this context a contrast was again drawn by the hilltop residents and the Warden between locals/pilgrims (especially from India) and international tourists. The former resisted paying the small fee and persistently used the forest, while tourists were consistent in their use of the toilet facilities. It was the pilgrims who were littering and polluting the site rather than the tourists, a refutation of the 1981 declaration by the Manila Christian Conference of Asia referred to above, even if the footsteps of the tourists were not motivated by religious devotion.

Changu Narayan and the PQTP

Following an assessment of the PQTP intervention at Svayambhunath a modified approach was developed for the project at Changu Narayan. The issues of pollution and littering were not as great, but many of the buildings, walls, stairs, and paths were in an even more dilapidated condition. In addition, about 200 priceless artifacts, including chariots more than 300 or 400 years old, stone carvings, and statues dating back to 1000 AD, and innumerable carvings and artifacts (stone, wood ,and metal) were simply lying around the site, suffering the depredations of time and weather with little or no protection: conservation was not extant. Much of the forest had disappeared and hillside erosion was evident. The lack of toilet facilities was a major concern. While it was a very active pilgrimage and tourism site, the indigenous community who had held custodianship of the site for centuries considered that it had little power to take remedial action. The same conflict with outside interests and government departments as at Svayambhu was evident at Changu Narayan. Rights of ownership or access to space was contested by different parties, as was the case in Svayambhunath, with "invasion" of social residential space by pilgrims and tourists alike a particular problem.

As with Svayambhu the process began with a series of public meetings to inform the community about the project and seek their support. While the village consisted of nine wards, in fact only those households constituting the community inhabiting the immediate precincts of the world heritage site were involved. This "community" was invited to suggest activities under the PQTP, and much of the resultant program derived from their proposals. It was thus much more of a bottom-up rather than a top-down planning process, with the community empowered from the beginning to participate in decision-making. Once consensus had been reached and the parameters of the program established, the PQTP team assisted the residents to elect a Community Development Committee (CDC). This was accepted by the government as having sole responsibility for implementing the project with the PQTP and coordinating efforts with line agencies such as the Archaeology Department and the Forestry Department. It was officially registered as a local NGO.

Under the Changu Narayan pilot project a more integrated community development approach was taken, although tourism development remained the point of access for facilitating social change. Empowerment was considered essential, and the responsibilities of the community were to be enhanced through the establishment of an elected representative community management organization (the Community Development Committee), the establishment of a Tourist Information Center controlled by the new Community Development Committee, and the organization by the community of an annual "Changu Narayan Tourism Festival" in addition to the numerous religious festivals.

A site-cleaning and garbage removal program initiated 2 years of intense activity, with the residents highly motivated to participate. Various construction activities transformed the site, and formerly abandoned *bajan patis* (traditional cultural performance stages and rest houses), with assistance from the Archaeology Department, became focal points for ongoing cultural activities associated with religious festivals. All 143 individual households within the site installed their own toilets, and stone paving replaced the mud paths. Beautification resulted in piles of garbage being replaced with gardens of colorful flowers, and with regular collection of rubbish bins the residents were more responsible towards rubbish disposal. A public car park, restaurant, and public toilets were constructed, set off by an impressive entrance gateway built in the traditional style. A successful Tourist Day festival was organized on February 6, 1998 and attracted more than 3000 visitors. Small curio/craft stalls funded under the Micro Credit Scheme were set up by village women, to sell locally produced items made as a result of the various training courses. The Tourist Information Center was functioning effectively, selling postcards, brochures, maps, and posters produced by the PQTP. Trained guides, who had benefited from English language tuition classes, were capable and competent communicators. Honoring a 1300-year-old tradition of looking upon visitors to the temple as honored guests, the CDC decided against an entrance fee. Nor were guide services charged, although visitors were invited to make voluntary donation for services rendered.

By early 1998 most project objectives had been achieved. The contests over space still continued but had diminished. The PQTP intervention had significantly improved the physical site and its hillsides and the village site management. Residents, pilgrims, and tourists all expressed satisfaction with the results. A striking although small example of resident "unconscious retaliation" had occurred in one instance, with the residents "invading" public space and transforming it into private space and space for social exchange among themselves. One third of the new car park, constructed specifically for pilgrims, tourists, and their transport as public space, was taken over by the villagers for spreading and drying their rice and millet, the paving representing the best warm and dry location for this process. To guard the grain against monkeys and ravens many of the women and children spent much of the day squatting in small communal groups among the grain, to the total exclusion of those for whom the space had been created! By mid-1998, however, the situation had changed. The Changu Narayan Tourist Information Center had closed. A brief excursion into Nepal's recent political history is necessary to understand the nature of the problem.

Decentralization and Dissonance at Changu Narayan

Over the past 20 years the Government of Nepal introduced a series of legislative measures designed to decentralize central administration and government services to the district and village level. Following the restoration of multiple-party democracy in 1990, the National Parliament introduced legislation to establish Village Development Committees (VDCs) and District Development Committees (DDCs), with responsibility for planning and implementing development activities at those levels. A key objective was to increase public participation in the development process. In 1990 this approach was strengthened with national NGOs and Community Based Organizations (CBOs) being sanctioned as partners of the two local government bodies in promoting development. The 1991 District Development Committee Act gave local government specific responsibility for development of specific sectors (such as district roads) and authority to contract support of any organization to do so, including NGOs and CBOs. Further moves to strengthen decentralization came with the passage in 1998 of the Local Self-Governance Act. This Act delegates authority and responsibility, and entrusts the means and resources to local authorities to make them more efficient and effective in local government, and to develop institutional mechanisms that are participatory and able to respond to the aspirations of the local people.

In Changu Narayan, the reliance of the PQTP on the newly formed CDC without involving the VDC in a substantive way inadvertently thrust the CDC into a power struggle with the VDC. The PQTP failed to take into account the contemporary political structure, which had modified the original political power structure of

the village and given authority to a wider unit than the community actually physically resident on Changu Narayan hill. Thus, while the hilltop residents had custodial responsibility for the temple site and were intimately and directly involved in
its day-to-day operations, they could only really exercise that responsibility under
the authority of and with the approval of the VDC. The channeling of PQTP funds
through the CDC *without formalized reference* to the VDC may be seen, in hindsight, to have challenged the primacy of the VDC, guaranteed by legislation, to
determine village-based development. The PQTP unintentionally gave one and a
half of the wards of Changu Narayan (i.e., the residents of the temple hilltop)
some exclusive rights and benefits not shared by the other seven and a half wards.
At the macro-community level the entire hilltop site became contested space, with
the VDC determined to assert its right to control that space over the residents
who actually lived within the space.

The VDC therefore took action to affirm its authority. An initial step was to pass
a motion in the VDC to close the CDC's Tourist Information Office, a simple enough
step because it had the support of seven of the nine wards' representatives. Perhaps more seriously, however, the VDC insisted on the introduction of a compulsory entrance fee of R60 for every visitor to Changu Narayan, a revenue-raising
exercise intended to benefit all 900 households in the village. It constructed a
tollgate across the entrance road just below the brow of the hill and set up its
own collection booth.

The difference on this issue of charging an entrance fee between the two Committees may be seen as an example of the ambivalence associated with some traditional theological values towards strangers. Buddhism, with its "encompassing tolerance," welcomes outsiders and relatively easily integrates them into its midst (E.
Cohen, 1998, p. 3). Hinduism, on the other hand, is stricter and will place bans on
entry by non-Hindus to many of its most sacred sites. At Changu Narayan, however,
there are religiously sanctioned rules of traditional hospitality, and for such reasons the CDC, as the host village occupying the space of the hilltop sacred site,
would prefer to treat tourists as "guests." By contrast, the VDC, most of whose
members reside outside the space of the sacred, view tourists as "customers" in
the context of the contemporary value of the "user pays" principle, who should
therefore be asked to pay (compulsory levying of fees). The District Officer, as
mediator in the dispute, has suggested a policy of not charging pilgrims and local
visitors to the site, but imposing an entry fee for tourists, as is the case at
Svayambhunath. This is widely practiced and accepted in many parts of the world
and is a compromise that is currently (June 1999) being explored by to the two
Committees.

In retrospect, the CDC established by the PQTP proved to be a partially inadequate vehicle for implementation of the project because of the intervention of
the VDC. However, given that the hilltop community had a centuries-old history of
custodianship of the site and a similar tradition of looking after visitors, it must
have appeared to the PQTP team as an eminently suitable repository of responsibility for the Project's execution. That has proved less successful than expected,
highlighting the need for a very thorough examination of the community-as-stake-
holder in the context of empowerment and for tourism initiatives to be integrated
into wider community development needs.

In the context of the assumed oneness or contiguity of locality/identity/community and the tendency to take that cohesion as self-evident, automatic, and complete, Watts (1992) reminds us that the failure of projects may frequently be based on an incomplete analysis of the actual situation. In the case of Changu Naraya, there was a facile mapping of cohesion onto territorially bounded space that excluded the greater part of the "community" as defined legally by the government under its decentralization legislation and socially by village residents. The fact that Newars are also divided by caste and religion as well (as locality) underlines the fact that "community" must not be interpreted as a whole. Empowerment is both a process and an outcome and, when used to assess community sustainability, it is important to understand that:

1. without the element of empowerment tourism development at the level of community will have difficulty achieving sustainability;
2. the exercise of traditional or legitimate empowerment by traditionally oriented communities will of itself be an ineffectual mechanism for attempting sustainable tourism development;
3. such traditional empowerment must be transformed into legal empowerment if sustainable tourism development is to be achieved;
4. empowerment for such communities will usually require environmental or institutional change to allow a genuine reallocation of power to ensure appropriate changes in the asymmetrical relationship of the community to the wider society; and
5. conversely, empowerment of indigenous communities cannot be "taken" by the communities concerned drawing only upon their own traditional resources but will require support and sanction by the state, if it is to avoid being short-lived.

In the case of both Svayambhunath and Changu Narayan, legislative action provided an environment for community-based empowerment while implementation requires a social process that extends well beyond the rhetoric of the political process. It is useful when assessing their sustainability to draw a distinction between the sustainability of the *sites* as attractors and the sustainability of the *management* (although both, of course, are mutually interdependent). The first is physical and the second is social and cultural. The empowerment of the indigenous Newar communities will necessarily be a vital part of the future management of these sites, even if at this point in time their shape and form cannot be finally determined. The identity of the Newar communities, their past and present and future, is inextricably linked to these two power places.

SECTION 5

CULTURE BROKERS

Chapter 21

The Culture Brokers

Valene L. Smith

Chester Seveck was a man of the past, born in 1890 along the coast north of Kotzebue. His father was an umelik *(captain of a whaling boat), and famous for having landed 22 bowhead, one 40 feet long. From him, Chester learned the traditional life skills. By age 18 he was already an experienced doghandler and that winter he sledged alone the 190 miles south to the gold fields at Nome to take frozen fish to hungry miners. He hoped to be an umelik like his father but times were changing. . . .*

At 17 Chester became a lay reader at the Episcopal Mission in Point Hope, and remained a staunch church member all his life but he also learned some shamanistic lore of Inuit angakoks. In later years, his peers considered him "different" because of his travels; some believed only a "powerful" angakok could have done so much in his life. There was jealousy and older Inuit were a little afraid of him.

Chester was the kind of young man you knew you could depend upon. In 1908 when the Federal government introduced reindeer into Alaska, Chester was invited to become a herder. This was his introduction to "White man's world" of paychecks and bureaucrats. He herded for 46 years and retired in 1954 with a government pension. Then he took up his new career as culture broker and tour guide.

Chester visited the Smithsonian Museum in Washington DC soon after the 1969 lunar landing, and saw the rocks Armstrong and Aldrin had brought back. He loved to tell tourists about his trip to the moon and the rocks he saw, because they were identical to the ones the astronauts had obtained. Inuit shamans sometimes did visit the spirit world for power to cure illness and group dissension. Inuit family sitting in a darkened igloo could hear them fly out through the smoke hole, and feel the whirlwind of their exit and re-entry. [Western skeptics might argue such extra-earth experiences were sleight-of-hand but traditional Inuit cosmology held the belief that shamans had such power. . . . see Weyer, 1969, p. 460.]

The tourists who visited Kotzebue between 1954 and 1980 found in Chester a charismatic living symbol of the Eskimo stories they had read as school chil-

dren. Thousands, perhaps millions, saw him (and Helen) on TV and in public appearances in Europe and Latin America and were inspired to visit Alaska, and Kotzebue, because of that marketing exposure. Chester was never a charlatan. He was a culture broker who independently decided the aspects of Inuit life he would share. He never spoke to tourists about "wife swapping" (sexual hospitality), incest, or homosexuality, as these topics were not openly discussed then in the guest's culture, either. He shared his knowledge of Inuit culture as he had lived it, as a "marginal man." The visitor-guests were richer for the cross-cultural understanding they gained of human adaptation to the Arctic while he guided them around Kotzebue.

Marginal Men and Women

Marginal men and women are cross-cultural mediators between Western and indigenous societies. Usually bilingual, some special circumstance (or interest) has afforded these individuals the opportunity to know, to move and to live in and between two cultures, as Chester did. A few other North Alaskan Inuit of his generation were also "marginal men" and understood Western ways. They became the 1960's political leaders who pioneered the Native Alaskan Lands Claims Settlement Act.

Outside metropolitan Kotzebue there are numerous Arctic locations where non-Inuit have chosen to live in the North as an alternative to urbanism. Some have investment capital to start up charter air services, or to construct lodges and promote hunting, fishing, and the wilderness experience. With long-term occupancy and close affiliation with Inuit staff, these settlers are other genera of "marginal men" and women affiliated with ecotourism. A somewhat parallel example includes Africa's "White hunters" who work closely with their native staff and interpret indigenous culture to their clients. Others may derive from an ethnic minority, as some Chinese have became the "marginal men" (or women) guides in Dyak villages of Borneo. These "go-betweens" are found in many locales and serve important functions of cultural interpretation, often with a level of detachment that is sometimes difficult for members of the indigenous cultures to attain. These bicultural informants fit the traditional interpretation of guides as pathfinders, mediators, and animators (E. Cohen, 1985).

The Culture Brokers

The term culture broker increasingly appears in the tourism literature but there has been little analysis of its significance. The discussion here identifies the responsibility of the culture broker as the mediator between hosts and guests, responsible for ethnic imaging and cultural trait selection. At the local level, guides are culture brokers, but as tourism has grown from a business to an industry, others including travel agents, government at all levels, and international agencies have assumed the leadership.

Webster's New World Dictionary of the English Language (1988) defines a broker as an "intermediary, or an interpreter, who negotiates between or brings together buyer and seller." A culture broker is the mediator between the demand and

the supply sides of tourism (Figure 21.1). The culture brokers are primary decision-makers, selectively identifying segments of the culture content to be shared
with outsiders, and many also serve as guides. Chester Seveck filled both roles.
First, as culture broker he chose from the entirety of Inuit culture those traits that
he felt would most interest the tourist, given his contact time with them was only
an hour or two. With a degree of ethnocentrism, his projected images should also
reflect well on Inuit society. Second, as guide he described the hunting skills, stewardship of the animals, and family values. He demonstrated male dancing, as a
hunter in pursuit of game. Helen showed the social dances of women, and demonstrated her skin sewing skills in the manufacture of Inuit fur boots (*mukluks*).
This local-level culture brokering is still operative in many areas of the world. The
quality of the experience relies heavily upon the integrity and knowledge of the
local guides. Chester benefited from his "marginal man" status, and the airlines
were able to offer the traveling public an unusual and quality experience.

On a regional scale, and dating to a century ago with Thomas Cook and his
peers, early travel agencies scouted for new destinations to extend their activities.
When they discovered something "new," as culture brokers they chose from a range
of visible culture traits one or two distinguishing characteristics to "define" this
society and used them in their advertising. When tour operators "discovered" Tana
Toraja in Sulawesi in the late 1960s (Crystal, 1977), three elements of this culture
were striking: the "thatched boat-like houses," the "princely heritage" of the people,
and their emphasis on elaborate rituals. "Princely heritage" was difficult to symbolize, and throughout Indonesia there are many dramatic house styles. Therefore,
the tour operators cum culture brokers established "hanging graves" filled with
mortuary statues as the definitive trait for Torajan culture. Kathleen Adams (1984,
p. 472), in her fieldwork in Sulawesi, recognized this arbitrary selection process,
and labeled the travel agents "brokers in ethnicity." As a consequence of the advertised emphasis on the death effigies, many tourists now ask Torajans about their
graves but almost none inquire about the houses or the significance of their
"princely" heritage. The emphasis on the "hanging graves" also had an unintended
effect on the world art market, for each wooden icon stolen from the graves is
now valued at US$30,000 or more as a collector's item. Torajan youth with little
conscience or interest in heritage are known to have removed the crudely carved

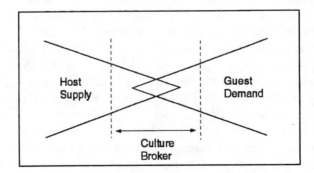

Figure 21.1. Culture brokers as mediators.

statues and sold them for small sums of money to buy their "aspirational wants" of T-shirts and Walkmans.

In yet another example, after NANA purchased the Kotzebue tour operation, the elected corporate leaders became the Inuit culture brokers in support of their own tourism enterprise. In deciding upon the type of exhibits for their Museum of the North, they chose to identify their Inuit ethnicity with the theme of animal and human migration from Asia into the New World. Alternately, they might have used their giant spirit, "Maniilaq," or they could have designed museum exhibits to illustrate their role as hosts of important Bering Sea trading rendezvous. Culture brokering on this level involves the conceptualization of culture norms, and a process of cultural selection and presentation.

Before Mass Tourism

Mass tourism began in the early 1970s. Prior to that time tourism was a relatively small-scale business. Individual travel agencies formed networks through international associations; hotels were primarily family owned and family operated. The essentials of tourism were independently handled with little supervision from governmental institutions.

The development of airplane travel into remote areas of the world, including the North American arctic, was greeted with great enthusiasm, for it meant access to new products including medicine, hunting supplies, and food, and gradually motorized generators and electrical gadgetry. "Bush" pilots did not negotiate for landing rights; they simply arrived. Arctic villages didn't float bonds to pay for an airport. Instead, to clear a runway, villagers gathered up stones and debris; the pilot laid out a perimeter of white-painted rocks and rigged a windsock. The usual terminal was a three-walled shack to provide weather protection. When Wien airline initiated tourism to Kotzebue in the late 1940s they bought an old warehouse from the local trading post, converted it to a dormitory, and the white station agent lived there and served as guide. In that era, when industrial nations listed their export earnings, they measured their worth in the heavy industries of iron and steel, mining and petrochemicals, followed by agriculture and manufacturing. Tourism was too insignificant to count.

Indicative of tourism in this era, in Hawaii in 1959 (the year of Hawaiian statehood, and the first jet flight to Europe but not to Hawaii) the Matson Steam Navigation Company, which operated the passenger liners and cargo ships between the US mainland and Hawaii, owned the four leading hotels on Waikiki Beach. They included the famed Royal Hawaiian, Surfrider, Moana, and Princess Ka'iulani, and none were over four stories in height. The 1959 visitor count to Hawaii was 250,000. The company was so discouraged by poor occupancy rates and the limited prospects for expanded tourism, even with advent of the airplane, they sold all four properties for US$17.65 million (Hibbard & Franzen, 1986). The number of visitors doubled within the next 5 years.

The institutionalization of tourism began in this era, and with it culture brokering was nationalized. Investment loans from the World Bank and International Monetary Fund to newly independent nations (Table 8.1) were granted on the premise that tourism was a potential source of employment and foreign exchange. The new postwar air carriers and their affiliate hotels now dealt with *governments* for traffic rights, construction of airports, and land for new hotels and other facilities. Governments became the cultural mediators—Do we want tourism? Will it benefit our country? Most nations took advantage of the loans and exercised their legal right to offer attractive inducements, including tax credits, and free or greatly reduced prices for land to attract airlines and hotel chains to serve their country.

Excitement and discussion on the future of tourism began to resonate and ripple. The American Anthropological Association symposium on tourism, which became the genesis for the first edition of *Hosts and Guests: The Anthropology of Tourism* (Smith, 1977), was held in 1974. That same year, the East–West Center in Honolulu sponsored a workshop to assess the impact of this (then) new business. The opening sentence to the resulting publication (Finney & Watson, 1975) asks, "Why do so many Pacific Island *governments* [emphasis ours] choose tourism as a major industry for economic development of their countries? (p. 1). Kloke (1975) opens his essay with "A number of South Pacific island *countries and territories* [emphasis ours] have made substantial commitments to the development of a new industry: international tourism" (p. 3). Robineau (1975) details the development of tourism to Tahiti by explaining that "until 1959, Tahiti could not be reached by plane except from Fiji over the 'coral route' . . . by seaplane via Apia in Western Samoa and Aitutaki in the Cook islands." "Since 1961, the opening of the Tahiti-Faaa international airport has made it possible for the big air lines to serve the territory," followed by the construction of the Club Mediterranée, and major hotels. He continues, "it was around 1965 that, in order to coordinate the Territory's tourist policy, a *Tourist Trade Development Office* [original emphasis] was erected. From that time on, a tourist policy was progressively elaborated and tourism was promoted to the rank of great pillars on which the Territory's economy was to repose" (pp. 61–75). The same era and publication carries the now-classic essay by Fijian John Samy (1975), "Crumbs from the Table? The Workers' Share in Tourism" in which he alleges that the development of "luxurious, multi-million dollar resort hotels creates not only resentment but also confirms prejudices" (pp. 111–124). Hiller (1975, pp. 238–246) pointed out that by 1972 the Caribbean was already the foremost region of the world depending for its development on the benefits of tourism. To illustrate his point, and the not-so-benign influence of government, he cites from a 1972 issue of *Travel Trade* (a North American travel industry journal) that the success of their industry depends on how the Caribbean Hotel Association "can persuade government it is in the overall interests of the islands' economy to grant exemptions and other assistance to the economy."

Government everywhere silently and effectively assumed control of tourism and became the national culture brokers, deciding when, how, and with whom they would interact in its development. Governments can do so, because only they have the legal right to control entry through their borders, to admit some individuals by grant of a visa and restrict others. Strongly Islamic nations still prohibit admittance to anyone whose passport contains an Israeli visa, irrespective of the traveler's religious affiliation. Saudi Arabia prohibited all tourists until 1998, and both China and Russia denied visitor visas to Westerners for decades after World War II.

Through their hirelings who generated policies and programs, governments initiated selective choices concerning the nature of their tourism in relation to their resources. As an example, the Seychelles islands are noted for their beautiful beaches and warm seas. In the late 1970s a German tour operator talked convincingly to government officials of the desirability of charter tourism—one plane a week would fill the hotel, ideal for noise abatement and limiting bus travel over their narrow roads. Several years later the government realized the extent of the financial leakage, as airline and hotel operations benefited the same company with virtually all the revenue. Guests were on full pension, just laid on the beach in the sun, and spent very little money in the community. The government subsequently cancelled the charter agreement, and the hotel was sold to a local company. The Tourist Board changed their promotion to upscale tourism using expensive small boutique "guest houses" and gourmet restaurants. The result was fewer visitors, but more revenue was more equitably distributed through the island (personal communication, Seychelles Tourist Board).

With control of tourism vested in government, including the mediating role of culture broker, reverberations began to echo. Kent (1975), discussing tourism in Hawaii as a "new kind of sugar" (a parody on their premier agricultural export) reports from the *Honolulu Advertiser*, "One morning recently, one Hawaiian resident remarked to another that the one-millionth tourist of the year would arrive in Honolulu by air that afternoon. 'Let's go out to the airport with a shotgun' was the response" (p. 169). Another comment from the same source describes a 1970 flyer distributed at the Honolulu airport, to discourage tourists, "Please, don't visit Hawaii until we can save what's left." But the official (government) 1974 Hawaii Visitor Bureau slogan read, "We've come a long way and it's important to keep the momentum going."

After Mass Tourism

The success of mass tourism, registered in arrivals and receipts, is illustrated best in the 1998 emergence of tourism as the leading source of foreign exports (Figure 21.2). The international emphasis of long-haul air carriers and multinational hotels chains further extended government authority at all levels. Competing airlines bid for traffic rights. Hotels sought land for convention centers, and subsequently cruise lines needed dock space, and bargained for cruise terminals that would increase local handicraft sales. Governments in turn allocated funds to NGOs to develop national images that would distinguish their culture and scenery. Culture brokering moved beyond mediating the hospitality needs of hosts and guests to selectively creating cultural icons (stereotypes) of national (or regional) destinations that would attract visitors.

The dynamics of this tourism growth eventually backfired, first in environmental degradation, either actual or potential, and second, as individuals and culture groups realized their voice of self-determination was fading, if not already lost. As noted in Chapter 14, numerous conferences revealed a heightened awareness of the necessity of landscape preservation. In addition, the Brundtland Report echoed across the world, mandating local input and advocating bottom-up administration. These were powerful wake-up calls, to break a spiral of unabated and undirected growth. From these movements a new international culture broker emerged, in the World Tourism Organization (WTO) and its affiliates: World Travel and Tour-

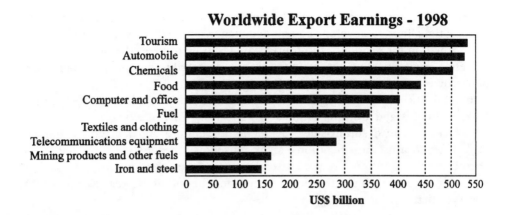

Figure 21.2. Worldwide export earnings: 1998. (Source: Tourism Highlights, 2000. WTO, reprinted with permission.)

ism Council (WTTC), Earth Council (EC), Green Globe, and LA21. Each entity has a mission statement, but in broad perspective WTO works toward mediating the sometimes flagrant competitiveness filled with disregard for everything except revenue. WTO addresses the needs of all member countries to participate in tourism. Their brokering for the supply side is to raise the standards of service through tourism training and education (their Themis program). They have also mediated cultural themes suitable for regional development, including Mundo Maya, the Silk Road, and the Slave Route. The centrality of these historic populations and their movements opens a vast range of individual ethnic symbols that can be effectively used for promotion. These new destinations will sustain increased employment in global areas where comparatively few tourists have traveled to date. As culture broker, WTO is broadening the geographic and cultural base of the supply side of tourism. Further, by training marginal workers for more skilled employment as hosts in tourism, those individuals are expected to ultimately enjoy a greater measure of discretionary income and leisure time. These employees, in turn, will become guests themselves, either at home or abroad, and support increased demand.

On the demand side, WTO is facilitating free movement for tourists (without visas), seeking to minimize terrorism and crime, and supporting expanded tourism among specific groups including the aged, handicapped, and youths.

Museums

Museums are increasing in importance as globalization appears to induce cultural homogenization. These heritage storehouses offer unique educational opportunities to the public, to school children, and especially to foreign tourists, all of whom are often drawn to them for visual validation of natural history and ethnography. The curators are culture brokers with multiple obligations: to provide historic time lines, to develop sequent occupancy, and to display natural resources as information for residents and tourists. In addition, to keep the museum active and encourage repeat visitations, curators are expected to mount special exhibits of narrower perspective but of timely importance.

Richard Kurin, Director of the Smithsonian (US National Museum) Center for Folklife Studies and Cultural Studies in *Reflections of a Culture Broker* (1997) introduces a theme of supply-side provider or "host culture" and demand-side guests, in relation to museum operations. Many museums are dependent on state-supported funding and must rely on attendance (in essence, popularity) as part of their evaluation, to secure the budget needs for the following year. Kurin (1997) observes that

> culture brokers study, understand and represent someone's culture (even sometimes their own) to non-specialized others through various means and media. 'Brokering' also captures the ideas that these representations are to some degree negotiated, dialogical, and driven by a variety of interests on behalf of the involved parties. (p. 19)

As Kurin documents, the development of displays can have controversial undercurrents. To prepare a Christmas exhibit in Jerusalem must involve representative input from Palestinians, Israelis, differing faiths, and also atheists. In the face of these contrasting philosophies curators as culture brokers must select from their collections the items to be shown and decide how they shall be displayed. The accompanying text and possible catalogs may provide an arena in which some of differing points of view can be detailed, further illustrating the mediation role of brokering. Special exhibits can be oriented toward age, gender, special interests, and timely topics such as wars and ethnic cleansing. The Anne Frank House in Amsterdam (see Chapter 16) has evolved over a 50-year period with differing emphases and interpretations. As Graburn and Mathers (2000, p. 691) affirm, "cultural interpretation *does* require expert mediation" [emphasis theirs], and "brokerage underscores the customer/client relationship."

Conclusion

Culture brokering is historically known as early as the 4th century AD, when local guides helped pilgrims find holy sites in Jerusalem (Sumption, 1975). The subsequent expansion of their activity as decision-makers is closely correlated with the growth of tourism and its increased politicalization. Now most culture brokers learn their craft in university courses. Many work in diverse offices, devising plans to heighten the visitor experience in ways that are environmentally sensitive. Others are professionally involved in tourism and guides are now professionally trained and licensed by virtually every host government. The emergent role of the WTO as global culture broker has set a new and higher performance standard for quality instead of kitsch, with emphasis on education at all levels. WTO programs, which are still new and formative, bode well for the future.

Chapter 22

Where Asia Wore A Smile: Lessons of Philippine Tourism Development

Linda K. Richter

The commitment to develop tourism is a policy decision fraught with politics but almost always couched in economic and social rhetoric. So it was in 1972, when President Ferdinand Marcos declared martial law in the Philippines and almost simultaneously declared that he was making tourism development a priority sector.

What followed was a transformation of Manila's skyline and the harnessing of this new policy sector to the President's political agenda. Perhaps no nation better exemplifies the use and abuse of tourism for political advantage than the Philippines. Prior to 1972, tourism had been a low-key interest, enjoying slow growth and modest expectations. All that changed after the onset of martial law.

Martial law was ostensibly declared to deal with Communist and Muslim insurgencies and labor and student unrest. The President also saw it as an opportunity to forge what he called a "New Society" of constitutional authoritarianism in which technocrats backed by Marcos would make the hard management and social decisions that the increasingly nationalist Congress was unwilling to pursue. Some critics ungenerously saw in the President's action a desire to postpone his tenure beyond his two-term limit, which would have expired in 1973. Press control, roundup of political opponents, and the dissolution of the Congress assured such criticisms had little exposure.

The President had a delicate problem. The situation had to be serious or else martial law would look like overkill, but the political environment also had to become generally stable quickly or foreign investment might dry up and foreign opposition to the "shattering of democracy" might emerge (Day, 1974). Tourism proved a useful response. It might seem counterintuitive to launch a tourism blitz upon declaring martial law, but President Marcos did just that. The government tourism slogan made martial law seem especially benign: "Where Asia Wears a Smile."

A Cabinet-level department was created to implement the new policy effort. In the next 8 years tourism arrivals quadrupled. No effort was spared to create a veneer of stability and attractiveness that might reflect positively on the Marcos

Presidency and the martial law era. With the hindsight of more than 25 years, it is clear that the policy proved ruinous and that succeeding administrations found in the politics of tourism their own opportunities and problems.

This chapter examines the Philippines primarily since 1972 as a case study in tourism development from which one can extrapolate some hard-won lessons that may prove helpful to other leaders and nations engaged in tourism development. Scores of nations are increasingly "banking" on tourism for economic and political gains. It can be a chastening experience unless authorities recognize that this new policy sector is no panacea, is volatile, and is extremely vulnerable to bad news from any quarter.

The Philippines paid dearly for the tourism development President Marcos launched, but it may still reap future benefits. Moreover, the lessons one can learn from the Philippines are not that tourism is bad, unworkable, or a mistaken strategy, but rather that tourism can unravel as fast as it develops and there are ways to assure that "Where Asia Wears a Smile" is more than a bittersweet slogan.

In the first section, six political "lessons" of Philippine tourism are laid out. These are derived from the Marcos era. They do not exhaust the insights one can take away from this period, but they highlight major points relevant to scores of other nations. In the second section the the Aquino and Ramos tourism policies are examined. The conclusion identifies continuing problems and opportunities for the Philippines in utilizing tourism for national development.

President Corazon Aquino, wife of Marcos' political rival who was assassinated in 1983, came to power in early 1986 following a discredited election, defections in the Philippine military, a popular uprising in Manila, and the forced exile of President Marcos. She governed during a time of great expectations, democratic resurgence, and political threats from both the left and the right.

In 1992, former General Fidel Ramos, who had served President Marcos until his 1986 defection and served Aquino as Secretary of Defense throughout her Presidency, became the first President elected under the new Constitution. He won a just-completed 6-year term with a very slim 24% plurality in a seven-way contest (Richter, 1993). The very different political environments of Aquino and Ramos allow one to assess the usefulness of the "lessons" of the Marcos period and to identify additional factors and constraints.

The Lessons of the Marcos Era: 1965–1986

Lesson One. Tourism Can Be a Versatile Tool of Political Leaders

President Marcos was not the first autocrat to see the tourist as a useful visitor. Franco of Spain in the 1930s also used tourism to soften the nation's fascist image (Pi-Sunyer, 1979). Most tourists stay in relatively few tourist areas and therefore what they see and do is controllable. Cleanliness, beautification, and security, a good exchange rate—these can be assured within tourist zones. Particularly under martial law, special courts assured tourists increased protection and criminals more severe sentences for crimes against visitors. Efforts to keep areas pristine were rewarded by favorable travelers' reactions that could be quoted at length in the locally controlled papers. Tourism could thus generate publicity for domestic consumption as well as the country's external reputation (Richter, 1980).

Tourists do not seek out political controversy but rather use the media for information about weather, the country's attractions, or news from home. They are typically unaware of what is being censored, what the real social and political conditions are, and the fate of dissident groups (Richter, 1980, 1982a).

Despite the fact that tourists generally avoid unpleasant topics, visitors still harbor the illusion that they've seen a destination. This is true even when they have moved in the narrowest of circles. Thus, the happy tourist is quite useful for his or her remarks about a trip because these impressions can generally be manipulated to reflect well on even the worst government.

Tourism proved politically useful in other ways as well. The typical development effort requires—as it did in the Philippines—the creation of a new infrastructure. The government can use the granting of loans and licenses as a marvelous opportunity for patronage. Under Marcos, government plans for phased development of tourism were shelved in favor of crash development that built in anticipation of influential mega-conventions. More than 12 five-star hotels were constructed in Manila in 1974–1976, though planners confidentially acknowledged it would be more than a decade before such capacity was needed.

The Philippines was not the first nation nor the last to use a prospective conference, fair, or mega-event as an excuse to bypass regulations and favor supporters, but the Philippines today stands as perhaps the saddest cautionary tale because of the lengths to which government institutions were raided to reward the President and his allies (Richter, 1989).

The facade of modernity did attract foreign aid and investment despite the fact that government insurance money was being used to build more luxury hotel rooms than public housing. While planners were horrified at the distortion of scarce resources, from the standpoint of the political elite, the crash development showcased the leadership and the ability of the government to transform the appearance of the key cities in ways readily apparent to outside investors, lending institutions, and loyal regime supporters.

Tourism also was a way to control real or imaginary opponents. A selective use of privatization policies by the President was justified in economic terms but primarily served the political advantage of the President. The crash hotel building and the changing fortunes of Philippine Airlines are just two examples of how the President proceeded (Richter, 1982a).

Lesson Two. Rhetoric Aside, Regime Politics Dominate Economic Policy

The Marcos government's primary objective was to turn around and stimulate Philippine tourism so that it would help legitimize the administration at home and abroad. Several key decisions illustrated the domination of political over economic considerations. First, the government launched the Balikbayan and the Reunion for Peace Programs. Both provided subsidized travel and preferential tourism benefits to Philippine visitors.

The Balikbayan Program was designed for those of Filipino ancestry and their relatives. The idea was to bring back those who had left the Philippines for a fresh look at the country under martial law. What was lost in money—most returning Filipinos stayed with relatives and did little touring—was more than made up in the use of statistics showing Filipinos flocking to the homeland. The Secretary of Tourism actually went so far as to declare martial law a tourist attraction (Richter, 1982b).

The Reunion for Peace program adopted a concept used by another formerly authoritarian government, the Republic of Korea. It subsidized the travel of former service personnel who had fought in the Philippines during World War II. Both groups could be assured to find the Philippines looking much better than they had remembered. Both groups had credibility in commenting upon the Philippine scene. Though most tourism based on nostalgia has "to sell the past to the future" (Dann, 1994, p. 65), in this case the sales job was to sell the present to representatives of the past.

Other decisions shaped the character of Philippine tourism in less benign ways. To boost tourist arrivals quickly, the Philippines unleashed a media blitz that promised "a tanned peach on every beach," that used suggestive advertising and the waiving of the curfew to facilitate a proliferation of sex tours to the islands, and that resulted in the development of pedophilia tours from several Western countries. The latter also stimulated the growth in child pornography videos.

To boost tourist investment from within the nation, the administration gave supporters up to 100% loans for hotel investment. When the banks balked at such loans, the government agreed to guarantee them. To garner foreign investments the government made still more enormous economic concessions.

This is a temptation most governments face in a competitive environment like tourism development; but insecure governments and poor nations are notoriously poor bargainers. The Philippines under President Marcos was both. To attract outside capital, investors were given great latitude, small equity requirements, tax holidays, guarantees of labor peace, waived or lax import restrictions. The political needs of the regime led to lopsided negotiations that brought few economic rewards.

Still, tourist arrivals soared. Measured only in arrivals, bed nights, and gross rather than net foreign exchange, tourism was a high-profile success—albeit not enough to fill up the new hotels. A succession of mega-events beginning with the 1976 IMF-World Bank meeting lured convention delegates with superb convention facilities and rock bottom rates (Richter, 1980).

Lesson Three. Luxury Tourism Often "Costs" Too Much

Under President and Imelda Marcos tourism marketing was targeted primarily for the "beautiful people," the sexually promiscuous male business traveler, and the politically useful. But there are problems with such a narrow focus. Lavish facilities for such clientele are costly to build, disproportionately need scarce foreign exchange for development and ongoing operations, exacerbate the "demonstration effect" on the population, lose value more quickly than modest facilities, and tend to use more capital than labor-intensive counterparts. As such they are a particular drag on developing nations.

The more affluent the tourism target, the more foreign exchange is lost in leakage for imports for the industry. Local products are seldom emphasized. Rather, the emphasis is on food, transport, entertainment, and facilities familiar to the guests. Once the regulations are waived for tourism imports there are no incentives for not importing items. For many Marcos cronies imports were lucrative not only for their tourism establishments but also as a way to obtain and then resell unneeded imports. Because there was no problem but rather an opportunity for the Marcos family and allies, the financial costs to the public were ignored.

The more affluent, "jet set" tourists the Marcos regime favored also reinforced the "demonstration effect"—the economic and social gap between hosts and guests. All this was happening in the context of worsening poverty for the average Filipino. Tourism was beginning to be controversial.

The more luxurious the tourism development, typically the less labor intensive it becomes, the shorter the time frame for maximizing high revenue returns, and the less flexibility tourism infrastructure has for alternative uses. It may seem strange that luxury tourism—particularly the large-scale five-star hotel—actually employs fewer people per guest than smaller establishments, but most studies bear this out. From self-service elevators to automated cleaning, food processing, and recreational services, luxury facilities need fewer personnel. Such establishments may also seek nonindigenous management in the entertainment and transportation sectors, with local people serving in menial jobs.

Luxury tourism, especially resort tourism, tends to follow a cycle of discovery, seasonal occupancy, and decline as newer resorts and destinations appear. Middle-class and less affluent charter tourism then comes in and gradually numbers are sustained only by massive cost-cutting. The very ostentatiousness, remoteness, and imports to sustain such establishments make it very difficult to switch to nontourism uses.

Lesson Four. Dependence on International Tourists Is Risky

Reliance on a few fickle international markets is dangerous. A nation's tourism industry needs a domestic market as well. The Philippines, in part because of the political interests of the Marcos regime, built its tourism during those years around the United States and Japan, the major aid-giving and corporate investors. The Philippine government was quite outspoken in stating it wanted influential visitors, not students, campers, or budget travelers. US tourists consisted overwhelmingly of Balikbayans now residing in the US and of US service personnel from the major bases then at Clark and Subic Bay.

Eighty-five percent of Japanese tourists were male and became associated with the public with the infamous sex tours. The Japanese were not necessarily more involved than other tourists in prostitution, but the language barrier and a propensity for organizing collective outings made their activities more obvious to the public, many of whom still remembered a brutal Japanese occupation during World War II (Benigno, 1993; Richter, 1994).

The Japanese government is unusually vigilant about the welfare of its citizens abroad and Japanese travelers are equally attentive to their government. In any event, Japanese tourism can turn on or turn off with alarming speed. A cholera scare or security issues can empty tourist establishments.

When international tourists for one reason or another did not come, there was no domestic tourism base to take up the slack. Precisely because the administration had made luxury tourism such a high-profile industry and had invested so much in it, the decline in tourists caused not only economic but political problems for the regime.

The government's reactions made matters worse. In desperation, the government became indiscriminate about the type of tourism that came. Certain towns became infamous for permitting child pornography and sex with international travelers. Then the government sought to keep Filipinos in the Philippines by levying heavy departure taxes. These met stiff resistance, in part because they were selectively applied. Both the public and the outbound tourist industry were furious.

Outbound Filipinos could not save the Philippine hotel industry even if they had been so inclined. The problem was overcapacity even if the international market had stabilized and grown slightly. The hotels were always on the verge of bankruptcy unless the government snagged a major convention. Because there were so many in financial danger, it was rather like the savings and loan scandal in the US in the mid-1980s. The hotels couldn't go under without dragging the economy down with it. As in the US scandal, the government took over much of the property and bailed out the rest. The political elite were not hurt. The Philippine economy and the government pension system were.

There were only feeble attempts to organize and promote domestic and student tourism and these were done largely for their public relations value. Even efforts such as Nayong Filipino, a cultural theme park, that highlights the religious and ethnic diversity of the Philippines was built next to the Manila international airport, making it clear just whom it was built to entertain and educate.

In fairness to the government, promoting domestic tourism is not easy in a developing nation short of forbidding nationals to travel abroad or strictly limiting such trips, as Korea and Taiwan did for years. Complicating domestic tourism in the Philippines are the logistics of traveling in a nation that is an archipelago frequently necessitating boat or air travel. Also, there is no tradition of religious pilgrimage except among the Muslim minority and that is directed toward taking the haj to Mecca!

The importance of domestic tourism in underdeveloped countries has been the subject of some debate. No one questions its desirability but rather the likelihood of it being successful (Archer, 1978; Wylie, 1993). Unless one is dealing with a nation like the US that has over 95% domestic tourism or a nation like India whose enormous size includes an upper class of over 40 million people and a tradition of religious pilgrimage, the domestic market is not readily substitutable in attractions and accommodations for the international one (Richter, 1989).

This is particularly true in the Philippines, where the problem is exacerbated by the way the industry was organized around affluent travelers, conventions, the military bases, and far-flung resorts. Prior to martial law some modest government-owned hotel and hostels were built in nonurban settings. They were successful with foreign and domestic travelers until political insurgencies since the late 1970s made their operation problematical.

Lesson Five: Tourism "Success" Is Not Necessarily Evidence of a Wise Development Strategy

Resources directed to tourism development must always be weighed against alternative uses of those monies, even when tourism itself seems to be profitable. Assessing the opportunity costs associated with one type of development strategy over another was not done in the Philippines. This was not because it couldn't be done. It could. The Philippines has sophisticated planners and economists. It wasn't done because the administration wanted to develop international tourism and it wanted an economic rationale for doing so.

The Philippine tourism industry was never a genuine success story. It was a facade of development; but it fooled many, which was after all the point as far as the government was concerned. The Secretary of Tourism, Jose Aspiras, was selected to head the World Tourism Organization for a time, so impressed was the travel industry with the Philippine "tourism miracle" (Richter, 1989). Even as late as 1993, there were some ready to give Aspiras a "lifetime achievement" award. The howls of protest in the now free press persuaded then-Congressman Aspiras to decline the award ("Aspiras Alibi," 1993; Benigno, 1993, p. 9).

Precisely because tourism is so manipulable, it is attractive as a measure of a nation's desirability. What tourism departments calculate—bed nights, length of stay, foreign exchange, convention use—are easily quantifiable and, as noted before, can be inflated with aggressive marketing, questionable promotions, and/or concessionary rates.

However, the industry's "success" also needs to be measured in terms of its impact on AIDs rates, prostitution, unwanted children, truancy, crime, and the exploitation of children for child labor, sex, and pornography. Yet, there is no mechanism or incentive in tourism departments anywhere in the world to monitor such developments. In many countries no government department tracks these issues. It is left to small, impoverished interest groups, churches, and human rights organizations to call attention to such problems (*Contours*, 1983–1995). Frequently, as under martial law in the Philippines, they cannot operate without harassment.

It was only when the negative impacts hurt the tourism industry, as in the case of AIDS or crime, that belated attention was paid. Even when governments have acted, typically their concern has been for the tourists' safety and health rather than the powerless child or the discredited prostitute.

Some will argue that this account is too harsh, that tourism can do much that is positive, by showcasing the arts and beauty of a country, providing a market for the performing arts and crafts, and generally enhancing opportunities for employment and the protection of otherwise economically nonviable places of historic or scenic value (Swain, 1993). This is, of course, true, but the characteristic measures of tourism "health" are too crude to assess this very well.

Still, politically it seems worthwhile that tourism foster such creative and artistic activities even in the absence of clear economic data as to its value. Such performances, crafts, and historical conservation become important if they are a means to sustain ways of life and skills central to the cultural identity of particular groups. This is especially important if, as with most minorities, they lack political influence except in terms of their collective identity and the value put on it by others.

Tourism has given tribal and Muslim groups in the Philippines more visibility than would probably have been possible without the industry. Indonesia is an even better example. An authoritarian Muslim government has been much more willing to exempt the Hindu island of Bali from its Islamization initiatives given its ability to exchange culture for cash through tourism. (It may also help that many Muslim communities have profound misgivings about the cultural impact of tourism!)

There are costs as well as opportunities to such tourism for all the groups involved. The culture and crafts will also be shaped by such exposure. The intrusiveness of strangers, bastardization of rituals, "airport art," and tacky souvenirs are endemic to mass tourism (Greenwood, 1989; Richter, 1989). Still, modernization, even without tourism, has had much the same impact. Further, one can be overly sentimental and romantic about other peoples' traditional lifestyles, while ignoring their desire to raise their standard of living (Harrison, 1993, pp. 19–34).

Lesson Six. Government Effectiveness Determines Tourism Viability

Effectiveness or what Samuel Huntington (1968) calls "political capacity" is not the same as whether government is "good" or "bad," democratic or authoritarian. It has to do with whether the government has the adaptability, resilience, cohesion, and skill to ensure order and guarantee basic services. In most developing nations such power does not penetrate the entire nation and may in some cases scarcely extend beyond the capital.

Stable and safe environments are important in ways the Philippine political elite tried to ignore (Richter, 1982a, 1989, 1993). In the Philippines, as in so many nations, tourism is promoted to provide the political and economic capital the government needs for development. Ironically, the industry requires a political capacity in place for law, security, and public interest legislation that is often sorely lacking. Studies from the Philippines and Thailand illustrate (Richter, 1989; R. Smith, 1992; V. Smith, 1992a) that too often sound plans are not implemented by government either because the resources or the necessary political will are absent to enforce meaningful regulations and critical standards.

Tourism not only needs political stability, it is more vulnerable to any form of insecurity than most policy areas. This is because it is built around the premise of pleasure. Even so-called adventure tourism is based on controlled excitement. The fragility of tourism has been demonstrated repeatedly over the last 15 years (Richter 1982a, 1989, 1993, 1997; Richter & Waugh, 1991). Tourism is a discretionary activity that can be pursued in scores of locales. That makes the industry both competitive and vulnerable.

Disaster, natural and man-made, can crush tourism. Disease, earthquakes, and typhoons ideally require competent emergency management skills, enforcement of sound health and safety codes, and a thorough risk assessment prior to tourism development and marketing.

A more common problem, however, relates to government expectations that tourism success will make the political system healthier and more secure. This almost never happens. Tourism, even well-developed tourism, is almost always destabilizing to some degree (Nunez, 1977). Hasty, ill-conceived development that accentuates the lifestyles of the elite and the foreign in contrast to the average people is a recipe for hostility.

Under President Marcos not only was there crash hotel development with few safeguards for the government financing involved, foreign aid also was diverted to build the properties that would be "owned" with little equity by those close to the regime. Few Filipinos could afford the grandiose hotels; those employed by the hotels were at the bottom of the employment ladder in most cases. Other government budgets at both the national and local level were raided to support the tourism effort. Prostitution soared (Richter, 1981).

All this tourism activity was taking place without public debate, in a country under martial law, at a time of enormous human rights abuses. Tourism became the target of the opposition. The "Light a Fire" movement torched several five-star hotels. The American Society of Travel Agents (ASTA) Conference was bombed, making a mockery of the speech President Marcos had just given the delegates on how rumors of unrest were media hyperbole! (Richter, 1989). In the insurgent South, Japanese tourists were kidnapped. And there was no backlash to the violence because few Filipinos had a stake in the industry, certainly none more than Marcos. Further, because most of those affected were primarily foreign, it was impossible to censor and control reports about what had happened. Tourism plummeted.

While attacks on tourists are rare, an industry that has thoughtlessly ignored the political and economic environment can be quickly undone. The Philippines also was an example of a more common political problem: general unrest and sporadic rebellion, even far from the tourist centers, may create an image that repels tourists. After the assassination of Marcos' rival, Benigno Aquino in 1983, capital flight, immigration to the US, and a falling GNP discouraged both business travel and discretionary visits.

Can these problems be avoided? Not entirely. However, tourism's contribution to the overall situation can be minimized. It is common for tourism planners to do attraction inventories in attempting to determine their tourism plans and priorities. As has been argued elsewhere (Richter, 1994), it is probably more important to do a political risk audit. Such an audit would attempt to assess political factors to be considered that may affect the pace, scale, and type of tourism that is desirable. For example, even quiet recognition of insurgencies could encourage planning and marketing that avoids such areas. In many parts of the Philippines tourism infrastructure is inaccessible because of Muslim separatist violence or other guerrilla activities. (Martin, 1994, pp. 36–37).

Since labor peace is critical to the industry, encouragement of indigenous hires, training, small-scale labor-intensive establishments, and progressive labor–management relations are important for securing popular protourism attitudes. Similarly, a slower pace of development and more modest facilities could have been less disturbing, provided more opportunities for adjustment and corrections, and proved less costly in both economic and psychological terms.

Even with a deteriorating situation, the tourism infrastructure would have been more capable of alternative uses for offices and apartments if it had not been built on such a luxurious scale and often in such remote areas. Ironically, in a country like the Philippines, even under a repressive regime, tourism development could have used resources better, assured more secure short-term success, and avoided tourism becoming the source of controversy it eventually became. Neither Marcos nor the Philippines benefited from the lavish excesses and the country is still coping with the tourism-related problems spawned in the Marcos era (Hall, 1992b; Richter, 1987a, 1987b, 1989, 1993) (see Chapter 10).

Learning the Lessons, Picking up the Pieces: Tourism Policy in the Aquino and Ramos Administrations

Tourism was not President Corazon Aquino's only (nor even major) problem when she came to power in February, 1986. President Marcos had stolen an election so blatantly that neither his own military, the public, nor the international community was willing to look the other way. His ouster was street theater at its finest. When he was finally whisked away to Hawaiian exile by the US military, Aquino took over a government whose very institutions had been disbanded or co-opted. Her political tasks were the restoration of democracy, the development of a new constitution, and the restoration of basic services (Richter, 1987b).

To do that, she had to simultaneously capitalize on any revenue-producing sector that could ease unemployment and garner precious foreign exchange. Tourism was a logical priority. Moreover, the government had become the largest owner of hotels in the country. As the five-star hotels went bankrupt in the 1980s, it was the government that was left holding the properties because the legal owners were the Marcos family or cronies without substantial equity in the properties. The hotels and resorts had to be made profitable either through the restoration of tourism and/or their sale to private bidders confident that the government could rejuvenate tourism.

There is evidence that the Aquino administration learned well the lessons of the Marcos era. But it wasn't easy to undo what should have been prevented in the first place. Three examples clearly demonstrate how difficult it is to correct problems of inept, corrupt, or socially flawed tourism.

First, the Aquino government tried to garner domestic and international confidence by adhering to a rule of law in the disposal of Marcos properties. An Assets Privatization Trust was established in 1986 that, along with other efforts, sought to sell nonperforming assets, which were mostly tourism properties or assets of the former President. Yet clear title to the properties was often difficult to obtain. In the meantime, 17 of the Marcos homes became tourist attractions open to the public. To encourage public trust, Aquino stipulated that funds collected would be used to fund the languishing agrarian reform program. Opportunities for joint ventures between the government and the private sector also made it less risky for investors to participate (Garcia, 1990, 1991).

Second, the tourism secretary struggled to get control over a bureaucracy bloated by patronage appointments from the Marcos era. In 1987, the number of employees was reduced from over 1300 to 700. Separation pay was generous and all procedures followed. Nonetheless, those fired filed a class action for reinstatement and won. In 1991, they were ordered back on the payroll with back pay! His successor, Secretary of Tourism Nazalina Lim, inherited a department with severe morale as well as financial problems (personal interview with Nazalina Lim, 1992).

Third, the government sought vigorously to reorient the marketing of the Philippines to put the emphasis on culture and scenic attractions rather than sex tours and pornography. De-sleazing was not an easy or particularly successful effort, but by 1986 there was an added urgency to the task: the threat of AIDS.

Tourist-generating governments were warned that pedophilia tours sent from their countries were not welcome. Individuals would be prosecuted in Philippine courts. Philippine communities, like Pagsanjan Falls, that had acquiesced to pedophilia activities were removed from government tourism brochures and maps (personal interview with Nazalina Lim, 1992). ECPAT, a child advocacy organization, remained critical of the government's approach, which they said singled out a few poor people for economic penalties, when it was poverty that had encouraged participation. The real offenders were seldom punished (personal interview with ECPAT, 1992).

Tourist promotions abroad and marketing efforts by the government junked suggestive posters and an emphasis on the beauty of Filipinas for more wholesome advertising. In conjunction with that, the government tried to discourage foreign men from acquiring mail-order brides or visiting the Philippines only to bring home a Filipina (Kruhse-MountBurton, 1990).

The Mayor of Manila was zealous in his crackdown on unsavory tourist belt establishments that encouraged prostitution, but there is evidence that the problem has moved elsewhere in the metropolitan area and is flourishing in Cebu (personal interview with Nazalina Lim and personal observation, 1992). Many upscale hotels continue to charge a "lady guest fee," though blatant advertising of sex tours in Japan and elsewhere has declined.

The Aquino administration applied Lesson One from the start. It demonstrated how tourism can serve to legitimize the new government even as it discredits the old one. Aquino needed tourism for many of the reasons Marcos did: to influence domestic and international political elite.

In her case, the agenda was to highlight the excesses of the Marcos years and contrast them with her own lifestyle and plans for the future. She hoped to project democratic values and economic good sense deserving of investor confidence and increased foreign aid. That was critical, for many influential leaders and investors had been badly burned by the Marcos debacle.

To do that, she took five steps. First, she refused to live in the bulletproof Malacanang Palace, but instead turned it into a museum of the Marcos excesses. There visitors could see Imelda's 1000 pairs of size 9 shoes, the 17 mink coats, the vault filled with empty jewelry boxes, and all the other luxuries somehow accrued on the President's $10,000 salary (personal tour, 1987). For 6 years, the Palace both earned money and demystified the Marcos family while providing a contrast to the more spartan lifestyle of Aquino.

Second, by putting the other 17 Marcos palaces on display she could again accentuate the corruption of her predecessor and earn some money until she could unload them. Third, Aquino and the story of her rise to power became a tourist attraction. The Department of Tourism developed a "Freedom Tour" that included stops at places in the Manila area that figured prominently in the overthrow of Marcos and in Aquino's personal history.

The DOT began a major promotional campaign aimed at criticizing the old regime while highlighting the new one. "Come to the New Philippines" demonstrated Aquino's adeptness in shaping the political uses of tourism to her own agenda, which fortunately for the Philippine people no longer included raids on the treasury or a personal financial link (Richter, 1987a).

Fourth, the government also attempted to diffuse economic opportunities in tourism and to enhance low-cost domestic and international tourism with a Home-Stay program. Unfortunately, the government could not provide enough training to help the fledgling entrepreneurs so the program remained small (personal interview with Nazalina Lim interview, 1987). Efforts were focused on social tourism and historical preservation, particularly at Corregidor and within the walls of Old Manila (Garrucho, 1989, p. 194).

The government was generally successful in assuring that tourism revenues subsidized other efforts like agrarian reform rather than negotiating bad deals for the sake of prestigious foreign investment. Import restrictions were tightened somewhat and duty-free stores were expanded to encourage more purchases within the country.

At first these initiatives seemed to work. Tourism improved after years of stagnation as the political system stabilized and the economy grew. Unfortunately, tourism in democratic regimes proved no more immune than in authoritarian ones to political unrest. Seven coup attempts during her 6-year term crippled Aquino's ability to do much more than hang on (Richter, 1990, p. 534; Richter, 1997).

While Aquino's government could not fully undo the errors of the Marcos period, it made an important start in insisting tourism pay its own way, that economic gains not be sacrificed to political expediency, and that national identity be tied to the culture not the exploitation of its women and children. She also made certain that tourism serve to legitimate her power and the extraconstitutional way it was acquired.

Ramos had just the opposite problem from Aquino. She took power in a euphoric environment with the press treating her almost as a saint. She could never fulfill the hopes of her followers and she soon would become a target for would-be usurpers. The Ramos administration ironically benefited from the low expectations held for it. Ramos was an earnest and colorless leader, elected in a seven-way presidential contest. He was not a "new" face, but rather was associated with both the Marcos and Aquino governments. Nevertheless, he presided over some major economic and political progress.

Ramos built on the tourism foundation laid by Aquino. He continued a Tourism Master Plan developed in 1991, which was designed to be a blueprint for tourism until 2010. (Chon & Oppermann, 1996, p. 35). He continued and expanded privatization efforts, sought to link tourism development with support for rural areas, and linked tourism to his ambitious "Philippine 2000" program.

The latter was designed to make the Philippines a Newly Industrialized Country (NIC) by the millennium. Within the program 19 key areas were identified as priorities because of the positive spillover effect they would have on the entire economy. Tourism was one of those so identified. Several of the infrastructure and transportation components benefited tourism, but more importantly they were integrated into the overall development of the nation.

There was also an attempt made to diffuse tourism development throughout the islands by promoting clusters of attractions in several areas. That had been done and undone during the Marcos years, but this time it was coupled with efforts to develop Cebu's international airport and other regional airports as a means of bypassing the polluted and crowded capital. So far, it has not worked. Over 92% of all international tourists continue to visit Manila, though arrivals to Cebu are encouraging (Gaborni, 1997a).

The President was also not able to diminish the problems associated with sex tourism. The sex industry once erroneously linked primarily to the US bases was always more closely tied to tourism. Currently, the upsurge in tourism has been matched with a dramatic rise in prostitution. In fact, as AIDS spread into Asia, the problem of child prostitution became much more serious. Increasingly younger and younger prostitutes are sought so that tourists feel less vulnerable to AIDS. In reality, it does not protect them and it certainly does not protect the children (Hall, 1992b; "Metro Manila Declared Hot Spot for HIV," 1994). By 1995, the United Nations Children's Fund estimated that there were over 100,000 child prostitutes in the Philippines, or 10% of the world total.

The Philippine government has encouraged tourist-generating nations to crack down on child abusers and has sent one high-profile sex tour boss to jail (Boseley, 1996, p. 7). The Internet and other global communications have facilitated the sex tour industry and the exploitation of children, making international efforts imperative. ECPAT and other international groups have kept up the pressure and publicity on the Philippine problem, but much more needs to be done.

What President Ramos did succeed in doing was to provide the political stability that allows tourism as well as other sectors to flourish. That is perhaps the most important lesson to be learned from his predecessors and surely the most difficult to assure. Under his tenure, international tourism arrivals reached 2.2 million (Gaborni, 1997a; WTO, 1997a).

Conclusion

Philippine tourism continues to struggle with the legacy of the Marcos era, but two successor governments have made clear to the public the high price of those policies. Lessons drawn from these policies have been important for shaping subsequent plans. Aquino particularly recognized the political usefulness of tourism (Lesson One) to legitimize her administration and discredit Marcos.

Both Aquino and Ramos, while supporting tourism rhetorically and financially, have sought to guarantee that tourism programs subsidize general development rather than vice versa (Lesson Two). They did this by decreasing government ownership of Philippine Airlines and hotel properties through privatization where possible. Ramos has also been adamant that tourism be strategically integrated into other public investments in infrastructure that benefit citizens as well as tourists.

Both leaders have deemphasized luxury tourism (Lesson Three) in favor of tourism programs targeted at a broader clientele. However, unloading the luxury hotels of the Marcos era continues to be a slow, costly process. Similarly, though Aquino recognized the desirability of a domestic tourism market and the fickleness of international tourism (Lesson Four), she inherited an infrastructure geared to foreign markets. She tried to control sex tourism, but undoing a thriving industry proved impossible. She was also dependent on the US and Japan, both countries central to tourism generally and prostitution specifically, for aid and assistance in controlling rebel factions.

Ramos, on the other hand, took office as the US bases were being dismantled. In the process, the radical left was losing a powerful symbol for organizing opposition to the government. He has not led on the sex tourism issue, but he has been a tireless advocate for new markets, including those for tourism. Currently, Japan and the US each generate less than 20% of the tourist arrivals—a much healthier balance than before (Kobayashi, 1997).

With less dependence on any one market, it should be possible to control sex tourism without crippling the tourist economy. However, Ramos' tenure (1992–1998) coincided with the enormous growth of the Internet, which has created an advertising outlet for sex tourism that has been increasingly difficult to control (ECPAT, 1997).

Finally, Aquino's policies demonstrated that the reverse of Lesson Five is also true: erratic tourism arrivals are not necessarily evidence of a poor development policy. She took many positive steps to foster tourism's role in Philippine development, but she did so at a time of great political unrest. Every coup attempt derailed tourism initiatives for months. She knew that overall government effectiveness determines tourism's viability more than mere attractions (Lesson Six), but her administration was trying to restore the economy, rehabilitate a political system, and garner international credibility even as two guerrilla movements and numerous military factions challenged her rule.

Ramos had fewer internal challenges and by the end of his tenure in 1998 his relentless protrade approach was paying political and economic dividends. However, the sudden financial crisis in East and Southeast Asia, which began in 1997, threatens the Philippine goal of Newly Industrialized Country status by the year 2000. Despite an erosion in the nation's economic prospects, the Philippines has not fallen as far or as fast as other nations in the region where speculative investments had been more prominent. Moreover, tourism to the Philippines continues despite a decline in intraregional arrivals.

The 1990s represented a new era for the Philippines in that the US no longer had bases in the Philippines. For the first time in over 350 years, no foreign troops were on Philippine soil. Conversion of the bases to nonmilitary use has accelerated. As the Philippines becomes more attractive for investment, it is hoped that the efforts of the Aquino and Ramos administrations to assure that tourism supports the growth of nontourist jobs will continue. Planned diversification is critical (Mak, 1993).

A new variable in Philippine tourism development is Joseph Estrada, the newly elected President of the Philippines. He was Vice-President under President Ramos, but he is from a different political party and his political moorings and background are far different from those of recent presidents. For example, he lacks a college education and is best known as a movie actor. Business elite are dismayed at his populist rhetoric while the powerful Catholic Church is horrified by his macho, womanizing image.

So far, Estrada has offered no clues as to the course he will pursue vis-à-vis tourism policy. His crackdown on crime while Vice-President was popular but not terribly successful. Based on his rhetoric, he is likely to be more sympathetic to tourist industry labor groups and to have around him confidantes less enamoured with external investment and more protective of indigenous businesses.

Finally, the Philippines is very much a part of the global effort to "reinvent government" through increased privatization and a major restructuring of the public sector to decentralize power. Both experiments are from outside modern Philippine culture and history, which has emphasized government involvement in the economy and until recently a highly centralized state (P. Kelly, 1997; Kobayashi, 1997). If the nation can develop wise tourism policies at all levels that integrate the industry into the broader needs of the population then the Philippines will provide still more lessons—this time in sustainable development—from which we can learn.

Chapter 23

Putting "Culture" Into Sustainable Tourism: Negotiating Tourism at Lake Balaton, Hungary

J. M. Tim Wallace

Recently, when an image seemed to be present in the glass windows of a new, Clearwater, FL, office building, someone interpreted the image to be an image of Mary, the mother of Christ. Soon thousands of people, often from far away, flocked daily to the location to marvel at what many perceived as a miracle. The visitors had defined the cultural significance of this site. Whether this site continues to develop as a tourist attraction depends on the guests continuing to value a certain interpretation of the site. Access and growth of the site will also depend on the commitment of the hosts to sustain the tourism at the site.

Sustainable tourism depends as much on hosts' and guests' cultural definition of a tourist destination as it does on the desire to protect the environment. The negotiation over the definition of a tourist destination has an impact on the environment and on the host culture and society. The removal of local people from a newly established "national park" directly affects the environment because park development may have more impact on the environment than previous human activities. Can tourism be sustainable, that is, can tourism be developed while minimizing changes to both the environment and the local culture and society? The degree to which sustainable development through tourism is possible depends on the negotiation among hosts and guests as to which interpretation of the touristic value and meaning of the destination predominates.

Defining Tourist Destinations: Guests Versus Hosts

Sometimes the guests have more control over the cultural destination of a site. When I traveled in 1995 with some Hungarian friends to Transylvania in Romania, I found another interesting destination that had been culturally constructed by tourists: Dracula's Castle (Bram Stoker's 1897 fictional mixing of Hungarian folk themes with a 13th century historical figure, Vlad Dracula, a Walachian Prince who had constructed an eerie castle on a desolate mountain in Transylvania, then part of Hungary). Before setting out from Hungary by car I had read a guidebook entry about Vlad's castle. Raised on a steady diet of Bela Lugosi and Boris Karlof horror movies, I insisted we see it during our excursion of this famous region.

Although the castle of Stoker's fictional Dracula was located near the Ukrainian border, it is the restored castle ruins of the historical Vlad in the village of Aref, central Romania, that has become the tourist attraction. As we got closer to Aref, my Hungarian friends kept asking Romanian ethnic Hungarians along the way to find the castle. Apparently, much was lost in the translation of "Dracula" to these local citizens, because they only scratched their heads in befuddlement at the question. Only with repeated reformulations of the question did people finally understand where we wanted to go. We knew we had finally arrived at the place when we saw the castle rising above a small village that was crowded with cars with foreign license plates and rife with handcraft booths. Official Romania is not happy with Vlad's association with Stoker's Dracula and so the interpretation signs in the castle only made favorable references to the historical Vlad, but the local tourist art entrepreneurs had no reservations. It was only here that the Stoker Dracula connection was made. I had finally found satisfaction after the long trip to Aref, because I wanted to believe that I had found and seen "Dracula's castle!" I had contributed to the construction of a tourist site with special meaning for the fictional Count Dracula's fans.

Another instructive case is the *Alarde* ritual of the Spanish town of Fuenterrabia described in a case study of Davyyd Greenwood (1989). The *Alarde* is an ancient, commemorative ritual re-creating the town's victory over besieging French forces in 1638. The color and pageantry of the ritual attracted lots of tourists, so many that in 1969 the municipal government decided that the ritual should be performed twice in the same day to give all the onlookers a chance to see it. This public recognition of the economic importance of the event to the town severely stunned many of the participants. Two years later, Greenwood reports, the *Alarde* ritual was on its last legs, abandoned by the dozens of volunteers who had supported the ritual every year.

By ordaining the *Alarde* a public event to attract outsiders into the town to spend money, the municipal government made it one more of Fuenterrabia's assets in the competitive tourism market. But this decision directly violated the *meaning* of the ritual, definitively destroying its authenticity and power for the people (Greenwood, 1989, p. 179). In this case the hosts who performed the ritual refused to renegotiate with the guests a culturally significant event that had become a tourist attraction. They preferred to abandon it rather than to change its meaning for the benefit of tourism.

Negotiating a Definition of a Tourist Destination

There are some cases where neither the hosts nor the guests have full control over the site's cultural definition. The interaction between hosts and guests is really the process of negotiation. It is in this context of constructing a cultural definition of a tourist destination that I would like to discuss the case of the Lake Balaton resort region in western Hungary. A review of this case shows that host communities who are heavily dependent on the economic component of the definition allow the guests to define the site. The hosts may accept or reject the guests' definition as long as they accept the consequences—that the tourists might not come back. Communities that have a diversified economy will be better able to control the cultural definition of their tourism destination. The host community may have initially defined their locality in specific ways, but once tourists have gained control over the definition of the site, changes to the site are dependent on the guests' reaction—in effect, a negotiation process. If protecting and sustaining the environment becomes a part of the negotiation, the level and mechanisms of environmental protection will be those that maintain or enhance numbers and/or spending levels of tourists.

Sustaining tourism does not mean protecting the natural environment, because decisions about environmental protection are made in political and economic contexts. As political and economic contexts change, and as the tourists change, what gets sustained may change, too. Sustainable tourism must include three basic elements: first, the cultural and economic significance of the site to the hosts; second, the value of the site to the guests; and third, the level of commitment and cooperation needed to maintain the site at a physical and cultural level acceptable to both hosts and guest. In the end, sustainable tourism depends on what is important to both the hosts and the guests. In the rest of this chapter, I will explain how Lake Balaton provides a clear example of how the cultural constructions and negotiations among hosts and guests over time affect the development of a nature-based, recreational tourism destination. The analysis presented here is based on three summers of ethnographic research largely between 1993 and 1995 at Lake Balaton and the surrounding region (Figure 23.1).

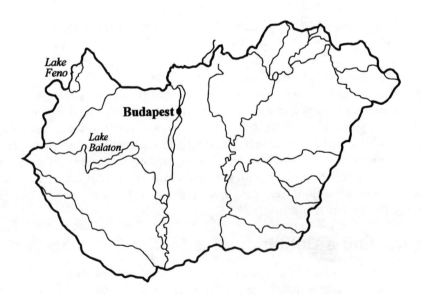

Figure 23.1. Map of modern Hungary with Lake Balaton. (Source: Martha Lampland, *The Object of Labor: Commodification in Socialist Hungary*. Chicago: University of Chicago Press, 1995)

Lake Balaton: The Hungarian Sea

Hungary is about the size of the state of Indiana and has a population of 10.2 million. There were at least two tourists for every Hungarian, since over 20.6 million international tourists visited Hungary in 1996, making it the fifth most popular tourist destination in Europe, and eighth in the world (Figure 23.2).

Earnings from tourism account for approximately 25% of total exports. Between 250,000 and 300,000 people are directly employed in tourism, and another 200,000–300,000 jobs in other sectors are indirectly connected to tourism (Eullul, 1994, p. 55).

Lake Balaton is Central and Western Europe's largest freshwater lake. It is located about 100 kilometers from Budapest and is reached by road and rail along both the hilly northern and flatter lower lying southern shores. After Budapest, it is Hungary's most visited tourist destination. According to the Central Statistical Office of Hungary, about 25% of all foreign tourists stay at Lake Balaton, usually spending more hotel nights there than tourists who visit Budapest (Kozponti Statisztikai Hivata, 1994a, p. 151). Nearly all the tourism is concentrated in a 6-week period from July to August. Its shallow depth, lack of waves, many "beach" areas, and wide array of diversions, restaurants, rooms, houses, and apartments to rent around the lake currently have made it a desirable attraction for Central European families seeking safe swimming sites for their young children during their summer vacations. Each town builds and controls its own *strand*, a small strip of green, grassy area giving access to an abbreviated 2-meter sandy shore in front of the lake's waters. During the high season the *strands* are very crowded with children running around the shore area, roasted bodies sizzling in the sun and dozens of snack shops with long lines of men in Speedo bathing suits stretching out in front of them. The principal attractions of the Balaton today are family-oriented, recreational activities connected with water: swimming, sunbathing, sailing, and relaxation.

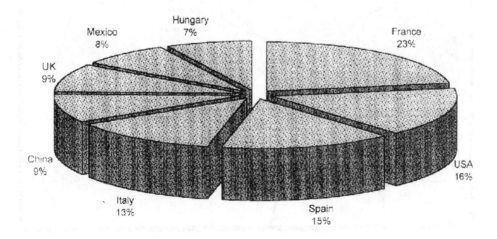

Figure 23.2. Top country destinations for international arrivals: 1996. (Source: WTO Tourism Highlights, 1997.)

Most of the guests in the high season are international, usually German speaking, who stay in private homes and apartments. Local officials estimate that only about 20% of all tourists stay in hotels. This makes it difficult to determine the exact number of tourists visiting Balaton, because most private citizens do not report income from their tourism lodging activities. It is estimated by local government biologists that about a million tourists a day visit Lake Balaton during the high season.

Geographically the lake is uniquely shaped. Its 598 square kilometers of surface space is elongated somewhat like a long zucchini cut in half. Except for Tihany (Figure 23.3), a small peninsula jutting into the water on the northeast shore (Figure 23.5), its width varies between 10 and 14 kilometers, while its length is 77 kilometers. The lake is very shallow throughout—averaging about 3 meters—except at Tihany where it is deepest at about 12 meters. The shallowness has distinct advantages and disadvantages. It warms quickly, from at least 16°C by mid-May

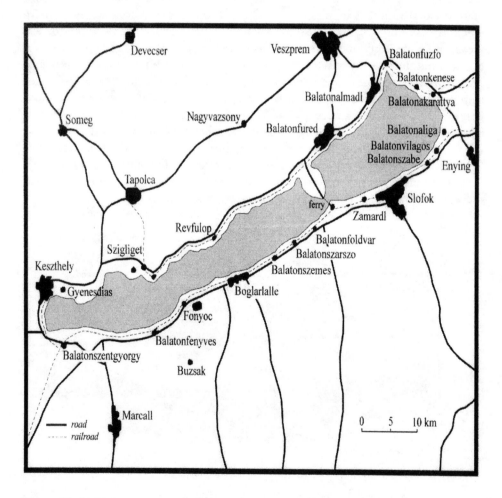

Figure 23.3. Map of Lake Balaton and surrounding towns. (Source: T. Sebestyon. *Balaton. **Budapest: Corvina, 1991.**)

through early October and as high as 25–27°C in mid summer. There are no waves and the depth changes very gradually, so parents generally need not worry much here about the safety of their children when they enter the water. The disadvantages also stem from its shallow depth. If the water gets too warm and stagnant, oxygen levels can get so low that massive fish kills occur. Tourists don't like to see dead fish floating by when they are swimming. The lake bottom sediment is so close to the surface that the swimming churns up the muddy bottom, making the water cloudy. Many tourists think muddy water is bad for them, but local people regard the lake's mud as mildly curative. The water warms the low mountains on the north shore and gives the region a near Mediterranean climate during the summer, making it ideal for vineyards.

Early History

Historically, the hilly northern shore has been noted for its vineyards, wines and fishing, while the flatter, marshier, boggier southern region was known for its grain and stud farms. The Romans introduced vineyards. Roman ships plied Lake Balaton—Lacus Pelso, as it was called on ancient Roman maps. Later, Slavs settled in the area and gave it its modern names.

The invading Magyars, not related to the Huns, arrived from Central Asia around 896 AD, eventually settling the old Slavic village sites or building new ones and constructing churches and monasteries. Alliance with the Austrians brought a baroque renaissance to the region, still reflected in many church buildings and in the religious art that adorns them (Keresztury, 1989, p. 1). One of the best examples of baroque architecture in the area is Festetics Castle, the palatial estate of the Festetics family from the 1700s through the end of World War I (Figure 23.4). They supplied the best racing and stud horses to the nobility of Europe. One of the oldest structures in the country still standing is the Abbey at Tihany (Figure 23.5), where the first document with writing in Hungarian was penned. There are many other important historical sites throughout the region.

The Beginning of Balaton Tourism

The history of the Balaton tourism begins on the north shore in Balatonfured in the late 18th century when the villagers had their lakeside thermal spring waters tested and certified that they were medicinal and hired a spa doctor. The golden age of the town, built around the spa treatment centers, began shortly thereafter as the prominent cultural and political figures of the era began to spend more time here. At the eastern end, the first Balaton steamer was put in operation out of the Balatonfured port in 1846, connecting with Szantod, a few kilometers from the modern city of Siofok. Later a ferry connected the northern and southern shores at the western end from Fonyod to Revfulop. Eventually another, separate rail line reached the towns on northern shore in 1909.

Keszthely (Figure 23.6), located at the western end of the lake, is considered by most Hungarians to be the cultural center and unofficial capital of the Balaton due to its size with 22,000 population; the large number of resident artists and academics; its 200-year-old agricultural university (Pannon Agartudomanyi Egyetem);

Figure 23.4. Festetics family palace near Keszthely. (Photo by Tim Wallace)

its Catholic Church's 13th century frescoes and the palatial mansion of the influential Festitics family (now a national museum).

From the Adriatic Sea to the Hungarian Sea

For much of the early modern period (18th and 19th centuries), the real Hungarian sea was the Adriatic Sea, as Hungarians controlled what is today Croatia within the Austro–Hungarian Empire. The wealthy of the era built their vacation homes there and spent summers enjoying the Adriatic sun and sea. During this time, the Balaton region was primarily agricultural. There were almost no bathing areas and what few tourists came were usually more interested in visiting and

Figure 23.5. The Abbey at Tihany overlooking Lake Balaton. (Photo by Tim Wallace)

relaxing in the spas, tasting the local wines, and fishing the dense reeds that surrounded the lake. This was to change dramatically, however, after World War I.

As punishment for their role in World War I, the Allies removed two thirds of the Hungarian territory and awarded it to Hungary's neighbors. Hungary was singled out for greater punishment than any of the other Axis allies. At one swoop of the pen, in a document called the Treaty of Trianon, Hungary's economy and national pride took a severe hit. Many historians say this lopsided concession was a major factor in Hungary's decision to participate in World War II as a German ally. With the creation of Slovenia and Croatia, an additional consequence of the Treaty was the removal of the Adriatic Sea coast as an internal tourist destination for Hungarians. The nobles and other wealthy Hungarians began to build more of their summer homes, cottages, and wine cellars around Lake Balaton, as the region started its growth as an important site for domestic tourism.

After the installation of the Communist governments in the postwar period, the fine estates, summer villas, large cottages, private resorts, and tracts of land were expropriated, nationalized, and redistributed to party officials and workers' unions. Up to this point, Balaton tourism had primarily been for the upper and emerging middle classes. After 1945, the government encouraged the construction of public resorts and holiday homes for the working classes. These actions changed the nature of the tourism around the lake and increased the density of both built structures and tourists within a short time. Reed and marsh strands were cut, beaches were built, and the rocky bottoms converted to sand. Homes, hotels, and restau-

Figure 23.6. Keszthely, cultural center of Lake Balaton. (Photo by Tim Wallace)

rants were built very close to the water line as Lake Balaton began to attract larger numbers of tourists from East European countries. Hungary was attractive to citizens from these countries because, arguably, it was the most prosperous and least restrictive country in the Warsaw Pact countries. Adding to the attractiveness of the sand, sea, and sun was the fact that goods often available only in the West could be purchased here. On the other hand, tourists from Western European countries found Hungary an inexpensive bargain, albeit one with a lower standard of tourism infrastructure. After the 1960s the Janos Kadar regime gradually relaxed travel restrictions on incoming tourists from both the East and the West (Borocz, 1996, p. 143). Western tourists made expenditures that satisfied a need for hard currencies, while the Warsaw Pact tourists brought a lower paying, higher volume of tourism. The potential disruptiveness of the Western tourist presence was gradually accepted as a consequence of economic realities.

Balaton From the 1980s

Lake Balaton's reputation as an inexpensive, mass tourist resort destination to swim, sunbathe, eat, drink, and relax was fixed by the 1980s. In 1980 Hungary recorded 10.45 million tourists. By 1990 that figure had doubled to 20.5 million (Hungarian Central Statistical Office, 1992, p. 164). Less restrictive tourism policies allowed travelers from Western countries to become much more numerous than before.

Lake Balaton also became an important meeting point for tourists from West and East Germany. It was easy for them to meet here and nearly impossible to do so in Germany. German tourists soon became the most important and highly visible tourists at Balaton, and Hungarian hosts adjusted their tourism programs accordingly, offering information in German, having German-speaking staff available, and improving the standard of services. Hungarians especially enjoyed the West Germans, whom they perceived as cultured and wealthy (and likely to spend a lot of money and be less demanding than the "less cultured" East Germans).

In the majority of commercial establishments tourist amenities were basic and far below international standards. Service was slow, uniform, and unresponsive. The few, major hotels in the region, often tied in with the spa resorts, were slightly better appointed with a more experienced staff only because their clientele were primarily from Western Europe. The vast majority of guests (ca. 80%) stayed in private homes and apartments (Borocz, 1996, p. 157).

The Hungarian political system after the 1956 revolution came to be known as "goulash communism," referring to an odd mixing of a state-dominated, socialist agricultural and industrial sector existing alongside a lively individual, informal, capitalist sector. Income from home activities was not regulated by the state. Individuals were able to acquire enough money to buy cars and small vacation homes, but were not allowed to invest in land. However, Balaton homeowners were able to rent their rooms, apartments, and vacation homes to tourists, keeping the cash from lodging transactions unrecorded. With 80% of all foreign tourists staying in noncommercial establishments, the income derived from lodging guests in the informal sector generated a growth and dependency on tourism among the working classes that had never been experienced before at Balaton.

The end of Soviet hegemony after 1989 also spelled another change for Balaton tourism. In the term of guests, fewer tourists from Warsaw Pact countries could afford to visit Hungary; West Germans suddenly did not need to visit their East German cousins, their cousins came to them. All travel restrictions were removed and Hungarians were easily able to go to Western European destinations for their holidays. The hosts now found themselves with a changing clientele and most of the paying tourists increasingly were East Germans. The length of the tourism season began to contract, decreasing from 2.5 months (mid-June to August) to about 5 weeks (July to mid-August).

Shortly after 1989, the economy changed, too, with Hungarians experiencing for the first time in decades high unemployment and inflation rates. The government could no longer afford the economic safety net they had provided everyone during the communist era (free education, health, generous retirement plans, employment for everyone, time off for informal sector activities, and so on), forcing Hungarians who previously had used their free market activities as an income supplement to rely on them as primary economic resources. The euphoria at the end of communism combined with the realization that the economy was changing led many of the people who owned property in Balaton to spruce up their homes and flats, construct new ones with renting in mind, open up new restaurants, and offer new services. Unfortunately, tourist arrivals in Hungary seemed to have peaked around 1993–1994 and have begun to level off and even show a small decline, especially at Lake Balaton. Recent investments are in jeopardy, even as people continue to clear scenic vistas to construct more rental houses. With the decrease of agricultural and manufacturing output and jobs, the privatization of the economy and the drastic cutback in government subsidies to individuals, tourism has become the backbone of the local economy. Dependency has replaced economic diversity.

The rapidity of tourism growth at Lake Balaton between 1960 and 1990 produced some very big environmental problems, especially in terms of the lake's water quality. The fact is there are too many tourists using Lake Balaton in the summer. The carrying capacity of Lake Balaton is about 600,000 tourists per day. In the summer, there are often over a million people using it. The problem cannot be corrected cheaply or easily. Even if it is fixed eventually, tourism receipts may have declined by that time anyway. Any decrease in tourism receipts would probably produce an economic crisis for thousands of Balaton residents.

The next section explains in some detail the environmental problems that may be leading to a crisis. I will try to outline the key factors contributing to it. In the process we will see how in the short run sustaining tourism is not necessarily compatible with sustaining development. Environmental planning for tourism growth should have occurred sooner than 1980. Even today, government officials in Hungary are doing little to repair the damages and not enough to prevent a worsening of the environmental problems.

The Ebb and Flow of Water Quality Issues in Balaton Tourism

Lake Balaton presents very complex issues in sustainable tourism when it comes to the physical environment. Sustaining the environmental component of tourism in the Lake Balaton case refers primarily to protecting water quality, the local fauna and flora, and the traditional landscape along the shore. All of the water quality problems are ultimately traced back to damaging human activities begun in the last century. At the outset of this discussion, it is important to keep in mind that until recently Lake Balaton was just another rural area in a country dominated by agriculture and animal husbandry. Balaton was not considered a mass tourism destination until the mid-20th century.

Lake Balaton is about 20,000 years old. The depth and size of the lake have changed significantly over the centuries. For example, the Medieval period was much wetter than today and Lake Balaton was much wider. As the rainfall declined, the formerly flooded areas became wetlands, important not only for bird and other mammal habitats but also the lake itself. The largest source of the lake's water, about 40–45%, is delivered via the Zala River from western Hungary snaking its way past large agricultural fields, water-hungry manufacturing plants, oilfields, and refineries. The rest of the water comes from rain running off the increasingly reed-bare campgrounds and resort-cluttered surrounding countryside. Hungarian limnologists (lake system biologists) observed the first serious signs of an impending water quality crisis around 1960. Excessive algae were seen at the western end, near Keszthely, where the Zala empties into the lake. The Kis-Balaton wetlands near Keszthely provided a natural filtration system for lake waters, removing pollutants and excessive nutrients from agricultural and livestock waste up river. In addition, the river water stayed long enough in the wetlands for it to separate its solid material and settle there. The heavy reed growth absorbed excess nutrients from its major water cleansing and sediment removal apparatus, a mechanism that limnologists (freshwater biologists) later decided was indispensable for the health of Lake Balaton. In effect, between 1860 and 1960 a hundred years of additional sediments and excess nutrients had been dumped into the Keszthely end of the lake as a result. This caused a toxic algae problem to arise. The algae also depleted the shallow lake of its normal oxygen levels, seriously affecting other marine life and causing massive fish kills (especially carp and eels) in later years.

The western end of the lake is currently the most polluted area. If this part of the lake is unhealthy, the whole lake will suffer eventually. Prior to 1800, the water around Keszthely was as clear as drinking water according to old documents. Deliberate draining to increase agricultural lands took place in the early 1920s, so that nearly all of what was once wetlands disappeared. This is an indication of the little importance most of the region had placed on tourism relative to agriculture and animal husbandry. As late as 1960, landowners and even the state tried to drain additional wetland areas. However, the marshy area closest to the lake mouth was never adequately suited to agriculture and was eventually abandoned. Unfortunately, the removal of wetlands had a disastrous effect on Lake Balaton.

A second environmental problem for the lake arose after the construction of the southern rail line in 1861. The tracks were built close to the lake—some places within about 50 meters of the shoreline. After the first flood, rail owners complained to the government. The response was the construction of a channel and dyke at Siofok to control the water's depth. Government engineers set the high level at 104.5 meters above sea level. Buildings and cottages were constructed nearby along the rail line. Now the lake level cannot be raised without flooding homes and businesses. Barring an unforeseen rainfall or drought of catastrophic proportions, the lake level will always be within a few centimeters of the high mark level. The shallowness of the lake reinforces the problems created by the destruction of the wetlands: lower oxygen levels and increased muddiness. Unfortunately, the worst effects of these two problems (lowered oxygen levels and muddiness) are more likely to occur at the height of the tourist season. The hotter it is, the less oxygen there is for the lake's aquatic creatures, sometimes provoking a massive fish kill as there was in 1994 when thousands of fish died during a July heat wave. The hot days also bring out more bathers, who are not happy seeing dead fish floating by as they wade in the very warm water with their children. In addition, the greater the number of bathers, the more the muddy sediment on the lake bottom is churned up, making the water cloudier and less appealing to tourists.

The third major environmental problem for the lake has been the disastrous leveling of the reed stands that existed for eons around the lake. Reeds soak up the excess nutrients flowing into the lake from fertilizers and other sources of nitrogen, slow the entrance of polluted runoff into the lake, protect delicate flora, serve as nests for birds and other animals, and in general contribute greatly to the overall biotic structure of the lake's complex ecosystem. The reeds were traditionally used as thatching for cottage roofs, a practice today mostly abandoned in favor of ceramic or asbestos tiling, although a few, newly restored homes are reusing them as an attraction for tourists looking for lodging in a more "authentic" Hungarian cottage.

Following the expropriation of the redistribution of properties around the shoreline, home and resort builders cut down reeds, which they saw as a nuisance, and planted trees. Dirt from the construction site often was just dumped into the lake. This sometimes added a few more meters to the shoreline property. Tree planting only worsened the problem, because their shade inhibited reed growth and allowed runoff to head into the lake unfiltered by denser plant life.

These three problems have together contributed to a significant decline in water quality. Although a major effort has been undertaken to solve some of these stubborn problems, my field school students in 1994 and 1995 could only find harsh adjectives for the lake's water. For example, one of them wrote in 1995, "The environmental problems of the lake become apparent when one looks at the nice, murky, brown color of the lake. This could be a devastating blow if the lake becomes so polluted that nobody wants to swim in it anymore" (Jaeger, 1995, p. 34). Another student wrote, "The water quality is poor and on any given day one may find dead fish floating or grounded on the beach" (Broomfield, 1995, p. 53). Although they generally did not mind sitting at the "beach" areas, most of them were reluctant to enter the water due to the dead fish, the cloudiness, and the water's stillness. They concluded they might contract some kind of a disease if they swam in it.

Germans, also, are uncomfortable with the same things and German newspapers monitor Balaton water quality to their readers. In 1994 and 1995 several German newspapers reported the Lake Balaton fish kills and cloudy water problems shortly before the German school holiday period. Both years Balaton business owners and residents reported noticeable declines in German tourist arrivals and length of stay. By their shorter visits or even their decision not to visit, German tourists were signaling their demand to Balaton hosts that maintenance of water quality was so important to them that they might not come back. In 1995 the Keszthely Bay was dredged to remove sediment. For the 1996 summer season, the Hungarian Water Authority tried to keep water levels as high as physically possible to lessen the possibility of fish kills and improve the color of the water. Recently, many towns are expanding the amount of *strand* area to give more space to sunbathers and children. Thus, it is clear that Hungarians took notice and are concerned about the situation.

The large scientific and water engineering communities have been doing research on Lake Balaton and monitoring its water quality for decades. But the combination of destruction of wetlands, fixing the water level, cutting the reeds, and building more small resorts, homes, and cottages up to the shoreline could produce an environmental crisis for the lake. Today, the infrastructure is so dense around the lake and in the Kis-Balaton it would be impossible to restore the lake to its pre-1800 environment. Nevertheless, the government has undertaken some projects to ameliorate the consequences of these human social, economic, and political decisions of the last 200 years. These include the reconstruction of the Kis-Balaton wetlands, the continued dredging of the Kis-Balaton Bay, and declaring much of the shoreline and wetlands as protected nature areas.

Germans and Austrians are far more interested in the recreational elements of the lake than are tourists from greater distances. Lake Balaton is relatively close to Germany, and Austria is a border state. German tourists want comfortable accommodations where they can relax and play, swim, sunbathe, eat, and drink, not unlike most American tourists visiting the beach towns of the US Atlantic, Pacific, and Gulf coastlines. They are not greatly interested in ethnic or cultural tourism. It is the very rare German tourist that can speak any Hungarian and few even attempt it. Balaton hosts and guests communicate in tourist German. The number of German-speaking tourists has become so great that most of the signage and restaurant menus are bilingual, and signs and menus in other languages are hard to find, much to the frustration of other foreign tourists.

Americans and British, in contrast, are much more interested in ethnic, cultural, and historical tourism. Eight times as many British tourists stay overnight in Keszthely as in Siofok, probably because Keszthely is noted in the guidebooks as the Balaton city with the most cultural attractions and programs. I once spoke with a Keszthely resident who taught English at the local university and moonlighted as a tour guide. She found British and American tourists to be remarkably different from Germans and Austrians in their touring preferences. On a weekend tour the latter wanted to taste the wine from north shore wine cellars, take a horse-drawn wagon ride through a picturesque village, visit the beach, and eat and drink throughout the afternoon and evening. The English speakers, in contrast, insisted on visiting as many churches, famous buildings, museums, and castle ruins as possible within a weekend. She said she far preferred guiding Germans because the "Brits and the Americans always leave me exhausted."

But there are many workaholic Germans that are so taken by the slower pace of life that they now seek to invest in a piece of it. They are changing the terms of negotiation over the definition of the site. The foreign purchase of the country vacation homes has become very common throughout Balaton communities, even in more distant areas such as the Kis-Balaton. Each summer seems to find more real estate for sale to foreigners and fewer native farmers staying behind. This is also having an interesting consequence for the physical environment. A colleague at the university in Keszthely found that his research is showing greater concentrations of native flora reappearing in fields around the Balaton. He attributed this occurrence to the large number of abandoned agricultural fields. He noted that in his recent travels in the area he found dozens of communities with abundant restored homes, newly painted with well-kept gardens. "Unfortunately, no one lived in them," he said. "They are like ghost towns," because the homes are owned by foreign guests who appear infrequently for a short vacation (Figure 23.7).

Tourism in the Kis-Balaton

About 20 years ago, prior to the wetlands reconstruction project in the Kis-Balaton, the national petroleum company, MOL, was digging for oil in Zalakaros, a small community near the Kis-Balaton. They found an underground hot spring instead. Hungarians love thermal baths, and soon construction was under way to convert this small farming community into a spa center. The Kis-Balaton reconstruction project, the beginning of tourism in this area, started in the 1980s. Sev-

Figure 23.7. Balaton farmhouse with thatched (reed) roof restored by German vacationers. (Photo by Tim Wallace)

eral farm communities sacrificed their land to this project, for which they received some financial compensation. Today, the wetlands project looks like a small lake in a very rural setting. Many species of birds have returned, white storks from Africa regularly return to summer over here, and various kinds of fish flourish in the waters. The peaceful, bucolic setting amidst old farming communities has attracted Austrian and German tourists seeking quite month-long vacations in a "natural" environment. At first, these tourists lodged with local families in their farmhouses. Recently, it has become very common for the tourists to buy a farmhouse, restore it, and use it as a vacation home. German families first find out about Hungarian village homes through advertisements in their newspapers. German and Hungarian real estate agents operate in the area to show them available homes for purchase.

More Cracks in the Negotiation

Balaton residents are not riveted by the prospect of forever serving German tourists. East Germans are especially resented, because they are seen as *declasse* proletarians and peasants without social graces. But the dislike of Germans is generally well cloaked, except among local youths in the 15–25 age range. We determined this by pairing field course participants with Hungarian students and asking them to interview together both hosts and guests during their 5-week program of study. On one occasion some Hungarian and American students were at a beach at Gyenesdias, a town near Keszthely. They wanted to interview Hungarian vacationers, but when they walked across the hot, crowded strand along the water's edge they were unable to find a single one. One of the Hungarian students remarked in a very serious tone to one of the Americans that the absence of Hungarians "makes the vacation town undesirable to him." He felt like a stranger in his own country (Massa, 1994, p. 119). Over and over again, the Americans reported a brooding sense of alienation among the young Hungarians with whom they were working.

It was clear from our research that local Balaton Hungarians responded more positively to tourists who took the time to learn some Hungarian words, wanted to visit cultural sites, and wished to participate in local customs. Hungarians were uncomfortable with the vertical, asymmetrical relationship characteristic of tourists who visit less developed countries. They preferred guests who were flexible in their expectations as to time, accommodations, and food and who were willing to treat Hungarian service personnel as guides to interpreting Hungarian culture, rather than as servants.

Conclusion: Processing and Sustaining Tourism

Tourism development is an ongoing process of negotiation, so it is inevitable that a tourist destination changes to fit the needs of both hosts and guests. Sometimes, the hosts are in control and sometimes the guests are in control. Sustainable tourism is a misnomer, as it assumes there is a single, original state at a particular moment in time when the destination was in its ideal environment, and social and cultural condition. Tourism is in the eye of the beholder—that is, the tourist, the hotel owner, the waiter, the real estate agent, the travel agent, the politician, the citizen, and so on.

One of the great fears of the Balaton residents dependent on tourism is that there will be massive fish kills in late June, just before the Germans arrive. A fish kill means a poor tourist season. Several poor tourist seasons in a row will hurt not only the hotel owners but the thousands of average residents who depend on the rental of the apartments and houses in order to survive inflation and difficult economic conditions. Residents want to know the secret for getting the "perfect" tourist—the one who is going to have the least impact and leave the most money. The negotiation between hosts and guests continues at Balaton. The post-1989 decline in agriculture and manufacturing in the region has made local residents overly dependent on tourism, so the hosts hold the upper hand for the moment in the definition of Balaton tourism. The national government is not committed to major changes in funding formulas to help Balaton. The problems afflicting Balaton are minor compared with the economic problems facing all Hungary. People living in other parts of the country where there are few tourists hope that some of the tourists visiting Balaton will come their way instead. The irony is that, on balance, fewer tourists at Balaton will probably have a positive effect on water quality and crowding, which may make the guests happy, but not the hosts who depend on tourism for income.

As the economy and the tourists change, so also will the cultural definition of Lake Balaton as a tourist destination change. If there are no tourists, then there is no tourist destination. However, when tourists arrive and interact with local residents, the process begins and starts to affect the social, cultural, and physical environment. Balaton is being tremendously affected by mass tourism. Few tourists stay in hotels. Most live in Hungarian homes and apartments and deal face to face with the hosts. These interactions saturate the day-to-day lives of the hosts throughout the summer, affecting the local culture to varying degrees. I was told by many of my Hungarian friends and acquaintances how nervously they awaited the arrival of the tourist season and how relieved they were when it was over.

Tourism in the 1980s and early 1990s had been confined primarily to the shores of the Balaton and only for a short 6–8-week season. Today, the purchase of vacation homes in areas distant from the Balaton shore is going to create perhaps more profound changes. As Butler (1990) points out, the true local environment can still be found in areas into which tourists do not penetrate,

> To disperse tourists in space and time, i.e., to extend the season to peaking, could and in some cases has, resulted in far more profound and permanent changes over a wider area, than when tourists are confined to small areas in huge numbers for clearly defined seasons. (Butler, 1992, p. 45)

Now, communities are even selling their vacant farmlands to foreigners seeking to build new houses. The Kis-Balaton will eventually become linked not only by the wetlands and the Zala River but also by the creeping development of these new residences to mass tourism at Lake Balaton. As one of my students recently asked rhetorically, "Will the Hungarian Sea become the Austro–German Hungarian Sea?" Just as English-speaking tourists are affecting the little Romanian village of Aref to find their fictional Dracula and tourists are seeing the Virgin Mary in an office building window in Clearwater, FL, so also the process of transformation of the Balaton continues as it has been doing for centuries since the time of the Romans. Sustainable tourism probably should not mean sustaining tourists, but rather assuring that the process of it be orderly, with minimal culture shock for the hosts. Hungarians must ask themselves how will they respond to these changes. "How should we sustain our Balaton? How do we retain our cultural heritage at Lake Balaton?" But if they change too much they also have to wonder "Will tourists come back again?" The cultural definition of a tourist destination is the result of a long process of negotiation among hosts and guests. Sometimes the former hold the upper hand and sometimes the latter do. There are multiple factors that determine whose definition takes priority, not the least of which are economic ones. As Hungary moves beyond the difficulties of the transition period of socialism to a new system, economic diversification may make it possible for Hungarians at Balaton to welcome tourists more on their own terms, or perhaps welcome a different kind of tourist. Even then, they will have to renegotiate the cultural definition of the Balaton.

Chapter 24

The Legend of Robin Hood: Myth, Inauthenticity, and Tourism Development in Nottingham, England

Myra Shackley

Myths and legends often form the basis of cultural tourism as in Nottingham (UK), whose tourism industry earns in excess of £256 million per year and employs 15,000 people, largely dependent upon themes based around the medieval story of Robin Hood. Despite doubts about the historical validity of the character, the legends and associated locations have been successfully packaged to attract a wide range of visitors. Visitors to Nottingham have an image of place derived largely from Robin Hood feature films, which have always been shot elsewhere. This, combined with the doubtful historical basis of the legend, may be thought to detract from the visitor experience at the destination, but in practice the reverse seems to be true. Visitors to Nottingham apparently either do not care whether the legend was authentic or expect Robin Hood to be a myth and are agreeably surprised to find some historical foundation. Nottingham's tourism received a measurable boost from the 1991 release of two Robin Hood films, but recent promotion has tried to diversify the cultural tourism product.

The Legend of Robin Hood

Nottinghamshire and Sherwood Forest are synonymous with the legendary medieval hero, Robin Hood, an outlaw dressed in Lincoln Green who supposedly robbed the rich to give to the poor. The accoutrements of the myth, characters such as Little John, Friar Tuck, Will Scarlett, and other Merry Men are familiar to all, and Robin is frequently depicted as an heroic figure standing up for oppressed peasantry. Despite skeptical claims that Robin Hood was actually the invention of sensation-seeking medieval minstrels (S. Davis, 1991) who tapped popular resentment, the character has remained universally popular for centuries regardless of its historical validity. Today, thanks to extensive film versions of the Robin Hood legend, the hero is both instantly recognizable and firmly stereotyped. It is, unfortunately, very difficult to identify the "real" Robin Hood who forms the background for the stories. Wandering outlaws of similar predilections certainly existed (J. Holt, 1982), but many authorities claim that Robin Hood merely represents an amalgam of different myths. In medieval times major stories of the day were told by traveling minstrels and the earliest written mention of Robin Hood occurs in a poem called "The Vision of William Concerning Piers Plowman" by William Lagland, considered to have been written around 1377. Several original ballads suggest that a Robin Hood character was active in the 13th century or even later (Dobson & Taylor, 1989), although a 16th century historian (coincidentally called John Major) wrote in 1521 that Robin Hood was active in the early 1190s during the reign of Richard I (the Lionheart). This 12th century identification has remained the most popular in cinematic representations. However, there is much contradictory evidence.

Nottinghamshire tradition says that Robin was a native of the village of Loxley in the 12th century, but this probably represents an amalgamation of two characters. Indeed, although Nottingham is the major area connected with the modern legend, in early ballads (Dobson & Taylor, 1989) much of the outlaw's life is set around the area of Barnesdale in Yorkshire. Other sites connecting Robin to Yorkshire include Kirklees Priory where he is supposed to have died and been buried. Nor are all the elements of the Robin Hood story contemporary. Maid Marion and Friar Tuck were later additions to the tale, the latter not appearing until the 1500s, probably as part of May Day plays. This has to cast some doubt on the validity of the claim that Robin Hood and Maid Marion were married in Edwinstowe Church, Nottingham, some 300 years earlier. However, Edwinstowe is still a major tourist attraction. The legend strongly identifies Robin with Sherwood Forest, fragments of which still exist today. In the 14th century primitive forests covered more than 30% of England with some, such as Sherwood, being owned by the King and guarded by royal rangers. Forestry laws were harsh and cruel, and the Robin Hood of legend defends oppressed local peasants both from rangers and from royal officials such as the Sheriff of Nottingham (Figure 24.1).

Robin Hood is one of the most popular film heroes of all time. Between 1908 and 1922 more than 26 major films have been made around the Robin Hood theme, starting with silent pictures, in addition to innumerable television series, commercials, cartoons, etc. (Turner, 1989). These have served to establish a picture both of the man and his contemporary environment in many people's minds, the exact image being related to the age of the consumer and thus to the film version with which they are most familiar. The most famous early portrayal is certainly the 1922 film *Robin Hood* starring Douglas Fairbanks, Jr. In 1938, Warner Brothers made *Adventures of Robin Hood* with Errol Flynn, widely regarded as the definitive Robin Hood movie. Most of the film was shot in Chico, CA, some 500 miles north of Hollywood. Ironically, part of the shooting did indeed take place in Sherwood Forest, although this was not the Nottinghamshire original but a Californian forest near Los Angeles that had been renamed at the time the 1922 film was being shot there.

Other significant Robin Hood films include *Robin and Marion* (1976, starring Sean Connery) and the 1973 animated Disney cartoon. In the UK the television

Figure 24.1. Statue of Robin Hood outside Nottingham Castle. (Photo by Myra Shackley)

Adventures of Robin Hood ran for 143 episodes between 1956 and 1960. By this time there can hardly have been anyone in the Western world who did not know what Robin Hood looked like or that he lived in Sherwood Forest, near Nottingham, and in recent years this association has formed the basis for most of Nottingham's tourism industry. This was greatly helped by the release (in 1991) of two films: *Robin Hood* (starring Patrick Bergin) and *Robin Hood Prince of Thieves* (with Kevin Costner). The latter was the more successful and was utilized as the basis for a massive Robin Hood promotion in Nottinghamshire despite the fact that none of it was shot in the county. Some of the landscape shots actually featured Hadrian's Wall and the Scottish lowlands.

Myths and Heritage Tourism

Myths and legends are frequently used as the basis for a heritage tourism product (Prentice, 1993). The visitor may be unaware that the character or story is invented. British examples include Scottish Highland tartans (a Victorian elaboration) and the creation of Sherlock Holmes (a fictional character). Perhaps the best parallel for Robin Hood comes with the legends of King Arthur and Camelot, equally historically doubtful but still the basis for much of Cornwall's cultural tourism product. Because contemporary images of a mythical or pseudohistorical character are generally derived from film or television portrayals, the potential tourist has a definite destination image that might differ markedly from the image he would have created in his own mind from reading a book. Many non-UK residents unfamiliar with such stories are unable to distinguish fact from fiction, hence the numbers of disappointed visitors each year trying to find the mythical 221b Baker Street, London residence of Sherlock Holmes.

In the case of Robin Hood, continuous media exposure has resulted in a firm image of both the character (complete with longbow, peaked hat with a feather, and green tunic) and his environment (the oakwoods of Sherwood Forest). Such pictures of the Greenwood, the battlements of Nottingham castle, and rural villages of medieval England create expectations in the minds of visitors that cannot possibly be realized, although they attract large numbers of visitors to Nottingham (Figure 24.2). As we know, destination images influence tourist behavior (Echtner & Ritchie, 1991) and strong positive images are preferred in the travel decision-making process (Woodside & Lysonski, 1989). Myths and legends are often used as the basis for a heritage tourism product and can create powerful and romantic subliminal images. When reinforced by heritage themes these are widely used to create images in advertising and may be combined into powerful marketing devices for tourism. Once at the destination, visitor satisfaction depends on a comparison between image and reality, which, in the case of Nottingham, might be thought to be disappointing (Chon, 1990). Myths are cultural products and as such may themselves become commoditized. It is often assumed that tourists desire culturally authentic, rather than potentially mythical, experiences, yet authenticity is a socially constructed concept. The tourist may be unable to recognize authenticity, making himself "damned to inauthenticity" in MacCannell's famous phrase (MacCannell, 1973). One could argue that the portrayal of mythical heritage is no less authentic than the staged authenticity of many tourist settings.

D. Pearce (1988) sees the term "image" as describing an overall mental picture or destination stereotype. Each individual will have a unique mental picture of the destination, although certain images will be held in common. In the case of Nottingham these shared images generally involve forests, castles with battlements and drawbridges, and medieval villages. The landscapes of today's Nottinghamshire are dominated by deserted coal tips and pitheads rather than castles, with the

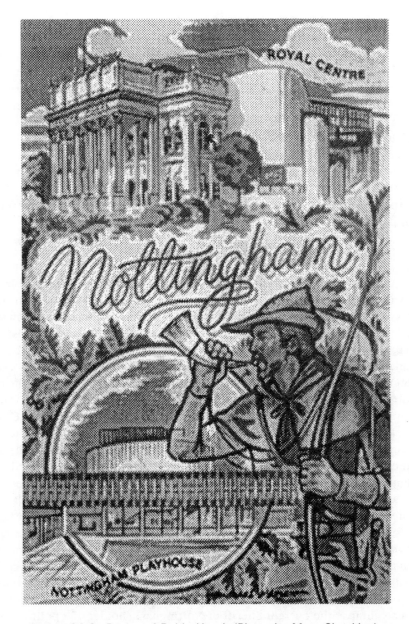

Figure 24.2. Poster of Robin Hood. (Photo by Myra Shackley)

heritage of the city center heavily influenced by the Industrial Revolution. This is not to say that nothing medieval survives but rather that it may take a determined visitor to find it.

The formation of this destination image begins with the development of a mental construct based upon a few impressions chosen from a flood of information. The potential visitor to Nottingham can thus make his own selection from a wide variety of potential images. In the early stages of image formation (Gunn, 1988) the image is generally formed from nontouristic information including general media, films, and books. Tourist information such as brochure literature forms a second stage. The destination image of Nottingham is particularly strong as a result of the Robin Hood films, although these are totally misleading, because none were actually made in the county. However, few tourists seem to be aware of this fact and are attracted to the area because of its associations with the legend rather than any landscape qualities. The association of Robin Hood with Nottingham is generally accepted quite uncritically.

Research suggests that the final phase of image formation is acquired after a visit has modified the image (Phelps, 1986). One might therefore expect that because the reality of Nottingham and Sherwood Forest falls so far short of expectations that it would affect the quality of the visitor experience. This, however, does not appear to be the case.

Nottingham and Robin Hood

Nottinghamshire has based a very successful tourism industry on Robin Hood and is now trying to use the positive image of place it has acquired from this process in the development of new products. At present, estimated tourism spending in the county exceeds £256 million per year (East Midlands Tourist Board [EMTB], 1993), attracting domestic visitors predominantly from London, the southeast and east Midlands. Overseas visitors are predominately German (18%), French (14.6%), or American (13.3%). Not surprisingly, attractions based around the theme of Robin Hood dominate Nottinghamshire's tourism product. Today's visitor is met by "Welcome to Nottinghamshire" "Robin Hood County" signs at the boundary and invited to visit nearly 50 sites that claim some association with the mythical outlaw. These include Nottingham Castle, which is marketed on its Robin Hood connotations although the medieval original was totally destroyed during the English Civil War and replaced by a Ducal mansion in 1679. It is now a museum and art gallery, which attracted 741,891 visitors in 1992 (EMTB, 1993). Another popular destination is the Sherwood Forest Visitor Centre, a favorite spot for walking in one of the few surviving remnants of the once extensive Sherwood Forest. This received major refurbishment in 1993 with the inevitable Robin Hood theme. The Major Oak, legendary haunt of Robin Hood's Merry Men, can still be seen, although foresters consider the tree to be no more than 300 years old and thus it postdates Robin Hood by anything up to 500 years. Visitors may also glimpse the current Sheriff of Nottingham (holder of a political office) or go to the Tales of Robin Hood, a purpose-built themed medieval adventure (appropriately located on Maid Marian Way in Nottingham) that opened in 1989 and attempts to recreate the atmosphere of 13th century Nottingham. Here a cable car ride takes visitors through forest settings in search of Robin Hood followed by extensive exhibits related to daily life in medieval times, plus a critical appraisal of the legend. There are also a number of related festivals and events, including the Robin Hood Festival (held in Sherwood Forest)), the Robin Hood Pageant (Nottingham Castle complete with jousting), and a new attraction, The World of Robin Hood, which opened in 1991 utilizing the scenery from the Kevin Costner film plus supplementary material from a failed heritage center called the Crusades Experience. Those still not satiated with the world's most famous outlaw can search for the church where he was supposedly married (at Edwinstowe) or Friar Tuck's Hut (at Rainworth).

The release of two major Robin Hood films in 1991 provided an opportunity to measure the effect of this boost to the destination image. Nottingham gained very considerable benefits from the Costner film and associated promotions despite having failed in a bid to attract the actor himself to Nottingham for the premier of the film. Sherwood Forest Visitor Centre received a 47% increase in inquiries directly after the film was released, and visitors to the Robin Hood Festival and Robin Hood Pageant increased by 20% and 27%, respectively. Inquiries and souvenir sales at Nottingham Tourist Information Centre increased by 45% between July and September (Nodding, Berresford, & Alexander, 1993). A special Robin Hood rate accommodation promotion generated £34,000 in bed nights plus additional spending, and an additional investment of £8,000 by the County Council on a promotional video generated free TV commercials worth £120,000 and greatly increased awareness of Nottinghamshire tourism.

In many ways, although Robin Hood has undeniably been a most successful ambassador for Nottinghamshire, the overemphasis on Greenwood products has made it difficult for marketeers to diversify. Nottingham has a lot else going for it, including major visitor attractions associated with Lord Byron and D. H. Lawrence, and an interesting industrial heritage based around lace making. The overpromotion of Robin Hood illustrates how heritage themes may swamp a region, becoming overworked and difficult to escape from. This theming reduces the complexity of urban history to a few instantly recognizable simple marketable devices. However, boredom thresholds differ between hosts and guests. Nottingham locals are tired of Robin Hood while visitors remain interested in seeing places associated with the legend.

Because of the failure of many Robin Hood sites to live up to their image, great attempts have been made to compensate. In the case of Nottingham Castle, for example, visitors often record disappointment and the management is trying to forestall this by providing extra information on the significance of the site in the English Civil War (Liepens, personal communication) and by opening new attractions such as the network of underground tunnels. The city won the UK award for Holiday Destination of the Year in 1993, partly for its Robin Hood promotions but also for events marking the 350th commemoration of the English Civil War and for the development of new attractions associated with Byron, Lawrence, and lace making. The Robin Hood theme is more extensively used in overseas marketing. Rod Nipper, Nottinghamshire's Principal Tourism Officer, said in 1994 in the course of a promotional visit to Arizona that "We found that Robin Hood was a particular attraction to Americans, but they had little idea of the geography of Britain." Despite the success of Robin Hood promotions, the limits of innovation have almost been reached. Today's promotions are increasingly trying to diversify and link Robin Hood with other local characters (including Byron and Lawrence) fighting against authority or institutions. But in the mind of the average visitor, particularly visitors from overseas who have no alternative images, Nottingham remains firmly associated with Robin Hood.

Does Authenticity Matter?

Within the UK Nottingham scores highly in most "quality of life" tests. It is famous as an urban shopping center, center of sporting excellence, and for having excellent pubs and nightclubs that cater to the huge student population (20% of citizens, during term). Recent unpublished surveys commissioned by Nottinghamshire councils suggest that visitors to Nottingham are generally motivated by an interest in history (particularly if they come from overseas). They are highly aware of the Robin Hood legends but not of the individual visitor attractions. They generally have an image of place that is generation dependent and usually formed by the Costner film or by the earlier Errol Flynn film, depending on their age. In the case of children, popular breakfast-cereal commercials with a Robin Hood theme are also significant in developing a mental picture. Visitors report high levels of satisfaction with all Robin Hood visitor attractions, except Nottingham Castle, which few realized had been destroyed. The most surprising result in recent surveys was that before their visit tourists had thought that Robin Hood was a mythological character (but didn't care). This conditioned their expectations of Nottinghamshire tourism and when they found that there was a reasonable historical basis for the Robin Hood legend they were pleasantly surprised. The net result was that expectations were exceeded and the visit rated as highly satisfactory. The inauthenticity of Robin Hood sites or the doubtful basis of the myth itself does not, apparently, matter to the heritage tourist. The crucial factor would appear to be the quality of the visitor experience. It would be possible to argue that the overpromotion of this mythical theme has led to commoditization of local culture (Greenwood, 1977), replacing authentic cultural products with staged authenticity (MacCannell, 1973). E. Cohen (1988) noted that not all tourists are seeking authenticity in the ethnographic sense and that recreational tourists are generally less concerned with authenticity and may be prepared to accept as authentic a cultural product or attraction that concerned cultural tourists (applying stricter criteria) may deem unauthentic. This is certainly true in Nottingham, where some tourists will see adequate evidence to support the myth but the majority will remain unconcerned. The staged product can be acceptable to some if it contains some resemblance to the real thing. The visitor may be aware that an attraction is not real but be able to achieve a high quality of experience by compliance with the fantasy. This, after all, is the reason for the success of historical recreations such as Colonial Williamsburg. What matters to Nottinghamshire visitors is not whether Robin Hood was a real character but whether they can have a good time trying to find out. And they can.

Chapter 25

European Union Cross-Border Cooperation: A New Tourism Dimension

Friedrich M. Zimmermann

The Austrian–Italian–Slovenian Three Borders Area is a perfect example of an area partitioned after World War I that is now attempting a common future under the new unified Europe. The European Union offers superb opportunities to develop multicultural tourism in peripheral areas such as Three Borders Area, where three major European ethnic groups (German, Italian, and Slavic), cultures, and languages meet. The unsuccessful bid for the Winter Olympics in 2006 (after a first try for 2002) united these disparate entities for the first time in history towards a common goal. Their coalition for a cause demonstrates the latent power of multinational cooperation for this unique location with its slogan "*Senza Confini*" ("Without Borders"). The creation of a transnational cross-border tourism region, rich in historical and cultural tradition and set amidst spectacular natural beauty, is a new research concept that holds promise for other European areas and elsewhere, such as idyllic but troubled Kashmir.

In contrast to its positive aspects of diverse cultures and natural beauty, the border area still retains strong national perspectives. However, the emerging economy of the European Union (EU) follows its own rules of internationalization despite public opinion. European history and tradition have created a variety of cultural identities. What will happen to the many cultures of Europe?

> European Culture is marked by its diversity: diversity of climate, countryside, architecture, language, beliefs, taste and artistic style. Such diversity must be protected, not diluted. It represents one of the chief sources of the wealth of our continent. But underlying this variety, there is an affinity, a family likeness, and a common European identity. Down through the ages the tension between the continent's cultural diversity and unity has helped to fuse ancient and modern, traditional and progressive, it [the culture] is undoubtedly a source of the greatness of the elements of our civilization. (European Community, 1983)

The Three Borders Area has been a region of long-standing tension and conflicts: the World War I battles at the Isonzo River, the fights over borders, the division into three nation states followed by forced nationalization and ethnic cleansing. The creation of a unified tourism region that will introduce theme-oriented tourist attractions into a peripheral area, and improve a stagnant economy, is a challenging research project.

The Research Team

The research to date has centered on a pilot area consisting of 12 communities along the European Union's internal borders between Austria and Italy and the external borders between Slovenia and Austria/Italy (Figure 25.1).

The research design is interdisciplinary, involving cooperation between two leading research institutions: the University of Graz Department of Human Geography and Regional Studies, and the University of Klagenfurt Department of Southeastern European History. Additional contributions have been made by the Geography Departments in Ljubljana (Slovenia) and Trieste (Italy), and tourism experts, decision-makers, and local opinion leaders added practical experience.

European Union Regional Policy and Tourism Development

Two important EU policies are very supportive and decisive for tourism development in the pilot region. First, the "European Union Regional Policies" initiated

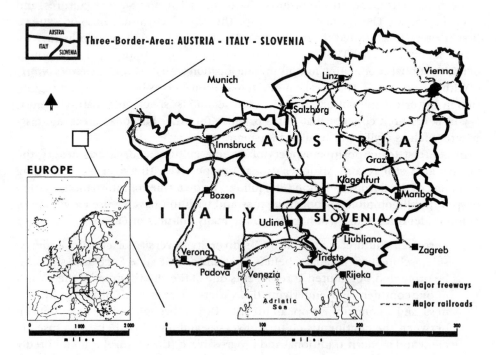

Figure 25.1. Location map of the Three Borders Area.

under the European Community (EC) Treaty (Rome, 1957) stated in part three, Title XIV, Article 130a:

> In order to promote its overall harmonious development, the Community shall develop and pursue its actions leading to the strengthening of its economic and social cohesion. In particular, the Community shall aim at reducing disparities between the levels of development of the various regions and the backwardness of the least favored regions, rural areas. (see also http://www.inforegio.org/wbpro/agenda2000/compare/04_en.htm)

Second, the EU is producing a new European culture, a "unity in diversity." Article 128 of the Treaty of Maastricht provided a framework that encourages the "flowering of the cultures of the Member States, while respecting their national and regional diversity," and "cooperation between Member States. . . ." Further, "The Community and the Member States shall foster cooperation with third countries and the competent international organizations in the sphere of culture, in particular the Council of Europe" (http://europa.eu.int/en/record/mt/title2.html).

The Historical Dimension of the Three Borders Area

During the national era of the 19th and early 20th centuries, several nation states developed in Europe. Separatist tendencies, national hegemony, and sharp political and cultural barriers continued for a long time (e.g., within the Austro-Hungarian Empire until 1918). The same tendencies occurred after the breakdown of communism in Central and Eastern Europe. Border regions became peripheral and economically marginal. In the course of European integration, these areas will find new challenges and new opportunities as border functions disappear.

The location of the Three Borders Area in a European context is characterized by centrality. Major traffic routes, freeways, and railroads meet here, connecting Northwestern Europe with the Balkans and Northeastern Europe with Italy and the Iberian Peninsula. The location is a crossroad of two major European trade routes and a living textbook of European history. Romans settled here, followed by Celtic-Roman tribes, the Slavs in the 6th and 7th centuries, Germanic settlers, and wars against the Turks in the 15th and 16th centuries. The French wars at the turn of the 18th and 19th centuries left major impacts in this area. World War I was disastrous. Between May 1915 and November 1917 the 12 "Isonzo battles" were fought and more than half a million soldiers—members of various European nations—were killed in this mountainous terrain. There are many remnants like museums, cemeteries, and literature commemorating these days (see Smith, Chapter 26).

Until World War I, this region was still a culturally diverse area of many languages. Nationalism, nationalization, and ethnic cleansing began after the peace treaty of St. Germain 1918-1919. This process was supported by Mussolini and Hitler and by the Yugoslav authorities after World War II. Contrasting political systems of Yugoslavia (Communist), Austria (neutral in 1955), and Italy (NATO and EC member) have caused political, cultural, and economic tensions. However, evidence of cross-border cooperation began with the opening of Yugoslavia's borders (mid-1960s), the independence of Slovenia in 1991, and the recent membership of Austria in the EU (1995). The meeting point of three European cultures, languages, and ethnic groups, shaped by centuries of European history, can be offered as the main tourism attraction for guests in the Three Borders Area.

Tourism Attractions Focusing on Culture and History

Trends in international tourism disfavor peripheral areas. The process of globalization in tourism has increased markedly since the late 1980s. Globally advertised bargains from airlines, hotel chains, and tour operators tend to benefit tourist sectors that can accommodate mass tourism, such as winter travel to Spain or the Canary Islands (see Selanniemi, Chapter 6). While large corporations cooperate with each other to their economic advantage, border regions have been disadvantaged. Small- and medium-scale enterprises are unable to compete on the international stage. Tourist motivations and destination preferences change; independent young singles and active senior citizens expect excitement, adventure, and entertainment; the price advantages of charter discounts (mass tourism) contrast with the relatively high prices of individual trips; the constant pressure for high quality, comfort, and innovation and the increasing importance of environmental issues add to the list. These industry trends create a need for action with new development strategies.

The Tourism Dimensions of the Three Borders Area

Tourism Supply

Tourism development in a peripheral area should introduce the concept of *complementary supply*. Three Borders Area has great potential for winter sports activities such as alpine skiing, snowboarding, and cross-country skiing, especially in an area that is less crowded than the major winter sports regions farther west (Figure 25.2). Additionally, ice-skating, sleigh-riding, indoor pools, and a casino can be offered. The facilities justify international winter sports events including world-cup ski-jumping, downhill racing, and a major cross-country skiing event across borders. The summer season offers national parks and other protected areas for hiking, mountain climbing, water-sports activities (rafting, kayaking, canoeing) cycling, mountain biking, golf, tennis, horseback riding, and parachuting.

The *accommodation sector* offers about 4000 rooms with regional differentiation. The Austrian section, located at the edge of the Corinthian Lake region, is based on small family-owned hotels and bed-and-breakfast establishments of average quality. The Slovenian part was developed under the Yugoslav government and is a planned tourism development area. Kranjska Gora especially could attain international status as a tourism destination. The war of independence in 1991, the conflicts in Bosnia and Herzegovina, as well as the recent conflict in Kosovo have had a tremendous impact on tourism in Slovenia. Not only was the number of tourists cut in half during the last couple of years, but also the privatization of formerly state-owned hotels led to a complete restructuring process in the region. Thus, large hotels have come under private company ownership and a huge number of small family-owned restaurants, hotels, and bed-and-breakfast enterprises have appeared. The Italian part of the region is characterized by a very limited

Figure 25.2. Skiing in the Three Borders Area. (Photo provided by Friedrich Zimmermann)

number of accommodations. However, the Italian region is well known as a second-home area for people living in southern Italy. Strategies for future cooperation among suppliers to provide services for various demand sectors are needed.

Tourism Demand

Parallel to the diversity of area attractions, tourism demand is also very diverse. The Austrian region annually hosts about 200,000 overnight stays: one third Austrian, one third German, and one third other foreigners. Activity in the Slovenian region peaked in 1990, when more than 700,000 overnight stays were registered but declined due to regional hostilities to fewer than 400,000 overnight stays in 1993. The guest count rebounded and by 1998 overnight stays reached 500,000 (50% of whom were domestic, 15% Italians, 10% Germans, 2% Austrians). The Italian region is dominantly short-term tourism, about 250,000 annual overnight stays, and day visits. Visitation to the Italian region tends towards stagnation, with a 40% domestic demand, followed by Slovenians and Austrians (about 10% each).

Strengths and Weaknesses

Natural beauty is one of the main components of the area within the Alpe-Adria Region. There are many natural areas, especially the Triglav National Park, nature parks, and protected areas. Limestone mountains with a very sensitive karst system also occur.

The Three Borders Area, located at a main transportation crossroads, has a very good *infrastructure*. International freeways make the region accessible for 20 million visitors within a radius of about 100 miles. The internal traffic system is well equipped, and there are attractive mountain roads with many panoramic views. Ski lifts for summer viewing and hiking are also available in all three parts of the region.

To date, *cultural attractions* have been marginal for tourism in the Three Borders Area. There is no one major site of international interest. However, various cultural attractions could be combined as regional day trip tours including the culture and history of the three major ethnic groups. This concept is inherent in the EU philosophy of national diversity in regional unity, and future cultural tourism will be dominated by a multicultural European approach in this region.

Organization and cooperation in the supraregional sense is not yet well developed. However, the bid for the 2006 Olympic Winter Games clearly demonstrates the vitality and validity of the cross-border projects that combine the Olympic concept with the present idea of a culturally and historically important Three Borders Area. At present, there are no cross-border *tourism* organizations, but the model for cooperation exists and needs to be reinforced.

Cross-Border Tourism as an Innovative European Concept

Holism and sustainability offer many new opportunities for small-scale tourism. In the past, tourism developed differently because it was heavily influenced by a national orientation with political/economic frameworks and varied recreation mentalities. Now the EU influence supports international competition, regional development strategies, and transnational cooperation. The former differences are of less importance. Postindustrial society favors a uniformity of tourism demand and supply. The application of tourism sustainability of small-scale tourism is especially suitable for peripheral areas as a special response to competition with transnational corporations that use aggressive tourism promotions.

Sustainable tourism needs multiple alliances and approaches. First, there should be a partnership between economy, society, and the environment. Decision-making must foster a democratic approach that includes the local population. The interests of both present *and* future generations should be considered with equal importance.

The peripheral location of the Three Borders Area offers a number of cooperative ideas and development options. Even though tourism to date is small scale, the area has great potential in terms of its untouched natural setting, the persistence of traditional lifestyles, and its historical uniqueness. The EU regional policy recognizes the need to provide external support for peripheral areas, and private investment is available from individual nations, states, and the EU for pilot projects. In the Three Borders Area, development must include the creation of cross-border nature protection areas, including expansion of Triglav National Park and comparable areas elsewhere in Italy and Austria. The existence of a unified administrative unit would increase the tourism exposure and marketability of the area as a summer tourist destination.

Cooperative marketing could offer various tourism packages with minimal new infrastructure. This integrated partnership might establish a type of holistic "Tourism Lifestyle," combining nature, history, culture, life, and economy that could bring new vitality to the region. Success for a sustainable tourism project will depend on strong political support. The 2006 Olympic Winter Games bid demonstrated that such support is attainable, and can overcome cross-border financial, legal, organizational, and social problems.

The Tourism Keystones

The tourism keystones, or unifying marketing themes, are designed to create a feeling of history, exemplified by the contemporary unification of a formerly divided region. Slogans such as "Europeus Sine Finibus," "A Region at the Crossroads of European History," or "Divided Past—Common Future" emphasize the cross-border tourism image favored by European Community Regional Policies. They can be marketed as *historical tours and adventure trips* by car or bus as well as *adventure trips by bike*.

Thematic hiking tours express different lifestyles during the experience of crossing borders. Hiking can offer recreation in a natural and/or cultural landscape for which slogans could be: "Unlimited Hiking Tours," "A Way for Everybody," "Hike Europe," or "All Ways Lead to Europe." Hiking paths could be designed according to thematic to thematic approaches: "A Bee's Hike," "Alpine Living and Lifestyles," or "A Day in the Life of a Soldier of the First World War," "A Day in the Life of a Miner," "A Day in the Life of a Hunter," or "A Day in the Life of a Smuggler."

The *winter sports* keystone follows the Olympic Games concept—the cross-border use of jointly regulated and promoted available resources. The Winter Olympics slogan "*Senza Confini*" ("Without Borders") confirms the desire and need to grow together within the region. The cooperative strategy could market a "Skiing Experience Without Borders."

Summer sport activities could also promote thematic regional images such as rafting golf, horseback riding, hiking and mountaineering, and regional spas and health centers. Advertising could feature "The Blue-White Waters of the Three Borders Area," "The Enjoyment of Adrenaline" (or maybe "The Adrenaline Experience"?), "Mountaineering Without Borders," "Triathlon in the Three Borders Area," and "Sports and Peace."

Multicultural food events should feature local, regional, and national food specialties, presented as "A Food Experience of Multiculturality." With an organized network of local restaurants offering specialties of Slovenia, Friuli, and Carinthia, the partnership could establish quality control and cooperate with local agriculture. Coordinated marketing could strengthen gourmet tourism.

Marketing Issues

As an international development project, marketing would include two target groups: residents of the outlying region and those close by. The wider target region would include the Adriatic region, the Carinthian Lake region, and the winter sports areas in Southern and Western Austria and Northern Italy. Short-term tourism and day trips would be appropriate for Italians living in Trieste, Udine, or Venice, Slovenians and Croatians living in Ljubljana, Maribor, Zagreb, and as far as Rijeka and Split, and Austrians living in Carinthia and Styria. Special packages could be marketed within a radius of 100 miles.

The stunning natural beauty and contrasts of the Three Borders Area holds appeal for long-distance visitors including Eastern Europeans (Hungarians, Czechs, Slovaks, Poles, and Russians), Scandinavians, Britons, or inhabitants of the BENELUX countries. Special discounts for student groups and the local population could lead to insights relating to market elasticity. To initiate marketing, representatives from the Three Borders Area communities must form a tourism promotion organization, develop detailed marketing plans, guarantee cooperation of the partner countries, and procure start-up funds. From this base, promotion will stimulate greater international awareness of the Three Borders Area.

Conclusion

Many border areas in Europe suffer economically as a result of being peripheral to the important economic centers. The Regional Policy of the EU recognizes these problems and supports structural changes that can benefit peripheral areas, and especially those that border Central and Eastern European countries. The Austrian-Italian–Slovenian border area is particularly well suited for development as a tourist region because of its uniqueness. Here, cultural and ethnic highlights, natural beauty, and an incredible history of war and conflict can be fused into a new type of sustainable tourism that will bring disparate European parts together in peace. The holistic approach that unites different societies and economies in partnership serves both today's needs and the interests of future generations. Tourism development features product clusters including those dealing with (1) historical tours, (2) mountain climbing and hiking, (3) winter sports, (4) adventurous summer activities, and (5) multicultural food events. The goal for Three Borders tourism is to overcome divisiveness by strengthening cultural pluralism or "Unity Through Multicultural Diversity."

SECTION 6

ISSUES OF THE 21st CENTURY

Chapter 26

Tourism Issues of the 21st Century

Valene L. Smith

At the Elder's Workshop (Inupiat Paitot) in 1976, three Inuit men, all in their 80's who had known or known of each other since childhood, sat with coffee cups in hand, remembering. . . . Chester Seveck, the tareurmiut (salt water man) from the coast; Joe Sun, a nunamiut (inland man) from the Kobuk River near tree-line where Indians once lived; and Puto Vestal who had worked in gold mining camps near Nome all his life quietly listened to these "men of the land." Joe Sun recalled,

> Wood was always one of our most precious possessions. If we couldn't find enough driftwood along the river (and Chester added, "or the beach"), someone must trade with the Indians who controlled access to the forests. We didn't trust the Indians. They called us "Eskimo" or "eaters of raw meat," so we named them "Irkillirk," or "eaters of body lice." My grandfather told stories about the old times [of his great-grandfather?] before. White men came, when Inuit and Indians had many wars. Indians waited until our men went hunting, then they sneaked in at night and threw torches into our igloos to set them afire. When the women and children ran out, Indians shot them with arrows, or took them prisoner. Then our men sneaked to their camp to set their tepees afire, killed the Indians, and rescued our women. It went on like that, back and forth, for a long time. Inuit wore "armor" or chest plates of caribou ribs to stop arrows. Later, Inuit men figured out a trap (like "land mines"). They buried tiny pieces of very sharp sticks in the ground before it froze; after snowfall you couldn't see them. When an Indian stepped on one, the point cut his moccasin and his foot. He went away howling. Of course we knew where to avoid the points, in a circle beyond the igloos. Later, I think it was before that Russian came [see Zagoskin, 1967], we knew we were killing each other off and soon there would be no one left, so some Inuit and Indian men met, and decided no more wars. Now, one Kotzebue man [Elwood Hunnicutt] is married to an Indian lady, and they have sixteen kids.

Puto had been turning pages in a little diary, then looked up, saying "Life is like a book, many chapters; you close one. . . ." He turned open a blank page, "I wonder what that page will write for my grandchildren?" (Inupiat Paitot field notes, January 1976)

Tourism as a global industry faces new challenges at the millennium, the most important of which is the need to look carefully at the Inuit's symbolic blank page, and plan for more expanded tourism. This chapter initially examines the three critical factors that will influence the future of tourism—namely (1) the economic and demographic factors that favor increased tourism and its global distribution; (2) the limited resources—namely energy and water—to sustain projected growth; and (3) the stewardship of fragile environments.

In addition to these fundamentals, globalization is creating new styles of tourism involving ethnicity in urban areas, a new exclusivity in wilderness regions, and expanded virtual tourism. Concerns for personal safety due to intensified terrorism and the global spread of disease are of increasing importance. The fact that tourism is now considered a human right calls attention to the widening disparity in access to tourism between rich and poor, and the need to provide tourism opportunities for the indigent.

Every nation needs to assess its own population growth in relation to resources, identify its capacity to provide quality vacation experiences for domestic as well as international visitors, and effectively plan its own commitment to tourism.

2000: A Psychological Time Marker

The year 2000 was a mental milestone or a bridge in time from which to assess the past and to speculate the future. In retrospect, the advent of modern mass tourism created an unprecedented awareness of travel impacts, and the subsequent research has provided a better foundation for tourism management than was true in 1970. The international bonding of government and industry through the World Tourism Organization, the World Travel and Tourism Council, the United Nations, and respective governments and their NGOs has provided an institutional framework. As a consequence, tourism has gained stature as an industry but also has become increasingly politicized as governments assume directional roles as culture brokers (Chapter 21) and use tourism as a tool to manage their economy (see Balance of Payments, below). Many countries, especially in the South Pacific, are now proactive in tourism planning, and recognize the need to support sustainable tourism development. They fund conservation and heritage projects, and support university and research institutes. There are more than 415 universities in 58 countries with tourism departments that provide tourism training, and 1213 researchers in 71 countries now ensure a cadre of potential teachers and qualified employees (Baretje, 2000, personal communication).

The ongoing "scientification" of tourism is well demonstrated by publication of the *Encyclopedia of Tourism* (Jafari, 2000) and the article "Annals and Tourism Evolving: Indexing 25 Years of Publication" (Swain, Brent, & Long, 1998). The latter examines Index headwords. Even the index of this volume identifies the breadth of studies in tourism. The most valuable single bibliographic source is the Centre

International de Recherches et d'Etudes Touristiques, 6 avenue du Grassi, 13100 Aix-en-Provence, France (available http://www.ciret-tourism.com).

Three recent milestones favoring further expansion of tourism have quietly been approved. The comprehensive Tourism Code of Ethics, which sets performance standards and provides mechanisms for redress, was approved by the WTO at their Santiago meeting in November 1999. Article 7 of this document describes tourism as a *human right* and is an important validation of leisure travel. The Tourism Satellite Accounts (see Introduction) were approved at the March 2000 United Nations Statistical Commission, giving tourism the distinction of the first industry to have UN-endorsed international standards for measuring its true economic impact. An important foundation has been structured, but the need now is constructive action at multiple levels of participation, using the strategy "Think Global, Act Local."

2000: A Technological Threshold

Technology at the millennium is transitioning from the Industrial Age of coal and petroleum to the Electronic-Cyberspace Age (see Chapter 1). This future, to be powered by innovative renewable fuels, is leading the world into the conquest of cosmic space and multiple other frontiers of technological change including wireless Internet, unprecedented use of DNA code, cloning, robotics, and artificial intelligence. The new technologies are already affecting our *worldview*: where we live and work, our concepts of governance, and our attitudes toward travel and recreation. Travel to the Moon and Mars will probably be realized within this century; travel to Deep Space (beyond our solar system) within this millennium. Technology can recreate any environment as virtual reality. The present time is exciting because we understand the processes involved in watching distances shrink as communication and transportation time bring destinations closer (see Figure 5).

The Critical Issues

Demographics

World population has more than doubled since the postwar 1950 baseline data of 2.5 million to reach 6.1 billion in 2000, and upward projections estimate 7.7 billion by 2020 and 9.4 billion by 2050 (Table 26.1). *Vision 2020* (WTO, 1998a) predicts international tourist arrivals in 2020 will increase by 240% to 1.6 billion arrivals, or nearly 21% of the entire world population will be traveling away from home each year. *Vision 2020* further suggests that this volume of international tourism is not evenly distributed, and that many individuals in the MDCs may make more than one (and possibly as many as four) international trip(s) per year. Thirty-two percent of travel will be long haul, transporting tourists to distant, even remote, destinations, and increasing their impact in the air and on the ground. Many air traffic corridors are already overcrowded, causing flight delays. To service these new tourists, European and American aircraft manufacturers have drawing board models for 650- and 800-passenger jumbo jets. With a domino effect, these giant craft will require longer runways, larger terminals, and more ground

Table 26.1. World Population, Urbanization, and International Arrivals: 1950–2050 (in billions)

Year	Population	Urban	% Urban Population	International Arrivals	% Total Arrivals
1950	2.5	0.8	30%	0.0025	1%
2000	6.1	2.9	47%	0.673	10.9%
2020	7.7	4.4	57%	1.6	21%
2050	9.4	6.5	69%	?	?

Source: UN census projections to 2020. Arrival figures are from Vision 2020 (WTO, 1998). Figures for 2050 Worldwatch extrapolations (Brown, Gardner, & Halweil, 1998, p. 44).

transport. In many instances, airport relocation to sites farther from urban centers is mandatory. The cumulative effect of larger populations that travel more and farther intensifies the pressures at destinations for recreational space and vacation activities. That pressure will be most heightened in the fragile environments of nature tourism.

In addition to this demographic increase, the future will be also influenced by three further factors:

1. virtually all industrial nations including China (as of May 1999) have now adopted a maximum 40-hour work week, ensuring more leisure time;
2. the new electronic technology that created jobs and prosperity in Asia, the US, and Europe also provides more discretionary income; and
3. the recognition of travel as a human right confirms positive social sanctions for travel.

Thus, the original definition of tourism as leisure time + discretionary income + positive sanctions is further validated for the future.

In the past 30 years, outbound tourism from the industrial West dominated and established then-new popular styles of tourism including mass tourism on motorcoach tours, the north–south flow to the sunbelts, the sun–sea–sand–sex beach and island resorts, adventure tourism, and cruising. Looking ahead, the emerging economies of Asia and their demographics suggest that, in the next decade or two, the Asian population will dominate tourism and the tourism styles will change in response to their cultural preferences. The psychographs of Asian travelers are different, and their importance is still little understood in the West. In part, Boracay (Chapter 10) is an evolutionary microcosm of Asian tourism that began with local householders hosting families of Western visitors for a beach vacation, and subsequently expanded to mass tourism involving Asians living in foreign-owned hotels on short, cheap air tours with emphasis on shopping. Alternately, the new emerging Asian cruise industry (Singh, 2000) follows the "fantasyland" theme using Carnival Cruises format of mega-ships, but is adapted to Asian cultural preferences. Short 3-, 4-, and 5-day cruises from Asian hubs emphasize shopping more than beaches or sightseeing, and the ships have larger casinos (and more electronic security) as well as private rooms for karaoke (http://www.starcruises.com).

Essentially half the present world population lives in Asia, in the area bounded by the five Asian mega-cities (Figure 26.1), and many more cities with large populations lie within this perimeter. The addition by 2020 of another 1.6 billion people, of whom almost half will be urban Asian, points vividly to new centers of mass tourism for which planning must begin now.

Population shifts (Table 26.2) illustrate that among the leading industrial nations (MDCs), only the US and the UK will have population increases in the next 50 years (the left-hand side of the table); all others decline. Among the LDCs, the greatest *percentages of growth* by 2050 are African (Ethiopia, Congo, Tanzania, and Nigeria), but the *greatest increases in numbers* of residents are Asian, led by India, China, and Pakistan. Rank as the "top 40" (the right-hand side of the table) is a WTO ranking of nations in terms of popularity as a destination (number of international arrivals) and as an earner and spender of foreign exchange. Comparing the two sides of Table 26.2 illustrates demographic growth in relation to tourism.

The US between 1990 and 1998 held No. 1 rank as an earner and spender nation but slipped in destination popularity from second to third place. The US also shows the greatest percentage of population growth and presumably will retain a leadership rank because of the popularity of its destination attractions. Increased domestic tourism plus increased international arrivals point to the need in America for serious recreation resource planning. Vehicular traffic to national parks such as Grand Canyon, Yellowstone, and Yosemite already exceeds comfortable carrying capacity.

In that same 8-year time span, China moved up from 12 to 6 in rank as a destination, from 25 to 7 in earnings, and from 40 to 10 as a tourism spending nation. WTO forecasts that by 2020 China will rank first as a destination, with 137 million international arrivals per year, and will rank fourth as a generating area. These projections become important as our data identify China's limited critical resources as well as the nation's new protourism policy.

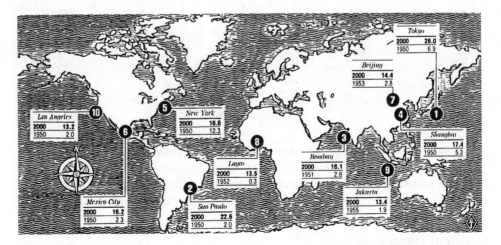

Figure 26.1. Mega-cities around the globe. (Source: United Nations, Elizabeth Traynor. Reprinted with permission of Dow Jones from *The Wall Street Journal*, December 11, 1997, p. A20)

Table 26.2. Population Shifts in MDCs and LDCs in 1998 With 2050 Projections and Selected Top 40 Countries as Destinations, Earners, and Spenders

Population Data (Millions)		Population Increase		Area	Rank Within Top 40					
					As Destination		As Earner		As Spender	
1998	2050	Millions	%		1990	1998	1990	1998	1990	1998
More Developed Countries (MDC)										
274	348	+74	+27	United States	2	3	1	1	1	1
147	114	−33	−22	Russia	17	13	23	16		11
126	110	−16	−13	Japan	28	32	17	25	33	
82	79	−12	−2	Germany	9	11	6	6	2	2
59	58	−1	−2	France	1	1	2	3	6	6
58	59	+1	+2	United Kingdom	7	5	5	5	4	4
57	42	−15	−26	Italy		4	4	3	2	5
Developing Countries (LDC)										
976	1533	+557	+57	India	12	6	33	34		
1255	1517	+262	+21	China			25	7	40	10
148	357	+209	+141	Pakistan						
122	339	+217	+178	Nigeria					37	38
168	243	+78	+47	Brazil	53	39	36	36	23	15
124	218	+94	+76	Bangladesh						
62	213	+151	+244	Ethiopia						
73	170	+97	+133	Iran						
49	165	+116	+237	Congo						
96	154	+58	+60	Mexico	8	7	10	14	12	23
66	115	+49	+74	Egypt	35	34	44	27		
32	89	+57	+178	Tanzania						

Source: Population figures from Brown et al., 1998, *Beyond Malthus: Sixteen Dimensions of the Population Problem* (World Watch Paper 143), "World's Top 40 Tourist Destinations," *Tourism Highlights* 1999, WTO, 2000.

No other country has shown comparable shifts, although Brazil is gaining in popularity as a destination and also as a spending nation. Some countries are listed because of their high percentages of population growth (Tanzania, Iran, and Congo) but have never appeared in the tourism "top 40" because political instability deters tourism.

Critical Resources

Gunn (1994), a widely recognized tourism planner, views tourism as a system or a series of integrated elements. Population dynamics is important but tourism growth that must be matched with the critical physical resources—energy and water—to sustain both a larger host population and increased numbers of visitors. A tourist destination requires a higher per capita share of both energy and water in comparison to the normal use. The after-dark entertainment industries with lighted signage and illumination are heavy power consumers. Tourist water consumption increases for laundry, swimming pools, and the decorative use of water in architectural and interior design.

Energy

Electric energy is vital to modern life and industry. Even the highly developed US energy network operates at maximum electrical output on days of high-energy demand for either heat (on unusually cold days) or air conditioning (during a heat wave). A mega-event scheduled in New York or Los Angeles during peak demand could be disastrous. New, costly, long-term facilities must be budgeted and built to accommodate the projected increasing domestic and tourist population. Elsewhere, especially in the LDCs (including China), rolling brownouts (limited electricity rotated around an area on a timed schedule) disrupt local services.

Coal was the primary energy source throughout most of the Industrial Revolution era, but coal is a known health hazard causing respiratory ailments and widespread air pollution. At least 800 million rural Chinese still use coal for cooking and the nation still generates 75% of its electricity from this source. Dunn (1999) reports that coal combustion is "the single largest source of CO_2 emissions . . . and greenhouse gases released by coal combustion play a significant role in destabilizing climate . . . extensive ecosystem damage, loss of species and other serious disruptions" (p. 17). The high incidence of air pollution from Asia (which crosses the North Pacific and reaches the West Coast of the US) is convincing the Chinese to shift to natural gas even at the considerable cost for new equipment.

Petroleum was second to coal as an Industrial Revolution energy fuel. The oil crises of 2000 with petroleum priced at US$35 per barrel or more is but a ripple preceding a tidal wave of disruptions, considering that oil production is near total global capacity. Geologists Campbell and Leberrere (1998) report that half the world petroleum supply was exhausted in the 20th century, and future production is expected to peak at 2010 and decline rather steeply thereafter. Because so many nations now depend on tourism as their primary income and employment source, the search for replacement energy is intense and diverse. New sources must be expandable to accommodate the ever-increasing demand.

Access to new fuels is an important reason for industrial development in space. The tourism space travel case study (Brent, Chapter 27) emphasizes the development of passenger travel. However, the new "race for space" is primarily rooted in potential industrial resources and land for colonization. Noteworthy among energy sources, Schmitt (2000) estimates that a single Atlantis shuttle load of helium-3 brought to earth from the moon could power all the energy needs of the US for a year.

Water

The role of water as a tourist resource dates to prehistory. Aboriginal peoples gathered at mineral springs to enjoy therapeutic baths as did the ancient Greeks and Romans, and travel agents continue to promote spa vacations. "It is for its great value to tourism that water quality and its protection must be seen by all sectors as absolutely essential to tourism's success—economically as well as socially and environmentally" (Gunn, 1994, p. 45).

Although critical shortages are not immediate, water is clearly an important 21st century issue. India, China, and the US are numerically ranked as the nations with the greatest potential water deficits (Postal, 1999), despite the fact that all have major watersheds and enormous river basins. With full realization that by 2050 her population may exceed 1.5 billion, China openly acknowledges the problem. China's present total water reserve is the sixth highest in the world but the per capita supply ranks 121st in the world, an amount equal to only one fourth of the world's per capita average (Xia, 2000, p. 6). If population pressure requires that water be allocated to cities rather than to irrigated farming, crop production and its high market value will suffer. The US once joked, some 40 years ago, about a futuristic plan to reroute the Yukon River from Alaska to southern California. Now that then-sleepy Los Angeles has grown into one of the world's mega-cities (Figure 26.1), this idea may reappear as a serious proposal. A similar and controversial project under consideration in China would divert part of the Yangtze River north to the now nearly dry Hai River basin, to sustain its agriculture. To find water on the moon and transport it to earth as ballast in returning space shuttles may not prove to be as ridiculous as it now sounds.

Environmental Stewardship

In 1900 only 10% of the world's population were city dwellers, but by 2000 that figure had increased to nearly 50% (Table 26.1). The presence of cities changes the landscape and reduces the amount of open land available for agriculture and for recreation. Each of the five mega-cities of Asia (Figure 26.1) currently exceed 10 million residents, but dozens of other cities in excess of 1 million are scattered through Asia from India to Korea. Further, the most rapidly urbanizing area of the world is sub-Saharan Africa (O'Meara, 1999, pp. 16–17). From these crowded urban cores, an eager humanity is waiting to pour out into international vacationlands, to enjoy the lifestyle of the Western tourists whose images they have seen on TV. Urban crowding is an incentive to spend discretionary funds on tourism, and has been encouraged by Japan and China to equalize balance of payments (see below).

The Japanese have traveled widely for several decades, and other Asians began their overseas travels dominantly in the 1990s. The Taiwanese are believed to have first ventured into the High Arctic on a Russian icebreaker in 1995. Taiwanese and Hong Kong Chinese began to arrive in Kotzebue in 1997 in such numbers that NANA felt obliged to hire a Chinese interpreter to serve them. Asian demand for beach resorts led to overdevelopment of Boracay, and many more Asian beaches in Vietnam, Malaysia, Thailand, Sabah, and Indonesia will certainly undergo similar expansion. African tourism will probably develop in another generation.

Balance of Payments

Asian cultures have traditionally fostered the philosophy of saving, not spending, their surplus income. However, in the new global economy in which national and international culture brokers increasingly politicize tourism, the economic value of tourism becomes a factor in international trade. In the 1980s, as overseas sales of Japanese products progressively increased that nation's favorable balance of payments, the Japanese government advocated more overseas tourism to partially equalize their income/debt ratios. The Chinese also recently adopted this policy, using overseas payments by Chinese tourists to help offset their mounting export income. The list of countries in which their workers may vacation first included contiguous Thailand and Malaysia, then Australia, and most recently the US. Chinese travel expenditures in these countries infuse money into the local economy and, with its multiplier effect, stimulates further purchase of Chinese manufactured goods. Tourism has become an export-import commodity, not just a host-guest exchange. As a product, tourism is subject to the criteria by which foreign manufactures such as automobiles or computers might be judged: quality, reliability, style, manufacturer guarantees, support services (here, NGOs, tourist boards, and consulates), and consumer satisfaction.

For the year 2000, China announced creation of three week-long holidays per year, the first in early May. In large numbers, urban Chinese enjoyed holidays by train to historic cities, gardens, and famous shrines, infusing urban wealth into rural poverty. During this week Chinese spent an estimated RMB 18 billion (US$2.068 billion) on travel, mostly for domestic tourism. Zhang (2000) suggests that the government supports this long holiday spending "as a means to stimulate consumption and further accelerate the entire national economic development," expressed in Chinese as *jiari jingji* ("holiday economy").

Cross-Cultural Values

Stewardship is a cultural construct, and conservation of public lands and wildlife is not a traditional global value. The increased industry promotion of ecotourism and adventure tourism for the expanding Asian market holds great appeal but threatens natural preserves. Lew (1998) observed many differences in the Asian–Pacific perception of ecotourism: "Despite the considerable literature defining what ecotourism is or should be, it is the practitioners [tour operators] who make ecotourism a tangible experience for their clients and destinations. In putting ecotourism into practice, they ensure that the often overlooked element of *a bottom line profit margin is calculated into the definition* of ecotourism [italics ours]. . . ." irrespective of "the loss of natural environment and traditional cultures that form the basis of many ecotour experiences. This is the price of the modernisation that most countries seek" (p. 93).

Hashimoto (2000) further emphasizes that the Chinese and the Japanese

> love nature and the natural phenomenon only if nature provides benefits for humans and not for nature itself . . . [they] do not understand human-nature relationship as it is understood in the West . . . that humans have to help conserve and renew while utilising the natural environment and resources. Such an anthropocentric view will encourage the exploitation of scenic beauty, and abundant natural biosphere as tourist attractions. Relying too heavily on "natural power" for maintenance and healing of environmental damage, and on technological 'quick fixes' may lead to long-term problems . . . it is an essential task for the tourism industry in these coun-

tries to understand and disseminate awareness of environmental issues sooner rather than later . . . failure to do so could be placing the environment in severe jeopardy. (p. 143)

The reality of this assessment has already occurred in Thailand where Twentieth Century Fox studio leased Maya Beach on Phi Leh Island (Thailand) to produce a 1999 film, *The Beach*. In violation of their own regulations, Thailand's Royal Forestry Department accepted a use fee of Bhat 4 million (about US$108,000), but did not set effective preservation standards. In preparation for filming, the island—described as one of the beautiful unspoiled islands in the Pacific—was transformed by bulldozing and the importation of nonnative plants to create a Hollywood version of "paradise." The issue stirred an international controversy from conservationists initiated by a Thai group who photographically documented the desecration (http:///www.uq.edu.au/-ppgredde/index.html).The circumstances illustrate in part the differing cultural concepts of environmental stewardship, and also demonstrate the electronic capability to monitor and mobilize public opinion in defense of sustainable use.

Stewardship by Exclusivity

"Travel has suddenly become such a huge industry that it's threatening to wreck the places we love" according to Tourtellot (2000, p. 110), senior editor of *National Geographic Traveler*. Tourtellot summarizes five options for possible stewardship: Spread Out; Concentrate; Limit Traffic by Quota, by Price, or by Lottery; Ban Access Entirely; and Raise Awareness. However, one of Tourtellot's sources identified the economic reality, "I've never seen a resource manager at the tourism-marketing table" (p. 119).

Tourism planning to protect environmental resources requires the coordination of government, tour operators, and service providers, as shown in efforts to protect the Great Barrier Reef (see Parker, Chapter 18). Two countries, Namibia and the Seychelles, have recently established environmental stewardship priorities, limiting tourists by price. Namibia, formerly Southwest Africa, was renamed for its formidable Namib desert when the country attained independence in 1990. The present government is eager to develop their tourism potential. However, due to water limitation they can serve a *maximum* of 1 million tourist arrivals per year. The Namibian Tourist Board worked with investors and developers to establish a "high-cost, low volume tourist base made up primarily of wealthy Europeans, Australasians and North Americans who have grown weary of the crime and crowded national parks in East Africa" (Swaney, 1999, p. 561). Namibian marketing is directed to these long-haul air travelers, but to avoid a criticism of exclusivity older, lower cost properties remain available for drive-in traffic from South Africa and Angola. This conservation-oriented decision is temporarily costly but long term it should preserve the Namibian desert landscape and its exotic wildlife.

The Seychelles (see Chapter 21) has boldly moved forward to create an autonomous private–public marketing organization to target the upscale market who want and can afford exclusivity. With resort room rates priced at US$1000 per night, the intent is to "place ourselves in a league different from other tropical islands" (Savy, 2000, p. 10). This new conservation strategy to "preserve some of the world's most idyllic islands for the enjoyment of tourists and the prosperity of residents for generations to come" permits only 180,000 annual visitors. The project is managed by Seychelles Tourism Management Authority (STMA), online January 2001.

Globalization

In the 1960s era that was the forerunner of mass tourism, corporations such as Hilton and Intercontinental Hotels, which were in business or had properties in multiple countries but were centered in one home nation, were termed *transnational*. This concept began to change as producer services in finance, consultancy, accounting, and advertising became *multinational* and stimulated broader-based international trade. As capital flowed by means of direct investment into industries, mining, and even agriculture in other countries, business became global. Most automobiles, for example, are no longer manufactured in a single plant but are assembled with component parts imported from specialty factories located in a number of countries. This development of an interactive world economy is now termed *globalization*. It has been accompanied by significant changes in political structure, including deregulation of the airlines and expansion of free trade under multilateral agreements such as the North American Free Trade Agreement (NAFTA), and the European Community (EC). The direct effects of cultural globalization were discussed in Section 1. The specific interest here is the correlation between globalization, urbanization, and tourism.

Urbanization

As the Industrial era and colonialism faded, many historic cities lost their aura of prosperity and greatness. Their central factories closed and jobs disappeared, leaving empty stores, abandoned churches, and vacant houses. Central business districts "died" as the population moved to the suburbs, started businesses, and patronized new shopping malls with their vast parking areas.

The New Cities

Globalization is widely discussed by social scientists who now see in cities the emergence of new nucleating cores to replace the vanishing nation-state. "Globalization entails a shift from two-dimensional Euclidian space with its centers and peripheries and sharp boundaries, to a multi-dimensional global space with unbounded, often discontinuous and interpenetrating sub-species" (Kearney, 1995, p. 549). As noted in Chapter 1, pre-World War II cities used to bear a national image in architecture, life style, and place names. The new cities build deterritorialized pinnacles of steel, glass, and mirror, termed "hyperspaces," in locations such as airports, franchised stores, and malls that are so detached from local referents as to have "monotonous universal qualities" (Eco, 1986).

Short and Kim (1999, p. 120) describe the new entrepreneurial city as less concerned with former values, such as promotion of local businesses, and more concerned with pro-growth activism, often termed the "growth machine" that believes "bigger is better." In pursuit of this goal, civic leaders may offer free land and tax incentives for new long-term growth enterprises (as national governments did in the 1970s). Cities now advertise for new businesses and new residents in newspapers, including the *Wall Street Journal* and the *Economist*, as well as in magazines as diverse as *Forbes, National Geographic Traveler*, and *Historic Preservation*. Cities adopt slogans, such as "Los Angeles: Capital of the Future," which advertises business opportunities, while others advertise quality of life, such as Miami, FL as "perfectly seasoned" (for retirement living) or Atlantic City, NJ, which proclaims itself as "American's favorite playground" (for tourism and gaming). These advertisements also attract new tourism.

Important to the development of the new cities are the information and best practices shared via their networks. In June 1996 representatives from 171 nations and 579 cities met in Istanbul at Habitat II (the second United Nations Conference on Human Settlements). Delegates signed a metropolitan version of Local Agenda 21 "to develop cities that are safer, healthier and more livable, equitable, sustainable and productive." The International Council on Local Environment Initiatives (ICLEI) serves as the clearinghouse, and in 1999 reported more than 2000 cities were engaged in Local Agenda 21, with more than 600 success stories, or "best practices" available for study.

Urban Tourism

As new global cities forge images as centers of political leadership, they attract several streams or categories of residents, four of which are particularly important to tourism: penturbia, internationalists, ethnic refugees, and urban poor.

Penturbia

Penturbia is the fifth urban movement in the US since 1735 AD (Lessinger, 1986). The first was migration within the original 13 colonies, followed by their grandchildren who spread into the Mississippi and Ohio valleys after 1790. After 1845, the third wave built industrial cities, and their grandchildren after 1900 fled to suburbia. Two generations later, after 1960, the Penturbians, wearied of commuting, began renovating abandoned warehouses in the urban cores as upscale townhouses and boutiques. They may even live "upstairs" in a view apartment where they can "go home to lunch, via elevator." Most like and support the cultural amenities of the city, and are important both to domestic and foreign tourism because they have no house or land to maintain.

The New "Internationalists"

The "new" city attracts top-echelon internationalists from global enterprises in finance, insurance, export–import, electronics, international airlines, and the arts. Often Echo Boomers in age, they are well educated, affluent and avant-garde. Many are single and may support alternative lifestyles or are married "dinks" (double income, no kids). They shun traditional ethnicity except as a veneer to their modeled culture of sophistication and political correctness. They have been instrumental in the development of new technology but find their professional interests are best served by globalization. Their urban presence is often defined by the boutiques and fine restaurants of renovated historic sites, including San Francisco's Ghiradelli Square (in the old chocolate factory), England's Ironbridge Gorge,

Capetown's Victoria and Albert Wharf, and in Australia, Sydney's Harbor and Opera district. They are also the Chinese of Shenzhen and other Economic Zones, and the Indians of the computer complex in Bangalore.

Ethnic Refugees

Late 20th century political turmoil in some developing countries led to liberalization of immigration policies (especially for "guest" workers, willing to accept minimal wages). Political refugees from former colonies flooded the "home" land. Others who were suddenly "stateless," "soilless," or victims of human rights violations sought haven wherever shelter was extended, including border refugee camps. The fortunate ones among them benefited from jet travel that speeded the flow of ethnic migration to cities such as New York and London where they filled the now-vacated rooms and opened businesses (Sassen, 1991). A rich and interesting literature describes the "Caribbeanization of the New York City" (Sutton, 1987), the Senegalese in Italy (Carter, 1995), the Turks in Germany (Mandel, 1991), and West Indians and Sikhs in England (Goulbourne, 1991).

A deterritorialization of culture progressed as these recent migrants formed ethnic enclaves built around the convenience of language, and proximity to ethnic food markets, to churches/synagogues/mosques/temples, and to friends and family. The presence of these often inner city ethnic entities further defines the influence of globalization. San Francisco's Chinatown (and the new Chinese community forming in Vancouver, British Columbia) is the largest Chinese "city" outside Asia; the Hispanic community of mega-city Los Angeles is the largest Latin "city" north of Mexico. Their folk festivals and craft fairs are major tourist attractions, and ultimately these urban newcomers also become important reserve storehouses of heritage that is often disappearing from a war-torn homeland.

Tourism and the Urban Poor

Globalization has not as yet erased the polarities between rich and poor. The wealthy can have tourism options whereas most urban poor do not (Sassen, 1998), and few tourism specialists have expressed concern with the tourism of poverty. Rural populations in Africa, Eastern Europe, and South America are often near, if not at, starvation levels, driven from traditional homes by hunger or by an emotional hungering for a better life in the city. Data from the Asian Development Bank (www.adb.org) suggest that, for China at least, the urban in-migrants benefited from increased life expectancy (+9%), access to culinary water (+50%) and sanitation (+120%), and five times (+500%) greater access to medical care. These ratios are not true, however, of many who live in the shanty towns and squatter's huts that ring the outskirts of Lima, Caracas, Rio, Harare, Dacca, and Djakarta, to name some of the most glaring. Attracted to the city in hope, some find jobs but many do not. For these homeless and hopeless, their avenue to escape is regrettably linked to crime, prostitution, and drugs, and not to pleasurable recreation because there is little or none provided or available to them.

If tourism is a human right, then the failure to provide recreation to everyone is a disgrace to a city and a blight on the industry. The editors of this volume are thoroughly mindful of the overwhelming problems resulting from the trauma of

ethnic cleansing, of starvation from weather-induced crop failure, and similar tragedies in which only basic needs can be minimally met. Beyond those tragic circumstances, there are avenues to provide recreation, and many are not costly. Communities are beginning to learn that funds invested in recreation are repaid by
decreased delinquency, less graffiti, fewer gangs, and more potential employees.

The London-based Overseas Development Institute (ODI) initiated a program:
Putting Poverty at the Heart of the Tourism Agenda (National Resource Perspective, March, 2000). Through proactive research and activities, they hope to halve
the number of people living in extreme poverty by donor-supported tourism master plans. ODI reports challenge the validity of nationally reported tourism growth
receipts because they lack economic sector analysis. The poverty-stricken currently benefit very little from national tourism development. Proposals to provide
training programs that will reach into slums to teach tourism job skills await implementation by WTO as well as ODI.

Volunteerism

To donate *gratis* one's time and talent to helping unknown people is a cultural
concept that is little known in Asia, Africa, and even Europe. Old World societies
relied on blood relatives as defined by membership in tribe, lineage, clan, and
family members to provide crisis support for illness and misfortune. Families who
had lived in the same villages, or on the same lands for generations, even centuries, maintained an important obligation of reciprocity and mutual aid.

In the Americas, the picture was different. Aside from the prehistoric migrations
of Native Americans, from the time of Cortes and the Conquest of Mexico (1521
AD), all new settlers irrespective of their origin in Europe, Africa, or Asia were
immigrants. Most came to the New World as *individuals*, leaving behind family
connections and reciprocity. To meet personal crises, lonely Americans turned to
neighbors for needed support, and the concept of community aid grew into the
now-international service organizations originally founded in America, including
Rotary International, Soroptimist, Kiwanis, Lion's Club, etc. Volunteerism is now
an integral part of the lifestyle and behavior of millions of Americans, many of
whom are retirees. Unpaid, these volunteers donate hours of time each week to
assist in hospitals, teach the illiterate, serve as teacher's aides in schools, feed the
homeless, and operate boys' and girls' recreational clubs. The new technology will
soon create larger numbers of retired workers in LDCs whose volunteer efforts
could similarly alleviate some hopelessness among the impoverished in their cities. Volunteerism is a cultural construct that can be implemented anywhere by
individuals who are motivated to reach out to others, as did Mother Teresa in
Calcutta to ease the pain of the dying.

Other Global Issues

The New Technologies

The Internet

The Internet is a powerful new factor in tourism that provides almost instantaneous access to current world tourism sources. The growing number of individu-

als who prefer to make their own travel arrangements via the Web soon discover a need for more knowledge of world geography as well as tourism services. The do-it-yourself search for cheaper airfares or last-minute bookings for unsold space on cruise vessels leads to poring over online advertisements for tours and hotels. However, the search is a rewarding exercise for many travelers who often benefit from the additional knowledge about their destinations. What used to be the excitement of going to the travel agency to obtain information and documents is now concentrated in their sense of self-satisfaction.

The travel industry clearly stands to benefit from increased Internet exposure. At a January 2000 WTO Tourism and Cyberspace symposium, panelists urged small enterprises to develop Web sites, which for modest cost enable them to reach global audiences at an advertising level never before attained. Small-scale entrepreneurs, especially home-stay owners in areas such as Pamukkale (see Chapter 12) or Bali (Dahles & Bras, 1999), could develop and have a marketing organization with more income security. "On Internet, content is not just king. Content is God. The more information you can give, the stronger you are" (McGovern, 2000, p. 15).

This newfound independence in making travel arrangements is not without risk. The world is a huge complex of places, some of which are not served by frequent transportation. Despite the listings of services (such as buses, dormitories, and cafes) in adventure travel magazines and guidebooks, on arrival travelers have found these facilities no longer exist. The convenience of self-planning faces at least two risks: quality control and fiscal responsibility. Unless the guest uses a reputable reservation service or a multinational hotel chain that requires regular site inspections, there are no guarantees of cleanliness or quality of the facilities. As Dann (1996) has repeatedly stressed, travel brochures are merely pieces of paper on which representations can be very misleading, and the mediated images of the Internet can be even more persuasive. Travel agents are the usual first line of traveler protection, and without that, Internet misrepresentation or fraud to individuals may become a legal issue. International litigation is an expensive and cumbersome process.

The Internet also offers the possibility of creating new centers of employment in rural and remote locations. Language facility and a Web site are the basic requirements to participate in global business and thus extend the economic benefits of tourism to outlying areas, often at less cost. Reservations for car rentals, hotel rooms, tours, and cruises can be handled from any geographic location given training and equipment.

Information Technology

Geographic Information Systems (GIS) are proving to be an invaluable new tool, to gather and map data on almost every aspect of land use important to tourism. When combined with the Global Positioning System (GPS), tourist attractions and services can be quickly and accurately located, and even emergency services can be dispatched to a site identified by a call from a cell phone. The pioneering journal *Information Technology & Tourism,* launched in 1998, is an important addition to the tourism literature and often draws directly from the GIS sources and data. Buhalis and Spada (2000) capture the essence of the information technologies (ITs) that "transform the tourism industry to the digital economy. The emergence of destination management systems (DMSs) as 'info-structures' enables destinations to disseminate comprehensive information about resources and services at destinations and local tourism products as well as to facilitate the planning, management, and marketing of regions as tourism entities or brands" (p. 41).

Virtual Tourism

The Internet has also helped to spawn the *virtual tourist*, or an armchair traveler who used to read travel books but now "surfs" his way to a destination, selecting routes and transportation, studying weather maps, and finally enjoying the colored (and sometimes animated) photos to dream of his stay—all with essentially no expense, no jetlag, and no threats to his personal security. Bristow (1999) suggests that virtual tourism may eventually become the "ultimate ecotourism," capable of incorporating the full range of human senses. Some museums have already developed this capacity, including the odors of decaying fish in Viking markets (at Maihaugen in Lillehammer, Norway and York, UK). MacCannell (Chapter 29), in the concluding case study, raises the penetrating question: if virtual reality is more authentic than reality, why should the tourist leave home?

Tourism students (and their professors) are also virtual tourists, gathering information about destinations to analyze its characteristics for their research and writing projects. Their use of the Internet may further instill an interest for *real* tourism, as did *National Geographic* and the stereopticon in the days of their grandparents.

In addition to theme parks, including Universal Studio where MacCannell has been engaged in research (see Chapter 29), HYPERPORTS are new commercial buildings. They will feature offices and state-of-the-art interactive platforms to display Business Solutions and Education products. The first HYPERPORT will be linked by footbridge to the Mall of America in Minneapolis, to take advantage of their 42 million annual visitors. The US$800 million building sited on 53 acres of land will be anchored by a 100,000-square-foot Sony display of their latest products. Using the theme of educational enrichment, the structural centerpiece will be Space and Discovery Park with a life-size replica of the International Space Station (ISS). Visitors can experience weightlessness and have virtual views of the Earth (Figure 27.2). Success of this ambitious project is expected to expand local tourism, lure more shoppers to the Mall of America, and stimulate construction of HYPERPORTS in other world locations. Space travel thus becomes a form of virtual tourism "shoppertainment."

Personal Security

Terrorism

Personal security is an element of mounting concern that has moved beyond criminal attacks and muggings for money and personal effects (see Chapter 28). The heightened terrorist activity of kidnapping and holding tourists hostage to barter their lives for armaments is a chilling deterrent to tourism in many unstable areas of the world. An individual tourist can observe the usual precautions of avoiding dark streets and high-crime areas of a city, but even tourist groups have little foreknowledge of raids on resorts. Unfortunately, incidents of terrorist attacks on tourists are often deliberately unreported or are downplayed, to protect local images and tourist income. The traveler's world is becoming progressively more dangerous, including "hacker" raids on computer software, that can disrupt air service, close airports, derail trains, and cause accidents.

Disease

The spread of contagious disease is of increasing concern as a consequence of tourism, and the rapid transit of infectious diseases between continents can occur in a matter of hours. "We live in a time where there exists a virtual viral superhighway, bringing people into contact with pathogens that affect our adaptation" (Armelagos, Barnes, & Lin, 1996, p. 7). Returning tourists as well as foreign visitors can introduce a new emerging disease that can affect large segments of the population. Many are mutant diseases that may be antibiotic resistant due to indiscriminate medical practices, including the use of subtherapeutic doses of antibiotics in animal feed. The incidence of HIV and AIDS in Africa, now spreading in part via tourism through shared needles and unprotected sex, becomes a tourist threat if hospitalization and blood transfusions are necessary.

Global warming is also identified as a "hidden health risk" (Epstein, 2000, pp. 50-67), contributing to the spread of diseases to higher elevations than normal, and under the influence of El Nino to areas that were normally arid. Threats of pulmonary infections such as hantavirus and West Nile virus are tourist deterrents.

The PEST Analysis

To complement our macro-view of tourism in the decades to come, Hall (2000, p. 88) has drafted a microperspective, or PEST (political, economic, social, technology) analysis of future trends in tourism (Table 26.3). Short term, it offers substantial guidelines with which to monitor and forecast change, and is a worthy addition to any discussion of the future of tourism.

The Future: War and Peace

More than a century ago, Inuit and Indians engaged in ethnic cleansing and used aboriginal equivalents of land mines to cripple their enemy. They finally agreed to a peace process and ceased fighting. Can the modern world also do so? "Peace is the pivotal issue . . . and how we handle this issue may determine whether or not humanity survives into the 21st century but also the quality of life for future generations and the biosphere, and even the course of human evolution" (Sponsel, 1994, p. 2).

Wars of the 18th and 19th centuries were fought on battlefields between armies composed of men trained and equipped for the purpose, and tourists watched its progress (Seaton, 1999). The 20th century wars progressively carried the conflict deeper into civilian space, damaging cities and destroying heritage sites, and unleashed the powerful potential of nuclear destruction. To these, the 21st century

Table 26.3. A PEST Analysis of Possible Future Trends for Tourism

<u>Political</u>
Short Term to 2005
- Ongoing emphasis on public–private partnerships in tourism
- Tourism continues to be given high political prominence because of its perceived economic and employment value
- Ongoing emphasis on free trade
- Continued financial support for tourism promotion
- Normalization of relations between Cuba and the US leads to dramatic tourism growth on the island

Mid-term 2006–2010
- Tourists increasingly subject to attack in some developing countries
- Increases resistance to free trade agreements as government subsidies are withdrawn, especially in Europe as assistance for rural tourism activities are reduced
- European Union continues to grow to include Eastern European nations

2011–2020
- Increased conflict between developing and developed countries over global economic development strategies as it becomes apparent to large numbers of the population in developing countries that they will never be able to have Western lifestyles due to population and resource constraints

<u>Economic</u>
Short Term to 2005
- Continued trade wars between Europe, Japan, and the US
- Continued growth of user-pays philosophy in visitor management
- Continued development of alliances between tourism/leisure/entertainment/sport/communication corporations

Mid-term 2006–2010
- Asian economic growth returns to early 1990 figures mainly due to the growth of the Chinese economy
- Formal horizontal and vertical integration between tourism/leisure/entertainment/sport/communication corporations
- Network strategies continue to be utilized by smaller, secondary tourism businesses

2001–2020
- Substantial free trade in APEC area
- Japan replaced as major tourism-generating market in Asia by China and India
- Economic growth targets come under increased pressure because of natural resource constraints; reduced economic growth and higher fuel costs lead to substantial reductions in the rate of world tourism growth

adds ethnic cleansing, biological warfare, child soldiers, and the threat of cyberwars, robotics, and space wars.

Anthropologist Jack Eller (1999) identifies a sociopolitical progression that may explain, at least in part, the military chronology of globalization. Nations as they existed until the outbreak of World War II were predominantly comprised of people who shared a common language, culture, and goals. The US identified its nationhood with the principle of the "melting pot" to which immigrants were attracted,

Table 26.3 continued.

Social
Short Term to 2005
- Continued growth in proportion of population over 55 in developed nations
- Continued growth of consumerism in Asian countries
- "Fast food" and restaurant sector continues to grow as less people prepare their own meals at home
- Increasing recognition by the tourism industry of the needs of single parent families
- Education standards continue to increase in the tourism industry

Mid-term 2006–2010
- Aging populations in developed countries increasingly have to rely on own funds rather than state pensions for their retirement
- Cruising continues to grow as a travel market as population ages
- Despite ongoing improvements in communication technology, business and conference travel continue to grow because of the desire for personal contact
- Educational travel continues to grow because of the need for lifelong learning skills and the continued reskilling required in the workplace

2011–2020
- Development of mass "health tourism" for the wealthier classes in the developed world as medical technology continues to lengthen life span of some
- Increasing focus on domestic and short-haul travel as cost of long-haul travel dramatically increases due to fuel costs
- Religious and spiritual-related travel increasingly important due to uncertainty and rapid change

Technology
Short Term to 2005
- Continued growth of Internet
- Reorientation of travel agencies as information brokers as increasing numbers of tourists book their own travel

Mid-term 2006–2010
- Widespread introduction of new generation double-decker jumbo jets further reinforcing development of "hub and spoke" transport patterns
- Dramatic growth in train travel in conjunction with air travel as high speed train systems continue to be integrated with aviation hubs
- Virtual tourism used to sell visits to destinations

2011–2020
- Increase cost of aviation fuel as world oil supplies come under increasing pressure, leading to dramatic impacts on visitor arrivals to long-haul destinations
- Public transport given renewed emphasis as price of fuel increases
- Air balloons increasingly used for commercial flights
- Space tourism commercially available

eager to assimilate into that larger whole. Americans were willing to pay the military price of war to defend the concept of equality beginning with their Civil War, to free the African slaves brought to this continent against their will. However, Canadian prime minister Trudeau, discussing Quebecois separatism, commented

Table 26.3 continued.

Environment

Short Term to 2005

- National parks and reserves continue to be established in order to promote tourism
- Biological diversity continues to diminish

Mit-term 2006–2010

- Water shortages start to curtail some resort developments in the southwest US
- Increasing restrictions placed on access to national parks due to impacts of large numbers of visitors—pricing used as a major tool
- Ongoing loss of biodiversity, rainforest areas particularly hard hit
- Damage to ozone leads to health warnings to international travelers to Australia, New Zealand, and southern South America because of increased danger of skin cancer

2011–2020

- Several island destinations in the Caribbean, the Indian Ocean, and the Pacific are evacuated due to sea level rise
- Freshwater shortages severely affect tourism development in many parts of the world
- Ski tourism in traditional alpine resorts in Europe, North America, and Australasia becomes increasingly expensive due to the unpredictability of snow cover
- Several significant species such as tiger, rhinoceros, elephants, pandas, chimpanzees, and guerrillas all but extinct save for their presence in privately run tourism sanctuaries

Source: Reproduced from C. Hall, 2000, "The Future of Tourism: A Personal Speculation," pp. 85–95 in *Tourism Recreation Research*, with permission.

in 1968, "Nationhood [is] little more than a state of mind" (cited in Eller, 2000, p. 346).

Slowly, and worldwide, that state of mind changed, as nations began to recognize in their midst special interest groups or the ethnicities defined as the "subjective symbolic or emblematic use of any aspect of culture [by a group], in order to differentiate themselves from another group" (DeVos, 1975, p. 16). These groups constructed individual and separatist social values, which Stavenhagen (1990) suggests "generally involve a clash of interests or a struggle over rights: rights to land, education, the use of a language, political representation, freedom of religion, the preservation of ethnic identity, and autonomy or self-determination" (p. 77). When such conflicts turn violent, as in ethnic cleansing, most tourists flee and do not return to visit refugee camps, to see the maimed and the orphaned whose conditions burden a society and further reduce the standard of living. Only the "danger tourists" in search of excitement, and the *thanatourists* who "travel to a location wholly, or partially, motivated by the desire for actual or symbolic encounters with death" are attracted to such grisly scenes (Seaton, 1999, p. 131).

By contrast, tourists have enshrined many war-related sites, such as the Anne Frank House (see Chapter 16) where *60 years* later tourists continue to visit the site of a book written by a child. MacCannell (1976, pp. 44–46) initially described this as a five-step process of sacralization, which involved:

1. the naming phase, for *preservation* of the site;
2. the *framing* and elevating of the site, giving it special recognition;
3. *enshrining* the site by some type of distinctive display;
4. *mechanical reproduction*, as scale models, postcards, and photos; and
5. *social reproduction*, or the naming of one's group, city, or region to identify themselves with this famous attraction.

Ethnic symbols are also sacralized and enshrined. Nothing is more French than the Tour Eiffel, more Indian than the Taj Mahal, or more American than the Statue of Liberty.

Wars leave as their legacy the largest assemblage of tourism attractions in the world (see Chapter 28) but they are best visited when there is peace.

The International Institute for Peace Through Tourism (http://www.iipt.org) works diligently to promote positive avenues to counter these negative trends.

> The world is becoming a global village in which people from different continents are made to feel like next door neighbors. In facilitating more authentic social relationships between individuals, tourism can help overcome many real prejudices, and foster new bonds of fraternity. In this sense tourism has become a real force for world peace. (Pope John Paul II, "Tourism: A vital force for peace," 1988, p. 13)

Chapter 27

From Kitty Hawk to the ISS Hilton

Maryann Brent

HAL, the Hilton Hotel programming team has arrived. They will integrate Hilton quality control requirements into Station's protocol. Please stand by for integration, HAL.

The year is 2025. HAL of the popular film and novel *2001: A Space Odyssey* (Arthur C. Clarke and Polaris Productions, 1968) is charged with monitoring Hilton's inventory and service provisions aboard International Space Station (ISS). Previous corporate images of Hilton luxury and comfort held over from the 20th century do not match the "campout" style on the ISS. By 2025, however, the concept of luxury no longer implies an extravagant use of natural resources. Let us hope that HAL's integration task will be productive and uneventful. HAL, what is the cost of a room for two with bath and a view?

Of all the "tourisms" one can think of, space tourism is certainly the ultimate among *rural* destinations. If one puts aside the idea of human activity in space as just an extension of Earth, the new islands in space could differ from Earth in important ways. The habitation of these new *places* and the proposition of space tourism present a unique opportunity for creating a community whose framework could minimize energy waste, environmental degradation, and litter. A parallel and perhaps more difficult part of the task relates to the drafting of interpersonal and intercultural protocols and ethics for living in confined isolated space. Time will tell if we are up to the challenge of grappling with the processes that lie ahead.

Space tourism lacks a history and it is puzzling to discuss a phenomenon that has not yet occurred. No wonder! Space travel was formerly reserved for a few elite government employees specifically trained in related technical and scientific areas that could accumulate several earned doctoral degrees. Guests were not invited. However, the situation is changing.

Some would argue that space tourism has indeed occurred. There are space camps for children (http://www.spacecamp.com/; http://www.legendcourt.co.uk/content/press/press_3.html) and adults (http://www.chez.com/neru/spacecp.htm; http://www.spacecamp.com/pc.htm; http://www.spacecamp.com/adultacad.htm).

Several tour companies specialize in the space experience by offering astronomy cruises, zero gravity (parabolic) flights, and suborbital flights aboard a Russian MiG25 (http://www.spaceadventures.com/). Two companies (http://www.spaceadventures.com/; http://www.microcadam.com/space/space.html) retain deposits in escrow for passengers who have reserved excursions to the edge of space (100 kilometers). The estimated inaugural date of this space tour is 2004. The tourists for these initial forays into space will be relatively wealthy and few in number. However, the mass tourism of space will occur rather later than 2004. Many advocates predict that mass space tourism will begin within 25–40 years. This chapter will attempt three things in anticipation of that outcome. It will attempt first of all to convince readers that space tourism and space exploration are a given. It will present selective descriptions about the space environment from the American and Russian space agency experiences. It will briefly touch on some problems that must be solved for successful exploration and successful commercial tourism.

The Persuasion

One hundred years ago, in 1900, there were few automobiles, many horse-drawn vehicles, and a goodly number of railroads. Three years later, man took flight at Kitty Hawk, NC. A mere 66 years intervened between that first successful flight (1903) and the development of global scheduled airline services and the visit of two Americans to the Moon in 1969. What an incredible leap of technology! Although national competition provided a reason for winning the race to the Moon in the 1960s, the growing influence of globalization might cause national competition to be less likely as an impetus for the next big step in space exploration. This is probable in light of the transnational aspect of the commercial space business community. How then will another big leap in technology happen? It will happen with cost reductions and the production of better engines and fuels. It is just a matter of a little more time.

Why Travel to Space?

We *are* already in outer space! Why travel beyond Earth's borders? That is another issue. Robotic missions are relatively inexpensive and well suited to scientific projects. We can use the savings to solve problems down here. Chapter 26 presented statistics relating to an alarming global population increase, a critical need for better stewardship of natural resources, the implications of instantaneous global communication and a global economy. In only one decade, for better or for worse, the Internet has radically diminished the consequences of geographical distance. The projected population count for the 21st century (10 billion) will seriously challenge our planet's sustainable limits, especially when considering the current reckless extraction of fossil fuels, forests, and potable water. The simultaneous doubling of the human population and depletion of physical resources are cause for alarm of themselves without even factoring in the consequences of cultural intolerance. Evidently we are running out of real estate.

In view of our serious earthly problems, NASA is sensitive to the argument that taxpayers' money will be squandered if they continue to send astronauts on scientific missions. Above all—why should NASA include tourists in the picture? Part of the response can be directed to the identity of the financiers. NASA and other national space agencies are no longer the exclusive financiers in the space industry. Commercial producers such as repair and maintenance crews, satellite launch companies, and space tour companies pursue the logic of markets and profit margins, not defense. Moreover, increasingly space-related projects (telescopes, space-based Earth photography, and the ISS) are transnational, whether government run, commercial, or a combination. Such expansion of the space industry to mixed uses and intricate financing has enriched both the motivations of the financiers and options for the clients. Thus, tax dollars are no longer the exclusive source of funding for space activity. Space operations are increasingly motivated by profit and commercial enterprise.

We need practice living in space! A few of us will soon inhabit space for periods of a few hours or days as tourists or repair technicians on the ISS. It is likely that biologists, physicians, or anthropologists will win grants to study aboard the ISS and eventually on a Mars Express for months or years at a time. If the work is of long duration, researchers will take their families. At this point, complex moral and cultural issues will arise. The experience gained from surviving independently in space will benefit the goals of exploration but it will also contribute to the general bank of scientific knowledge for all living creatures. Observations of the ozone layer, planetary geology, weather tracking, and the behavior of materials and human beings in a confined microgravity environment will directly contribute to the quality of our life on Earth.

The late Carl Sagan (1994), in a hypothetical search for intelligent life on Earth, provided a series of descriptions of Earth in progressively larger scale. While resolutions of 100 kilometers revealed only oceans and large topographical features, a closer look provided clues to the possibility of intelligent life:

> When you examine the Earth at about 100-meter resolution, . . . (m)any of the devegetated smudges are revealed to have an underlying checkerboard geometry. These are the planet's cities. . . . When you take pictures at a meter resolution or better, you find that the crisscrossing straight lines within the cities and the long straight lines that join them with other cities are filled with streamlined, multicolored beings a few meters in length, politely running one behind the other in long, slow orderly procession. They are very patient. One stream of beings stops so another stream can continue at right angles. Periodically, the favor is returned. At night, they turn on two bright lights in front so they can see where they're going. Some, a privileged few, go into little houses when their workday is done and retire for the night. Most are homeless and sleep in the streets.
>
> At last! You've detected the source of all the technology, the dominant life-forms on the planet. The streets of the cities and the roadways of the countryside are evidently built for their benefit. You might believe that you were really beginning to understand life on Earth. And perhaps you'd be right. (pp. 71–72)

Emissions from automobile air conditioners and exhaust are a significant source of photochemical pollution, which has been linked to ozone thinning. One hopes that the wide distribution of our automobile technology or any other specific activity will be checked if it bears a serious ecological risk. Models for disastrous consequences of such predicaments include the decline of the Roman Empire and the population collapse on Easter Island. In the case of Rome, the lifestyle required the importation of human and natural resources and manufactured goods from near and distant colonies, and the colonies required administration. There are arguments for the Empire's inability to administer its extensive territory as well as poisoned drinking water owing to lead that leached into the aqueducts and a variety of other factors. By contrast, Easter Island increasingly isolated itself. The focus on statue production distracted the population from the impacts of deforestation. Deforestation prevented boat building, which was crucial for fishing (high-quality protein) and the possibility of trade (the exchange of products and ideas). By the 1800s, the Easter Islanders were trapped on a barren island with few goods or skills to trade, creeping starvation, and rampant disease (Bahn & Flenley, 1992). A critical loss of natural and human resources occurred relatively quickly in both cases and could have been prevented. These are important lessons to keep in mind because our human community could very possibly "shoot itself in the foot." Thus, methodical sky watching from Earth and Earth observation from satellites can acquaint us with our "place" in the solar system and our relationship to our environment. Sky watching, Earth observation, and space exploration can contribute to our local–global health and well being and prevent an ecological catastrophe on our Earth Island if we act wisely.

What We Already Know: Selected Experiences

Recent Vehicles and Launch Systems

Commercial success demands high reliability. When translated into technical requirements, success means reusability and new types of fuel. The solid fuels currently used on the Shuttle are too hazardous for tourism because they cannot be aborted after ignition. The new rocketplane designs use safer fuels and avoid bearing the weight of both jet and rocket fuel at takeoff by various creative means. Some designs require rocketplanes to be carried on the underbelly of a jet (or towed by a jet) to rocket altitude. Other designs allow for the rocketplane to be fueled aloft. Space Access and Kelly Space permit the rocket capsule to eject from the nose of the jet plane. All of these designs work in principle. However, the requirements for technical dependability, stable economics, and passenger safety require meticulous design, testing, and redesign. The process is costly and time consuming (Figure 27.1).

The reusability requirement evokes the Victorian virtues of tidiness and thrift. Over the years, discarded launch stages from NASA and the Russian Space Agency contributed to suborbital or orbital debris. Rocket booster stages were purposely designed to fall into Earth's oceans, but man-made debris has occasionally damaged satellites or spaceships. For-profit businesses can afford neither the extravagance nor the risk associated with such littering. For this reason, the space vehicles currently in development and/or production feature reusable single-stage or two-stage launches with a variety of propulsion technologies. Specific propulsion technologies will not be addressed here. However, the selected new vehicle designs might be of interest (Table 27.1).

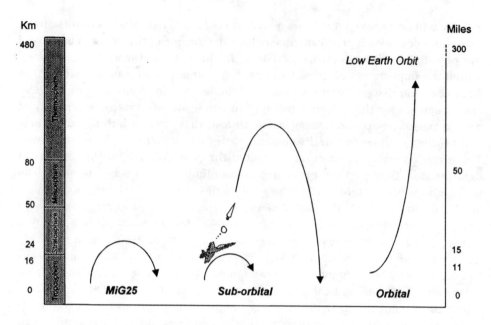

Figure 27.1. Suborbital and orbital travel.

Accommodations and Biomedical Issues

Space hotels will be constructed for space and on planetary bodies. Although the partial gravity existing on planetary bodies makes them seem to be the logical choice, most hotel designs thus far have illustrated a preference for orbital space locations. The impacts on human physiology will vary according to the degree of gravity experienced and the duration of visits. This section will explore hospitality, the associated biomedical issues, and selected hotel designs currently in production.

Gravity

The popular media have focused on "zero" gravity that one can experience in space. In fact, zero gravity in the natural world is a misnomer. The gravities of the Sun, planets, and moons exert an influence on each other relative to their proximity. While Shuttle video recordings of "floating" astronauts imply a total lack of gravity, there is a mere 10% reduction in Earth gravity at 400 miles [within low Earth orbit (LEO)]. The term LEO refers to a distance range of 50–400 miles from Earth. A 10% reduction in gravity does not explain the condition of weightlessness. Then why are astronauts depicted as floating about their spacecraft? The experience of weightlessness in LEO results from *freefall* (http:// microgravity.nasa.gov/wimg.html), the condition of continuous falling when in orbit around a planetary body. The continuous falling occurs because the outward (centrifugal) force from the launch and gravity force from the planet exactly cancel each other at a *central point* in the spacecraft.

Supposing that a human being is placed exactly in the center of the spacecraft, his/her arms, legs, head, and most of the torso extending beyond the hypothetical

Table 27.1. Space Vehicle Characteristics

Stages	Name	Financier/Builder	Nationality	Takeoff/Landing	No. Crew/ No. Passengers	Vehicle Design	Suborbital or Orbital
Single-stage	Ascender	Private/Bristol Spaceplanes Limited	UK	horizontal/horizontal	2/2	Jet and rocket engines in one plane	suborbital
	Roton	Scaled Composites/ Roton Rocket Company	US	vertical/vertical	piloted	space helicopter	orbital
	Venture Star/ X-33	NASA/Lockheed	US	vertical/horizontal			
Two-stage	K-1	Kistler Aerospace	US				
	Eclipse Astroliner	NASA/Kelly Space and Technology	US	horizontal/horizontal	piloted	Rocketplane towed, glides to Earth	suborbital and orbital
	Space Lifter	?/Vela Technology	US	horizontal/horizontal		Rocketplane carried on underbelly of jet	
	Pioneer Pathfinder		US	horizontal/horizontal	2/	Jet and rocket engines in one plane, which is refueled aloft by a tanker	suborbital
	Sea Launch	Boeing, KB Yuzhnoye/ POYuzhmash,RSC Engia, Kvaerner Maritime	US, Ukraine, Russia, Norway	vertical/?		Zenit booster vehicle, floating converted oil platform and command ship	

central point would be subject to outward or gravitational forces. Thus, the weight-less condition is not uniformly perfect. Another term, also a misnomer, for the weightless experience during orbital travel is *microgravity*. This nearly weight-less condition caused by freefall, sometimes called microgravity or very near zero gravity, produces some biomedical effects of which space passengers should be aware. Thus, it is appropriate to explain what happens to the human body in re-duced gravity conditions. The following information concerning the effect of microgravity on the human body and human perceptions has been condensed from the core textbook prepared for students of the International Space Univer-sity, Strasbourg, France: *Keys to Space: An Interdisciplinary Approach to Space Studies* (1999; see also http://www.isunet.edu/IS/Library/Publications/home.html).

The Human Body: Bones, Blood, Muscle, and Perception

Surprisingly, the most common complaint in microgravity is lodging foreign bodies in the eye. This happens because dust particles do not "settle," and the use of goggles has been an effective solution. While biomedical responses to microgravity do not bear serious consequences for healthy individuals, some of the responses could limit one's enjoyment. Thus, the comfort of passengers during this unique experience depends upon the presentation of information to passen-gers, careful forethought and preparation by passengers, and the scheduling of balanced social and individual activities for passengers by their tour company.

Because we have evolved in Earth's gravity, a sudden reduction in gravity pro-duces startling changes in our bodies. Bones immediately adapt by releasing cal-cium into the blood because the body senses that its weight-bearing "struts" are no longer necessary (Churchill, 1999a). The blood calcium is carried off to the kidneys and released in the urine. Increased urination also reduces blood volume.

Veins, the less elastic (more "baggy") blood vessels, accommodate a greater vol-ume of blood in the lower body in normal gravity (Churchill, 1999b). When gravity disappears and the body reduces blood volume in the veins of the lower body, the veins collapse. As a result of the fluid loss, the legs become much slimmer than usual. In fact, all body fluids move toward the upper torso and head because there is no longer a force pulling them *down*. The increased fluid volume in the chest and around the heart causes the heart to beat faster, because it has to move more volume than normal. In orbital space, increased heart rate is a normal occurrence.

Increased fluid volume in the head causes fullness in the sinuses and the possi-bility of headaches or sleeplessness. The face loses its normal contours and takes on a rounded look (Churchill, 1999c). Other adaptations include decreased red blood cell production and the decreased effectiveness of antibiotics. The body's adaptations to microgravity are reversible upon return to Earth gravity conditions. Discomfort owing to these adaptive changes can be mitigated in orbit with pre-scribed or over-the-counter drugs, physical exercise, or, for extended visits, thera-peutic equipment.

Perceptual Changes

Neurovestibular function in the inner ear (the biological center for balance and movement referents) becomes confused, because there is no reference for *up* or *down* (Clement, 1999). This change can cause nausea initially but rarely persists for more than 2 days. The interruption of circadian rhythms could also produce dysphoria (flat mood) or gastrointestinal disturbances. This last condition, not limited to space flight, can also occur during very long airplane flights to distant and exotic places on Earth's surface.

Long-Duration Visits

The knowledge acquired from the long-duration space visits of the American and Russian space programs has been used by NASA and RSA (the Russian Space Agency) in protocols for health maintenance while in orbit and upon return to Earth. During visits of more than a few days, a consistent regimen of weight-bearing exercises prevents bone calcium loss (Churchill, 1999a). The effects of fluid redistribution can be alleviated with the usual remedies for headaches or sinus problems. The diuresis (excessive urination) slows automatically after 48–72 hours. Before returning to Earth, however, astronauts load fluids to avoid sensations of dizziness and weakness after landing. It will be important for tourists to understand how their bodies will react to microgravity during short- and long-duration voyages. Prudent tour companies will prepare them with advance information and avail them of sensible scheduling and remedies.

Hotels

There are several hotel designs for LEO accommodations. Two in particular distinguish themselves here: Robert Bigelow's Lunar Cruise Ship and the ISS Hilton. Robert Bigelow, the Las Vegas developer, has personally invested US$500,000,000 for a Las Vegas spaceport, an industrial space platform with hotel, and translunar cruise ship (http://www.hobbyspace.com/Tourism/index.html#Bigelow). To date, he is the only hotel designer who has actually appropriated funds for a project. His company, Bigelow Aerospace, employs former NASA and aerospace scientists and engineers to design and build the lunar fly-by cruiser. The concept of a party ship in space is intriguing. Hotel construction will renovate jettisoned Shuttle fuel tanks for accommodations.

The story of the Russian space station MIR is indicative of the intense interest in space tourism. The 14-year old MIR was to have been the first "space hotel" financed by a Netherlands-based Mircorp who planned to rent it out for advertising and promotional uses (URL http://www.mircorp.com/). Dennis Tito, an American space engineer, paid US$20 million to be its first guest and the first *paid* "space tourist" in a week-long visit. When the Russians decided to de-orbit the aging craft in February 2001, the funds already paid by Tito were reallocated. He received cosmonaut training at the Russian space base, Star City, then rode on a Russian Soyuz rocket for his much-publicized week aboard the ISS. He returned to earth May 6, 2001, reporting to various media, "I wish I could have stayed a month" and encouraging others to "live their dream." The physical and social infrastructure for human presence beyond Earth's boundaries has clearly been crossed, with exciting developments to follow. Peter Diamandis of the X-Prize Foundation predicts "the first trillionaires will be made in space" (personal communication).

Other Space Businesses

The purported reason for ISS' existence is a multinational infrastructure for scientific research in space. After the original construction work, ISS will require staff transportation, supplies, repairs, and maintenance. The original objectives may be expanded or ISS may ultimately become a base for more distant exploration. In consideration of all of these issues, ISS and satellite communication and observation companies will require certain services such as launch services, spaceports on Earth, space freight/passenger delivery transportation, and on-site factories (http://www.spacebusiness.com/; http://www.spacearchive.org/). Most of these services currently exist owing to the national space agency programs and they are being expanded for commercial launch enterprises.

Problems to Solve

The Funding Conundrum

Funding space projects is a delicate challenge, because proponents of space exploration cannot necessarily rely on government funding. The first mandate of national governments has been the protection of citizens living within their boundaries, and government-funded programs are appropriate only as they concern the national security. Because the principal threat to American national security concluded with the conclusion of the Cold War, the government has not been able to rationalize adequately the enormous expense of continued human space exploration. ISS as a transnational enterprise is an apparent exception. An important alternative funding for space exploration has emerged in private and commercial sectors.

Private and commercial financing (Wall Street) are difficult to obtain without the assurance of profits. A reliable prediction of future profits cannot be established without a profit history. A profit history includes a record of successful commercial activity that has earned a profit. This circular problem has thwarted the development of many worthwhile space businesses. At the first conference hosted by the Space Transportation Association and its Space Travel and Tourism Division (June, 1999, Washington, DC), Apollo 11 astronaut "Buzz" Aldrin expressed frustration at the diminished American presence in space during the past 30 years: "Had we continued with 1% of the national budget [as during the 'space race'], we would have walked on Mars 10 years ago" (Aldrin, 1999, personal communication).

While critics believe that public space exploration will divert funding from social programs, Aldrin reminded conference attendees that NASA used only 3% of the figure allotted to social programs during the "space race." He further remarked that "[Apollo 11 cost] one third of what we spend annually on alcohol or cosmetics. We bet more on horse races in any given year than NASA spent on the entire Apollo Project" (Aldrin, 1999, personal communication).

Aldrin proposed that a space lottery could successfully fund space exploration. Technically, such a lottery is illegal at present. If lotteries with space travel prizes are pursued as a means of financing exploration, laws would have to be changed.

However, space businesses are emerging despite the funding problem, largely from the efforts of a small group of passionate individuals and supportive foundations. Among these are the space societies, providing opportunities for discussion; philanthropy, providing capital; media attention, which disseminates information; and the X-Prize, which offers a cash incentive and media attention.

The X-Prize

Prizes have advanced science and commerce for centuries, and prize winners have achieved the status of heroes. Precedents include announcements by the English Parliament of a prize for measuring longitude (1714) and the French hotel developer, Raymond Orteig, for the first solo transatlantic flight between New York and Paris (1919). The longitude prize of £10,000, won by John Harrison, was directly responsible for development of the precision clocks that allowed accurate navigational plotting. Political jealousy caused Harrison's payment to be delayed until 1773, when King George III directed Parliament to acknowledge Harrison's contribution. The prize for the first solo transatlantic flight, won by Charles Lindbergh in 1927, dispelled the fear of flying over water and advanced the world's freight and passenger airline industry. In this century, prizes for competitive sports (fighting, racing) have become gigantic industries. Since 1996, the X-Prize has offered a cash prize of US$10 million to a commercial enterprise that flies three passengers to 100 kilometers, returns them safely to Earth, and repeats the trip within 2 weeks (http://www.xprize.org). Founder Peter Diamandis expects the prize to generate a billion dollar space industry.

At press time, 17 companies are competing, and a winner is anticipated by 2004. Financing and testing the prototypes has delayed an earlier winner, which must hold an outstanding launch success rate—much better than NASA during the Space Race era. The process, however, is very expensive. Adventure tourists will happily pay high prices that include development costs in exchange for the excitement of new experiences despite perceptions of risk (http://www.spacefuture.com/archive/demand_for_space_tourism_in_america_and_japan.shtml; http://www.spacefuture.com/archive/general_public_space_travel_and_tourism.shtml #APPENDIX A). By contrast, mass tourists, who possess a low tolerance for risk and smaller bank accounts, will take safety and reliability for granted. Market analysts expect this second wave of space visitors to generate the highest profits, even though per-passenger costs will be much lower than for the initial market. Meanwhile, X-Prize participants continue the testing, the iterations, and the financial struggle.

Space Policy and Law

During the Cold War, regulations relating to space activity were determined by international treaties between governments. These space-related agreements are a subcategory of international law and refer to the activities of governments, international organizations, and individuals. The foundation of space law is the Outer Space Treaty, drafted by the United Nations and signed in 1967. The main principles of the Outer Space Treaty address liability (the burden of liability rests with the launching country), the prohibition against weapons of mass destruction in space, nonsovereignty, and universal freedom of access.

However, space navigation law is now developing a new framework to accommodate the changing role of national governments (research in place of defense) and an expanding international commercial activity. Commercial activities may or may not overlap governmental activity and include telecommunications, remote sensing, global position sensing, space debris, and the ISS. For example, the US recently enacted the Commercial Space Act of 1998 (http://geo.arc.nasa.gov/sge/

landsat/sec107.html), which is an example of national space law. The Commercial Space Act of 1998 provides for licensing commercial space vehicles and their payloads and for liability (up to US$1.5 billion). In the US, the governing body for commercial space transportation is the Federal Aviation Administration (FAA), while the Air Force and related agencies will begin to assume some responsibility for research and development of military space technology and policy. Thus, a true split in function is currently emerging in the US. Other countries such as Japan, Australia, UK, Russia, and Sweden have also enacted national space documents.

Whereas in the past legal issues have been linked to defense and the activities of national space agencies, new commercial activities, including tourism, require a greatly expanded legal framework. Space law addresses activities in space as well as the launch, the return, and rescue of astronauts and launched objects, property rights, liability, certification of vehicles, and registration of launched objects. In the event of damage, there are complex differences between the legal treatment of damage occurring on the surface of the Earth or in space. Often the language of the documents is ambiguous, and where it is reasonably clear, the law has not been tested. One major current inadequacy in international law concerns the ambiguity of language relating to the mining of resources from planetary bodies such as asteroids, the Moon, or Mars. The resources considered desirable include minerals and hydrocarbons (for construction and energy generation) and helium-3 (for energy generation) but it is currently unclear if mining is illegal according to the 1979 Moon Treaty (http://lunar.arc.nasa.gov/science/results/lunarice/moon.html). Article 7 prohibits the disruption of the lunar environment. Article 11 states that the Moon and its natural resources are the common heritage of mankind and an international regime should govern the exploitation of the natural resources of the Moon. The Moon Agreement is an outdated document whose issues must be revisited. Specifically, the issue of resource extraction and use must be clarified, because mining will be absolutely necessary for progress in exploration, habitation, and tourism site construction.

Who is liable if three countries jointly launch a craft that damages a satellite and the satellite subsequently deorbits and causes further damage? Are the original three owners or the satellite owner liable? In the case of the Russian satellite Cosmos 954 that returned to Earth and landed in Canada, Russia denied liability but compensated Canada with an undisclosed amount for damages. The case was never heard in a court of law. Such laws also relate to tourist vehicles and must be brought up to date.

What of space travel insurance for tourists? It is definitely needed but does not currently exist. What about space debris? This issue is very important and can refer both to natural debris and man-made debris. How does one responsibly decommission old equipment in space? Space law must define its limits and continue to respond to the complex nature of international and national involvement.

By the Way, Where Does Space Begin?

The United Nations' International Space Flight Organization will address registration, international standards, and the zoning of space. However, the boundary between the atmosphere of the Earth and outer space has not yet been defined in international law (http://www.spacelaw.com.au/). Some academic suggestions for the beginning of space include: the lowest altitude of an orbiting satellite or the atmospheric density (mass/volume) of a particular gas. Insurance requirements make the first definition unfeasible while the irregular nature of Earth's atmosphere rules out the second. While the "beginning of space" issue has not yet been resolved in international law, some individual countries use the power of the launch vehicle (ability) as the identifier of space rather than the location of a satellite, payload, or space station. The current popular definition for tourism purposes uses location: a distance of 100 kilometers from Earth, which is a low (nearby) practical orbital height for these short-duration flights.

Staunch Supporters

People offer many reasons for exploring and inhabiting outer space. Robert Zubrin, Buzz Aldrin, and Peter Diamandis all vividly remember the Apollo years (1967–1972) and expected a human presence on Mars decades ago. These men are exceedingly impatient for advances in space travel. Zubrin is president of the Mars Society (http://www.marssociety.org/) and designer of Mars Direct, a workable plan for a 3-year Mars project at a cost of US$20 billion (as opposed to the US$450 billion rejected by the US Congress in 1989). One of Zubrin's hallmarks is the use of materials and resources present on Mars to produce food, fuel, building materials, and air, instead of transporting all of the supplies. Aldrin is one of the American heroes who first walked on the Moon (1969) and founder of Starcraft Boosters (http://www.starbooster.com/), a space cargo delivery system. His reusable spacecraft, StarBooster, could eventually be used as a space people-mover system. NASA has invited Starcraft Boosters to participate in the plans for the new Shuttle architecture (Brekke, 2000). Peter Diamandis is founder of the X-Prize Foundation, physician, astronautical engineer, former head of International Microspace (a satellite launch company), and board member of the International Space University (http://www.isunet.edu/). These people work unceasingly for the success of commercial space businesses and space exploration, and there are many others. At conferences related to commercial uses of space, space tourism, or civilian space transportation, they are omnipresent and they are driven. Why?

Earth has been called the cradle of human civilization, but we cannot stay in the cradle forever. Although *Homo sapiens* has existed for 150,000 or 2 million years (depending on the criteria used) (Tattersall, 2000), only in *this* century has the speed of human travel shifted from a range of 4–50 miles per hour by carriage or railroad to 35,000 miles per hour during shuttle reentry. Successive transportation technologies have increased our speed and distance exponentially. This astonishing shift will certainly impact the human experience beyond mere travel activity. Perhaps at this point the appropriate question is not *if* we will explore, colonize, and send tourists to space, but *when*. In fact, the process has already begun.

Conclusions

This chapter has addressed an event that has not yet occurred: mass space tourism. Even though a few travelers have paid for a few hours or a few days of the

Figure 27.1. Earth rising over the Moon's horizon. (Reprinted courtesy of National Aeronautical Space Administration)

space experience, space tourism has not *yet* begun in earnest. That will only occur with scheduled departures and standardized arrangements. At the mention of space tourism, some roll their eyes in disbelief, some are apprehensive, and some are eager. No matter which reaction is encountered, space exploration and space tourism are sure to occur. We are beginning to reach out beyond our Earth (Figure 27.2).

Acknowledgments—The author would like to express appreciation to Sir Arthur Clarke for his vision and to the Arthur C. Clarke Foundation and the International Space University 1998 Summer Session scholarship fund for the unique opportunity of learning about space.

Chapter 28

Hostility and Hospitality: War and Terrorism

Valene L. Smith

Hospitality, or caring for guests with kindness and solicitude, is a relationship usually won through trust and friendship, but one that can be quickly shattered by mistrust or overt antisocial acts. Hostilities directed toward tourists take many forms, from rudeness and verbal abuse to violence that threaten their possessions, even their person. The study of crime, war, and terrorism in relation to tourism is still relatively new but is of increasing importance because of the negative economic impacts on tourist receipts. This case study analyzes these three forms of hostilities and their relation to tourism, first as an immediate interruption or deterrent to tourist travel, and second, in terms of the respective tourist markers that become attractions, sometimes even tourist destinations.

Crime

To prey upon the vulnerability of travelers is an ancient and lawless profession. Whether termed pickpockets, robbers, dacoits, or highwaymen, the brigands raided caravans on the historic Silk Road; pirates looted Spanish galleons for their New World gold; and criminals now mug tourists in airport parking lots. Theft, which may be accompanied by murder to deter recognition of identity, is a direct attack upon the victim to obtain his/her possessions, and is often a crime of opportunity. Individuals who publicly display small items of value (rolls of money, expensive jewelry, cameras, and laptops) invite theft, especially in communities where poverty prevails or professional thieves regularly operate. In local eyes, the traveler is (comparatively) rich and an easy target due to his/her lack of familiarity with the area, with body language, and other behavioral cues.

Repetitive crime sounds a tourism alarm. A series of car thefts in Miami, FL (which coincidentally involved German tourists driving rental cars away from the airport after their arrival), received widespread media coverage in Europe and North America. The incidents raised deep concern among Florida tourism officials because of the negative impact on the hospitality reputation of the area. Remedial action was prompt and nationwide, and included the removal of all stickers or labels that identified the vehicles as rental cars. Better maps were prepared to direct travelers to major highways for access to urban cores or accommodations. In 1999 in a country seriously impacted by inflation created by the Asian economic crisis, tourists in Bangkok were advised not to hire unknown taxis at the airport because of several murders.

Travelers, especially foreign tourists, are easily identifiable as targets. Because most are short-term visitors, especially in resort locations such as Hawaii and other island destinations, time is the ally of the criminal. Even if the victim files a police report and the perpetrator is ultimately apprehended, the victim may have already departed for home, or be unable to remain to prosecute. To protect their reputation, Hawaiian authorities consolidated efforts of police, airlines, and hotels to provide gratis services for major victims to return to the island to prosecute, as a warning to other would-be thieves that tourism provides no immunity for crime.

The tourist markers associated with crime are usually short term and local unless related to well-known individuals or exceptional circumstances. Tourists to Washington, DC, often visit the theater where President Lincoln was assassinated and are treated to a detailed explanation of the event. Conspiracy theories concerning the deaths of world figures John F. Kennedy and Princess Diane will continue to attract tourists and the curious to the sites of their deaths. Even fictional crimes, as in the Agatha Christie novel, *Murder on the Orient Express,* or the purported crimes investigated by the master detective, Sherlock Holmes, have become marketing tools to promote special interest guided tours featuring crimes, including the infamous vampire castle in Romania (mentioned by Wallace in Chapter 23). In general, however, crimes are personal events principally remembered by the victim, and only a few become tourist markers to generate long-term or mass tourism.

War

Throughout world history, war as the primary time marker of society has played such an important role in the lives of generations of people that the accumulated war-related tourist markers now constitute the world's largest single category of tourist sites, destinations, and activities. Included in this list are battlefields, cemeteries, war memorials, peace parks, historic warships, museums and libraries, reenactments, motion pictures, plays, martial music, toy soldiers, flags, jewelry, ruined buildings, and victory arches. Tourists visit the battlefields at Troy, Waterloo, Gettysburg, Gallipoli, Normandy, and Kuwait, to name only a few, where heroes earned their reputations and legends of bravery became books to fill libraries. For centuries, to serve God (as a Crusader) and country (as a solider) brought honor to house and homeland. To preserve family wealth, primogeniture inheritance gave to the eldest son the family home and its lands, and committed a second son to the army and a third to the Church.

If the nature and style of war change as now appears probable, the implications of this transition and its effect on new tourism markers appropriately places the topic among the tourism issues of the 21st century.

The Temporal Nature of War

Wars were historically fought for control over land, place (geographic site), resources, and population. Although often described euphemistically as wars of revolution, unification, liberation, intervention, or peacekeeping, the real goals of conflict remain constant. Anthropologist Turney-High (1981) studied war as a social process and defined it as, "War is a state of mind and a legal condition . . . the essence of which is to introduce turbulence and crisis into another social system while attempting to prevent a lack of equilibrium within the we-group" (p. 19).

The social process generates three war phases common to both aggressor or aggrieved:

- *Before the war* is a period of relatively predictable everyday living when social and cultural events based on heritage or tradition continue and the status quo prevails; there may be a growing unease concerning economic and political stability as war clouds gather, with mounting uncertainly about the future. Military preparedness activates.
- *During the war* is marked by militarization creating emotional insecurity and fear for the safety of self and loved ones. Wars make enormous drains on resources and often cause food and fuel shortages and rationing. Modern wars are progressively invasive into civilian space and create dislocation, refugees, and mass murder. War is a matter of personal anguish, bodily injury, psychological trauma, and fear for the future in terms of its outcome, relocation, reunification of families, and the tragedies of loss of life, of property, and security.
- *After the war* becomes a period of reassessment: to consolidate old or form new social networks, depending on the outcome of the war, and the respective roles as victor and vanquished (and possible refugee status). It includes a period of reflection, for remembrance, for physical and mental healing. Victory brings laurels but at a cost of lives lost and spent resources; for the vanquished there is loss of liberty and land. For both, there is loss of family leaving widows, orphans, and the disabled dependent on society for survival. Everyone looks back to the "good times, before the war."

As birth, marriage, and death are the ritual markers for an individual's personal life cycle, wars are the important time markers of society. Most nations are born from earlier wars; nations mature and eventually die usually as the outcome of war. Meanwhile, their citizens also mark their lives by its three stages, and thus strengthen the tourism markers of remembrance, reunion, and the lessons taught by war, "lest we forget."

The emotional intensity of war cuts so deeply into the human psyche that it generates powerful desires to honor bravery and sacrifice, to commend leadership and duty, and to hallow sacred ground in remembrance. This outpouring of sentiment helps to stabilize society, forging action from reaction by the construction of monuments, many of which later serve as tourist markers. However, the precise nature of those markers is best identified in terms of the level or type of warfare (Figure 28.1), which include, tribal wars, national wars, global wars, and

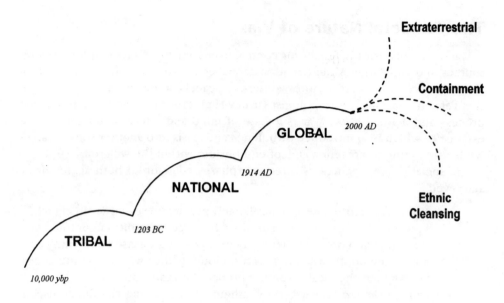

Figure 28.1. The war cycle.

three forms of postmillennial wars: ethnic cleansing, containment and intervention, and extraterrestrial conflicts.

Tribal Warfare

Tribal wars were fought between aboriginal peoples, generally for the same reasons as modern wars, for control of land, place, resources, and population. Carol Ember (1978), using data from the Human Relation Area File, estimated that at least 90% of the world's aboriginal tribes had engaged in some form of warfare. The Inuit who are now members of NANA once fought their inland Indian neighbors for access to the wooded forest of the taiga, for building materials and firewood. Although some driftwood washed up on the shores of Kotzebue Sound, it was not plentiful, and wood was in great demand for a quick fire, and for building sledges and as house supports. The sites and tales of battle and personal honorifics were well known to Inuit a hundred years ago but such knowledge is now essentially lost as three generations have attended public schools and no longer recount oral history. The Inuit war relic tourist markers are limited to exhibits of caribou "slat armor" in museums fortunate to own sample specimens.

More detailed scenarios of tribal war are available about the Kapuoka of Papua New Guinea (Pospisil, 1978) and the Yanomamo of Brazil (Chagnon, 1983). The nature of war in both groups is recorded in documentary film, sometimes shown on public television. New Zealand Maori often perform their ancient war dances as tourist entertainment.

National Wars: 1203 BC Onwards

National wars began in the 11th century BC with the Trojan Wars and siege of Troy, when political organization was sufficiently developed to endow leadership with power to conscript civilians into an army, and the ability to provide logistical support for the duration of the conflict. Wars are said to have influenced sociocultural evolution by increasing social differentiation and integration (Ferguson, 1994). The emergent unified population acclaimed public heroes whose exploits became legendary, and glorified war sacrifices made for God and country. By modern standards, the first national wars were small in scale and fought on battlefields while wives or other family members often waited on the sidelines for the temporary truce that would permit removal of the wounded or dead. At times these were gentlemanly wars, with a truce declared for Christmas day; under other circumstances, troops looted, raped, and burned. Towner (1996) notes that until the time of Napoleon in 1815, wars were announced sufficiently in advance so travelers could vacate the sites. Foreigners might be inconvenienced by the need to rearrange their itinerary but some in the vicinity of Waterloo chose to stay and watch the battle (Seaton, 1999). *Thanatourism* (dark tourism) or preoccupation with death and dying may prove to be another tourist marker.

The history of national wars fill many volumes for each country, and school children labor to master the list of names and dates deemed essential for a proper education. Those pages paint global images of great armies led by powerful men whose exploits changed the course of history: Julius Caesar, Peter the Great, George Washington, Simon Bolivar, Genghis Khan, and Wellington. The memorabilia of their wars fill countless museums and libraries, and for most, there are also visible markers, including victory arches, the Winter Palace and galleries in the Hermitage, Washington's stately home of Mount Vernon, and Trafalgar Square where hundreds meet each day to lunch and visit, under the shadow of the monument honoring a decisive naval battle. China proudly advertises her two most noted icons (and tourist attractions) both of which are military: The Great Wall, and the Terra Cotta soldiers.

National wars also inspired martial and commemorative music, dramatic plays, poetry, and military cemeteries with perpetual flames and honor guards, and on-site battlefield museums where visitors can study the strategies and walk the ramparts and trenches. Monumental figures of men on horseback are erected in town squares, and streets are renamed to commemorate important victories or generals. These tourist markers may extend back for centuries, including the much-visited archaeological site, the battlefield of Troy made famous by Homer in his epic poems (circa 800 BC). In the US, social groups have spontaneously formed to study the Civil War (1861–1865), and have outfitted themselves with authentic-style uniforms, small arms, and even cannons to be used in reenactments. Some of these mock battles that may last 2 days are held in locations hundreds of miles distant from the original battle site, and attract crowds that number in the thousands. The topic has become so popular that individuals have turned it into a presentation to offer as "shoppertainment" in the malls (Figure 28.2).

In 1864 Henri Dunant founded the Red Cross and initiated the Convention for the Amelioration of the Wounded in Time of War. It established protection for the wounded and their ministering personnel using the Red Cross as a symbol of aid. As nations signed the convention, a new concept of peace joined war as a tourism marker followed by the construction of peace monuments, museums, and peace parks.

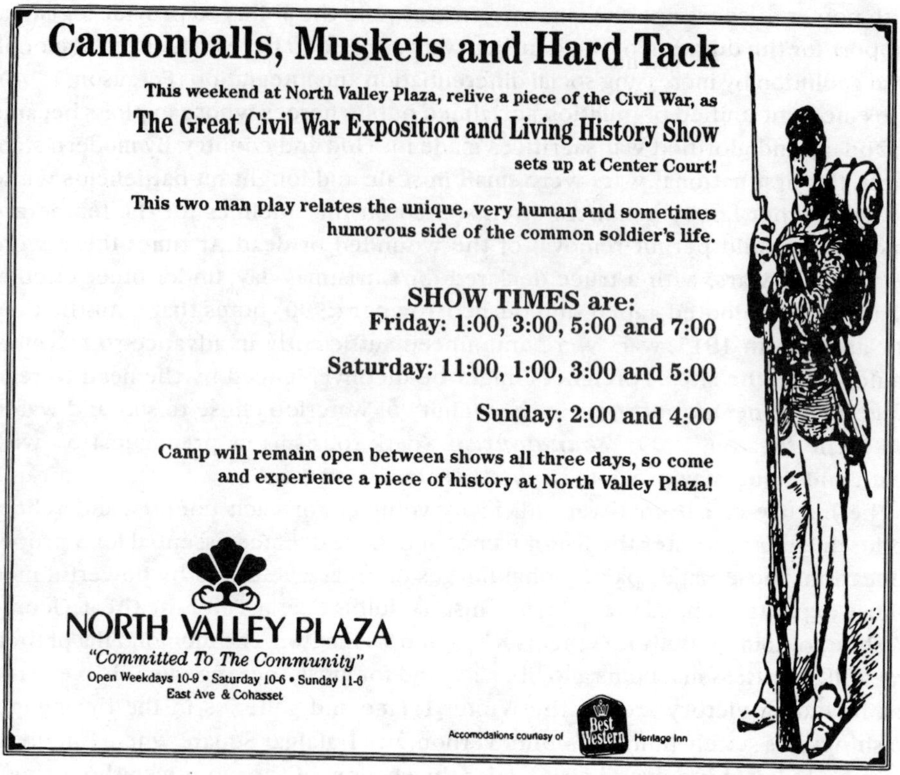

Figure 28.2. Military "shoppertainment." (From *Chico Enterprise Record*, June 13, 1999. Reprinted with permission.)

Global Wars

The first World War (1914–1918), termed then the Great War and The War to End Wars, did not live up to its name but it did radically alter the structure of war. The new technology included the first use of turreted tanks on half-tracks and Big Bertha cannons that dropped large shells on cities, in the first real invasion of the city as civilian residential space. The field of battle went skyward, initially with planes for aerial reconnaissance and later for bombardment. In 1915 the first submarine casualty was a passenger liner, the *Lusitania*, sunk by the Germans. Soldiers from overseas colonies—men who had never expected to travel abroad—were suddenly fighting in the European countryside, and families back home mourned their absence and their losses. Memorials to their service, mostly columns inscribed with their names, stand in city parks in towns around the world.

The war markers expanded in scope, due in large part to the new photography and newsreels, which although days late and jerky, gave black-and-white reality to spectators far from the battle scene. War heroes became international heroes, including ace fighter pilots Blue Max and Red Baron, and monuments to foreign generals were mounted in national sites of prominence.

The importance of World War II, the war to Make the World Safe for Democracy, to postindustrial mass tourism is discussed in Chapter 1 and need not be repeated here. Innovations in military hardware included the German development of the V-1 jet-powered missiles and *Blitzkrieg* tactics, while the American Norden bombsight and larger aircraft extended the battle lines directly into the cities of Europe, and ultimately to Asia. The use of nuclear bombs triggered fears for the future.

World War II generated more heroes, more statues, and more movies. Paramount among differences between this war and its predecessors are two new tourism identifiers: first, visitor attendance at Holocaust sites and museums, including the Nazi concentration camps, and the Anne Frank House; second, the number of military unit reunions, held in the US and, more importantly, abroad. Convenient air transportation made it possible for men of many units to renew their military bonding at every 5-year reunion. Frequently discussed but seldom documented is the emotional bond between military buddies under fire, which is a formidable time marker and personal rite of passage. The veterans gather to achieve closure on what, for most, was the defining event in their lives; to be recognized; to validate what they did; to look up old friends; and, increasingly, to de-demonize the enemy. And many vets take group tours to reestablish the camaraderie they knew as young men. (Col. Hal Ryder, quoted in Jordan, 1997, p. 13)

The June 6, 1994 memorial marking the 50th anniversary of the Normandy landing of Allied troops in France is believed to be the largest single-day mega-event ever held, and a milestone celebration of war and tourism.

Wars of the 21st Century

The Gulf War in 1991 was the transitioning military engagement between global wars and the future, for it demonstrated significant new military capabilities. Civilians anywhere in the world with television access could watch the war "live" as if inside a stealth bomber pin-pointing its firepower on a strategic target. Long-range missiles were launched from ships or shore, with little or no danger to the crew. In the 6 days of the Gulf War, more explosive tonnage was dropped on Iraq than the combined explosives deployed by all countries during World War II (Dollahan, 1998, personal communication). In the 4 days of Desert Fox operations in November 1998, the explosive tonnage dropped on Iraq again exceeded that of its predecessor, the Gulf War. High-altitude photography and computer graphics informed the world of troop deployment and the accuracy of the strikes. The planning and strategy of the war became public, accompanied by extensive quasi-military briefings. The "hero general" appeared frequently on TV, to express his hope that the engagement could be brought to a timely end without loss of life.

Tourist markers, a decade later? The dust had barely settled in Kuwait until the first handful of curious tourists arrived. This was a United Nations war, with many nations contributing military units, with an American general serving as supreme commander. As an international, interagency activity, war was not "formally declared." This shift established global rather than national priorities, and reduced the personal identity of national participation. To date, no peace treaty has been negotiated or signed. Instead, intermittent bombing continues.

Diller and Scofidio (1994, p. 19) call attention to the changing monetary obligations. The 1918 Treaty of Versailles levied war reparations *to be paid to the victors*. In a profound philosophical shift, in World War II *the victors paid the costs* to rebuild the damaged cities and industries. In the Gulf War, in Israel where "war is fueled by tourism within war," the *defending countries* are asked to pay. These authors correctly note that Israel lives in a state of permanent war, and it is the tourist receipts on which their national defense budget depends. When tourist income disappeared during the Gulf War, Israel billed the US for direct damages from Iraqi Scud missiles in the amount of US$200 million and an additional US$400 million for lost revenues from tourism.

Kosovo 1999 is a still more indeterminate engagement— as a first NATO joint military action, and the first international military intervention into intrastate ethnic conflicts. Peacekeeping or "the nonviolent use of third-party armed forces to maintain peace among belligerents" (Carment & James, 1998, p. 301) emerges as a function of a potential international military police. No such body currently exists nor have ground rules for engagement been defined. Too often, the armed forces that to date have been deployed to neutralize local conflicts and pressure militants to a negotiated peace have been locally perceived as partisan "belligerents and end up as targets of the side they appear to oppose" (p. 303). Soldiers operating under these conditions, in Somalia and Bosnia, earned no public acclaim or hero status at home, and tourist markers for future attractions are dubious. Given the economic malaise, destroyed properties and plight of refugees, prospects for a war-related hospitality industry are minimal, and rejuvenation of preconflict tourism may be years distant.

Terrorism and Ethnic Cleansing

The distinction between terrorism and ethnic cleansing as a 21st century form of war is now minimal, as minority ethnicities press their claims for recognition and power to the point of genocide. It is fruitful to examine their structure and motivations.

Terrorism

In the decade since the Gulf War, terrorism has greatly increased. Supporters sought to overthrow what were once national goals, and pitted temporary warriors against legal police and military authority. Warriors differ from soldiers, as they are usually free to join and drop out, are commonly unpaid, owe allegiance to a cause and a leader, and are seldom governed by constitutional or legal precepts. Wahab (1996), an Egyptian tourism specialist and lawyer, astutely observed, "Terrorism is an unsigned message of violence without content and sent to a person with an unknown address. It represents an opinion that is not endorsed by the population majority . . . and is an aggressive movement that lies outside the constitutional and legal framework of the state" (p. 178).

The concept of small voluntary groups who fight together in support of a cause is not new. In many ways, the legendary Robin Hood and his Merry Men (see Shackley, Chapter 24) were terrorists fighting against the established social order, as are contemporary groups such as the *Sentero Luminoso* (Shining Path) currently in Latin America, the Palestinian *Hamas*, or the followers of terrorist leader Osama Bin Laden.

Terrorist groups who use tourists to advance their political agenda are a major concern for host governments that are heavily dependent upon tourism revenues, and must ensure the safety of their guests. Richter and Waugh (1986) predicted this relationship between terrorism and tourism would increase "not because the problem is new but because the political and economic ramifications are immense and likely to grow larger" (p. 238). An important purpose of some terrorists is to economically cripple a targeted nation in its ability to provide essential services, and thereby possibly effect a collapse of government. This type of terrorism is an important part of what Borneman (1998) terms the "disintegrating political order," the boundaries of which lay in nationhood. Egypt is typical of nations with a high population density and low tax base that now rely on tourism income to meet annual expenses. To preserve the hospitality image, the government maintains moderate political positions in the Arab–Israeli conflict, as well as with reference to Islamic fundamentalism. Their neutrality invites political dissension. Using the "soft target" tactic and striking at a very popular tourist destination, the November 1997 terrorist gunfire on tourists visiting the historic temple of Queen Hatshepsut in Upper Egypt killed 58 persons and attained world media coverage. Alarmed by the possibility of further immediate attacks, tourism operators cancelled succeeding tours. Overseas governments, to ensure the safety of their traveling citizens, evacuated some clients then traveling elsewhere in Egypt (Butler, 1999). Tourism came to a standstill but, with promises of more security guards, the usual winter sun-seekers gradually returned the Egyptian tourist industry to normalcy in the subsequent year.

Terrorist street bombings that occur almost routinely in destinations of stress such as Northern Ireland deter travelers, but the area was never a major international tourism center and these ongoing occurrences to date have not been directly tourist related. In a study of Israel, a nation heavily dependent upon tourism income to maintain essential services, Krakover (1999) found that tourists apparently have short memories and do not personally identify with such random street events. In the short term, tourism moderately declines following a publicized attack, but within 6 weeks the area in question returns to full tourist visitation. Where organized terrorism operates on a larger scale, tourists are considered "soft targets" because they frequent areas that are very public, hard to defend, and the international media coverage serves terrorists particularly well (Sonmez & Graefe, 1998a, p. 115). Hijacking of airplanes and the holding of tourists as hostages with demands for armaments in exchange for their lives are public acts that excite government attention.

Tribes in northern Dubai successfully used their (well-treated) hostages to bargain their government for additional needed services, but not all hostages have been so lucky. Business travelers in Latin America are frequent targets, and their parent companies add the costly insurance premiums to meet ransom demands to the expense of doing business in the area. Here, kidnap terrorism has proved to be financially profitable in funding their illegal activities but, true to their criminal intent and the need to protect terrorist identity, the industrial hostage often does not survive the kidnapping.

Unlike a crime scene where spectators may gather, few tourists visit a terrorist site. A sense of chill seems to prevail, especially because terrorist groups commonly stage a memorial event on the first (and subsequent) anniversaries of the original attack. In general, terrorism leaves few permanent tourist markers. Except for family and friends of the deceased, there is little emotional attachment to the event or its site. Tourists seldom seek Lockerbie, Scotland, as a destination and the site of the 1988 bomb-induced crash of Pan-American Flight 103—an event that economically bankrupted this pioneering global airline and politically embarrassed the US. To date, terrorist attacks have been unnerving to local residents because they are so unpredictable in time and place. But few foreign visitors pay heed to possibilities of terrorist activity except in locations where tourist hostages have been killed, as in Kashmir. The attitude seems to be: with hundreds of flights every day, which airliner will be hijacked?

Ethnic Cleansing

As a form of war, ethnic cleansing is a return to tribalism, and negates much of the prevalent humanism in Western thought that validates the human soul. Such warfare is inhumane but not new. The Nanking Massacre of 1935 killed over 300,000 in one city in a few days, and most of the world knew nothing of it until the 1990s. Stalin ordered the extermination of over 1 million Ukrainians who refused to hand over their lands for collective farms, and the world said nothing. The Killing Days in Cambodia reputedly obliterated some 2.5 million people, but the world took no action. The actual count of Chinese killed under the Gang of Four may never be known but has been estimated at 10 million. Again, the world said nothing. Such behavior is possibly excusable under atheistic communism and Asian theologies, but the question begs scholarly scrutiny by social scientists in relation to Christian ethics if not Judaic–Christian–Islamic belief, and secular humanism.

The ethnic cleansing, which has become apparent in the 1990s, especially in central tribal Africa and among the ethnic groups of former Yugoslavia, shares some parallels with terrorism, as an attack on central government. It differs because the goal is not to destroy the government but, rather, to elevate and propel one ethnicity into positions of control. To do so, the most effective means is to eliminate their competitors by gunfire, by ravaged land, and by driving them out as refugees. The legal military and police are often divided against themselves, and "intervention and peacekeeping in the absence of peace" (Fortman, Martin, & Rooussel, 1998, pp. 147-150) has become a trial by fire. Existing entities including the UN, NATO, and EC have been unable to maintain adequate humanitarian assistance, let alone develop effective containment, then remediate ethnic conflict.

In 2000, some 51 nations were torn by ethnic conflict, which surged after the end of the Cold War thanks to the ready availability of leftover small arms, grenades, and landmines. Some 12 countries, including 7 in Europe, manufacture and sell assault rifles, machine guns, and grenade launchers. As Boutwell and Klare (2000, pp. 48-53) point out, a few hundred machine guns and mortars will supply a small army that can take over an entire country and kill or wound hundreds of thousands of civilians. Two social and psychological factors support ethnic cleansing: first, armed conflict bonds partisans to a common cause and, second, it offers to them opportunities for upward social mobility and status among their peers, and "terrorist" rank as warriors, recognized by both brethren and enemies. War has indeed changed, moving from the battlefield to city streets, farms, and churches.

This new form of war is also noteworthy for the number of abducted children who "disappear" from families or off the streets and, after paramilitary training, reappear as child soldiers. Some gun-bearers are as young as age 5 and 6, and a group of 12 year olds led the ethnic Karma rebel group in Myanmar (former Burma) in an aborted effort to storm and hold a hospital in December 1999 (Boothby & Knudsen, 2000).

Another significant dimension is the emergence of *Danger Tourism*, represented by individuals who voluntarily seek out and visit sites of political turmoil and ethnic battles. Predominantly younger Echo Boomers and Generation X in age, they exchange information about their adventures and activities through a favored Web site (http://www.fieldingtravel.com/blackflag/) and its chat room. Their destinations include Timor, Djakarta, and Somalia where they can see "the action" and buy the status-symbol T-shirts, "I was at the riots of. . . ."

Their motivations are varied and unclear but may be an age-related rite of passage comparable to military service but lacking its compulsory duties and potential risk. Unlike the Lincoln Brigade, who volunteered to fight in the Spanish Revolution in the 1930s, these observers are noncombatants and chose ethnic cleansing over terrorism because the activities in the former are more predictable, prolonged, and less dangerous. Adams (2000) suggests that their "web-based dialogues are read by cyber-voyagers, and presumably their representations of the places they visit are digested and amplified by websurfers round the globe." Thus, their interpretation of events to a larger audience is usually different from the established media, and their on-site comments "can play a role in the rearticulation of indigenous ethnic sensibilities."

Ethnic cleansing leaves as tourism markers the mass graves of immediacy, the sordid pictures in holocaust museums, and occasional memorials with intellectual and spiritual depth. At Nanking, against the backdrop of the mammoth stone bas-reliefs of torture and death, stands a small plain stone column given by a former Japanese soldier whose conscience compelled this simple but profound public penitence for the pain his behavior had caused. At Lidice, a Czech village whose population was annihilated in World War II by a single Nazi coup, the postwar community became a rose garden that blooms from the blood of the erased as a symbol of rebirth and beauty. At some future date the names of leaders who ordered this barbarism may be written in the annals of history but the events are seared on the memories of residual survivors, to constitute the basis of violent future reciprocity. As Zimmermann noted in the case study on Cross-Border Tourism (Chapter 25), the existence of ancient battlegrounds proved to be a stumbling block in developing new peaceful tourism.

Civil Disturbances in the 21st Century

Military budgets and training in almost every nation presume that conflicts will continue, and will require international forces, and possibly mercenary armies, reducing personal allegiance to family and unit. The potential for increased civil disturbances including war, ethnic cleansing, and terrorism are rooted in the competition of a progressively larger population competing for diminishing resources: land, food, water, and energy.

Military Intervention and Containment

The efforts to control civilian violence through introduction of third-party forces have not yet proved effective. The US army points out that every war during the 1990s, excluding the Gulf War, has involved action in urban environments "in places such as Somalia, Haiti and Bosnia, we've fought a three-block war in urban settings" (Kitfield, 1998). In possible preparation for further action, the US has established eight simulated urban centers for training the MOUT (Military Operations on Urban Terrain) and, like the US Marine Corps, is investigating the use of robots "to clear mine fields, locate snipers, or detect chemical and biological weapons." Missiles that resemble birds (in size and shape) are being developed to destroy a single room, rather than a building or a city block. Hero figures in these new armed forces are nameless and faceless warriors or intervention police clad in hooded bulletproof garb and gas masks. Members of Generation X who have become desensitized to violence as they practice and gain skill in lethal video games seem unlikely to create tourist markers to honor unknown "fallen."

Star Wars

The conquest of space is fraught with questions pertaining to missile defense systems and the fictionalized television and motion pictures versions of Star Wars. Sovereignty, or control of space resources for colonies and industrial products, will be a central issue to be resolved in terms of then prevailing geopolitical philosophy. Can space be a "common ground," like oceans and atmosphere, and "international" as 20th century scientists have sought to define Antarctica? Or will territoriality be invoked with boundaries linked to land-based Earth domains, to be defended against spatial ethnicities? Some initial cosmic policies will probably be established in this 21st century. Star Wars may generate a new genre of military leadership revered as global heroes who defend our planet against Martians or other unknown creatures. The tourist markers may well be stored in a computer "chip." Providing hospitality aboard an ISS environment where even the host population are in-migrants and not native to "space" poses many new adjustments (V. Smith, 2000).

Cyberwars

Cyberwars present other challenges that to date have been essentially rhetoric but have the capacity to turn lethal. Insurgent groups can establish a Net presence, disseminate propaganda, by-pass established news services, and sway public opinion. During the Kosovo war, journalists who were unable to attend official press conferences received disinformation by e-mail from presumed legitimate sources. According to *Newsweek* ("Hackers Hit Military Computers," 1999), 3 days after the onset of Kosovo bombing, hackers in Belgrade "attacked" NATO headquarters with e-mail-bearing viruses; the US Defense Department reported more than 100 attempted break-ins on their computers every day. To date, none of these cyber invasions has been successful but cyberwar clearly holds the potential for future fatalities. Unseen and unknown illegal or terrorist cyber warriors could access and control biological and nuclear weapons of mass destruction, and leave no record of power or leadership.

Conclusion

War has been an important activity throughout human history, and despite its destruction, wars created a social, economic, and political heritage that varied according to national or ethnic context. Tourism markers reinforced local societal values, and through sacralization and enshrinement, many such as the L'Arc de Triomphe in Paris became world famous visitor attractions. Many tourists learned and better understood history through visitation at sites and shrines including battlefields and holocaust museums. Visitors at Hiroshima and Nagasaki are awed by the visual evidence of nuclear destruction.

Technological change has continuously altered the nature and effects of war, making it more pervasive and destructive. As the implements of war become more mechanized and robotic, the tourism markers seem increasingly depersonalized. A heat-seeking warhead or a terrain-guided stealth plane no longer even bears the name of its inventor or manufacturer. Increasingly tourism has turned to the historic, the traditional, and to heritage because those markers have a personal identity in contrast to the "hyperspaces" described for globalization. We are led to question: does ethnic cleansing replaces war as globalization replaces nationhood? If so, what new 21st century tourist markers will replace statues, tombs, and monuments as the honorific symbols of remembrance? Some old markers of former respectability will be destroyed, as when the Russians toppled and smashed their vast collection of Lenin statues when communism was abandoned as their political philosophy. Tourism markers thus need to be recognized and understood as significant mirrors of social and political perspective.

Chapter 29

Remarks on the Commodification of Cultures

Dean MacCannell

Much of my work is about the tourist *attraction* and the motivation to leave home, to experience *otherness*. I have tried to describe the ways Western institutions of modern mass tourism produce, and attempt to satisfy, the need for otherness. What appears before us is the spectacle of the great success of tourism to establish itself worldwide, a spectacle in which we all have *bit parts*. But this success is also accompanied by a feeling of loss of the sense of discovery and adventure that one might have experienced traveling before everything was laid out in advance by the travel industry.

There have been many changes in formerly remote places as a result of their having become popular tourist destinations. Can tourism (or anthropology for that matter) ever overcome the awkward and difficult quality of cross-cultural understanding in settings that are organized for tourist visits? And there are real, not just philosophical, problems of authenticity? Can faraway places be experienced as *authentic* or *natural* when they are constructed, artificial habitats made entirely for tourists to visit?

A culture of tourism has emerged on a global base, with the same hotels and the similar theme parks at every major destination. Students who came late to tourism research call the same cultural complex *postmodernity*. The key characteristic of the culture of tourism is that every place on Earth is theoretically a *destination* and every tourist destination begins to resemble every other destination and that tourist "destinations" increasingly resemble *home*, the place where the tourists are from. A question that emerges from this evolution is whether tourism itself, in its drive to homogenize the travel experience and the destination, will eventually destroy the reason to travel.

Tourism, whether we are the tourist or the host, profoundly influences the ways we define place, *foreignness*, and ourselves. Tourism began as an acknowledgment, perhaps even a celebration, of an almost sacred connection between peoples, places, and their symbols: Switzerland and its Alps, Africa and its animals, Egypt and its

Pyramids, London and its Bridge, Japan and Mount Fuji. It will become evident that tourism has ended up as something quite different.

Why Leave Home

There are two quite different reasons for trying to "get away from it *all*." Some tourists leave home for the purpose of *doing nothing*, or having a good time, playing with vacation friends, relaxing in the hot springs, lying on the beach, being entertained. For some, to be a tourist can mean a week at a nearby low-budget vacation camp, while for others it involves a distant quest for exotic nature or cultures and the kind of travel undertaken by explorers. These latter may shun the night life and the beach, undertaking visits to shrines, remote villages, and natural monuments, ultimately turning their vacation into a kind of work, perhaps more rigorous than their actual work. The different varieties of tourist experience may be correlated with the social class of the tourist, but money is not an absolutely determining factor. Hitchhiking students from the West, with very little money, seek exotic experiences on every continent. They have made "hippie" a word that appears in almost all the world's languages.

What the two types of tourist (recreational vs. explorer) have in common is they feel they must undertake their quest for *otherness*, or for pleasure, away from home. The common denominator of tourism in all its forms is that it constitutes a break from the daily distractions and responsibilities of home and work. Ideally, when the tourists are away from home and in the presence of the attraction, certain values and pleasures may become a kind of *total experience*. This could be a sense of absolute freedom from care and utter relaxation on a perfect beach in the South Pacific. It could be a release from ordinary social constraints at a weekend holiday motel. It might be a near loss of self in a remote peasant village where ancient cultural traditions are still followed precisely. Perhaps it is a feeling of sublime awe at the site of a former natural or historic catastrophe or miracle—gazing upon Mount Fuji for the first time, or the Egyptian pyramids, for example. Such *magical* experiences are bracketed by the tour. They are ritually separated from everyday existence. They are heightened moments. One goes only to return home.

But tourism today does not resemble the first trips organized by the British inventor of guided tours, Thomas Cook. The earliest organized tours reduced the uncertainty of travel, but the early tourists were exposed to hardships and risks similar to those faced by explorers and mountaineers. There are striking images of women on the first Cook's Tour to Switzerland, in long skirts, down on their hands and knees, crossing glacial crevices bridged by narrow wooden boards. These images stand in sharp contrast to the motor coach slowdown at an Alpine viewpoint with through-the-window-only photo opportunities.

In the early days of packaged tourism, *getting there* was as much a part of the experience of spiritual displacement as arrival at the destination. The tourist could feel the undulations of the sea or the mountain path, experience the changes in temperature, hear and smell sharply etched local sensations en route. Progress toward a destination was a series of arrivals and departures, each constituting itself as a distinct experience. Even the mode of conveyance—steam railway, sailing ship, horse-drawn omnibus, rickshaw—was integral to the succession of differences one felt each step away from home. Today, any sense of traversing space, especially space that is marked by local distinction, is almost absent from the travel experience. Travel by air and high-speed motorways is marked mainly by the passage of time and the droning of engines partially masked by a music system. The experiences one has going between any two points on the face of the Earth are increasingly similar. They do not resemble earlier travel so much as they reproduce the experience of sitting in hospital waiting rooms. Now it is possible to travel around the world without leaving a globally unified protective envelop in which ticketing, banking, hotels, restaurants, airport lounges, shopping areas, tour buses, and the planes themselves are utterly uniform. Only superficial decorative appliqué seeks to remind the tourist of former local specificity: "This used to be Tahiti, or Kansas."

As travel becomes increasingly homogeneous and generic, the tourists, for their part, become nostalgic for any travel experience that might be classified as *real* or *authentic*. Thus, a second order of tourism is built on the first, a kind of *antitourism*, which promises *real* as opposed to *tourist* experiences. Tour company entrepreneurs provide fly-and-walk trips to the North Pole, opportunity to retrace Darwin's travels in the Galapagos, Cannibal Tours up the Sepik River in New Guinea, ecotourism in the Yucatan, visits to Yurts in Outer Mongolia.

Even in these exotic destinations, it is still necessary to question the opposition traveler versus *tourist*. When the tourist is in an "exotic" place, the consequences of a bus or a plane not showing up on time may be more interesting. The tourist might have to spend the night sleeping outdoors rather than staying in an inferior stopover hotel or trying to nap in an airport lounge. But the fact remains that even in the most exotic destinations, the itinerary has been worked out in advance, and the local arrangements, however crude these may be, have been made by the tour operators. The villagers en route know in advance that the tourists are coming and have prepared for them. The tourists may take a turn on the back of an ostrich or an elephant, but mainly they ride in four-wheel-drive vehicles. Wealthy *ecotourists* from the US visiting Central America in search of unspoiled nature, authentic *primitives*, and undiscovered archaeological sites famously arrive in leather upholstered, air-conditioned Land Rovers with concert hall-quality stereo systems. This kind of adventuresome travel increasingly resembles staying at home flipping through the pages of a magazine, or rock climbing tethered from above on the plywood cliffs in a sporting goods shop.

Travel, in the sense of adventure and discovery, implies selecting one's own route, using the same modes of transportation as used by the local people, and working out one's eating and sleeping arrangements on the spot rather than in advance. As such, it is now very rare. When it does occur, the traveler on every continent is likely to trip across and fall into grooves already well worn by tourists. The traveler would be hard-pressed to find a place anywhere in the world that is not already set up in advance to accommodate him. In San Francisco, tourists ride *real* cable cars, not just the cute little rubber tired copies of cable cars used by the sightseeing companies; not just the *tourist* cable cars. In Switzerland, tourists are once again conveyed to the entrance of their hotel in a horse-drawn omnibus. And in Virtual Reality, the tourist no longer watches passively as Luke Skywalker defends the universe; he takes over the controls of the Millennium Falcon and *defends the universe* himself.

Is it Possible to Experience "Otherness" While on Tour?

The worldwide distribution of images of local places, peoples, and monuments once supplied much of the motive for touristic travel. The first contact a tourist had with a destination was not the place itself but with a story about it in a magazine or encyclopedia, its picture on a calendar, a colorful brochure obtained at a travel agency, or perhaps an informational movie travelogue or video. The proliferation of touristic imagery was great even before the information age. Charles Dickens, in what appears to be hyperbole, makes a factual observation: "There is, probably, not a famous picture or statue in all Italy, but could easily be buried under a mountain of printed paper devoted to dissertations on it" (*Pictures From Italy*). Having seen a picture or read an account of the Egyptian pyramids, the Swiss Alps, Japanese pearl divers, the Northern Lights, etc., one would want to go to see for himself or herself.

This has always been the kernel of the touristic motive to travel—the desire to be where I am not. The motive is conditional in that it does not involve a permanent removal from one's everyday life. It is only a temporary change premised on the assumption of a safe return home. The motive may be stated as a simple desire to experience other peoples' ways of life, to see a famous attraction or monument for oneself, to discover if a beach lives up to the claims that have been made for it. But at least in the West, there is also an element of desire to become identified with the paradoxical combination of remoteness, inaccessibility, mysteriousness, and fame of the site. The act of touristic travel begins with an image, a dream, or a memory in which the tourist places himself or herself at an attraction. The actual experience at the attraction is a different matter altogether.

Any thought one might have entertained about getting to know the life of the native peoples as it is actually lived, or discovering for oneself the actual feelings and textures of a famous stone wall or monument, or becoming identified with the remoteness and mystery of the place, quickly give way to the realization that the dominant element in every tourist landscape are the tourists. The *others* one meets in tourist settings are other tourists and local workers whose job it is to serve tourists. The primary experience will not be of the place so much as it will be a collection of often insensitive and off-the-point reactions to the place expressed by one's fellow tourists, and forced conviviality-for-hire of tourist service workers. Each tourist goes to the destination wanting to see it as a picture-perfect image of itself; a perfect picture just like the one in the travel agency but now with *me* in it. They come away with the realization that literally thousands of other tourists have preceded them with a similar dream and millions more will follow. Even the most remote attractions, the *unspoiled* highland villages of primitive peoples, accessible only to those who are willing to walk for several days, are entirely organized around their function as an attraction.

Tourism Changes its Destinations

The past 150 years can be characterized as a period during which the character of the destination has changed radically. The changes that have occurred go well beyond the construction of hotels, airports, and restaurants to accommodate tourists. Local traditions are modified to make them more attractive to tourists. Religious observances are transformed into tourist spectacles. For example, the crocodile ritual performed for tourists by the Iatmul people of the Sepik region in New Guinea has been shortened from 3 days to under 45 minutes, and performed not annually, but upon the arrival of the cruise ship. Wherever tourists are found, there is an emergent culture of tourism made from fragments of the local cultures that tourism destroyed.

An obvious effect of this evolution has been to infuse tourist destinations with anxiety. Each destination desperately attempts to mark and market itself as having distinction, an *identity*. What occurs is not local specificity, but countless variations on the theme of *generic locality*, a kind of stressful existence that might be called "trying to be distinctive for tourists." Even places with great former distinction feel the need to remake themselves according to the tourist formula. In the West, historic leaders and folk heroes reappear as cartoon figures; a version of a French meal is served at McDonald's in Paris; someone wearing a Beefeater costume hands out informational brochures in London. Every other day or week is set aside to engage tourists in a celebration of "historic" or "mythic" events of little current interest to local people.

There is a characteristic transformation of places where the local and the global are linked through tourism. First, a place of work, for example, a beach where small fishing boats were hauled out, nets repaired, today's successes and failures discussed and tomorrow's activities planned, becomes a *work display* for tourists. The entire scene becomes an object of touristic consumption to be taken in as an example of *the picturesque* with a message: work is *natural*; work is *beautiful*; work is *picturesque*. Perhaps some famous people, or *beautiful people*, members of the international elite leisure class, *discover* the *unspoiled* beach village. After initial contact between the tourists and the locals it is no longer necessary for any fishing or associated activities to take place, so long as some of the boats, nets, and fishermen remain photogenically arrayed as a reminder of their former purpose. Eventually, the picturesque elements are selectively integrated into the decoration of the beach bars and discos, which will retain a traditional seafaring theme. A place of work becomes a place of entertainment. The fishermen, or their children, are now integrated into the global economy as service workers for international tourists. Everywhere local practices and traditions are hollowed out thus to make a place for this new kind of work.

The Culture of Tourism Is Becoming World Culture

The erosion of the specificity of tourist destinations in favor of a homogeneous culture of tourism is the result of the transformation of local economies as described above and also of the movement and displacement of millions of natural historical and cultural objects, including the things that tourists once had to travel to see. It is no longer a matter of removing and assembling representative examples of artifacts and practices of diverse other peoples in museums of ethnology. Entire human habitats are now constructed from actual and imagined mementos of *otherness*. With the possible exception of deep wilderness and a few precious religious shrines, every tourist attraction now meets the tourist more than halfway. The attractions are on tour.

This phenomenon begins, but does not stop, with the "World Tour" of the entourage and elaborate stage settings of international rock-and-roll superstars, or the "Treasures of Ancient Egypt." It extends to entire habitats for tourists. Disneyland, a large and complex system of attractions, was once thought to be a "place," considered by many the most representative symbol of US culture. It was the only place the Russian Premier, Nikita Khruschchev, asked to see when he visited the US during the Cold War in the 1960s. Now Disneyland itself has traveled to France and Japan, not to mention Florida. Some of the most famous and venerable monuments of nature and culture have been moved or reproduced in a new location. Hearst Castle on the California coast was constructed from entire palaces, abbeys, and convents purchased in Europe by the newspaper multimillionaire, William Randolph Hearst, then disassembled, crated, and shipped to the US for reassembly. Even in its original use as a home, it functioned mainly as an attraction and transformed its famous owner into a kind of tourist in his own house. The underwater habitat of the entire Pacific Rim, including representative species of plants and animals, is faithfully reproduced in the massive "Ring of Fire" aquarium in Osaka. The original London Bridge has been moved to a resort town in the Arizona desert. Even the everyday life of peasant villagers worldwide is subject to these displacements. At "Little World" in Japan one finds entire Greek, African, Thai, and American Indian villages, including some of their inhabitants, functioning as both a theme park and a living ethnological museum.

The drive to embrace everything that once secured a sense of "locality" or local distinction, everything that was once symbolic of cultural or natural distinction, is central to tourism. At the end of this drive, we predictably find the reproduction and redistribution of markers of locality to the point that the local is killed by the very desire to embrace it. The culture of tourism may eventually be seen as the millennial stage of colonialism and Empire. During the early phases of colonialism and Empire, global powers marked their dominance by bringing things back from campaigns that could be displayed in the Capital. Napoleon took an obelisk from Egypt and had it erected in Paris. The Greek (so called "Elgin") marbles are still displayed in the British Museum. Of course, these objects continue to be important tourist attractions that seem to resemble contemporary displaced imagery in tourist settings—the re-creation *of the Paris Experience* in a Las Vegas Casino-Hotel, for example. The difference is that the earlier displaced symbols have the dignity of marking actual historical events, however egregious that history might have been. Their contemporary relatives mark nothing but the power of global capital to efface history and to construct generic localities, or to package identity.

The version of tourism produced by global capital has, in effect, declared itself as capable of producing, reproducing, buying, selling, and moving anything and anyone whatsoever to anyplace whatsoever. It does not restrict itself to a few spoils of military victory. Walt Disney built replicas of the Caribbean Sea and the Matterhorn at his Disneyland in California, and attempted to bring Abraham Lincoln back from the dead. These displacements are of such a magnitude that it is almost impossible to think they were conceived by humans. Only a "God of Tourism" could imagine replacing the Matterhorn, or resuscitating a dead president.

The drive to reproduce the past, nature, and other cultures seems to be motivated by a limitless appetite for more otherness, but it is an otherness that is under control, a comforting otherness, an otherness that has been domesticated. The latex alligators at Disneyland mount ferocious *attacks* on boats carrying tourists. Thus, they respond to our ideas about the *being* of alligators much better than the real alligators sleeping motionless in a river or a zoo. Disney alligators are, at once, *more realistic* than real alligators and safe to be around. The *automatronic* Mr. Lincoln is shorter in stature than the original, delivers a boring speech, and appears to be somewhat palsied in his gestures. He comes off as quite a bit like our leaders of today. He certainly does not measure up to the genius of his creator, Mr. Disney.

When everything has been moved out of time and out of place, recontextualized and domesticated, tourism is no longer a mere vacation activity, an entertainment. It becomes the primary engine of myth and culture in the making. With sufficient capital accumulation, in Las Vegas for example, or the West Edmonton Mall in Canada, it is no longer necessary to attach this engine to existing social, physical, or historical arrangements. At the West Edmonton Mall (now emulated on a grander scale at the Mall of America) one finds Parisian Boulevards, an indoor lake with penguins, a submarine ride and replicas of Columbus's ship, a reconstruction of New Orleans' Bourbon Street, performing dolphins, Siberian tigers, a 19th century iron bridge from England. The culture of tourism has established itself to the point that it is possible to create entire tourist habitats. It has become a phenomenon in itself, capable of self-reproduction. Any distinction that might have once held between the resort vacation camp, theme park, shopping mall, and the city can be broken down by tourism. Now these various functions or sites of formerly specialized activities have blended and merged into single universal *architecture of pleasure*. Constructed *historical* and man-made *natural* places are being built throughout the Western world and beyond, often replacing the *actual* historical and natural places they pretend to emulate.

Does the Change in Tourism Lead to a Change in the Motive to Travel?

In the West, when Cook arranged the first group tours of Switzerland and Egypt, when the first vacation camps were built, the tourists, the destinations, and the motives were clearly different than they are today. *Tourist* was a temporary identity available and desirable to the industrial middle class and upper working class. In the late 19th century members of the new middle class obtained *disposable income* and some free time that would allow them (with the assistance of some smart entrepreneurs) to mock up a bourgeois version of the Grand Tour. This same moment was also one of bittersweet alienation and nostalgia for the new industrial bourgeoisie. Comfortable at home but still alienated, the tour became their special expressive form. Having recently sacrificed traditions and land use incompatible with the requirements of career success in the industrial age, these early tourists longed for cultural distinction, *unspoiled* natural beauty, strong and authentic relations with the family, the past, the soil. Tourism, travel, sightseeing, and the guided tour to historic and natural shrines responds to these longings and desires. The tour, as a pastiche of fragments of culture, history, and landscape, mirrored the loss and detachment the new bourgeois consciousness imagined itself to have experienced. The greater the career success, the greater the sense of loss, the more elaborate and extensive the tour must be. The early tourists went literally to the ends of the Earth in search of tokens of unspoiled nature, authenticity, and tradition missing in their own lives, but still visible in the lives of others.

As each place visited by the tourists increasingly resembles every other place, a process driven by tourism itself, the original motives no longer apply. A Londoner need not travel to Egypt to buy magnificent replicas of Egyptian artifacts. They are available for sale in the London Museum gift shop. Egypt in London (or New York, or Tokyo) is becoming as ubiquitous as a Londoner, a New Yorker, or a Nihongo speaker in Egypt. Each major city of the world and much of the hinterland has become fully transformed by the international culture of tourism to the point that the ethnic neighborhoods, theme parks, shopping malls, restaurants, and natural attractions of one's own city and region are no more or less *other* than those of touristic destinations around the world.

The everyday life of the international middle class is now fully colonized by global capital in a touristic cultural form. The adolescent tourist in the US no longer dreams of a summer bicycle tour around Europe, at least not in innocent isolation from the manipulative gaze of global capital. An entire commercial complex has grown up around the European-style bicycle. There are things to buy: spandex clothing, special shoes, smoother gear change mechanisms, sport water bottles. Moreover, there is no particular reason to go to Europe as "European-style" bicycling experiences are now marketed worldwide. The best Japanese restaurants in San Francisco have branches in Osaka and Milan. As the places one can visit increasingly resemble the place where one is coming from, the motive for travel necessarily becomes narcissistic or a matter of pure vanity: one travels only to have traveled.

Tourists are evolving into pure consumers, spending billions and ending up with nothing to show for it. When a tourist from London travels to Egypt to *take in the sights*, the act no longer leaves any tangible trace, except perhaps in his conversations: "Oh yes, I've been there." It is possible to travel around the world, seeing all the important sights, spending enormous quantities of money, and return home with nothing but a bag of dirty laundry. Nothing was produced for purposes of exchange to be carried home, used up, or resold. Typically and ideally, while on tour, every purchase made by the tourist is of services or consumables provided by the international travel and hotel industry: food and drink, a night's lodging, soap, throwaway chop sticks; other things immediately converted to waste. Even the lightweight things that are locally made by and for tourists—the souvenirs, postcards, and photographs—end up stashed in boxes at the back of closets, a difficult kind of rubbish that can neither be used nor disposed of.

Will the Reason for International Travel Eventually Disappear?

There are contradictions at the heart of international tourism that are now appearing as internal barriers to its future development.

First, international tourism is vulnerable as a result of its own previous success and excess. When the culture of tourism succeeds in replacing local culture, it becomes increasingly difficult to distinguish between destinations. The more each place comes to resemble someplace close to home, and the more tourist experience resembles everyday experience, the more difficult it becomes to justify travel. The Paris theme park, the Los Angeles theme Park, the Tokyo theme park, the Orlando theme park are all operated by the same company and staffed by the same cartoon figures. The international culture of tourism increasingly resembles a kind of corporate, high-technology feudalism in which the nation-state gives way to a few tightly controlled corporations that exercise control over work, leisure, and knowledge of the world and the place of the individual in it. The production and marketing of *experiences* as the characteristic commodity of late capitalism may have reached the saturation point.

Second, international travel and tourism is vulnerable to increasing acceptance of *virtuality* and to the realization that media images of *otherness* are often superior to actual experience. The media always get further *behind the scenes* than one can actually go as a tourist. Also, the more one travels, the more one realizes that actual experience in tourist settings is always highly staged and manipulated. Therefore, it is not much different from mediated experience, except that the mediated experience is usually better than the so-called *real* experience. Mickey Mouse on screen is enormously more entertaining than the actor in the Mickey Mouse suit at Disneyland.

Third, potentially exacerbating these internal problems are at least two important externalities. The first is that a relatively minor reversal in the world economy can quickly relieve the international middle class of its discretionary money. Certainly touristic travel would be among the first *sacrifices* the international middle class would make. The second is that tourist destinations are also vulnerable to civil unrest and natural disasters.

The Next Tourism

How did it occur that the world's largest industry could leave itself open to collapse at the moment of its greatest expansion? If the seeds of its destruction have been planted, they are certainly being nurtured by its overinvolvement with those aspects of culture that are dead and dying: with colorful peasantry, unspoiled rain forests, outmoded forms of work, with ancient Egypt, Rome, or Greece. International tourism embraces death and dying not as history but as entertainment.

Under these conditions, it would be surprising if the cultural subjects that emerge from tourism were anything but stillborn. On the *right*, it is becoming increasingly difficult for the human subject to think itself as anything different from, or other than, its place in an organization. There is no expressed desire except for that which can be satisfied by a good paying job. As organizations become larger and more powerful, and as every community is increasingly composed of decontextualized, generic symbols of *place*, everyday existence becomes a kind of frenzy of boredom. On the *left*, the subject is supposed to be nothing more than its micro-identities (e.g., feminist, or Third world, or gay, or heterosexual white male). The only ideological common ground is tourism. Left and right, imagination departs. The tourists now depend on someone else—perhaps it is Walt Disney, or the new virtual reality factories, or the police of political correctness—to do their dreaming for them. We should consider the consequences. A life that is lived without imagination, or one in which all the imagery is supplied by others, resembles a kind of living death.

Still, it is premature to assume that tourism has no future other than collapse. Tourism is logically self-canceling, but that does not necessarily mean that it will go into decline. The international culture of tourism would not be the first death cult humankind has devised for itself.

It comes down to the question: As every destination comes increasingly to resemble every other destination, why leave home? The answer is not obvious and requires a logic of its own, a touristic logic. Tourism literally makes one's own place, one's "home," into the ultimate destination. The tourist's home may be without style or distinction—just another postmodern box with superficial styling references *to the local* provided by a design studio. Eventually, when the transformation of global culture is complete, the "home" may be no different from any of the places visited on the tourist's itinerary, except for its singular designation as the point of origin and final destination.

In such a world, rigid and homogeneous, leaving home is the only way to mark it as distinct from other places; it may not be different from other places, but at least it is the place you are "from." You may never be able to change your social position but you can travel as a kind of simple-minded literalization of social and geographic mobility. Real mobility is no longer technically possible once every move takes the traveler to a place no different from the place he just left. What the tourist discovers is that "home" is deeply arbitrary even if it seems to be the point of origin and final destination. This realization can serve either to kill tourism, so we can start to live again, or it will make touristic travel all the more frenzied. What better way of marking status differences in a world in which we must "stay in our places" than having visited just about every place? As tourists we come home, making "our place" the most important place of all. At the same time, our social standing is nicely inflated without the embarrassment of a heap of status objects that unfortunately can also be symptoms of insecurity. On his return home, the tourist can enjoy a kind of euphoria of pseudosuperiority that is not dependent on any specific "thing." He can be "worldly" or "traveled," which are now entirely content free and *duty free* designations.

Summary

Tourism has been the ground for the production of a new global culture. In the name of tourism, capital and modernized peoples have been deployed to the most remote regions of the world. Tourism has coated almost the entire world with decorative traces of the cultures it has consumed. Its reach is extensive, but it has yet to find the majority of the world's peoples. Most of the people in the world at this moment are not tourists, nor do they earn their living by serving tourists. They are subsistence agriculturalists, living just beyond the reach of tourism in Africa, Latin America, China, India. (The persistence of cultures just beyond the reach of global tourism and capital is not to be taken for granted, however, just as the chapters in this volume make abundantly clear.)

The questions that I raised in *The Tourist: A New Theory of the Leisure Class* (MacCannell, 1989b) are entirely inappropriate and out of place when they are applied to this other half of the world's people, which constitutes a living critique of the anxieties associated with tourism and postmodernity. Paralleling and opposing the movements of the tourists, during the last 25 years there has been a rapid increase of the movements of nontourists from formerly remote regions of the world into centers of wealth and power: the African, Caribbean, and Asian diasporas; the flight of peasant refugees from Central America; the migrations of agricultural and other guest workers; Southeast Asian Boat People. The question of whether these people are having an *authentic travel experience* is an insult. The tourist follows the officially marked path, while for the refugee and the homeless, the marked path, the road, the sidewalk, the trail, the reserved seat on a scheduled flight, is only one way of going from place to place, and not necessarily the way that offers them the least resistance. The refugee may even feel the need to stay off the road for purposes of movement, or to use the road for something else. They may harvest it for information, for example. They travel by gripping onto the skids of helicopters, onto sides of trains and buses, hiding in cargo bays of planes and boats, walking through enemy territory at night, hiring smugglers to sneak them across international borders. They do not know where they will rest or eat, or even if they will rest or eat. They become separated from family members traveling with them sometimes for months or forever. They cannot be certain of their destination. These are not *virtual* experiences, designed to produce a sensation of a thrill or fear. They are real and consequential. The one defining certainty is precisely the opposite of that of the tourist: they know they cannot return home.

The tourist can no more prove himself than the refugee or the homeless can exist as other than proof of intense commitment to survival, to life. In their very drive to represent themselves as *community*, in their makeover that refers to *tradition*, the places tourists live and visit all the more perfectly become nameless and placeless.

There are still vital grounds for human celebration on a global scale, but they have nothing to do with the institutions of mass tourism as these have evolved. They would involve celebrating the survival strategies and creative adaptations of the immigrants displaced by the movement of global capital. We should be trying to invent a new celebration of otherness, one that honors life, not death, one that focuses on current creative work, not just the creative work of the past. Can we acknowledge those among us who must make new homes in alien environments, invent new family, work, and community arrangements? Not the peoples, places, and things destroyed by industrial society and memorialized by modern tourism during its first 150 years. Not the world as it used to be, but the new world that is emerging from the humus of the old, its heroes and heroines, their struggles, their acts of epic bravery, their arts.

If we were to do so, we would soon discover that the field of the absolute other is not half a world away, but only a few miles, or blocks, or inches.

Contributors

Maryann Brent is a native of the eastern United States, with a background in modern languages and is a Certified Travel Counselor (CTC) in the travel industry. In 1997 she completed the Ph.D. in Geography at the University of Waterloo in Ontario, and served as co-editor of the 25-year Special Index Issue, *Annals of Tourism Research* (1999). Current research includes the application of ArcView (GIS) to tourism research, space tourism at International Space University, and resort morphology.

Magalí Daltabuit is a Mexican biological/environmental anthropologist and full-time researcher at the Centro Regional de Investigaciónes Multidisciplinarias (Cuernavaca) of the Universidad Nacional Autónoma de México. She has a long history of research and fieldwork in southern Mexico, Belize, and Guatemala studying biocultural adaptations to rapid change. Her publications include monographs and articles on Maya women's health, nutrition, and work, migration and the environment, and the challenge of ecotourism. She has co-authored several papers with R. Brooke Thomas and Oriol Pi-Sunyer.

Michael Fagence teaches and researches at the University of Queensland, Brisbane, Australia. His principal fields of interest fall within the scope of tourism planning, with recent research focusing on the means available in planning to minimize the impact of tourism development on special cultural groups such as the Old Order Amish and Mennonites.

Nelson H. H. Graburn was born in England and studied anthropology at Cambridge, McGill, and the University of Chicago. Since 1964, he has taught Anthropology at the University of California, Berkeley, where he is also Curator at the Hearst Museum of Anthropology. His research interests include the study of tourism, museums, arts, identity, and representation. He has carried out fieldwork in Japan and among the Indians of Canada and the Inuit (Eskimos) of Canada, Greenland, and Alaska.

Rudi Hartmann teaches tourism at the University of Colorado at Denver. He received his Ph.D. from the Technical University of Munich (1983) and has been affiliated with the Clark University, University of California at Berkeley, and the University of Lund, Sweden. His research interests include sustainability of recreational resources and spatial patterns, dynamics, and impacts of tourism development.

Robin Heath is a native of Zimbabwe (formerly Southern Rhodesia) whose grandparents entered the country in the 1890s. After teaching in high schools for a number of years and the University of Rhodesia, she became interested in tourism research during her tenure as Research Officer at the Institute of Social and Economic Research, University of Durban-Westville, KwaZulu-Natal. Presently, she is

Senior Lecturer in the Geography Department of the University of Zimbabwe, where she teaches tourism and recreation and pursues research activity.

Jafar Jafari is professor of Hospitality and Tourism at the University of Wisconsin-Stout. Founder and Editor of *Annals of Tourism Research*, and founding president of International Academy for the Study of Tourism, his career is highlighted by the publication of the *Encyclopedia of Tourism* and participation in multiple World Tourism Organization conferences and other symposia reflective of his global scholarly interests.

Dean MacCannell is professor and Chair of Landscape Architecture at the University of California, Davis. He is author of *The Tourist: A New Theory of the Leisure Class* (1976/1999), *Empty Meeting Grounds* (1992), and over 50 articles and monographs on cultural analysis and criticism. His work on tourism has been featured in a BBC miniseries, *The Tourist* (1996).

Steven Parker is professor of Political Science at the University of Nevada, Las Vegas. He specializes in the subject of natural resource policy, as it applies to tourism. His research has focused on the United States, Australia, the Netherlands, Antilles, Papua New Guinea, Mexico, and Palau.

Oriol Pi-Sunyer is professor of Anthropology at the University of Massachusetts, Amherst. His interests in tourism date to the early 1970s when he returned to his native Catalonia. Tourism research in Mexico began in the late 1980s with the recognition that the situation in Quintana Roo shares significant features with the early phases of mass tourism in the Mediterranean. Together with R. Brooke Thomas and Magalí Daltabuit he has written several pieces that explore the dimensions of mass tourism in southern Mexico. One of his major theoretical concerns is the relationship between structures of power and forms of representation

Roel Puijk is associate professor at the Faculty of Culture, Media and Social Sciences, Lillehammer College (Norway). He has carried out studies on local development and tourism based on fieldwork in France and Norway. In addition, he has worked in media research and conducted studies on the production of television in Norwegian television and on the international mediation of the Lillehammer Winter Olympics.

Linda K. Richter is professor of political science at Kansas State University, where she teaches public policy and public administration with area specialties in South and Southeast Asia. She has authored three books and over 40 articles on tourism policy issues including national policies, gender issues, heritage, and health issues in tourism. She is currently associate editor of *Annals of Tourism Research* and the International Academy of the Study of Tourism.

Tom Selänniemi from Helsinki, Finland, holds a Ph.D. in Cultural Anthropology and is the Manager for Sustainable Tourism at Finnair Travel Services as well as Lecturer at the Finnish Network University for Tourism Studies. His main research interests are the anthropology of tourists, mass tourism and sustainability, ethnographic methods in tourism research, and the "secular pilgrimages" of cultural tourists.

Myra Shackley is professor of Culture Resource Management at Nottingham Trent University and directs their Centre for Tourism and Visitor Management. She was trained as an archaeologist and geographer and has research interests in the management of protected areas, indigenous people, and historic sites in response to tourism impacts. Myra has carried out field research throughout the Developing World and published 11 books, of which the most recent are *Wildlife Tourism* (1996) and *Visitor Management; Case Studies From World Heritage Sites*.

Valene L. Smith, Ph.D., is Research Professor at California State University, Chico and a peripatetic tourism anthropologist with sustained interests in ethnotourism and marginal lands (arctic, deserts, and tropics). A certified counselor (CTC) in the travel industry, this volume reflects her duality of academic training and work experience as tour operator and guide. Research interests include the history and development of tourism; concerns for its future as a global industry, to protect marginal lands as world population increases with expanded recreational needs; and space tourism.

Trevor H. B. Sofield, Ph.D. in Anthropology, is Professor and Head, School of Tourism Studies, University of Tasmania, Launceston, Australia. The former editor of *Pacific Tourism Review*, his major research interests include ecologically sustainable tourism, regional and heritage tourism, and development of tourism in LDCs. His tourism research consultancies include the World Bank, UNDP (Nepal), UNESCO (heritage tourism), and Government of China.

Margaret Byrne Swain is affiliated with the Anthropology Department at the University of California, Davis. Her research interests combine the issues of gender, ethnicity, and tourism, and her primary field site is in Yunnan, China. At Davis, she coordinates the Gender and Global Issues program and related projects, including the 1997 international conference Gender/Tourism/Fun.

R. Brooke Thomas is professor of Anthropology at the University of Massachusetts, Amherst. Since the 1960s, he has conducted research on biological adaptations of the Andean Quechua of Peru. In the 1990s, he studied the impact of mass tourism on the Lowland Maya of the Mexican state of Quintana Roo. He is committed to linking approaches derived from human adaptability and political economy in an analysis of impoverishment, particularly in indigenous societies. For some years, he has collaborated in research and publication with Oriol Pi-Sunyer and Magalí Daltabuit.

William J. Trousdale is the founder and president of EcoPlan International, a Canadian economic and planning firm based in Vancouver BC (www.ecoplanintl.com). He holds degrees in economics and resource planning from Colorado College and the University of British Columbia, respectively. A certified professional planner in the US and Canada, he has worked throughout North and South America and Asia. His work with decision analysis and sustainable tourism has earned awards and international recognition. Other professional interests include environmental policy and evaluation, impact assessment, feasibility analysis, economic development, and aboriginal development issues.

Charles F. Urbanowicz received his Ph.D. in Anthropology in 1972 from the University of Oregon and taught at the University of Minnesota in 1972–1973 and then joined the faculty at California State University, Chico, where he is a professor of Anthropology. Part of Charlie's earlier research of the 1970s, dealing with the Polynesian Kingdom of Tonga, appeared in earlier editions of *Hosts and Guests: The Anthropology of Tourism,* and he is extremely delighted that Valene, a colleague and friend for more than a quarter of a century, invited him to contribute to this current edition.

Anne Marie Van Broeck holds a Ph.D. in Anthropology from Catholic University of Leuven, Belgium. She has taught at the University in Colombia (where she also did research on terrorism) and is current Head of Undergraduate Programs in Tourism Studies at Cozumel campus, Universidad de Quintana Roo, Mexico.

J. M. Tim Wallace is an associate professor in the Department of Sociology and Anthropology at North Carolina State University. His most recent research has been in Costa Rica working on issues of sustainable development and tourism in rural areas. Other recent research includes a social impact assessment of an ecotourism project in Madagascar designed to protect lemurs.

Friedrich M. Zimmermann is professor of Human Geography and Regional Science and chair of the Department of Geography at the University of Graz, Austria. He is an experienced researcher in the fields of regional development and regional studies, using sustainable and holistic approaches to study the effects of regional policies in Europe. Additionally, he is an expert in tourism planning and prognosis and consultant for private and public institutions.

Bibliography

Aaker, D., Kumar, V., & Day, G. (1995). *Marketing research* (5th ed.). New York: John Wiley.

Abracosa, R., & Ortolano, I. (1987). Environmental impact assessment in the Philippines: 1977-1985. *Environmental Impact Assessment Review, 7,* 293-310.

Abt, V. (1986). *The business of risk: Commercial gambling in mainstream America.* Lawrence, KS: University of Kansas.

Adams, K. M. (1984). "Come to Tana Toraja, Land of the Heavenly Kings." Travel agents as brokers in ethnicity. *Annals of Tourism Research, 11*(3), 469-485.

Adams, K. M. (2000). Danger-zone tourism: Prospects and problematics for tourism in tumultuous times. In H. Chang, P. Teas, & T. Chang (Eds.), *Interconnected worlds: Tourism is Southeast Asia.* Amsterdam: Elsevier Science.

Ahlsmith, S. (1999, November). Marketing to diversity. *Travel Counselor,* 37-39.

Ahmad, Y., & Sammy, G. (1985). *Guidelines to environmental impact assessment in developing countries.* London: UNEP.

AIEST (1991). *Quality tourism: Concept of a sustainable tourism development; Harmonizing economical, social and ecological interests.* Berne, Switzerland: Association Internationale d'Experts Scientifique du Tourisme.

Allport, G. (1954). *The nature of prejudice.* Reading, MA: Addison Wesley.

Amnesty International. (1993). *Bosnia Herzegovina: Rape and sexual abuse by armed forces.* New York: Author.

Andereck, K. (1997). Territorial functioning in a tourism setting. *Annals of Tourism Research, 24,* 706-720.

Anderlea, G. (1953). *Trends and prospects of Latin American tourism.* Geneva: International Institute of Scientific Travel Research.

Anderson, B. (1991). *Imagined communities* (rev. ed.). London: Verso.

Anne Frank House. (1995). *The restoration of the Anne Frank House: House with a story.* Amsterdam: Author.

Annis, S. (1987). *God and production in a Guatemala town.* Austin: University of Texas Press.

Appadurai, A. (1990). Disjunction and differences in the global cultural economy. *Theory, Culture and Society, 7,* 295-310.

Appadurai, A. (1996). *Modernity at large: Cultural dimensions of globalization.* Minneapolis: University of Minnesota Press.

Archer, B. (1978). Domestic tourism as a development factor. *Annals of Tourism Research, 5,* 126-141.

Archer, B., & Cooper, C. (1994). The positive and negative impacts of tourism. In W. Theobald (Ed.), *Global tourism: The next decade* (pp. 73-91). Oxford: Butterworth-Heinemann.

Archer, B., & Fletcher, J. (1990). Multiplier analysis in tourism. In *Cahier de tourisme.* Centre des Etudes Touristiques, Universite de Droit, d'Economie et des Sciences.

Aridjis, H. (1994, January 5). Slaves and guerrillas, forests and blood. *The New York Times,* p. A15.

Armelagos, G., Barnes, K., & Lin, J. (1996). Disease in human evolution: The re-emergence of infectious diseases in the third epidemiological transition. *Anthro Notes, 18*(3), 1-7.

Ashley, C., Boyd, C., & Good, H. (2000, March). Pro poor tourism: Putting poverty at the heart of the tourism agenda. In *Natural resource perspective 15*. London: Overseas Development Institute.

Ashworth, G. (1992). Tourism policy and planning for a quality urban environment: The case of heritage tourism. In H. Briassoulis & J. van der Straaten (Eds.), *Tourism and the environment: Regional, economic and policy issues* (pp. 109-120). Dordrecht, The Netherlands: Kluwer Academic.

Ashworth, G., & Dietvorst, A. (1995). *Tourism and spatial transformations: Implications for policy and planning*. Oxford: CAB.

Ashworth, G., & Turnbridge, J. (2000). *The tourist-historic city: Retrospect and prospect of managing the heritage city*. Amsterdam: Elsevier Science.

Asia Development Bank. (1991). *Environmental evaluation of coastal zone projects: Methods and approaches* (Paper #8). Manila.

Asian Development Bank. (1997). *Key indicators of developing Asian and Pacific countries*. Singapore: Author.

Asian Women's Liberation. (1980). Prostitution tourism [Special issue]. *3*, 1-33.

Aspiras alibi. (1993, September 22). *Manila Standard*.

Association Internationale d'Experts Scientifique du Tourisme. (1991). *Quality tourism: Concept of a sustainable tourism development; harmonizing economical, social and ecological interests*. Berne, Switzerland: Author.

Association Mondiale pour la Formation Professionelle Touristique. (1990). *Capacitation turistica: Seminaro Latinoamericano*. Madrid: Author.

Atkinson, H., Berry, A., & Jarvis, R. (1995). *Business accounting for hospitality and tourism*. London: Thomson Business Press.

Aveling, R., & Wilson, R. (1992). *Tourism in the habitat of the great apes: Costs and benefits*. Paper presented at the 4th World Congress on National Park and Protected Areas, Caracas, Venezuela, February 10-21.

Bahadur Bista, D. (1999). And then there was man. In L. Chengyal & K. Moran. (Eds.) *Nepal* (pp. 79-90). Basingstoke: APA Publications.

Bahn, P., & Flenley, J. (1992). *Easter Island, earth island*. London: Thames & Hudson.

Banskota, K., Sharma, B., Neupane, I., & Gyawali, P. (1995). *A rapid assessment of the Quality Tourism Project*. Kathmandu: CREST.

Baretje, R. (2001). Centre International de Recherches et d'Etudes (CIRET), 6 avenue de Grassi, 13100 Aix-en-Provence, France.

Barfield, R. (1994). The devil's horsemen: Steppe nomadic warfare in historical perspective. In S. Reyna & R. Downs (Eds.), *Studying war: Anthropological perspectives* (pp. 157-184). Langhorne, PA: Gordon and Breach Science Publishers.

Barkin, D. (1989). Environmental degradation and productive transformation in Mexico: The contradictions of crisis management. *Yearbook, Conference of Latin American Geographers, 15*, 3-12.

Barnet, R., & Cavanaugh, J. (1996). Homogenization of global culture. In J. Mander & E. Goldsmith (Eds.), *The case against the global economy and for a turn toward the local* (pp. 71-77). San Francisco: Sierra Club Books.

Barth, F. (Ed.). (1969). *Ethnic groups and boundaries: The social organization of culture difference*. Oslo: Universitetsforlaget.

Barton, D. (1999, November 27). Thrill ride. *The Sacramento Bee*, p. 1.

Bårtvedt, R. (1984). *Vor gode brae ogsa i sommer beskuet af hoiformemme oine*. University of Bergen.

Baum, R. (1993). *Human resources in international tourism*. Oxford: Butterworth and Heinemann.

Baum, T. (1994). *Human resources management for the European tourism and hospitality*. Oxford: Butterworth and Heinemann.

Baum, T. (1999). The decline of the traditional North Atlantic fisheries and tourism's response: The cases of Iceland and Newfoundland. *Current Issues in Tourism, 2*, 47-67.

Beard, J., & Ragheb, M. (1983). Measuring leisure satisfaction. *Journal of Leisure Research, 15*, 219-228.

Beckett, J. (1996). Exploring the possible impact of current and future IT developments on university teaching and learning processes. *International Journal of Hospitality Management, 15*, 137-154.

Beer, J. (1993). *Packaged experience: Japanese overseas tourism in Asia.* Doctoral dissertation, University of California, Berkeley.

Behlmer, R. (1963). *The adventures of Robin Hood* (the Screen Play and Background of the 1938 Warner Brothers Picture). Wisconsin: University of Wisconsin Press.

Beltran, A. (1979). *Regions of refuge* (Monograph #12). Washington, DC: Society for Applied Anthropology.

Benigno, T. (1993). Blunder of an award. *Philippine Star*, p. 9.

Bernstein, P. (1996). *Against the gods: The remarkable story of risk.* New York: John Wiley & Sons.

Bertke, M. (1994). *Tourism in the West Balaton area including Kis-Balaton from an American perspective: Final report of the American Hungarian student summer 1994 program.* Raleigh, NC: North Carolina State University.

Bertman, S. (1998). *Hyperculture: The human cost of speed.* New York: Praeger Trade.

Bhattacharyya, D. (1997). Mediating India: An analysis of a guidebook. *Annals of Tourism Research, 24*, 371-389.

Biddlecomb, C. (1981). *Pacific tourism: Contrasts in values and expectations.* Pacific Conference of Churches.

Binkley, C. (1998, April 1). Gamble on Las Vegas hotel-casinos may not pay off. *The Wall Street Journal*, p. B6.

Bisset, R. (1987). Methods for environmental impact assessment: A selective survey with case studies. In A. Biwas & Q. Geping (Eds.), *Environmental impact assessment for developing countries* (pp. 3-64). London: Tycooly International.

Black, A. (1996). Negotiating the tourist gaze: The example of Malta. In J. Boissevain (Ed.), *Coping with tourists: European reactions to mass tourism* (pp. 112-142). Providence and Oxford: Berghahn Books.

Blow, B. (1920). *California highways: A descriptive record of road development by the state and by such counties as have paved highways.* San Francisco: H. S. Crocker.

Boissevain, J. (1996). *Coping with tourists.* Providence, RI: Berghahn Books.

Boldender, J. (1980). *Guidelines on tourism investment.* Madrid: World Tourism Organization.

Boldender, J., & Gerty, M. (1992). *Guidelines on tourism investment.* Madrid: World Tourism Organization.

Boldender, J., & Ward, T. (1987). *An examination of tourism investment incentives.* Madrid: World Tourism Organization.

Bond, C. (1995, July). If you can't bear to part with it, open a new museum. *Smithsonian*, 90-97.

Boniface, B., & Cooper, C. (1994). *The geography of travel and tourism.* London: Heinemann.

Boniface, P., & Fowler, P. (1993). *Heritage and tourism in 'the global village.'* London: Routledge.

Boo, E. (1990). *Ecotourism: Potentials and pitfalls* (Volumes 1 and 2: World Wildlife Fund). Lancaster: Wickersham Printing Company.

Boo, E. (1994). *The ecotourism boom: Planning for development and management, wildlands and human needs.* Washington, DC: World Wildlife Fund.

Booth, C. (1998, October 26). In with the new: Gaming is waning, so the neon city is on the remake. *Time*, 152(17).

Boothby, N., & Knudsen, C. (2000, June). Children of the gun. *Scientific American*, 60-65.

Boothroyd, P. (1990). On using environmental assessment to promote fair sustainable development. In P. Jacobs & B. Sadler (Eds.), *Sustainable development and environmental assessment perspectives on planning for a common future* (pp. 143-155). Hull, Quebec, Canada: CEARC.

Bordas, M. (1994). *Competitiveness of tourist destinations in long distance markets.* Aix-en-Provence: Etudes et Memoires, Centre des Hautes Etudes Touristiques.

Borman, R. (1999). Cofan: Story of the Forest people and the outsiders. *Cultural Survival Quarterly, 23*(2), 48-50.

Borneman, J. (1998). *Subversions of international order: Studies in the political anthropology of culture.* Albany, NY: State University of New York Press.

Borocz, J. (1996). *Leisure migration: A sociological study on tourism.* Oxford, UK: Pergamon Press.

Boseley, S. (1996, October 20). Manila jails child sex tour boss. *Guardian Weekly.*

Bourdieu, P. (1989). *Distinction: A social critique of the judgement of taste.* London: Routledge & Kegan.

Boutwell, J., & Klare, M. (2000, June). Waging a new kind of war. *Scientific American*, 48-53.

Bowman, G. (1991). The politics of tour guiding: Israeli and Palestinian guides in Israel and the Occupied Territories. In D. Harrison (Ed.), *Tourism and the less-developed countries* (pp. 121-134). London: Belhaven Press.

Braham, B. (1988). *Computer systems in the hotel and catering industry* (Vol. 18). London: Casell.

Brandenburg, R. (1964). *The making of Mexico.* Englewood Cliffs, NJ: Prentice Hall.

Bratton, R., Go, F., & Ritchie, B. (Eds.). (1991). *New Horizons in Tourism and Hospitality Education, Training and Research, Conference Proceedings*, World Tourism Education and Research Center, University of Calgary, Canada, July 2-5.

Brechin, S., West, P., Harmon, D., & Kutay, K. (1991). Resident peoples and protected areas: A framework for inquiry. In P. West & S. Brechin (Eds.), *Resident peoples and national parks: Social dilemmas and strategies in international conservation* (pp. 5-28). Tucson: University of Arizona Press.

Brekke, D. (2000, January). Who needs NASA? *Wired, 8*, 118-128.

Brent, M. (1997). *Coastal resort morphology as a response to transportation technology.* Doctoral dissertation, University of Waterloo, Ontario, Canada.

Briassoulis, H., & van der Straaten. J. (Eds.). (1992). *Tourism and the environment: Regional, economic and policy issue.* Dordrecht, The Netherlands: Kluwer Academic.

Brillantes, A. (1991). *The Philippine local government code of 1991: Issues and concerns in the environmental sector.* Philippines: Delos Reyes Printing Press Laguna College.

Bristow, R. (1999). Commentary: Virtual tourism—the ultimate ecotourism? *Tourism Geographies, 1*(2), 218-225.

Britton, R. (1977). Making tourism more supportive of small state development: The case of St. Vincent. *Annals of Tourism Research, 4*, 268-277.

Britton, S. (1982). The political economy of tourism in the third world. *Annals of Tourism Research, 9*, 331-358.

Brohman, J. (1996). New directions in tourism for third world development. *Annals of Tourism Research, 23*, 48-70.

Broomfield, T. (1995). Tourism in Zala county. In T. Wallace (Ed.), *Tourism issues for Hungary's western Balaton region* (pp. 51-58). Raleigh, NC: North Carolina State University.

Brown, D. (1996). Genuine fakes. In T. Selwyn (Ed.), *The tourist image: Myths and myth making in tourism* (pp. 33-47). Chichester: John Wiley & Sons.

Brown, D. (1999). Mayas and tourists in the Maya world. *Human Organization, 58*(3), 295-304.

Brown, L. (1973). Rich countries and poor in a finite, interdependent world. *Daedalus, 104*, 153-164.

Brown, L., Gardner, G., & Halweil, B. (1998). *Beyond Malthus: Sixteen dimensions of the population problem* (World-Watch Paper 143). Washington, DC: World-Watch Institute.

Bruner, E. (1996). Tourism in Ghana: The representation of slavery and the return of the black diaspora. *American Anthropologist, 98*, 290-304.

Brush, S. (1993). Indigenous knowledge of biological resources as intellectual property rights: The role of anthropology. *American Anthropologist, 95*, 653-686.

Buck, R. (1978). Boundary maintenance revisited: Tourist experience in an Old Order Amish community. *Rural Sociology, 43*, 221-234.

Buck, R., & Alleman, T. (1979). Tourist enterprise concentration and Old Order Amish survival: Explorations in productive coexistence. *Journal of Travel Research, 18*, 15-20.

Buergermeister, J., D'Amore, L., Jafari, J., & Pearce, D. (1992). New horizons in tourism hospitality education. *Annals of Tourism Research, 1*(9), 139-142.

Buhalis, D., & Spada, A. (2000). Destination management systems: Criteria for success—an exploratory research. *Information Technology & Tourism, 3*(1), 41-55.

Buhalis, D., Tjoa, A. Min, & Jafari, J. (Eds.). (1998). *Information and communications technologies in tourism*. Vienna and New York: Springer.

Bull, A. (1991). *The economics of travel and tourism*. Melbourne: Longman.

Bull, A. (1994). *The economics of travel and tourism*. London: Pitman.

Burkart, B. (1999). Navigation by lifestage. *Travel Counselor, 9*, 18-20.

Butler, R. (1974). Problems in the prediction of tourist development: A theoretical approach. In J. Matznetter (Ed.), *Studies in the geography of tourism, 17* (pp. 49-64). Frankfurt/Main: Johann Wolfgang Goethe-Universitat.

Butler, R. (1980). The concept of a tourist area cycle of evolution: Implications for the management of resources. *The Canadian Geographer, 24*, 5-12.

Butler, R. (1990). Tourism, heritage and sustainable development. In J. Nelson & S. Woodley (Eds.), *Heritage conservation and sustainable development* (pp. 49-66). Waterloo, ON: Heritage Resources Center, University of Waterloo.

Butler, R. (1991). West Edmonton mall as a tourist attraction. *The Canadian Geographer, 35*, 287-295.

Butler, R. (1992). Alternative tourism: The thin edge of the wedge. In V. Smith & W. Eadington (Eds.), *Tourism alternatives: Potentials and problems in the development of tourism* (pp. 31-46). Philadelphia, PA: University of Pennsylvania Press.

Butler, R. (1993). Tourism: An evolutionary perspective. In J. Nelson, R. Butler, & G. Wall (Eds.), *Tourism and sustainable development: Monitoring, planning and managing* (pp. 27-43). Waterloo, ON: University of Waterloo.

Butler, R. (1999). *After the war: Ethnic tourism to Lebanon*. Paper presented at the Annual Meeting of the Association of American Geographers, Honolulu, Hawaii, March 23-25.

Butler, R., & Hinch, T. (1996). *Tourism and indigenous peoples*. London: International Thomson Business Press.

Butler, R., & Pearce, D. (Eds.). (1995). *Change in tourism: People, places, processes*. London: Routledge.

Butler, R., & Wall, G. (1988). Formation of the international academy for the study of tourism. *Annals of Tourism Research, 15*, 572-574.

Buznard, J. (1993). *The beaten track: European tourism, literature, and the ways to culture, 1800-1918*. Oxford: Oxford University Press.

Byrnes, N. (1999, June 14). Few icebergs on the horizon. *Business Week*, pp. 80-83.

Callahan, R. (1998). Ethnic politics and tourism: A British case study. *Annals of Tourism Research, 25*, 818-836.

Camire, D. (1996, October 14). Voters in 8 states to decide gaming issues. *Reno Gazette-Journal*, p. 1F.

Campbell, C. (1990). *The romantic ethic and the spirit of modern consumerism*. Oxford: Basil Blackwell.

Campbell, C., & Laberrere, J. (1998, March). The end of cheap oil. *Scientific American*.

Campbell, R. (1988). Busman's holiday—or the best surprise is no surprise. *Kroeber Anthropological Society Papers, 67-68*, 12-19.

Cann, C., Churchill, S., & Edgerton, R. (1999). Response of bone and muscle systems to spaceflight. In A. Houston & M. Rycroft (Eds.), *Keys to space: An interdisciplinary approach to space studies* (pp. 22-29). Boston: McGraw-Hill.

Cantwell, J. (1889). A narrative account of the exploration of the Kowak River, Alaska. In *Report of the cruises of the revenue marine steamer Corwin in the Arctic Ocean in the year 1884*. Washington, DC: Government Printing Office.

Cardenas, C. (1990, April 1). For Mexico, freedom before free trade. *The New York Times*, p. E.

Carment, D., & James, P. (1998). Ethnic conflict: An appraisal. In D. Carment & P. James (Eds.), *Peace in the midst of wars* (pp. 298-317). Columbia, SC: University of South Carolina Press.

Carneiro, R. (1994). War and peace: Alternating realities in human history. In S. Reyna & R. Downs (Eds.), *Studying war: Anthropological perspectives* (pp. 3-29). Langhorne, PA: Gordon and Breach Science Publishers.

Carpenter, R., & Maragos, J. (1989). *How to assess environmental impacts on tropical islands and coastal areas*. Honolulu: East-West Center and Asian Development Bank.

Carson, R. (1962). *Silent spring*. Greenwich: Fawcett.

Carter, D. (1995). *Invisible cities: Touba Turin, Senegalese transnational migrants in northern Italy*. Minneapolis, MN: University of Minnesota Press.

Cater, E., & Lowman,. G. (1994). *Ecotourism: A sustainable option?* London: John Wiley & Sons.

Celaya, R., & Owen, E. (1993). *Let's go: The budget guide to Mexico 1993*. New York: St. Martin's Press.

Chagnon, N. (1983). *Yanomano: The fierce people* (3rd ed.). New York: Holt, Rinehart & Winston.

Chant, S. (1992). Tourism in Latin America: Perspectives from Mexico and Costa Rica. In D. Harrison (Ed.), *Tourism in less developed countries*. London: Belhaven Press.

Chevalier, J. (1983). There is nothing simple about simple commodity production. *The Journal of Peasant Studies, 10*, 153-186.

Chief Eagle. (1990). *Dolls by Charles Chief Eagle*. Rapid City, SD: U.S. Department of the Interior, Indian Arts and Crafts Board, Sioux Indian Museum and Crafts Center.

Child, G., & Child, R. (1990). An historical perspective of sustainable wildlife utilisation. In *Conference Proceedings, 18th IUCN General Assembly, Workshop #7: Sustained Utilization of Wildlife*. Perth, Australia.

Child, R., & Heath, R. (1990). *Outdoor recreational patterns amongst the residents of Harare, Zimbabwe*. Harare, Zimbabwe: University of Zimbabwe.

Chitepo, V. (1986). Opening address. In R. Heath (Ed.), *Tourism in tourist areas of Zimbabwe. Proceedings of the 1985 Conference of the Geographical Association of Zimbabwe*, Lake McIlwaine, Zimbabwe.

Chon, K. (1990). The role of destination image in tourism: A review and discussion. *The Tourist Review, 2*, 2-9.

Chon, K., & Oppermann, M. (1996). Convention participation decision-making process.

Annals of Tourism Research, 24, 178-191.

Choris, L. (1822). *Voyage pittoresque autour du monde.* Paris: Didot.

Chow, W. (1980). Integrating tourism with rural development. *Annals of Tourism Research,* 7, 584-607.

Christaller, W. (1966). *Central places in southern Germany.* Englewood Cliffs, NJ: Prentice-Hall, Inc.

Christiansen, E. (1993a). Industry rebounds with 8.4% handle gain. *International Gaming & Wagering Business, 14*(7), 12-35.

Christiansen, E. (1993b). Revenues soar to $30 billion. *International Gaming & Wagering Business, 14*(8), 12-35.

Churchill, S. (1999a). Effect of weight-bearing exercise on bone loss. In A. Houston & M. Rycroft (Eds.), *Keys to space:An interdisciplinary approach to space studies* (pp. 22-29). Boston: McGraw-Hill.

Churchill, S.. (1999b). Response of cardiovascular system to spaceflight. In A. Houston & M. Rycroft (Eds.), *Keys to space:An interdisciplinary approach to space studies* (pp. 30-34). Boston: McGraw-Hill.

Churchill, S. (1999c). Introduction to human space life sciences. In A. Houston & M. Rycroft (Eds.), *Keys to space:An interdisciplinary approach to space studies* (pp. 13-21). Boston: McGraw-Hill.

Clarke, A., & Kubrick, S. (1968). *2001:A space odyssey.* Hollywood: Polaris Productions.

Classon, J., Godfrey, K., & Goodey, B. (1995). *Towards visitor impact management:Visitor impacts, carrying capacity and management responses in Europe's historic towns and cities.* London: Avebury.

Clement, G. (1999). Space neuroscience. In A. Houston & M. Rycroft (Eds.), *Keys to space: An interdisciplinary approach to space studies* (pp. 35-42). Boston: McGraw-Hill.

Clement, H. (1961). *The future of tourism in the Pacific and Far East.* Washington, DC: US Government Printing Office.

Clendinnen, I. (1987). *Ambivalent conquests.* Cambridge: Cambridge University Press.

Cleveland, D. (1994, March). Can science and advocacy coexist? *The Ethics of Sustainable Development Anthropology Newsletter,* 9-10.

Cline, H. (1962). *Mexico, revolution to evolution, 1940-1960.* London: Oxford University Press.

Coccosis, H., & Nijkamp, P. (1995). *Sustainable tourism development.* London: Avebury-Gower.

Cohen, C. (1994). Marketing paradise, making nation. *Annals of Tourism Research, 22,* 404-421.

Cohen, E. (1972). Toward a sociology of international tourism. *Social Research, 39*(2), 164-182

Cohen, E. (1973). Nomads from affluence: Notes on the phenomenon of drifter tourism. *International Journal of Comparative Sociology, 14,* 89-103.

Cohen, E. (1978). The impact of tourism on the physical environment. *Annals of Tourism Research, 2,* 215-237.

Cohen, E. (1979a). A phenomenology of tourist experiences. *Sociology, 13,* 179-201.

Cohen, E. (1979b). Sociology of tourism [Special issue]. *Annals of Tourism Research, 1 & 2.*

Cohen, E. (1979c). The impact of tourism on the hill tribes of northern Thailand. *Internationales Asienforum, 1,* 5-38.

Cohen, E. (1984). The sociology of tourism: Approaches, issues and findings. *Annual Review of Sociology, 10,* 374-392.

Cohen, E. (1985). Tourist guides: Pathfinds, mediators and animator [Special issue]. *Annals of Tourism Research, 12*(1).

Cohen, E. (1988). Authenticity and commoditization in tourism. *Annals of Tourism Research, 15*, 371-386.

Cohen, E. (1992). Pilgrimage centers: Concentric and excentric. *Annals of Tourism Research, 19*(1), 35-50.

Cohen, E. (1993a). Tourist arts [Special issue]. *Annals of Tourism Research, 20*.

Cohen, E. (1993b). Introduction: Investigating tourist arts. *Annals of Tourism Research, 20*, 1-8.

Cohen, E. (1993c). The heterogeneization of tourist art. *Annals of Tourism Research, 20*, 138-163.

Cohen, E. (1998). Tourism and religions: A comparative perspective. *Pacific Tourism Review, 2*(1), 1-10.

Collier, G. (1994). *Basta! Land and the Zapatista rebellion in Chiapas*. Oakland, CA: Food First.

Collins, J. (1996, May 25-June 7)). American eagle seen as dominating region. *Caribbean Week*, p. 62.

Collins, M. (1991). *Ecotourism in the Yucatan Peninsula of Mexico*. Syracuse, NY: SUNY ESF-IEPP Publication.

Colvin, J. (1991). The scientist and ecotourism? Bridging the gap. In J. Kusler (Ed.), *Ecotourism and resource conservation: A collection of papers compiled by Jon. A. Kusler* (pp. 575-581). Madison, WI: Omnipress.

Comfort, M. (1964). *Conrad N. Hilton, hotelier*. Minneapolis: T. S. Dennison & Company.

Compton, P. (1991). Hungary. In D. Hall (Ed.), *Tourism and economic development in Eastern Europe and the Soviet Union* (pp. 173-189). London: Belhaven Press.

Conforti, J. (1996). Ghettos as tourism attractions. *Annals of Tourism Research, 23*, 830-842.

Connor, M. (1993). Indian gaming: Prosperity, controversy. *International Gaming & Wagering Business, 14*(3), 8-12.

Connor, M. (1995). Casino catalyst: Has tribal gaming spurred casino legalization nationwide? *International Gaming & Wagering Business, 16*(3), 66-68.

Connor, M. (1997). The waiting game. *International Gaming & Wagering Business, 18*(3), 62-65.

Contours: Concerns for Tourism Thailand. (1983-1995). Bangkok: ECTWT.

Cook, S. (1993). Craft commodity production, market diversity, and differential rewards in Mexican capitalism today. In J. Nash (Ed.), *Crafts in the world market* (pp. 59-83). Albany, NY: State University of New York Press.

Cook, S. (1999). *Outlook for travel and tourism*. Washington, DC: Travel Industry of America.

Cothran, D., & Cothran, C. (1998). Promise or political risk for Mexican tourism. *Annals of Tourism Research, 25*, 477-497.

Cox, D. (1998, March 26). Boomtown expansion gets final approval. *Reno Gazette-Journal*, pp. 1A, 3A.

Cox, K. (1999). A futurist perspective for space: Discovering, shaping and influencing our intention in earth/space. In *Conference Proceedings, International Space Conference*. Los Angeles, September.

Crang, M. (1996). Magic kingdom or a quixotic quest for authenticity? *Annals of Tourism Research, 23*, 415-431.

Crick, M. (1989). Representations of international tourism in the social sciences: Sun sex, sights, savings and servility. *Annual Review of Anthropology, 18*, 307-344.

Crystal, D. (1997). *English as a global language*. Cambridge: Cambridge University Press.

Crystal, E. (1977). Tourism in Toraja (Sulesi, Indonesia). In V. Smith (Ed.), *Hosts and guests: The anthropology of tourism* (pp. 109-126). Philadelphia: University of Pennsylvania Press.

Cultural Survival Quarterly. (1999a). Indigenous rights and self-determination in Mexico [Special issue]. *23*(4).

Cultural Survival Quarterly. (1999b). Visions of the future: The prospect for reconciliation [Special issue]. *23*(4).

Dahles, H. (1998). Redefining Amsterdam as a tourist destination. *Annals of Tourism Research, 25,* 55-69.

Dahles, H., & Bras, K. (1999). *Tourism & small entrepreneurs. Development, national policy, and entrepreneurial culture: Indonesian cases.* New York: Cognizant Communication Corporation.

Daltabuit, M. (1992). *Mujeres Mayas, trabajo, nutricion y fecundidad.* Mexico, DF: UNAM, Instituto de Investigaciones Antropologicas.

Daltabuit, M. (1996). *Ecoturismo y desarollo sustentable: Impacto en comunidades rurales de la frontera sur.* Cuernavaca, Morelos, Mexico: CRIM/UNAM, Instituto de Investigaciones Antropologicas.

Daltabuit, M., & Pi-Sunyer, O. (1990). Tourism development in Quintana Roo, Mexico. *Cultural Survival Quarterly, 14,* 9-13.

Daltabuit, M., Rios, A., & Perez, F. (1988). *Coba: Estrategias adaptivas de tres familias Mayas.* Mexico, DF: UNAM, Instituteo de Investigaciones Antropologicas.

D'Amore, L., & Anunza, T. (1986). International terrorism: Implications and challenge for global tourism. *Business Quarterly, 11,* 20-29.

D'Amore, L., & Jafari, J. (Eds.). (1988). *Tourism—a vital force for peace.* First Global Peace Conference, June 3, 1988. Montreal, Canada: IIPT.

Daniel, Y. (1996). Tourism dance performances. *Annals of Tourism Research, 23,* 780-797.

Dann, G. (1981). Tourist motivation: An appraisal. *Annals of Tourism Research, 8,* 170-219.

Dann, G. (1991). Tourism and sociocultural change in the Caribbean. *Annals of Tourism Research, 18,* 337-338.

Dann, G. (1994). Tourism: The nostalgia industry of the future. In W. Theobald (Ed.), *Global tourism: The next decade* (pp. 55-67). Oxford: Butterworth-Heinemann.

Dann, G. (1996). *The language of tourism.* Wallingford, Oxon: CAB International.

Dann, G., Nash, D., & Pearce, P. (1988). Methodology in tourism research. *Annals of Tourism Research, 15,* 1-28.

Dash, J. (2000, January 2). Fly me to the Moon. *The Sacramento Bee,* p. J.

Davidson, T. (1994). What are travel and tourism? Are they really an industry? In W. Theobald (Ed.), *Global tourism: The next decade* (pp. 20-26). Oxford: Butterworth-Heinemann.

Davis, C. (1995, January 30). American Indians offer casino funding. *Pacific Business News,* p. 1.

Davis, H. (1967). Investing in tourism. *Finance and Development, 4,* 1-8.

Davis, J., & Otterstrom, S. (1998). Growth of Indian gaming in the United States of America. In K. Meyer-Arendt & R. Hartmann (Eds.), *Casing gambling in America: Origins, trends, and impacts* (pp. 53-66). New York: Cognizant Communication Corp.

Davis, S. (1991). *Robin Hood's England.* Washington, DC: Time Travelers Press.

Day, B. (1974). *The Philippines: Shattered showcase of democracy in Asia.* New York: M. Evans and Co.

DeGroote, P. (1982). Toerisme in de Derde Wereld. In P. DeGroote (Ed.), *Mongraphie: Refertan vor Geoteor's tweede integratieweekend,* unpublished conference proceedings, September 24-26.

de Holan, P., & Phillips, N. (1997). Sun, sand, and hard currency: Tourism in Cuba. *Annals of Tourism Research, 24,* 777-795.

DeKadt, E. (1976). *Tourism: Passport to development.* New York: Oxford University Press.

Deller, S., Marcouiller, D., & Green, G. (1997). Recreational housing and local government finance. *Annals of Tourism Research, 24,* 687-705.

Department of Tourism. (1991). *Tourism master plan for the Philippines.* Manila: Government of the Philippines.

DeVos, G. (1975). Ethnic pluralism: Conflict and accommodation. In G. DeVos & L. Romanucci-Ross (Eds.), *Ethnic identity: Continuities and change* (pp. 5-41). Palo Alto: Mayfield.

DeVries, J. (1976). *The economy of Europe in an age of crisis, 1600-1750.* Cambridge: Cambridge University Press.

Di Benedetto, C., & Bojanic, D. (1993). Tourism area life cycle extensions. *Annals of Tourism Research, 20,* 557-570.

DiChristina, M. (1999a, June). Star travelers. *Popular Science,* 54-59.

DiChristina, M. (1999b, November). Highway through space. *Popular Science,* 66-70.

Dieke, P. (Ed.). (2000). *The political economy of tourism in Africa.* New York: Cognizant Communication Corp.

Dieng, I., & Bugnicourt, J. (1982). *Touristes-Roi en Afrique.* Paris: Editions Karthala.

Diller, E., & Scofidio, R. (1994). *Back to the front: Tourisms of war.* Basse-Normandie, France: FPAC.

Distel, B. (1993). Erinnerung und Aufklaerung—die KZ-Gedenkstaette Dachau 60 jahre nach der errichtung des konzentrationslagers [Preserving the memory and providing education at the Dachau memorial site and museum sixty years after the establishment of the concentration camp]. In *Didaktische arbeit in KZ-gedenkstaetten* (pp. 22-28). Munchen: Bayerische landeszentrale fuer politische bildung.

Doberstein, B. (1993). Environmental impact assessment and urban solid waste management: EIA reform and sustainable development in Denpasar, Bali. *The Indian Geographic Journal, 58.*

Dobson, R., & Taylor, J. (1989). *Rymes of Robin Hood: An introduction to the English outlaw.* London: Allan Sutton.

Dogan, H. (1990). Forms of adjustment: Sociocultural impacts of tourism. *Annals of Tourism Research 16*(2), 216-236.

Doganis, R. (1985). *Flying off course: The economics of international airlines.* London: George Allen and Unwin.

Doganis, R. (1992). *The airport business.* London: Routledge.

Douglas, N. (1997). Applying the life cycle model to Melanesia. *Annals of Tourism Research, 24,* 1-22.

Dowman, K., & Bubriski, K. (1995). *Power places of Kathmandu: Hindu and Buddhist holy sites in the sacred valley of Nepal.* London: Thames & Hudson.

Downes, J., &. Paton, T. (Eds.). 1993). *Travel agency law.* London: Pitman.

Ducille, A. (1994). Dyes and dolls: Multicultural Barbie and the merchandising of difference. *A Journal of Feminist Cultural Studies, 6,* 46-68.

Duffield, B., & Long, J. (1981). Tourism in the highlands and islands of Scotland: Rewards and conflicts. *Annals of Tourism Research, 8,* 403-431.

Dulles, F. (1952). *A history of recreation: America learns to play.* New York: Appleton Century Crofts.

Dunkel, D. (1984). Tourism and the environment—a review of the literature and issues. *Environmental Sociology, 37,* 5-18.

Dunn, S. (1999). King Coal's weakening grip on power. *World-Watch, 12*(5), 10-19.

Durkheim, E. (1912). *Elementary forms of religious life* (J. Swain, Trans.). London: Allen and Unwin.

Durning, A. (1992). *How much is enough?* New York: W. W. Norton & Company.

Dworin, P. (1994). Going strong 30 years later. *International Gaming & Wagering Business, 15*(3), 8.

Dwyer, L., & Forsyth, P. (1998). Economic significance of cruise tourism. *Annals of Tourism Research, 25*, 393–415.

Eadington, W. (1992). *Recent national trends in the casino gaming industry and their implications for the economy of Nevada*. Reno: University of Nevada.

Eady, W. (1995). The use of GIS in environmental assessment. *Impact Assessment, 13*, 199–206.

East Midlands Tourist Board. (1993). *1992-1993 annual report*. Lincoln, England: Author.

Environmentally Critical Areas Network. (1992). *Strategic environmental plan for Palawan*. Philippines: Government of the Philippines.

Echtner, C., & Jamal, T. (1997). The disciplinary dilemma of tourism studies. *Annals of Tourism Research, 24*, 868–883.

Echtner, C., & Ritchie, J. (1991). The meaning and measurement of destination image. *Journal of Tourism Studies, 2*, 2–12.

Eco, H. (1986). *Travels in hyperreality*. New York: Harcourt Brace Jovanovich.

ECPAT. (1997, July). Australia: End child prostitution, pornography and trafficking. Newsletter, 10(1).

Ecumenical Coalition on Third World Tourism. (1988). *Tourism: An ecumenical concern. The story of the ecumenical coalition on third world tourism*. Thailand: Author.

Edgell, D. (1990). *International tourism policy*. New York: Van Nostrand Reinhold.

Edgell, D. (1999). *Tourism policy: The next millennium*. Champaign, IL: Sagamore Publishing.

Edwards, J., Llurdes, I. & Coit, J. (1996). Mines and quarries: Industrial heritage tourism. *Annals of Tourism Research, 23*, 341–363.

Eller, J. (1999). *From culture to ethnicity to conflict: An anthropological perspective on international ethnic conflict*. Ann Arbor, MI: The University of Michigan Press.

Ellul, A. (1994). *Tourism and environment in European countries*. Strasbourg, France: Steering Committee for Conservation and Management of the Environment.

Ember, C. (1978). Myths about hunter-gatherers. *Ethnology, 17*, 439–448.

English, P. (1986). *The great escape? An examination of north-south tourism*. Ottawa: The North-South Institute.

Enloe, C. (1989). *Bananas, beaches and bases*. Berkeley and Los Angeles: University of California Press.

Epstein, P. (2000, August). Is global warming harmful to health? *Scientific American*, 50–57.

Erisman, H. (1983). Tourism and cultural dependency in the West Indies. *Annals of Tourism Research, 10*, 337–361.

Escobar, A. (1995). *Encountering development: The making and unmaking of the Third World*. Princeton: Princeton University Press.

European Community. (1983). *The community of culture*. Brussels: European Union.

Falk, P. (1994). *The consuming body*. London: Sage.

Fame, A. (1991). *Undoing the social towards a deconstructive sociology*. Buckingham: Open University Press.

Farrell, B., & McLellan, R. (1987). Tourism and physical environment [Special issue]. *Annals of Tourism Research, 14*.

Farrell, B., & Runyon, D. (1991). Ecology and tourism. *Annals of Tourism Research, 18*, 26–40.

Farriss, N. (1984). *Maya society under colonial rule*. Princeton, NJ: Princeton University Press.

Fash, W. (1991). *Scribes, warriors and kings: The city of Copan and the ancient Maya*. London: Thames and Hudson, Ltd.

Fayos Sola, E. (1996). *Organizada por la Asociacion Espanola de Directores de Hotel con la Colaboracion de la Organizacion Mundial del Turismo y FITUR 96*. Madrid:World Tourism Organization.

Feder, E. (1971). *The rape of the peasantry*. New York:Anchor Books.

Fedler,A., & Iso-Ahola, S. (1987). Interrelationships of leisure, recreation and tourism. *Annals of Tourism Research, 14*, 311-313.

Ferda, F. (1991). *Expert systems for environmental screening*. Laxenburg,Austria: International Institute for Applied Systems Analysis.

Ferguson, B. (1994). The general consequences of war. In S. Reyna & R. Downs (Eds.), *Studying war:Anthropological perspectives* (pp. 85-112). Langhorne, PA: Gordon and Breach Science Publishers.

Feyerabend,A. (1997). *Coming or going:An examination of reverse culture shock in the 'tourism as ritual' theory* (unpublished paper). Berkeley: University of California.

Findlay, J. (1986). *People of chance: Gambling in American society from Jamestown to Las Vegas*. Oxford: Oxford University Press.

Fine, E., & Speer. J. (1985) Tour guide performances as sight sacralization. *Annals of Tourism Research, 12*, 73-95.

Finney, B., &Watson, K., (Eds.). (1975). *A new kind of sugar:Tourism in the Pacific*. Honolulu: East-West Center.

Fodness, D., & Murray, B. (1997).Tourist information search. *Annals of Tourism Research, 24*, 503-523.

FONATUR. (1993). *Panel aeropuerto:Estudio continuo de visitantes pro via aerea*. Mexico, DF: Fonatur: Subdireccion General de Comercializacion.

Forbes, H. (1997). *Ethnic conflict: Commerce, culture and the contact hypothesis*. New Haven, CT:Yale University Press.

Formanek-Brunell, M. (1993). *Made to play house: Dolls and the commercialization of American girlhood, 1830-1930*. New Haven, CT:Yale University Press.

Fortman, M., Martin, P., & Roussel, S. (1998).Trial by fire: International actors and organizations in the Yugoslav crisis. In D. Carment & P. James (Eds.), *Peace in the midst of wars* (pp. 126-162). Columbia, SC: University of South Carolina Press.

Foster, D. (1985). *Travel and tourism management*. London: Macmillan.

Foster, G. (1988). *Tzintzuntzan:Mexican peasants in a changing world*. Prospect Heights, IL:Waveland Press.

Foster, J. (1964).The sociological consequences of tourism. *International Journal of Comparative Sociology, 5*, 217-227.

Foucault, M. (1980). Power/knowledge. In C. Gordon (Ed.), *Selected interviews and other writings 1972-1977*. New York: Pantheon Books.

Frank, O., & Pressle, M. (Eds.). (1995). *The diary of a young girl: Definitive edition*. New York: Doubleday.

Fratkin, E., & Wu, T. (1997, Fall). Maasai and Barabaig herders struggle for land rights in Kenya and Tanzania, *Cultural Survival Quarterly, 21*(3), 55-61.

Frechtling, D. (1996). *Practical tourism forecasting*. London: Butterworth-Heinemann.

Frey, N. (1998). *Pilgrim stories: On and off the road to Santiago*. Berkeley, CA: University of California Press.

Fridgen, J. (1991). *Dimensions of tourism*. East Lansing, MI:The AHMA Educational Institute.

Friedl, E. (1964). Lagging emulation in post-peasant society. *American Anthropologist, 66*, 569-586.

Funnell, C. (1975). *By the beautiful Sea:The rise and high times of that American resort: Atlantic City*. New York: Knopf.

Gaborni, J. (1997a,August). Leaping over hurdles. *Asia Travel Trade*, 22-23.

Gaborni, J. (1997b, October). Boom time in Manila. *Asia Travel Trade*, 22-24.

Galeotti, I. (1969). *Industrialization of tourism in developing areas*. Madrid: World Tourism Organization.

Garbarino, M. (1977). *Sociocultural theory in anthropology: A short history*. New York: Holt, Rhinehart and Winston.

Garcia, R. (1990). *Fookien Times yearbook 1990*. Manila: Fookien Times.

Garcia, R. (1991). *Fookien Times yearbook 1991*. Manila: Fookien Times.

Garrett, L. (2000). *Betrayal of trust: The collapse of global public health*. New York: Hyperion.

Garrett, W. (1989, October) La ruta Maya. *National Geographic Magazine*, 442-479.

Garrucho, P. (1989). *Fookien Times yearbook 1989*. Manila: Fookien Times.

Gartner, W. (1996). *Tourism development. Principles, processes and policies*. New York: Van Nostrand Reinhold.

Gebhart, F. (1999, November). Changing all the rules. *Travel Counselor*, 8-10.

Geddes, H. (1996). *Mass media and cultural identity among the Yucatecan Maya: The constitution of global, national and local subjects* (Paper accepted for publication). Studies in Latin American Society.

Gee, C., & Lurie, M. (Eds.). (1993). *The story of the Pacific Asia Travel Association*. San Francisco: Pacific Asia Travel Association.

Gee, C., Makens, J., & Choy, D. (Eds.). (1984). *The travel industry* (2nd ed.). New York: Van Nostrand Reinhold.

Geertz, C. (1994). Life on the edge. *The New York Review of Books*, 3-4.

Gellner, D., & Quigley, D. (Eds.). (1995). *Contested hierarchies: A collaborative ethnography of caste among the Newars of the Kathmandu Valley*. Oxford: Clarendon Press.

Getz, D. (1991). *Festivals, special events, and tourism*. New York: Van Nostrand Reinhold.

Getz, D. (1993). Tourist shopping villages. *Tourism Management, 14*, 15-26.

Getz, D. (1997). *Event management & event tourism*. New York: Cognizant Communication Corp.

Getz, D. (2000). *Explore wine tourism: Management, development & destinations*. New York: Cognizant Communication Corp.

Giaroleto, L. (1988). *Strategic airline management*. London: Pitman Publishing.

Giddens, A. (1990). *The consequences of modernity*. Cambridge: Polity Press.

Giddings, J. (1960). The archaeology of Bering Strait. *Current Anthropology, 1*, 121-138.

Gilbert, D. (1990). Conceptual issues in the meaning of tourism. In C. Cooper (Ed.), *Progress in tourism, recreation and hospitality management* (pp. 4-27). London: Belhaven.

Gilpin, A. (1995). *Environmental impact assessment (EIA): Cutting edge for the twenty-first century*. Cambridge: Cambridge University Press.

Ginsburg, F. (1994). Embedded aesthetics: Creating a discursive space for indigenous media. *Cultural Anthropology, 9*, 365-382.

Giuliano, G. (1986). Land use impacts of transportation investments: Highway and transit. In S. Hanson (Ed.), *The geography of urban transportation* (pp. 274-279). New York: The Guilford Press.

Glade, W., & Anderson, C. (1963). *The political economy of Mexico*. Madison, WI: The University of Wisconsin Press.

Gnoth, J. (1997). Tourism motivation and expectation formation. *Annals of Tourism Research, 24*, 283-304.

Go, F., & Pine, R. (Eds.). (1995). *Globalisation strategy in the hotel industry*. London: Thomson Business Press.

Goeldner, C., Ritchie, B., & McIntosh, R. (Eds.). (1999). *Tourism: Principles, practices, and philosophies* (8th ed.). New York: John Wiley & Sons, Inc.

Goffman, E. (1967). *Interaction ritual*. New York: Doubleday.

Golden, T. (1994a, January 3). Mexican troops battling rebels. *The New York Times*, p. A1.

Golden,T. (1994b, January 4). Rebels determined 'to build socialism.' *The New York Times*, p.A1.

Gonzalez, J. (1994). A partnership for social reform: Government and private sectors for the social reform agenda. *STAC Report, 6*, 2.

Goodall, B., & Ashworth, G. (Eds.). (1988). *Marketing in the tourism industry: The promotion of destination regions.* London: Groom Helms.

Goodrich, J. (1988). The holiday maker. *Journal of Travel Research, 27*, 55-56.

Goodwin, M., Miller, K., & Witten, S. (1996). *Fodor's net travel.* New York: Michael Wolff.

Gopsill's Atlantic City Directory. (1886). Philadelphia, PA: James Gopsill's Sons.

Gordon, B. (1998). Warfare and tourism: Paris in World War II. *Annals of Tourism Research, 25*, 616-638.

Gordon, D. (1978, April 22). Mexico survey. *The Economist.*

Gottlieb, A. (1982). Americans' vacations. *Annals of Tourism Research, 9*, 165-187.

Gottmanm J. (1964). *Megalopolis: The urbanized northeastern seaboard of the United States.* Cambridge, MA: The MIT Press.

Goulbourne, H. (1991). *Ethnicity and nationalism in Post-Imperial Britain.* Cambridge: Cambridge University Press.

Gould, P., & White, R. (1986). *Mental maps.* Boston: Allen & Unwin.

Graburn, H. (1983). The anthropology of tourism [Special issue]. *Annals of Tourism Research, 10.*

Graburn, H., & Jafari, J. (1991). Introduction: Tourism social science. *Annals of Tourism Research, 18*, 1-11.

Graburn, N. (1976). *Ethnic and tourist arts: Cultural expressions from the fourth world.* Berkeley, CA: University of California Press.

Graburn, N. (1977). Tourism: The sacred journey. In V. Smith (Ed.), *Hosts and guests: The anthropology of tourism* (pp. 17-32). Philadelphia, PA: University of Pennsylvania Press.

Graburn, N. (1995a). The past in the present in Japan: Nostalgia and neo-traditionalism in contemporary Japanese domestic tourism. In R. Butler & D. Pearce (Eds.), *Changes in tourism: People, places, processes* (Chap. 4). London: Routledge.

Graburn, N. (1995b). Tourism modernity and nostalgia. In A. Ahmed & C. Shore (Eds.), *The future of anthropology: Its relevance to the contemporary world* (pp. 158-178). London: Athlone Press.

Graburn, N., & Delugan, R. (1995). Review of June Nash, Ed., *Crafts in the world market. American Ethnologist, 22*, 215.

Graburn, N., & Mathers, K. (2000). Museums inside and out [Book review]. *Current Anthropology, 41*(4). 691-692.

Gray, H. (1982). Economics of international tourism [Special issue]. *Annals of Tourism Research, 9.*

Green, B., & Chalip, L. (1998). Sport tourism as the celebration of subculture. *Annals of Tourism Research, 25*, 275-291.

Greenwood, D. (1972). Tourism as an agent of change: A Spanish Basque case. *Ethnology, 11*, 80-91.

Greenwood, D. (1977). Culture by the pound: An anthropological perspective on tourism as cultural commoditization. In V. Smith (Ed.), *Hosts and guests: The anthropology of tourism* (pp. 171-186). Philadelphia, PA: University of Pennsylvania Press.

Greenwood, D. (1989). Culture by the pound: An anthropological perspective on tourism as cultural commoditization. In V. Smith (Ed.), *Hosts and guests: The anthropology of tourism* (2nd ed., pp. 171-185). Philadelphia, PA: University of Pennsylvania Press.

Gunn, C. (1988). *Vacationscapes: Designing tourist regions.* New York: Van Nostrand Reinhold.

Gunn, C. (Ed.). (1994). *Tourism planning: Basics, concepts, cases* (3rd ed.). London and

Washington:Taylor & Francis.

Gunn, C. (1995). *America's tourism explosion and its modern fallout.* Unpublished manuscript.

Gunther, K. (1999). Can local communities conserve wildlife? CAMPFIRE in Zimbabwe. *Cultural Survival Quarterly, 4,* 69-72.

Gupta, A., & Ferguson, J. (Eds.). (1997). *Culture power place: Explorations in critical anthropology.* London: Duke University Press.

Hackers hit military computers. (1999, October 11). *Newsweek,* p. 20.

Hadsell, V. (1993). *Hungry? Eat a Cruise Ship!* San Anselmo, CA: Center for Responsible Tourism.

Hall, C. (1991). Tourism as the subject of post-graduate dissertations in Australia. *Annals of Tourism Research, 18,* 520-523.

Hall, C. (1992a). *Hallmark tourist events: Impacts, management & planning.* London: Belhaven Press.

Hall, C. (1992b). Sex tourism in south-east Asia. In D. Harrison (Ed.), *Tourism and the less developed countries* (pp. 64-74). London: Belhaven.

Hall, C. (1994). *Tourism and politics: Policy, power and place.* Chichester, West Sussex: Wiley and Sons.

Hall, C. (1998). Historical antecedents of sustainable development and ecotourism: New labels on old bottles? In C. Hall & A. Lew (Eds.), *Sustainable tourism: A geographical perspective* (pp. 13-24). New York: Addison Wesley Longman Ltd.

Hall, C. (2000). The future of tourism: a personal speculation. *Tourism Recreation Research, 25*(1), 85-96.

Hall, C., & Jenkins, J. (1995). *Tourism and public policy.* London: Routledge.

Hall, C., & Lew, A. (Eds.). (1998). *Sustainable tourism: A geographical perspective.* New York: Addison Wesley Longman Ltd.

Hall, C., & McArthur, S.(Eds.). (1996). *Heritage management in Australia and New Zealand: The human dimension.* Oxford: Oxford University Press.:

Hamilton, A. (1990). Fear and desire: Aborigenes, Asians, and the national imaginary. *Australian Culture History, 6,* 92-112.

Hamilton Paterson, J. (1996. January). A watery grave. *Outside,* 31-39.

Hampton, M. (1998). Backpacker tourism and economic development. *Annals of Tourism Research, 25,* 639-660.

Hanefors, M., & Larsson, L. (1989). *Fardledaren: Turismkunskap for Front Personal.* Malmo: Liber.

Hanefors, M., & Larsson, L. (1993). Video strategies used by tour operators: What is really communicated? *Tourism Management, 14,* 27-33.

Hanlon, P. (1995). *Global airlines: Competition in a transnational industry.* London: Butterworth-Heinemann.

Hanna, N. (1989). *Tropical beach handbook (BMW).* London: Fourth Estate.

Harrell-Bond, B. (1978). *A window on an outside world: Tourism as development in the Gambia.* Hanover, NH: American University Field Staff.

Harrington, N. (1974). The legacy of Caribbean history and tourism. *Annals of Tourism Research, 2,* 13-25.

Harris, K. (1996). International hospitality marketing on the internet: Project 'interweave.' *International Journal of Hospitality Management, 1,* 155-163.

Harris, P. (1995). *Accounting and finance in the international hospitality industry.* London: Butterworth-Heinemann.

Harrison, D. (1993). Bulgarian tourism: A state of uncertainty. *Annals of Tourism Research, 20,* 519-534.

Harrison, J. (1997). Museums and touristic expectations. *Annals of Tourism Research, 24,*

23-40.

Hartmann, R. (1992). Dachau revisited: Tourism to the memorial site and museum of the former concentration camp. In T. Singh, et al. (Eds.), *Tourism environment: Nature, culture, economy* (pp. 183-190). New Delhi: Inter-India Publications.

Hartmann, R. (1998). Dealing with Dachau in geographic education. In H. Brodsky (Ed.), *Land and community: Geography in Jewish studies* (pp. 357-369). Bethesda, MD: University of Maryland Press.

Hashimoto, A. (2000). Environmental perception and sense of responsibility of the tourism industry in Mainland China, Taiwan and Japan. *Journal of Sustainable Development, 8*(2), 131-146.

Hastings, J. (1988). Time out of time: Life crises and schooner sailing in the Pacific. *Kroeber Anthropological Society Papers, 67-68*, 42-54.

Hawkins, D., &. Ritchie, J. (Eds.). (1991). *World travel and tourism review: Indicators, trends and forecasts.* Wallingford: CAB International.

Headland, R. (1994). Historical development of Antarctic tourism. *Annals of Tourism Research, 21*, 269-280.

Heath, E., & Wall, G. (1992). *Marketing tourism destinations: A strategic planning approach.* New York: John Wiley.

Heath, H. (1994). Impressions of western Balaton. In T. Wallace (Ed.), *Tourism issues for Hungary's western Balaton region* (pp. 92-98). Raleigh, NC: North Carolina State University.

Helber Engineering. (1984). *Resort development concept plan for Boracay Island, Philippines* (Unpublished report). Honolulu.

Hibbard, D., & Franzen, D. (1986). *The view from Diamond Head: From royal residence to urban resort.* Honolulu: Editions Limited.

Hichcock, M., King, V., & Parnwell, M. (1993). *Tourism in south-east Asia.* London: Routledge.

Hill, R. (1993). Indian gaming allows tribes to rediscover and protect their traditions. *Indian Gaming, 3*(10), 3, 17.

Hill, R. (1994). The future of Indian gaming. *Cultural Survival Quarterly, 17*(4), 61.

Hiller, H., (1975). The organization and marketing of tourism. In B. Finney & K. Watson (Eds.), *A new kind of sugar: Tourism in the Pacific* (pp. 237-246). Honolulu: East-West Center.

Hirshey, G. (1994, July 17). Gambling nation. *The New York Times Magazine*, pp. 34-50.

Hobsbawm, E. (1973). Peasants and politics. *Journal of Peasant Studies, 1*, 3-22.

Hoffman, M. (1991). *The world almanac and book of facts.* New York: Pharos Books.

Hokanson, D. (1988). *The Lincoln highway: Main street across America.* Iowa City, IA: University of Iowa Press.

Holden, A. (1990). *A big deal: A year as a professional poker player.* New York: Viking.

Holloway, C. (1994). *The business of tourism.* Plymouth: Pitman.

Holloway, C., & Robinson, C. (1995). *Marketing for tourism* (3rd ed.). London: Longman.

Holmes, D. (1989). *Cultural disenchantments.* Princeton, NJ: Princeton University Press.

Holt, J. (1982). *Robin Hood.* London: Thames and Hudson.

Holtz, S. (1990). Environmental assessment and sustainable development: Exploring the relationship. In P. Jacobs & B. Sadler (Eds.), *Sustainable development and environmental assessment: Perspectives on planning for a common future* (pp. 93-104). Hull, Quebec, Canada: CEARC.

Hong, E. (1985). *See the third world while it lasts: The social and environmental impact of tourism with special reference to Malaysia.* Penang, Malaysia: Consumers' Association of Penang.

Honigmann, J. (1976). *The development of anthropology.* Homewood, IL: The Dorsey Press.

Horner, A. (1993). Tourism arts in Africa before tourism. *Annals of Tourism Research, 20*,

52-63.

Horner, S., & Swarbrooke, J. (1996). *Marketing tourism, hospitality and leisure in Europe*. London: Thomson Business Press.

Hostetler, J. (1968). *Amish society*. Baltimore, MD: Johns Hopkins Press.

Houston, A., & Rycroft, M. (Eds.). (1999). *Keys to space: An interdisciplinary approach to space studies*. Boston: McGraw-Hill.

Hovinen, G. (1995). Heritage issues in urban tourism. *Tourism Management, 16*, 381-388.

Hoyt, H. (1939). *The structure and growth of residential neighborhoods in American cities*. Washington, DC: Federal Housing Administration.

Hubert, H., & Mauss, M. (1898). *Sacrifice: Its nature and functions* (W. Halls, Trans.). London: Cohen & West.

Hudman, L. (1981). *Directory of tourism education programs*. Wheaton: Merton House Publishing.

Hudman, L., & Hawkins, D. (1990). *Tourism in contemporary society*. Old Tappan, NJ: Prentice Hall.

Hudson, B. (1998). Waterfalls: Resources for tourism. *Annals of Tourism Research, 25*, 958-973.

Hughey, M. (Ed.). (1998). *New tribalisms: The resurgence of race and ethnicity*. New York: New York City Press.

Hugill, P. (1985). The rediscovery of America: Elite automobile tourism. *Annals of Tourism Research, 12*, 435-448.

Hungarian Central Statistical Office. (1992). *Hungarian statistical handbook: 1991*. Budapest: Statiqum Publishing and Printing Company, Ltd.

Hungarian Central Statistical Office. (1996). *Statistical handbook of Hungary: 1995*. Budapest: Central Statistical Printing Office.

Hunt, E., & Nash, J. (1967). Local and territorial units. In M. Nash (Ed.), *Social anthropology* (pp. 253-282). Chicago: University of Chicago Press.

Hunt, J., & Layne, D. (1991). Evolution of travel and tourism terminology and definitions. *Journal of Travel Research, 24*, 7-11.

Hunter, C. (1997). Sustainable tourism as an adaptive paradigm. *Annals of Tourism Research, 24*, 850-867.

Hunter, C., & Green, H. (1995). *Tourism and the environment: A sustainable relationship* (rev. ed.). New York: Routledge.

Huntington, S. (1968). *Political order in changing societies*. New Haven: Yale University Press.

Huse, M., Gustavsen, T., & Almedal, S. (1998). Tourism impact comparisons among Norwegian towns. *Annals of Tourism Research, 25*, 721-738.

Inkpen, G. (1994). *Information technology for travel and tourism*. London: Pitman.

Inskeep, E. (1991). *Tourism planning: An integrated and sustainable approach*. New York: Van Nostrand Reinhold.

Inskeep, E. (1994). *National and regional tourism planning*. London: Routledge.

Ioannides, D. (1995). Planning for international tourism in less developed countries: Towards sustainability? *Journal of Planning Literature, 9*, 235-254.

Instituto Nacional de Estadistica. (1991). *1990 census*. Mexico, DF: Author.

International Bank for Reconstruction and Development. (1966). *The economic eevelopment of Morocco*. Baltimore, MD: John Hopkins Press.

International Union of Official Travel Organization. (1966a). *Economic review of world tourism*. Madrid: World Tourism Organization.

International Union of Official Travel Organization. (1966b). *Pilot study of Africa's tourism prospects*. Madrid: World Tourism Organization.

International Union of Official Travel Organization. (1968). *Tourism and national eco-*

nomic development. Madrid: World Tourism Organization.

Jaakson, R. (1996). Tourism in transition in post-soviet Estonia. *Annals of Tourism Research, 23*, 617-634.

Jackowski, A., & Smith, V. (1992). Polish pilgrim-tourists. *Annals of Tourism Research, 19*(1), 92-106.

Jackson, G., & Morpeth, N. (1999). Local Agenda 21 and community participation in tourism policy and planning: Future or fallacy. *Current Issues in Tourism, 2*(1), 1-38.

Jacobsen, C., & Cohen, A. (1986). The power of social collectivism: Towards an integrative conceptualization and operationalization. *British Journal of Sociology, 37*(1), 106-121.

Jacobsen, J. (1997). The making of an attraction: The case of North Cape. *Annals of Tourism Research, 24*, 341-356.

Jaeger, A. (1995). *Tourism issues for Hungary's western Balaton region: Final reports of participants in the 1995 North Carolina State University summer ethnographic field school in Hungary.* Raleigh, NC: North Carolina State University, Department of Sociology and Anthropology.

Jafari, J. (1974). Socioeconomic costs of tourism to developing countries. *Annals of Tourism Research, 1*, 227-262.

Jafari, J. (1975). Special edition commemorating the 50th anniversary of WTO [Special issue]. *Annals of Tourism Research, 2*.

Jafari, J. (1977). Jamaica: Why don't you stop and say hello. *Annals of Tourism Research, 4*, 295-298.

Jafari, J. (1983). Understanding the structure of tourism. In C. Eddystone (Ed.), *Tourism and culture: A comparative perspective* (pp. 65-84). New Orleans: The University of New Orleans.

Jafari, J. (1987). Tourism models: The sociocultural aspects. *Tourism Management, 8*, 67-68.

Jafari, J. (1988a). Introduction. In L. D'Amore & J. Jafari (Eds.), *Tourism: A vital force for peace* (pp. 3-6). Montreal: L. J. D'Amore and Associates.

Jafari, J. (1988b). Soft tourism. *Tourism Management, 9*, 82-84.

Jafari, J. (1990). Research and scholarship: The basis of tourism education. *The Journal of Tourism Studies, 1*, 33-41.

Jafari, J. (1991). Mediterranean congress on sociology of tourism. *Annals of Tourism Research, 18*, 668-669.

Jafari, J. (1992). Tourism peoples and their cultures. *Sociolgia Urbana e Ruralo, 13*, 149-159.

Jafari, J. (1994). Structure of tourism: Three models. In S. Witt & L. Mountinho (Eds.), *Tourism marketing and management handbook* (2nd ed., pp. 1-7). New York: Prentice Hall.

Jafari, J. (1997a). Tourism and culture: An inquiry into paradoxes. In *Proceedings of a UNESCO round table on Culture, Tourism, Development: Critical Issues for the 21st Century.* Paris: UNESCO.

Jafari, J. (1997b). Tourismification of the profession: Chameleon job names across the industry. *Progress in Tourism and Hospitality Research, 3*(3), 175-181.

Jafari, J. (Ed.). (2000). *Encyclopedia of tourism.* London: Routledge.

Jafari, J., & Aaser, D. (1988). Tourism as the subject of doctoral dissertations. *Annals of Tourism Research, 15*, 407-429.

Jafari, J., & Pizam, A. (1996). Tourism management. In M. Warner (Editor-in Chief), *International encyclopedia of business and management* (pp. 4903-4913). London: Routledge.

Jafari, J., & Ritchie, B. (1981). Toward a framework for education: Problems and prospects. *Annals of Tourism Research, 8*, 13-34.

Jafari, J., & Toepper, L. (1984). *Cooperative tourism effort: A joint NTO-industry-academe action program.* San Francisco: Pacific Asia Travel Association.

Jafari, J., & Wayne, S. (1992). WTO general assembly. *Annals of Tourism Research, 19,* 579-580.

Jakle, J. (1981). Touring by automobile in 1932: The American West as stereotype. *Annals of Tourism Research, 8,* 591-595.

Jakle, J. (1985). *The tourist: Travel in twentieth century North America.* Lincoln, NE: University of Nebraska Press.

Janiskee, R. (1996). Historic houses and special events. *Annals of Tourism Research, 23,* 398-414.

Jansen-Verbeke, M. (1991). Tourism in Europe on the eve of 1992. *Annals of Tourism Research, 18,* 529-533.

Jansen-Verbeke, M., & van Rekom, J. (1996). Scanning museum visitors. *Annals of Tourism Research, 23,* 364-375.

Jeans, D. (1990). Beach resort morphology in England and Australia: A review and extension. In P. Fabbri (Ed.), *Recreational uses of coastal areas.* Dordrecht, The Netherlands: Kluwer Academic Publishers.

Jenkins, C. (1997). Tourism educational systems, institutions and curricula: Standardisations and certification. In *Human capital in the tourism industry of the twenty-first century* (pp. 220-226). Madrid: World Tourism Organization.

Johansson, A., & Nyberg, L. (1996). Tourism conference on safety and establishment of a center. *Annals of Tourism Research, 23,* 724-725.

Johnson, G. (1999, April 28). Make room in the sky for a 650-seat 'cruise ship.' *Chico Enterprise Record,* p. D6.

Johnson, I. (1997, December 11). China's new containment policy: Fighting the rise of megacities. *The Wall Street Journal,* p. A20.

Johnson, P., & Thomas, B. (1992a). *Choice and demand in tourism.* London: Mansell.

Johnson, P., & Thomas, B. (1992b). *Perspectives on tourism policy.* London: Mansell.

Johnston, B. (1995). Share the dream: Dolls and fabrics of Peru. *Dollmaker's Journal, 3,* 13.

Johnston, C., Liu, J., & Din, K. (1991). Coastal and marine tourism. *Annals of Tourism Research, 18,* 523.

Johnston, D. (1992). *Temples of chance: How America Inc. bought out Murder Inc. to win control of the casino business.* New York: Doubleday.

Johnston, J. (1995). *Tourism issues for Hungary's western Balaton region: Final reports of participants in the 1995 North Carolina State University summer ethnographic field school in Hungary.* Raleigh, NC: North Carolina State University, Department of Sociology and Anthropology.

Jokinen, E., & Veilola, S. (1994). The body in tourism: Touring contemporary research in tourism. In J. Jardel (Ed.), *Le tourisme international entre tradition et modernite.* Nice, France: Actes du Colloque International, Laboratoire d'ethnologie.

Jones, K. (1999, November). *Travel Counselor,* p. 9.

Jones, L. (1993, June 28). Ecotourism: Can it save the world? *Travel Counselor,* 52-56.

Jones, P., & Pizam, A. (1993). *The international hospitality industry: Organisational and operational issues.* London: Longman.

Jones, R. (1981). Poker and the American dream. In W. Arens & S. Montague (Eds.), *The American dimension: Cultural myths and social realities* (2nd ed., pp. 27-35). Sherman Oaks, CA: Alfred Publishing Co.

Jordan, M. (1997). War and remembrance: Germany targets the power and popularity of nostalgia tours. *Outbound, 4*(1), 12-14.

Julien, B. (1995). Current and future directions for structured impact assessments. *Impact Assessment, 13,* 403-433.

Kahn, H. (1999). Some past, present and future trends in the travel industry. *Travel Trade*, 16-17.

Kearney, M. (1995). The local and the global: The anthropology of globalization and transnationalism. *Annual Review of Anthropology, 24*, 547-65.

Kekec. (1990). *Pamukkale "Hierapolis."* Istanbul, Turkey: Hitit. Color.

Kelly, J. (1993). *An archaeological guide to Mexico's Yucatan Peninsula.* Norman, OK: University of Oklahoma.

Kelly, M. (1998). Jordan's potential tourism development. *Annals of Tourism Research, 25*, 904-918.

Kelly, P. (1997). Globalization, power and the politics of scale in the Philippines. *Geoforum, 28*, 151-171.

Kent, N. (1975). A new kind of sugar. In B. Finney & K. Watson (Eds.), *A new kind of sugar: Tourism in the Pacific* (pp. 168-198). Santa Cruz, CA: Center for South Pacific Studies, University of California, Santa Cruz.

Kent, N. (1983). *Hawaii: Islands under the influence.* New York: Monthly Review Press.

Keresztury, D. (1989). Introduction. In S. Karoly (Ed.), *Balaton* (pp. 1-2). Budapest: Officina Nova.

Khan, M., Olsen, M., & Var, T. (1993). *VNR's encyclopedia of hospitality and tourism.* New York: Van Nostrand Reinhold.

Kinnaird, V., & Hall, D. (1994). *Tourism: A gender analysis.* Chichester, West Sussex: Wiley & Sons.

Kintz, E. (1990). *Life under the tropical canopy.* Fort Worth, TX: Holt, Rinehart & Winston.

Kirshenblatt-Gimblett, B. (1998). *Destination culture: Tourism, museums and heritage.* Berkeley: University of California Press.

Kistler, W. (1999, January). Humanity's future in space. *The Futurist, 43*-46.

Kitfield, J. (1998). War in the urban jungles. *Air Force Magazine, 81*, 72-76.

Klenosky, D., & Gitelson, R. (1998). Travel agents' destination recommendations. *Annals of Tourism Research, 25*, 661-674.

Kloke, C. (1975). South Pacific economies and tourism. In B. Finney & K. Watson, (Eds.), *A new kind of sugar: Tourism in the Pacific* (pp. 3-26). Honolulu: East-West Center.

Kmet, M. (1998, April 6). Marketing pays off for the Mayan region. *Travel Age*, 18-21.

Knowles, T. (1996). *Corporate strategy for hospitality.* London: Longman.

Kobayashi, H. (1997). *Political economy of tourism development in southeast Asia.* Canberra: Australian National University.

Kolltveit, B. (1980). *Over fjord og fjell: Hardanger Sunnhordlandske Dampskipsselskap 1880-1980.* Bergen: HSD.

Kolltveit, D. (1987). (Bygdeboknemnda). Ulvik, Gards—og aettesoga. *Ulvik herad.*

Kontogeorgopoulos, N. (1998). Accommodation employment patterns and opportunities. *Annals of Tourism Research, 25*, 314-339.

Kottak, C. (1990). *Prime-time society: An anthropological analysis of television and culture.* Belmont, CA: Wordsworth Publishing Company.

Kowinski, W. S. (1985). *The malling of America.* New York: William Morrow Co.

Kozponti Statisztikai Hivatal. (1994a). *Yearbook of tourism 1993.* Budapest: Author.

Kozponti Statisztikai Hivatal. (1994b). *Zala Megye Statisztikai Evkonyve 1993.* Zalaegerszeg: Kozponti Statisztikai Hivatal Zala Megyei Igazgatosaga.

Krapf, K. (1963). *Tourism as a factor in economic development: Role and importance of international tourism.* New York: United Nations.

Krakover, S. (1999). *The effect of terror on the flow of tourists to Israel.* Paper presented at the Annual Meeting of the Association of American Geographers, Honolulu, HI, March 23-27.

Kraybill, D. (1989). *The riddle of Amish culture.* Baltimore, MD: Johns Hopkins Press.

Krech, D., Crutchfield, R., & Ballachey, E. (1962). *Examples of twelve types of appeals. Individual in society*. p. 77. New York: McGraw-Hill Book Company.

Krippendorf, J. (1986). Tourism in the system of industrial society. *Annals of Tourism Research, 13*, 517-532.

Krippendorf, J. (1987). *The holiday makers: Understanding the impact of leisure and travel*. London: Heinemann.

Krippendorf, J. (1991). Towards new tourism policies. In S. Medlik (Ed.), *Managing tourism* (pp. 307-318). London: Butterworth-Heinemann.

Kruhse-MountBurton, S. (1990) Australian men and sex tourism in southeast Asia. In M. Lanfant et al. (Eds.), *International tourism—identity and change* (pp. 192-204). London: Sage.

Kurin, R. (1997). *Reflections of a culture broker: A view from the Smithsonian*. Washington, DC: Smithsonian Institution Press.

Lalli, M. (1994, February). Dolls with a mission. *Doll Reader*, 54-57.

Lalli, S. (1997). A peculiar institution. In J. Sheehan (Ed.), *The players: The men who made Las Vegas* (pp. 1-22). Reno/Las Vegas: University of Nevada Press.

Lampland, M. (1995). *The object of labor commodification in socialist Hungary*. Chicago: University of Chicago Press.

Landa, D. (1941). Relacion de las cosas de Yucatan (Ms 1566). In A. Tozzer (Ed. and Trans.), *Papers of the Peabody Museum, 18* (p. 98). Cambridge, MA: Harvard University Press.

Lanfant, M. (1991). The ISA tourism group seminar. *Annals of Tourism Research, 18*, 335-336.

Lanfant, M., Allcock, J., & Bruner, E. (1995). *International tourism: Identity and change*. London: Sage Studies in International Sociology.

Lardner, J. (1999, December 20) World-class workaholics. *U.S. News and World Report, 18*(127), 42-48.

Lavery, P. (Ed.). (1974). *Recreational geography*. Newton Abbot, Devon: Douglas David & Charles Limited.

Lavery, P., & Van Doren, C. (1990). *Travel and tourism: A North American-European perspective*. Huntington, UK: Elm Publications.

Law, C. (1993). *Urban tourism: Attracting visitors to large cities*. London: Mansell.

Lawmakers aim to bar Indian lottery. (1995, March 11). *The Sacramento Bee*, p. A25.

Lawson, F. (1995). *Hotels and resorts: Planning, design and refurbishment*. London: Butterworth-Heinemann.

Lea, J. (1988). *Tourism development in the third world*. New York: Routledge, Chapman and Hall.

Leach, E. (1961). *Rethinking anthropology*. London: Athlone Press, University of London.

Leach, E. (Ed.). (1982). *Rethinking anthropology*. New York: Athlone Press.

League of Nations. (1936). *Survey of tourist traffic considered as an international economic factor*. New York: United Nations.

Lee, D., & Snepenger, D. (1992). An ecotourism assessment of Tortuguero, Costa Rica. *Annals of Tourism Research, 19*, 367-370.

Lee, R. (1978). Who owns boardwalk: The structure of control in the tourist industry of Yucatan. In V. Smith, (Ed.), *Tourism and economic change* (pp. 19-35). Williamsburg, VA: William and Mary Press.

Leinberger, C., & Lockwood, C. (1986, October). How business is reshaping America. *The Atlantic*, 43-52.

Leiper, N. (1979). The framework of tourism: Towards a definition of tourism, tourist and the tourist industry. *Annals of Tourism Research, 6*, 390-407.

Lekeny, D. (1995). A political economy of Asian sex tourism. *Annals of Tourism Research, 22*, 367-384.

Lem, W. (1994). Class politics, cultural politics. *Critique of Anthropology, 14*, 393–417.

Lengyel, N. (1993). *A Balatoni Turizmus Fejlesztesi Koncepcioja.* Budapest: Orszagos Idegenforgalmi Hivatal.

Lessinger, J. (1986). *Regions of opportunity.* New York: Random House.

Letsie, N. (1991). Development of tourism in the SADCC region. In L. Pfotenhauer (Ed.), *Tourism in Botswana* (Proceedings of a symposium held in Gaborone, Botswana October 19, 1990). Gaborene, Botswana: Botswana Society.

Lew, A. (1998). The Asia Pacific ecotourism industry: Putting sustainable tourism into practice. In C. Hall & A. Lew (Eds.), *Sustainable tourism: A geographical perspective.* London: Addison Wesley Longman.

Lew, A., & Van Otten, G. (1998). *Tourism and gaming on American Indian lands.* New York: Cognizant Communication Corp.

Lew, A., & Yu, L. (1995). *Tourism in China: Geographic, political, and economic perspectives.* Boulder, CO: Westview Press.

Lewis, T. (1995). Buddhist merchants in Kathmandu: The Asan Twah market and Uray social organization. In D. Gellner & D. Quigley (Eds.), *Contested hierarchies: A collaborative ethnography of caste among the Newars of the Kathmandu Valley* (pp. 39–79). Oxford: Clarendon Press.

Lickorish, L., & Kershaw, A. (1958). *The travel trade.* London: Practical Press.

Liggett, B. (1995, January 19). Gaming QA, best bets. *The Reno Gazette-Journal*, p. 19.

Lindberg, K., & Hawkins, D. (Eds.). (1993). *Ecotourism: A guide for planners and managers.* Bennington, VT: Ecotourism Society.

Lindberg, K., McCool, S., & Stankey, G. (1997). Rethinking carrying capacity. *Annals of Tourism Research, 24*(2), 461–465.

Lipman, G. (1999). In *Using tourism satellite accounts to reach the bottom line.* Madrid: World Tourism Organization.

Littrell, M., Anderson, L., & Brown, P. (1993). What makes a craft souvenir authentic? *Annals of Tourism Research, 20*, 197–215.

Liu, J. (1999). *The economic impact of Hawaii cultural attractions on the local economy.* Paper presented at the 95th annual meting of the Association of American Geographers, March 23–25, Honolulu, HI.

Loban, S. (1998). Designing effective documents for destination information systems. In D. Buhalis, A. Min Tjoa, & J. Jafari (Eds.), *Information and communications technologies in tourism* (pp. 73–83). Vienna and New York: Springer.

Locke, J. (1999). Religions of Nepal. In L. Chengyal & K. Moran (Eds.), *Nepal.* Basingstoke: APA Publications.

Lockwood, A., & Jones, P. (1988). *The management of hotel operations.* London: Cassell.

Long, V. (1993a). Monkey business: Mixing tourism with ecology. *Business Mexico, 3*, 23–26.

Long, V. (1993b). Techniques for socially sustainable tourism development: Lessons from Mexico. In J. Nelson, R. Butler, & G. Wall (Eds.), *Tourism and sustainable development: Monitoring, planning* (pp. 201–218). Waterloo, Ontario, Canada: University of Waterloo, Heritages Resources Center.

Long, V., & Wall, G. (1996). Successful tourism in Nusa Lembongan, Indonesia. *Tourism Management, 17*, 43–50.

Lore of the Inupiat ["The Elders Speak"] (Three volume work). (1989/1990/1992). Kotzebue, Alaska: Northwest Arctic Burrough School District.

Lowenthal, D. (1962). Tourists and thermalists. *Geographical Review, 52*, 124–127.

Lowenthal, D. (1985). *The past is a foreign country.* Cambridge: Cambridge University Press.

Luhrman, D. (1997, January 28). *WTO top ten.* Madrid: World Tourism Organization.

Lukashina, N., Amirkhanov, M., Anisimov, V., & Trunev, A. (1996). Tourism and environmental degradation in Sochi, Russia. *Annals of Tourism Research, 23*, 654-665.

Lundberg, D. (1995). *Tourism economics.* New York: John Wiley & Sons.

Luthy, D. (1994). The origin and growth of Amish tourism. In D. Kraybill & M. Olshan (Eds.), *The Amish struggle with modernity* (pp. 113-129). Hanover: University Press of New England.

MacCannell, D. (1973). Staged authenticity: Arrangements of social space in tourist settings. *American Journal of Sociology, 79*, 589-603.

MacCannell, D. (1976). *The tourist: A new theory of the leisure class.* London: Macmillan.

MacCannell, D. (1989a). Semiotics of tourism [Special issue]. *Annals of Tourism Research, 16.*

MacCannell, D. (1989b). *The tourist: A new theory of the leisure class.* New York: Schocken Books.

MacDonald, M. (1994). *Tourism in the west Balaton area including Kis Balaton from an American perspective: Final report of the American Hungarian student summer 1994 program.* Raleigh, NC: North Carolina State University.

Madsen Camacho, M. (1996). Dissenting workers and social control: A case study of the hotel industry in Huatulco, Oaxaca. *Human Organization, 55*(1), 33-40.

Mak, J. (1993). Exacting resort developers to create non- tourism jobs. *Annals of Tourism Research, 22*, 250-261.

Malinoski, B. (1922). *Argonauts of the western Pacific.* New York: E. F. Dutton & Co.

Mallari, A., & Enote, J. (1996). Maintaining control: Culture and tourism in the pueblo of Zuni. In M. Price (Ed.), *People and tourism in fragile environments* (pp. 19-32). Chichester: John Wiley & Sons, Ltd.

Mancini, M. (1999, November). Who are you? Untangling the baby boomers identity crisis. *Travel Counselor,* 12-16.

Mandel, R. (1991). Foreigners in the fatherland: Turkish immigrant workers in Germany. In C. Guerin-Gonzalez & C. Strikwerda (Eds.), *The politics of immigrant workers: Labor activism and migration in the world economy since 1830.* New York: Holmes &Meier.

Manning, S. (1997, November 20). Looking for a truly sensual experience? Mall offers much more than shopping. *Enterprise Record,* p. C6.

Mansperger, M. (1995). Tourism and cultural change in small-scale societies. *Human Organization, 54*, 87-94.

Marcuse, H. (1990). Das ehemalige konzentrationslager Dachau. Der muehevolle weg zur gedenkstaette 1945-68 (The former Dachau concentration camp: The difficult path to memorial site and museum). *Dachauer hefte*, 182-205.

Marcuse, H. (1999). *Forgetting genocide: Remembering Dachau.* New York: Cambridge University Press.

Markwell, K. (1997). Dimensions of photography in a nature-based tour. *Annals of Tourism Research, 24*, 131-155.

Marsh, G. (1864). *Man and nature or physical geography as modified by human nature* (edited 1965, D. Lowenthal). Cambridge, MA: Harvard University Belknap Press.

Martin, R. (1994, February 17). Resurgent Islam. *Far Eastern Economic Review*, 36-37.

Maslow, A. (1970). *Motivation and personality* (2nd ed.). New York: Harper and Row.

Massa, P. (1994). *Tourism in the west Balaton area including Kis Balaton from an American perspective: Final report of the American Hungarian student summer 1994 program.* Raleigh, NC: North Carolina State Universtiy.

Mastny, L. (2000). Coming to terms with the Arctic. *World-Watch, 13*, 24-36.

Mathieson, A., & Wall, G. (1982). *Tourism: Economic, physical and social impacts.* London and New York: Longman Group Ltd.

Matthews, H. (1977). Radicals and third world tourism. A Caribbean focus. *Annals of Tour-*

ism Research, 5, 20-29.

McElroy, J., & de Albuquerque, K. (1998). Tourism penetration index in small Caribbean islands. *Annals of Tourism Research, 25,* 145-168.

McGahey, S. (1994). Ugly Korean travelers documented abroad. *Business Korea, 12*(1), 65-67.

McGarty, C. (1995). *Dietary delocalization in a Yucatecan resort community: Junk food in paradise.* Amherst, MA: University of Massachusetts.

McGovern, G. (2000). Tourism sector urged to get online fast. *WTO News, 1,* 15.

McIntosh, A. (1998). Mixing methods: putting the tourist at the forefront of tourism research. *Tourism Analysis, 3,* 121-127.

McIntosh, I. (1999). Ecotourism: A boon for indigenous people? *Cultural Survival Quarterly, 3,* 3.

McIntosh, R. (1977). *Tourism: Principles, practices, philosophies* (2nd ed.). Columbus, OH: Grid.

McIntosh, R., Goeldner, C., & Ritchie, B. (1994). *Tourism: Principles, practices, philosophies* (7th ed.). New York: John Wiley & Sons.

McIntyre, G. (1993). *Sustainable tourism development: Guide for local planners.* Madrid: World Tourism Organization.

McKay, N. (1991). The meaning of good faith in the Indian gaming regulatory act. *Gonzaga Law Review, 27*(3), 471-486.

McKercher, B. (1996). Differences between tourism and recreation in parks. *Annals of Tourism Research, 23,* 563-575.

McLaren, D. (1998). *Rethinking tourism and ecotravel: The paving of paradise and what you can do to it.* West Hartford, CT: Kumarian Press, Inc.

McLaren, D. (1999). The history of indigenous peoples and tourism. *Cultural Survival Quarterly, 23*(2), 27-30.

McNaughton, K. (1995). *Tourism issues for Hungary's western Balaton region: Final reports of participants in the 1995 North Carolina State University summer ethnographic field school in Hungary.* Raleigh, NC: North Carolina State University, Department of Sociology and Anthropology.

Medlik, S. (Ed.). (1991). *Managing tourism.* Oxford: Butterworth-Heineman.

Medlik, S. (1993). *Dictionary of travel, tourism and hospitality.* Oxford: Butterworth-Heinemann.

Meethan, K. (1996). Consuming (in) the civilized city. *Annals of Tourism Research, 23,* 322-340.

Metro Manila declared hot spot for HIV. (1994, December 30). *Philippine News,* p. A.

Meyer-Arendt, K. (1987). *Resort evolution along the Gulf of Mexico littoral: Historical, morphological and environmental aspects.* Doctoral dissertation, Louisiana State University.

Meyer-Arendt, K., &. Hartmann, R. (Eds.). (1998). *Casino gambling in America: Origins, trends and impacts.* New York: Cognizant Communication Corp.

Meyer-Arendt, K., Sambrook, R., & Kermath, B. (1992, September). Seaside resorts in the Dominican Republic: A typology. *The Journal of Geography,* 218-225.

Middleton, V. (Ed.). *The constitutions of Latin America.* Chicago, IL: Henry Regnery.

Mieczkowski, Z. (1995). *Environmental issues of tourism and recreation.* Lanham, MD: University Press of America.

Mill, P., & Morrison, A. (1985). *The tourism system: An introductory text.* Englewood Cliffs, NJ: Prentice Hall International Editions.

Miller, C. (1994). The social impacts of televised media among the Yucatec Maya. Unpublished manuscript.

Miniter, R. (1997, July 17). Too many elephants. *Wall Street Journal,* p. A22.

Mintz, S. (1985). *Sweetness and power: The place of sugar in modern history.* New York: Viking Penguin.

Mitchell, C., Nolan, R., & Hohol, F. (1993). Tourism and community economic development: A case study of St. Jacobs, Ontario. In D. Bruce & M. Whitla (Eds.), *Tourism strategies for rural development* (pp. 16-25). Sackville, NB: Mount Allison University.

Mitchell, J. (Ed.). (2000). *Crucibles of hazard: Mega-cities and disasters in transition.* New York: United Nations University Press.

Mitchell, L. (1979). Geography of tourism [Special issue]. *Annals of Tourism Research, 6.*

Mitchell, S. (1998). *Official guide to the generations.* Ithaca, NY: New Strategist Publications.

Mok, C., & Lam, T. (1997). A model of tourists shopping propensity: A case of Taiwanese visitors to Hong Kong. *Pacific Tourism Review, 1,* 137-128.

Montanari, A., & Williams, A. (1995). *European tourism: Regions, spaces and restructuring.* London: Wiley & Sons.

Moscardo, G. (1996). Mindful visitors: Heritage and tourism. *Annals of Tourism Research, 23,* 376-397.

Moscardo, G., & Pearce, P. (1999). Understanding ethnic tourists. *Annals of Tourism Research, 26,* 416-434.

Much, M. (1998, January 26). Gambling. *Investor's Business Daily,* p. B14.

Mueller, M. (1998). *Anne Frank: The biography.* New York: Metropolitan Books Henry Holt and Company, Inc.

Murphy, J., Forrest, E., & Vatring, C. (1996a, February). Restaurant marketing on the worldwide web. *Cornell Hotel and Restaurant Administration Quarterly,* 61-71.

Murphy, J., Forrest, E., Vatring, C., & Brymer, R. (1996b, June). Hotel management and marketing on the internet. *Cornell Hotel and Restaurant Administration Quarterly,* 70-82.

Murphy, P. (1985). *Tourism: A community approach.* New York and London: Routledge.

Murphy, P. (1998). Tourism and sustainable development, In W. Theobald, (Ed.), *Global tourism: The next decade* (pp. 173-190). Oxford: Butterworth-Heinemann..

Myers, C. (1965). *Education and national development in Mexico.* Princeton, NJ: Princeton University.

Nash, D. (1979). The rise and fall of an aristocratic tourist culture—Nice: 1763-1936. *Annals of Tourism Research, 6,* 61-65.

Nash, D. (1981). Tourism as an anthropological subject. *Current Anthropology, 22,* 461-481.

Nash, D. (1996). *Anthropology of tourism.* Oxford: Elsevier Science.

Nash, D., & Smith, V. (1991). Anthropology and tourism. *Annals of Tourism Research, 18,* 12-25.

Nash, J. (1993). Introduction: Traditional arts and changing markets in Middle America. In J. Nash (Ed.), *Crafts in the world market.* Albany, NY: State University of New York Press.

Nash, M. (1967). *Machine age Maya* (rev. ed.). Chicago, IL: The University of Chicago Press.

National Economic and Development Authority. (1992). *National physical framework plan 1993-2022.* Government of the Philippines.

National Resource Perspective. (2000). *Pro-poor tourism strategies.* London: Overseas Development Institute.

Nazim, M., & Polunin, N. (1993). *Environmental challenges: From Stockholm to Rio and beyond.* Lahore, Pakistan: Energy and Environmental Society of Pakistan & Geneva, Switzerland: Foundation for Environmental Conservation.

Nelson, J., Butler, R., & Wall, G. (1992). *Tourism and sustainable development: Monitoring, planning, managing.* Waterloo, ON: Heritage Resources Centre, University of Waterloo.

Nettle, D., & Romaine, S. (2000). *Vanishing voices: The extinction of the world's languages*. Oxford: University Press.

Nicholson, T. (1997). *Tourism development and community: Four Philippine case studies in Boracay, Samal, Mariduque, and Davao*. Quezon City: VSO Philippines.

Nickerson, N. (1995). Tourism and gambling content analysis. *Annals of Tourism Research, 22*, 53–66.

Nodding, P., Berresford, J., & Alexander, M. (1993). *Live the legend in Robin Hood country* [Submission to UK Tourism Marketing Awards]. London: The Tourism Society.

Noricks, J. (1984). The poker story: An American subculture. *The University Journal, California State University, Chico, 24*, 29–31.

Nugent, S. (1994). Invisible Amazonia and the aftermath of conquest: A coda to the quincentenary celebrations. *Journal of Historical Sociology, 7*, 224–241.

Nunez, T. (1977). Touristic studies in anthropological perspective. In V. Smith (Ed.), *Hosts and guests: The anthropology of tourism* (pp. 207–216). Oxford: Basil Blackwell.

Nuryanti, W. (1996). Heritage and postmodern tourism. *Annals of Tourism Research, 23*, 249–260.

Nyamaphene, K. (1985). Prevention of land use conflict in Zimbabawe's marginal lands. *Land Use Policy, 2*, 323–326.

O'Connor, P. (1995). *Using computers in hospitality*. London: Cassell.

Ogilvie, F. (1933). *The tourism movement: An economic study*. Westminster: P. S. King and Sons.

Okey, R. (1987). Trekking in nature's terrarium. *Americas, 39*, 8–13.

Olsen, M., Teare, R., & Gummesson, E. (1995). *Service quality in hospitality organizations*. London: Cassell.

Olshan, M. (1994). Amish cottage industries as trojan horse. In D. Kraybill & M. Olshan (Eds.), *The Amish struggle with modernity* (pp. 133–146). Hanover: University Press of New England.

O'Meara, M. (1999). *Reinventing cities for people and the planet* (Worldwatch Paper No. 47). Washington, DC: Worldwatch Institute.

Oppermann, M. (1998). *Sex tourism and prostitution: Aspects of leisure, recreation, and work*. New York: Cognizant Communication Corp.

Oppermann, M., & Chon, K. (1997). Convention participation decision-making process. *Annals of Tourism Research, 24*, 178–191.

Orams, M. (1999). *Marine tourism: Development, impacts and management*. London: Routledge.

Orkin, M. (1991). *Can you win? The real odds for casino gambling, sports betting and lotteries*. New York: Freeman & Co.

Ortner, S. (1995). Resistance and the problem of ethnographic refusal. *Comparative Studies in Society and History, 37*, 173–193.

Orwall, B. (1998, September 21). Coming to famous theme parks: Troubleland. *Wall Street Journal*, pp. B1, B6.

Osborne, W. (1994, December). The ethical symbiosis between anthropologists and the peoples they study. *Anthropology Newsletter, 1*, 6.

Oster, P. (1990). *The Mexicans*. New York: Harper and Row.

Oswalt, W. (1979). *Eskimos and explorers*. Novato, CA: Chandler & Sharp Publishers, Inc.

Owen, G. (1994). *Accounting for hospitality, tourism and leisure*. London: Pitman.

Pace, R. (1993). First time televiewing in Amazonia: Television acculturation in Gurupa, Brazil. *Ethnology, 32*, 187–205.

Packard, V. (1960). *The waste makers*. New York: David Mc Kay.

Page, S. (Ed.). (1994). *Urba*. London: Routledge.

Page, S., & Meyer, D. (1996). Tourist accidents: An exploratory analysis. *Annals of Tourism*

Research, 23, 666-690.

Palawan Council for Sustainable Development. (1993). *Guidelines for tourism-oriented establishment in the province of Palawan* (Rep. No. R.A. 7611). Philippines: Government of the Philippines.

Pannett, A. (1992). *Principles of hotel and catering law.* London: Cassell.

Parnwell, M. (1993). Environmental issues and tourism in Thailand. In M. Hichkock, V. King, & M. Parnwell (Eds.), *Tourism in South East Asia.* London: Routledge.

Passport Cancun (20th ed.). (1994). Cancun: Apoyo Promocional.

Patterson, K. (1996). As Mexico develops tourist sector, locals push for greater control. *The Christian Science Monitor.*

Pattullo, P. (1996). *Last resorts: The cost of tourism in the Caribbean.* Kingston, Jamaica: Ian Randle.

Peacock, M. (1995). *Information technology in hospitality.* London: Cassell.

Pearce, D. (1987). Coastal tourism. *Annals of Tourism Research, 14,* 278-279.

Pearce, D. (1988). Economics, equity and sustainable development. *Futures, 20,* 598-605.

Pearce, D. (1992). *Tourist organisations.* London: Pitman.

Pearce, D. (1995). *Tourism today: A geographical analysis* (2nd ed.). Essex: Longman.

Pearce, D. (1998). Tourism development in Paris: Public intervention. *Annals of Tourism Research, 25,* 457-476.

Pearce, D., & Butler, R. (Eds.). (1992). *Methodological and conceptual issues in tourism research.* London: Routledge.

Pearce, D., & Butler, R. (Eds.). (1993). *Tourism research: Critiques and challenges.* London: Routledge.

Pearce, P. (1982). *The social psychology of tourist behavior.* Oxford: Pergamon Press.

Pearce, P. (1988). *The Ulysses factor: Evaluating visitors in tourist settings.* New York: Springer-Verlag.

Pearce, P. (1993). Fundamentals of tourist motivation. In D. Pearce & R. Butler (Eds.), *Tourism research: Critiques and challenges* (pp. 113-134). London and New York: Routledge.

Peck, J., & Lepie, A. (1989). Tourism and development in three North Carolina coastal towns. In V. Smith, (Ed.), *Hosts and guests: The anthropology of tourism* (2nd ed., pp. 203-222). Philadelphia: University of Pennsylvania Press.

Peppelenbosch, P., & Tempelman, G. (1989). The pros and cons of international tourism to the third world. In T. Singh, H. Theuns, & F. Go (Eds.), *Toward appropriate tourism? The case of developing countries* (pp. 23-34). Frankfurt, Germany: Peter Lang.

Perduek, R. (1988). Tourism and commercial recreation. In L. Barnett (Ed.), *Research about leisure: Past, present and future* (pp. 162-173). Champaign, IL: Sagamore Publishing.

Perez, L. (1973). Aspects of underdevelopment: Tourism in the West Indies. *Science and Society, 37,* 473-480.

Perez Taylor, R. (1994). *Entre al tradicion y la modernidad: Antropologia de la memoria colectiva.* University of Barcelona: Faculty of Geography and History, Department of Social Anthropology.

Peters, M. (1969). *International tourism: The economics and development of international tourist trade.* London: Hutchison and Company.

Petersen, W. (1997). *Ethnicity counts.* New Brunswick, NJ: Transaction Publishers.

Peterson, C., McCarthy, C., & Bosselman, F. (1999). *Managing tourism growth—issues and applications.* Covelo, CA: Island Press.

Phelps, A. (1986, September). Holiday destination image—the problem of assessment: An example developed in Menorca. *Tourism Management,* 168-180.

Phillips, R. (1995). Why not tourist art? Significant silences in native American museum representation. In G. Prakash (Ed.), *After colonialism* (pp. 98-125). Princeton, NJ: Princeton University Press.

Picard, M., & Wood, R. (Eds.). (1997). *Tourism, ethnicity and the state in Asian and Pacific societies.* Honolulu: University of Hawaii Press.

Pi-Sunyer, O. (1973). Tourism and its discontents: The impact of a new industry on a Catalan community. *Studies in European Society, 1*, 11-20.

Pi-Sunyer, O. (1979). The politics of tourism in Catalonia. *Mediterranean Studies, 1*, 46-69.

Pigram, J. (1993). Planning for tourism in rural areas: Bridging the policy implementation gap. In P. Pearce & R. Butler (Eds.), *Tourism research: Critiques and challenges* (pp. 156-174). London and New York: Routledge.

Pitman, D. (1987). *The mobil guide to the national parks of Zimbabwe.* Harare, Zimbabwe: Modus.

Pizam, A. (1980). The management of tourism [Special issue]. *Annals of Tourism Research, 7.*

Pizam, A., & Mansfeld, Y. (Eds.). (1996). *Tourism, crime and international security issues.* New York: John Wiley & Sons.

Place, S. (1991). Nature tourism and rural development in Tortuguero. *Annals of Tourism Research, 18*, 186-201.

Place, S. (1998). How sustainable is ecotourism in Costa Rica? In C. Hall & A. Lew (Eds.), *Sustainable tourism: A geographical perspective* (pp. 107-118). Essex, UK: Addison-Wesley-Longman, Ltd.

Plevin, N. (1995, November 18). Zuni's choice: Banning outsiders creates power struggle within. *The New Mexican*, pp. A1, A4.

Plog, S. (1974, November). Why destinations rise and fall in popularity. *Cornell Hotel and Restaurant Administration Quarterly*, 11-13.

Plog, S. (1991). Psychographic positions of destinations. In *Leisure travel* (p. 83). New York: John Wiley & Sons.

Plog, S. (1994). Leisure travel: An extraordinary industry faces superordinary problems. In W. Theobald (Ed.), *Global tourism* (pp. 40-54). Oxford: Butterworth-Heinemann.

Plog, S. (1998). Why destination preservation makes economic sense. In W. Theobald (Ed.), *Global tourism* (2nd ed., pp. 251-266). Oxford: Butterworth-Heinemann.

Poirer, R. (1997). Political risk analysis and tourism. *Annals of Tourism Research, 24*, 675-686.

Polpl, W., & Lavery, P. (1993). *Tourism in Europe: Structures and developments.* Oxford: CAB International.

Poon, A. (1993). *Tourism, technology and competitive strategies.* Oxford: CAB International.

Posey, D. (1991). Effecting international change. *Cultural Survival Quarterly, 15*, 29-35.

Pospisil, L. (1978). *The Kapauku Papuans and their law* (2nd ed.). New York: Holt, Rinehart, Winston.

Postal, S. (1999). When the world's wells run dry. *WorldWatch, 13*(5), 30-38.

Poustie, M., Geddes, N., Stewart, W., & Ross, J. (1996). *Hospitality and tourism law.* London: Thomson Business Press.

Powers, T. (1974). *Appraising international tourism projects.* Washington, DC: Inter-American Development Bank.

Prentice, R. (1993). *Tourism and heritage attractions.* London: Routledge.

Prentice, R., Witt, S., & Hamer, C. (1998). Tourism as experience: The case of heritage parks. *Annals of Tourism Research, 25*, 1-24.

Priestley, G., & Mundet, L. (1998). The post-stagnation phase of the resort cycle. *Annals of Tourism Research, 25*, 85-111.

Priestly, J. (1951). On doing nothing. In W. Williams (Ed.), *A book of English essays* (pp. 341-350). London: Penguin Books.

Prieto, J. (1954). *Tourism and the balance of payments*. Madrid: Ministerio de Informacion y Turismo.

Puijk, R. (1996). Dealing with fish and tourists: A case study from northern Norway. In J. Boissevain (Ed.), *Coping with tourists: European reactions to mass tourism* (pp. 204-226). Providence/Oxford: Berghahn Books.

Quezada, E. (1940). Quinze dias con el senor Presidente de la Nacion por el territorio de Quintana Roo. Excelsion. In V. Rojas (1969), *The Maya of east central Quintana Roo* (pp. 247-248, Monograph No. 55). Washington, DC: Carnegie Institute.

Quick, P. (1991). Travel and tourism in national economies: Present and future. In D. Hawkins & B. Ritchie (Eds.), *World travel and tourism review* (pp. 72-77). Oxford: CAB International.

Quigley, D. (1995). Conclusion: Caste organization and the ancient city. In Gellner, D. & Quigley, D. (Eds.), *Contested hierarchies of collaborative ethnography of caste among the Newars of the Kathmandu Valley* (pp. 293-327). Oxford: Clarendon Press.

Rainey, F. (1947). The whale hunters of Tigara. In *Anthropological papers of the American Museum of Natural History, XLL*. New York: American Museum of Natural History.

Ray, D. (1975). *The Eskimos of Bering Straits*. Seattle, WA: University of Washington Press.

Redekop, C. (1988). *Mennonite identity*. Lanham, MD: University of America Press.

Redfield, R. (1947). The folk society. *American Journal of Sociology, 52*, 295-298.

Redfield, R., & Villa Rojas, A. (1962). *Chan Com: A Maya village*. Chicago, IL: University of Chicago Press.

Reed, M. (1997). Power relations and community-based tourism planning. *Annals of Tourism Research, 24*, 566-591.

Reed, N. (1964). *The Caste War of Yucatan*. Stanford, CA: Stanford University Press.

Reese, W. (1981, May-June). Travel and tourism in the American west after 1865. *American Book Collector, 2-12*.

Reiley, M. (1996). *Human resource management: A guide to personnel management in the hotel and industries*. London: Butterworth-Heinemann.

Relph, E. (1986). *Place and placelessness*. London: Pion Ltd.

Renner, M. (1996). *Fighting for survival: Environmental decline, social conflict and the new age of insecurity*. New York: W. W. Norton & Company.

Renshaw, M. (1992). *The travel agent*. Sunderland: Centre for Travel and Tourism, Business Education Publishers Ltd.

Rescan Consultants, Inc. (1993). Windy craggy qualitative risk assessment. In *Interim report on Tatshenshini/Alsek land use, British Columbia* (Vol. 2, Appendices). Vancouver: Commission on Resources and Environment.

Richter, L. (1980). The political uses of tourism: A Philippine case study. *Journal of Developing Areas, 14*, 237-257.

Richter, L. (1981, April). Tourism by decree. *Southeast Asia Chronicle*, p. 78.

Richter, L. (1982a). *Land reform and tourism development: Policy making in the Philippines*. Cambridge, MA: Schenkman Publishing Co.

Richter, L. (1982b, November). Philippine policies toward Filipino Americans. *Asian Thought and Society*.

Richter, L. (1987a). Public bureaucracy in post Marcos Philippines. *Southeast Asian Journal of Social Science, 15*, 55-77.

Richter, L. (1987b). Philippine politics from Marcos to Aquino. In C. Lande (Ed.), *Rebuilding a nation: Philippine challenges and American politics*. Washington, DC: Washington Institute Press.

Richter, L. (1989). *The politics of tourism in Asia*. Honolulu, HI: University of Hawaii Press.

Richter, L. (1990). Exploring theories of female leadership in south and southeast Asia. *Pacific Affairs, 63*, 524-540.

Richter, L. (1992). Political instability and tourism in the third world. In D. Harrison (Ed.), *Tourism in less developed countries* (pp. 35-46). London: Belhaven Press.

Richter, L. (1993). Tourism and policy-making in southeast Asia. In M. Hitchcock, V. King, & M. Parnwell (Eds.), *Tourism in southeast Asia*. London: Routledge Press.

Richter, L. (1994). The political fragility of tourism. *Teoros, Revue de recherche en tourisme, 13*, 12-15.

Richter, L. (1996). Changing directions in Philippine policy formation and implementation. *Crossroad: The Journal of Southeast Asian Studies, 9*.

Richter, L. (1997). After political turmoil: Rebuilding tourism in three Asian countries. In *Conference Proceedings, War, Terrorism and Tourism* (p. 54), September 25-27, Dubrovnik, Croatia.

Richter, L., & Nash, D. (1992). Methodological and conceptual issues in tourism research. *Annals of Tourism Research, 19*, 371-372.

Richter, L., & Waugh, W. (1986). Terrorism and tourism as logical companions. In S. Medlik (Ed.), *Managing tourism* (pp. 318-327). Oxford: Butterworth-Heinemann.

Riding, A. (1986). *Distant neighbors*. New York: Vintage Books.

Riley, R., Baker, D., & Van Doren, C. (1998). Movie induced tourism. *Annals of Tourism Research, 25*, 919-935.

Rimmington, M., & Kozak, M. (1997). Developments in information technology: Implication for the tourism industry and tourism marketing. *Anatolia: An International Journal of Tourism and Hospitality Research, 8*, 59-80.

Ritchie, B. (1981). Tourism education [Special issue]. *Annals of Tourism Research, 8*.

Ritchie, B., & Goeldner, C. (Eds.). (1987). *Travel, tourism and hospitality research*. New York: John Wiley.

Ritchie, B., & Goeldner, C. (Eds.). (1994). *Travel tourism and hospitality research* (rev. ed.). New York: John Wiley.

Robb, J. (1998). Tourism and legends: Archaeology of heritage. *Annals of Tourism Research, 25*, 579-596.

Robineau, C. (1975). The Tahitian economy and tourism. In B. Finney & K. Watson, *A new kind of sugar: Tourism in the Pacific* (pp. 61-78). Honolulu: East-West Center.

Rodenburg, E. (1980). The effects of scale on economic development: Tourism in Bali. *Annals of Tourism Research, 7*, 177-196.

Rodrigo, C. (1993, May 17). Sheraton enters gaming industry. *Pacific Business News*, p. 2.

Rogers, E. (1962). *The diffusion of innovations* (4th ed.). New York: Free Press.

Romero, J. (1993). Things I probably shouldn't say, but will anyway. *International Gaming & Wagering Business, 14*, 8.

Rose, I. (1991). The rise and fall of the third wave: Gambling will be outlawed in forty years. In W. Eadington & J. Cronelium (Eds.), *Gambling and public policy: International perspectives* (pp. 65-86). Reno, NV: University of Nevada.

Rosenbaum, B. (1993). With our heads bowed: The dynamics of gender in a Maya community. In *Series on Culture and Society, Institute for Meso-American Studies*. Albany, NY: State University of New York, distributed by University of Texas Press.

Ross, G. (1997). Career stress responses among hospitality employees. *Annals of Tourism Research, 24*, 41-51.

Roughan, J. (1990). Villager, the resource owner! Terrorist? In M. Miller & J. Auyong (Eds.), *Proceedings of the 1990 Congress on Coastal and Marine Tourism* (Vol. 2, pp. 440-446). Newport, OR: National Coastal Resources & Development Institute.

RP turnaround noted worldwide. (1994, April-June). *STAC Report, 6*(2), 6-7.

Ryan, C. (1992a). Crime, violence, terrorism and tourism. *Tourism Management, 14*, 173-183.

Ryan, C. (1992b). *Recreational tourism*. London: Routledge.

Ryan, C. (1995). *Researching tourist satisfaction.* London: Routledge.

Ryan, C. (1998). The travel career ladder: An appraisal. *Annals of Tourism Research, 25,* 936-957.

Ryan, C., & Crotts, J. (1997). Carving and tourism: A Maori perspective. *Annals of Tourism Research, 24,* 898-918.

Ryan, C., & Glendon, I. (1998). Application of leisure motivation scale to tourism. *Annals of Tourism Research, 25,* 169-184.

Ryan, C., & Page, S. (2000). *Tourism management towards the new millennium.* Amsterdam: Elsevier Science.

Ryan, S. (1990). *Ethnic conflict and international relations.* Aldershot, UK: Dartmouth Publishing Co.

Sadler, B. (1990). Appendix 1: Synopsis of the round table discussions. In P. Jacobs & B. Sadler (Eds.), *Sustainable development and environmental assessement: Perspectives on planning for a common future.* Hull, Quebec, Canada: CEARC.

Sagan, C. (1994). *Pale blue dot: A vision of the human future in space.* New York: Random House.

Salamone, F. (1997). Authenticity in tourism: The San Angel Inns. *Annals of Tourism Research, 24,* 305-321.

Salgado, W. (2000). *Migrations: Humanity in transition.* New York: Aperture.

Samy, J. (1975). Crumbs from the table? The worker' share in tourism. In B. Finney & K. Watson (Eds.), *A new kind of sugar: Tourism in the Pacific* (pp. 111-124). Honolulu: East-West Center.

Sanborn Map & Publishing Ltd. (1886). Atlantic City, New Jersey map. New York: Author.

Sassen, S. (1991). *The global city: New York, London, Tokyo.* Princeton, NJ: Princeton University Press.

Satre, P. (1993). *The Harrah's survey of U.S. casino gaming entertainment.* Memphis, TN: Harrah's Entertainment.

Satre, P. (1994). *The Harrah's survey of U.S. casino entertainment.* Memphis, TN: Harrah's Entertainment.

Satre, P. (1995). *Harrah's survey of casino entertainment.* Memphis, TN: Harrah's Entertainment.

Savy, F. (2000). Seychelles preserving paradise. *WTO News, 2,* 10-11.

Scarne, J. (1965). *Scarne on cards.* New York: Signet.

Schmid, A. (1988). *Political terrorism.* New York: North-Holland Publishing Co.

Schmitt, H. (2000). Moon's helium-3 could power earth [Quoted on-line]. http:// www.space.com/science astronomy/helium3_0006/30.html

Scholes, F., & Roys, R. (1948). *The Maya Chontal Indians of Acalan Tixchel.* Washington, DC: Carnegie Institution of Washington.

Seaton, A. (1999). War and thanatourism: Waterloo 1815-1914. *Annals of Tourism Research, 26,* 130-150.

Seaton, A., & Bennett, M. (1996). *Marketing tourism products: Concepts, issues and cases.* London: Thomson Business Press.

Seaton, A., Wood, R., Dieke, P., & Jenkins, C. (Eds.). (1994). *Tourism—the state of the art: The Strathclyde symposium.* England: Wiley and Sons.

Sebestyon, T. (1991). *Balaton.* Budapest: Corvina.

Selänniemi, T. (1994a). A charter trip to sacred places—individual mass tourism. In J. Jardel (Ed.), *Le tourisme international entre tradition et modernite* (pp. 335-340). Nice, France: University de Nice, Laboratoire d'ethnologie.

Selänniemi, T. (1994b). *Heritage and the tourist: From quick glimpses to devotional visits.* RC50 Sociology of Tourism. XIIth World Congress of Sociology, Bielefeld, Germany.

Selänniemi, T. (1994c). *Pakettimatka pyhaan paikkaan—suomalaisturistit Ateenassa* (A charter trip to a sacred place—Finnish tourists in Athens). Jyvaskyla: Jyvaskylan yliopisto, etnologian laitos (University of Jyvaskyla).

Selänniemi, T. (1996a). *Beneath, between and beyond the paradigms: Looking down on the tourist in the sociology of tourism.* Paper presented at the International Sociological Association RC50A symposium, Paradigms in Tourism Research, Jyvaskyla, Finland, 4-7 July.

Selänniemi (1996b). *Matka Ikuiseen Kesaan. Kulttuuriantropologinen Nakokulma Suomalaisten Etelanmatkailuun* (A journey to the eternal summer: An anthropological perspective on Finnish sunlust tourism). Helsinki: SKS.

Selänniemi, T. (1997). The mind in the museum, the body on the beach: Place and authenticity in mass tourism. In W. Nuryanti (Ed.), *Tourism and culture. Toward a sustainable future: Balancing conservation and development.* Yogyakarta: Gadjah Mada University Press.

Selwyn, T. (1990). Postgraduate studies in the sociology and anthropology of tourism. *Annals of Tourism Research, 17,* 637-638.

Selwyn, T. (1996). *The tourist image: Myths and myth making in tourism.* London: John Wiley.

Seveck, C. (1973). *Longest reindeer herder: A true life story of an Alaskan Eskimo covering the period from 1890 to 1973* (2nd ed.). Anchorage: Arctic Circle Enterprises.

Shackley, M. (1996). Too much room at the inn? *Annals of Tourism Research, 23,* 449-462.

Sharpley, R. (1994). *Tourism, tourists and society.* England: ELM Publications.

Shaw, G., & Williams, A. (1994). *Critical issues in tourism.* Oxford: Blackwell.

Sheldon, A. (1987). *God and production in a Guatemalan town.* Austin, TX: University of Texas Press.

Sheldon, P. (1997). *Tourism information technology.* Oxford: CAB International.

Sheldon, P., & Collison, F. (1990). Faculty review criteria in tourism hospitality. *Annals of Tourism Research, 17,* 556-567.

Shirouzu, N. (1997, October 21). Shopping malls, American-style, await Japanese. *Wall Street Journal*, p. A5A.

Short, J., & Kim, Y. (1999). *Globalization and the city.* New York: Longman.

Sigaux, G. (1966). *History of tourism* (J. White, Trans.). London: Leisure Arts.

Simon Property Group. (1995). *Mall of America impact study.* Indianapolis, IN: Author.

Simpson, E. (1937). *The Ejido: Mexico's way out.* Chapel Hill, NC: University of North Carolina Press.

Sinclair, M., & Stabler, M. (Eds.). (1991). *The tourism industry: An international analysis.* Oxford: CAB International.

Singh, A. (2000). The Asia Pacific cruise line industry: Current trends, opportunities and future outlook. *Tourism Recreation Research, 25*(2), 49-62.

Singh, T., & Singh, S. (Eds.). (1999). *Tourism development in critical environments.* New York: Cognizant Communication Corp.

Singh, T., Theuns, H., & Go, F. (1989). *Toward appropriate tourism: The case of developing countries.* Frankfurt, Germany: Peter Lang.

Sirakaya, E. (1997). Attitudinal compliance with ecotourism guidelines. *Annals of Tourism Research, 24,* 919-950.

Skomal, S. (1994, May). Lessons of the field: Ethics in fieldwork. *Anthropology Newsletter, 1,* 4.

Slusser, M. (1982). *Nepal mandala: A cultural study of the Kathmandu Valley.* Princeton, NJ: Princeton University Press.

Smith, M., & Krannich, R. (1998). Tourism dependence and resident attitudes. *Annals of Tourism Research, 25,* 783-802.

Smith, R. (1992). Beach resort evolution: Implications for planning. *Annals of Tourism*

Research, 19(2), 304-322.

Smith, S. (Ed.). (1995). *Tourism analysis: A handbook* (2nd ed.). Essex: Longman.

Smith, V. (1966). *Kotzebue: A modern Alaska Eskimo community.* Ph.D. dissertation, University of Utah, Department of Anthropology.

Smith, V. (1976). *Inupiat Paitot* (Elders' Workshop) (unpublished field notes). Kotzebue, AK.

Smith, V. (Ed.). (1977). *Hosts and guests: The anthropology of tourism.* Philadelphia, PA: The University of Pennsylvania Press.

Smith, V. (1978). Renascent Alaskan Eskimo Ethnicity: Inupiat Paitot 1976. In *Actes du XLII congres international des Americanistes, Congres du Centenaire* (pp. 227-237). Paris: Fondation Singer-Polignac.

Smith, V. (1979). Women: The taste-makers in tourism. *Annals of Tourism Research, 6,* 49-60.

Smith, V. (1980). Tourism and development: Anthropological perspectives [Special issue]. *Annals of Tourism Research, 7.*

Smith, V. (Ed.). (1989a). *Hosts and guests: The anthropology of tourism* (2nd ed.). Philadelphia, PA: University of Pennsylvania Press.

Smith, V. (1989b). Introduction. In V. Smith (Ed.), *Hosts and guests: The anthropology of tourism* (2nd ed., pp. 1-17). Philadelphia, PA: University of Pennsylvania Press.

Smith, V. (1992a). Boracay, Philippines: A case study. In V. Smith & W. Eadington (Eds.), *Tourism alternatives: Potential and problems in the development of tourism* (pp. 135-141). Philadelphia, PA: University of Pennsylvania Press.

Smith, V. (1992b). Pilgrimage and tourism: The quest in guest [Special issue]. *Annals of Tourism Research, 19.*

Smith, V. (1994). Privatization in the third world: Small-scale tourism enterprises. In W. Theobald (Ed.), *Global tourism: The next decade* (pp. 163-173). Oxford: Butterworth-Heinemann.

Smith, V. (1996a). War and its tourist attractions. In A. Pizam & Y. Mansfeld (Eds.), *Tourism, crime and international security issues* (pp. 247-264). New York: John Wiley & Sons.

Smith, V. (1996b). Indigenous tourism: The four Hs. In R. Butler & T. Hinch (Eds.), *Tourism and indigenous peoples* (pp. 284-307). London: International Thomson Business Press.

Smith, V. (1996c). The Inuit as hosts: Heritage and wilderness tourism in Nunavut. In M. Price (Ed.), *People and tourism in fragile environments* (pp. 33-50). Chichester: John Wiley & Sons, Ltd.

Smith, V. (1998). War and tourism: An American ethnography. *Annals of Tourism Research, 25,* 202-227.

Smith, V. (2000). Space tourism: the 21st century "frontier." *Tourism Recreation Research, 25*(3), 5-15.

Smith, V., & Eadington, W. (Eds.). (1992). *Tourism alternatives: Potentials and problems in the development of tourism.* Philadelphia, PA: University of Pennsylvania Press.

Sofield, R. (1990). The impact of tourism development on traditional socio-cultural values in the South Pacific: Conflict, co-existence and symbiosis. In M. Miller & J. Auyong (Eds.), *Proceedings of the 1990 Congress on Coastal and Marine Tourism.* Newport, OR: National Coastal Resources & Development Institute.

Sofield, T., & Li, F. (1998). Tourism development and cultural policies in China. *Annals of Tourism Research, 25,* 362-392.

Sonmez, S. (1998). Tourism, terrorism, and political instability. *Annals of Tourism Research, 25,* 416-456.

Sonmez, S., & Graefe, A. (1998). Influence of terrorism risk on foreign tourism decisions. *Annals of Tourism Research, 25,* 112-144.

Sonmez, S., & Tarlow, P. (1998). Managing tourism crises resulting from terrorism and crime.

In *International Conference, War, Terrorism, Tourism: Times of Crisis and Recovery* (pp. 21-23). September 25-27, 1997, Dubrovnik, Croatia.

Spanier, D. (1992). *Welcome to the pleasuredome: Inside Las Vegas.* Las Vegas, NV: University of Nevada Press.

Sponsel, L. (1994). The mutual relevance of anthropology and peace studies. In L. Sponsel & T. Gregor (Eds.), *The anthropology of peace and nonviolence* (pp. 1-36). Boulder, CO: Lynne Rienner Publishers, Inc.

Srisang, K. (1989). The ecumenical coalition on third world tourism. *Annals of Tourism Research, 16,* 119-121.

Stansfield, C. (1971). The nature of seafront development and social status of seaside resorts. *Society and Leisure, 4,* 117-150.

Stansfield, C. (1978). Atlantic City and the resort cycle: Background to the legalization of gambling. *Annals of Tourism Research, 5*(2), 238-251.

Stansfield, C., & Rickert, J. (1970). The recreation business district. *Journal of Leisure Research, 2,* 213-225.

Stanton, M. (1989). The Polynesian Cultural Center: A multi-ethnic model of seven Pacific cultures. In V. Smith (Ed.), *Hosts and guests: The anthropology of tourism* (pp. 247-264). Philadelphia, PA: University of Pennsylvania Press.

Stearns, J. (1996, November 21). Tourists like Reno, but rivals gain. *Reno Gazette-Journal,* p. E1.

Stearns, J. (1997a, March 19). Megaresorts put mega pressure on northern Nevada. *Reno Gazette-Journal,* p. A1.

Stearns, J. (1997b, March 20). Saturated market dampens Reno future. *Reno Gazette-Journal,* p. A1.

Stephen, L. (1993). Weaving in the fast lane: Class, ethnicity and gender in Zapotec craft commercialization. In J. Nash (Ed.), *Crafts in the world market* (pp. 25-58). Albany, NY: State University of New York Press.

Stephenson, G. (1989). Knowledge browsing—front ends to statistical databases. In J. Rafanelli & S. Klensin (Eds.), *Proceedings of the Fourth International Working Conference on Statistical and Scientific Data Base Management* (pp. 327-337). New York: Springer.

Sternberg, E. (1997). The iconography of the tourism experience. *Annals of Tourism Research, 24,* 951-969.

Stonich, S. (1998). Political ecology of tourism. *Annals of Tourism Research, 25,* 25-54.

Stonich, S. (2000). *The other side of paradise: Tourism, conservation and development in the Bay Islands.* New York: Cognizant Communication Corp.

Strauss, N. (1999, June 27). On night music died, many to blame for mayhem. *New York Times,* p. A1.

Stringer, P. (1984). Social psychology and tourism [Special issue]. *Annals of Tourism Research, 11.*

Strong, M. (1993). The moral dimension of prosperity. Cited in *WTTC Viewpoint, 1*(2), p. 8.

Stymeist, D. (1996). Transformation of Vilavilairevo in tourism. *Annals of Tourism Research, 23,* 1-18.

Sumption, J. (1975). *Pilgrimage: An image of mediaeval religion.* Totowa, NJ: Bowman & Littlefield.

Sutton, C. (1987). The Caribbeanization of New York City and the emergence of a transational socio-cultural system. In C. Sutton & E. Chaney (Eds.), *Caribbean life in New York City: Sociocultural dimensions* (pp. 25-29). Staten Island, NY: Cenentary Migration Studies.

Swain, M. (1990). Commoditizing ethnicity in southwest China. *Cultural Survival Quarterly, 14,* 26-29.

Swain, M. (1993). Women producers of ethnic arts. *Annals of Tourism Research, 20,* 32-

51.

Swain, M. (1994). *Ashima:A tale of Sani identity and the Chinese civilizing project.* Paper presented at Association for Asian Studies Annual Meeting. Boston, March.

Swain, M. (1995). A comparison of state and private artisan production for tourism in Yunnan. In A. Lew & L. Yu (Eds.), *Tourism in China* (pp. 223-233). Boulder, CO: Westview Press.

Swain, M., Brent, M., & Long, V. (1998). Annals and tourism evolving: Indexing 25 years of publication. *Annals of Tourism Research, 25*(Suppl.), 991-1014.

Swaney, D. (1992). *Zimbabwe, Botswana & Namibia.* Hawthorn, Vic., Australia: Lonely Planet.

Swaney, D. (1999). *Zimbabwe, Botswana & Namibia.* Oakland: Lonely Planet.

Swarbrook, J. (1995). *The development and management of visitor attractions.* London: Butterworth-Heinemann.

Sweetman, B. (1999, June). Runway to space. *Popular Science,* 72-77.

Syratt, G. (1995). *Manual of travel agency practice.* London: Butterworth-Heinemann.

Tabatchnaia-Tamirisa, N., Loke, M., Leung, P., & Tucker, K. (1997). Energy and tourism in Hawaii. *Annals of Tourism Research, 24,* 390-401.

Tansey, K. (1999, April 26). Agency name reflects vision of its owner. *Travel Weekly,* 81.

Taplin, J., & Qiu, M. (1997). Car trip attraction and route choice in Australia. *Annals of Tourism Research, 24,* 624-637.

Tattersall, I. (2000, January). Once we were not alone. *Scientific American, 282*(1), 56-62.

Taussig, M. (1987). *Shamanism, colonialism and the wild man: A study in terror and healing.* Chicago: University of Chicago Press.

Taylor, G. (1998). Styles of travel. In W. Theobald (Ed.), *Global tourism* (2nd ed., pp. 267-277). Oxford: Butterworth-Heinemann.

Teare, R., & Olsen, M. (1991). *International hospitality management: Corporate strategy in practice.* London: Pitman.

Teare, R., Adams, D., & Messenger, S. (1992). *Managing projects in hospitality organisations.* London: Cassell.

Teas, J. (1988). I'm studying monkeys. What do you do? Youth and travelers in Nepal. *Kroeber Anthropological Society Papers, 67-68,* 35-41.

Telfer, D., & Wall, G. (1996). Linkages between tourism and food production. *Annals of Tourism Research, 23,* 635-653.

Teo, P., & Yeoh, G. (1997). Remaking local heritage for tourism. *Annals of Tourism Research, 24,* 192-213.

Testa, R. (1992). *After the fire: The destruction of Lancaster County Amish.* Hanover: University Press of New England.

Teye, V. (1988). Geography and tourism at the AAG meeting. *Annals of Tourism Research, 15,* 567-569.

The Minority Traveler. (1996). Washington, DC: Travel Industry Association of America.

The world's most expensive cruise. (1981, January 11). *Wall Street Journal,* p. A1.

Theobald, W. (1994). *Global tourism: The next decade.* Oxford: Butterworth-Heinemann.

Theobald, W. (1998). *Global tourism: The next decade* (2nd ed.). Oxford: Butterworth-Heineman.

Theroux, P. (1975). *Great railway bazaar: By train through Asia.* New York: Houghton Mifflin.

Theroux, P. (1993). *The happy isles of Oceania: Paddling the Pacific.* New York: Ballentine Books.

Thomas, J. (1964, August) Eighteen important travel motivations. What makes people travel. *ASTA Travel News,* 64-65.

Thomas, K. (1983). *Man and the natural world: Changing attitudes in England, 1500-*

1800. London: Lane.

Thompson, E. (1966). *The making of the English working class*. New York: Random House.

Thompson, G. (1998, March 25). Adelson blasts LVCVA, competitors, union. *Las Vegas Sun*, pp. A1, A5.

Timothy, D., & Wall, G. (1997). Selling to tourists: Indonesian street vendors. *Annals of Tourism Research, 24*, 322–340.

Tjostheim, I., & Eide, J.-O. (1998). A case study of an on-line auction for the world wide web. In D. Buhalis, A. Min Tjoa, & J. Jafari (Eds.), *Information and communications technologies in tourism* (pp. 149–161). Vienna and New York: Springer.

Tobin, B. (1974). The bicycle boom of the 1890s: The development of private transportation and the birth of the modern tourist. *Journal of Popular Culture, 8*, 838–49.

Tooman, L. (1997). Applications of the life-cycle model in tourism. *Annals of Tourism Research, 24*, 214–234.

Tourism: A Vital Force for Peace. (1988). First Global Conference. 3680 rue de la Montagne, Montreal, P.Q. Canada H3G 2A8

Tourism Canada. (1990). *An action strategy for sustainable tourism development: Globe '90*. Ottawa: Author.

Tourism Review Steering Committee. (1997). *Review of the marine tourism industry in the Great Barrier Reef world heritage area*. Townsville, Australia: Great Barrier Reef Marine Park Authority.

Tourtellot, J. (1999, July/August). The two faces of tourism. *National Geographic Traveler*, 98–109.

Tourtellot, J. (2000, October). The tourism wars. *National Geographic Traveler*, 110–119.

Towner, J. (1996). *An historical geography of recreation and tourism in the Western world 1540–1940*. Chichester: John Wiley & Sons.

Travel and Tourism Research Association. (1991). *Tourism: Building credibility for a credible industry*. Salt Lake City, UT: Author.

Travel Industry of America. (2000). *The minority traveler* (2nd ed.). Washington, DC: Author.

Travel Industry of America. (2001). *Profile of travelers who participate in gambling*. Washington, DC: Author.

Travis, J. (1993). *The rise of the Devon seaside resorts 1750–1900*. Exeter: University of Exeter Press.

Trease, G. (1967). *The grand tour*. London: Heinemann.

Tremblay, P. (1998). The economic organization of tourism. *Annals of Tourism Research, 25*, 837–859.

Tribe, J. (1995). *The economics of leisure and tourism: Environments, markets and impacts*. London: Butterworth-Heinemann.

Tribe, J. (1997). The indiscipline of tourism. *Annals of Tourism Research, 24*, 638–657.

Trousdale, W. (1996). *Sustainable tourism planning: A case study of Guimaras, Philippines*. Vancourver, BC: Centre for Human Settlements.

Trousdale, W. (1999). Governance in context: Boracay island, Philippines. *Annals of Tourism Research, 26*, (840–867).

Tsing, A. (1993). *In the realm of the diamond queen: Marginality in an out-of-the-way place*. Princeton, NJ: Princeton University Press.

Tunbridge, J.. & Ashworth, G. (1996). *Dissonant heritage: The management of the past as a resource in conflict*. New York: Wiley.

Turner, D. (1989). *Robin of the movies: The cinematic history of the legendary outlaw of Sherwood*. Kingswinford, England: Yeoman Publishing.

Turner, F. (1967). *Taking the cure*. London: Michael Joseph.

Turner, F. (1920). *The frontier in American history*. New York: Holt, Rinehart and Winston.

Turner, J. (1969). *Barbarous Mexico*. Austin: University of Texas Press. (Original work published 1910)

Turner, L., & Ash, J. (1976). *The golden hordes: International tourism and the pleasure periphery*. New York: St. Martin's Press.

Turner, V. (1969). *The ritual process*. Chicago: Aldine.

Turner, V. (1973). The center out there: The pilgrim's goal. *History of Religion, 12*(3), 191-230.

Turner, V. (1974). Liminal to liminoid in play, flow and ritual: An essay in comparative symbology. *Rice University Studies, 60*, 53-92.

Turner, V. (1978). *Dramas, fields and metaphors*. Ithaca, NY: Cornell University Press.

Turner, V., & Turner, E. (1978). *Image and pilgrimage in Christian culture*. New York: Columbia University Press.

Turney-High, H. (1971). *Primitive war*. Columbia, SC: University of South Carolina Press.

Turney High, H. (1981). *The military: The theory of land warfare as behavioral science*. West Hanover, MA: The Christopher Publishing House.

UNESCO. (1976). The effects of tourism and sociocultural values. *Annals of Tourism Research, 4*, 74-105.

United Nations. (1954). *The population of Central America (including Mexico), 1950-1980*. New York: Department of Social Affairs, Population Division.

United Nations Committee on Sustainable Development. (1999). *Report CSD-7*. Geneva: United Nations.

United Nations Development Programme. (1994). *1994 Project document: Establishing partnership for quality tourism*. Kathmandu: Author.

Urbanowicz, C. (1989). Tourism in Tonga revisited: Continued troubled times? In V. Smith (Ed.), *Hosts and guests: The anthropology of tourism* (2nd ed., pp. 105-117). Philadelphia, PA: University of Pennsylvania Press.

Urbanowicz, C. (1998). *Gambling (gaming) in the United States of America from an anthropological perspective*. Paper presented at the International Congress of Anthropological and Ethnological Sciences, July 27-August 1, Williamsburg, VA.

Urry, J (1990). *The tourist gaze: Leisure and travel in contemporary societies*. London: Sage.

US Travel Data Center. (1996). *The minority traveler*. Washington, DC: Travel Industry Association of America.

Vaagbo, O. (1993). *Den Norske Turkulturen*. Oslo: FIFRO.

Valdez, N. (1996). Land reform and the two faces of development in rural Mexico. *Political and Legal Anthropology Review, 19*(2), 109-126.

Van den Berghe, P. (1994). *The quest for the other: Ethnic tourism in San Cristobal, Mexico*. Seattle, WA: University of Washington Press.

Van den Berghe, P. (1995). Marketing Mayas: Ethnic tourism promotion in Mexico. *Annals of Tourism Research, 22*, 568-588.

Van den Berghe, P., & Keyes, C. (1984). Tourism and ethnicity [Special issue]. *Annals of Tourism Research, 11*.

Van Gennep, A. (1960). *The rites of passage* (M. Vizedom & G. Caffee, Trans.). Chicago: The University of Chicago Press. (Original work published 1909)

Van Mechelen, N. (1991). *Dolls by Nadine Van Mechelen*. Browning, MT: U.S. Department of the Interior, Indian Arts and Crafts Board, and Museum of the Plains Indian and Crafts Center.

Var, T. (1991). Sustainable tourism development. *Annals of Tourism Research, 18*, 327-329.

Varkonyi, J. (1992). *Balaton: Lake of style and spectacle*. Budapest: Hungarian Tourist Board.

Veijola, S., & Jokinen, E. (1994). The body in tourism theory. *Culture & Society, 11*, 125-

151.

Venison, P. (1983). *Managing hotels.* London: Butterworth-Heinemann.

Vera, R. (1991). Sembrarn de hoteles el corredor Cancun Tulum, sin importar poblacion y ecologia. *Proceso 789,* 20-22.

Vernon, R. (1963). *The dilemma of Mexico's development.* Cambridge, MA: Harvard University Press.

Villa Rojas, A. (1945). *The Maya of east central Quintana Roo.* Washington, DC: Carnegie Institution of Washington.

Villa Rojas, A. (1969). The Maya of Yucatan. In R. Wauchope (Gen. Ed.), *Handbook of Middle American Indians* (Vol. 8, pp. 244-275). Austin, TX: University of Texas Press.

Vukonic, B. (1996). *Tourism and religion.* Exeter: Pergamon Press.

Wachenfeld, D., Oliver, J., & Morrissey, J. (1998). *State of the Great Barrier Reef world heritage area.* Townsville, Australia: Great Barrier Reef Marine Park Authority.

Wagner, U. (1977). Out of time and place—mass tourism and charter trips. *Ethnos, 42,* 38-52.

Wagner, U. (1981). Tourism in the Gambia: Development and dependency? *Ethnos, 3-4,* 190-206.

Wahab, S. (1972). An introduction to tourism theory. *IUOTO Research Journal, 1,* 34-43.

Wahab, S. (1975). *Tourism management.* London: Tourism International Press.

Wahab, S. (1996). Tourism and terrorism: Synthesis of the probiem with emphasis on Egypt. In A. Pizam & Y. Mansfeld (Eds.), *Tourism, crime and international security issues* (pp. 175-186). Chichester: John Wiley & Sons.

Wahnschafft, R. (1982). Formal and informal tourism sectors: A case study in Pattaya, Thailand. *Annals of Tourism Research, 9,* 429-451.

Waitt, G. (1999). Naturalizing the 'primitive': A critique of marketing Australia's indigenous population as 'hunters-gatherers.' *Tourism Geographics, 1*(2), 142-164.

Wakefield, J. (2000, January). Book me a double—with a view of Venus. *Wired, 8,* 132-134.

Wall, F., & Butler, R. (1985). The evolution of tourism: Historical perspectives [Special issue]. *Annals of Tourism Research, 12.*

Wall, G. (1974). Car owners and holiday activities. In P. Lavery (Ed.), *Recreational geography.* Newton Abbot, Devon: David & Charles.

Wall, G. (1993). Towards a tourism typology. In J. Nelson, R. Butler, & G. Wall (Eds.), *Tourism and sustainable development: Monitoring, planning, managing* (pp. 45-58). Waterloo, ON: Heritage Resources Centre, University of Waterloo.

Wall, G. (1996). Perspectives on tourism in selected Balinese villages. *Annals of Tourism Research, 23,* 123-137.

Wallace, G. (1993). Visitor management: Lessons from Galapagos National Park. In K. Lindberg & D. Hawkins (Eds.), *Ecotourism: A guide for planners and managers* (pp. 55-81). Bennington, VT: Ecotourism Society.

Walle, A. (1996). Habits of thought and cultural tourism. *Annals of Tourism Research, 23,* 874-890.

Walle, A. (1997a). Pursuing risk or insight: Marketing adventures. *Annals of Tourism Research, 24,* 265-282.

Walle, A. (1997b). Quantitative versus qualitative tourism research. *Annals of Tourism Research, 24,* 524-336.

Walle, A. (1998). *Cultural tourism: A strategic focus.* Boulder, CO: Westview Press.

Wallerstein, N., & Bernstein, E., (1988). Empowerment education: Freire's ideas adapted to health education. *Health Education Quarterly, 15*(4), 379-394.

Walton, J. (1983). *The English seaside resort: A social history 1750-1914.* Leicester: Leicester University Press.

Wang, F. (1993). *Guanyu Fazhan Luyoushiye de Qingkuang Baogao* (A status report about the development of tourism enterprise). Shilin: Lunan Yizu Autonomous County Tourism Bureau.

Ward, B., & Dillon, M. (1991). *Guidelines to hotel and leisure project financing.* Madrid: World Tourism Organization.

Ward, B., Wells, J., & Kennedy, M. (1991). *Tourism education.* National conference, University of Canberra. Canberra, Australia: Bureau of Tourism Research.

Water, S. (1967). *Tourism: A new path to economic improvement in developing nations.* New York: Child and Water, Inc.

Waters, S. (annual). *Travel industry world yearbook: The big picture.* New York: Child and Waters.

Waters, S. (1969). New light on the multiplier effect in analyzing the impact of tourism spending. *World Travel, 89,* 29–32.

Watts, M. (1992). Space for everything (a commentary). *Cultural Anthropology, 7*(1), 115–129.

Wauchope, R. (1969). *Handbook of Middle American Indians.* Austin, TX: University of Texas Press.

Weaver, C. (1998). Peripheries of the periphery: Tourism in Tobago and Barbuda. *Annals of Tourism Research, 25,* 292–313.

Weaver, D. (1998a). *Ecotourism in the less developed world.* London: CAB International.

Weaver, D. (1998b). *The tourism–war nexus: A life cycle approach.* Paper presented at the Australian Tourism and Hospitality Research Conference, February 10–14, Goldcoast, Queensland, Australia.

Weber, M. (1978). *The theory of social and economic organization.* New York: The Free Press. (Original work published 1946).

Webster's 1988 new world dictionary of the English language (3rd college ed.). (1988). New York: Simon & Schuster.

Weiler, B., & Hall, C. (1992). *Special interest tourism.* London: Belhaven Press.

Weiss, G. (1977). The problem of development in the non-western world. *American Anthropologist, 79,* 887–893.

Weissmann, J. (1993). Upping the ante: Allowing Indian tribes to sue states in federal court under the Indian gaming regulatory act. *The George Washington Law Review, 6*(1), 123–161.

Wenkam, R. (1975). The pacific tourist blight. *Annals of Tourism Research, 3,* 68–77.

Wetterau, B. (1990). *The New York Public Library book of chronologies.* New York: Stonesong Press.

Weyer, E. (1969). *The Eskimos: Their environment and folkways.* Hamden, CT: Archon Books.

Wheatcroft, S. (1994). *Aviation and tourism policies: Balancing the benefits.* London: Routledge.

Whelan, T. (1991). *Nature tourism.* Washington, DC: Island Press.

White, J. (1967). *History of tourism.* London: Leisure Art.

White, M. (1999a, September 23). Hilton Hotels studying feasibility of building a resort in space. *The Sacramento Bee,* p. E.

White, M. (1999b, September 24). Space: The final frontier of tourism? *Globe and Mail,* p. M.

Wilen, J. (1998, March 28). Internet gamers ask for betting regulation. *Reno Gazette-Journal,* p. B10.

Wilkening, D. (1999, August 16). Study: Agents need to become 'convenience providers.' *Travel Weekly,* 24.

Wilkie, J. (1970). *The Mexican Revolution: Federal expenditure and social change since 1910.* Berkeley, CA: University of California Press.

Wilkinson, P. (1996). Graphical images of the commonwealth Caribbean: The tourist area cycle of evolution. In L. Harrison & W. Husbands (Eds.), *Practicing responsible tourism: International case studies in tourism planning, policy, and development* (pp. 16-40). Toronto: John Wiley & Sons, Inc.

Wilkinson, P. (1997). *Tourism policy & planning: Case studies from the commonwealth Caribbean.* New York: Cognizant Communication Corp.

Williams, A., & Shaw, G. (1991). *Tourism and economic development: Western European experiences* (2nd ed.) London: Belhaven Press.

Williams, P. (1991). Tourism, technology and the environment. *Annals of Tourism Research, 18,* 330-331.

Williams, P., & Gill, A. (1991). *Carrying capacity management in tourism settings: A tourism growth management process.* Burnaby, British Columbia: Simon Fraser University, Centre for Tourism Policy and Research.

Williams, P., & Gill, A. (1998). Tourism carrying capacity management issues. In W. Theobald (Ed.), *Global tourism* (2nd ed., pp. 231-246). Oxford: Butterworth-Heinemann.

Williams, P., Penrose, R., & Hawkes, S. (1998). Shared decision-making in tourism land use planning. *Annals of Tourism Research, 25,* 860-889.

Williamson, R. (1999). The international fur ban and public policy advocacy: The significance of Inuit cultural persistence. *Practicing Anthropology, 21,* 2-8.

Wilson, D. (1997). Paradoxes of tourism in Goa. *Annals of Tourism Research, 24,* 52-75.

Wilson, K. (1998). Market/industry confusion in tourism economic analyses. *Annals of Tourism Research, 25,* 803-817.

Winthrop, R. (1999). The real world, the dilemmas of tradition. *Practicing Anthropology, 21*(3), 34-35.

Witt, S., & Moutinho, L. (1989). *Tourism marketing and management handbook.* New York: Prentice-Hall.

Witt, S., & Moutinho, L. (1994). *The tourism marketing and management handbook* (2nd ed.) Hemel Hempstead: Prentice-Hall.

Wober, K. (1998). Measuring tourism managers' information needs by tracking and analyzing the tourism web site statistics. In D. Buhalis, A. Min Tjoa, & J. Jafari (Eds.), *Information and communications technologies in tourism* (pp. 26-35). Vienna and New York: Springer.

Wolf, E. (1957). Closed corporate peasant communities in Mesoamerica and central Java. *Southwestern Journal of Anthropology, 13,* 1-18.

Wolf, E., & Hansen, E. (1972). *The human condition in Latin America.* New York: Oxford University Press.

Wolfe, R. (1952). Wasaga Beach: The divorce from the geographic environment. *Canadian Geographer, 2,* 58-65.

Wolfe, R. (1966). Recreational travel—the new migration. *Canadian Geographer, 10,* 1-14.

Wolfe, R. (1982). Recreational travel—the new migration revisited. *Ontario Geography, 19,* 103-124.

Wolff, C. (1992). Documenting the past: Dolls help to preserve Tibetan culture. *The Cloth Doll, 9,* 26-29.

Wood, R. (1994). *Organisational behaviour for hospitality management.* London: Butterworth-Heinemann.

Woodside, A., & Lysonski, S. (1989). A general model of traveller destination choice. *Journal of Travel Research, 17,* 8-14.

World Bank. (1991). *The World Bank operational manual.* Washington, DC: Author.

World Bank. (1994). *World development report 1994.* Washington and New York: World Bank and Oxford University Press.

World Commission on Environment and Development. (1987). *Our common future* (The Brundtland Report). London: Oxford University Press.

World Tourism Organization. (1991a). *International conference on travel and tourism statistics*. Madrid:Author.

World Tourism Organization. (1991b). General assembly round tables: Education and training. *WTO News*, 4-5.

World Tourism Organization. (1992). *The world directory of tourism education and training institutions*. Madrid:Author.

World Tourism Organization. (1993). *Recommendations on tourism statistics*. Madrid: Author.

World Tourism Organization. (1994). *Global tourism forecasts to the year 2000 and beyond*. Madrid:Author.

World Tourism Organization. (1996a). *World's top tourism destinations 1995*. Madrid:Author.

World Tourism Organization. (1996b). *What tourism managers need to know:A practical guide to the development and use of indicators of sustainable tourism*. Madrid: Author.

World Tourism Organization. (1997a). *Tourism highlights 1997*. Madrid:Author.

World Tourism Organization. (1997b). *Human capital in the tourism industry of the 21st century*. Madrid:Author.

World Tourism Organization. (1998). *Vision 2020*. Madrid:Author.

World Tourism Organization. (1999a). *Using tourism satellite accounts to reach the bottome line. World: Proving the economic importance of tourism*. Madrid:Author.

World Tourism Organization. (1999b). *Tourism highlights 1998*. Madrid:Author.

World Tourism Organization. (2000a). *Tourism highlights 1999*. Madrid:Author.

World Tourism Organization. (2000b). *Global code of ethics for tourism* (Adopted by the General Assembly of the World Tourism Organization). Madrid:Author.

World Tourism Organization/United Nations Environmental Programme. (1992). *Guidelines: Development of national parks and protected areas for tourism*. Madrid: Author.

World Travel and Tourism Council. (1993). *Travel and tourism:A new economic perspective*. Brussels:Author.

World Travel and Tourism Council. (1998). *Annual report*. Brussels:Author.

World Travel and Tourism Council. (1999). *Steps to success: Global good practices in travel and tourism human resources* (3rd ed.). North Vancouver, BC, Canada:World Travel & Tourism Human Resource Centre, Capilano College.

World travel and tourism review (Vol. 1). (1991). Oxford: CAB International.

Wylie, R. (1993). Domestic tourism revisited. *Annals of Tourism Research, 20*, 216-229.

Xia, L. (2000, August). Heeding nature's warnings. *China Today, 49*(8), 6-9.

Xiao, H. (1997). Tourism and leisure in China:A tale of two cities. *Annals of Tourism Research, 24*, 357-370.

Yale, P. (1995). *The business of tour operators*. London: Pitman.

Yamashita, S., Din, K., & Eades, J. (1997). *Tourism and cultural development in Asia and Oceania*. Kuala Lumpur, Malaysia: Universiti Kebangsaan Malaysia.

Yoshihashi, P. (1993, October 22). The gambling industry rakes it in as casinos spread across the U.S. *The Wall Street Journal*, pp. 1, 9.

Young, G. (1973). *Tourism: Blessing or blight?* Harmondsworth: Penguin Books.

Young, J. (1993). *The texture of memory: Holocaust memorials and meaning*. New Haven:Yale University Press.

Yunnan International Non-government Organization Society. (1993). *Yunnan International Non-government Organization Society:A brief introduction*. Kunming, Yunnan.

Yunnan Sheng Luyouju. (1993). *Yunnan Luyou Tongji Ziliao, 1992* (Yunnan tourism statistical data). Kunming, Yunnan.

Zagoskin, V. (1967). *Lieutenant Zagoskin's travels in Russian America, 1842–1844. The first ethnographic and geographic investigations in the Yukon and Kuskokwim Valleys of Alaska* (H. N. Michael, Ed., P. Rainey, Trans. Arctic Institute of North America. Anthropology of the North. Translations from Russian Sources, No. 7). Toronto: University of Toronto Press.

Zalatan, A. (1998). Wives' involvement in tourism decision processes. *Annals of Tourism Research, 25*, 890–903.

Zeppel, H. (1998). "Come share our culture": Marketing aboriginal tourism in Australia. *Pacific Tourism Review, 2*(1), 83–90.

Zhang, G. (2000, May 10). *Holiday economy.* Email message to Tri-net@hawaii.edu from hmzhang@inet.polyu.edu.hk

Zinmaya, L. (1989). Some recent trends in tourism arrivals in Zimbabwe. *Geography, 74*, 62–65.

Note: Listed below are additional information sources

Air Canada. http://www.aircanada.ca/home.html

Caribbean Studies Assocation. http://www.fiu.edu/~lacc/csa98/

Caribbean Tourism Organization. http://www.travelfile.com/www/custom/1/012/3837/cto.html

Earth Council. Home page. www.ecouncil.ac.cr/rio/focus/summary/business.htm

Grenada Board of Tourism. http://www.travelgrenada.com/index.html

Grenada Carnival. htto://www.travelgrenada.com/carnival.htm

Human Relations Area Files. http://www.yale.edu/hraf

Institute fur Film und Bild in Wissenschaft und Unterrecht. (VHS cassettes). Call Numbers: Available Inter-library Loan: California State University-Chico:

> Begegnungen in Kenya (English narration-VHS) CSUC call Number G155K4B552
> Turisten in Sri Lanka (English narration-VHS) CSUC call Number G155S65B553
> Blickwechsel das andere Mexico (Spanish narration-VHS) CSUC Call Number G155M6B553

Island Resources Foundation. http://www.irf.org

Island Resources Foundation Library holdings catalogue search. http://www.unesco.org/ioc/isisdb/html/irfsearch.htm

Journal of Sport Tourism. http://www.free-press.com/journals/jst/

Lonely Planet. http://lonelyplanet.com.au.

Notting Hill Carnival 1997. http://www.nottinghillcarnival.net.uk/carnival.htm

Rene Waksberg's Tourism Research Links. http://www.geocities.com/ResearchTriangle/9481/tourism.htm

St. Lucia Mirror. http://www.stluciamirror.com/

The George Washington University Tourism and Hospitality Review. http://www.sha.cornell.edu/pubs/

The Nation. http://www.thenation.com

Travel Grenada. http://www.travelgrenada.com/maps.htm

United Nations Economic Commission on Latin America and the Caribbean (ECLAC). Caribbean links. http://community.wow.net.eclac/CARLINKS/home.htm

United Nations Economic Commission on Latin America and the Caribbean (ECLAC). Caribbean news. http://community.wow.net/eclac/CARNEWS/carnews.htm

United Nations Economic Commission on Latin America and the Caribbean (ECLAC). Caribbean sustainable development. http://community.wow.net/eclac/home.htm

WWW.Carnaval.Com http://www.carnaval.com/sitemap.htm

Index